EPILEGOMENA
TO THE STUDY OF
GREEK RELIGION

and

THEMIS

EPILEGOMENA TO THE STUDY OF GREEK RELIGION

and

THEMIS

A Study of the Social Origins of Greek Religion

BY JANE ELLEN HARRISON

UNIVERSITY BOOKS New Hyde Park, New York

EPILEGOMENA

TO

HOPE

In Remembrance of
Spanish Nights and Days

ای دل ز غبار جسم اگر پاک شوی
تو روح مجردی بر افلاك شوی
عرش است نشیمن تو شرمت بادا
كائی و مقیم خطهٔ خاك شوی

THEMIS

TO

GILBERT MURRAY
χαριστήριον

CONTENTS

PREFACE

THESE *Epilegomena* are the sequel to my two books *Prolegomena* and *Themis*. I have tried here to summarize as briefly as possible the results of many years' work on the origins of Greek Religion, and to indicate the bearing of these results on religious questions of to-day.

For the new material offered I am largely indebted to the psychological work of Jung and Freud and to the less well known writings of the greatest of Russian philosophers Vladímir Solovióv.

J. E. H.

NEWNHAM COLLEGE.
July 29, 1921.

I

PRIMITIVE RITUAL

ἔφυγον κακόν εὗρον ἄμεινον

THE little township of Chaeronea in Boeotia, Plutarch's birth-place, saw enacted year by year a strange and very ancient cere-monial[1]. It was called "The Driving out of Famine"[2]. A household slave was driven out of doors with rods of *agnus castus*, a willow-like plant, and over him were pronounced the words "Out with Famine, in with Health and Wealth." The Archon for the year performed the ceremony at the Common Hearth which was in intent the Town Hall of the community and each householder performed it separately for his own house. Plutarch himself per-formed it at the Common Hearth when he was Archon. There was present, he tells us, a large concourse of people and when all was over he and his friends discussed the matter at dinner.

I have chosen this ceremony out of thousands of others because it expresses with singular directness and simplicity what is, I think, the very pith and marrow of primitive religion. The religious im-pulse is directed, if I am right, primarily to one end and one only, *the conservation and promotion of life*. This end is served in two ways, one negative, one positive, by the riddance of whatever is conceived to be hostile and by the enhancement of whatever is conceived of as favourable to life. Religious rites are primarily of two kinds and two only, of *expulsion* and *impulsion*. Primitive man has before him, in order that he may live, the old dual task to get rid of evil, to secure good. Evil is to him of course mainly hunger and barrenness. Good is food and fertility. The Hebrew word for "good" meant originally good to eat[3]. The word was pri-marily applied to ripe fruits; it meant luscious, succulent. Hunger and barrenness he tries by endless varying rites to carry out, to expel, to kill; he curses it, he mourns over it, he has ceremonies

[1] Plut. *Symp.* VI. 8. 1.

[2] "καλεῖται δὲ βουλίμου ἐξέλασις." Βούλιμος is sometimes translated "Ox-hunger," but from Plutarch's discussion with his friends it is clear that this may be mere popular etymology. They agreed however that the strange archaic word meant a great and public famine.

[3] See J. E. Harrison, *Themis*, pp. 139, 280.

of death and lamentation ($\pi \acute{\epsilon} \nu \theta \epsilon a$). Food and fertility and growth he welcomes, he rejoices over; he has ceremonies of working producing, exerting ($\ddot{o}\rho\gamma\iota a$).

But, and this is important, the two notions are never very sharply sundered, they are but two faces of the same thought, or rather will, the "will to live." Beating, at the first glance, looks like mere expulsion of evil—you "beat the mischief out of" a child[1]. But certain ritual prescriptions show another face. In Lithuania[2] the Easter Beating must be inflicted with a twig or branch of birch on which the green leaves have just sprouted. Endless care is taken to secure this. If the birch branches do not bud in time the birch rods are kept in warm water for days—if even then they do not bud they are artificially heated in a stove pipe. In Orlagau in Thuringia the custom is called "whipping with fresh green," and the spoken words tell the same tale: "Good morning! Fresh Green! Long life! You must give us a bright thaler." All is to be fresh, new, bright, living. It is the induction by contagion of new vitality and fertility. In Plutarch's ceremony, be it noted, the slave is beaten with rods of *agnus castus*, a plant much in use in ancient "medicine" as a fertility charm.

This double-edged aspect of ritual comes out rather beautifully in the bonfire festivals that survive to-day. Leaping over a bonfire, dancing round it, is still by the peasantry of modern Europe supposed to bring fertility, or as they would say "Good luck," to man and beast and crops. In Franche-Comté[3] a bonfire is lighted on the Eve of Twelfth Night and while the bonfire blazes the people dance round it crying "Good Year come back! Bread and Wine come back!" Here we have it would seem pure *impulsion*, the bringing in of good. But behind lurks *expulsion*. The word "bonfire" is not, as used to be held, *bon-feu*, good fire, *feu de joie*; it is bane or bone fire, a fire for burning up old bones and rubbish of every kind. Purification and the rubbish-heap first, and only later, because of the splendid blaze, a glow like the life-giving sun, jollification, fertility, impulsion. Humanity, thank God! seems

---

[1] See J. E. Harrison, *Prolegomena*, p. 100 ff.

[2] Frazer, *Golden Bough*, Part VI, "The Scapegoat," p. 271.

[3] "Scapegoat," p. 316; and for fertilizing action of bonfires see *Balder the Beautiful*, 1. 188, 336.

never satisfied to rest in negation. Out of riddance springs inevitably and almost instantly magical induction; out of destruction, construction; out of purification and abstinence, sanctification. The history of man's religious development from superstitious fear to faith and hope and charity is largely the history of the shift from *bone fire* to *bon-feu*.

Aristotle[1] with his inspired amazing insight saw and said that poetry had two forms: *praise* which issued in hymns and heroic poetry (ἐγκώμια), *blame* which yielded iambic satire (ψόγους). Aristotle could not and did not know that these two modes arose out of two ritual forms. The ritual of expulsion, riddance, cursing and finally purification issues in the literature of blame, the ritual of induction, of blessing, of magical fertilization in the literature of praise. It is all summed up in the old ritual formula: "Out with Famine, in with Health and Wealth." We analyse and distinguish, but at bottom is the one double-edged impulse, the impulse towards life.

The twofold aspect of ritual, negative and positive, for *expulsion* and *impulsion*, is very clearly seen in two ritual implements in use among the Greeks, the Gorgoneion and the Liknon or Winnowing Fan.

The Gorgoneion[2] is the head of a Gorgon, but the head was there before the beast. This Gorgoneion is in fact nothing but a ritual mask, a grinning face with glaring eyes, protruding beast-like tusks and pendent tongue. The Greek used the Gorgoneion for what he called "prophylactic" purposes, that is to scare away all evil things, his enemies in the flesh and his ghostly foes. He placed it over his house, hung it over his oven and wore it on his shield, doubtless—though here for the Greeks precise evidence fails us—he danced with it as a mask in his ritual dances. Most anthropological museums contain specimens of Gorgoneion-like masks used by savages for ritual dances; such masks have the characteristic tusks and protruding pendent tongue. The protruding tongue is but the gesture of the street-boy of to-day by which he marks contempt and disgust. The origin is not so much

---

[1] *Poet.* iv. 7.

[2] Hastings, *Encyclopaedia of Religion and Ethics*, *s.v.* "Gorgoneion."

the idea of showing disgust as of ejecting a hurtful substance from the mouth. If we give it its Greek name it is *apoptuic* rather than *apotropaic*, its gist is to get rid of rather than to avert. The Gorgon with its upstanding hair is a constant monument of the religion of Fear, it is Terror incarnate.

Very different in its functions was the *liknon*[1] or winnowing-fan. Yet in origin it was closely analogous. The word in Greek for the winnowing-fan is πτύον, i.e. the spitter, that which throws up, disgorges, rejects the chaff and keeps the grain. The *liknon* became to the Greeks the great symbol and vehicle of purification physical and spiritual. But unlike the Gorgoneion it was wholly alien to the emotions of aversion and fear. It purified in order to promote growth and fertility. Its association with grain made this symbolism easy and natural. Its shape—it was a shoe-shaped basket—helped. The shoe-shaped basket was used not only for actual winnowing but, shovel-like, for the carrying of both grain and fruits. It was a purifier because it was a winnower; it was a fertility charm because it was a basket for first-fruits. Hence we find it used as a cradle for the new-born child, we find it held over the head of the initiate at the Eleusinian mysteries, we find it carried in marriage processions. At Athenian weddings a boy, both of whose parents were alive, carried a *liknon* full of loaves and pronounced the words: "Bad have I fled, better have I found"[2]. In fact as an old lexicographer[3] tells us the *liknon* is serviceable for every rite of initiation and every sacrifice. It must needs be so, for it embodies as the marriage formulary shows the essence of all ritual expulsion and impulsion.

It is probable that at this point an objection may arise in the mind of the reader. The ceremony at Chaeronea is, he will say, a curious old rite or custom, interesting in its way but not religious in the sense in which we use the word now. The objection is partly valid. In the sense in which we use the word now the rite of Chaeronea is not religious, that is to say it is not worship addressed to a god, it is not worship conducted by a priest, it is not worship held in a church. The object of this discussion is to

[1] J. E. Harrison, "Mystica Vannus Iacchi," in *Journal of Hellenic Studies*, xxiii. (1903) 292–324, and xxiv. (1904) 241–254, resumed in Hastings, *Encyclopaedia, s.v.* "Fan."

[2] Ps. Plut. *Prov. Alec.* xvi.   [3] Harpocration, *s.v.* "λίκνον."

show the constantly shifting nature of the notion of religion which, being, if my contention be right, a function of our human nature, grows and shifts with human growth. But, and this is important, Plutarch an educated Greek regarded the Chaeronea rite as religious. He calls it a *sacrifice* ($\theta\upsilon\sigma\acute{\iota}\alpha$), a sacred act, a word that came in late Greek to cover any and every religious doing. Now Plutarch was not only a highly educated but a deeply religious man. A great deal of his strenuous life was devoted to the study and elucidation of religious thought and practice, his greatest woman friend Clea was a priestess of Isis and all his life long he remained profoundly pious. What Plutarch called a " sacrifice " was we may be sure in his eyes religious.

The Chaeronea rite then was to Plutarch religious, yet it contained and implied no god. The kindred rite at Athens, the expulsion of the *pharmakoi* or scapegoats, became " associated with " the worship of Apollo, but Apollo is no integral part of it. Pretty well all over the world we find rites of expulsion and impulsion, but they involve no divinity. We must face at the outset the fact that religion does not presuppose a god. This, even if we confine ourselves to modern times, is plain enough. Buddhism claims perhaps more worshippers than any other religion, more than Mahomedanism, more than Judaism, more than Christianity. No one denies to Buddhism the name of religion, yet Buddhism is godless, pure atheism. It is at once its strength and for popular purposes its weakness.

That the Chaeronea rite is as godless as priestless is clear enough. The civil officer, the Archon, expels the slave and pronounces the expulsion of Famine and the incoming of Health and Wealth; that is all. The action is what we call "magical," it is the attempt directly to control natural facts and forces without appeal to any supposed divine being for his intervention. Plutarch, intimately acquainted with the worship of the gods, surrounded by the imposing figures of the Olympians, yet does not hesitate to call a magical ceremony religious, and we hold him to be right.

Is there then no distinction between religion and magic? There is, and it is a distinction very simple but all important; religion is social, magic is or may be individual, religion is of the group however small, magic of the single unit. The methods of all very early religions are necessarily magical, i.e. godless, but they are consecrated, made religious by their being practised for the common weal. The essence of magic is the *opus operatum*, the act effective in itself. Baptism and the consecration of the elements in the Eucharist are rites primarily magical, though much contaminated by theological sanction; they are religious because they are social, practised openly for the common weal. By this definition the Chaeronea rite is seen to be magical and hence atheistic, but though atheistic it is deeply religious. The Archon practises it at the Common Hearth for the whole township; the householder at home for his family. In both cases we are concerned with a group and a group function—the action is social.

The discovery of its social origin[1] is perhaps the greatest advance yet made in the scientific study of religion. The notion of social origin upsets so many modern individualistic convictions and prejudices that it is sure to meet with some hostility. The discovery has been a long slow process and was only made possible by recent scientific examination of religious phenomena among primitive peoples. The new and unexpected facts disclosed by this examination—facts which have bit by bit revolutionized our whole outlook—may conveniently be grouped under four heads:

    (1) Totem, Tabu and Exogamy.
    (2) Initiation Ceremonies.
    (3) The Medicine-Man and King-God.
    (4) The Fertility-Play or Year-Drama.

By a brief examination of these groups of facts it will become clear (1) that religion is a social factor and can only properly be studied in relation to social structure; (2) that the idea of a god is a bye-product arising out of rites and sanctities, a bye-product of high importance but non-essential; (3) that the function of religion is to conserve the common life physical and spiritual, this function being sometimes aided sometimes hindered by the idea of a god.

   [1] The discovery was first formulated by the genius of Emil Durkheim in his brief paper, "De la définition des phénomènes religieux," in the *Année Sociologique* of 1898. His theory has been since expanded in his *The Elementary Forms of the Religious Life*, English edition, by J. W. Swain.

(1) Totem, Tabu and Exogamy.

The word *totem*[1] means not plant or animal but simply family, group or tribe. It is important to grasp this clearly as the supposed kinship of man with various plants and animals is a fact so odd that it has arrested undue attention and tended to obscure the real significance of the totem. Besides the idea of family or group the word totem is also used for a family mark. Thus the primal notion of a totem is a group distinguished by a common label or badge. The totem animal is always a group of animals not an individual animal, the totem relation is always the relation of a group of men to a group of animals or plants, the primary gist of totemism is the *distinction of groups*.

How this distinction of groups came to be of such intense religious significance we shall see in a moment. For the present it is interesting to note that as the totem animal—the tribal animal—long precedes the animal god, so in Greek religion Moira-*partition*[2] preceded and overruled the whole Olympian system.

Totemism is then mainly and primarily an affirmation of group unity. Primitive man thinks or rather feels in terms of his group: the group is his universe. So much perhaps our latter-day parochialism or patriotism might teach us. Totems are not worshipped, they are not definite deities propitiated with prayer and sacrifice, but it is easy to see that from the focus of attention on the totem animal or plant they may be the stuff of which pagan divinity is made. The "making of a god" is a stage at which we have not yet arrived. It is enough to note for the present that the totem is the collective symbol, the badge of distinction, the representa-

---

[1] For the whole subject of Totemism see Dr Frazer's *Totemism*, 1887, and his *Totemism and Exogamy*, 4 vols., 1910; E. Durkheim, *The Elementary Forms of the Religious Life*; S. Freud, *Totem und Tabu*, 1913. Dr Frazer holds that exogamy arose independently of totemism and that totemism is the earlier of the two; he gives up the hope of discovering the origin of exogamy and believes he has caught the secret of totemism. Dr Durkheim holds that totemism and exogamy are inextricably intertwined: that the one cannot exist save as an unmeaning survival without the other. He stresses here as elsewhere the group aspect. Dr Freud adopts mainly the same position as Dr Durkheim, stressing and more fully explaining the *tabu* element. The view here expressed is based on Durkheim and Freud.

[2] For *Moira* in relation to social organization see F. M. Cornford, *From Religion to Philosophy*.

tion of a family or group unity as distinct from other unities, a totem marks out, separates, differentiates. That such a badge or mark may become an intense emotional focus is self-evident; we have only to think of the passionate devotion inspired to-day by the colours. Once chosen and set up, such a badge is an emotional focus but we are left with the further question, where was the need of such a badge, the vital necessity of distinction, separation. Primitive man has no *natural* need for social order, for division and classification; what made him invent a totem and elaborate its attendant irksome system of tabus? The need must have been intense, imperative, essential to the conservation of life. To find this need we must go back to the beginning of society.

Human society with all its civilization is based on the family, the "promiscuous herd" as starting point is a theorist's dream. This primal family consisted of an adult male, one or more females and their children. This same primal family is observable even among the higher quadrupeds. With gorillas one adult male only is observable in each band. So long as the children are young all is well, and if all the children were females no difficulty would arise. The father simply marries his daughters as he married their mother. There is no "natural" instinct of repulsion against incest. Primitive man has no hygienic conscience for the next generation. Indeed, be the stock healthy, no need for such conscience exists. It is when the young male offspring grow up to maturity that trouble begins. The single oldest or strongest dominant male is confronted by his own sons as rivals[1]. He may not, probably does not, know them to be his sons, knowledge of the fact of fatherhood is comparatively late, but they are young males, inevitable rivals. If he is to keep his wives to himself he must kill these rivals or expel them. His rule is—no other male to touch the females of his camp, the result—expulsion of adolescent sons, i.e. exogamy.

It seems an *impasse*. Perpetual reiterated expulsion of all the young forces of the family. In time it is true the young males may and do conquer, the old father grows old and weak, the sons band together and slay him, but it is only themselves to retell

---

[1] Andrew Lang, "The Family," in *Custom and Myth*, 1884, p. 245. Darwin, *Descent of Man*, II. 362.

the old hideous story of sexual jealousy. Advance in civilization is forbidden for cooperation is impossible.

But there were other forces at work. The mother counted for something, the young males were to her not merely as to their father, young males, they were sons. The higher quadrupeds have longer infancy and this would foster affection even in the father. The eldest son not very much younger than his father would have little chance, he would be surely killed or expelled, but the youngest born when his father's passions were ebbing might have better luck. Moreover man *is* a social animal and his brain is highly developed, he must have vaguely hungered after peace and consequent plenty, killing your sons would pall after a time. The next step, *the* crucial step, the beginning of all our morality was taken— man began to impose tabus, and thereby arrived at a sort of social contract.

Tabu is never an artificial strengthening of an instinctive repulsion, it cuts clean across individual desire. It is easy to see what was the nature of the first tabu. It was made in the interests of the Father. Weary at last of the expulsion and slaying of sons, conscious that the day would come when they would in turn slay or disable him, he made terms with them on the basis of a tabu. You may stay at home on condition that you do not touch my wives or at least certain of my wives, your mother and your sisters or some of them are to you tabu. And if tabu they must be marked as such, they must carry on their bodies a totem badge or mark of avoidance. This system of distinction once started branched out of course into endless complexities with which we are not concerned. The primal cardinal fact is that totemism consists in group distinction, that it functions through tabu and that it takes its rise in perhaps the strongest or at least the fiercest of human impulses in sex jealousy. Here, as so often elsewhere, the fabric of Church and State[1] rests on a basis of savage animal impulse, crossed by the dawnings of a social impulse.

The tabus of the primal family have left their traces in the curious survivals among savages known as Avoidance[2]. It seems

---

[1] See J. G. Frazer, *Psyche's Task*, passim.

[2] See J. J. Atkinson, *Primal Law*, 1903. The theory of the origin of exogamy in the jealousy of the Sire is due to Mr Atkinson, but he does not connect this with totemism.

odd and inexplicable to us that a brother may not speak to or
even see his sister. The arrangement is, among the houseless
nomads of Australia, inconvenient and to our thinking absolutely
senseless. But in the light of the primal tabu on all sisters it is
clear enough. The sister if she catch sight of her brother by accident in the bush is well advised to fall flat on her face.

Moreover, and this is an interesting point, we find the echo of
the old savage primal family in Greek mythology. Before Zeus
reigned there was an older dynasty—that of Kronos, and before
Kronos was Ouranos the Heaven, mated to Gaia the Earth. Ouranos
hated his children and slew them, but Kronos the *youngest* son
conspired against his father and emasculated him and reigned in
his stead. The story repeats itself in varying form from generation
to generation. Kronos in his turn devours his own children as fast
as they are born, knowing that he was fated to be deprived of his
kingdom by one of them. Rhea the mother devised a plan by
which she might save her *youngest born* Zeus, who reigned there-
after in his father's stead. In these stories it is the kingship that
is emphasized, but it is clear that behind lies the jealousy of the Sire.

This explanation of the totem as essentially a group badge
adopted to mark exclusions and facilitate tabus made necessary
by the Sire's jealousy clears up much that has long been mysterious.
The totem animal once chosen may as a rule not be killed and
eaten, but on certain solemn occasions by common consent he
is killed and he is eaten. From that solemn slaying is traceable all
the long series of sacrifices and sacraments. Just so the father—
for whom indeed the totem animal is in a sense surrogate—cannot
and may not be slain. But in the old family system, as we have
seen, by common consent and insurrection of the brothers he was
slain. This slaying, at first an inevitable outrage, may well have
crystallized into a custom. Whether the old Sire was ever eaten
by way of incorporating his exceptional powers may remain uncertain. But in the slaying of the father we have at least the germ
of the later sacrifice of the king-god.

Further, light is thrown by this explanation on the curious
attitude of mind towards the totem, which Freud[1] has called
Ambivalenz, the attitude that is of mingled attraction and repul-

---

[1] *Op. cit.*, the term was originated by Bleuler.

sion, desire and shrinking, which is the very gist and marrow of tabu. This *Ambivalenz* is characteristic of the feeling of the son to the father, and of all savages towards tabued objects. It is the attitude of obedience to a non-natural prohibition, the desire remaining while the prohibition holds. It disappears when the rationality of a prohibition is fully recognized, but it survives in diseased neurotic consciences charged with the atmosphere of repressed desire. Tabu is the first categorical imperative and is the parent of sanctity, that sanctity which long preceded divinity. Holiness has just this character of *Ambivalenz*; the thing that is *sacer* as Robertson Smith long ago recognized is impure as well as pure, a danger as well as a safeguard, it attracts and repels. Now-a-days we think of things holy as things divine, either gods themselves or things especially associated with divinity, but sanctity to primitive man meant something quite other, it meant the thing tabued, whether person or plant or animal, the tabu being imposed by the group protecting itself against the individual. Sin, sanctity, repentance, purification, all the notions we feel to be so intensely and characteristically religious took their rise at least in tabu.

Especially does this conjoint notion of tabu and totemism explain the sanctity of animals and plants and the rise of plant and animal gods. On any other showing it is not easy to understand why a man should worship the plant or animal which he can any time kill and eat. He might admire it, and feel curiosity as to its wondrous ways, he might if it were fierce and strong feel fear of it, but he would not feel that special blend of awe and attraction which we call worship. But given that an animal or plant has been chosen as a totem, all becomes simple. It may have been quite accidentally that the thing chosen was plant or animal. The choice was natural as man's attention is much engaged by plants and animals but it was not essential, as is shown by the fact that almost any natural object may become a totem, and even some objects that are artificial. Given then that an animal or plant is chosen as a totem, it becomes the sign manual of tabu, it is hedged round with prohibitions, it becomes a thing apart, marked by the group with sanctity, remote from daily use. It is not the plant or animal that is useful to him or that feeds him that the savage will tend to worship. It is the plant or animal tabued. From the tabued animal or plant to the sacred animal or plant and from the sacred to the divine the steps are easy.

Moreover plants and animals are of high, indeed the highest importance in totemistic rites. So high is this importance that it has led some observers to see in these plant and animal rites the actual origin of the sanctity of the totem. This we believe to be mistaken, sanctity arises primarily in tabu.

Turning to totemistic rites their object is clear enough. They are uniformly what we have called *impulsive* or inductive. Their object is to produce and enhance life, the multiplication of such totem plants and animals as are good for food. The ceremonies are known among some Australians as *Intichiuma*[1] and this name has become current. They are also known as *mbatgalkatiuma*, which means "to fecundate" or to "put in good condition." The Intichiuma are celebrated just before the rainy season. The rain is important because the savage has grasped the all important fact that life depends on moisture. This life-giving moisture will be sought and found in various ways according to physical conditions. In Egypt religious ceremonial will centre not on rain-making but on the Nile. In Greece we shall have rain-making ceremonies and the cult of springs and small rivers. In Australia as soon as the rains arrive, vegetation springs up as though by magic and animals multiply. It is the great religious season of the year.

The rites celebrated are mainly mimetic dances. All over the world, in the magico-religious stage, primitive man dances where we should pray or praise. This is inevitable though at first surprising. He cannot pray, he knows of no one to pray to. He must *act* directly—try to get what he wants by doing it. His dances are in the main, in so far as they are not merely the outlet of pent up emotion, *mimetic*. He does in pantomime what he wishes done. He wants to multiply his totem, so he imitates the actions of this totem—he jumps like a kangaroo, he screeches like a bat, he croaks like a frog, he imitates the birth of a Witchetty grub. Only a kangaroo man can cause kangaroos to multiply and though

---

[1] The best summary and analysis of the *Intichiuma* rites is found in Durkheim, *The Elementary Forms of the Religious Life*, p. 326, based of course on Spencer and Gillen and Strehlow's investigations.

he may not, save in solemn sacrament, eat kangaroo himself, he performs the kangaroo ceremonies that other totem groups may eat and they will do the like for him. Rain is often imitated and caused by the sprinkling of drops of blood or the shaking of white down to simulate clouds.

And here a point of great importance must be noted. These pantomimic rites have all one object, the promotion of life by means of food, but they are separable into two groups, the one purely imitative, just described, the other imitative but also commemorative. The one looks forward, the other back[1]. The commemorative rite looks back to the ancestors of the tribe and re-enacts their doings, it represents the mythical history of the tribe. The past is made to live again by means of a veritable dramatic representation. Now here the intent is manifestly not the direct impulsion of fertility but the strengthening of solidarity. So important however is the *indirect* action of this strengthening of solidarity that to omit the performance of the ancestor rites would inevitably bring bad luck. There could be no better instance of the intense religious importance of the group. No group can function with its full force unless it invokes tradition. Here in these commemorative ancestor rites we have the dawn of true religious notions of high importance, the idea of immortality, the idea of group immortality as preceding individual immortality, the idea of ancestor worship which springs straight out of ancestor commemoration and is a powerful factor in the making of the anthropomorphic god.

Totemism and tabu have given us in embryo our main religious conceptions, the ideas of sanctity, of sacrament, of sin, of sacrifice, of animal and plant worship, of immortality and ancestor worship. We have seen them emerge in close conjunction with social structure, and this no longer surprises us. If religious impulse be the impulse to the conservation and promotion of the group life, and that life depends for its conservation on some sort of social contract, the dependence of religion on social structure is inherent and

---

[1] For the detailed psychological analysis of rites both commemorative and anticipative, see J. E. Harrison, *Themis*, chapter II, "On the Dithyramb, the δρώμενον and the Drama," and more simply, *Ancient Art and Ritual*, chapter II, "Pantomime Dances."

essential. Rites not only procure the means of life but they are the means whereby the social group periodically reaffirms itself.

To watch the further development of these embryo notions we pass to our second head.

(2) INITIATION CEREMONIES.

Initiation ceremonies are but a specialized form of the fertility ceremonies described under the name Intichiuma. When the novices are initiated a series of ceremonies are performed before them which reproduce even in minute particulars the rites of the Intichiuma. The mechanism of the rites is often identical, but the initiation rites are marked off by two peculiarities which it is all important to note. These are (1) the initiation rite is into the tribe, it is of far wider import than the totem ceremony; (2) the initiation rite is concerned with the human element in the tribe, it has not for its direct object the fertilization of either animal or plant. Its object is, as the savage himself frequently says, "to make or manufacture a man."

The detailed ceremonies of initiation are variable and cannot be discussed here[1]. We can only emphasize the main gist of the rite and this has been well summed up in the formulary *rite de passage*, rite of transition from one stage to another. It has been ably observed[2] that all ceremonies concerned directly with the welfare of man have this transition character, ceremonies of birth, of puberty, of marriage and of death are all alike in mechanism, they all facilitate the passage from one state to another, they are all of expulsion and impulsion, they ward off the dangers of the transit and enhance its benefits. The *rite de passage* on which primitive man focussed his attention was emphatically the rite of puberty or maturity, his transit from childhood when he was a useless encumbrance to manhood when he took upon himself the two main duties of savage maturity, he became a warrior and a father, he defended the present generation and engendered the next.

[1] A collection convenient for the general reader will be found in Hutton Webster, *Secret Societies*, 1908, and see the article "Initiation," by Goblet d'Alviella in Hastings, *Encyclopaedia of Religion and Ethics*, and H. Schurtz, *Altersklassen und Männerbunde*, 1902.

[2] Van Gennep, *Rites de passage*, 1909.

The attention of explorers was at first drawn to initiation rites, mainly because of the horrible sufferings endured by the novices. These sufferings were in part tests of endurance such as are imposed now-a-days by boys when they initiate a new school-fellow. More important and indeed cardinal is the fact that in initiation ceremonies the death of the novice is almost always simulated and sometimes actually caused. This death is followed by a resurrection. All the various mummeries of death and resurrection[1], often bloody and disgusting enough, simulate and therefore to the savage mind stimulate the passage from the old life to the new. But the simulated death has another aim, distinctly social, that is to emphasize the solidarity of the tribe, only by his simulated death can the boy be brought into contact and made one with his ancestors. They it is who instruct him in the tribal secrets, the old men of the tribe who initiate him are often positively disguised as ancestors. Thus we see in Initiation as in the Intichiuma the two elements, commemoration of ancestors as well as magical mimesis.

Initiation, it will be remembered, is of the tribe not of the totem. In initiation the youth is brought into relation with a larger unit, and this larger unit is figured to him by a Great Spirit[2], a very near approach to what we call a god. If the totem replaces the old Sire so this Great Spirit replaces for the time his peculiar totem and is figured as the father of all the members of different totems who constitute the tribe. Thus among the Euahlayi the Great Spirit is called Baiame and in this tribe it is related that the various totems were only the names given to the different parts of Baiame's body and this is but a simple figurative way of saying that the Great Spirit is the synthesis of all the totems and consequently a sort of presentation of the idea or rather sentiment of tribal unity. These Great Spirits found among so many primitive peoples were, it was at first thought, mere borrowings from Christianity taken over from missionaries. But the fact that the Great Spirit is found uniformly not in totem rites but in tribal initiations shows clearly that the Great Spirit is the outcome and expression of a special social structure. He had his origin in those rites which it was his function to represent.

[1] Frazer, *Golden Bough*, xi. 225, "The Ritual of Death and Resurrection."
[2] Durkheim, *Elementary Forms*, p. 294 ff.

Initiation was to the savage *the* rite of paramount importance. Other *rites de passage* were performed at the other crises of a man's life but they all paled before the maturity rite. Birth was scarcely accounted an event for religious sanction, marriage followed as a corollary from initiation and death itself was a *rite de passage*, when the dead man passed over to join the dead members of his tribe in another world[1]. Moreover death itself is not a crisis so clearly marked as with us, a man dies socially when he ceases to be able to dance his tribal dances. The notion of death as an initiation has left manifest traces in Greek religion. That to die is to be initiated into the "Higher Mysteries" was to the Greek a literal fact. This initiation was consummated by a Sacred Marriage with the Earth Mother. Hence it is not surprising that as Artemidorus[2] observes: "if sick men dream of marriage it is a foreboding of death," for "all the accompaniments of marriage are exactly the same as those of death," and again, "marriage and death have universally been held by mankind to be 'fulfilments' (τέλη)." The Greek word for *initiation* (τελετή) tells its own tale, it means not entering in, but completion, accomplishment, fulfilment, its cognate (τέλειος) means "grown up." The great Eleusinian mysteries were primarily the rite of man's maturity side by side with rites to promote the maturity of earth's fruits[3].

Birth, puberty, marriage, death were to the savage and in large measure to the whole ancient world all crises of life to be attended by rites of initiation, *rites de passage*. He did not formulate their similarity but he felt it and expressed it by the similarity of rites; all were the occasion of rites of expulsion, to free life from evil, and even more of impulsion, to promote life's welfare. But before we pass to the next point we must emphasize the peculiar social structure out of which initiation rites sprang. We have left behind us the old family group with the dominant sire and even the totem group which succeeded it is less prominent. We have advanced to the tribe. The important social feature in tribal initiation is the band of young men confronted by the band of elder men, as initiators. We have an oligarchy rather than an

---

[1] R. Hertz, "La Représentation Collective de la Mort," in *Année Sociologique,* x. (1905–06) 88.

[2] *Oneirocr.* ii. 49 and 65; for the whole subject of the analogy of death and marriage rites, see J. C. Lawson, *Modern Greek Folk Lore,* 1910, p. 590.

[3] Hastings, *Encyclopaedia of Religion and Ethics,* "Initiation" (Greek).

autocracy. Moreover, whereas totem-rites focus on nutrition, initiation rites focus on sex.

It was long a puzzle in Greek religion why Dionysos should always be attended by a *thiasos*, a band of dancing revellers. Zeus and the other Olympian divinities had no such attendants. The question was only made more complex yet more pressing by the discovery that this band of revellers of young men dancing was closely paralleled in other cults. Greece had not only Satyrs, it had also Kouretes, Korybantes, Titanes, Seilenoi, Bacchoi, Rome had its dancing priests, its Salii, far-off India had its dancing Maruts, half daimon half man[1]. The riddle was read for Greece by the discovery in Crete of the Hymn to the Kouretes[2], a ritual hymn containing very early material; it is sung by a band of armed dancers and they invoke their leader, the Greatest Kouros, to come for the year and to leap for fields of fruit and for fleecy flocks and *for young citizens*. The Kouretes are the young men just come to maturity, just initiated into the fertility dance of their tribe; they invoke their leader as lord of moisture and life, or as they say, "Lord of all that is wet and gleaming." The band of initiate youths are the prototypes of all the Satyrs and Seilenoi, the Salii and Maruts of Europe and Asia, they too are the parents of the still surviving mummers and sword-dancers of village feasts[3].

The cult of the Kouretes was at home in Crete and the great central worship of the Mother goddess. In the bridal chamber ($\theta a\lambda \acute{a}\mu \epsilon v\mu a$) of Crete the young men, before they might win their earthly brides, were initiated to the Mountain Mother[4] and became symbolically her consorts or husbands. Marriage is *the* mystery *par excellence*. The ceremony was of prime importance as securing alike her fertility and theirs. Thus it will be seen that the Kouretes reflect a matrilinear social structure, the condition that naturally arises when parentage is precarious and often untraceable. Such a social structure focuses its attention on Mother and Child rather than on Father. The Child grows up into the young initiated man

[1] Hastings, *Encyclopaedia*, "Kouretes and Korybantes"; Leopold v. Schroeder, *Mysterium und Mimus im Rig-Veda*, 1908.

[2] J. E. Harrison, *Themis*, pp. 1–49.

[3] E. K. Chambers, *The Mediaeval Stage*, pp. 182–204.

[4] A. B. Cook, *Zeus*, 1913, p. 650; Hastings, *Encyclopaedia*, "Mountain Mother."

and the young initiated man becomes the consort of the perennial mother. The Kouretes in the Hymn tend the holy child and this is with magical intent, they marry that the land may be fertile, they tend the child that their own children may be nurtured. Then as the religious instinct develops they project from their own body a leader, a Greatest Kouros, to whom they hand over the functions they themselves performed. But this process will become more clear at a later stage in the argument. In like fashion the religious rites of the Satyrs centre round the Mother Semele, the Phrygo-Thracian Earth goddess, and in like fashion the Satyrs project from their band the arch-satyr Dionysos; the *thiasos* is before the god.

So far we have seen that the social factor which shaped and conditioned religious notions was the *group*, first the totem-group then the tribal-group. We have now to watch the emergence and development of the *individual* as social factor and to mark its influence on ritual and religious thinking. This brings us to our third stage.

(3) The Medicine-Man and King-God.

The old Byzantine scholar Tzetzes has bequeathed to a tardily thankful posterity this remarkable statement:

Zeuses the ancients used to call their kings.

He feels it to be noteworthy for, in slightly altered words, he repeats it six several times. Yet for eight centuries it lay, a neglected fossil. Scholars of course were conscious of a doctrine known as the "divine right of kings." They remembered that Dr Johnson was taken to Queen Anne, was touched by Queen Anne for scrofula. Virgil they knew tells how the mad and blasphemous Salmoneus King of Thessaly was blasted because he dared to counterfeit the thunder and lightning. But it occurred to no one[1] that Salmoneus *qua* king was doing his regular business, that in the eyes of his people he *was* Zeus and *had* to make the weather.

What then is this divinity that "doth hedge a king"? How could the notion arise when kings are born and die and sleep and wake and eat and drink like the rest of us? The answer is found

---

[1] Attention was, I believe, first called to the passage in Tzetzes and the true explanation given by Mr A. B. Cook, *Classical Review*, 1903–1904.

in the origin of the kingship. How did kings come to be? The answer may seem obvious. The king is the strongest man of the tribe. This simple solution like so many obvious answers is wrong or at least not wholly right. It is the answer of what Dr Frazer[1] calls the "armchair philosopher with his feet on the fender," and not of the man who seeks his facts among the savages of to-day in Uganda, in Malay, in Central Australia, in Japan. Here and there a strong man by sheer physical force may enjoy a certain dominance, but mere strength will not suffice for a king, the savage is ruled rather by hope and fear than force, the king must have magic behind him. The personality of king and god alike develop out of the head medicine-man, and the business of the head medicine-man as we have seen is to be food-producer and rain-maker. The king then is the head medicine-man and, delightful corollary, his fetishes are the regalia, the possession of which, as for example among the Southern Celebes, *carries with it the right to the throne.* These regalia may be almost anything, a weapon, a bit of stone or wood, or queer shaped fruit, best of all *a bit of the body of a former king* like the relic of a saint.

In the Australian ceremonies of the Intichiuma, it will be remembered, the ancestors of the tribe were commemorated in pantomime. When the magical functions of the tribe are focused on one individual, the king, the ancestors are not forgotten. Among the Matabeles of South Africa[2] the king each year offers sacrifices at the festival of the new fruits which ends the annual tribal dances. On these occasions "*he prays to the spirits of his forefathers and to his own spirit.*" There is, it will be noted, no god involved, only the forefathers and himself the head medicine-man. In Southern Nigeria[3] one of the petty kings gave this account of himself and certainly he does not figure as "the strong man." "The whole town forced me to be head chief. They hanged the big juju (or fetish of the buffalo's horns) round my neck.....It is an old custom that the head-chief here shall never leave his compound. I have been shut up ten years, but being an old man I don't miss my freedom. I am the oldest man of the town and they

---

[1] My instances are all taken from Dr Frazer's *Lectures on the Early History of the Kingship,* 1905.

[2] Frazer, *op. cit.* p. 32.   [3] *Op. cit.* p. 118.

keep me here to look after the jujus and to conduct the rites
celebrated when women are about to give birth to children, and
other ceremonies of the same kind. By the observance and performance of these ceremonies I bring game to the hunter, cause
the young crop to be good, bring fish to the fisherman, and make
rain to fall. So they bring me meat, yams, fish. To make rain,
I drink water and squirt it out and pray to our big deities. If I
were to go outside this compound I should fall down dead on
returning to the hut. My wives cut my hair and nails and take
great care of the parings." Here the mention of the "big deities"
shows the dawn of the priestly go-between, but otherwise we have
just an old medicine-man, a centre of tribal sanctities.

These puppet kings though intensely divine are really rather
the slaves and tools of their people than their lords. This is shown
not only by their tedious trammelled lives hedged round by tabus
but in poignant fashion by their tragic deaths[1]. In his life he must
be what the Greeks called ἀμύμων, "blameless," that is flawless
in his physical life, because on his integrity and vitality depended
the life of his people and of all those natural things on which that
people's life depended. Fertility, flocks and herds, rain and sunshine depended on the king's life, if that life waned pestilence and
famine would certainly ensue. So by inexorable savage logic, the
king must never be allowed to grow enfeebled, he must, if needs
be, be put to death to save his life, Sometimes the king himself
is put to death by common consent of the tribe like the ancient
Sire, sometimes by proxy it is the king's son, sometimes a sacred
beast in whom the king is incarnate—survival of the totem, sometimes a chance stranger regarded as a kind of divine apparition,
sometimes merely a representative puppet. In some form or
another "it is expedient that one man shall die for the people"
and to be efficacious that man must be sacred, divine. Hence all the
manifold rites of death and burial of the gods which puzzled the
pious Plutarch[2] so sadly. Rites of "tearing to pieces," "resurrections," "regenerations," of "deaths and dismemberments," rites
which he knew took place not only in Egypt or Asia Minor but
in connection with his own god Dionysos. Plutarch would fain

---

[1] Frazer, *Golden Bough*, III. "The Dying God."
[2] *De Iside et Osiride*, 69–71.

think of his gods as Olympians, serene, beneficent, immortal, but being an honest man he cannot blink facts. He is like some kindly Anglican called upon suddenly on Ash Wednesday to curse his neighbours instead of blessing them.

The sanctity of the king-god's life, the supreme importance of conserving it, survives in the ritual of the Roman Church to-day, in the custom of burning Incense. Ask a Roman priest, or indeed any educated person, what is the significance of Incense[1]. He will tell you it is part of the regular ritual of the Mass, that it is a symbol of purification, of consecration—that Incense mounts like prayer to heaven and, what not. All this Incense has come to mean, but the use of Incense dates from the time of the Pharaohs, and to the priest of Pharaoh's time Incense spelt something simpler and more substantial. The Egyptian wanted to keep his king alive. The king had been his benefactor during life, why lose his benefactions by death? To keep the king alive the Egyptian mummified the corpse, and also made portrait statues of exact and marvellous similitude. But something was wanting. The statue lacked the moisture, the juices of life, the aroma, the smell of the living man—a smell of which the Egyptian with his liberal use of unguents and perfumes was vividly conscious. To supply the deficiency of moisture he poured out libations, to give the aroma he burnt Incense and his custom spread well nigh over the whole civilized world.

It may seem at first sight to be of little consequence whether magical functions were distributed among a group of initiated men or focused in the "person of a single king." Possibly even the transition might seem a loss. For the dominance of a democratic body of full grown men we substitute a single autocrat. History has however shown everywhere that real freedom begins with the emergence of the gifted individual, the democracy of the whole tribe is but a democracy in name, it is really the tyranny of a gerontocracy, of the old men who initiate the young men and forcibly impose the tradition of the tribe. With the medicine-king arose a certain though very limited scope for the forces of personality and also, as the medicine-man was the depository of such experimental science as the tribe possessed, his elevation to the

[1] G. Elliot Smith, *The Evolution of the Dragon.* Manchester University Press.

kingship was in some sense the first beginning of "endowment" of research.

But for religion the momentous step taken by the institution of the kingship was that henceforward sanctities tended to become personalities. The notions of tabu and sanctity became incarnate in a person—the king as incarnate tabu and magic is undoubtedly the father of the pagan god. We shall later see that our modern notion of divinity, though owing much of its anthropomorphism to pagan gods, has also other roots. This notion that the sacred, the divine, was human-shaped is perhaps the most momentous step, for better for worse, that the religious imagination has ever taken. How such a step came to be taken, that is how the god developed out of the human king, will be best seen when we examine our last stage or stratum, the Fertility Play or Year Drama.

(4) THE FERTILITY PLAY OR YEAR DRAMA.

At Viza, the ancient Bizue in Thrace, some eight hours to the North of Salmydessus on the Black Sea, may still be seen[1] a folk-play which by its very simplicity and even baldness makes singularly clear its original magical intent. The masqueraders assemble early in the morning. They are two men wearing masks, goat-skin caps and bells, one of them sometimes differentiated by a blackened face, two boys disguised as girls, an old woman carrying a baby in a basket and a sort of chorus of gipsies and gendarmes. The masqueraders after the fashion of mummers in England and elsewhere go from house to house demanding food and money and singing songs of blessing on the generous house-holders. One of them carries a phallos with which he knocks at the doors. All the characters dance together, some brandishing drawn swords, and an obscene pantomime is acted on straw heaps in front of the house by two men, one disguised as a woman. Then follows a sort of preliminary act, the mock forging of a ploughshare by the "smith" and his wife, the yoking of the plough which is drawn round the village square and the sowing of seed.

Next comes the play proper. The old woman Babo comes in

[1] It was seen by Mr R. M. Dawkins in 1906; see "The Modern Carnival in Thrace and the Cult of Dionysos," *J.H.S.* XXVI. (1906) 191, and A. J. B. Wace, "North Greek Festivals," *B.S.A.* XVI. (1909–1910) 232.

with the baby in the *likno* or cradle-basket. She declares that "the baby is getting too big for the basket." The child has a huge appetite, demands food and drink and finally calls for a wife. One of the girls is then pursued by one of the men and brought to the child, now grown to maturity, as bride. At this point comes a notable interruption; before the wedding can take place, the second man comes in as antagonist to hinder the wedding. A fight ensues and ultimately the antagonist is shot down by the original bridegroom. The slayer traces a line round the supposed slain indicating a grave. He then pretends to flay the dead man. Meantime the other bride raises a loud lament and throws herself over the prostrate body. In the lament the slayer and the rest of the actors join. Then follows the parody of a Christian funeral. Suddenly the dead man comes to life, gets up and the play proper ends.

The play proper is followed by a plough ceremony similar to the plough prelude. This time the two brides are yoked to the plough and drag it twice round the village square. While the plough is being dragged chorus and spectators cry aloud: *May wheat be ten piastres the bushel! Rye, five piastres the basket! Barley, three piastres the bushel! Amen, O God, that the poor may eat! Yea, O God, that poor folk be filled!*

The intent of the whole ritual could not be clearer, it is a fertility drama "that the poor may eat." The central notion is the same as that of the rite at Chaeronea, "Out with Hunger, in with Health and Wealth," only the primary notion has become amplified and humanized, it has become a cycle of the life of man and the life of the year.

In that cycle two events are cardinal. The Fight (*agon*) and the Death swiftly followed by the Resurrection. The Fight in variant forms is world-wide and the Fight of Summer and Winter variously disguised, the Fight of the Old Year and the New, of Darkness and Light, the Fight of the Old King with the Young, of the Father with the Son, of the Hero with the Monster. The great Agon dwindles down into a Tug of War widely practised as a magical Fertility Rite.

The Death and Resurrection have the like magical intent, and here the essential rite is the Resurrection, the Death is but the necessary preliminary. Sometimes as in the rites of Tammuz and

Adonis[1] the lamentations over the death develop so portentously that they tend to obscure the rite of resurrection, but the rite is always there, witness the ritual hymn to Adonis; after the long lamentation comes:

> Where grass was not, there grass is eaten,
> Where water was not, water is drunk,
> Where cattle sheds are not, cattle sheds are built.

For those who see in these Year-Daimons or Vegetation Spirits only actual men, definite heroes who died and were buried in particular tombs, these resurrection rites present a serious difficulty; the actual historical hero does die and is buried, he does not rise again. If the rites of the folk-drama are purely commemorative then why introduce a resurrection ceremony? If these rites are, as we believe them to be[2], the utterance of man's ardent desire and the commemoration with magical intent of nature's annual doings, all is clear. The annual course of nature knows an annual resurrection and on its happening all man's life and prosperity depend.

Of recent years research over the most widespread areas has brought to light in very singular and convincing fashion the tenacity and vitality of the Folk-Play or Fertility Drama[3]. It survives not only in children's games and peasant festivals but in the forms or moulds that it has lent to literature. Among the Rig-Veda hymns for example it has been shown[4] that certain dialogue poems go back undoubtedly to a primitive form of ritual drama, the intent here, as elsewhere, being purely magical, the stimulation of powers of fertility in man and cattle, or the letting loose for the like purpose of the powers of rain and moisture of springs and rivers. Behind the literary hymn form lie the fertility dances of the armed daimons, the Salii, the Maruts of ancient India.

More familiar and perhaps to us more convincing is the fact that Greek Tragedy owes to this Fertility Drama not indeed its material but the form in which that material is cast. After a detailed examination of the plays and fragments Professor

[1] Langdon, *Tammuz and Ishtar*, p. 23.

[2] We do not for a moment deny that the rites often and indeed usually crystallize about an historical kernel as e.g. in the Christian religion

[3] For the whole subject see E. K. Chambers, *The Mediaeval Stage*, for May Games, Sword Dances and Mummers' Play, vol. I. pp. 160–227. Clarendon Press, 1903.

[4] Leopold von Schroeder, *Mysterium und Mimus im Rig-Veda*. Leipzig, 1908.

Murray[1] has come to the conclusion—and few now gainsay him—
that while the contents of the plots come from the heroic saga the
ritual forms in which that content is cast derive straight from
the *dromena* the doings of the Year-Daimon. Such forms are the
Prologue, the Agon, the Pathos, the Messenger's Speech, the Threnos or Lamentation, the Anagnorisis or Recognition and the final
Theophany. Certain of these forms, notably the Agon, survive
in the Sacred Games of the Greeks, but here for the most part
in shadowy fashion since they are well nigh submerged by a
growing athleticism. Tragedy which took its plots, its content
from the heroic saga, from the lives and struggles of individual
heroes, ended in death, because in this world the human individual
knows no resurrection. Comedy[2] is nearer to the original folk-
play and finds its consummation in a revel and a marriage.

Still more strange is it to find the ritual mould surviving even
in the plays of Shakespeare[3]. The Hamlet-saga like the Orestes-
saga has behind it the ancient and world-wide battle of Summer
and Winter, of the Old King and the New, of Life and Death, of
Fertility and Barrenness; behind the tragic fooling, as behind the
Old King Oedipus is the figure of the scapegoat, the whole tragic
katharsis rests on the expulsion of evil in the ritual of the spring—
Renouveau. The examination of the elder Eddic poems[4] shows
that the theory of their origin in primitive ritual drama correlates
a number of facts which else appear meaningless and unrelated.
Finally and perhaps most strangely of all it has recently been
shown[5] that the legend of the Holy Grail has a like ritual foundation. In the Grail literature "we possess a unique example of the
restatement of an ancient and august Ritual in terms of imperishable Romance."

The question of the influence of folk-plays and fertility dramas
on various forms of literature has now long passed beyond the

[1] "Excursus on the Ritual Forms preserved in Greek Tragedy," in *Themis*,
p. 341.

[2] F. M. Cornford, *The Origin of Attic Comedy*, 1914, and "The Origin of the
Olympic Games," being chapter VII of *Themis*.

[3] *Hamlet and Orestes*. The Annual Shakespeare Lecture before the British
Academy, 1914. Gilbert Murray.

[4] Bertha S. Phillpotts, *The Elder Edda and Ancient Scandinavian Drama*,
p. 198. Cambridge University Press, 1920.

[5] Jessie L. Weston, *From Ritual to Romance*. Cambridge University Press,
1920.

region of conjecture. It is firmly based on fact and widely accepted. It would be a delight to follow it into further fields[1] but the task before us now is quite other. We have to note not the evolution of literature but the primitive beginnings of theology, to mark how the god rose out of the rite.

The ritual dance then is dead, but its ghost still lives on in Seville Cathedral[2] and wakes to a feeble fluttering life three times a year. At the Festival of Corpus Christi, during the Octave of the Immaculate Conception and during the three days of Carnival (when I had the good fortune to see it) the ritual dance is danced in the Holy of Holies behind the great gold grille immediately in front of the High Altar. It is danced by the so-called Seises or groups of choristers. Their number has now dwindled to two groups of five.

This dance of the Seises has been to the Church the cause of no small embarrassment and she has frequently but so far vainly sought to abolish it. She admits that its origin is "perdue dans la nuit des temps." It is frankly pagan and we can scarcely avoid the conjecture that it took its origin in the dances of the Kouretes in Crete in honour of the Mother and the Son. At Carnival, when I saw it, the dance took place after Vespers. The song with which the dance was accompanied was a prayer to the Sun, but it was to the setting, not as with the Kouretes the rising Sun. It was a prayer for light and healing. The dance is now attenuated to a single formal step. It is decorous even prim in character. But the fading light, the wondrous setting, above all, the harsh plangent Spanish voices of the boy singers are strangely moving. It is a sight once seen never forgotten. Great Pan is dead but his ghost still dances.

[1] I would here record my conviction which I hope to establish in another connection that the widespread legend, Don Juan, arose from a fertility ritual. As a similar survival may be noted the Passion play of Hasan and Husain, still annually enacted in Persia and India. Taking its rise undoubtedly in a historical fact, it is cast in the form of a ritual drama.

[2] All that is known of the history of this strange survival is set down by Don Simón de la Rosa y Lopez in his *Los Seises de la Catedral de Sevilla*, 1904. The modern music which now accompanies the dance is published in *Baile de Seises en la Catedral de Sevilla*, para piano con letra por D. Hilarion Eslava, Sevilla.

II

PRIMITIVE THEOLOGY

"God is my desire." Tolstoi.

In all the primitive ritual so far examined, in the rites of Totemism, of Initiation Ceremonies, the King-God and the Fertility Drama, one surprising fact stands out clean and clear; we have nothing that we in our modern sense of the words could call the worship of a god—of sanctity we have abundance, of divinity nothing. Yet all the while if we examine the matter closely there are present elements which must and did go to the making of a god. Only it is important to grasp at the outset firmly this fact, that it is possible to have a living and vigorous religion without a theology.

Man, the psychologists tell us, is essentially an image-maker[1]. He cannot perform the simplest operation without forming of it some sort of correlative idea. It has been much disputed whether the myth arises out of the rite or the rite out of the myth, whether a man thinks something because he does it or does it because he thinks it. As a matter of fact the two operations arose together and are practically inseparable. An animal first perceives, perception immediately sets up reaction, that reaction is two-fold, perception sets up action in the body, representation in the mind. A rite is not of course the same as a simple action. A rite is—it must never be forgotten—an action *re*done (commemorative) or *pre*done (anticipatory and magical). There is therefore always in a rite a certain tension either of remembrance or anticipation and this tension emphasizes the emotion and leads on to representation[2].

It is moreover, psychology tells us, mainly from delayed reactions that representation springs. In animals who act from what we call instinct action follows immediately or at least swiftly on perception, but in man where the nervous system is more complex perception is not immediately transformed into action, there

[1] For the analysis of magic and its dependence on 'free ideas' see my *Alpha and Omega*, pp. 187–195.

[2] I have elsewhere analysed the psychology of the δρώμενον or rite. See *Themis*, pp. 42–49, and my *Ancient Art and Ritual*, in the Home University Library, pp. 35–44.

is an interval for choice between several possible courses. Perception is pent up and, helped by emotion, becomes conscious representation. In this momentary halt between perception and reaction all our images, ideas, in fact our whole mental life, is built up. If we were a mass of well combined instincts, that is if the cycle of perception and action were instantly fulfilled, we should have no representation and hence no art and no theology. In fact in a word religious presentation, mythology or theology, as we like to call it, springs like ritual from arrested, unsatisfied desire[1]. We figure to ourselves what we want, we create an image and that image is our god.

A god so projected *is* part of the worshipper and is felt and realized as such; divinity has not yet separated off from humanity. The dancer in the sacred rite cannot be said to worship his god, he lives him, experiences him. The worshipper at this stage might communicate with his god, he would not offer him sacrificial gifts or prayer. The question arises, by what process did severance take place? We cannot answer with certainty, but two points suggest themselves. The process of personification led to severance and personification was undoubtedly helped by two things: (1) the existence of a leader to the band of worshippers, (2) the making of puppets and images.

Collective group-emotion is strong, but, dominant though it be, it might never be strong enough to induce personification but for a nucleus of actual fact. The band of dancers has a leader, that leader is in a sense separate and about him emotion focuses. Once elected as representative spokesman and chief-dancer, he is in a sense insulated; the rest of the band regard him with contemplation and some incipient awe, he is sacred and on the way to become separately divine. He is what the Greeks called a δαιμόνων ἀγούμενος, *leader of daimons*, and not far from being the accomplished *theos* or god. In this matter we are on safe ground for in the famous *Hymn of the Kouretes* Zeus himself as chief dancer is addressed as Greatest Kouros or Young Man, head of the initiate band[2].

---

[1] This remains equally true if, with the new psychological school of "Behaviourists," we regard the primitive element in desire as an impulse away from the actual rather than an attraction towards the ideal. See Bertrand Russell, *Analysis of Mind*, p. 68.

[2] See *Themis*, pp. 30–49.

The seasonal character of all these rites helped on the process of personification that led to severance. A perception that is *recurrent* is apt to lead on to a *conception*. The plural generates the abstract. The recurrent May-Kings and Jack-o'-the-Greens and Deaths get a kind of permanent separate life of their own and become separate beings. In this way they help to beget a kind of daimon or spirit; from being annual they became a sort of perennial though not yet immortal god. We are apt to think and speak of the King of the May or the Death as "personifying the Spirit of Vegetation" or of Death. But primitive man does not first conceive an abstraction and then embody it. The process is the reverse. He first *per*ceives the actual leader and then helped by frequent repetitions *con*ceives a daimon of the dance.

There is another practical help to the determination and stability of his image. We find in many rites an actual puppet or animal refashioned or rechosen from year to year. The puppet or animal is a nucleus, a focus for emotions and floating conceptions. If the puppet be a human doll the daimon will take human form, if an animal the god will be theriomorphic. Out of the puppet arose the idol and to the idol certainly among the Greeks the gods owe much of the beauty and the fixity of their forms. Moreover the puppet necessarily fosters the notion of separateness. You may identify yourself with the leader of the band, the common dance and song compel that, but, though the puppet is the focus of your emotion, you know it is *not* you, you are outside it, you contemplate it and you may ultimately worship it. "Le dieu c'est le désir extériorisé, personnifié"[1].

This analysis of the making of a god lends to our outlook on religion generally a singular unity and clarity. Primitive ritual we saw concerned itself with the conservation and furtherance of life, with the nurture of the individual and the reproduction of the race. It was the expression in action of the will to live, the "desire to have life and to have it more abundantly." What ritual expresses in action theology utters in concomitant representation, the gods are images of desire. Religion then in these its two aspects is no longer an attitude towards the unseen and unknown but an emotion towards the known and experienced; it is the

[1] E. Doutté, *Magie et Religion*, 1909, p. 601.

offspring not of fear but of desire, the gods are human will and passion incarnate. It is only when the god is separated from the rite that he dies down into a sterile, immobile perfection[1].

The daimon is born of the rite and with the rite which begat him he is doomed. The gradual dwindling and death of the rite is inevitable. Magic is found again and again to be a failure. It does not bring the expected help and bit by bit it is discredited. According to Dr Frazer it is out of this discrediting of magic that religion is born. Finding himself helpless in the face of natural powers man tries to pull the strings of higher powers and so obtain control. He imagines gods and tries to influence them by prayer and sacrifice. More recent psychology would state the case otherwise. The rite fails but the daimon projected from the rite remains. The presentation once made still holds the imagination. But because of the failure of the rite the presentation is as it were cut loose. Out of this desolate, dehumanized daimon bit by bit develops the god. He is segregated aloof from the worshipper, but he is made in the image of that worshipper, so must be approached by human means, known by experience to be valid with other human beings, and such are prayer, praise and sacrifice.

This separation of god from worshipper, this segregation of the image from the imagination that begot it, is manifestly a late and somewhat artificial stage, but in most religions it develops into a doctrine and even hardens into something of a dogma. Man utterly forgets that his gods are man-begotten and he stresses the gulf that separates him from his own image and presentation. This is very notable in Greek religion. The Greeks being a people of high imaginative power are at the mercy of their own imaginations. Pindar is instant in stressing the gulf that separates humanity from divinity. To seek to become even *like* the gods to him as a Greek savoured of insolence. "Strive not thou to become a god"[2]. "Desire not thou soul of mine, life of the immortals"[3]. And yet oddly enough the old reality and actuality even in Greek religion again and again crops up. Man hungers to be one again with the image he has himself made. The old kinship pulls at

---

[1] See *Themis*, chapter x. "The Olympians."
[2] Pind. *Ol.* v. 58.   [3] Pind. *Pyth.* III. 59.

him. So in the mystery religions the goal is always reunion with the divine. To the initiate it is said at last: "Thou art become God from Man"[1]. Nothing short of this contents him.

At first it would seem as if this stage of religion in which the image of the god is completely projected and segregated, a stage which for convenience sake we may call *Olympianism*[2], is, even if inevitable, a set back. These projected "Olympians" though they are ideals are by no means ideal; they reflect the passions of their worshippers and not infrequently lag behind them in morality. Jahweh is even more unbridled, licentious, vengeful than his people. The average Athenian would have been ashamed to emulate the amours of Zeus. Moreover the fact that these Olympians are completely segregated, that they are the vehicles of all sorts of primitive tabus and sanctities, even the detail that they are lodged in separate and sacred houses, removes them from all chance of wholesome criticism: "Shall not the Judge of all the world do right?"

What then is the biological function of this theology? Does it in any way serve the purposes of life?

Recent psychology is ready with an answer simple and illuminating. In this way.

We recognize now-a-days two types of thinking. The first which Jung[3] calls "directed thinking" is what we normally mean by thinking. It "imitates reality and seeks to direct it." It is exhausting and is the sort of thinking employed in all scientific research; it looks for adaptations and creates innovations. With that type of thought, which is comparatively late in development, though in embryo it may have existed from the outset, we have little to do in religion.

The second kind of thought is what is called "dream or phantasy-thinking." It turns away from reality and sets free subjective wishes. In regard to adaptation, because of its neglect of reality, it is wholly unproductive. Giving free rein to impulse as it does, it is not exhausting. Freud calls this sort of mind-functioning the "pleasure and pain principle," it is ontogenetically older than

---

[1] Orphic Gold Tablet. See *Prolegomena*, p. 663.

[2] For a detailed analysis of *Olympianism* and its contrast with daimon-worship see two chapters, ix. and x., in *Themis*, "From Daimon to Olympian" and "The Olympians."

[3] *Psychology of the Unconscious*, translated by B. M. Hinkle, 1919.

directed thinking, it is typified by the mental operations of children and savages and by those of adults in their dreams, reveries and mental disorders.

It is from this early infantile type of dream or phantasy-thinking engendered by the fertility rite that primitive theology and mythology spring. They do not seek adaptation to fact, they turn away from reality and utter unfulfilled desire. "The gods *are* libido," says Jung boldly. If we may be allowed to substitute for the word *libido* with its offensive and misleading connotations some such term as "vital impulse," Jung's proposition may be accepted of all the primitive divinities[1]. We imagine what we lack, the "dying resurrected gods and heroes are but the projected hopes and fears of humanity." The older mind still buried in all of us, the mind of dream-fantasies is, and always has been, incessantly weaving dream-images of imaginary wish fulfilment. The soul in self-defence, unable as yet to adapt itself to its environment, finding that Fate withholds satisfaction in the visible world, would fain

> —grasp this sorry scheme of things entire
> And having shattered it to bits
> Remould it nearer to the heart's desire.

And the imaged agent of this remoulding is the god, "our own vast image, glory crowned."

In like manner arises the myth. The myth is not an attempted explanation of either facts or rites. Its origin is not in "directed thinking," it is not rationalization. The myth is a fragment of the soul life, the dream-thinking of the people, as the dream is the myth of the individual[2]. As Freud says, "it is probable that myths correspond to the distorted residue of the wish phantasies of whole nations, the secularized dreams of young humanity." Mythical tradition it would seem does not set forth any actual account of old events—that is the function of legend—but rather myth acts in such a way that it always reveals a wish-thought common to humanity and constantly rejuvenated.

What then is the biological function of theology and myth?

We hear much now-a-days of the danger of "suppressed com-

---

[1] In every divinity two factors are observable (1) the "vital impulse" common to all natures, (2) the projection of human desire.

[2] See W. H. R. Rivers, "Dreams and Primitive Culture" in *Bulletin of John Rylands Library, Manchester*, vol IV. 3 and 4, p. 387.

plexes." It is indeed in the discovery of the danger of these complexes and the methods of their cure that the main originality of the Freudian school consists. Man finds himself in inevitable conflict with some and often many elements of his environment; he shirks the conflict. Just because it is harassing and depressing he forcibly drives it out of his conscious life. But his unconscious life is beyond his control. Into that unconscious stratum the conflict sinks and lives there an uninterrupted life. Now the function of religion is to prevent, to render needless just this suppression of conflict. Man has made for himself representations of beings stronger and more splendid than himself, he has lost all sense that they are really projections of his own desire and to these beings he hands over his conflict, he no longer needs to banish the conflict into the unconscious but gods will see to it and fight on his side: "God is our refuge and strength," "Casting all your care upon Him for He careth for you." The function of theology is to keep the conflict that would be submerged in the sphere of the conscious and prevent its development into a mischievous subliminal complex. Theology thus is seen to have high biological value. Probably but for its aid man long before he developed sufficient reason to adapt himself to his environment must have gone under.

It will readily be seen that for this purpose of refuge a god of the Olympian type serves best. A god of the daimon type is too near, too intimate for relief. The more completely segregated is the god the better he serves as safety valve. Modern psychology has in truth dived deep into the "ocean of insanity upon which the little barque of human reason insecurely floats"[1], and knowing this insecurity and this frailty modern psychology teaches us to be careful how we lightly tamper with the faiths of others, how we try to rid a man of what may seem to us a burden unbearable but may be to him an incalculable solace and relief. And further the new psychology sets theology in a new and kinder light. Those of us who are free-thinkers used to think of it rationalistically as a bundle of dead errors, or at best as a subject dead and dry. But conceive of it in this new light and theology becomes a subject

---

[1] Bertrand Russell, *The practice and theory of Bolshevism*, p. 127.

of passionate and absorbing interest, it is the science of the images of human desire, impulse, aspiration.

Our consideration of primitive theology has then led to the same conclusion as our consideration of primitive ritual. They are in fact but two faces or modes of the same impulse—the impulse to the conservation of life. Personification, theology is but a natural, inevitable utterance of human desire. As Shakespeare had it long ago

> Such tricks hath strong imagination,
> That, if it would but apprehend some joy,
> It comprehends some bringer of that joy.

It is not surprising therefore that recent writers on religion should tend to define religion itself in terms no longer of knowledge and belief but in terms of life. Thus in *The Tree of Life*[1] Ernest Crawley writes, the permanent source of religion is "the instructive affirmation of life," and again, "the primary function of religion is to affirm and consecrate life." Religion "consecrates also the means of life....it surrounds with an insulation of taboo those critical moments and periods in which the sources of life are in danger—birth, puberty, marriage, sickness and death." God is in very literal truth the Desire of the Nations[2]. "In its widest sense," says a recent American writer[3], "religion means for any species that degree of interest that it can experience in what makes for its own continuity," and more explicitly: "Religion is the greatest thing in the world of living men. *Twentieth century religion is an enlightened consciousness of the impulse that makes for species continuity, and an intelligent concern for all the values that minister to this end.*" How far such a statement is adequate we have now to consider.

---

[1] Pp. 258 and 270.

[2] I do not propose here even to resume my discussion of *mana* in *Themis*, pp. 65–69, and *Alpha and Omega*, pp. 167–173. It is sufficiently obvious that Freud's *libido* and primitive *mana* are roughly commensurate. To primitive man the stuff of the world is neither mental nor material but—as to the new psychologists—a neutral stuff or force out of which both are compounded. See Bertrand Russell, *Analysis of Mind*, passim—a book which only appeared when these sheets were in proof.

[3] Orlando O. Norris in "What is Religion," from *The American Schoolmaster*, Jan. 1919. Ypsilanti, Michigan.

III

THE RELIGION OF TO-DAY[1]

VIA CRUCIS, VIA LUCIS

PRIMITIVE RITUAL, the ritual of Totemism, of King-Gods, of Initiation Ceremonies, of Fertility Dramas, is dead to-day or lingers on only among remote savages and in obscure country haunts. It has been driven out inch by inch by science, by "directed" as opposed to phantasy thinking. The ritual even of sacrifice that once played so large a part in man's life is dead and even the custom of prayer for material goods languishes. In like fashion primitive divinities, daimons of the year, have died with the rites that begot them, and divinities of the "Olympian" type are losing their hold. They are seen for what they are, *objets d'art*, creations of man's imagination, they no longer are incumbent on man's life, imposing an obligation of obedience; as ideals they may command adoration, they can no longer compel worship[2]. Jahweh is seen to be a projection of Hebrew desire and takes his place side by side with Zeus, Poseidon and Apollo. Is this then the end? Is our twentieth century religion only an "enlightened consciousness of the impulse that makes for species continuity," and as such is it best rechristened Science?

The essence of Modernism the Pope himself has told us is Immanence, and the statement is instructive. Immanence is of course no new thing, it is as old as S. Augustine[3]. "I have gone astray," he says, "like a Sheep that was lost, seeking thee with great anxiety without, when yet thou art within, and dwelleth in my soul, if it desire thy presence. I wandered about the Villages and Streets of the City of this world, enquiring for thee everywhere, and found thee not: because I expected to meet that abroad which all the while I had at home....." And thus, after consulting the creatures abroad, "I came home at last, descended

[1] Some portion of this chapter was read before the Society of 'Heretics' on Feb. 27, 1921.

[2] For this distinction between art and religion, see my *Ancient Art and Ritual*, p. 227.

[3] *Meditations*, trans. Stanhope, 1704, p. 224.

into myself," and at last, "Thanks to that light, which discovered thee to Me and Me to myself. For in finding and in knowing myself I find and know thee." There lives no mystic who has not experienced Immanence, and assuredly to S. Augustine the City of God is the City of Mansoul. So now-a-days God is no longer envisaged as external, as Creator, King, Judge, Ruler, Lawgiver, or even as Father and Saviour, nor even as the "Friend behind phenomena," He has gone inward, He has become the "undying human memory, the increasing human will." Henceforth the Kingdom of God is within us[1].

For the new Immanentist, creeds have become all but insignificant, they are to him not living expressions of truth apprehended but ancient barriers, dams artificially built to stem the inrush of living waters. The whole centre of gravity has in fact shifted from authority to experience. The new Immanence is nearer akin to the old daimon-dance than to any ordered Olympian ritual of prayer and sacrifice. It is very near to that primal mystery, the impulse of life, which it was the function of primitive religion to conserve. Are we then to accept this solution that the Immanent God is nothing but the mystery of the whole of things and that the function of modern religion is the realization of self within the limits of the community? And if so why seek for god rather within the limits of the human self than in external nature? The answer is that only there can we find him. In the natural world we find mystery enough, but also laws appealing to our minds, in the biological world we find a law which is eternal change, in the world of the human spirit alone we find the functions of value and choice and these functions are religious. Primitive religion aimed at the impulsion and conservation of life; the religion of to-day aims at the bettering of life, by the exercise of the function of choice and the practice of asceticism. After this fashion.

The core and essence of religion to-day is the practice of asceticism. Concerned as we have been hitherto with religion as the impulsion of life this may seem almost a paradox; it is really a very simple and obvious truth. Physical life once secured by civilization and the general advance of science, religion turns not

---

[1] See J. E. Harrison, *Rationalism and Reaction*, Conway Memorial Lecture, 1919, p. 19.

to the impulsion of life but to its betterment, and the betterment of life involves asceticism—the expulsion of evil. And be it remembered asceticism as we have already seen lies at the very basis of primitive religion in the form of tabu. Tabu in primitive days was imposed by the group in the interests of the group[1], tabu to-day in the form of asceticism is imposed by the individual in the interests of his own spiritual life, of what we call his soul.

Perhaps it needed a Russian philosopher writing in the Russian tongue to see this simple truth and get at the true biological function of asceticism, for language always thinks ahead of conscious ratiocination. The Russians have two ways of making the simple statement, "I am ashamed." They say either "to me is shame," literally, "to me is cold shuddering," or "to me is consciousness"[2], "I am conscious." To the Russian and to the greatest of their philosophers, Solovióv, shame is the sign manual of human consciousness and shame issues in asceticism. The normal animal save where artificialized by man knows no shame. Bodily facts, whether of nutrition or sex, have for him no embarrassment. Of such facts man is and perennially has been ashamed, not because they are *morally* wrong, i.e. non-social—they are in fact highly social and necessary—but simply because they are of his animal body, they are what S. Paul calls "carnal." Shame is to man at once his means of salvation and his high prerogative.

This new religion, this bettering of life, involves conflict. It is the setting of the will towards what Bergson calls the "ascending wave" of the *élan vital* against the descending wave which he calls matter. We belong in part to that descending wave, hence the conflict, its pull is always upon us even to the rending of flesh and spirit. The conflict cannot be avoided. It belongs to the conscious part of us. Psycho-analysis has its work to do. But,

[1] The social character of religion has been well brought out and possibly somewhat over-emphasized in a recent book by George Willis Cooke, *The Social Evolution of Religion*. Boston, 1920.

[2] МНѢ СТЫДНО or МНѢ СОВѢСТНО. A good general account of Solovióv's life and philosophy which have had immense influence in Russia will be found in J. B. Séverac, *Vladimir Solovióv*, in the series *Grands philosophes français et étrangers*, published by Louis Michaud. One important work appears in English under the title of *The Justification of the Good*, translated by Natalie A. Duddington. Constable.

when all your suppressed complexes have been dragged to light and all your subconscious dunghill is spaded out in front of you, your conscious self has still to choose the higher and refuse the lower. It is useless to deny like a Christian Scientist the fact that evil, i.e. the lesser good, exists—we must frankly face its existence and refuse participation.

But why should the flesh be shameful? This is the cardinal question. Simply because there is in man something else which is rarer, finer, what we call "better," than the flesh—that is the spirit. Simply because in the eternal nature of things *the better is the enemy of the good*, the better is ashamed of the good. Simply because we are, as human beings, conscious of a scale of values, a lower and a higher, a better and a worse. This scale of values we find not in external nature but in our own souls, and in our own souls henceforth is our religion—our conduct towards others is matter for our morality. Asceticism is the setting out of the soul towards the higher value. Religion means to us now, at least to me, not cosmology, not a story told to account for how things are, not ritual or theology, the various projections of our own unsatisfied desire; religion means a way of life possible because we are not only animals but human animals; it means the sense that you and I are good but that we can and mean to be better, and that in order to be better we will if need be—and need is—practise asceticism, suffer sharp pain and desolation in the death, the crucifixion of animal desires. All religion in all time is concerned with life, the religion of to-day with the betterment of life.

But, thank Heaven, asceticism is not all or chiefly that depressing thing, negation. The negations of the Decalogue died with the jealous God who dictated them—died, that is, as religious impulses. The new Immanence is vital, creative, it says: "you, that is the best in you, is one with God, *is* God, your work *is* the divine activity, 'whatsoever thy hand findeth to do do it with thy might.'" In the old days most religiously minded people were troubled by the thought that they were not "devoting themselves to others"; self-sacrifice was felt to be incumbent, the only road to peace. Hence the constant itch for philanthropy. Now religion says all things are possible and permissible, only remember there is a better as well as a good. The instincts are good and remain the prime motors to thought. The personal emotions are good, the best of which the spiritually undeveloped are capable, yet in the exercise of these you but strengthen your selfhood. But in science, that is the disinterested search after truth, in art which is creative self-absorption, you lose yourself in something bigger and more permanent and these henceforth rank as of the highest religious value.

Asceticism is then not only resistance to the descending wave, it is also, it is chiefly, the rising on the upward wave, buoyant, triumphant. To the Greek asceticism is "the attuning of an instrument," not the mortification of the flesh. It is just the "training or discipline that is necessary for eminence in art, in athletics as for eminence in virtue. The Greek words ἄσκησις, ἀρετή level these distinctions"[1].

To conclude, it is in the spirit of the purest religion that a poet tells of the ascetic—a poet who at least for a time renounced human for discarnate joy—Keats, who, to quote the words of a recent critic[2], was "great in his actual poetic achievement, great in his possession of the rarest faculty of all, the power and the desire to make his nature single, to refine his own being, in the words of Anton Chehov, 'to squeeze the slave out of himself.'"

Keats writes to his sister-in-law:

Notwithstanding your happiness and your recommendations I hope I shall never marry. Though the most beautiful creature were waiting for me at the end of a journey or a walk, though the carpet were of silk, the curtain of the morning clouds, the chairs stuffed with cygnets' down, the food manna, the wine above claret, the windows opening on Winandermere, I should not feel—or rather my happiness would not be so fine, as my solitude is sublime.

There, instead of what I have described, there is a sublimity to welcome me home. The roaring of the wind is my wife and the stars through my window-pane are my children.....I feel more and more every day, as my imagination strengthens, that I do not live in this world alone, but in a thousand worlds. No sooner am I alone than shapes of epic greatness are stationed around me and serve my spirit the office which is equivalent to a king's bodyguard.

[1] J. A. K. Thomson, *Greeks and Barbarians*, p. 110.
[2] Mr Middleton Murry, *Nation and Athenaeum*, Feb. 26, 1921.

And yet, he ends:

> I have not the least contempt for my species. . . . and my greatest elevations of soul leave me every time more humbled.

Is this asceticism a thing cold and dead? Hear Keats again:

> There is an awful warmth about my heart—like a load of immortality.

An awful warmth about his heart. Yes, and an awful light about his head. *Via Crucis, Via Lucis.*

CHAPTER I.

THE HYMN OF THE KOURETES.

Ζεῦ πάντων ἀρχά,
πάντων ἁγήτωρ,
Ζεῦ, coι πέμπω ταύταν γμνων ἀρχάν.

ZEUS, the Father of Gods and Men, was born, men fabled,
in the island of Crete. So far there was substantial agreement.
It may be that this uniformity reflects some half-unconscious
tradition that in Crete were the beginnings of that faith and
practice which if it cannot be called Hellenic religion was at least
the substratum on which Hellenic religion was based. No one
now thinks he can have an adequate knowledge of Greek art without a study of the Mycenaean and Minoan periods, and, since the
roots of religion strike as deep as or deeper than the roots of art,
no one now will approach the study of the Olympian Zeus without
seeking for the origin of the god in his reputed birth-place.

By the most fortunate of chances, at Palaikastro on the eastern
coast of Crete, just the very material needed for this study has come
to light, a ritual Hymn commemorating the birth of the infant
Zeus. The Hymn itself is, as will be seen, late, but it embodies
very early material, material indeed so primitive that we seem at
last to get back to the very beginnings of Greek religion, to a
way of thinking that is not in our sense religious at all, but that
demonstrably leads on to religious faith and practice. This
primitive mode of faith and practice it is, I believe, of the first
importance that we should grasp and as fully as may be realise.
It lets us see myth as well as ritual in the making, it will even
disclose certain elements that lie deep embedded in early
Greek philosophy. The new, or at least partially new, outlook
opened by the Hymn is easy to misconceive, and, in the first flush

of discovery, easy perhaps to over-emphasize. It needs patient
scrutiny and some effort of the historical imagination. To such
a scrutiny and to conclusions arising from it the following chapters
will be devoted.

Before the meaning of the Hymn is discussed the circumstances
of its finding must be made clear. This Hymn, about which our
main enquiry into the origins of Greek religion will centre, was
not found at Knossos nor even at Phaestos, places whose names
are now in every man's mouth, but at the remote seaport town of
Palaikastro, a name familiar only to archaeologists. If Palaikastro
should ever be a household word to classical scholars in general, it
will be as the place of the finding of this Hymn. The marshy
plain out of which Palaikastro rises is almost certainly the ancient
Heleia, known to us through inscriptions[1] as a tract of land over
which the dwellers in Itanos and Hierapytna disputed. Near to
Heleia these same inscriptions tell us lay the sanctuary of
Diktaean Zeus.

Our Hymn bids the god come to Dikte. The two great
mountain peaks of Crete, Ida and Dikte, both claimed to be the
birth-place of Zeus. Dikte, though less splendid and dominant,
has the earlier and better claim. Hesiod[2], our earliest authority,
places the birth-story at Lyktos on the north-western spur of
Dikte.

> To Lyktos first she came, bearing the child
> As black night swiftly fell.

There is a shade of suspicious emphasis on the 'first,' as of one
whose orthodoxy is impeached. When the glory of Cnossos overshadowed and overwhelmed lesser and earlier sanctities, Ida was
necessarily supreme, and it required some courage to support the
claims of Dikte. Diodorus[3] with true theological tact combines
the two stories: the god was born indeed on Dikte but educated
by the Kouretes on Mount Ida.

---

[1] Dittenberger, II. 929, line 37 Ἰτάνιοι πόλιν οἰκοῦντες ἐπιθαλάσσιον χώραν ἔχοντες προγονικὴν γειτονοῦσαν τῶι τοῦ Διὸς τοῦ Δικταίου ἱερῶι, and see lines 45 and 65.
[2] Hes. *Theog.* 481
ἔνθα μὲν ἵκτο φέρουσα θοὴν διὰ νύκτα μέλαιναν
πρώτην ἐς Λύκτον.
[3] v. 70 κατὰ δὲ τὴν Ἴδην, ἐν ᾗ συνέβη τραφῆναι τὸν θεόν...ἀνδρωθέντα δ' αὐτὸν φασι πρῶτον πόλιν κτίσαι περὶ τὴν Δίκταν, ὅπου καὶ τὴν γένεσιν αὐτοῦ γενέσθαι μυθολογοῦσιν....

But Palaikastro, as a glance at the map[1] in Fig. 1 will show, is not Dikte—not even near Dikte. All eastern Crete with its towns of Itanos and Praisos, where dwelt the Eteokretans, and the modern sites of Zakro and Palaikastro are cut off from the mountain mass of Dikte by the low narrow isthmus[2] that joins

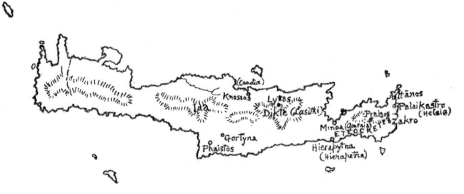

Fɪɢ. 1. Map of Crete.

the trading towns of Minoa (Gournia) and Hierapytna (Hierapetra). How comes it then that in remote Palaikastro Diktaean Zeus is worshipped, that in Palaikastro the ruins of his temple have come to light? This brings us to the question of chronology.

Strabo[3] in discussing the origin of Cretan institutions makes an interesting remark. 'Among the Cretans,' he says, 'when their warlike cities, and especially that of Knossos, were ravaged, certain of their customs were kept up among the inhabitants of Lyttos and Gortyna and other of the lesser towns rather than by the Knossians.' Here we have much history in a nutshell. Conspicuous cities pay the toll of their splendour. Palaikastro is but a lesser town (πολίχνιον): there we may hope to find customs surviving that had died down at Knossos.

In the Hymn before us just such customs are enshrined. The actual stele was engraved in the second or third century after

---

[1] Reproduced with slight modifications from *B.S.A.* vɪɪɪ. p. 287, Fig. 1.

[2] Strabo, x. 475 πλατυτάτη δὲ κατὰ τὸ μέσον ἐστί, πάλιν δ' ἐντεῦθεν εἰς στενώτερον τοῦ προτέρου συμπίπτουσιν ἰσθμὸν αἱ ἠόνες περὶ ἑξήκοντα σταδίων, τὸν ἀπὸ Μινῴας τῆς Λυττίων εἰς Ἱεράπυτναν καὶ τὸ Λιβυκὸν πέλαγος.

[3] Strabo, x. 481 κακωθεισῶν τῶν πόλεων καὶ μάλιστα τῆς Κνωσσίων, τῶν πολεμικῶν· μεῖναι δέ τινα τῶν νομίμων παρὰ Λυττίοις καὶ Γορτυνίοις καὶ ἄλλοις τισὶ πολιχνίοις μᾶλλον ἢ παρ' ἐκείνοις. Clement, citing as his authority the *Nostoi* of Antikleides, says that human sacrifice was offered by the Lyctii, a Cretan tribe (Book ɪɪɪ. 4).

Christ[1]; that is clear from the very cursive character of the letters.
But the poem inscribed is much earlier, probably about 300 B.C.
We have oddly enough two copies on the back and face of the
same stone.   It seems to have presented serious difficulties to the
stone-mason.   The first copy whether from another stone or from
a MS. was so faulty that it had to be redone.   This looks as if
matter and language were unfamiliar.   For some reason which
now escapes us, an old ritual hymn was revived.   How far it was
rewritten we cannot now say.   Its material is, as will presently be
shown, primaeval; we cannot date it, it is *νόμιμον*.

The cave on Dikte where Zeus was born has been identified
and thoroughly excavated[2].   It is a large double cavern about
500 feet above the modern village of Psychro in the upland of
Lasithi.   Lyttos, of which the ruins still remain, lies on one spur
of the north-western peak of Dikte (Lasithi); on the opposite spur
is the Psychro cave.   In the lowest stratum of the deposit in the
cave is found Kamares ware, above that Mycenaean ware, and so
on in regular sequence to the geometric period, i.e. about the
eighth century B.C.   After that, save in quite sporadic cases the
votive offerings cease.   It is impossible to avoid the conclusion
that the cult in the cave came to an end.   Dikte it is probable was
superseded by Ida.   In a treaty[3] between Lyttos and Olous, Zeus
is sworn by, but his title is *Βιδάτας* 'Zeus of Ida,' not *Δικταῖος*.
On his own mountain 'He of Dikte' was superseded.

Central Crete in her public documents swears by Zeus of Ida,
but a little group of cities in the remote eastern district held to
the earlier cult.   Itanos, the northernmost of the towns on the
east coast, was said to have been founded by one of the Kouretes.
In an inscription[4] found on the modern site (Erimopolis) the
citizens swear first of all by Zeus Diktaios and Hera and the gods
in Dikte.   At Eteokretan Praisos, Strabo[5], quoting Staphylos,
says there was the sanctuary of Diktaean Zeus.   Athenaeus[6]

[1] See Prof. Bosanquet, *B.S.A.* xv. 1908—1909, p. 347, and Prof. Gilbert Murray, p. 364.
[2] For full description see Mr D. G. Hogarth, *The Dictaean Cave, B.S.A.* vi. p. 94 and especially p. 115.
[3] *C.I.A.* ii. 549, and see R. C. Bosanquet, *op. cit.* p. 349.
[4] Blass (in Collitz-Bechtel, iii².), 5058 [Τά]δε ὤμοσαν τοι Ἰτάνιοι πά[ντες] Δία Δικταῖον καὶ Ἥραν καὶ θ[εο]ὺς τοὺς ἐν Δίκται καὶ....
[5] Strabo, x. 475 ...ὧν (τῶν Ἐτεοκρήτων) εἶναι πολίχνιον Πρᾶσον ὅπου τὸ τοῦ Δικταίου Διὸς ἱερόν.   For an inscription of Praisos in which 'Diktaios' may be with great probability restored see Prof. Bosanquet, *op. cit.* p. 350.
[6] Athen. ix. 375, quoting Agathocles, Μυθεύουσιν ἐν Κρήτῃ γενέσθαι τὴν Διὸς

notes that the Praisians sacrifice *to* a sow, and he connects the custom with the 'unspeakable sacrifice' which took place on Dikte in commemoration of the fact that Zeus was suckled by a sow. Settlers from Hierapytna[1] take their oath by two Zeuses, Zeus Oratrios and Zeus Diktaios.

It is clear then that though in classical days central Crete was dominated by the Zeus of Ida, Zeus of Dikte[2], whose worship went on during the bronze and iron ages in the great cave at Lyttos, was a living power in the eastern and especially the north-eastern extremity of Crete.

Zeus of Ida might and did dominate central Crete, but in the eastern and especially the north-eastern extremities Zeus of Dikte, Zeus of the Birth-cave, lived on in classical and even post-classical days. His was a name to swear by and at Palaikastro he had a temple and a precinct. It is this temple that has been recovered for us by the excavations of the British School[3] carried on in 1902—1905. These excavations have abundantly shown that in the third Late-Minoan period (after 1500 B.C.) Palaikastro was the seat of a ruling prince, after Knossos, Phaistos and Gournia had been destroyed. Not a stone of the temple was standing, but from architectural fragments found scattered on the site some notion of its size and its decoration can be gleaned. The temenos wall[4] can be traced for about thirty-six metres. The temple stood not as the Hellenic temples of Troy and Mycenae at the summit of the hill, but on a platform artificially levelled, about half-way down. The bulk of the votive offerings belong to the archaic period and show that the sanctuary was in full prosperity from the seventh to the fifth century B.C. Bronze shields of the same style and date as those found in the cave on Mt. Ida have also come to light.

τέκνωσιν ἐπὶ τῆς Δίκτης ἐν ᾗ καὶ ἀπόρρητος γίνεται θυσία...Πραίσιοι δὲ καὶ ἱερὰ ῥέζουσιν ὑὶ καὶ αὕτη προτελὴς αὐτοῖς ἡ θυσία νενόμισται.

[1] Blass, 5039 Ὀμνύω τὰν Ἐστίαν καὶ Ζῆνα Ὀράτριον καὶ Ζῆνα Δικταῖον.

[2] It is even probable that the name of Dikte was transferred to one of the peaks, perhaps the cone of Modhi near Praisos and Palaikastro. Strabo expressly states that Dikte is only 100 stadia from Salmonion, the north-east promontory of Crete, and that it is not 'as Aratus alleges' near Ida, but distant from it 1000 stadia towards the east. Aratus is probably describing the old Dikte of the cave. Strabo must intend some more easterly peak. The conjecture is due to Prof. Bosanquet, *op. cit.* p. 351.

[3] See *Excavations at Palaikastro*, iv. *B.S.A.* xi. p. 299, Pl. ix.—xv.

[4] This temenos wall is mentioned in an inscription (Dittenberger, ii. 929, l. 75) τὸ δὲ ἱερὸν καὶ τὸν περίβολον αὐτοῦ ἰδίοις σημείοις καὶ περιοικοδομήμασιν περιεχόμενον.

The three main fragments of the inscribed Hymn were found a little to the south of the temple in a deep pocket of earth and stones which had been dug right down into the Minoan strata, probably in some recent search for building stones. The missing pieces were carefully searched for over the whole field of excavation, but they have either been destroyed or carried away as building material. They may still come to light built into churches or houses in the neighbourhood. More than half the stele is missing, but, thanks to the fact that there are two copies of the text back and front, not nearly half of the text. One of the fragments, that which contains the opening lines in the fair copy, is reproduced in Fig. 2.

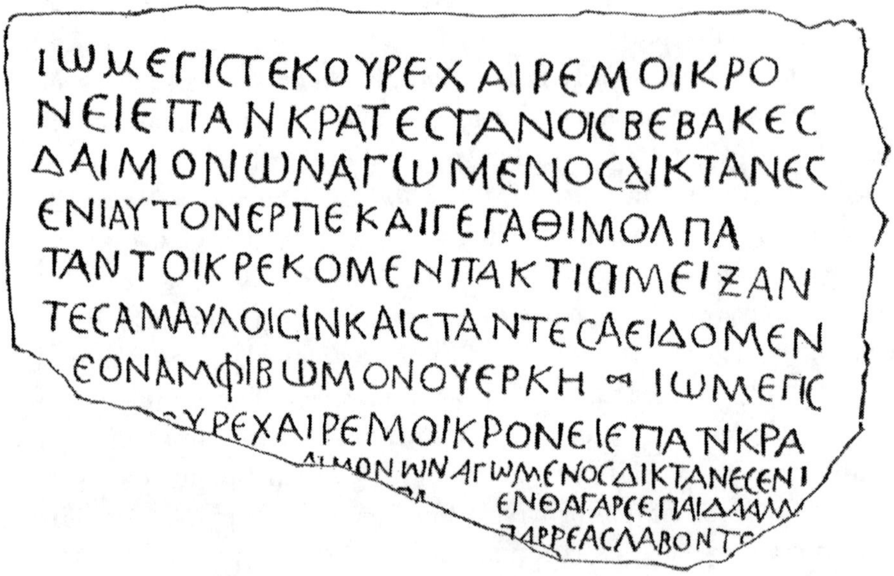

FIG. 2. Fragment of Hymn of the Kouretes.

For what precise occasion our Hymn was written we shall probably never know, but the fact that it was found near a temple of Diktaean Zeus in a place remote from Dikte, the significant fact too of the double copy, show clearly that the Hymn is essentially a revival, and that we may expect to find in it fossilised ways of thinking. This will emerge more clearly in the sequel. We must first consider the general structure and character of the Hymn. The text[1] is as follows.

[1] As restored by Prof. Gilbert Murray. See *B.S.A.* xv. 1908—1909, p. 357.

RESTORED TEXT.

Ἰώ,
Μέγιστε Κοῦρε, χαῖρέ μοι,
Κρόνιε, παγκρατὲς γάνους,
βέβακες
5 δαιμόνων ἀγώμενος·
Δίκταν ἐς ἐνιαυτὸν ἕρ-
    πε καὶ γέγαθι μολπᾷ,

Τάν τοι κρέκομεν πακτίσι
μείξαντες ἄμ’ αὐλοῖσιν,
10 καὶ στάντες ἀείδομεν τεὸν
    ἀμφὶ βωμὸν εὐερκῆ.
Ἰώ, κ.τ.λ.

Ἔνθα γὰρ σέ, παῖδ’ ἄμβροτον,
ἀσπιδ[ηφόροι τροφῆες]
15 παρ Ῥέας λαβόντες πόδα
    κ[ρούοντες ἀπέκρυψαν].
Ἰώ, κ.τ.λ.

. . . . .

TRANSLATION.

‘Io, Kouros most Great, I give thee hail, Kronian, Lord of all
that is wet and gleaming, thou art come at the head of thy
Daimones. To Dikte for the Year, Oh, march, and rejoice in the
dance and song,

That we make to thee with harps and pipes mingled together,
and sing as we come to a stand at thy well-fenced altar.

Io, etc.

For here the shielded Nurturers took thee, a child immortal,
from Rhea, and with noise of beating feet hid thee away.

Io, etc.

. . . .

RESTORED TEXT (*continued*).

```
       .    .    .    .
20     .    .    .    .
       .    .    . τâ]ς καλᾶς Ἀο(ῦ)ς              ◡  ⏜ — —
       Ἰώ, κ.τ.λ.
       [*Ὧραι δὲ βρ]ύον κατῆτος           — — ◡ ◡   ⏜ ◡ — ⏝
       καὶ βροτο(ὺ)ς Δίκα κατῆχε          ⏜ ◡ — ⏝   ⏜ ◡ — ⏝
25     [πάντα τ' ἄγρι' ἄμφεπ]ε ζῴ'        ⏜ ◡ — ◡   ⏜ ◡ — ⏝
       ἁ φίλολβος Εἰρήνα.                 ⏜ ◡ — ◡   ⏜ — —
       Ἰώ, κ.τ.λ.
       *Α[μιν θόρε, κὲς στα]μνία,          ⏜ ◡ — —   ⏜ — ◡ ◡
       καὶ θόρ' εὔποκ' ἐ[ς ποίμνια,       ⏜ ◡ — ◡   ⏜ — ◡ ◡
30     κὲς λήϊ]α καρπῶν θόρε,             ⏜ — ◡ ◡   ⏜ — ◡ ◡
       κὲς τελεσ[φόρους σίμβλους.]        ⏜ ◡ — ◡   ⏜ — —
       Ἰώ, κ.τ.λ.
       Θόρε κὲς] πόληας ἁμῶν,             ⏜ ◡ — ◡   ⏜ — ◡ ◡
       κὲς ποντοφόρο(υ)ς νᾶας,            ⏜ — ◡ ◡   ⏜ — ⏝
35     θόρε κὲς [νεοὺς πολ]είτας,         ⏝ ◡ — —   ⏜ ◡ — ⏝
       θόρε κὲς Θέμιν κ[αλάν].            ⏝ ◡ — ◡   ⏜ — —
```

TRANSLATION (*continued*).

       .   .   .   . of fair dawn ?

Io, etc.

And the Horai began to be fruitful year by year (?) and
Dikè to possess mankind, and all wild living things were held
about by wealth-loving Peace.

Io, etc.

To us also leap for full jars, and leap for fleecy flocks, and leap
for fields of fruit, and for hives to bring increase.

Io, etc.

Leap for our Cities, and leap for our sea-borne ships, and leap
for our young citizens and for goodly Themis.'

Our Hymn is obviously a Hymn of Invocation of a ritual type fairly well known[1], though the instances extant are unfortunately rare. It opens with a refrain in ordinary lyric (di-iambic)[2] metre and this refrain is repeated before each of the (di-trochaic) stanzas. The structure of the Hymn is of importance and should be clearly realised. It falls into three parts.

First we have in the refrain the actual invocation; the god is addressed by his various titles and instructed how, where and when to come—he is invoked as 'Kouros most Great,' as 'Kronian[3],' as 'Lord of all that is wet and gleaming[4]'—it is

---

[1] Our earliest instance is the invocation of the Bull-god by the women of Elis; the Delphic Paean to Dithyrambos presents a later and closer analogy. See p. 205 and also my *Prolegomena*, pp. 438 and 417.

[2] I call the metre of the refrain iambic because this seems simplest. But of course the difference between iambics and trochees is often only nominal. Wilamowitz considers it more consonant with the rest of the hymn to scan trochaically:

ἰ-ώ, μέγιστε Κοῦρε,	— — ‿ ‿ ‿ — ‿
χαῖρέ μοι, Κρόνειε, (sic lapis)	— ‿ — ‿ — ‿
παγκρατὲς γάνος, βέβακες	— ‿ — ‿ — ‿ — —
δαιμόνων ἀγώμενος,	— ‿ — — — ‿
Δίκταν [ἐς] ἐνιαυτὸν ἔρπε	— — ‿ ‿ — ‿ — ‿
καὶ γέγαθι μολπᾷ,	— ‿ — ‿ — —

This involves treating ἰ‿ώ as = a cretic, keeping the very questionable form Κρόνειε (Κρονεῖον = temple of Kronos in Pap. Grenf. I. 11 is of course different): and deleting ἐς before ἐνιαυτόν. Otherwise it has great advantages. (G.M.)

[3] The order of the words is, I think, conclusive against taking μέγιστε Κοῦρε Κρόνιε together, 'greatest Kronian youth,' 'greatest son of Kronos.' (G.M.)

[4] Both reading and translation are doubtful. Wilamowitz and Mr A. B. Cook independently suggest γάνος. The stone has γάνους three times, which is strong evidence of what the stone-cutter meant to write, and is not really weakened by the fact that in one case the Υ is crowded in between the Ο and Σ, as if it had been omitted and then inserted; παγκρατὲς γάνος, 'Almighty Gleam' or 'Radiance,' would be simple and good: but παγκρατὲς γάνους seems to be quite good Greek for 'Lord of all γάνος.' Any compound of -κρατής would take the genitive, like ἐγκρατής, ἀκρατής. Cf. the gen. with παμμήτωρ, παναίτιος, πάνδοκος.

But what is the meaning of γάνος? The Etymologicum Magnum has a gloss: γάνος: ὕδωρ χάρμα φῶς λίπος αὐγή λευκότης λαμπηδών. 'γάνος: *water joy light grease gleam candor fulgor*.' (I am reduced to Latin for the last two equivalents.) It starts with 'water' and it ends with 'light' or 'gleam.' I translate '*wet and gleaming*.'

It has been suggested by Mr Cook that perhaps the Kouros is only Lord of the Bright Sky, like a Sun God, and that γάνος is *hoc sublime candens*, The Aether. Now it is quite true that γάνος never means simply *water*, without any 'gleam,' while instances can easily be found in which it means only 'gleam' or 'glory' with no sense of wetness, e.g. Aesch. *Ag.* 579 λάφυρα—δόμοις ἐπασσάλευσαν ἀρχαῖον γάνος. If the context required it we could certainly leave out the wetness. But (1) the wetness is normally present: it is κρηναῖον γάνος, Ἀσωποῦ γάνος, βότρυος or ἀμπέλου γάνος, ξουθῆς μελίσσης γάνος, γάνος Ἠριδανοῖο and the like; and (2) the context here seems to me not to reject but rather to welcome the connotation of moisture. It is not mere sunlight that the Kouros brings; it is fruitful Spring as a whole, with dew and showers and young sap as well as sunshine. Γάνος in its ordinary sense exactly hits off the required meaning; see pp. 173—175. (G.M.)

in these capacities he is wanted and expected. He is further bidden to come at the head of his *Daimones*, he is to come to Dikte and for the year, he is to come marching and rejoicing. So far for the god.

Next by an easy transition we have a statement of the ritual performed. The god is adjured to rejoice in the dance and song which the worshippers make to him 'with harps and pipes mingled together, and which they sing as they come to a stand at his well-fenced altar.' We have clearly a ritual dance accompanying a song. The reason, or rather the occasion, of this dance and song is next stated. We have in fact what would usually be called an 'aetiological' myth. The worshippers dance round the altar of the Kouros because 'here the shielded Nurturers took the Kouros, an immortal child from Rhea, and with noise of beating feet hid him away.'

Next follows a lamentable gap. When the text re-emerges we are midway in the third factor, the statement of the benefits which resulted from the events recounted in the myth, benefits which clearly it is expected will be renewed in the annual restatement and ritual re-enactment of this myth. The coming Seasons are to be fruitful, Dikè is to possess mankind, the Kouros by leaping in conjunction with his worshippers is to bring fertility for flocks and fields, prosperity to cities and sea-borne ships, and young citizens.

The full gist of the Hymn will not appear till all three factors have been examined in detail, but already, at the first superficial glance, we note certain characteristics of a Hymn of Invocation that may help to its understanding. The god invoked is not present, not there in a temple ready waiting to be worshipped; he is bidden to come, and apparently his coming, and as we shall later see his very existence, depends on the ritual that invokes him. Moreover the words addressed to him are not, as we should expect and find in the ordinary worship addressed to an Olympian, a prayer, but an injunction, a command, 'come,' 'leap.' Strangest of all, the god it would seem performs the same ritual as his worshippers, and it is by performing that ritual that he is able to confer his blessings. He leaps when his attendant worshippers leap and the land is fertile. All this as will later appear lands us in a region rather of magic than religion.

It will now be necessary to examine in detail the three[1] factors of the Hymn—the introductory refrain, the aetiological[2] myth, and what for convenience we may call 'the resultant blessings.' The gist of the ritual will be found in the second factor, the aetiological myth, but we begin with the first.

1. The Invocation.

Μέγιστε Κοῦρε, χαῖρέ μοι,
Κρόνιε.

The opening words are enough to startle the seven mythological sleepers. From the circumstances of the finding of the Hymn in the temple of Diktaean Zeus and from the title Kronian, it is clear that Zeus[3] the Father of gods and men, is addressed as 'Kouros most Great,' greatest of grown-up youths. To our unaccustomed ears the title sounds strange and barely reverent. 'Father,' still more 'Mother,' and even 'Babe' are to us holy words, but a full-grown youth has to us no connotation of sanctity. Moreover the words Full-grown Youth go ill with 'Kronian,' a title of reverend association. How these two dissonant titles come to be unequally yoked together will appear in the sequel.

When the Hymn was first discovered, the opening words as was natural at once arrested attention, but—so crusted and stiffened is the mind with traditional thinking—the full significance of the title could not at first be seen. Zeus the Father was firmly rooted in our minds, so it was natural at first to think, here we have the young Zeus, Zeus the Divine Son. The Christian religion has accustomed us to a god as Son. But it should at once be noted, Kouros is not υἱός, not *son*, nor is it even παῖς, *child*. Kouros connotes[4] no relationship to a parent, it is simply

---

[1] The first two factors only will be examined at this point; the third factor, the 'resultant blessings and their relation to Themis,' is reserved for chapter x.

[2] I use the current term 'aetiological' provisionally, for convenience. Its inadequacy will be shown later, p. 329.

[3] It should, however, be definitely noted at the outset, for the fact is of cardinal importance, that nowhere, neither in the refrain nor in the body of the poem, does the actual name *Zeus* appear.

[4] The word κοῦρος is of course often used as the rough equivalent of παῖς or υἱός, cf. Eur. *El.* 463 τῷ Μαίας ἀγροτῆρι κούρῳ, but I suspect that in this and similar passages it covers an earlier and different relation.

young man just come to maturity. Hence it is that Kouros with a capital is in English practically untranslatable save by periphrasis. 'Greatest of Youths' is intolerably clumsy, 'Prince of Youths,' which perhaps might serve, introduces an alien association. Nothing is more stimulating to enquiry than an untranslatable word, since underlying it we may hope to find something new, unknown. We have no sacred Kouros now, we have got to rediscover what caused the sanctity of the Kouros[1]. We shall find it in the aetiological myth, but before we examine this, another statement in the Invocation yet remains and one scarcely less surprising.

The Kouros, the young Zeus, is hailed as coming 'at the head of his *daimones*' (δαιμόνων ἀγώμενος). This brings us to a curious and, for our investigation, cardinal point. Nowhere save in this Hymn do we hear of Zeus with attendant *daimones*[2]. He stands always alone, aloof, approached with awe, utterly delimited from his worshippers. One god only, Dionysos, and he but a half-bred Olympian, is attended by *daimones*. We can scarcely picture Dionysos without his attendant *thiasos*, be they holy women, Maenads, be they the revel rout of Satyrs. We think of this *thiasos* of *daimones* as attendants, inferior persons, pale reflections, emanations as it were from the god himself. It seems appropriate that he should be surrounded by attendants (προπόλοι): superior persons, high officials, always are. If this be all, how strange, how even unseemly is it that Zeus, the supreme god, Father of Gods and Men, should have no *thiasos*, no escort. The Hymn brings us face to face with the fact that Zeus once had a *thiasos*, once when he was a young man, a Kouros. When he grew up to be the Father, it seems, he lost his *thiasos* and has gone about unattended ever since. If we can once seize the meaning of this *thiasos* and its relation to the god we shall have gone far to understand the making of Greek theology.

[1] Some survivals of initiation-rites and of the Kouros idea will be considered in chapters IX. and X.
[2] Mr Cook kindly reminds me that this rule has one singular and beautiful exception. In the *Phaedrus* of Plato (246 E) we read ὁ μὲν δὴ μέγας ἡγεμὼν ἐν οὐρανῷ Ζεύς...πρῶτος πορεύεται...τῷ δ' ἕπεται στρατιὰ θεῶν τε καὶ δαιμόνων...θεῖον χοροῦ.... The passage reads almost like a reminiscence of a ritual-procession similar to that headed by the greatest Kouros (δαιμόνων ἀγώμενος).

2. THE AETIOLOGICAL MYTH.

The presence of the Kouros is confidently claimed and with it all the blessings to flocks and herds that attend his coming. The god will come, *is* come, to Dikte for the year and the produce of the year; and the reason is clearly stated. The worshippers 'come to a stand' at the altar and there recite and probably enact the myth.

For here the shielded Nurturers took thee, a child immortal and with noise of beating feet hid thee away.

The text at this point is unfortunately defective[1], but enough remains to make it clear, beyond the possibility of doubt, that the story told is the familiar myth of the birth of Zeus and his nurture by the Kouretes[2]. The myth is obviously 'aetiological.' The worshippers of the Kouros say they invoke the Kouros because of the myth (ἔνθα γάρ). We may of course safely invert the order of things, the myth arose out of or rather together with the ritual, not the ritual out of the myth.

The myth of the birth of Zeus and its ritual enactment is recounted by Strabo[3] as follows. After mentioning the mysteries of Demeter and Dionysos, he says, 'These things in general and the sacred ceremonies of Zeus in particular, are performed with orgiastic rites and with assistance of attendants (προπόλοι) similar to the Satyrs that attend Dionysos. *These attendants they call Kouretes;* they are certain young men who perform armed movements accompanied by dancing. *They allege as their reason the myth about the birth of Zeus,* in which Kronos is introduced with his habit of swallowing his children immediately after birth, and Rhea trying to conceal her birth-pangs and to get the new-born child out of the way and doing her utmost to save it. With a view to this she enlists the help of the Kouretes. They surround the goddess and with drums and with the din of other instruments

---

[1] Prof. Murray writes, *op. cit.* p. 359 "'L. 14 ἀσπιδ[ηφόροι Κούρητες] Bosanquet.' The sense seems certain but the metrical license – – – ⏑ for – ⏑ ⏑ ⏔ is doubtful and does not occur elsewhere in the hymn. Hence I prefer τροφῆες: ἀσπίδ[εσσι | Κού ⏑ ρητες] however would correspond neatly with μείξαντες ἅμ' | αὐ ⏑ λοῖσιν.''

[2] In the similar ritual at Ephesus as Prof. Murray points out (*op. cit.* p. 359) the Kouretes in like fashion 'come to a stand' round the altar. See Strabo, p. 640, init. ὄρος, ὅπου στάντας φασὶ τοὺς Κούρητας τῷ ψόφῳ τῶν ὅπλων ἐκπλῆξαι.... For particulars of this ritual see p. 246.

[3] x. 468 ...προστησάμενοι μῦθον τὸν περὶ τῆς τοῦ Διὸς γενέσεως, ἐν ᾧ τὸν μὲν Κρόνον εἰσάγουσιν εἰθισμένον καταπίνειν τὰ τέκνα κ.τ.λ.

try to strike terror into Kronos and to escape notice whilst trying to filch away the child. The child is then given over to them to be reared with the same care by which it was rescued.'

A little earlier in his discussion of the functions of the Kouretes he says[1] they are '*daimones* or attendants (προπόλοι) on the gods, similar to Satyroi, Seilenoi, Bacchoi and Tityroi, and this is expressly stated by those who hand down the tradition of Cretan and Phrygian ceremonies, these being involved with certain sacred rites, some of them mystical, others relating to the child-nurture of Zeus and the orgiastic rites of the Mother of the Gods in Phrygia and in the region about the Trojan Ida.

Strabo thought that the child reared and protected by the Kouretes was Zeus, but our ritual Hymn knows him only as Kouros. It need not therefore surprise us that the Kouros appears elsewhere with other names. He is sometimes Dionysos, sometimes Zagreus.

The mysteries of Dionysos (Zagreus) are, says Clement of Alexandria, 'utterly inhuman.' He then proceeds to recount them. Utterly inhuman they are as Clement understood or rather utterly misunderstood them: very human indeed, social and civilising through and through if my interpretation be correct, so human and social that a very considerable portion of humanity thinks it well to practise analogous rites to-day.

Let Clement[2] tell his story:

'The mysteries of Dionysos are wholly inhuman, for while he was still a child and the Kouretes were dancing round him their armed dance the Titans came stealthily upon him and lured him with childish toys and tore him limb from limb while he was yet a babe. Thus does the Thracian Orpheus, the poet of the Rite recount.

The cones, the rhombos and the limb-bending toys,
And the fair gold apples of the Hesperides.'

---

[1] x. 466 ...τοιούτους γάρ τινας δαίμονας ἢ προπόλους θεῶν τοὺς Κουρῆτας φασὶν οἱ παραδόντες τὰ Κρητικὰ καὶ τὰ Φρύγια, ἱερουργίαις τισιν ἐμπεπλεγμένα ταῖς μὲν μυστικαῖς ταῖς δ' ἄλλαις περί τε τὴν τοῦ Διὸς παιδοτροφίαν τὴν ἐν Κρήτῃ καὶ τοὺς τῆς μητρὸς τῶν θεῶν ὀργιασμοὺς ἐν τῇ Φρυγίᾳ καὶ τοῖς περὶ τὴν Ἴδην τὴν Τρωικὴν τόποις.

[2] Abel, *Orphica*, 196 τὰ γὰρ Διονύσου μυστήρια τέλεον ἀπάνθρωπα, ὃν εἰσέτι παῖδα ὄντα, ἐνόπλῳ κινήσει περιχορευόντων Κουρήτων, δόλῳ δὲ ὑποδύντων Τιτάνων, ἀπατήσαντες παιδαριώδεσιν ἀθύρμασιν, οὗτοι δὴ οἱ Τιτᾶνες διέσπασαν, ἔτι νηπίαχον ὄντα, ὡς ὁ τῆς τελετῆς ποιητὴς Ὀρφεύς φησιν ὁ Θρᾴκιος.

κῶνος καὶ ῥόμβος καὶ παίγνια καμπεσίγυια
μῆλά τε χρύσεα καλὰ παρ' Ἑσπερίδων λιγυφώνων.

Other authorities add other details. The wicked Titans who stole the child away were painted over with white clay, gypsum[1] (τίτανος). Moreover, and this is of cardinal importance, there is a sequel to the story. After the child has been made away with (ἀφανισμός), swallowed by his father (τεκνοφαγία) or torn to pieces (διασπαραγμός), he comes back to life again : there is a coming to life again (ἀναβίωσις), a resurrection (παλιγγενεσία)[2], how and when we are not told. Some said[3] the child's heart was saved and then put back into a figure made of gypsum. In some versions[4] the wicked giants or white-clay-men are struck[5] with lightning by Zeus and burnt to ashes and from these ashes sprang the human race.

The cardinal elements of the story whether told of the infant Zeus, Dionysos, Zagreus or the Kouros are :

(1) A child is taken from his mother and carefully tended by men called Kouretes. To guard him they dance over him an armed dance (παιδοτροφία).

(2) The child is hidden, made away with, killed, dismembered by men sometimes called Titans, 'white-clay-men' (ἀφανισμός, σπαραγμός).

(3) The child reappears, is brought to life again. Sometimes this is effected by the white-clay-men, sometimes the child reappears as a white-clay-man himself, his heart being put into a figure of gypsum (ἀναβίωσις, παλιγγενεσία).

Of these elements only the first, the Child-Nurture, appears in the Hymn. This need not surprise us. Literature, even hieratic literature, tends to expurgate savage material, the death and

---

[1] Harpocrat. *s.v.* ἀπομάττων : ὡς ἄρα οἱ Τιτᾶνες τὸν Διόνυσον ἐλυμήναντο γύψῳ καταπλασάμενοι.

[2] Plut. *De Is. et Os.* xxxv. and *De Ei ap. Delph.* ix. Διόνυσον δὲ καὶ Ζαγρέα καὶ Νυκτέλιον καὶ Ἰσοδαίτην αὐτὸν ὀνομάζουσι, καὶ φθοράς τινας καὶ ἀφανισμούς, καὶ τὰς ἀναβιώσεις καὶ παλιγγενεσίας, οἰκεῖα ταῖς εἰρημέναις μεταβολαῖς αἰνίγματα καὶ μυθεύματα παραίνουσι.

[3] Firmicus Mat. *De Err. Prof. Relig.* 6 ...imaginem eius ex gypso plastico opere perfecit et cor pueri, ex quo facinus fuerat sorore deferente detectum, in ea parte plastae conlocat, qua pectoris fuerant lineamenta formata. Possibly the *imago* may have been like the παίγνια καμπεσίγυια and similar in character to the jointed terracotta dolls with movable arms and legs, found in Greek tombs.

[4] The sources for all these details are collected in Abel's *Orphica*, pp. 224 ff. and in Lobeck's *Aglaophamus*, pp. 553 ff. The Zagreus story is told in minute detail in the *Dionysiaka* of Nonnus, vi. 155 ff.

[5] The thunder-element in the story and the myth of the swallowing of the thunder-stone by Kronos will be discussed in chapter iii.

resurrection ritual was well enough as a mystery, but in the third century A.D. not for publication even in a ritual Hymn.

In the study of Greek religion it is all important that the clear distinction should be realized between the comparatively permanent element of the ritual and the shifting manifold character of the myth. In the case before us we have a uniform ritual, the elements of which we have disentangled—the armed dance over the child, the mimic death and rebirth; but the myth shifts; it is told variously of Zagreus, Dionysos, Zeus, and there is every variety of detail as to how the child is mimetically killed and how the resurrection is effected. To understand the religious intent of the whole complex it is all important to seize on the permanent ritual factors.

This does not, however, imply, as is sometimes supposed, that ritual is prior to myth; they probably arose together. Ritual is the utterance of an emotion, a thing felt, in *action*, myth in words or thoughts. They arise *pari passu*. The myth is not at first *aetiological*, it does not arise to give a reason; it is representative, another form of utterance, of expression. When the emotion that started the ritual has died down and the ritual though hallowed by tradition seems unmeaning, a reason is sought in the myth and it is regarded as aetiological[1].

We have now to ask what is the meaning of this extraordinary ritual. Why is a child or young man subjected to mimic rites of death and resurrection?

The orthodox explanation is that the child is a sort of vegetation spirit or corn-baby, torn to pieces in winter, revived in spring. I do not deny that in the myth there is an element of Corn- or rather Year-baby, but the explanation cannot be regarded as satisfactory, as it fails to explain the Kouretes, and the Titans disguised with white clay.

I offer a simpler and I think more complete explanation. Every single element, however seemingly preposterous, in both the ritual and myth of Zagreus can be explained I believe by the analogy of *primitive rites of tribal initiation*.

---

[1] This point will become clearer when (in chapter II.) the psychology of the δρώμενον, the ritual act, is examined. The general relation of myth to ritual is reserved for chapter VIII.

This I had long suspected because of the white-clay-men.
These I have already fully discussed elsewhere[1] and I need now
only briefly resume what is necessary for the immediate argument.
The word Titanes (white-clay-men) comes of course from τῐ́τᾰνος,
white earth or clay, gypsum. The Titanes, the white-clay-men,
were later, regardless of quantity, mythologized into Tītānes,
Titans, giants. Harpocration[2], explaining the word ἀπομάττων,
says that the Titans, when they tore Dionysos to pieces, were
covered with a coat of gypsum in order that they might not be
recognized. Later, people when they were initiated went on
doing the same thing and for the same reason that most people
do most things nowadays, because 'it was the thing to do.'
Nonnus[3] also says that the Titans were 'whitened with mystic
gypsum.'

A coat of white paint was a means of making yourself up as a
bogey or ghost; by disguising your real character as a common
human man you reinforced your normal personality. A coat of
white or sometimes black paint is the frequent disguise of savages
to-day when in ceremonies of initiation for the edification of their
juniors they counterfeit their tribal ancestors.

The Titans then, the white-clay-men, are real men dressed up
as bogies to perform initiation rites. It is only later when their
meaning is forgotten that they are explained as Tītānes, mythological giants. Thus much was clear to me years ago: i.e. that
under the myth of Zagreus lay some form of initiation rite. What
I then did not see, though my blindness seems to me now almost
incredible, was the significance of the child and the toys[4] and
above all why the child was first killed and then brought back
to life.

Again light came to me unexpectedly from a paper kindly sent

---

[1] *Prolegomena*, p. 492.

[2] ἐκμιμούμενοι τὰ μυθολογούμενα παρ' ἐνίοις, ὡς ἄρα οἱ Τιτᾶνες τὸν Διόνυσον
ἐλυμήναντο γύψῳ καταπλασάμενοι ἐπὶ τῷ μὴ γνώριμοι γενέσθαι. τοῦτο μὲν οὖν τὸ
ἔθνος ἐκλιπεῖν, πηλῷ δὲ ὕστερον καταπλάττεσθαι νομίμου χάριν.

[3] Nonn. *Dionys.* XXVII. 228

ἐλευκαίνοντο δὲ γύψῳ
μυστιπόλῳ.

[4] A child's 'toys' in antiquity were apt to be much more than mere playthings.
They were charms inductive of good, prophylactic against evil, influences. Thus
crepundia, from *crepere* 'to rattle,' served to amuse the child but also to protect
him. For this whole subject see R. Wünsch, *Charms and Amulets,* in Hastings'
Encyclopaedia of Religion and Ethics.

to me by Dr Frazer[1] containing an account of certain initiation ceremonies among the Wiradthuri tribe of New South Wales. This account must be briefly resumed :

'At a certain stage in the initiation ceremonies of these tribes the women and children huddled together and were securely covered up with blankets and bushes. Then a number of men came from the sacred ground where the initiation ceremonies were performed. Some of them swung bull-roarers, and some of them took up lighted sticks from a fire, and threw them over the women and children " to make them believe that Dhuramoolan had tried to burn them." At a later period of the ceremonies the boys were similarly covered up with blankets, a large fire was kindled near them, and when the roaring of the wood and the crackling of the flames became audible, several old men began to swing bull-roarers, and the lads were told that Dhuramoolan was about to burn them. These performances were explained by a legend that Dhuramoolan, a powerful being, whose voice sounded like the rumbling of distant thunder, had been charged by a still more powerful being called Baiamai, with the duty of taking the boys away into the bush and instructing them in all the laws, traditions, and customs of the community. So Dhuramoolan pretended that he always killed the boys, cut them up, and burnt them to ashes, after which he moulded the ashes into human shape, and restored them to life as new beings.'

With the Cretan ritual in our minds it is clear that the Wiradthuri rites present more than an analogy; *mutato nomine* the account might have been written of Zagreus.

I have chosen the account of the Wiradthuri out of countless other instances, because in it we have the definite statement that the boys were burnt to ashes and Zagreus-like remodelled again in human shape. But everywhere, in Africa, in America, in Australia, in the South Pacific Islands, we come upon what is practically the same sequence of ceremonies. When a boy is initiated, that is when he passes from childhood to adolescence, this pantomime, this terrifying (ἔκπληξις), this pretended killing of the child, this

---

[1] *On some Ceremonies of the Central Australian Tribes*, Melbourne, 1901. Dr Frazer's authority is R. H. Matthews, *The Burbung of the Wiradthuri Tribes*, Journal of Anthropological Institute, xxv. (1896), pp. 297 f., 308, 311.

painting him with clay and bringing him back to life again as a young man, is everywhere enacted. Till the boy has died and come to life again, till he has utterly 'put away childish things' he cannot be a full member of the tribe, he may not know the tribal secrets or dance the tribal dances, he may not handle bull-roarers, he cannot perform any of the functions of the full-grown man.

At and through his initiation the boy is brought into close communion with his tribal ancestors: he becomes socialized, part of the body politic. Henceforth he belongs to something bigger, more potent, more lasting, than his own individual existence: he is part of the stream of the totemic life, one with the generations before and yet to come.

So vital, so crucial is the change that the savage exhausts his imagination and his ingenuity in his emphasis of death and new birth. It is not enough to be killed, you must be torn to pieces or burnt to ashes. Above all you must utterly forget your past life. The precautions taken to secure this completeness of death and resurrection and consequent oblivion are sometimes disgusting enough. Murder is carefully counterfeited with the help of bladders of blood and the like. Sometimes the details are amusing: not only does the boy forget his own name that in this his social baptism he may receive a new one, but he does not know his own mother, he has forgotten how to speak and can only stammer, he cannot even swallow, he has to be artificially fed. He cannot come in straight at the door but must stumble in backwards. If he forgets and stupidly recognizes his mother or eats his food like a Christian he is taken back and 'huskinawed' again[1]. All this is of course much more than mere pretence, it is a method of powerful suggestion.

The ritual, then, commemorated and perhaps in part enacted in our Hymn is the ritual of tribal Initiation. The Kouretes are Young Men who have been initiated themselves and will initiate others, will instruct them in tribal duties and tribal dances, will

---

[1] For details as to Death and Resurrection elements in Initiation Ceremonies see H. Schurtz, *Altersklassen und Männerbünde*, 1902; H. Webster, *Primitive Secret Societies*, 1908; H. Hubert and M. Mauss, *Mélanges d'Histoire des Religions*, 1909, pp. 144 ff.; A. van Gennep, *Les Rites de Passage*, 1909, pp. 93 ff.; L. Lévy-Bruhl, *Les fonctions mentales dans les Sociétés Inférieures*, 1910, pp. 409 ff.; and, especially, Dr J. G. Frazer, *Golden Bough*[2], iii. pp. 423 ff. and *Totemism and Exogamy*, iv. p. 228.

steal them away from their mothers, conceal them, make away
with them by some pretended death and finally bring them back
as new-born, grown youths, full members of their tribe. The word
Koures is simply a specialized derivative of Kouros, as γυμνής of
γυμνός, and perhaps γόης of γόος. It is, like Kouros, a word
impossible to translate, because we have lost the social condition
expressed. Young Men (*Kouroi*) we know, but Initiated Young
Men (*Kouretes*) are gone for ever.

The Kouretes are young men full-grown, but it will have been
already noted that in the Hymn we have a child, and in the
Zagreus myth a babe[1]. This brings us to an important point. It
is not only the passage from childhood to adolescence that among
savages is marked by rites of initiation, of death and resurrection.
As Monsieur van Gennep[2] has well shown in his suggestive book,
the ceremonies that accompany each successive stage of life,
ceremonies, i.e. of birth, of marriage, of ordination as a medicine-
man, and finally of death, are, no less than the ceremonies of
adolescence, one and all *Rites de Passage*, ceremonies of transition,
of going out from the old and going in to the new[3].

Myths, then, which embody the hiding, slaying and bringing to
life again of a child or young man, may reflect almost any form of
initiation rite. It is not always possible to distinguish very clearly.
Later[4] we shall see that the Kouretes had to do with a rite of the
initiation of a sort of medicine-man, a rite nearer akin to our
Ordination than to either Baptism or Confirmation. When the
Greeks lost touch with the tribal customs which involved the rite
of adolescence, we may suspect that they invented or at least
emphasized Infant-Initiation. Later theologians entirely forgot
the Kouros, and even the infant Zeus presented somewhat of a
difficulty if not a scandal. A babe is rather the attribute of the

---

[1] Thus Nonnus, *Dionysiaka*, vi. 179
       ἄλλοτε ποικιλόμορφον ἔην βρέφος, ἄλλοτε κούρῳ
       εἴκελος οἰστρηθέντι,
whereas Lucretius, ii. 635
                    Dictaeos referunt Curetas...
                    Cum *pueri* circum *puerum*.
[2] *Les Rites de Passage*, Paris, 1909.
[3] For the psychology of initiation rites see Mr Marett's very interesting analysis
in *The Birth of Humility*, Inaugural Lecture before the University of Oxford, 1910.
[4] Chapter iii.

divine Mother than the divine Father, and in patriarchal times, once the cult of the Mother was overshadowed, the infant Zeus needed apology. He was consigned to 'local legend' and was held to be due to '*contaminatio* with the child Dionysos.'

A clear and striking instance of a Second Birth in early childhood is reported by Mr and Mrs Routledge[1] as practised among the Akikúyu of British East Africa. It is known as 'To be Born Again' or 'To be Born of a Goat,' and takes place when the boy is about ten years old or even younger if the father can afford the necessary goat for sacrifice. The goat is killed, a piece of skin cut in a circle and passed over one shoulder of the candidate and under the other arm. No men are allowed inside the hut, but women are present. The mother sits on a hide on the floor with the boy between her knees, the goat's gut is passed round the woman and brought in front of the boy. The woman groans as in labour, another woman cuts the gut, and the boy imitates the cry of a new-born infant, the women present all applaud and afterwards the assistant and the mother wash the boy. That night the boy sleeps in the same hut as the mother. On the second day the boy stays with his mother in the homestead. On the third day food is brought, and the relatives and friends come to a feast in the evening, but no native beer is drunk. After all is over the hut is swept out. The boy again sleeps in the mother's hut, and that night the father sleeps in the hut also.'

The Akikúyu rite presents one feature of great interest. The boy is 'Born of a Goat.' It is nowhere stated that he is called a Goat, but the child of a goat must surely in some sense have been regarded as a Kid. We are irresistibly reminded of the Kid-Dionysos (Eriphios)[2], of the Horned Child[3] and of the Baby Minotaur. The notion lingers on in the beautiful thought that at Baptism a child becomes one of the lambs of Christ the Lamb of God. At present among the Akikúyu the boy who is 'Born

---

[1] *With a Prehistoric Race*, 1910, p. 151. Neither Mr nor Mrs Routledge could obtain permission actually to witness the rite. The custom is one of the oldest among the Akikúyu customs and universal among them. There is great reluctance to talk of the ceremony, and the knowledge of it was only obtained from natives who had broken with their own traditions and come under the influence of Christianity. Till a boy has been born again he cannot assist at the burial rites of his father. He is not part of the clan.

[2] Hesych. *s.v.*   [3] See p. 130.

of a Goat' is regarded as fit to tend goats, but behind a ceremony so emphatic and so expensive must, it would seem, lie some more serious significance[1].

The Akikúyu rite contains no mimic death. Death indeed seems scarcely an integral part of initiation, it is only a preparation for, an emphasis of, the new Life[2]. But an element like this of a striking and dramatic nature tends in myth sometimes to swamp the really integral factor. We hear more for example of the sufferings ($\pi\acute{a}\theta\eta$) of Dionysos than of his rebirth; the death of the child in such myths as those of Atreus and Thyestes, Demeter and Demophon[3] obscures the element of Resurrection. But there can be little doubt that originally the New Birth and Resurrection lay behind. Lucian[4] in his account of the strange solecisms committed by dancers says that he remembers how a man who was supposed to be 'dancing the Birth of Zeus and the Child-Eating of Kronos actually *danced by mistake the calamities of Thyestes,* deceived by their similarity.' The mistake is at least highly suggestive; the ritual dance of the two myths must have been almost identical.

Anthropologists have been sometimes blamed[5], and perhaps with justice, for the fiendish glee with which, as though they were Christian Fathers, they seize on barbarous survivals in Greek religion or literature. Zagreus dismembered by the Titans, the cannibal feasts of Thyestes and Lycaon, Demeter burning Demophon—these and a host of other stories are 'survivals of human sacrifice[6].' It is only a little anthropology that is a dangerous thing. Men will kill and eat each other and especially their enemies for many and diverse reasons, but actual Human Gift-Sacrifice, and especially child-sacrifice, is rare among savages. Many a cannibal is a kind and good father; adorned with a

[1] For theriomorphs and the inclusion of the animal in the tribe see p. 125 ff.

[2] The Orphic Hymn, xxxviii. 14, misunderstanding inverts the sequence. The Kouretes are ...τροφέες τε καὶ αὖτ' ὀλετῆρες.

[3] Mr W. R. Halliday has shown clearly that the story of Demeter passing Demophon through the fire is the survival of an infant initiation-rite. See p. 34, note 2.

[4] *de Salt.* 80 τὰς γὰρ γονὰς ὀρχούμενός τις καὶ τὴν τοῦ Κρόνου τεκνοφαγίαν παρῳρχεῖτο καὶ τὰς Θυέστου συμφορὰς τῷ ὁμοίῳ παρηγμένος.

[5] See Prof. Murray, *Olympian Houses* in Albany Review, 1907, p. 205.

[6] A like explanation is often given of the rites of the Lupercalia, but see Warde-Fowler, *Roman Festivals*, p. 316 'The youths were never actually killed but were the figures in a kind of acted parable.'

necklace of skulls he will sit playing with the child on his knee. But, rare though Human Sacrifice is, and rarer still its survivals, the mock slaying of a boy in initiation rites is so common as to be almost universal, and in a large number of instances it is the memory of this mock slaying, misunderstood, that survives. By way of placation, of palinode, we offer to the humanist the mysteries of Zagreus made harmless, humanized by anthropology. Dhura-moolan '*pretended* that he killed the boys.'

Primarily then the Kouretes are, in their capacity of Initiators, Child-Nurturers, Guardians (Παιδοτρόφοι, Φύλακες). Strabo[1] is on this point emphatic. 'In the Cretan discourses,' he says, 'the Kouretes are called the nurses and guardians of Zeus,' and again[2]

Fig. 3.

in trying to explain the word Kouretes he says, 'they were so called either because they were young and boys, or because of their rearing of Zeus.' They earned this title, he adds, through being 'as it were Satyrs attendant on Zeus....' In the light of this initiation nurture the other functions of the Kouretes fall easily and naturally into place.

The Kouretes are *armed and orgiastic dancers* (ὀρχηστῆρες ἀσπιδηφόροι). Strabo[3] says they are certain youths who execute

---

[1] x. 472 ἐν δὲ τοῖς Κρητικοῖς λόγοις οἱ Κουρῆτες Διὸς τροφεῖς λέγονται καὶ φύλακες.
[2] x. 468 ὥσθ' οἱ Κουρῆτες ἤτοι διὰ τὸ νέοι καὶ κόροι ὄντες ὑπουργεῖν ἢ διὰ τὸ κουρο-
τροφεῖν τὸν Δία (λέγεται γὰρ ἀμφοτέρως) ταύτης ἠξιώθησαν τῆς προσηγορίας, οἱονεὶ
Σάτυροί τινες ὄντες περὶ τὸν Δία.
[3] op. cit.

movements in armour; it is especially as inspired dancers that they fulfil their function as ministers in sacred rites. 'They inspire terror by armed dances accompanied by noise and hubbub of timbrels and clashing arms and also by the sound of the flute and shouting.' Nursing young children or even drilling young boys are functions that seem to us scarcely congruous with the dancing of armed dances. On the terracotta relief[1] in Fig. 3 we see the Kouretes armed with shields and short spears dancing over the infant Zeus, and if we try to realize the scene at all it seems to us absurd, calculated rather to scare the child to death than to defend him. But the Kouretes as Initiators continue their incongruous functions. Pantomimic dancing is of the essence of each and every mystery function. To disclose the mysteries is as Lucian[2] puts it 'to dance out the mysteries.' Instruction among savage peoples is always imparted in more or less mimetic dances[3]. At initiation you learn certain dances which confer on you definite social status. When a man is too old to dance, he hands over his dance to another and a younger, and he then among some tribes ceases to exist socially. His funeral when he dies is celebrated with scanty and perfunctory rites; having lost his dance he is a negligible social unit[4].

The dances taught to boys at initiation are frequently if not always *armed* dances. These are not necessarily warlike. The accoutrement of spear and shield was in part decorative, in part a provision for making the necessary hubbub. What a Koures in ancient days must have looked like may be gathered from Fig. 4[5], a photograph taken of the peculiar dance with song (μολπή) of the neophytes among the Akikúyu prior to their initiation as men. Conspicuous in their dancing gear are the great ceremonial dancing shields and the long staves. They are painted in zigzag with white paint, and wear tails and skins of monkey and wild cat. To be allowed to dance it is essential that a boy be 'painted

---

[1] *Annali d. Inst.* xii. (1840), Tav. d' agg. K. I am uncertain where the relief now is. E. Braun, who publishes it, says it passed from the Palazzo Colonna to royal castle of Agliè near Turin.

[2] *Pisc.* 33 ἥν τινα καὶ τῶν μεμυημένων ἰδὼν ἐξαγορεύοντα τοῖν θεοῖν τὰ ἀπόρρητα καὶ ἐξορχούμενον ἀγανακτήσω....

[3] Webster, *op. cit.* pp. 50, 51.

[4] R. Hertz, *Contribution à une étude sur la représentation collective de la mort.* Année Sociologique, x. 1905–6.

[5] W. S. and K. Routledge, *With a Prehistoric People*, 1910, Pl. cviii. Reproduced by kind permission of Mr and Mrs Routledge.

with a particular pattern' of divine institution, 'he must wear a particular dress and carry certain articles[1].'

The ancient Kouretes were not merely young men; they were half divine, *Daimones*. The Kouros in the Hymn is bidden to come at the head of his *Daimones* (δαιμόνων ἀγώμενος). As *daimones* the Kouretes resembled, Strabo[2] says, Satyrs, Seilenoi, Bacchoi, Tityroi. Divine but not quite gods, they are as we shall

Fɪɢ. 4.

presently see the stuff of which ancient gods are made. Hesiod[3], and Hesiod only, calls them actually gods. He tells of

> ...the worthless idle race of Satyrs
> And the gods, Kouretes, lovers of sport and dancing.

[1] *op. cit.* p. 156.
[2] x. 466 ἔοικε δὲ μᾶλλον τῷ περὶ Σατύρων καὶ Σειληνῶν καὶ Βακχῶν καὶ Τιτύρων λόγῳ.
[3] *Frg.* cxxɪx.

> καὶ γένος οὐτιδανῶν Σατύρων καὶ ἀμηχανοεργῶν
> Κουρῆτες τε Θεοί, φιλοπαίγμονες ὀρχηστῆρες.

In the light of initiation ceremonies we understand why the Kouretes and Korybantes though they are real live youths are yet regarded as δαίμονες, as half divine, as possessed (ἔνθεοι), enthusiastic, ecstatic, and why their ceremonies are characterized by Strabo[1] as orgiastic. The precise meaning of orgies will concern us later; for the present it is enough to note that in most savage mysteries it is a main part of the duty of initiators to impersonate gods or demons. The initiators dress up as the ancestral ghosts of the tribe, sometimes even wearing the actual skulls[2] of their ancestors, and in this disguise dance round the catechumens and terrify them half out of their senses. It is only when fully initiated that the boys learn that these terrific figures are not spirits at all but just their living uncles and cousins[3]. The secret is never imparted to women and children. To do so would be death.

As δαίμονες whether wholly or half divine the Kouretes *have all manner of magical capacities*. These capacities are by Strabo rather implied than expressly stated and are especially noticeable in their Phrygian equivalents, Korybantes. The Korybantes bind and release men from spells, they induce madness and heal it. The chorus asks[4] the love-sick Phaedra

> Is this some Spirit, O child of man?
> Doth Hecat hold thee perchance, or Pan?
> Doth She of the Mountains work her ban,
> Or the dread Corybantes bind thee?

The Kouretes are also, as all primitive magicians are, seers (μάντεις). When Minos in Crete lost his son Glaukos he sent for the Kouretes to discover where the child was hidden[5]. Closely akin to this magical aspect is the fact that they are metal-workers[6]. Among primitive people metallurgy is an uncanny craft, and the smith is half medicine man. The metal-working side of these

---

[1] x. 465 ὡς δὲ τύπῳ εἰπεῖν καὶ κατὰ τὸ πλέον ἐνθουσιαστικούς τινας καὶ Βακχικούς.

[2] H. Schurtz, *Altersklassen und Männerbünde*, 1902, p. 38. For the functions of ancestral ghosts see chapter 273.

[3] H. Webster, *Primitive Secret Societies*, pp. 101 and 187.

[4] Eur. *Hip.* 141

> ἦ σύ γ᾽ ἔνθεος, ὦ κούρα,
> εἴτ᾽ ἐκ Πανὸς εἴθ᾽ Ἑκάτας
> ἢ σεμνῶν Κορυβάντων φοι-
> τᾶς ἢ ματρὸς ὀρείας;

[5] Apollod. 3. 2. 2.

[6] Soph. *ap.* Strabo, x. 473 says of the Idaean Daktyls οἳ σίδηρόν τε ἐξεῦρον καὶ εἰργάσαντο πρῶτοι καὶ ἄλλα πολλὰ τῶν πρὸς τὸν βίον χρησίμων.

figures comes out best in the kindred Daktyls and Telchines. A step more and the magicians become Culture-Heroes, inventors of all the arts of life, house-building, bee-keeping, shield-making and the like[1]. As culture-heroes they attend the Kouros in the Hymn. This development of the *daimon* and the culture-hero will be discussed later.

Just such functions are performed to-day among primitive peoples by the Initiated Young Man. If the investigations of recent anthropologists[2] are correct, it is not so much about the family and the domestic hearth that the beginnings of the arts cluster, as about the institution known as the Man's House[3]. Here, unencumbered by woman, man practises and develops his diverse crafts, makes his weapons, his boats, his sacred images, his dancing masks. Even after marriage when he counts as an elderly man he returns to the Man's House[4] to keep in touch with civilization and the outside world. He is a Culture-Hero in the making.

To resume the results of our enquiry.

The worshippers in the Hymn invoke a Kouros who is obviously but a reflection or impersonation of the body of Kouretes. They 'allege as their reason' an aetiological myth. This myth on examination turns out to be but the mythical representation of a rite of mimic death and resurrection practised at a ceremony of initiation. Now the Kouros and the Kouretes[5] are figures that belong to cultus; they are what would in common parlance be

---

[1] Diod. Sic. v. 64. Idaean Daktyls are described as γόητες who superintend ἐπῳδὰς καὶ τελετὰς καὶ μυστήρια. They invent fire and the use of iron. The magical functions of the Kouretes and their aspect as medicine-men will be discussed in chapter iii.

[2] See especially H. Schurtz, *Altersklassen und Männerbünde*, p. 48.

[3] H. Webster, *Primitive Secret Societies*, ch. i. The ancient Kouretes seem to have had a sort of Man's House at Messene; it was a *megaron* not a temple. See Pausanias, iv. 31. 7 Κουρήτων μέγαρον ἔνθα ζῷα τὰ πάντα ὁμοίως καθαγίζουσιν.

[4] That institutions analogous to those of the Man's House among savages lived on in Crete we have abundant evidence in Strabo's account (x. 483) of Cretan institutions. The Ἀγέλαι with their ἄρχοντες, the συσσίτια, the ἀνδρεῖα, clearly belong to the same social morphology as the Männerhaus. It is probable that the ἁρπαγή and the custom ἀποκρύπτειν τὸν παῖδα (Strabo, 483) is a misunderstanding and in part a corruption of primitive initiation ceremonies. For a discussion of some part of these Cretan customs and their religious origin see Dr E. Bethe, *Die dorische Knabenliebe, ihre Ethik und ihre Idee* in Rhein. Mus. LXII. p. 438.

[5] For the meagre survivals of the actual worship of the Kouretes in historical times as attested by inscription see Prof. Bosanquet, *op. cit.* p. 353.

called religious.   We are face to face with the fact, startling
enough, that these religious figures arise, not from any 'religious
instinct,' not from any innate tendency to prayer and praise, *but
straight out of a social custom*.   Themis and Dike, invoked
by the Kouretes, lie at the undifferentiated beginnings of things
when social spelt religious.   They are not late abstractions, but
primitive realities and sanctities[1].

This contradicts, it is clear, many preconceived notions.   We
are accustomed to regard religion as a matter intensely spiritual
and individual.   Such undoubtedly it tends to become, but in its
origin, in the case under investigation, it is not spiritual and
individual, but social and collective.   But for the existence of a
tribe or group of some kind, a ceremony of initiation would be
impossible.   The surprise is all the greater because the particular
doctrine in question, that of the New Birth, is usually held to be
late and due to 'Orphic,' i.e. quasi Oriental influence.   It is held
to have affinities with Christianity, and is a doctrine passionately
adhered to by many sects and establishments in the present day.
It may indeed—in some form or another—as Conversion or as
Regeneration—be said to be *the* religious doctrine par excellence.

Now it has of late been frequently pointed out that the god
in some sense always 'reflects' the worshipper, takes on the
colour of his habits and his thoughts.   The morality of a god is
not often much in advance of that of his worshippers, and sometimes it lags considerably behind.   The social structure is also, it
is allowed, in some sense reflected in the god: a matriarchal
society will worship a Mother and a Son, a patriarchal society will
tend to have a cult of the Father.   All this is true, but the truth
lies much deeper.   Not only does the god reflect the thoughts,
social conditions, morality and the like, but in its origin his
substance when analysed turns out to be just nothing but the
representation, the utterance, the emphasis of these imaginations,
these emotions, arising out of particular social conditions.

Long ago Robertson Smith[2] noted that among the ancient
Semites or indeed everywhere antique religion 'was essentially an
affair of the community rather than of individuals'; the benefits
expected from the gods were of a public character, affecting the

---

[1] For fuller discussion of this point see chapter x.
[2] *Religion of the Semites*, 1889, pp. 211, 240.

whole community, especially fruitful seasons, increase of flocks and herds, and success in war. The individual sufferer, who to us is the special object of Divine protection, was more or less an outcast[1]. 'Hannah with her sad face and silent petition was a strange figure at the sanctuary of Shiloh; the leper and the mourner alike were unclean and shut out from the exercises of religion as well as from the privileges of social life.' But necessarily at the time when Robertson Smith wrote he conceived of a god as something existing independently of the community, though very closely related. This brings us to our last point.

So long as religion was defined by its object it was, to the detriment of science, confused with theology. It was currently supposed that religion was a kind of instinct of the soul after some sort of god or spirit or—as the doctrine became more rarefied —some innate power of apprehending the infinite[2]. The blunder here made was an elementary one, and took small account of facts. The most widespread and perhaps potent of all religions, Buddhism, knows no god. The error arose partly from ignorance or carelessness as to facts, and partly from the mistake in method common to all pre-scientific enquiry, the mistake of starting with a general term *religion* of which the enquirers had a preconceived idea, and then trying to fit into it any facts that came to hand.

In the present enquiry we shall at the outset attempt no definition of the term *religion*, but we shall collect the facts that admittedly are religious and see from what human activities they appear to have sprung. The Kouros and the Kouretes are such facts. They sprang, we have just seen, from certain social interests and activities. The worshippers, or rather the social agents, are prior to the god. The ritual act, what the Greeks called the δρώμενον, is prior to the divinity. The psychological genesis of the δρώμενον will be examined in the next chapter.

[1] It is when the old tribal sanctions are broken down that Aidos and Nemesis of and for the individual come into force. See Prof. Murray, *Rise of the Greek Epic*[2], p. 103.

[2] This error, originated I believe by Max Müller and adopted with various modifications and extensions by M. Réville in his *Prolégomènes à l'histoire des religions*, and by Morris Jastrow in his *Study of Religions*, has been well exposed by Prof. Durkheim in his article *De la définition des phénomènes religieux* in Année Sociologique, II. (1898), pp. 4 ff.

Note to p. 17. I withdraw the etymology of Titanes (white-clay-men) in favour of F. Solmseu's explanation of Titanes as Kings. See *Indogermanische Forschungen*, 1912, xxx. 35 and Mr A. B. Cook, *Zeus*, I. p. 655. For the function of the King-God in relation to the Fertility-Drama and the part he played in the development of the Eniautos-Daimon see my *Epilegomena*, pp. 18–26.

CHAPTER II.

THE DITHYRAMB, THE ΔΡΩΜΕΝΟΝ AND THE DRAMA.

ΘΙΑϹΕΥΕΤΑΙ ΨΥΧΑΝ.

WE have seen the Kouros grow out of the band of his attendants the Kouretes, yet the Kouretes and the Kouros remain
figures somewhat alien and remote, belonging to a bygone
civilization, only to be realized by comparison with barbarous
analogies. We have further seen or rather suspected that in the
thiasos of Dionysos, in his attendant Satyrs, the band of *daimones*
who attended the Kouros found its closest analogy. This clue if
followed leads to a conclusion as unlooked for as it is illuminating
—Dionysos is the Kouros. The Cretan cult of the Kouretes and
the Thracian religion of Dionysos are substantially one.

Anyone entering the theatre of Dionysos for the first time will
probably seat himself at once in the great chair of the high priest
of Dionysos, midway in the front row of the spectators' seats.
Immediately opposite him, as his Baedeker will inform him, is
the logeion or 'stage,' as it is usually though incorrectly called,
of Phaedrus[1]. He will be told that this 'stage' is late, dating not
earlier than the time of Septimius Severus (193–211 A.D.), and, in
his haste to search for the traces of the ancient circular orchestra,
he may be inclined to pass it by; yet he will do well to give to
the sculptured frieze that decorates it a passing glance. On the
first slab to the right of the steps (Fig. 5) is represented as is
fitting the birth of the god to whom the theatre is consecrate,
Dionysos. The birth is just accomplished. Zeus is seated in the

---

[1] For archaeological details see my *Mythology and Monuments of Ancient Athens*,
p. 282.

centre; opposite him Hermes stands, holding the new-born child; to either side stands a nude guardian figure holding a shield. Who are the armed guardians?   Who but the *Kouretes*?

The seated Zeus on the relief is full grown, no longer a Kouros; he is Father of the new-born child—he is the familiar Zeus of classical theology, Father of Gods and men.   Yet he is attended by the Kouretes.   Why this shift of functions, this transformation of character?   Why this blend of Cretan and Theban mythology? We shall find the answer it may be in the subject of the present chapter, the myth and ritual of the Dithyramb.

'Dithyramb,' like 'Kouros' and 'Kouretes,' is a word of somewhat remote and obscure association.   We think of a Dithyramb not as a god, but as a form of lyric, full of thrill in its very

Fig. 5.

name, but excited, exotic, apt to become licentious.   It is with the form rather than the content of the Dithyramb that the modern commentator is mainly concerned.   The very name might by now have sunk into obscurity as a mere curiosity for specialists, but for one fact which most intimately concerns us.   We are told on the best authority[1] that the Dithyramb gave birth to a literary offspring greater, more vital than itself—to tragedy.   The beginnings of drama and of primitive magical rites are, we shall presently see, intertwined at the very roots.   It is then of the first importance that we should grasp as far as may be the nature and origin of the Dithyramb.

[1] This authority has recently been called in question. See Prof. Ridgeway, *Origin of Tragedy*, 1910, *passim*.

Aristotle in a famous sentence has left us his views as to the origin of tragedy. 'Tragedy—as also Comedy,' he says in the *Poetics*[1], 'was at first mere improvisation. *The one originated with the leaders of the dithyramb*, the other with those of the phallic songs which are still in use in many of our cities.' Dithyramb and drama alike may seem for the moment alien to the subject of our last chapter, but it will soon appear that an enquiry into their origin and interaction will throw fresh light on the relations between the Kouros and the Kouretes, and will go far to illuminate the strange conjunction of the stage of Phaedrus.

What then is the Dithyramb? What element in it caused this parting of the ways between it and comedy? Something there must have been that differentiated it out from the common phallic mime, some seed of beauty and solemn significance that was to blossom into tragedy, there to find what Aristotle[2] calls its φύσις, and then to cease.

Plato[3] is our single and sufficient direct authority. In discussing the various sorts of odes he says, 'Some are prayers to the gods, and these are called by the title *hymns*; others of an opposite sort might best be called *dirges*, another sort are *paeans*, and another—the birth of Dionysos I suppose—is called *Dithyramb.*' Plato throws out this all-important statement with a touch of indifference (οἶμαι), as of a thing accredited, but too technical to be interesting. Scholars[4], guiltless of any knowledge of initiation-ceremonies, have usually assumed that Plato has been misled by the false etymology of the Double Door. Is it not at least as possible that this false etymology arose, in part of course from the form of an ancient ritual title misunderstood, but in greater part from the fact that Plato's statement is literally true, that the Dithyramb was originally the *Song of the Birth*?

---

1 iv. 12 γενομένη (δ') οὖν ἀπ' ἀρχῆς αὐτοσχεδιαστική, καὶ αὐτὴ καὶ ἡ κωμῳδία, καὶ ἡ μὲν ἀπὸ τῶν ἐξαρχόντων τὸν διθύραμβον, ἡ δὲ ἀπὸ τῶν τὰ φαλλικὰ ἃ ἔτι καὶ νῦν ἐν πολλαῖς τῶν πόλεων διαμένει νομιζόμενα.

2 *op. cit.* καὶ πολλὰς μεταβολὰς μεταβαλοῦσα ἡ τραγῳδία ἐπαύσατο ἐπεὶ ἔσχε τὴν αὑτῆς φύσιν.

3 *Legg.* 700 B ...καὶ παίωνες ἕτερον καὶ ἄλλο Διονύσου γένεσις, οἶμαι, διθύραμβος λεγόμενος.

4 See especially Crusius in Pauly Wissowa, *Real-Encyclopädie, s.v.* Dithyrambos, p. 1208. See also my *Prolegomena,* pp. 412 and 437—445, where the sources for the Dithyramb as Birth-Song are collected but the connection with the New Birth and Initiation Rites is not understood.

Timotheos, tradition said, wrote a Dithyramb called the Birth-pangs of Semele (Σεμέλης ὠδῖνες), and of a Dithyramb by Pindar we possess a beautiful fragment (p. 203) which tells of the Birth of Bromios from Semele in the spring-time. But the best evidence of the truth of Plato's statement comes to us from the *Bacchae*[1] of Euripides. The Bacchos has been bound and led off to the dungeon; all seems lost; and the chorus makes its supreme appeal to Thebes not to disallow the worship of the god. They chant the story of his miraculous double birth, from which, they think, his title of Dithyrambos, He-of-the-Twofold-Door, is derived.

> Acheloüs' roaming daughter,
> Holy Dirce, virgin water,
> Bathed he not of old in thee,
> The Babe of God, the Mystery?
> When from out the fire immortal
>   To himself his God did take him,
>   To his own flesh, and bespake him:
> 'Enter now life's second portal,
>   Motherless Mystery; lo, I break
>   Mine own body for thy sake,
>   Thou of the Twofold Door, and seal thee
>   Mine, O Bromios'—thus he spake—
>   'And to this thy land reveal thee.'

I have quoted Prof. Gilbert Murray's version because it renders so convincingly the stately, almost stiff, dogmatic, ritual tone of the hymn, its formalism which suddenly at the end of the strophe breaks into tender and delicate poetry. This strange and beautiful song, we are asked to believe, arose not out of ancient ritual, but from a grotesque fable based on a false etymology. scholars are a race strangely credulous. Once the suggestion made, it is surely evident that we have in the song the reflection, the presentation, of rites of initiation seen or heard of by Euripides among the Bacchants of Macedonia. It is even probable, I think, that actual pronouncements from actual ritual formularies are quoted.

The child is snatched by its father Zeus from the immortal

---

[1] *v.* 518 ff.

ὅτε μηρῷ πυρὸς ἐξ ἀ-
θανάτου Ζεὺς ὁ τεκὼν ἥρ-
πασέ νιν τάδ' ἀναβοάσας·
Ἴθι, Διθύραμβ', ἐμὰν ἄρ-
σενα τάνδε βᾶθι νηδύν·
ἀναφαίνω σε τόδ', ὦ Βάκ-
χιε, Θήβαις ὀνομάζειν.

fire—an allusion of course to the Epiphany of Zeus in the Thunderstorm.　But the 'immortal fire' also reflects an initiation-rite of
purgation by fire, a rite which, in weakened form, lasted on to
classical times in the ἀμφιδρόμια[1], or 'Running round the fire,'
performed when the child was from five to seven days old.　Such
a rite lies at the back of the story of Demeter and Demophon[2].
The goddess would have made the child 'deathless and ageless
for all his days'; by day she anointed him with ambrosia, by night
she hid him in the strength of fire like a brand.　The expression
'the strength of fire' (πυρὸς μένος) explains the gist of the rite.
The child is weak and helpless, exposed to every kind of evil
chance and sorcery.　In fire is a great strength, and the child
must be put in contact with this strength to catch its contagion
and grow strong.　The water rite, baptism, has the same intent.
Water too is full of sanctity, of force, of *mana*; through water
comes the birth into a new life.　In the hymn of the Bacchae it
almost looks as if the water, the bathing in Dirke, might be for
the quenching of the burning child, but that is not the original
notion.　The baptism of water and the baptism of fire are to the
same end, the magical acquisition of ghostly strength.　In ancient
Christian ritual before the candidate was immersed a blazing
torch was thrust down into the font.　The emphasis was rather
on regeneration than purification.

　　The child then is purified, or rather perhaps we should say
strengthened and revitalized, by fire and water; new and stronger
life is put into him.　Yet another rite remains of singular significance, and it is introduced with emphasis[3].　The Father-god
'cries aloud' (ἀναβοάσας)[4].　This loud, clear, emphatic utterance
makes us expect some weighty ritual pronouncement, and such a
pronouncement immediately follows : *Come, O Dithyrambos, enter*

---

[1] For sources see Pauly-Wissowa, *s.v.*
[2] *Hom. Hymn* II. 239 νύκτας δὲ κρύπτεσκε πυρὸς μένει ἠΰτε δαλόν.　See Mr R. W.
Halliday, *Note on Homeric Hymn to Demeter*, 239 ff. in Class. Rev. 1911, p. 8.
[3] Eur. *Bacch.* 526

> ἴθι, Διθύραμβ', ἐμὰν ἄρ-
> σενα τάνδε βᾶθι νηδύν·
> ἀναφαίνω σε τόδ', ὦ Βάκ-
> χιε, Θήβαις ὀνομάζειν.

[4] βοή, originally βοϝή, the lowing of cattle, seems to be a regular ritual word.
Pindar (*Ol.* XIII. 25) calls the Dithyramb βοηλάτας, and in the account in the
Philosophoumena, ed. Cruice, 1860, p. 170, of the mystic birth in the Eleusinian
Mysteries it is said of the Hierophant βοᾷ καὶ κέκραγε λέγων, ἱερὸν ἔτεκε πότνια
κοῦρον, Βριμὼ Βριμόν.

this my male womb. The child is to be born anew, not of his mother Semele, but of his father Zeus, and—significant fact—his Epiphany at Thebes is to be marked by the new name Dithyrambos, common to child and Birth-song alike. What does it all mean?

Taken at its face value it is of course nonsense. The God Dithyrambos is born of his mother, well and good. He was not, could not be, born again of his father. Birth belongs to the category of facts that cannot be repeated. How then is the second birth explained by scholars? Until quite lately it was left at its face value: it was nonsense, only it was 'poetical' nonsense. Moreover it was a mystery, and into a mystery it was perhaps as well not to look too closely. By an ancient *mystery* people used to understand something enacted in secret, and probably offensive. To the word *mystery* we now attach a perfectly definite meaning. A *mystery* is a rite, a δρώμενον enacted with magical intent. It is secret, not because it is indecent, but because it is intensely social, decent and entirely sacred.

When the critical spirit awoke, and it was felt that some definite meaning must be attached to the second birth of the Dithyramb, the next suggestion was that it embodied a social shift from matriarchy to patriarchy. This was a step in the right direction because it was an attempt to see in a religious dogma the utterance, the projection of a social fact; but the explanation, though it has elements of truth, is, I now feel[1], inadequate. The shift from matriarchy to patriarchy never crystallized into a rite, never burst into a ritual hymn.

The birth from the father cannot be real; it must therefore be sham, or to speak more elegantly, it must be mimetic. When we examine later the nature and psychology of a δρώμενον it will be seen that all rites *quâ* rites are mimetic, but the rite of the New Birth is in its essence *the* mimetic rite *par excellence.* After our discussion of the Kouretes the gist of this mimetic rite needs no further elucidation. The New Birth of the Dithyramb, like the New Birth of the Kouros, reflects a tribal rite of initiation, and in both cases we have a blend of two sorts of rites, the rites

---

[1] As such I explained it in my *Prolegomena,* p. 411. The explanation was I believe first offered by Bachofen in his *Mutterrecht.*

of infancy, the rites of adolescence.   One point however requires further emphasis.

In the case of the Kouros the child is taken from its mother, in the case of the Dithyramb it is actually re-born from the thigh of its father.   In both cases the intent is the same, but in the case of the Dithyramb it is far more emphatically expressed.   The birth from the male womb is to rid the child from the infection of his mother—to turn him from a woman-thing into a man-thing. Woman to primitive man is a thing at once weak and magical, to be oppressed, yet feared.   She is charged with powers of child-bearing denied to man, powers only half understood, forces of attraction, but also of danger and repulsion, forces that all over the world seem to fill him with dim terror.   The attitude of man to woman, and, though perhaps in a less degree, of woman to man, is still to-day essentially magical.

Man cannot escape being born of woman, but he can, and, if he is wise, will, as soon as he comes to manhood, perform cere-monies of riddance and purgation.   Initiation rites teem with such ceremonies, and savage life is everywhere hampered by sex taboos[1].   Among the tribes of Western Victoria if a boy is caught eating a female opossum he is severely punished; it will make him 'like a girl,' that is peevish and discontented.   Among the Narrinyeri during initiation a boy may not eat any food that has even belonged to a woman; everything he possesses becomes like himself—'narumbe,' taboo to women, sacred from their touch. If he eats with a woman he will grow ugly and become grey. Among the Kugis a woman with child—who naturally at that time is doubly a woman—may not even give food to her husband. If such a woman among the Indians of Guiana eat of game caught by hounds, the hounds will become so emasculate that they will never be able to hunt again.

The Kouretes, it will be remembered[2], take the child from the mother, Rhea.   At Sparta, Plutarch[3] tells us—and Dorian Sparta

---

[1] The few examples I give are taken from the large collection made by E. Crawley, *The Mystic Rose, A study of primitive marriage*, pp. 166–7.   See also Dr Frazer, *Golden Bough*[2], vol. I. 326, III. 204 ff.

[2] p. 13.

[3] *Vit. Lyc.* XVI.   The Lesche seems to be the Greek equivalent of the 'Man's House.'   See p. 27.   For a similar Boeotian custom see Sophocles, *Oed. Tyr.* 1035.

is, as much as Crete, the home of primitive custom—at Sparta it was not left even to the father, much less to the mother, to decide what children he would rear; he was obliged to bring the child to a place called the *Lesche*, there to be examined by the most ancient men of the tribe to see if he was stout and strong and fit to be a tribesman. If he was weakly he was thrown down a crag of Taÿgetos. It must have been an anxious time for many a mother, and that anxiety is, it may be, in part reflected in the many stories of mothers who hide their child directly after birth. Rhea hides Zeus from Kronos. Auge[1] has a child by Heracles and conceals him. Evadne[2] hid her child amid the reeds in a dim thicket, and 'his tender body was bedewed with the gleam of pansy flowers purple and gold, and no man had seen him or heard of him though he was now born five days.' Stories of this type, where the child is hid by the mother from fear of the father, have hitherto been explained[3] by some story of a divine father and the mother's fear of the human father's anger.

The child, whether concealed or acknowledged, might remain with its mother for a time. She will practise on it her mother-rites. She will, perhaps, like the Spartan[4] mother, wash her baby with wine to strengthen it. She will certainly bathe or sprinkle it with holy water and pass it through the fire. She may wean it from her own breast and feed it with honey and alien milk, but, sooner or later, the day of separation is at hand. The Kouretes of the tribe will come and will take him away, will hide him for weeks or months in the bush, will clothe him in strange clothes, teach him strange dances and strange lore, and bring him back all changed, with a new soul, the soul of his tribe, his mother's child no more, trained it may be henceforth to scorn or spit at her. He belongs from henceforth to his father and to the Man's House.

Nowhere have I been able to find among savage tribes any mimic birth from the father[5], that is any strict parallel to the

---

[1] Paus. VIII. 4. 8.
[2] Pind. *Ol.* VI. 52

τοὶ δ' οὔτ' ἂν ἀκοῦσαι
οὔτ' ἰδεῖν εὔχοντο πεμπταῖον γεγεναμένον · ἀλλ' ἐν
κέκρυπτο γὰρ σχοίνῳ βατίᾳ ἐν ἀπειράτῳ.

[3] The new explanation offered here was suggested to me by Mr F. M. Cornford.
[4] Plutarch, *op. cit.*
[5] The customs of the *Couvade* which might seem to belong here can I think be otherwise better explained.

mimic birth of Dithyrambos from the thigh of Zeus, though, such is the secrecy about initiation rites, that a ceremony of this kind may well exist unrecorded and only wait observation.   But at the initiation rites known as the *Bora*[1] in New South Wales the 'surrender of the boys by their mother is dramatically represented. A circle is marked out, the mothers of those to be initiated stand just outside it, the boys are bidden to enter the circle, and thus magically pass from the women to the men of the tribe.

The δρώμενον then that underlies the ritual of the Dithyramb and of the Kouros is one and the same, the rite of the New Birth. This is the cardinal doctrine of the *Bacchae*.   That is why in their hour of supreme peril they invoke the Dithyramb.   It is against this rite of the New Birth that Pentheus blasphemes.   It is to that Rite personified as Purity, Sanctity, Holiness, that the Bacchants raise their Hymn[2]:

> Thou Immaculate on high,
> Thou Recording Purity.

The Hymn of the New Birth becomes a god *Dithyrambos*, the Rite of Purification becomes a goddess Purity—*Hosia*, and Purity outraged is near akin to the Dike later (*v.* 1015) invoked. Both are guardians of τὰ νόμιμα.

It has been seen that the Kouros is but the projection of the Kouretes; it is equally manifest that Dionysos is but his thiasos incarnate.   But here instantly a difficulty presents itself.   Dionysos, the Bacchos, has a thiasos of Bacchae.   But how can a thiasos of women project a young male god?   They cannot and do not.   Who then do they worship, what divine figure is their utterance?   They tell us themselves; they shout it at us in a splendid ritual song.

In the first chorus they chant the praise of Thebes, birthplace of the Dithyramb son of Semele:

> All hail, O Thebes, thou nurse of Semelê!
> With Semelê's wild ivy crown thy towers[3].

---

[1] Webster, *Primitive Secret Societies*, p. 21, quoting Matthews.

[2] *v.* 170 Ὁσία πότνα θεῶν. For ὁσία with the meaning 'rite of initiation,' see *Hom. Hymn to Demeter*, 211 δεξαμένη δ' ὁσίης ἐπέβη πολυπότνια Δηώ. In offering this interpretation, and in what follows as to the Bacchants, I do not mean to imply that Euripides was always fully conscious of the primitive material which lay behind his plot.

[3] *Eur. Bacch.* 105   ὦ Σεμέλας τροφοὶ Θῆ-
βαι, στεφανοῦσθε κισσῷ.

Then in the antistrophe they turn and sing, of what? Of Crete and the Kouretes, of Mother Rhea and the Child Zeus[1].

> Hail thou, O Nurse of Zeus, O Caverned Haunt,
>   Where fierce arms clanged to guard God's cradle rare.
> For thee of old some crested Corybant
>   First woke in Cretan air,
> The wild orb of our orgies,
>   Our Timbrel.

The chorus has neither sense nor antiphonal structure of meaning, save that the worship of the Dithyramb was one with the worship of the Kouros. The priest of Dionysos as he sat in his great seat and looked across at the 'stage of Phaedrus' with its seated Zeus, its new-born Dionysos, its attendant Kouretes, would remember and understand.

And, that there may be no mistake, the chorus insist that the ritual gear of Dionysos is the ritual gear of the Mother:

> The timbrel, the timbrel was another's,
>   And back to mother Rhea must it wend.
> And to our holy singing from the Mother's,
>   The mad Satyrs carried it to blend
>   In the dancing and the cheer
>   Of our third and perfect Year,
> And it serves Dionysos in the end[2].

The Bacchants are not indicating the analogy between two cults as though they were a parcel of commentators making marginal notes. Half mad with excitement they shout aloud the dogmas of their most holy religion—the religion of the Mother and the Child.

The Maenads are the mothers and therefore the nurses of the holy child; only a decadent civilization separates the figures of mother and nurse. As nurses they rear the holy child till the armed, full-grown men take him away to their new Child-Rearing

---

[1] Eur. *Bacch.* 119

ὦ θαλάμευμα Κουρή-
των ζάθεοί τε Κρήτας
Διογενέτορες ἔναυλοι.

[2] v. 130

παρὰ δὲ μαινόμενοι Σάτυροι
ματέρος ἐξανύσαντο θεᾶς,
    ἐς δὲ χορεύματα
συνῆψαν τριετηρίδων,
    αἷς χαίρει Διόνυσος.

(παιδοτροφία). As nurses they are thrice familiar. In Homer[1] the god has his nurses (τιθῆναι), chased by Lykoörgos:

> Through Nysa's goodly land
> He Dionysos' Nursing Nymphs did chase.

Sophocles in the *Oedipus at Colonos*[2] knows of the Nurses:

> Footless sacred shadowy thicket, where a myriad berries grow,
> Where no heat of the sun may enter, neither wind of the winter blow,
> Where the Reveller Dionysos with his Nursing Nymphs will go.

At Delphi, Plutarch[3] tells us, the Thyiades, nurses of Dionysos, wake up the child Dionysos in the cradle.

The Bacchants are the Mothers; that is why at their coming they have magical power to make the whole earth blossom:

> Oh burst in bloom of wreathing bryony,
> Berries and leaves and flowers[4].

It is not only the 'wild white maids,' but the young mothers with babes at home who are out upon the mountains:

> And one a young fawn held, and one a wild
> Wolf cub, and fed them with white milk, and smiled
> In love, young mothers with a mother's heart,
> And babes at home forgotten[5]!

At the touch of their wands, from the rocks break out streams of wine and water, and milk and honey[6].

It is at the great service of the Mothers on Mount Cithaeron that the whole of creation moves and stirs and lives:

> All the mountain felt
> And worshipped with them, and the wild things knelt
> And ramped, and gloried, and the wilderness
> Was filled with moving voices and dim stress[7].

It is against the religion of the Bacchants, as Nurses and Mothers of all that is, that Pentheus rages, charging them, the Mothers, with license, banning their great service of Aphrodite.

---

[1] *Il.* VI. 129
> ὅς ποτε μαινομένοιο Διωνύσοιο τιθήνας
> σεῦε κατ' ἠγάθεον Νυσήϊον.

[2] v. 679
> ἵν' ὁ βακχιώτας
> ἀεὶ Διόνυσος ἐμβατεύει
> θεαῖς ἀμφιπολῶν τιθήναις.

[3] *De Isid. et Os.* ...ὅταν αἱ Θυιάδες ἐγείρωσι τὸν Λικνίτην. For Dionysos Liknites see *Prolegomena*, p. 402.

[4] Eur. *Bacch.* 107
> βρύετε, βρύετε, χλοήρει
> μίλακι καλλικάρπῳ κ.τ.λ.

[5] v. 699.   [6] v. 705.   [7] v. 726.

And, appealing to their most holy Rite of the New Birth, they turn and answer his foul-mouthed blasphemy in that song of increase and grace and peace unspeakable[1]:

> Where is the Home for me?
>   O Cyprus set in the sea,
> Aphrodite's home in the soft sea-foam
>   Would I could wend to thee;

and, in the awful irony of the end, it is by his mother's hand that Pentheus is torn to pieces.

The attitude of Pentheus seems to us blasphemous, intolerable; yet if we reflect calmly it is not hard to see how it arose. The divine figures of Mother and Child reflect the social conditions of a matriarchal group with its rite of adolescent initiation; its factors are the mother, the child and the tribe, the child as babe and later as Kouros. But when, chiefly through the accumulation of property, matriarchy passes and patriarchy takes its place, the relation of mother to child is less prominent; the child is viewed as part of the property of the father. Moreover with the decay of matriarchy, initiation ceremonies lose their pristine significance. It is not hard to see that, given women worshippers and a young male god grown to adolescence, the relation of son to mother might be misconceived as that of lover to bride. We find the same misunderstanding of matriarchal conditions in the parallel figures of Adonis and Aphrodite.

The memory of primitive matriarchal conditions often survives rather curiously in mythology. Dionysos is not alone. Again and again we have stories of this god or that who is 'reared by the Nymphs.' Apollo tells Hermes how the Thriae, the bee-maidens, reared him in a glade of Parnassos; they taught him soothsaying while he tended his kine, and—he adds naively—

> my father took no heed[2].

So far then it has been established that behind the Dithyramb lay a rite, a δρώμενον, and that rite was one of group initiation. Further it has been seen that the group belonged to the social

---

[1] Eur. *Bacch.* 402, adopting the Oxford text; for other readings and views see Dr Verrall, *The Bacchants of Euripides*, p. 155.

[2] *Hom. Hymn to Hermes*, 557

> πατὴρ δ' ἐμὸς οὐκ ἀλέγιζεν.

structure known as matriarchal, a structure reflected in the divine
figures of Mother and Babe or Kouros, rather than in that of
Father and Son. We shall have later to consider more closely
how the divine figure developed from the human institution; but
first it is all-important that we should examine and if possible
define the precise nature of a δρώμενον. We shall then be in a
position to see more clearly how from the particular δρώμενον
under consideration, the Dithyramb, arose, on the one hand, for
theology, a god, on the other, if Aristotle be right, for art, the
drama[1].

Etymologically δρώμενα are of course *things done*[2]. It is,
however, at once evident that the word in its technical use as
meaning religious rites, *sacra*, does not apply to all things done.
The eating of your dinner, the digesting of your food, are assuredly
things done, and very important things, but they are not δρώμενα.
Nor does a thing done become a δρώμενον simply because it is
done socially, collectively; a large number of persons may eat and
digest their dinner collectively, yet the act remains secular. What
is it that adds the sanctity[3], that makes the act in our sense
religious?

First the act must be strongly felt about, must cause or be
caused by a keen emotion. The great events of life, birth,
adolescence, marriage, death, do not incessantly repeat themselves;
it is about these events that religion largely focuses. When the
getting of certain foods was irregular and precarious, a source of
anxiety and joy, the eating of such foods was apt to be religious
and protected by taboos. The regular rising and setting of sun
and moon and stars, because regular, cause little or no emotion;
but religion early focused on things of tension and terror, the
thunderstorm and the monsoon. Such manifestations cause vivid
reactions. Tension finds relief in excited movement; you dance
and leap for fear, for joy, for sheer psychological relief. It is this

---

[1] In the present chapter the first only of these questions will be considered, the
genesis of the god from the δρώμενον. The relation of drama to the Dithyramb is
reserved for chapters VII. and VIII., and see Prof. Murray's Excursus after chapter VIII.

[2] In the specialized sense of 'rites' δρώμενα consist of two factors (a) the thing
done, the δρώμενον proper, and (b) the thing *said*, τὸ λεγόμενον. The thing *said*,
which is the element of myth, will be considered later, p. 327.

[3] The notion of sanctity will be further analysed in chapter III.

excited doing, this dancing, that is the very kernel of both drama and δρώμενον. Our Kouretes were dancers (ὀρχηστῆρες).

A high emotional tension is best caused and maintained by a thing felt socially. The individual in a savage tribe has but a thin and meagre personality. If he dances alone he will not dance long; but if his whole tribe dances together he will dance the live-long night and his emotion will mount to passion, to ecstasy. Save for the χόρος, the band, there would be no drama and no δρώμενον. Emotion socialized, felt collectively, is emotion intensified and rendered permanent. Intellectually the group is weak; everyone knows this who has ever sat on a committee and arrived at a confused compromise. Emotionally the group is strong; everyone knows this who has felt the thrill of speaking to or acting with a great multitude.

The next step or rather notion implied is all important. A δρώμενον is as we said not simply a thing done, not even a thing excitedly and socially done. What is it then? It is a thing *re*-done or *pre*-done, a thing enacted or represented. It is sometimes *re*-done, commemorative, sometimes *pre*-done, anticipatory, and both elements seem to go to its religiousness. When a tribe comes back from war or from hunting, or even from a journey, from any experience in fact that from novelty or intensity causes strong emotion, the men will, if successful, recount and dance their experiences to the women and children at home. Such a dance we should perhaps scarcely call religious, but when the doings of dead chiefs in the past or ancestors are commemorated, when the dance is made public and social, and causes strong emotion, it takes on a religious colour[1]. The important point to note is that the hunting, fighting, or what not, the thing done, is never religious; the thing re-done with heightened emotion is on the way to become so. The element of action re-done, imitated, the element of μίμησις, is, I think, essential. In all religion, as in all art, there is this element of make-believe. Not the attempt to deceive, but a desire to *re*-live, to *re*-present.

Why do we 'represent' things at all; why do we not just do them and have done with it? This is a curious point. The

---

[1] This element of commemoration in the δρώμενον will be more fully examined when we reach the question of the relation of hero-worship to the drama (chapter VIII.).

occasion, though scarcely the cause, of these representations is
fairly clear. Psychologists tell us that representations, ideas,
imaginations, all the intellectual, conceptual factors in our life
are mainly due to deferred reactions. If an impulse finds instantly
its appropriate satisfaction, there is no representation. It is out
of the delay, just the space between the impulse and the reaction,
that all our mental life, our images, ideas, our consciousness, our
will, most of all our religion, arise. If we were utterly, instantly
satisfied, if we were a mass of well contrived instincts, we
should have no representations, no memory, no μίμησις, no
δρώμενα, no drama. Art and religion alike spring from unsatisfied desire[1].

Another point should be noted. When the men return from
the war, the hunt, the journey, and *re*-enact their doings, they
are at first undoubtedly representing a particular action that
actually has taken place. Their drama is history or at least
narrative; they say in effect, such and such a thing *did* happen
in the past. Everything with the savage begins in this *particular*
way. But, it is easy to see that, if the dramatic commemoration
be often repeated, the action tends to cut itself loose from the
particular in which it arose and become generalized, abstracted as
it were. The particular hunt, journey, battle, is in the lapse of
time forgotten or supplanted by a succession of similar hunts,
journeys, battles, and the dance comes to commemorate and
embody hunting, journeying, fighting. Like children they play
not at a funeral, but at 'funerals,' births, battles, what not. To
put it grammatically, the singular comes first, but the singular
gets you no further. The plural detaches you from the single
concrete fact; and all the world over, the plural, the *neuter* plural
as we call it, begets the abstract. Moreover, the time is no longer
particular, it is undefined, not what happened but what happens.
Such a dance generalized, universalized, is material for the next
stage, the dance *pre*-done.

The religious character of μίμησις comes out perhaps more
clearly when the action is *pre*-done, for here we are closely neigh-
boured by magic. A tribe about to go to war will dance a war

---

[1] For the function of imitation in the development of religious rites see Dr P.
Beck, *Die Nachahmung und ihre Bedeutung für Psychologie und Völkerkunde*,
Leipzig, 1904.

dance, men about to start out hunting will catch their game in pantomime. Such cases are specially instructive because it is fairly clear that the drama or δρώμενον here is a sort of precipitated desire, a discharge of pent-up emotion. The thought of the hunt, the desire to catch the game or kill the enemy cannot find expression yet in the actual act; it grows and accumulates by inhibition till at last the exasperated nerves and muscles can bear it no longer and it breaks out into mimetic, anticipatory action. Mimetic, not of what you see done by another, but of what you desire to do yourself.

Now so far in these mimetic rites, whether commemorative or anticipatory or magical, though they cover a large portion of the ceremonies that when practised by savage peoples we call religious, there is certainly nothing present that by any straining of language can be called a god, nothing equivalent to what *we* mean now-a-days by worship. In the Hymn of the Kouretes, as has already been noted, though the god is there as Kouros, he is not worshipped; there is no praise, nor prayer, nor sacrifice, he is simply bidden to come and to 'leap,' he and his attendants. The all-important question must now be asked, how did this figure of the god arise? The answer has been in part anticipated in the account of the Kouros.

The Dithyramb, we are always told, was not the outpouring of an individual inspired singer, but rather a choric dance, the dance and song of a band. As singing a Birth-Song the band must have been a band of youths just initiated or about to be initiated, dancing an excited mimetic dance; but in less specialized rites it might be a war-dance, a rain-dance, a thunder-dance. The dancers dancing together utter their conjoint desire, their delight, their terror, in steps and gestures, in cries of fear or joy or lamentation, in shrieks of war. In so uttering they inevitably emphasize and intensify it. Moreover being a collective emotion it is necessarily felt as something more than the experience of the individual, as something dominant and external. The dancers themselves by every means in their power seek to heighten this effect. They sink their own personality and by the wearing of masks and disguises, by dancing to a common rhythm, above all by the common excitement, they become emotionally one, a true congregation, not a collection of individuals. The emotion they feel collectively, the thing that is more than any individual emotion, they externalize, project; it is the raw material of god-head. Primitive gods are to a large extent collective enthusiasms, uttered, formulated. *Le dieu c'est le désir extériorisé, personnifié*[1].

Strong and dominant though this collective emotion is, it might never crystallize into anything like a personality but for a nucleus of actual fact. Democratic or oligarchic though primitive peoples tend to be, the band of dancers, the χόρος, has for practical convenience a leader, an ἔξαρχος[2]. The Kouretes have a 'greatest Kourês'; an inscription[3] from Ephesos mentions not only a college of Kouretes, but an official known as a Chief Koures (πρωτοκούρης). Among the officials of the *thiasos* of Iobacchoi[4] at Athens, whose club-rules have come down to us intact, is an archbacchos (ἀρχίβακχος).

Having chosen as spokesman, leader and representative a πρωτοκούρης, a *praesul* or chief dancer, they differentiate him to the utmost, make him their vicar, and then draw off. Their attitude becomes gradually one of contemplation and respect; community of emotion ceases. More and more the chorus become interested spectators, at first wholly sympathetic, later critical. Theatrically speaking they become an audience, religiously, the worshippers of a god. The process of severance between god and worshipper, actor and audience, is slow. Actual worship, of prayer and praise and sacrifice, denotes that the severance is complete; ritual such as that of the Kouretes, in which the god is 'summoned' and bidden to leap, denotes an intermediate stage when he is merely representative and felt to be of like passions though of higher potency than his summoner. Gradually the chorus loses all sense that the god is themselves, he is utterly projected, no longer chief daemon (δαιμόνων ἀγούμενος), but unique and aloof, a perfected θεός. Strong emotion collectively experienced begets this illusion of objective reality; each worshipper is conscious of something in his emotion not himself, stronger than himself. He

---

[1] See E. Doutté, *Magie et Religion*, 1909, p. 601; for other elements that go to the making of a god see chapter III.

[2] Cf. Aristotle, *loc. cit.*, ἀπὸ τῶν ἐξαρχόντων τοῦ Διθυράμβου, and Euripides, *Bacch.* 140 ὁ δ' ἔξαρχος Βρόμιος.

[3] Dittenberger, *Syll.* I.² 1861, 1.

[4] See my *Prolegomena*, pp. 656 and 475.

does not know it is the force of collective suggestion, he calls it a god. As Philo[1] puts it, 'Bacchic and Korybantic worshippers rave until they actually *see* what they desire.'

This process of projection, of deification, is much helped by what we may perhaps call the story-telling instinct. The god like his worshipper must have a life-history. We hear much of the sufferings ($\pi\acute{a}\theta\eta$) of Dionysos. They are of course primarily the projected $\pi\acute{a}\theta\eta$ of his worshippers; the worshippers have passed through the rite of Second Birth, have endured the death that issues in resurrection; therefore the god is Twice-Born. But once the life-history projected, it tends to consolidate the figure of the god and to define his personality, to crystallize and clear it of all demonic vagueness. Even in the time of the Christian fathers[2] it was realized that the great festivals of the gods were commemorations of the events of a god's life—his birth, his marriage, his exploits, sufferings, death. They used this undoubted fact as an argument to show that the gods were but divinized men, whose deeds ($\acute{a}\theta\lambda a$) were solemnly commemorated. What the Christian fathers necessarily could not realize was that it was the social life of the group rather than the individual that became the object of religious representation.

Nowhere so clearly as in the religion of Dionysos do we see the steps of the making of the god, and nowhere is this religion so vividly presented to the imagination as in the *Bacchae* of Euripides. The very vividness, the oneness of the perception, seen with the single intention of the poet, makes it to us hard of apprehension and has rendered necessary the cold psychological analysis just attempted.

The question is often raised—is the Bacchos the god Dionysos himself or merely a human leader, an adept, an impostor, as Pentheus held? He is one and both, human and divine, because, as we have seen, divinity at its very source is human. In the *Bacchae*

---

[1] *de vit. contemplat.* 2, p. 473 M. οἱ βακχευόμενοι καὶ κορυβαντῶντες ἐνθουσιάζουσι μέχρις ἂν τὸ ποθούμενον ἴδωσιν. See Rohde, *Psyche*, p. 304.

[2] See S. August. *de civitat. dei*, VII. 18 Unicuique eorum...ex ejus ingenio, moribus, actibus, casibus, sacra et solennia constituta. Lactantius, *Divin. instit.* v. 20 Ipsos ritus...vel ex rebus gestis hominum, vel ex casibus, vel etiam ex mortibus natos. Ludorum celebrationes deorum festa sunt, siquidem ob natales eorum vel templorum novorum dedicationes sunt constituti, and see VI. 20. The question of the life-history of the god, that is the orderly sequence of his festivals, will be discussed when we come to the ἐνιαυτός, p. 331.

we catch the god in the three stages of his making, stages that shift with the changing scenes. He is a human leader, an ἔξαρχος, ὁ δ᾽ ἔξαρχος Βρόμιος[1]; he is half divinized, a *daimon* more than mortal, ὁ δαίμων ὁ Διὸς παῖς[2]. In the prologue he has no *thiasos*, he is alone, cut loose from the χορός that projected him, a full-blown Olympian Θεός.

Full-blown but never full-grown. Unlike Zeus he rarely quite grows up; Father-hood is never of his essence. Always through the *Bacchae* he is the young male god with tender face and fair curled hair. What seemed to Pentheus in his ignorance a base effeminacy is but the young bloom and glory of the Kouros. His name, of which philologists seem at last to have reached the interpretation, tells the same tale; he is Dionysos[3], Zeus-Young-Man, Zeus Kouros. As Bacchos he is but the incarnate cry of his *thiasos*, Iacchos[4]. So the god Paean is but the paean, the song projected.

We have been told perhaps too often that the essence of the Bacchic as contrasted with the Olympian religion is the doctrine of union and communion with the god. Now at last we see why: Bacchic religion is based on the collective emotion of the *thiasos*. Its god is a projection of group-unity. Dr Verrall in his essay on the *Bacchants of Euripides*[5] hits the mark in one trenchant, illuminating bit of translation, 'The rapture of the initiated,' he says, 'lies essentially in this: "*his soul is congregationalized,*"

$$\Theta\iota\alpha\sigma\epsilon\acute{\upsilon}\epsilon\tau\alpha\iota\ \psi\upsilon\chi\acute{\alpha}\nu.\,'$$

The Olympians are, as will later[6] appear, the last product of rationalism, of individualistic thinking; the *thiasos* has projected them utterly. Cut off from the very source of their life and being, the emotion of the *thiasos*, they desiccate and die. Dionysos with his *thiasos* is still—Comus, still trails behind him the glory of the old group ecstasy.

---

[1] Eur. *Bacch.* 140.

[2] *v.* 416.

[3] See Kretschmer, *Aus der Anomia*, 1890, p. 25 thess. Διόνυσος *Διό(σ)νυσος, sk. snuš-ā, ahd. snura, lat. nurus, gr. νυός (*σνυσός). The notion that Dionysos was a young Zeus survived into late days. Thus the scholiast on Apollonius Rhodius (ɪ. 917) says οἱ δὲ δύο πρότερον εἶναι τοὺς Καβείρους, Δία τε πρεσβύτερον καὶ Διόνυσον νεώτερον.

[4] Bacchos = Iacchos = ϝιϝακχος, see Prellwitz, *Etymologisches Wörterbuch*, p. 191; for Iacchos see my *Prolegomena*, p. 541.

[5] p. 39.   [6] Chapter x.

To resume. So far we have seen that the religion of the Kouros and the Kouretes, and of Dionysos and his *thiasos* are substantially the same. Both are the reflection of a group religion and of social conditions which are matriarchal and emphasize the figures of Mother and Child. The cardinal doctrine of both religions is the doctrine of the New Birth, and this doctrine is the reflection of the rite of social initiation. One element in the making of a god we have seen to be the projection of collective emotion, the reaction of man on his fellow man. But man does not sit in the void reacting on his fellow man; we have now to consider his reaction on the world of nature that surrounds him.

Note to p. 32. For a recent view of the Dithyramb see W. M. Calder, 'The Dithyramb an Anatolian Dirge,' *Classical Review*, 1922, p. 11.

Note to p. 37. For Initiation Ceremonies see my *Epilegomena*, pp. 14 ff.

Note to p. 48. I adhere firmly to my view expressed here and p. 27 that the Kouros of the Palaikastro Hymn is in origin but the *projection* of the worshipping Kouretes, but I should like to call the attention of every reader to an interesting and wholly opposed interpretation put forward by Mr A. B. Cook. It will be found buried in Appendix B of *Zeus* II. part II. pp. 931 and 932. Mr Cook objects to my identification of *Creator Spiritus* with *spiritus creatorum*. Yes—there is the whole controversy in a neat nutshell! though Creator Spiritus is not the epithet I should myself apply to Zeus.

CHAPTER III.

THE KOURETES, THE THUNDER-RITES AND *MANA*.

τὰ δὲ πάντα οἰακίζει κεραγνόc.

Cὴ γὰρ ἡ βαcιλεία καὶ ἡ δύναμιc καὶ ἡ δόξα εἰc τοὺc αἰῶναc.

We have not yet done with the Kouretes. A fragment of the *Cretans* of Euripides preserved for us by Porphyry[1] in his treatise on Vegetarianism contains a somewhat detailed account of a ceremonial conducted by them which is of high importance for our argument. It has certain analogies to the rites of New Birth already described, but presents also certain notable differences. It is of peculiar interest because in it are described rites of the Kouretes which culminate in the initiation of a Bacchos. This confirms the substantial identity of Bacchic and Kouretic rites which has been established in the last two chapters.

For a moment let us see where the fragment must have stood in the lost play. The evidence is in part drawn from another recently discovered fragment[2].

We are in the palace of Minos in Crete. A child has been born to the royal house, a portent, the monstrous Minotaur. Minos is troubled, he will purify the palace, will ask the meaning of the portent. The whole scene reminds us of another lost play of Euripides, *Melanippe the Wise*[3], where the portentous twins are born and Melanippe in her famous, rationalizing, truly Euripidean

---

[1] *de Abst.* iv. 19; Nauck, *Frg.* 472. For the whole fragment see my *Prolegomena*, chapter x.

[2] *Berliner Klassikertexte*, v. 2 *Gr. Dichterfragmente* (2), 1907, p. 73. See also G. Körte, *Die Kreter des Euripides*, in Hist. u. Phil. Aufsätze; E. Curtius, Berlin, 1884, p. 195; and A. Kappelmacher, *Zu den Kreten des Euripides*, Wiener Eranos, 50 Vers. Graz, 1909.

[3] Nauck, *Frg.* 484.

speech, explains that the order of the cosmos is fixed and that such things as portents cannot be. Minos then sends for the priests and medicine men, the Idaean Daktyls, presumably to purify the palace and bring peace and understanding. They leave their secret sanctuary on Ida—the strange manner of its building they describe, they come in white robes to the terror-stricken palace and in solemn anapaests tell of the manner of their life on Mount Ida and of the initiation ceremonies that have made them what they are and have given them authority to cleanse and interpret.

Their avowal of ritual acts performed on Mount Ida is as follows:

> There in one pure stream
> My days have run, the servant I
>   Initiate of Idaean Jove;
>   Where midnight Zagreus roves, I rove.
> I have endured his thunder-cry,
>
> Fulfilled his red and bleeding feasts;
>   Held the Great Mother's mountain flame;
>   Enhallowed I and named by name
> A Bacchos of the Mailed Priests.
>
> Robed in pure white I have borne me clean
>   From man's vile birth and coffined clay
>   And exiled from my lips alway
> Touch of all meat where Life hath been[1].

The analogies between these rites and the initiation rites discussed in the last chapter are obvious. We have here as there to do with mysteries performed by the 'mailed priests,' the Kouretes, and these mysteries are mysteries of Zagreus, and of the Great Mother, and of Zeus. But, be it noted, it is Idaean, not Diktaean Zeus whom the Kouretes now serve. This leads us to suspect—what is indeed I believe the fact—that we have to do with initiation ceremonies of a later and more highly developed type, initiation ceremonies not merely tribal and social, whether

---

[1]   ἁγνὸν δὲ βίον τείνων ἐξ οὗ
   Διὸς Ἰδαίου μύστης γενόμην
   καὶ νυκτιπόλου Ζαγρέως βροντὰς
   τούς τ' ὠμοφάγους δαῖτας τελέσας
   μητρί τ' ὀρείῳ δᾷδας ἀνασχὼν
   καὶ κουρήτων
   βάκχος ἐκλήθην ὁσιωθείς.

The text is Nauck's, save for the addition of τε in line 4—τούς τ' ὠμοφάγους. The translation is by Prof. Murray. With his sanction I have substituted the word 'enhallowed' for 'I am set free' in stanza two.

of infancy or adolescence, but ceremonies that have become in the later sense mysteries, rites to which only a chosen few were admitted. This seems clear from the asceticism of the avowal in the last lines. It is obvious that the whole of the initiated youth of a tribe would not be vegetarians, nor could they preserve life-long ceremonial purity from the contagion of child-birth and funerals. Moreover the initiated man in these rites was, when fully consecrated, called a Bacchos, and the Bacchoi were always a select congregation. Plato[1] tells us that those concerned with rites of initiation used to say

> Few are the Bacchoi, many bear the Wand.

It may be conjectured that the rite here administered by the Kouretes was some sort of rite of ordination of a medicine-man. In this connection it is interesting to note that Epimenides of Crete, the typical medicine-man of antiquity, was called by his contemporaries the 'new Koures.' Plutarch[2] in his account of the purification of Athens in the days of Solon says of Epimenides that he was a man of Phaistos, son of the nymph Balte, 'beloved of the gods,' and 'an adept in religious matters dealing with the lore of orgiastic and initiation rites.' It was because of this that he was reputed to be son of a nymph and gained his title of Koures. Koures, as has already been noted, can only mean *Young Man in a specialized sense.* We may conjecture—though it is only a conjecture—that the Kouretes were Young Men selected from the general band of initiated youths. One of their functions was, it appears, the consecration of the Bacchoi.

Plutarch naturally regards Epimenides as 'dear to the gods,' and an adept in matters religious, but the traditions that gathered round his name are those of magic and medicine rather than of religion. He is credited[3] indeed, and perhaps rightly, with the authorship of a *Theogony* as well as an *Argonautika*, a *Kretika*,

---

[1] *Phaed.* 69 c εἰσὶ γὰρ δὴ φασὶν οἱ περὶ τὰς τελετὰς ναρθηκοφόροι μὲν πολλοί, Βάκχοι δέ τε παῦροι. Olympiodorus *ad loc.* attributes a hexameter to this effect to Orpheus. See my *Prolegomena,* p. 474.

[2] *Vit. Solon.* XII. ...ἧκεν ἐκ Κρήτης Ἐπιμενίδης ὁ Φαίστιος....Ἐδόκει δέ τις εἶναι θεοφιλὴς καὶ σοφὸς περὶ τὰ θεῖα τὴν ἐνθουσιαστικὴν καὶ τελεστικὴν σοφίαν, διὸ καὶ παῖδα νύμφης ὄνομα Βάλτης καὶ Κούρητα νέον αὐτὸν οἱ τότε ἄνθρωποι προσηγόρευον. Diogenes cites the Ὅμοια of Myronianos as authority for the title of Koures: φησὶν ὅτι Κούρητα αὐτὸν ἐκάλουν Κρῆτες. For the name of the nymph Balte or Blaste see Pauly Wissowa, *s.v.*

[3] Diog. Laert. *Vit. Epim.* I. 111.

Purifications, Sacrifices, and *Oracles,* and, notable fact, a *Birth of the Kouretes and Korybantes*; but when we come to his life and acts his true inwardness as a medicine-man emerges. His career begins, in orthodox fashion, with a long magical sleep[1]. He was tending sheep, and turning aside to rest in the shade of a cave he fell asleep; after fifty-seven years he woke, looked for his sheep, met his younger brother, now a grey-haired man, and learnt the truth.

The long sleep is usually taken as just one of the marvels of the life of Epimenides. The real significance lies deeper. The cave in which he went to sleep was no chance cave; it was the cave of Diktaean Zeus. The sleep was no chance sleep; it was the sleep of initiation. We gather this from the account left us by Maximus of Tyre[2]. He tells us that Epimenides was not only a marvellous adept in religious matters, but also that he got his skill not by learning, and described a long sleep in which *he had a dream for his teacher.* The same authority tells us[3] that Epimenides said when he was lying at mid-day in the cave of Diktaean Zeus a deep sleep of many years befell him, and he met with the gods and divine intercourse and Truth and Justice.

Maximus found this a hard saying (λόγον πιστεύεσθαι χαλεπόν), but in the light of savage parallels the difficulty disappears. Round the figure of Epimenides the new Koures are crystallized the ordinary initiation-experiences of a medicine-man to-day. Among the tribes of Alice Springs, in Central Australia[4], if a man will become a medicine-man he must sleep, and must sleep in a special sacred cave. When he feels a call he leaves the camp and goes alone till he comes to the mouth of the cave. Here with considerable trepidation he lies down to sleep, not venturing to go inside lest he should be spirited away for ever. Next morning the *Iruntarinia* or spirit-people are supposed to come, make a hole in his tongue, pierce his head from ear to ear, carry him into the depths of the cave and there remove his internal organs and provide him with a new set. The hole is actually there

---

[1] *loc. cit.* 109. The sources for Epimenides are collected by Diels, *Fragmente d. Vorsokratiker,* II. pp. 489 ff. See also Pauly Wissowa, *s.v.*

[2] c. 22, p. 224. Diels, *Fragmente,* II. p. 494 δεινὸς δὲ ἦν ταῦτα (τὰ θεῖα) οὐ μαθών, ἀλλ' ὕπνον αὐτῶι διηγεῖτο μακρὸν καὶ ὄνειρον διδάσκαλον.

[3] c. 28, p. 286 ...⟨μέσης γὰρ⟩ ἡμέρας ἐν Δικταίου Διὸς τῶι ἄντρωι κείμενος ὕπνωι βαθεῖ ἔτη συχνὰ ὄναρ ἔφη ἐντυχεῖν αὐτὸς θεοῖς καὶ θεῶν λόγοις καὶ Ἀληθείαι καὶ Δίκηι.

[4] Spencer and Gillen, *Native Tribes of Central Australia,* p. 523.

when the man emerges from the cave. The rest of course happens
in the man's dream or trance. Among some peoples[1] the necessary
initiation-sleep is induced by a sleeping draught.

The rites we are about to examine are then not rites of simple
tribal initiation, but rather rites of initiation practised by the
Kouretes in perhaps a later stage of their development as a
magical fraternity. The Kouretes are now well on their way
to become *daimones*; they will presently become actual gods
(θεοί), as in Hesiod[2]. Diogenes[3] says that some reported that the
Kretans 'sacrificed to Epimenides as to a god.' In historical
times both Crete and Thera had a cult of the Kouretes. The
colonists of Hierapytna[4] swear not only by a long list of Olympians,
but by the Kouretes, the Nymphs, and the Korybantes. From
the mountain village of Hagia Barbaria, on the way to Gortys, has
come an inscription[5] in which 'Ertaios, son of Amnatos, to the
Kouretes, guardians of kine, fulfils his word and makes a thank-
offering.' Much earlier are the rock inscriptions in Thera[6], where
the Koures, to whom dedication is made, has his name spelt with
the ancient Koppa. From medicine-man to god was not, as will
later be seen, a far cry.

Before we proceed to examine the rites of the medicine-man,
the Bacchos, a passage in Diodorus[7] must be examined, which
bears on the relation between adolescence and ordination rites.
After a long discussion of Cretan mythology he says

The Cretans, in alleging that they handed on from Crete to other peoples
the dues of the gods, their sacrifices, and the rites appertaining to mysteries,
bring forward this point as being to their thinking the chief piece of evidence.
The rite of initiation at Eleusis, which is perhaps the most celebrated of all,
and the rite of Samothrace, among the Cicones, whence came Orpheus, its
inventor, are all imparted as mysteries; whereas in Crete, at Knossos, from

---

[1] Webster, *Primitive Secret Societies*, p. 174: among the tribes of the Lower Congo.
[2] See *supra*, p. 25.   [3] *op. cit.* 20.   [4] Blass in Collitz-Bechtel, 5039.
[5] 'Ε]ρταῖος 'Αμνάτου Κώρησι τοῖς πρὸ καρταιπόδων (ἀ)ρὰν καὶ (χα)ρι(σ)τηλον, de Sanctis,
Mon. dei Lincei, XVIII. (1908), p. 178. For the cult of the Kouretes see Prof. Bosanquet, *B.S.A.* xv. (1908–1909), p. 351 and H. v. Gaertingen, *Inschriften von Priene*
1906, p. 136, no. 186, where an inscribed basis commemorates a certain Apollodorus
as ἱερητεύοντα βασιλεῖ καὶ Κούρησιν. For the worship of Zeus Kretagenes and the
Kouretes in Karian towns, see Le Bas, *Inschriften*, III. 338, 394, 406.
[6] *I.G.I.M.A.* III. 354 ff.
[7] v. 77 ...τοῦτο φέρουσιν, ὡς οἴονται, μέγιστον τεκμήριον· τήν τε γὰρ παρ' Ἀθηναίοις
ἐν Ἐλευσῖνι γινομένην τελετήν, ἐπιφανεστάτην σχεδὸν οὖσαν ἁπασῶν καὶ τὴν ἐν Σαμοθράκῃ
καὶ τὴν ἐν Θρᾴκῃ ἐν τοῖς Κίκοσιν, ὅθεν ὁ καταδείξας Ὀρφεὺς ἦν, μυστικῶς παραδίδοσθαι,
κατὰ δὲ τὴν Κρήτην ἐν Κνωσῷ νόμιμον ἐξ ἀρχαίων εἶναι φανερῶς τὰς τελετὰς ταύτας
πᾶσι παραδίδοσθαι, καὶ τὰ παρὰ τοῖς ἄλλοις ἐν ἀπορρήτῳ παραδιδόμενα παρ' αὑτοῖς μηδένα
κρύπτειν τῶν βουλομένων τὰ τοιαῦτα γινώσκειν.

ancient days it was the custom that these rites should be imparted openly to all, and things that among other people were communicated in dead secrecy (ἐν ἀπορρήτῳ) among the Cretans, they said, no one concealed from anyone who wished to know such matters.

What seems to be behind this rather obscure statement is this. Initiation-rites of adolescence, as contrasted with initiation-rites of a magical fraternity, are comparatively public and open[1]. Every tribesman has a right to be initiated; nearly every tribesman *is* initiated and knows the secrets of initiation. A magical fraternity on the other hand is always more or less of a secret society. The rites of both sets of initiation are closely analogous[2]. They centre round the new birth, that is the new set of social relations, the new soul, and are figured by real sleep or mimic death. The rites of adolescence, and probably what we have called mother-rites, are primary, the magical fraternity-rites a later development. Crete, the mother of initiation-rites in the Ægean, kept the memory of her adolescence-rites and their comparative publicity, but when her initiation-rites passed to Greece proper and to Thrace, they had reached the magical fraternity stage. They were not only mysteries, but mysterious.

In the rites described by Euripides we have no mention of a new birth, though perhaps this is implied by the new name given, 'Bacchos.' The candidate has to hold aloft the torches of the Mountain Mother, and he has to accomplish two things, the Feasts of Raw Flesh and the Thunders of night-wandering Zagreus. The torch-light dance or procession upon the mountains (ὀρει-βάσια) is sufficiently known from the *Bacchae*. The Feasts of Raw Flesh (ὠμοφαγία) will be later discussed[3]. It is the first-named rite, the rite of the *Thunders* (βρονταί), which has long been held to be unintelligible, and on which we must now focus our attention. It will provide us with material for a sensible advance in the understanding of the origins of Greek and any other religion.

---

[1] This has been clearly brought out by M. Lévy-Bruhl in his *Fonctions Mentales dans les Sociétés Inférieures*, p. 417, entirely without reference to the passage of Diodorus, 'l'initiation des novices en général est imposée à tous, *elle est relativement publique*....'

[2] Lévy-Bruhl, *op. cit.* p. 417 'la ressemblance entre les épreuves de l'initiation des sorciers ou shamans et celles de l'initiation des novices de la tribu en général est frappante.'

[3] *Prolegomena*, pp. 479—497. A full discussion of the ὠμοφαγία will come best when we reach the question of sacrifice in chapter v.

THE RITE OF THE 'THUNDERS.'

καὶ νυκτιπόλου Ζαγρέως βροντὰς
.   .   .   .   . τελέσας.

'Having accomplished the Thunders of night-wandering
Zagreus.' What are the Thunders, and how can they be
accomplished? No answer was forthcoming, so not unnaturally
scholars proceeded to emend βροντάς[1]. Following Prof. Gilbert
Murray's advice I kept the text[2] and waited for further evidence
as to its interpretation.

Light came from an unexpected quarter. In investigating
thunderbolts I was referred to a passage, again, oddly enough, in
Porphyry. Pythagoras, Porphyry[3] tells us, in the course of his
journey from Asia Minor to Italy came to Crete. There he met
on landing some of the Mystae of Morgos, one of the Idaean
Daktyls, by whom he was initiated into their rites. The first rite
he underwent at their hands was purification, and this purification
was effected by—the thunderbolt or thunder-stone.

A thunder-stone[4] is not so strange an implement of purification
as it might at first sight appear. Celts or stone-axes over a large
portion of the civilized world are, by a strange blunder, taken to
be thunderbolts—weapons shot down by the sky-god. Such

---

[1] Porphyry (*De Abst.* iv. 19), who preserves the fragment for us—as a text on
which to preach vegetarianism—has βροντάς. The MSS. follow him with the
exception of the Leipzig MS., which has βρορás. Lobeck (see Nauck, *ad loc.*)
suggests σπονδάς, which may be rejected as of impossible violence. Valens reads
βιοτάς, which is feeble in sense. The most plausible suggestion is Diels' βούτας =
ox-herd. Dieterich (*De Hymnis Orphicis*, p. 11) accepts βούτας, holding βροντάς
to be hopeless: 'perperam traditur βροντάς praeclare emendavit Dielesius.' The
praeclare is juster than the *perperam*. Wilamowitz-Moellendorff (*Griechische
Dichterfragmente*, p. 77, note 1) follows Diels, interpreting βούτας as βουκόλος.
The temptation to adopt βούτας is severe. In the *omophagia* a wild bull was
hunted and eaten; the bull-forms of Dionysos are familiar, his followers are known
to have been called βουκόλοι, at Athens we have a βουκολεῖον, and indeed an actual
βούτης (Butes) worshipped in the Erechtheion. But had the original reading been
βούτας it is hard to see why the unintelligible βροντάς should have been substituted.

[2] *Prolegomena*, p. 480, note 1.

[3] *Vit. Pyth.* 17 Κρήτης δ' ἐπιβὰς τοῖς Μόργου μύσταις ἑνὸς τῶν Ἰδαίων Δακτύλων, ὑφ'
ἂν καὶ ἐκαθάρθη τῇ κεραυνίᾳ λίθῳ.

[4] For the superstitions that gather round *thunder-stones*, and for celts as supposed
thunder-stones, see H. Martin's *La Foudre dans l'Antiquité*, 1866, and P. Saint Yve's
Talismans et reliques tombés du ciel, in Revue des Etudes Ethnographiques et
Sociologiques, 1909, p. 1. See also Sir John Evans, *Ancient Stone Implements*,
p. 59, E. B. Tylor, *Early History of Man*, 2nd edit. p. 226, and Cartailhac, *L'âge de
pierre dans les souvenirs et superstitions populaires*.

stones are called to-day by the modern Greek peasant 'lightning-axes' (ἀστροπελέκια, a shortened form of ἀστραπσπελέκια[1]). Great is their value as charms against thunder, *similia similibus*, to keep milk sweet, to cure rheumatism and the like.

The celt reproduced in Fig. 6 is a curious illustration of the use of these supposed thunder-stones in mysteries. It was found in the Argolid, and is now in the Central Museum at Athens. The inscription[2] cannot be interpreted, and is probably of the *Abraxas* order, but it is clear that the scene represented has to do with Mithraic mysteries. We have the slaying of the holy bull, and, below, a figure that looks like a Roman soldier bearing a rod surmounted by an eagle, is received by a priest: the soldier is probably qualifying to become an 'Eagle.'

FIG. 6.

Porphyry[3] then goes on to enumerate the various ceremonies gone through during initiation. Pythagoras had to wear a wreath of black wool, to lie face foremost near the sea for a whole night and, finally, like Epimenides, to go down into the cave of Idaean Zeus, probably a great underground cavern on Mount Dikte. There he had to spend thrice nine days, and then at last he was allowed to gaze on the throne which year by year was draped for Zeus. There was on Dikte a tomb as well as a throne, since Porphyry tells us that Pythagoras engraved an inscription on it as follows: 'Pythagoras to Zeus'—and the beginning of what he wrote was:

Here died Zan and lies buried, whom they call Zeus,

---

[1] Prof. Bosanquet kindly tells me that in Crete stone-axes are specially abundant on the mountains. Near Palaikastro many are picked up on the now denuded limestone.

[2] This inscription is inaccurately reproduced by Perrot and Chipiez, *Grèce Primitive*, vol. VI. p. 119, Fig. 5. The first four letters as given by them are Βάκχ, which led me to hope that the word inscribed was Βάκχος, but Mr R. M. Dawkins was good enough to examine the actual stone and to send me the inscription corrected. The drawing in Fig. 6, with the correct inscription, I owe to the kindness of Mrs Hugh Stewart.

[3] *Loc. cit. supra* ἔωθεν μὲν παρὰ θαλάττῃ πρηνὴς ἐκταθείς, νύκτωρ δὲ παρὰ ποταμῷ ἀρνειοῦ μέλανος μαλλοῖς ἐστεφανωμένος. εἰς δὲ τὸ Ἰδαῖον καλούμενον ἄντρον καταβὰς ἔρια ἔχων μέλανα τὰς νομιζομένας τρὶς ἐννέα ἡμέρας ἐκεῖ διέτριψεν καὶ καθήγισεν τῷ Διὶ τόν

an inscription which reminds us of another divine being whose tomb Zeus took over:

Here died Pikos and lies buried, who is also Zeus[1].

After all these solemnities the final apocalypse of an empty throne falls rather flat. Why is the throne draped if it is to remain empty? Was the throne really empty? Probably not. Zeus in human shape was not seated thereon, otherwise we should have been told, but his throne may on certain occasions have been tenanted by a symbol as awe-inspiring as, or even more than, himself,—his thunderbolt.

The two coins in Fig. 7 suggest this[2]. The first is from Seleukeia Pieria[3], the date probably early in the first century B.C.

Silver Tetradrachm of Seleukeia
Pieria.

Denarius of Antoninus
Pius. Rev.

Fig. 7.

The reverse shows a large thunderbolt with fillet attached, lying on a cushion on a throne; the legend is ΣΕΛΕΥΚΕΩΝ ΤΗΣ ΙΕΡΑΣ ΚΑΙ ΑΥΤΟΝΟΜΟΥ. The turreted head on the obverse is supposed to be the Tyche of Seleukeia. The second coin figured is a denarius of Antoninus Pius, and also shows a thunderbolt resting on a spread throne. Closely analogous in idea, though

τε στορνύμενον αὐτῷ κατ' ἔτος θρόνον ἐθεάσατο, ἐπίγραμμά τ' ἐνεχάραξεν ἐπὶ τῷ τάφῳ ἐπιγράψας 'Πυθαγόρας τῷ Διί,' οὗ ἡ ἀρχή· ˚Ωδε θανὼν κεῖται Ζάν, ὃν Δία κικλήσκουσιν.

[1] Suidas, s.v. Πῖκος· ἐνθάδε κεῖται θανών...Πῖκος ὁ καὶ Ζεύς. See p. 109.

[2] The coins reproduced are in the possession of Mr A. B. Cook, and will be discussed in his forthcoming book on *Zeus*. He very kindly allows me to anticipate their publication.

[3] Cf. *Brit. Mus. Cat. Gk. Coins, Syria,* pp. 270 f. Pl. xxxii. 6 and 8. The thunder-cult of Seleukeia Pieria is well known. Appian in his *History of Syria* (c. 56) says of the inhabitants of Seleukeia θρήσκουσι καὶ ὑμνοῦσι καὶ νῦν Κεραυνόν. Keraunos had annually appointed priests, κεραυνοφόροι, with whom may perhaps be compared the λιθοφόρος, who had a seat in the Dionysiac theatre at Athens. See my *Myth. and Mon. Ancient Athens,* p. 274.

not in style, is a Graeco-Roman relief (Fig. 8), now in the museum at Mantua[1]. Here again we have the spread throne, the thunderbolt; the only addition is an eagle.

The thunderbolt was to the primitive Greek not the symbol or attribute of the god, but itself the divine thing, the embodiment and vehicle of the god. As such, long after Zeus had taken on full human form in literature, it held its place in cultus, not as a weapon in the hand of the human god, but actually occupying his throne. This identity of the two is specially manifest in the

Fig. 8.

figure of the infant Zagreus. In the terracotta relief from the Palazzo Colonna, reproduced in Fig. 3, we have seen three dancing Kouretes or Korybantes who clash their shields over the infant Zeus. Near him, lying on the ground, is a thunderbolt, his vehicle, his equivalent rather than his attribute.

The human child completely replaces the thunderbolt. On the ivory relief[2] from Milan (Fig. 9) the child is seated on the throne once held by the thunderbolt. This relief though late embodies a primitive form of the myth. It is matriarchal and tribal in sentiment. We have the Mother and Child, the Kouretes and their correlatives the Satyrs, but the Father is nowhere represented.

The fact that child and thunder-stone were one and the same was deep-rooted in myth as well as ritual. Hesiod[3] knew it,

---

[1] E. Braun, *Kunstmythologie*, Taf. 6.
[2] *Arch. Zeit.* 1846, Taf. 38; with this relief may be compared the child on the throne in the coin of Magnesia, p. 241.
[3] Hes. *Theog.* 485 τῷ δὲ σπαργανίσασα μέγαν λίθον ἐγγυάλιξεν.

FIG. 9. Ivory relief from Milan.

at least subconsciously.   When
Kronos was about to swallow
Zeus, what is it that Rhea gives
him and that he really swallowed?
A stone in swaddling clothes.   On
the well-known relief[1] on the
Capitoline altar Rhea is figured
with the swaddled stone in her
hands, offering it to Kronos.
When the appointed time came
'that stone which he had swallowed last he vomited forth first
and Zeus set it up in goodly
Pytho as a sign and a marvel[2].'
In goodly Pytho it was seen by
Pausanias[3]; it was anointed with
oil day by day, and had a yearly
festival. It was not till the stone
was vomited up that the thunder
and lightning were let loose[4].
Long before Zeus was Zeus,
thunder and lightning were, in a
sense to be considered presently,
divine potencies, their vehicle
was a thunder-stone; by such a
thunder-stone was Pythagoras
purified, on such a thunder-stone
did he gaze in the Diktaean
cave.

[1] Overbeck, *Kunstmythologie*, Atlas iii.
24.

[2] Hes. *Theog.* 496

πρῶτον δ' ἐξείμεσσε λίθον, πύματον κατα-
    πίνων·
τὸν μὲν Ζεὺς στήριξε κατὰ χθονὸς εὐρυ-
    οδείης
Πυθοῖ ἐν ἀγαθέῃ γυάλοις ὑπο Παρνησοῖο
σῆμ' ἔμεν ἐξοπίσω θαῦμα θνητοῖσι βρο-
    τοῖσιν.

[3] x. 24. 7.

[4] See Prof. Gilbert Murray's illuminating analysis and interpretation of the
confused Hesiodic account in *Anthropology
and the Classics*, p. 86.

Given then a rite in which the catechumen is purified by a thunder-stone and which has for its culmination the probable, if not certain, ἀνακάλυψις of a thunderbolt on a throne, was it in human nature not to heighten the dramatic effect by adding the sound of simulated thunder?

Here again we are not left to conjecture: we have definite evidence that in certain mystery-rites thunder was actually imitated by bull-voiced mimes, by drums and other apparatus. Strabo[1] in his account of the Kouretes mentions that Aeschylus[2] in the lost *Edoni* says that the instruments of Kotys were used by the Thracians in their orgies of Dionysos. Kotys is but a Thraco-Phrygian form of the Mountain Mother to whom the Cretan mystic expressly states he held aloft the torches. She was variously called Kotys, Bendis, Rhea, Kybele. After describing the din made by the 'mountain gear' of Kotyto, the maddening hum of the *bombykes*, the clash of the bronze cymbals and the twang of strings, Aeschylus goes on '*And bull-voices roar thereto from somewhere out of the unseen, fearful semblances, and from a drum an image as it were of thunder underground is borne on the air heavy with dread.*'

Real thunder cannot be had to order; mimic thunder can, and we know was. Nor is it easy to imagine a more efficient instrument of ἔκπληξις. We know the very instrument with which in ancient days mimic thunder was manufactured, the famous Bull-roarer or ῥόμβος, the sound of whose whirring is mystical, awe-inspiring, and truly religious. It is like nothing in the world but itself, perhaps the nearest approach is the ominous sound of a rising storm-wind or angry imminent thunder. The rhombos is carefully described by the scholiast[3] on Clement of Alexandria in commenting on the passage quoted above, in which he describes 'the wholly inhuman mysteries of Dionysos Zagreus.' The rhombos, says the scholiast, is 'a bit of wood to which a string

[1] x. 470.
[2] Nauck, *Frg.* 57

ταυρόφθογγοι δ' ὑπομυκῶνταί
ποθεν ἐξ ἀφανοῦς φοβεροὶ μῖμοι
τυπάνου δ' εἰκὼν ὥσθ' ὑπογαίου
βροντῆς φέρεται βαρυταρβής.

[3] *Ad* Clemens Alex. *Cohort.* p. 5 'Κῶνος καὶ ῥόμβος' ξυλάριον οὗ ἐξῆπται τὸ σπαρτίον καὶ ἐν ταῖς τελεταῖς ἐδονεῖτο ἵνα ῥοιξῇ. See Lobeck, *Aglaoph.* p. 700. The scholiast professes to explain κῶνος but as Mr A. B. Cook kindly pointed out to me κῶνος is obviously some form of spinning top. The object described as a bit of wood with a string through it is obviously a rhombos or Bull-Roarer. The

is tied, and it is whirled round and round at initiation-rites to make a whirring sound.'

In the mysteries of Zagreus, then, as practised by the Kouretes and Idaean Daktyls, the initiated man (1) was purified by a thunderbolt, (2) heard mimic thunder, (3) probably beheld a thunderbolt on a throne. After these experiences, he may, I think, fairly be said to have 'accomplished the Thunders.'

To elucidate the general principle of man's reaction on the outside world, which is the main object of the present chapter, we could examine no better instance than the Thunder-Rites.

The Thunder-Rites of Zagreus occur, it has been seen, in the initiation of a Bacchos or medicine-man. It will be remembered that among the Wiradthuri they occur during rites of adolescence. After what has been said of the analogy between the two this is not surprising. When the gist of the Thunder-Rite has been once grasped it will be abundantly clear that at any and every ceremony of initiation a Thunder-Rite is appropriate.

What purpose do they serve? What is their religious function?

The Greeks, says a Christian Father, worship ($\theta\epsilon\rho\alpha\pi\epsilon\acute{\upsilon}o\upsilon\sigma\iota$) the thunderbolt. The statement causes us something of a shock. The Greeks of classical days regarded the thunderbolt as the weapon of Zeus the Sky-God, as his attribute, but assuredly they did not regard the thunder as itself a full-blown personal god[1]. Nor does the Christian Father say they did. All he states is that they 'worshipped' the thunderbolt, that is, had a cult of it, tended it, attended to it, made it the object of 'religious' care.

Religion has been defined as 'l'ensemble des pratiques qui concernent les choses sacrées'; so far as it goes the definition is excellent, but it only pushes the difficulty a step further back.

bibliography of the Bull-Roarer is fully given by Dr Frazer, *Golden Bough²*, vol. III. note 1. The first to draw attention to the importance of the savage Bull-Roarer in connection with Greek initiation-rites was Mr Andrew Lang, *Custom and Myth*, 1884, pp. 39—41, 51—55. To the authorities here given must now be added the valuable papers by Mr R. R. Marett, *Savage Supreme Beings and the Bull-Roarer* in Hibbert Journal, Jan. 1910, and M. van Gennep, *Mythes et Légendes d'Australie*, Introduction, pp. lxviii ff.

[1] In imperial days a personal Keraunos was made the object of a definite cult in our sense. In remote Arcadia Pausanias notes (VIII. 29. 1) that on the Alpheios they offered sacrifice to Lightnings, Storms and Thunders ($\theta\acute{\upsilon}o\upsilon\sigma\iota\nu$ Ἀστραπαῖς καὶ Θυέλλαις καὶ Βρονταῖς). Appian (*Syr.* 58) writes φασὶ δὲ αὐτῷ (Seleukos Nikator) τὰς Σελευκείας οἰκίζοντι τὴν μὲν ἐπὶ τῇ θαλάσσῃ διοσημίαν ἡγήσασθαι κεραυνοῦ καὶ διὰ τοῦτο θεὸν αὐτοῖς Κεραυνὸν ἔθετο, καὶ θρησκεύουσι καὶ ὑμνοῦσι καὶ νῦν Κεραυνόν.

The cardinal question remains, what do we mean by the word *sacred*[1]?

In bygone days the answer would have been prompt and simple, the thunderbolt is sacred because it belonged to a god. The god is presupposed and from him comes the sanctity. We now know, from a study of the customs and representations of primitive peoples, that, broadly speaking, the reverse is true, a thing is regarded as sacred, and out of that sanctity, given certain conditions, emerges a *daimon* and ultimately a god. *Le sacré, c'est le père du dieu.* This comes out very clearly in the attitude of the Wiradthuri towards the Bull-Roarer.

Before initiation no boy may behold a Bull-Roarer. He and the women hear from a distance the awful unearthly whirring sound. At the moment of initiation the novices are closely covered with blankets and the fearsome din breaks upon them in complete darkness. The roaring, boys and women are told, represents the muttering of thunder, and the thunder—this is the important point—is the voice of Dhuramoolan. 'Thunder,' said Umbara headman of the Yuin tribe[2], 'is the voice of Him (and he pointed upwards to the sky) calling on the rain to fall and everything to grow up new.'

Now here we have the Bull-Roarer explained, for the edification of the women and children, as a more or less anthropomorphic being, a kind of Sky-God; but note this important point. When the boy is actually initiated the central mystery takes the form of a revelation (ἀποκάλυψις) of the Bull-Roarer, the boy sees and handles it, and learns to twirl it; it is not, he finds, the voice of Dhuramoolan the Sky-God, it is a Bull-Roarer. Women and children must be told the myth of Dhuramoolan, but the grown man has done with theology. Now we should expect that with the god will go the sanctity. Not at all; the sanctity did not arise from the god, and it survives him. Wherein resides the sanctity?

The sanctity of the Bull-Roarer and of all sacred things will be found I think at the outset to contain two factors, the sense

[1] E. Durkheim, *Définition des phénomènes religieux*, p. 17, in Année Sociologique, II. (1898).

[2] Here and throughout my discussion of the Bull-Roarer I am much indebted to Mr R. R. Marett's *Savage Supreme Beings and the Bull-Roarer*, Hibbert Journal, Jan. 1910.

of fear or perhaps it would be better called awe, and the sense of force, power, effectiveness. The awesomeness of the Bull-Roarer is known to all who have heard it; it possesses in a high degree the quality of uncanniness. Heard in the open sunlight it sends a shudder through even modern nerves; on temperaments more primitive, more excitable, more suggestible, heard in the darkness of the rites of 'night-haunting Zagreus' its effect might well be one of frenzy[1].

'The feare of things invisible is the naturall seed of Religion,' said Hobbes, and he spoke truly, but his statement requires some modification or rather amplification. It is not the fear of the individual savage that begets religion, it is fear felt together, fear emphasized, qualified, by a sort of social sanction. Moreover fear does not quite express the emotion felt. It is rather awe, and awe contains in it the element of wonder as well as fear[2]; awe is on the way to be reverence, and reverence is essentially religious. It is remote entirely from mere blind panic, it is of the nature of attraction rather than repulsion. The Point Barrow natives[3] are afraid of the Aurora Borealis, they think it may strike them in the back of the neck. So they brandish knives and throw filth to drive it away. It is a little difficult to call the act religious. The famous *Primus in orbe deos fecit timor* of Lucretius is the truth, but not the whole truth. Moreover the fear which has gone to the making of religion is at least as much social as physical[4].

This brings us to the second factor in sanctity, the factor which I think differentiates awe from mere fear, the recognition of force, power, effectiveness. This comes out very clearly in the case of the Bull-Roarer. The Bull-Roarer has of course in itself no power, but its roaring is like the roaring of thunder, and to this day a Bull-Roarer is called in Scotland a 'thunner spell.' Because the Bull-Roarer makes the sound of thunder, has the same quality

---

[1] Æsch. *Frg. Edoni*, Nauck, *Frg.* 57 μανίας ἐπαγωγὸν ὁμοκλάν.

[2] As to the individual psychology of religion I follow mainly Mr W. McDougall, *An Introduction to Social Psychology*; see especially the excellent chapter (XIII.) on *The Instinctive Bases of Religion*.

[3] Marett, *Threshold of Religion*, p. 15, from Murdoch, *Point Barrow Expedition*, p. 432.

[4] For this religion of fear and wonder Mr Marett (*op. cit.* p. 13) suggests the name *teratism*, which would be excellent but that it leaves no place for the gentler forces of fertility.

as thunder, that is, psychologically *produces the same reactions*, it *is* thunder.

To us a thunderstorm is mainly a thing of terror, a thing to be avoided, a thing 'not to go out in.' We get abundant and superabundant rain without thunderstorms. But an occasional drought broken up by thunderstorms helps us to realize what thunder and the Bull-Roarer which makes thunder mean to the Central Australian, where 'a thunderstorm causes the desert to blossom as a rose truly as if by magic[1].' The thunder, as the headman said, 'caused the rain to fall and everything to grow up new.' Now we realize its virtue in the adolescence rite; it gives the boys 'more power,' they not only grow up, but grow up new. The Bull-Roarer is as it were the rite incarnate. The Bull-Roarer is the vehicle not of a god or even of a spirit, but of unformulated uncanny force, what Mr Lang[2] calls a 'Powerful Awful.'

The awful, the uncanny, the unknown, is within man rather than without. In all excited states, whatever be the stimulant, whether of sex or intoxication, or vehement motion as in dancing, man is conscious of a potency beyond himself, yet within himself, he feels himself possessed, not by a personal god—he is not yet ἔνθεος—but by an exalted power. The power within him he does not, cannot, at first clearly distinguish from the power without, and the fusion and confusion is naturally helped when the emotion is felt collectively in the group. This fusion of internal will and energy with external power[3] is of the very essence of the notion of sanctity and is admirably seen in the Bull-Roarer. The initiated boy when taught to twirl the Bull-Roarer feels himself actually making the Thunder, his will and energy and action conspire with its uncanny potency. There is no clear severance; he is conscious of control, he can alter the pace and thereby the weird sounds, he is a Thunder-maker and we are landed straight into Magic.

---

[1] Mr R. R. Marett, *op. cit.* p. 406, and Howitt, *The Native Tribes of South-East Australia*, 1904, p. 538.

[2] See *Preanimistic Religion*, The Contemporary Review, 1909, p. 589. Mr Lang denies a pre-Animistic stage of religion. The case for pre-Animism is well stated by Mr E. Clodd in his *Pre-Animistic Stages in Religion*, a paper read before the Third International Congress for the History of Religions at Oxford, 1908.

[3] It will be seen in chapter v., when we come to discuss totemism and sacrifice, that primitive man's lack of power to draw intellectual distinctions lies at the back of many religious phenomena.

But before examining Magic it is interesting to note that this notion of the 'sacred' which we have resolved into the fearful and the effective, and have seen to be the result of man's emotion projected into external nature, is wide-spread among primitive peoples and has given rise to an instructive terminology. It is indeed in examining this terminology that we best seize and fix the Protean shape of the 'sacred.' We have so far focused attention on the Bull-Roarer because it is a singularly illuminating instance of sanctity, and of a sanctity actually observable in Greece, but we must now extend the field of vision to a more comprehensive sanctity as expressed in savage languages. Almost all savages have some word by which they express a force or power which seems to them uncanny, something which arrests their attention and rouses in them a feeling of awe. One or two of these words will repay a closer investigation.

We begin with the word *orenda*[1] in use among the Iroquois of North America, which in some ways seems least mysterious, nearest to ordinary natural power. A man's *orenda* is his power to do things, almost his personality, yet remaining impersonal. A man who hunts well has much *orenda*; when a man is in a rage great is his *orenda*. A man's *orenda* is very like the Greek θυμός and μένος, bodily life, vigour, passion, power, the virtue that is in you to feel and do, also to know, for it is by his *orenda* that the medicine-man learns the secrets of the future. *Orenda* is nowise confined to man. It is further the material of magical action. When a storm is brewing the rain-maker is preparing its *orenda*. *Orenda* is in the notes of birds. A shy bird hard to catch has fine *orenda*. The *orenda* of man is pitted against the *orenda* of his prey; the *orenda* of one man in battle or in games is pitted against that of another. The *orenda* of the rabbit controls the snow and fixes the depth to which it is to fall. *Orenda* is often, as already seen, like a mere natural force, but here we see its non-natural side. Again when the maize is ripening the Iroquois knows the real, natural cause, the sun's heat. But he knows more; it is the cigala makes the sun to shine and the

---

[1] E. S. Hartland, *Presidential Address to Anthropological Section of British Association*, York, 1906, p. 5, quoting J. N. B. Hewitt in *American Anthropologist*, N.S. IV. p. 38.

cigala does it by chirping, by uttering his *orenda*. Generally *orenda* seems to be good, but if a man has died from witchcraft, 'an evil *orenda* has struck him.'

The *mana*[1] of the Melanesians is very like *orenda*, but seems to be somewhat more specialized[2]. All men do not possess *mana*, though it seems mainly to originate in personal human beings. Spirits and ghosts are apt to possess *mana*, but all ghosts do not possess it, only ghosts that are specially potent, *Tindalos*. The word *mana* is adjective as well as substantive, it is indeed very adjectival in its nature, qualities seem almost like specialized forms of *mana*[3]. A man's social position depends mainly on the amount of *mana* he has, either naturally or by virtue[4] of ceremonies of initiation. All this sounds rather abstract, yet on the other hand *mana* has a certain fluid substantiveness. It can be communicated from stone to stone. Asked to describe *mana* one savage will say it is 'heavy,' another that it is 'hot,' a third that it is 'strange, uncommon.' A man finds a queer looking stone, puts it near his yams or in his pig-sty, pigs and yams prosper, clearly the stone had *mana* for pigs and yams. Sometimes it seems to stand for mere vague greatness. In Mangarevan any number over forty is *mana mana mana*, aptly rendered by Mr Marett[5] as an 'awful' lot. Here we have the unknown bordering on the supernatural, though as has been well remarked nothing to the savage is so natural as the 'supernatural.' Perhaps the term super-usual would be safer as having no connotation of 'natural law.'

This vague force in man and in almost everything is constantly trembling on the verge of personality. The medicine-men of the Australian Dieri[6] are *Kutchi*; when one of the Dieri sees a circling dust-storm near the camp great is his terror, for there is *Kutchi*. He hurls his boomerang and kills *Kutchi* and flies for terror afterwards. '*Kutchi* growl along a me, by and by me tumble down.'

---

[1] Codrington, *The Melanesians*, 1891, pp. 118—120 and p. 192.

[2] Any attempt to distinguish between the *mana*, *orenda* and the like is evidently precarious, since we are liable to be misled by the emphasis on special usages of the word as noted by particular observers.

[3] W. R. Halliday, *The Force of Initiative in Magical Conflict*, in Folk-Lore XXI. (1910), p. 148.

[4] Miss Hope Mirrlees calls my attention to Chaucer's use of the word *vertu*, with meanings closely analogous to those of *mana* and almost as various.

[5] *Threshold of Religion*, p. 122.

[6] Howitt, *Native Tribes of South-East Australia*, p. 446.

Here is a self-projected terror on the way to become a god. Yet we cannot, even though we supply him with a capital letter and a personal pronoun, call *Kutchi* really a god; *Kutchi* is a general term for the 'superusual.' So the Kaffir *unkulunkulu* is translated as 'the old, old one' or 'the great, great one' and the heart of the orthodox anthropologist leaps up to meet a primitive, personal god, an All-Father, 'Savage Supreme Being'; yet we are assured by those most at home in the language and thought of the Kaffirs that *unkulunkulu* in its native form implies no personality.

The savage, like the child, passes from the particular to the general; the mature and civilized mind well supplied with ready-made abstractions is apt to start from generalities. To the savage this stone or tree or yam has *mana* or *orenda*, that is what concerns him; but gradually,—and this is another high road to impersonation—from the multitude of things that have *mana*, there arises the notion of a sort of *continuum* of *mana*, a world of unseen power lying behind the visible universe, a world which is the sphere, as will be seen, of magical activity and the medium of mysticism. The mystical element, the oneness and continuousness comes out very clearly in the notion of Wa-kon'-da among the Sioux Indians. This *continuum*, rather felt than formulated, is perhaps primitive man's first effort at generalization[1].

The conception of Wa-kon'-da has been so carefully observed and the rites connected with it recorded in detail by Miss Alice Fletcher during thirty years' residence among the Omaha Indians that it will be best briefly to resume her account. The Wa-kon'-da rites and beliefs are specially instructive to us because thunder, from the sanctity of which our enquiry began, is one of the most usual and significant manifestations of Wa-kon'-da. 'The Omahas regard all animate and inanimate forms, all phenomena, as pervaded by a common life, which was continuous and similar to the will-power they were conscious of in themselves. This mysterious power in all things they called Wa-kon'-da, and through it all things were related to man, and to each other. In the idea of the continuity of life, a relation was maintained between the seen

---

[1] It does not follow that the conception of *mana* belonged to the most primitive stratum of Melanesian culture; see Dr Rivers in his presidential address to the Anthropological Section of the British Association, 1911, p. 5.

and the unseen, the dead and the living, and also between the fragment of anything and its entirety[1].'

Any man may at any time seek to obtain Wa-kon'-da by the 'rite of the vision.' He will go out alone, will fast, chant incantations, seek to fall into a trance, till finally he sees some object, a feather, a tuft of hair, a small black stone—the symbol of thunder, or a pebble which represents water. This object henceforward he will carry about with him. To him it is henceforth, not an object of worship, but a sort of credential, a pledge, a fragment as it were of Wa-kon'-da, connecting him with the whole power represented by whatever form appeared to him in his vision. Certain religious societies were based on these visions. The men to whom a bear had appeared formed the Bear society, those to whom the black stone appeared became the Thunder society.

Miss Fletcher constantly insists that Wa-kon'-da is not a person. Yet Wakon'-da is very human; it can pity, man can appeal to it, adjure its help. Wa-kon'-da is invisible. 'No man,' said the tribal elder, 'has ever seen Wa-kon'-da.' Perhaps the nearest we can get to understanding Wa-kon'-da is to think of it as life—invisible life—too all-pervading ever to be personal. This comes out very clearly in the initiation-rites of the Omaha. It has already been noted that in examining religious facts we have to take account not only of man's reactions to and relations with his fellow-men, but also of his reactions to and relations with the non-human world, the external universe. It is to induce and safeguard these relations that the Omaha initiations to be now considered are largely devised.

The first initiation takes place on the fourth day after birth. Before it takes place the child is regarded as part of its mother, it has no separate existence, no personal name. The rite is one of introduction to the cosmos. To the sun and moon, the thunder and the clouds, the hills, the earth, the beasts, the water, the

---

[1] A. C. Fletcher, *The Significance of the Scalp-Lock*, Journal of Anthropological Studies, xxvii. (1897–8), p. 436. It is Miss Fletcher's admirable practice to have her accounts of ritual, etc., retranslated into Omaha and to submit them for criticism to some elder among the natives; the danger of misconception is thereby minimized.

formal announcement is made that a new life is among them; they are asked, or rather adjured, to accept and cherish it. The refrain after each clause comes :

> Consent ye, consent ye all, I implore.

The second rite comes when the child is between two and three years old. It is specially significant in relation to the notion of Wa-kon'-da. When the child first speaks, first walks, it is regarded as a manifestation of life, of Wa-kon'-da. The speaking and walking are in fact called Wa-kon'-da. It is only these *first* manifestations that are so called. If later a child falls sick and gets better the restored life is never called Wa-kon'-da. This second ceremony differs from the first in that it is also an initiation into the tribe. It takes place 'after the first thunder in the spring-time, when the grass is well up and the birds singing.'

The only ritual necessary for the child, boy or girl, is a pair of new moccasins, now to be worn for the first time. Great sanctity attaches to these moccasins, they cannot be given away or exchanged. The mother comes with her child to the sacred hut set up for the purpose, but the child must enter it alone, bearing his moccasins. Then follow six incantations, each ending with a roll of mimic thunder in a minor key. During the first song powers are invoked to come from the four cardinal points. During the second song a tuft of hair is shorn from the crown of the child's head and laid by the priest in a sacred case: but as we learn from the words of the song addressed to the Thunder as Grandfather, the lock and with it the life of the child pass into the keeping of the Thunder :

> Grandfather! there far above, on high,
> The hair like a shadow dark flashes before you.

In the third song it is proclaimed that the power of death as well as life lies with Wa-kon'-da :

> What time I will, then only then,
>   A man lies dead a gruesome thing,
> What time I will, then, suddenly,
>   A man lies dead a gruesome thing.
>
>   (The Thunder rolls.)

The fourth song accompanies the putting on of the moccasins; its gist is:

> In this place has the truth been declared to you,
> Now therefore arise! go forth in its strength.

So far the main element of the rite is consecration to the thunder-god, the supreme Wa-kon'-da. Next comes a ceremony the gist of which, like the earlier ceremony, is to naturalize the child in the universe. Boys only are consecrated to the thunder-spirit, who is also the war-spirit; but the next ceremony is open to girls. It is called Dhi-ku-win-he, 'Turning the child.' The priest takes the child to the east of the fire in the hut, then lifting it by the shoulders carries it to the south, lets its feet rest on a stone or buffalo skull, a sort of omphalos placed there for the purpose. There the priest turns the child completely round, then carries it to the west, the north, the east again, turning it upon the stone at each point while the fifth song is sung:

> Turned by the winds goes the one I send yonder,
> Yonder he goes who is whirled by the wind,
> Goes where the four hills of life and the four winds are standing,
> There in the midst of the winds do I send him,
> Into the midst of the winds, standing there.
>
> > (The Thunder rolls.)

The stone and grass laid on it and the buffalo skull stand for earth; the four hills are the four stages of life. Up till now the child bore its cradle name. It now takes its *ni-ki-e* name which relates it to its gens. After the turning of the child its *ni-ki-e* name is announced by the priest with a kind of primitive *Benedicite omnia opera*:

> Ye hills, grass, trees—ye creeping things both great and small—I bid you hear! This child has thrown away its cradle name. *Hi-e.*

The ceremony ends with a fire invocation. The priest picks up the bunches of grass, dashes them to the ground, where they burst into flames, and as the flames light up the sacred lodge the child is dismissed, while the priest sings:

> O hot red fire hasten,
> O haste ye flames to come,
> Come speedily to help me.

The whole gist of this 'Turning ceremony' is the placing of the child 'in the midst of' those elements that bring life, health, fruitfulness, success, in a word Wa-kon'-da.   Very early in life the child has 'accomplished the Thunders.'

An examination of the words *orenda, mana* and Wa-kon'-da has helped us to realize what is meant by the word 'sacred' and also in what sense it is possible to 'worship' or rather to 'attend to' the thunder without any presupposition of a personal thunder-god.   It remains to ask—Is this notion of 'sacred' as something charged with force and fear confined to primitive terminology or does it survive in the speech of civilized peoples?   The Sanscrit word Brahman[1] means to us a holy man of high caste, but if we go back to Vedic texts we find that *bráhman* in the neuter means 'charm, rite, formulary, prayer.'   The caste of the Brahmans is nothing but the men who have *bráhman*, and this is the force, the inside power, by which both men and gods act.   Certain texts further define *bráhman* as the substance, the heart, the great essence of things (*pratyantam*), that which is most inward.   This essence of things is the god Brahmâ.   In a word the *bráhman* of ritual, the power or efficacity felt by the worshipper is transformed by the Hindu, if he is a theologian, into a god, if he is a philo-sopher, into a metaphysical entity.   The mystic by the practice of *yoga, union, becomes bráhman* and has thereby attained a magical omnipotence.

Where the Indian loses himself in metaphysics, the Greek, being an artist, delights himself with an *agalma*, the image, the imagination of a personal god.   But he too starts from Wa-kon'-da of the crudest kind, from strength and force.   Hesiod[2] in his conscious self is thoroughly orthodox, his theology is emphatically and even noisily Olympian.   Zeus is to him human-shaped, Father of gods and men, Zeus who knoweth imperishable counsels.   But the theology of Hesiod[3] is all confused and tangled with the flotsam and jetsam of earlier ages, weltering up unawares from subconscious depths :

> Styx, Ocean's daughter did with Pallas wed ;
> Zelos, fair-ankled Nike did she bear
> Within his halls, and next the glorious twain,

[1] See Hubert et Mauss, *Théorie générale de la Magie*, in Année Sociologique, VII. (1902–3), p. 117.
[2] For the κράτος τε βία τε of Hesiod see Professor Gilbert Murray's illuminating account in *Anthropology and the Classics*, p. 74.
[3] *Theog.* 383.

> Power and Force. Not any house of Zeus
> Is reft of them, nor seat. When he goes forth
> They follow, hard behind, and by the throne
> Of Zeus, Loud-thunderer, stablish they their seat.

Kratos and Bia, Power and Force, are shadow-figures in a mature, flesh and blood theology. They affect us as strange or superfluous. Once more they meet us in the *Prometheus Bound*, and, though now completely humanized, they strike the same strange chill. Hesiod, we are told, abounds in 'abstractions,' 'personifications' of qualities. Rather his verse is full of reminiscences, resurgences of early pre-anthropomorphic faith; he is haunted by the spirits of ghostly *mana* and *orenda* and Wa-kon'-da and *bráhman*. Styx, Cold Shudder, Petrifaction, is married to Pallas, who, as we shall later[1] find, began life as a thunderbolt. Cold Shudder, Fear of the Uncanny, almost *Tabu*, brings forth Eager Effort (Ζηλός) and Achievement; Dominance (Nike), and Power and Force are added to the strange phantom crew. We seem to have the confused, half forgotten psychology of a thunderstorm.

In this connection it is interesting to note that Kratos, Force, is sometimes almost specialized into thunder. It is *the* strength of Zeus. The process of specialization can be watched. When in the *Oedipus Rex*[2] the chorus adjures Zeus to blast the Plague-God they pray, 'O Thou who wieldest the forces (κράτη) of the fire-bearing Lightnings, O Father Zeus.' In the later writer, Cornutus[3], Kratos is used as the actual equivalent of the thunderbolt: 'and the *Kratos* which he holds in his right hand.'

In the first two chapters we established as a main element in religion collective emotion, man's reaction on his fellow-man. In the present chapter we have dwelt chiefly on man's reaction to the universe. We have seen his emotion extend itself, project itself into natural phenomena, and noted how this projection

[1] p. 87.
[2] v. 200   ὦ τᾶν πυρφόρων
           ἀστραπᾶν κράτη νέμων,
           ἅ Ζεῦ πάτερ, ὑπὸ σῷ φθίσον κεραυνῷ.
[3] Cornut. 10. 13 τὸ δὲ κράτος ὃ ἐν δεξιᾷ χειρὶ κατέχει. I am indebted for this reference to Dr Usener's *Keraunos* in Rhein. Mus. LX. (1905), p. 12.

begets in him such conceptions as *mana*, *orenda*, Wa-kon'-da, Kratos and Bia. We now pass to man's attempt, at first collective, then individual, to control these forces, to what we might conveniently call the manipulation of *mana*[1], or, to use current phraseology, we pass to the consideration of magic and its negative social counterpart *tabu*.

[1] I have adopted *mana* rather than Wa-kon'-da as a general term for impersonal force because it is already current and also because its content is perhaps somewhat less specialized and mystical.

Note to p. 64. For the psychology of the religion of fear see my *Epilegomena*, pp. 1—6.

CHAPTER IV.

MAGIC.

εὐδαίμων τε καὶ ὄλβιος ὃς τάδε πάντα
εἰδὼς ἐργάζηται ἀναίτιος ἀθανάτοισιν,
ὄρνιθας κρίνων καὶ ὑπερβασίας ἀλεείνων.

(a) MAGIC AND TABU.

THE word μαγεία from which our word magic is derived, was, among the Greeks of classical days, never really at home. Plato[1] on the one occasion that he uses it thinks it necessary to add a definition, and this definition, we shall see, is highly significant. In the first dialogue that bears the name of *Alcibiades* Socrates is urging on Alcibiades to an exceptionally high standard of conduct and education. Such a standard is best (he says) exemplified by the training of the Spartan and Persian kings. 'When the young prince is fourteen years old he is given into the charge of certain persons who are called the "Royal paedagogues." These are four Persians in the flower of their age who are selected as being reputed foremost in certain virtues: one is the wisest, one the most just, one the most prudent, one the bravest. Of these the one who is wisest teaches the magic (μαγείαν) of Zoroaster the son of Horomazos'; and then to our surprise Socrates adds by way of explanation, 'the art of the magician is the service (θεραπεία) of the gods. The same man gives instruction in kingly duties' (τὰ βασιλικά).

---

[1] Or the author of the *Alcibiades*, 122 B ὧν ὁ μὲν (ὁ σοφώτατος) μαγείαν τε διδάσκει τὴν Ζωροάστρου τοῦ Ὡρομάζου· ἔστι δὲ τοῦτο θεῶν θεραπεία· διδάσκει δὲ καὶ τὰ βασιλικά.

'Mageia' is the service of the gods, and the same man who teaches 'mageia' teaches kingly duties. No statement could well be more contrary to current feeling about magic. We associate magic rather with demons than with gods, and we picture it as practised by ignorant old women, hole and corner charlatans, or lovers insane through passion. We know that certain 'magical practices' survived among the Greeks, but when asked for instances we do not call to mind kings and potentates, we think of Phaedra's old nurse in the *Hippolytus*, of Simaetha desolate and desperate, of Thessalian witches dragging down the moon, of things and people outside the pale, at war with the powers that be, whether of earth or heaven. Yet in primitive days in Greece, as in Persia, magic had to do, if not with divinities (θεοί), yet at least with things divine, with sanctities (τὰ θεῖα), and not less certainly a knowledge of magic was assuredly part of the necessary equipment of a king (τὰ βασιλικά). The king as magician will be considered in the next section. For the present we have to deal with the manipulation of sanctities by the tribe or by its representative, the medicine-man. We shall find that the attitude towards *mana* is a two-fold one, the positive attitude which is magic, the negative which is *tabu*[1].

The design in Fig. 10 is from the fragment of a 'Dipylon' amphora[2] found in the excavations on the site of the Kynosarges gymnasium on the left bank of the Ilissos below the spring of Kallirrhoë. Most of the vases found in the 'Dipylon' tombs on this site were claimed by the owner of the land and are now inaccessible, but by great good fortune this fragment fell to the excavators, and is now preserved in the British School at Athens.

Happily the class of vases known from the first place of their finding as 'Dipylon' can be dated within narrow limits. Their ornamentation is characteristically geometric, and they belong to a period extending from *circ.* 900—700 B.C. Our fragment is a

---

[1] Mr Marett, *Threshold of Religion*, p. 114, prefers to call *tabu* a negative *mana*.

[2] J. P. Droop, 'Dipylon vases from the Kynosarges site,' *B.S.A.* XII. (1905–6), p. 81, Figs. 1 and 2. The fragment has been discussed by M. Th. Reinach, *Itanos et l'Inventio Scuti*, Revue de l'Histoire des Religions, LX. (1909), p. 324, in relation to the shield and thunder-ceremonies, but not, I think, quite rightly interpreted.

specimen of somewhat advanced style[1], and we may safely place
it at about 800—700 B.C.

The centre of the design is occupied by a rectangular table or
altar; on it is a large indented Mycenaean shield, apparently
made of some sort of wicker-work.   To the right is a seated man
holding in either hand an implement[2] for which hitherto archaeologists have found no name.   From the implement in the man's
right hand comes a zigzag pattern.   A similar pattern also seems
to issue from his right thigh.   It is probable that to the left of
the table or altar another man was seated, as the remains of a
latticed seat are clearly visible, and also the remains of a
zigzag pattern corresponding to that issuing from the topmost
implement.

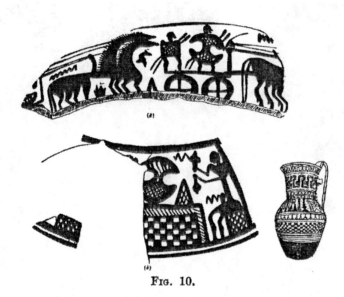

FIG. 10.

It has been conjectured that the man is 'worshipping' the
shield.   The shield is undoubtedly sacred, its prominent position
on the altar shows that, and it confers sanctity on the place where
it is set up.   Its full significance will be shown later.   But the
man is not 'worshipping' it.   If he were, common reverence would
demand that he should stand up, and somehow salute the object

[1] For the chronology of Dipylon vases see F. Poulsen, *Die Dipylon-Gräber und
die Dipylonvasen*, Leipzig, 1905, and S. Wide, *Geometrische Vasen*, Jahrb. d. Arch.
Inst. XII. (1897), 195.   Our fragment is placed by Mr Droop in Dr Wide's Class II (a).
[2] There is a crack in the vase between the two hands, but Mr Woodward of the
British School, who has kindly re-examined the original of the fragment for me,
thinks it improbable that the two objects formed one implement.

of his worship. But here he is complacently seated, manipulating the odd implements in his hands. Odd to us they are, and no classical archaeologist offered any explanation; but to an anthropologist[1] skilled in the knowledge of savage gear they are thrice familiar. They are primitive musical instruments, part of the normal equipment of the medicine-man. They are gourd-rattles.

A glance at the series of gourd-rattles in Fig. 11 brings immediate conviction. To the right (*a*) is a natural pear-shaped gourd from W. Africa, simply dried with the seeds inside acting as pellets. The middle design (*b*) is from a gourd pierced through

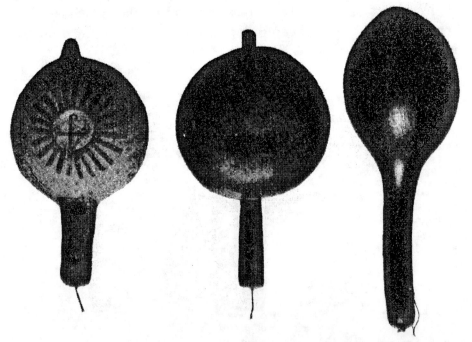

| (*c*) Pottery-rattle. Moki of Arizona. | (*b*) Gourd-rattle with stick. Zuñi of New Mexico. | (*a*) Natural Gourd-rattle. W. Africa. |

Fig. 11.

with a wooden handle. It is from the Zuñi tribe in New Mexico. In the third design (*c*) the rattle has been copied in pottery, the protuberance at the top being copied from the stick handle in the

[1] I sent a photograph of the Dipylon fragment to Mr Balfour at the Pitt Rivers Museum, Oxford, asking if he could explain the implements, and he at once wrote, 'I think they must be a pair of hollow rattles, perhaps of gourd, a very common form over the world, and one surviving in modern Sudan.' I publish drawings of the three instances in Fig. 11 by his kind permission. Mr R. W. Halliday kindly tells me that in the Anthropological Museum at Berlin are a number of these ritual rattles, some gourds, some made of wood, some double, some and more frequently single.

conservative fashion usual in the making of such implements. This third example is from the Moki tribe in Arizona[1].

Our babies still play with rattles; our priests no longer use them in their ritual, and it surprises us a little to see a grown man ceremonially seated before an altar enthusiastically working two rattles. Why does he work them? Not, as might be thought, to make thunder; they are not Bull-Roarers. The shake of an actual gourd-rattle tells us instantly what the man is doing. The soft plash is unmistakable. *He is making rain*; making it in the simplest yet most magical fashion. The rain may come accompanied by thunder and lightning. A zigzag of lightning comes from the topmost rattle[2] and from the man's thigh, but what he is actually making is rain—you can hear it falling.

Our medicine-man's method of rain-making is simple and handy—just a pair of rattles. We know of another rain-maker— this time a king—whose apparatus was more complex. 'Salmoneus,' Apollodorus tells us, 'said that he himself was Zeus, and he took away from Zeus his sacrifices and ordered men to sacrifice to him.' Of course he did nothing of the sort: there was no Zeus, there were no sacrifices. What he really did, Apollodorus[3] tells us in the next sentence, he made the weather: 'he fastened bronze cauldrons by straps of hide to his chariot and dragged them after him and said that he was thundering, and threw up blazing torches into the sky and said that he was lightening.'

Orthodox theology by the mouth of Vergil[4] proclaims Salmoneus a half mad criminal, a blasphemous king who counterfeits the

---

[1] In Arizona magical rain-making still goes on. By the kindness of Miss H. E. Allen, of Bryn Mawr College, I am possessed of a pottery figure of a rain-maker. He holds in front of him a vase to receive the rain about to fall. Figures of this kind are still in use, Miss Allen tells me, as rain-makers, but in the neighbouring towns 'they are already sold as chimney-piece ornaments.'

[2] These zigzags occur on 'Dipylon' vases where no rain-making ceremony is depicted. It is not therefore absolutely certain that they represent lightning, but it is highly probable. A zigzag pattern is used to decorate a votive double-axe on 'palace' pottery, and the connection of the double-axe with lightning is well known. See *B.S.A.* VII. (1900-1), Fig. 15, p. 53, and Mr A. B. Cook, *Class. Rev.* 1903, p. 406. It has been suggested to me by Miss Gertrude Elles that the zigzag pattern may represent simply rain. A zigzag line is the Egyptian hieroglyph for water. If so the rain issuing from the body of the rain-maker is illustrated by Aristophanes, *Nubes*, 372.

[3] I. 9. 7 ἔλεγε γὰρ ἑαυτὸν εἶναι Δία καὶ τὰς ἐκείνου θυσίας ἀφελόμενος ἑαυτῷ προσέτασσε θύειν, καὶ βύρσας μὲν ἐξηραμμένας ἐξ ἅρματος μετὰ λεβήτων χαλκῶν σύρων, ἔλεγε βροντᾶν, βάλλων δὲ εἰς οὐρανὸν αἰθομένας λαμπάδας ἔλεγεν ἀστράπτειν.

[4] *Æn.* VI. 585.

thunder of Zeus, and as such condemned to eternal blasting in Hades.

> Salmoneus saw I cruel payment making
> For that he mocked the lightning and the thunder
> Of Jove in high Olympus. His four steeds
> Bore him aloft : shaking a fiery torch
> Through the Greek folk, midway in Elis town
> In triumph went he—for himself, mad man,
> He claimed God's rights. The inimitable bolt
> He mimicked and the storm cloud with the beat
> Of brass and clashing horse hooves.

Even the kindly Plutarch[1] feels that on such as imitate thunder and lightning God justly looks askance, but he adds,

Fig. 12.

pleasantly, 'to those who imitate him in virtue, God gives a share of his Eunomia and Dike.'

Vergil describes the mad and blasphemous king as though he was an Olympian victor, and as such Salmoneus is depicted on the vase-painting from the fifth century krater[2] in Fig. 12. The central figure, Salmoneus, both holds and wears a wreath, and is all decked about with olive sprigs and fillets. In his right hand is

---

[1] *Ad princip. inerud.* 780 F νεμεσᾷ γὰρ ὁ θεὸς τοῖς ἀπομιμουμένοις βροντὰς καὶ κεραυνοὺς καὶ ἀκτινοβολίας. ἀκτινοβολία probably means 'sunshine.'

[2] Now in Chicago, published by Prof. Ernest Gardner in the *American Journal of Archeology*, III. (1899), 331, pl. 4, and wrongly, I think, interpreted as the madness of Athamas.

a thunderbolt, in his left he uplifts a sword as though threatening the sky, which is about to discharge its thunderbolts. That he is a victor[1] is made certain by the figure of Nike behind him. She raises her hand as though in deprecation. Even for an Olympic victor Salmoneus goes rather far.

Vergil and the vase-painter alike think of Salmoneus as at Olympia in Elis; there it was fabled he perished, he and his people, blasted by the thunderbolt. But we learn from Apollodorus that before he ruled in Elis he dwelt in a country more primitive and always the home of magic, Pelasgian Thessaly[2]. From Thessaly comes to us an account of a curious rain-making ceremony not attributed to Salmoneus but well in line with his method of making the thunder. Antigonos of Karystos[3], in his *Account of Marvellous Things*, says that at Krannon there was kept a bronze waggon, and 'when the land suffered from drought they shook it by way of praying the god for rain, and it was said rain came.'

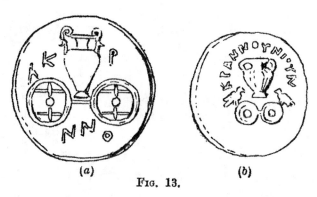

(a)   (b)

Fig. 13.

Antigonos is rather vague as to what was actually done. They shook or agitated the waggon (ἢν σείοντες). The type of some bronze coins[4] of Krannon (Κρανουνίων) of which two specimens

---

[1] This point has been very clearly brought out by Mr A. B. Cook in his discussion of the vase in the *Class. Rev.* XVII. (1903), p. 275.

[2] At some time or other the kingdom and cult of Salmoneus must have passed to Crete and settled on the N.W. promontory of Salmonium or Sammonium. An Athena Salmonia occurs in an inscription dealing with Hierapytna. See Th. Reinach, *Rev. de l'Hist. des Religions*, LX. (1909), p. 177[3].

[3] *Hist. Mirab.* xv. Ἐν δὲ Κράννωνι τῆς Θετταλίας δύο φασὶν μόνον εἶναι κόρακας· διὸ καὶ ἐπὶ τῶν προξενιῶν τῶν ἀναγραφομένων τὸ παράσημον τῆς πόλεως...ὑπογράφονται δύο κόρακες ἐφ' ἁμαξίου χαλκοῦ, διὰ τὸ μηδέποτε πλείους τούτων ὦφθαι. ἡ δὲ ἅμαξα προσπαρακεῖται διὰ τοιαύτην αἰτίαν· ξένον γὰρ ἴσως ἂν καὶ τοῦτο φανείη. ἔστιν αὐτοῖς ἀνακειμένη χαλκῆ, ἢν ὅταν αὐχμὸς ᾖ σείοντες ὕδωρ αἰτοῦνται τὸν θεὸν καὶ φασι γίνεσθαι.

[4] Reproduced *Meisterwerken*, p. 259, by Dr Furtwängler, to whom I owe the reference. In the English edition of the book, the very interesting excursus on Ge praying for rain is unfortunately omitted.

are reproduced in Fig. 13 makes it all clear. In (*a*) we have a primitive waggon, just two wheels with a cross pole—on it an amphora, doubtless filled with water. The coin is not earlier than 400 B.C.[1], and the shape of the high-handled amphora is late, but the primitive wheels show that an old type is revived. In coin (*b*) the wheels are just rude pierced disks on which are perched the rain-birds, the crows or ravens.

On these coins of Krannon we have then as the device of the city (παράσημον), as a traditional ceremony, public, honourable, a magical ceremony for the making of rain. This is a fact of paramount importance. Magic was no hole and corner practice[2] but an affair of public ritual, performed with full social sanction. We have in fact a state of things like that which Socrates attributed to the Persians, a social phase in which magic was the service (θεραπεία) of the gods; instruction about it might well be given as part of the duties of a king (τὰ βασιλικά); in a word magic was of the state, not of the individual. What exactly is this public social magic?

In the light of the three last chapters the nature and origin of magic is not hard to realize. First and foremost magic is a δρώμενον, a thing predone. The rain-maker jingles his rattle and shakes his water-cart, he *does* something. Language[3] here speaks clearly enough. The Latin *factura* is magical 'making,' witchcraft; the Sanskrit *krtya* is doing and magic; the Greek ἐργάζεσθαι is used of ritual operations of a magical character. The German *zauber* is connected with O.H.G. *zouwan*, Gothic *tanyan*, to do. The doing is sometimes that form of doing which we call speaking; γόης the Greek enchanter, is but a specialized howler; the Hebrew *dabar* does not distinguish between word and deed. Of whatever kind the action, the essence of magic is

I'll do, and I'll do, and I'll do.

[1] See Head, *Historia Nummorum*, p. 250.
[2] I do not for a moment deny that magic *came to be* a matter of hole and corner rites, nor that, broadly speaking, one distinction between religion and magic is that magic concerns itself with the weal of the individual, religion with that of the community, but I am here dealing with a stage prior to this differentiation.
[3] H. Osthoff, *Allerhand Zauber etymologisch beleuchtet* in Bezzenberger's *Beiträge*, xxiv. 109, and H. Osthoff in *Archiv f. Relig.* 1908, p. 60, for ἐργάζεσθαι; see also Tylor, *Early History of Mankind*, 1878, p. 135.

But this deed, this thing done, is not the beginning. Behind it lies desire, hope, if we like to call it so, faith. Our word 'credo' is, sound for sound, the Vedic[1] ç*raddhā*, and ç*raddhā* means to 'set one's heart on.' *Le désir c'est le père du dieu* is true in part, but the god has other ancestors; *le désir c'est le père de la sorcellerie* might be taken without qualification. Man, say the wise Upanishads, is altogether desire (*kāma*): as is his desire so is his insight (*kratu*), as is his insight so is his deed (*karma*).

This oneness of desire and deed, which the Indian mystic emphasizes, comes out very clearly in the simplest forms of magic when the magical act is only an uttered desire. You are becalmed, you can do nothing, think of nothing but the wind that will not come. The thought of it possesses you, obsesses you, till the tension on your nerves is too much, your longing will out; the wind will not whistle for you, you whistle for the wind. Your first whistle is sheer, incarnate longing, but, as it came after long waiting, perhaps the wind really does rise. Next time the nerve paths are ready prepared, a habit is set up, a private, it may be public, ritual is inaugurated.

In the case of whistling for the wind we have an element of μίμησις; you long for, you think intensely of, the wind, and you make a wind-sound; but some other cases are simpler, their content is nothing but the one element of emotional discharge. You get a letter that hurts you, you tear it up instantly. You do this not because you think you are tearing up the writer, but just because you are hurt, and hurt nerves seek muscular discharge. You get a letter that heals you and you keep it, you hold it tight in your hand, you even, if you are a real savage, put it to your lips, simply because you act on the instinct to clutch what is life to you. The simplest case of all is Mr Marett's famous bull[2]. A man escapes from an enraged bull leaving his coat, the bull goes on goring the coat. Of course, as Mr Marett prudently observes, 'it is very hard to know what is going on in the bull's mind,' but one may guess that the bull does not act in obedience to a mistaken application of the laws of association; he is simply letting loose his rage on something that happens to be goreable.

[1] See Maurice Bloomfield, *Religion of the Veda*, 1908, pp. 186 and 261.
[2] *Threshold of Religion*, p. 44.

The mainspring then of magic is emotion, desire—whether constructive or destructive—emotion, however, essentially not passive but active. But though any theory of magic which starts rather from the intellect than from the will, which thinks to find its roots in the 'mental framework and constitution' of man is doomed to failure, it would be a great mistake to suppose that magic contains nothing of intellectual effort, no theory whatever. The last chapter was devoted to this theory, or perhaps we might almost call it category of thought, to that notion of awfulness and force informed by collective emotion, variously called Wakon'-da, *orenda, mana. Mana, orenda,* Wakon'-da are not the origin of magic —that lies as we have seen in will and emotion—but they are the medium in which as it were magic acts and its vehicle. As we saw in the case of Wakon'-da, this medium makes a sort of spiritualized unity behind the visible differentiation of thought, it joins not only man and man, but man and all living things, all material things possessed by it, it is the link between the whole and its severed part. Things can affect each other not by analogy, because like affects like, but by that deeper thing *participation*[1], in a common life that serves for link. A deer and a feather and the plant *kikuli* are all one, says the Huichol Indian. Absurd, says the civilized rationalist, they belong to different classes, concepts utterly differentiated by difference in qualities. But the wise savage knows better, they have all one quintessence, one life, and that mystical life produces in him the same reactions of awe and hope; they are to him one.

The fundamental presupposition of magic, says Dr Frazer, is identical with that of science, and it consists of a 'faith, implicit, but real and firm, in the order and uniformity of nature[2].' The fundamental presupposition of all but the most rudimentary magic, that in which the action is almost purely a reaction, as in the case of the torn letter, an action rather bordering on magic than actually magical—the fundamental presupposition is, not the order and uniformity of nature, not a thing mechanical, but a belief in something like the omnipresence of life, of power, something analogous to the Stoic conception of the world as a living animal, a thing not to be coerced and restrained, but reverently wooed, a thing not immutable at all, but waxing and waning,

---

[1] Lévy-Bruhl, *Les fonctions mentales*, 1910, p. 69.
[2] *The Golden Bough*[2], I. p. 61.

above all not calculable and observable, but wilful and mysterious, a thing a man learns to know not by experiment but by initiation, a thing not of 'a natural law' but mystical entirely, halting always between an essence and a personality. Without this belief in *mana*, Wa-kon'-da, there would be acts of psychological discharge, but there could scarcely be a system of magic[1].

This notion of the continuous medium in which magic can act, and which anything like advanced magic seems to presuppose, is in a sense an abstraction or at least a pluralization, and must have been a gradual growth. One of the means and methods of its growth it is possible to trace. This brings us back to our medicine-man on the Dipylon fragment.

In the centre of the design, as already noted, is a great 'Mycenaean' shield, not *worshipped*, for the medicine-man, as we have seen, is making rain on his own account, but manifestly, from its place on the altar, 'sacred.' Why is the shield sacred? The prompt answer will probably be returned, 'because it is the shield of a god'—perhaps of the sky-god. We have the usual *a priori* anthropomorphism. Man conceives of god in his own image. Savage man is a warrior, so his god is a warrior. He has a battle-axe, a shield. The battle-axe, the shield are sacred, divine, because they are the weapons, the attributes, of a war-*god*. Because in our theology we have borrowed from the Semites the Lord is a Man of War, because to us, 'there is none other that fighteth for us,' we straightway impose a war-god on the savage and the primitive Greek. Let us look at facts—savage facts first.

The Omaha, arch-spiritualists as they are, believe they can act on, they can direct, such Wa-kon'-da as they have by a sort of immediate telepathy on their fellows. They have a word for this —*Wa-zhiñ-dhe-dhe, wazhiñ*, directive energy, *dhe-dhe*, to send[2]; by

---

[1] See especially MM. Hubert et Mauss, *Theorie Générale de la Magie*, Année Sociologique, 1902–3, p. 108.

[2] Miss Alice Fletcher, *On the import of the totem among the Omahas*, Proceedings of the American Assoc. for the Advancement of Science, 1897, p. 326. See also *Notes on certain beliefs concerning Will-Power among the Siouan tribes*, a paper read by Miss Fletcher before the American Association for the Advancement of Science, Buffalo Meeting, Aug. 1896. For my knowledge of this interesting paper I am indebted to the kindness of Dr A. C. Haddon.

singing certain songs you can send will and power to a friend to help him in a race or a game, or strength and courage to a warrior in battle.   But peoples less spiritualized cling to the outward and visible sign.   An Arunta native 'sings' over a stick or a stone or a spear, and thereby gives it what he calls Arungquiltha, a magical dangerous evil power.   The object itself, a thin flake of flint attached to a spear thrower and carefully painted, is called Arungquiltha; the property is not distinguished from the vehicle.   It is left in the sun for some days, and the men visit it daily and sing over it a request to kill the intended victim, 'Go straight, go straight, kill him.'   By and by, if the Arungquiltha is successful, they hear a noise like a crash of thunder, and then they know that, in the form of a great spear the Arungquiltha has gone straight to the man, mutilating and thus killing him[1].

A tool is but an extension, an amplification, of a man's personality.   If the savage feels that he can get Wa-kon'-da, surely that Wa-kon'-da can pass into that outer personality which is his tool, his weapon.   We hear it passing as he 'sings' the Arungquiltha. It is, M. Bergson[2] has taught us, characteristic of man as intelligent rather than instinctive that he is a tool-user, *Homo faber*.   The other animals have tools indeed, beaks and paws of which they make marvellous use, but these instruments are parts of the animal who uses them, they are organic.   A very intelligent animal like an elephant can use a tool, he cannot make one.   It is the fabricated tool, inorganic, separate, adaptable, apt to serve the remoter rather than the immediate end, that marks the intelligence of man.   This separation, this adaptability, this superiority of function in the tool, primitive man did not analyse, but he found that with his tool he had more *mana* than without; he could send his *mana* out further, he was bigger and more splendid; so the tool, the weapon, became *per se* sacred, not because it was the instrument of a god, but because it was the extension and emphasis of a man.

We must then clear our minds of all notion that the hoplolatry of the Greeks implies anthropomorphism.   The shield on the altar is sacred *because it is a shield*, a tool, a defensive weapon,

---

[1] Spencer and Gillen, *The Native Tribes of Central Australia*, 1899, p. 548.

[2] *L'Évolution Créatrice*, p. 151, 'L'intelligence, envisagée dans ce qui en paraît être la démarche originelle, est la faculté de fabriquer des objets artificiels, en particulier des outils à faire des outils et d'en varier indéfiniment la fabrication.'

part of a man's personality, charged with magical force, spreading the contagion of its *mana* by its very presence. Not less sacred are the tools of the medicine-man, the rain-rattles.

In the light of this notion of the tool, the weapon as part of a man's personality, many a funeral custom becomes clear[1]. A warrior's weapons, a medicine-man's gear, a woman's cooking utensils and her baskets, are buried with them. We think it is because they will want them in the next world. It is not quite that; we are nearer the truth when we say it is from sentiment. The tools a man used are part of him, of his life, of his *mana*. What life, what *mana*, have joined together, let not man nor death put asunder.

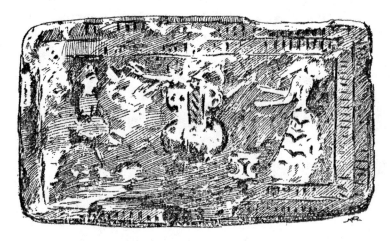

Fig. 14.

A weapon then does not of necessity owe its sanctity to a god; rather in one case, the actual case before us, we can see before our very eyes a god grow up out of a weapon. Pallas Athena, Guardian, Promachos, of her city, is altogether human; but what of the Palladion? The Palladia have always one characteristic, they are sky-fallen (διοπετεῖς)[2]. They are πάλτα, things hurled,

---

[1] See Lévy-Bruhl, 'Les Fonctions Mentales dans les Sociétés Inférieures,' p. 384, and R. Hertz, *La Représentation collective de la Mort* in Année Sociologique, x. 1905–6. In the matter of tools, etc. as part of the personality of a man I am glad to find my view has been anticipated by Mr A. B. Cook in a paper on *Greek Votive Offering* in Folk-Lore xiv. 1903, p. 278. Mr Cook quotes as his psychological authority Lotze in the *Microcosmus* i. 136. My view is only an application to the savage of William James's view of personality in general; see his *Principles of Psychology* i. p. 292.

[2] See M. Theodor Reinach's brilliant articles *Itanos et l'Inventio Scuti*, no. ii. p. 331, in Revue de l'Histoire des Religions, lx. 1909.

cast down; the lightning is the hurled fire (παλτὸν πῦρ). Pallas then is but another form of *Keraunos*—the thunderbolt hurled. According to ancient thinking, that which slays can save; so the Palladion which was the slayer became the Saviour, the Shield. In the well-known fresco from Mycenae[1] in Fig. 14 we see the Shield, half humanized, as the object of an actual cult; before it is a portable altar, to either side a woman worshipper. But it is not the goddess Pallas Athena who lends sanctity to the Palladion, it is the sanctity of the Palladion that begets the godhead of Pallas Athena.

This question of the sanctity of the weapon itself as a vehicle of *mana* and an extension of man's personality is important for our adequate understanding of the thunder-cult among the Greeks. The Greek of classical days normally conceived of thunder not as a vague force but as a definite weapon, a bolt wielded by Zeus. Hesiod's great account of a thunderstorm finishes thus[2]:

> Turmoil and dust the winds belched out and thunder
> And lightning and the smoking thunderbolt,
> Shafts of great Zeus.

Here and elsewhere we have three factors in a thunderstorm, thunder itself, the noise heard (βροντή), lightning, the flash seen (στεροπή), and a third thing, κεραυνός, which we translate 'thunderbolt.' All three are shafts, κῆλα, of mighty Zeus. Mighty Zeus we may dismiss. He is the product of a late anthropomorphism, but the three sorts of 'shaft' mentioned are interesting. Thunder is a reality, a sound actually heard, lightning no less a reality, actually seen, but the third shaft—the thunderbolt? There is no such thing. Yet by a sort of irony it is the non-existent thunderbolt that Greek art most frequently depicts[3].

The word translated 'shafts,' κῆλα, is an interesting one. It is used only in the plural and of the weapons of a god, and twice it occurs in descriptions of the weather. In the Hesiod passage

---

[1] Ἐφημερὶς Ἀρχ. 1887, Pl. x. 2.

[2] Hes. *Theog.* 708

> σὺν δ' ἄνεμοι ἔνοσίν τε κονίην τ' ἐσφαράγιζον,
> βροντήν τε στεροπήν τε καὶ αἰθαλόεντα κεραυνὸν
> κῆλα Διὸς μεγάλοιο.

[3] For the various forms, bird, flower, etc., in which Greek art depicts the thunderbolt, see P. Jacobsthal, *Der Blitz in der Orientalischen und Griechischen Kunst*, 1906.

we have seen it used of thunder and lightning; in the *Iliad*[1], when Zeus the Counsellor hath begun to snow he shows forth there his shafts, his κῆλα to men.   The shafts of Apollo[2] when he rains the plague nine days long upon the Greek host are κῆλα, which makes it probable that they were originally the avenging darts of the outraged Sun.   When Hesiod numbers κεραυνός among the κῆλα, he is of course quite unaware that they are practically the same word, κῆλα and κεραυνός both from a root[3] meaning to 'smash.' Neither word commits us definitely to any notion of a particular missile; both simply mean 'destroyers, smashers.'

We know now-a-days, though most of us vaguely enough, that a thunderstorm is somehow due to a 'discharge of electricity.' When a man is 'struck by lightning' he 'dies of an electric shock.'   But how should primitive man know that?   Meteorology is the last of the sciences.   He sees the black cloud rising, he feels a horrible oppression in the sultry air, he hears unearthly rumblings and watches flashes of lightning play across the sky.   Finally he hears a noise over his head like a cart-load of bricks; earth and sky, as Hesiod describes it, are jumbled together with an unspeakable din and he gives up all for lost.   Presently it is all over, the sun is shining, the trees glistening, the earth refreshed and glad.   If that were all, he might think there had been 'plenty devil about,' or if he was an optimist much *mana* and Wa-kon'-da. But when he goes into the bush he finds a great tree split and charred, or the body of his best friend lying on the road dead, distorted.   Something has struck the tree and the man and smashed them; there have been κῆλα, destroying weapons, about, clubs or battle-axes or sharp pointed arrows that slay.

This notion of the thunderbolt, the weapon, was fostered but not I think started by a popular and widespread error.   We have seen that in the mysteries of the Idaean Daktyls, Pythagoras was

[1] XII. 280

ὦρετο μητίετα Ζεὺς
νιφέμεν ἀνθρώποισι πιφαυσκόμενος τὰ Ϝὰ κῆλα.

[2] *Il.* I. 53

ἐννῆμαρ μὲν ἀνὰ στρατὸν ᾤχετο κῆλα θεοῖο.
Sunbeams in the Anthology (*Anth. Pal.* XIV. 139) are χρύσεα κῆλα.

[3] The root çar, which gives Sanskrit çṛnâ‘ti, he breaks, destroys, and çaljâ-s, arrow-point, Gk. κῆλον and κεραΐζειν (κεραϜίζειν), to destroy, where the primitive meaning comes out.   See for κῆλον, Meyer, *Handbuch d. Gr. Etymologie*, II, p. 440; for κεραυνός, II. p. 362.   Pindar, Mr Cornford points out to me, plays on the diverse meanings of κῆλα and κηλεῖν in his κῆλα δὲ καὶ | δαιμόνων θέλγει φρένας (*Pyth.* I. 20). The weapons of the gods are magical to hurt and heal.

purified by a thunder-stone and that this thunder-stone was in all probability nothing but a black stone *celt*, the simplest form of stone-age axe. The wide-spread delusion that these *celts* were thunderbolts cannot have taken hold of men's minds till a time when their real use as ordinary axes was forgotten. It cannot therefore have been very primitive, though it is almost world-wide. The double axe, πέλεκυς, as will later be seen, was assuredly in Crete and other parts of the Ægean a sacred object, but the *normal* weapon which is the normal art-form of the thunderbolt is not a double axe. It is more of the nature of a double pointed dart, a *bidens*. The special form of weapon taken to represent the thunderbolt is however a matter of secondary importance. The essential fact is that thunder was regarded not only as a *force* (κράτος), a sort of incarnate *mana* or Wa-kon'-da, but as that extension of human force which is a destructive weapon (κεραυνός).

So far then we have considered magic as the manipulation of *mana*. Man tries to handle this mysterious force, a force partly within him, partly without, for his own ends—he tries to make thunder, mainly that it may rain and the earth may bring forth her fruits. But the thunder as destructive weapon has brought us face to face with another aspect of, or rather perhaps attitude towards, *mana*, that attitude towards things that is summed up in the word *tabu*. *Tabu*, avoidance, scruple, some authorities would have us think, is of the very essence of religion. M. Salomon Reinach[1] proposes to define religion as *un ensemble de scrupules qui font obstacle au libre exercice de nos facultés.* This seems to me a somewhat serious misconception. It is to put *tabu* before *mana*, a negative aspect before a positive conviction. It is true that the Latin word *religio*[2], from which our word comes, means 'to consider, to be careful about, to attend to,' it is the opposite of *negligere*, but attention is not *tabu*. We shall get a clearer notion of the real gist of *tabu* and its intimate inextricable relation with *mana* if we study a certain special form of Greek thunder-cult.

[1] *Orpheus*, p. 4. M. Reinach does not of course ignore the *mana* element, but his emphasis on the negative, *tabu*, side, is, I think, misleading.

[2] For an excellent analysis of *religio* see W. Otto, *Religio und Superstitio*, in Archiv f. Religionswissenschaft XII. (1909), p. 533, and XIV. (1911), p. 406.

In Greece a place that was struck by lightning became an ἄβατον, a spot not to be trodden on, unapproachable. On the Acropolis at Thebes were to be seen, Pausanias[1] tells us, the bridal chambers of Harmonia and Semele—and even to his day, Pausanias adds, no one was allowed to set foot in the chamber of Semele. And why? The other name for these *tabu*-ed places speaks clearly—they were ἐνηλύσια, *places of coming.* This Pollux tells us, is the name given to places on which a bolt from heaven has descended. The *Etymologicum Magnum* adds that such places were dedicated to Zeus the Descender (Καταιβάτῃ), and were called ἄβατα and ἄδυτα. In the ἄβατον at Thebes, 'along with the thunderbolt which was hurled on the bridal chamber of Semele, there fell a log from heaven, and they say that Polydorus adorned this log with bronze and called it *Dionysos' Kadmos.*'

Here we see unmistakeably the meaning of *tabu*: it is an attitude towards *mana*; something full of *mana*, instinct, alive with Wa-kon'-da, has fallen from heaven to earth and that spot of earth becomes charged as it were with an electric potency, that spot of earth must in common prudence for the common good be fenced about. It becomes a *Horkos*, an enclosed sanctity[2]. When theologians, busy with their full-blown Olympians, forgot the old notion of *mana*, the double-edged sanctity, they invented the vulgar story that Semele was blasted for impiety, for idle curiosity; but the old local legend remembered that the thunderstorm was the bridal of Earth and Sky, of Gaia-Semele and Ouranos-Keraunos, and that from that wedding sprang the thunder-child Bromios.

On the Acropolis of Athens as on the Acropolis at Thebes, and probably in early days on every high place, there was a Place of Coming—and it shows us a new characteristic of these ἄβατα. They were not only fenced in as *tabu*, but they were left open to the sky, 'hypaethral,' left in communication as it were with the source of their *mana*, their sanctity, which might pour in upon them anew any time. In the north porch of the Erechtheion are the marks of a trident[3]. In examining the roof of this north

---

[1] IX. 12. 3 ...καὶ ἐς ἡμᾶς ἔτι ἄβατον φυλάσσουσιν ἀνθρώποις.

[2] See Professor Gilbert Murray, *Rise of the Greek Epic*, p. 265 'The word *Horkos* which we translate an oath, really means "a fence," or "something that shuts you in."'

[3] See my *Primitive Athens*, 1906, p. 59.

porch it has been found that immediately above the trident-mark
an opening in the roof had been purposely left : the architectural
traces are clear.   But what does Poseidon want with a hole in the
roof?   It is no good to a sea-god.   It is every good to a lightning-
god, and before Poseidon took to the sea he was Erechtheus the
Smiter, the Earth-shaker; this trident was the weapon of his
striking, his *fulmen trisulcum*.   Lightning-struck places are to
the Latins *bidentalia*[1], consecrated by the *bidens*, the two-bladed
thunderbolt, a sanctity more potent than any tender two-toothed
lamb.

Rome gives us not only the *bidentalia*, but a clear case of the
hypaethral ἄβατον in the shrine of old Terminus.   Ovid[2] tells us
that, when the new Capitol was being built, a whole multitude of
divinities were consulted by augury as to whether they would
withdraw to make place for Jupiter.   They tactfully consented,
all but .old Terminus, the sacred boundary-stone.   He stood fast,
remaining in his shrine, and 'still possesses a temple in common
with mighty Jupiter.'

> And still, that he may see only heaven's signs,
> In the roof above him is a little hole.

Servius[3] in commenting on a passage in Vergil says, in the
Capitoline temple the part of the roof immediately above the very
stone of Terminus was open, for to Terminus it is not allowable to
sacrifice save in the open air.   The reason lies a little deeper.
Terminus was just an old thunder-stone, a διοπετὲς ἄγαλμα, a
Palladion; he had come down from the sky and naturally he
liked to look up at it, more *mana* to him!   All sky-gods felt the
same, Fulgur, Caelum, Sol and Luna were, Vitruvius[4] tells us,
worshipped in hypaethral temples.

Thebes, we have seen, had its ἄβατον, its place of *mana* and
tabu; at Thebes was born the thunder-child Bromios.   The
Bacchae of Euripides is hard enough to understand anyhow, but
we cannot even begin its understanding till we realize that the
roots of its plot lie deep in things primitive, in the terror and

---

[1] See H. Usener, *Keraunos*, Rhein. Mus. LX. 1905, p. 22.
[2] *Fast.* II. 667
> Nunc quoque, se supra ne quid nisi sidera cernat,
> Exiguum templi tecta foramen habent.
[3] *ad Æn.* IX. 448.   [4] I. 2. 5.

beauty, the blasting and the blessing of the thunderstorm, the
magic of *mana*, the sanctity of *tabu*.

The keynote is struck in the first words of the prologue.
Dionysos enters, so quietly, yet against a background of thunder
and lightning.

> Behold God's son is come unto this land
> Of Thebes—even I, Dionysos, whom the brand
> Of heaven's hot splendour lit to life—when she
> Who bore me, Cadmus' daughter, Semele,
> Died here[1]

He sees the ἄβατον of his mother, from which is rising faint smoke
through the vine leaves.

> There by the castle's side
> I see the place, the Tomb of the Lightning's Bride,
> The wreck of smouldering chambers, and the great
> Faint wreaths of fire undying[2].

The god knows this ἄβατον, though unapproachable, is no monument of shame, but of grace, of glory unspeakable.

> Aye, Cadmus hath done well, in purity
> He keeps the place apart, inviolate,
> His daughter's sanctuary, and I have set
> My green and clustered vines to robe it round[3].

The sacrilege of the later version of the story is horrible to
think of.

All through the play there are hauntings of lightning and
thunder. The sudden fiery apparitions are not merely ' poetical,'
in honour of any and every god; they are primitive, and of the
actual lightning-cultus of the land. And above all, the great
Epiphany of the Lightning is but the leaping forth afresh of the
fire from Semele's Tomb.

> Unveil the Lightning's eye; arouse
> The Fire that sleeps, against this house,

and then the measure changes, and to arrest attention come the
two solemn emphatic syllables ἀ, ἀ.

> O saw ye, marked ye there the flame
>   From Semele's enhallowed sod
> Awakened? Yea, the Death that came
> Ablaze from heaven of old, the same
> Hot splendour of the shaft of God[4].

---

[1] Eur. *Bacch.* 1.   [2] *v.* 6.
[3] *v.* 10.   [4] *v.* 596.

And again on Cithaeron we have the awful stillness before the
storm, the mysterious voice and then the Epiphany of the pillar
of fire,

> So spake he and there came
> 'Twixt earth and sky a pillar of high flame
> And silence took the air—and no leaf stirred
> In all the dell[1].

Euripides is a realist, but he is a poet, and the stuff he is
dealing with is very primitive. His persons are also *personae*,
masks[2]. Behind his very human and vividly conceived realities are
shadowy shapes of earlier days, powers and portents (τείρεα) of
earth and heaven, Pentheus the dragon's seed and Bromios the
thunder and lightning. It is in part this strange blend of two
worlds, two ways of thinking, that lends to the *Bacchae* its amazing
beauty.

The Thunder-Rites have made clear to us the two-fold attitude
of man towards *mana*, his active attitude in magic, his negative
attitude in *tabu*. We have further seen how in the thunder
as weapon, we have an extension of man's personality, a bridge,
as it were, between the emotion and desire within a man, his own
internal *mana* and that *mana* of the outside world he is trying
to manipulate. We have now to consider other developments
of magic which have left clear traces of their influence on Greek
mythology and cultus, especially the magic of birds and its relation to the medicine-king, and the control of both over not only
thunder but the weather generally.

(*b*) MEDICINE-BIRD AND MEDICINE KING.

From Homer magic has been expurgated[3]; that does not
surprise us. It is to Hesiod that we look for primitive superstitions, for it is Hesiod who deals with those 'Works,' those
doings of man that are, we have seen, so closely intertwined with
the beginnings of magic. Of magic in Hesiod there is no express

---

[1] Eur. *Bacch.* 1082.
[2] See Mr F. M. Cornford, *Thucydides Mythistoricus*, p. 141.
[3] For the absence of magic and other 'Beastly Devices of the Heathen,' from
Homer, see Mr Andrew Lang, 'Homer and Anthropology,' in *Anthropology and*

mention[1], and of actual magical rites we hear nothing, though *tabus* abound; but of magical ways of thinking, thinly veiled by Olympian orthodoxy, the *Works and Days* are full, and for the understanding of the magical attitude we can have no better helper than Hesiod.

Hesiod ends his *Works and Days*[2] with the words that stand at the head of this Chapter:

> Lucky and bless'd is he, who, knowing all these things,
> Toils in the fields, blameless before the Immortals,
> *Knowing in birds and not overstepping tabus.*

Here we have the Whole Duty of Man, positive and negative, at least of Hesiod's holy or pious man, his θεῖος ἀνήρ, which might perhaps be translated *man of sanctities*[3]. His θεῖος ἀνήρ Hesiod characterizes as πεπνυμένα εἰδώς, 'Knowing the things of the spirit,' the man who is good about *mana*[4].

Hesiod is of course a convinced and most conscientious theologian of the Olympian school. Tradition says he was born at Kyme in Æolis, and his father migrated to Askra on the slopes of Mt Helikon. Anyhow his 'epos of plain teaching[5],' like the Homeric epos of romance and war, moves formally and consciously in front of a background of Ionian Olympian gods, whom everywhere he is concerned to glorify and defend. But far more clearly than in Homer these gods are seen to be, however much revered, an artificial background. Thus in the lines before us the pious man is to be 'blameless before the immortals,' but, when it came

---

the Classics, edited by E. Marett, 1908, p. 44. For its emergence in Hesiod and the Rejected Epics, see Prof. Gilbert Murray, 'Anthropology in the Greek Epic Tradition outside Homer,' in the same volume, p. 66.

[1] My attention was drawn to this curious fact by Mr D. S. Robertson. It may be that magic by the time of Hesiod was too uncanny for discussion.

[2] *v.* 825

> εὐδαίμων τε καὶ ὄλβιος ὃς τάδε πάντα
> εἰδὼς ἐργάζηται ἀναίτιος ἀθανάτοισιν
> ὄρνιθας κρίνων καὶ ὑπερβασίας ἀλεείνων.

[3] *Op.* 731

> ...θεῖος ἀνήρ, πεπνυμένα εἰδώς,

for the meaning of θεῖος as 'magical' and θεός as primarily 'medicine-man,' see Prof. Gilbert Murray, *Anthropology and the Classics,* p. 79, and for the connection of these and other words with magic and the root θεσ, see my *Prolegomena,* pp. 49 and 137.

[4] The definition of the ὄλβιος in Hesiod contrasts strangely with that of Pindar (frag. 137) with its other-worldliness,

> Ὄλβιος ὅστις ἰδὼν κεῖν' εἶσ' ὑπὸ χθόν· οἶδε μὲν βίου τελευτάν,
> οἶδεν δὲ διόσδοτον ἀρχάν.

[5] See Prof. Gilbert Murray, *Literature of Ancient Greece,* 1897, p. 53.

to real definition of his duties, these duties are, not to glorify Athena or to offer burnt sacrifice to Zeus, they are not prayer or praise or sacrifice in any form, but simply the observance of sanctities, *attentions*, positive and negative. He is to be 'knowing in birds and not overstepping tabus.'

In the *Theogony* Hesiod is learned and theological, in the *Works and Days* he is practical and religious. He is the small Boeotian farmer, and the small Boeotian farmer had his living to earn and enough to do to earn it, without greatly concerning himself with theogonies and the like, which must have seemed to him but 'genealogies and foolish questions' or at best matter for the learned, leisured subjects for 'Sunday reading.' The small Boeotian farmer is not a sceptic but a man hard pressed by practical necessities. What really concerns him is the weather and the crops and the season; *how* he must till the earth and *when*, that is the *Works* and the *Days*. With all this to know, with the weather to watch and tabus to attend to, with all the lucky and unlucky things to be done and not done, a man had his hands full and had not much time for brooding over Athena, goddess of light and reason, or Apollo with his silver bow.

We think of Helicon as the fountain of inspiration, as the mountain of the Muses, where, circling and surging, 'they bathe their shining limbs in Hippocrene and dance ever with soft feet around the violet spring.' So does Hesiod in the *prooemium* to the *Theogony* which is at once local and Homeric, Boeotian and Ionian. But the real Helicon of Hesiod's father! 'He made his dwelling near Helicon in a sorry township, even Askra *bad in winter, insufferable in summer, never good*[1].' In Helicon it was all you could do to keep body and soul together by ceaseless industry and thrift, by endless 'watching out,' by tireless observance of the signs of earth and heaven. Year in, year out, the Boeotian farmer must keep his weather eye open.

You must watch the House-carrier[2], the snail, because, when he crawls up the plants from the ground, fleeing from the Pleiades,

---

[1] Hes. *Op.* 640

Ἄσκρῃ χεῖμα κακῇ θέρει ἀργαλέῃ οὐδέ ποτ' ἐσθλῇ.

[2] v. 572

ἀλλ' ὁπότ' ἂν φερέοικος ἀπὸ χθονὸς ἂμ φυτὰ βαίνῃ
Πληιάδας φεύγων, τότε δὴ σκάφος οὐκέτι οἰνέων.

Mr A. B. Cook has pointed out (*Class. Rev.* VIII. p. 381) that these descriptive names, such as 'House-Carrier,' 'Boneless One,' 'No-Hair,' are comparable to the *tabu* on the proper name of some totem-animals.

it is no longer seasonable to dig about the vines. The snail 'fleeing
from the Pleiades'—a strange conjunction of earth and heaven.
We are in a world truly magical where anything can 'participate
with' and, in a sense, be the cause of anything else. If you are
a woman, you must watch to see 'when the soaring spider weaveth
her web in the full day,' and when 'the Wise One, the ant,
gathereth her heap.' You will find that it is on the 12th day
of the waxing moon and then is it well that a woman should set
up her loom and lay the beginning of her work[1]. But first and
foremost you should watch the birds who are so near the heavenly
signs, the τείρεα, and who must know more than man. This
watching of the birds we are accustomed to call the 'science of
augury'; we shall presently see that in its origin it is pure magic,
'pure *doing*; the magical birds *make* the weather before they
portend it[2].'

> Take heed what time thou hearest the voice of the crane
> Who, year by year, from out the clouds on high
> Clangs shrilly, for her voice bringeth the sign
> For ploughing and the time of winter's rain,
> And bites the heart of him that hath no ox[3].

If the warning of the crane be neglected there is yet for the
late plougher another chance of which already we have learnt:

> And if thou ploughest late, this be thy charm:
> When first the cuckoo cuckoos in the oak,
> Gladdening men's hearts over the boundless earth,
> Then may Zeus rain[4].

Again the advice to the Vine-grower:

> But when Zeus hath accomplished sixty days
> After the solstice, then Arkturos leaves
> Okeanos' holy stream, and first doth rise
> In radiance at the twilight. After him
> Comes the shrill swallow, daughter of Pandion,
> Uprising with the rising of the spring.
> Before she comes, prune thou thy vines. 'Tis best[5].

The short practical mandates cut sharply in through the poetry
and all the lovely blend of bird and constellation, which are alike
τείρεα, heavenly signs.

On a black-figured vase in the Vatican[6] (Fig. 15) we have the
scene of the coming of the swallow. We have a group of men and

---

[1] Hes. *Op.* 776.
[2] I owe this suggestion and much help in the matter of bird-magic to the
kindness of Mr Halliday.
[3] v. 450.   [4] v. 486.   [5] v. 564.
[6] From a photograph. See Baumeister, *Denkmäler*, III. Fig. 2128, p. 1935.

boys all glad and eager to welcome her. The first boy says 'Look, there's a swallow' (ἰδοὺ χελιδών); a man answers 'by Herakles, so there is' (νὴ τὸν Ἡρακλέα); another boy exclaims 'There she goes' (αὑτηὶ); and then 'Spring has come' (ἔαρ ἤδη).

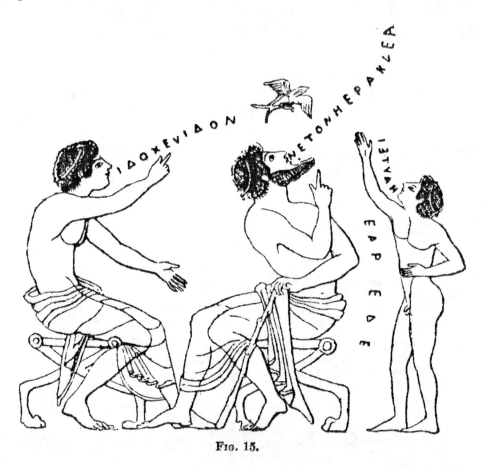

FIG. 15.

I have advisedly translated ὄρνιθας κρίνων 'knowing in *birds*,' rather than 'reading or discriminating *omens*.' A convention in construing and even in literary translation prevails, that the word ὄρνις, whenever it has anything to do with presage, is to be translated *omen*. The habit seems to me at once ugly and slipshod. All the colour and atmosphere of the word ὄρνις is thereby lost; lost because with us the word omen is no more a wingéd word. It is safer, I think, to translate ὄρνις as bird, and realise by a slight mental effort that to the Greek a 'bird' is ominous.

The classical scholar is in no danger of forgetting the wider and derived meaning of ὄρνις. Aristophanes[1] is always at hand to remind him :

> An ox or an ass that may happen to pass,
> A voice in the street or a slave that you meet,
> A name or a word by chance over-heard,
> If you deem it an omen, *you call it a bird.*

The danger is that we should forget the simple fact to which the use of ὄρνις, and οἰωνός, and the Latin *aves* bears such overwhelming testimony, namely that among Greeks and Romans alike the watching of birds, their flight, their notes, their habits, their migrations were in all mantic art a primary factor.

The mantic weather-bird precedes the prophetic god. The claim put forward by the chorus of Birds[2] is just:

> We are Delphi, Ammon, Dodona, in fine
> We are every oracular temple and shrine...
> If birds are your omens, it clearly will follow
> That birds are the proper prophetic Apollo.

Nor is this mere comedy. In a primitive religion to introduce new gods is to introduce new birds. When Pentheus is raging against Teiresias, the ancient mantic priest, who will support the new Bacchic religion, he says

> 'Tis thou hast planned
> This work, Teiresias, 'tis thou must set
> Another altar and another yet
> Amongst us, *watch new birds*[3].

The remembrance of the mantic birds was never lost at Delphi. The vase-painting in Fig. 16[4] shows us the Delphic omphalos decked with sprays and fillets, Apollo to the right with his staff of mantic bay, Artemis to the left with blazing torch. Between them, perched on the oracular stone itself, a holy bird.

If Hesiod had been pressed as to why birds were ominous, why they could help man by foretelling to him the coming of spring or the falling of rain, he would no doubt have fallen back on his Olympian gods. The gods had given the birds this power, the eagle was the messenger of Zeus, the raven of Apollo, the owl of Athena. He would not quite have called them as we do now *attributes*, but he would have thought of them, if pressed, as

---

[1] *Aves*, 719, trans. Rogers.   [2] *v*. 716.
[3] Eur. *Bacch.* 256.   [4] *Annali dell' Arch. Inst.* 1865, Tav. d' agg.

heralds of his immortals. This view is almost inevitable as long
as the bird is regarded as an omen pure and simple, as merely
portending the weather, the said weather being made or at least
arranged by some one else. There are not wanting signs however
that, beneath this notion of birds as portents, there lies an earlier
stratum of thought in which birds were regarded not merely as

FIG. 16.

portending the weather but as potencies who actually make it,
not, that is, as messengers but as magicians. This early way of
thinking comes out most clearly in the case of a bird who never
became the 'attribute' of any Olympian, the homely woodpecker.

In the *Birds* of Aristophanes the Hoopoe asks Euelpides if
the birds ought not by rights to have the kingdom, since, as he
has admitted, they were there before Kronos and the Titans, yes,
and before Earth herself[1]. Yes! by Apollo, says Euelpides, they
certainly ought and you had better be trimming up your beaks,
for you can't expect that

> Zeus the pretender
> 'll make haste to surrender
> The Woodpecker's sceptre he stole[2].

[1] Ar. *Aves*, 468
> ἀρχαιότεροι πρότεροί τε Κρόνου καὶ Τιτάνων ἐγένεσθε
> καὶ γῆς.

[2] Ar. *Aves*, 478
> πάνυ τοίνυν χρὴ ῥύγχος βόσκειν·
> οὐκ ἀποδώσει ταχέως ὁ Ζεὺς τὸ σκῆπτρον τῷ δρυκολάπτῃ.

Peisthetairos and Euelpides go on to explain how divers birds were kings in divers

Zeus stole the sceptre from the woodpecker in Greece but too effectively. The tradition of *Keleos* the old king of Eleusis[1] lived on; but who remembers that he was the rain-bird, the green woodpecker living at Woodpecker-town (Keleai), the woodpecker who yaffles in our copses to-day? In German mythology[2] he survives, but as miscreant not as king. The woodpecker was ordered by God to dig a well. He refused, fearing to soil his fine clothes. God cursed him for his idleness. He was never again to drink from a pond and must always cry *giet, giet* (giess) for rain. The many thirst-stories found in folk-lore all point to rain-birds.

It was in Italy not Greece that the royal woodpecker lived on, and it is there that we shall find him realize his function not as omen-bird but as magician-king, not portending the weather but actually making it.

The design in Fig. 17 is from a gem, a carnelian now in the Berlin Museum[3]. A bird, who for the moment shall be nameless, is perched on a post round which is coiled a snake[4]. At the foot is a ram slain in sacrifice. A young warrior carrying a shield stands before the bird with upraised hand as though saluting it or asking a question. The interpretation of the gem, though it has analogies to the scene on the Hagia Triada sarcophagos to be later discussed[5], must have remained pure conjecture, but for a passage in Denys of Halicarnassos as follows:

Fig. 17.

Three hundred stadia further (in the country of the Apennines) is Tiora, called Matiene. Here there is said to have been an oracle of Mars of great antiquity. It is reported to have been similar in character to the fabled oracle at Dodona, except that, whereas at Dodona it was said that a dove

---

lands: the cock in Persia, the kite among certain Greeks, the cuckoo among the Phenicians; and this is why birds are wont to sit upon their sceptres.

[1] Paus. II. 14. 2. Another mystery-priest is Trochilus, the wren, P. I. 14. 2. For classical references to birds here and elsewhere see D'Arcy Thompson, *A Glossary of Greek Birds*.

[2] Grimm, *Teutonic Mythology*, II. p. 674.

[3] Furtwängler, *Ant. Gem*, pl. XXIV. 10, p. 119.

[4] The snake, I think, marks the post as, like the tree, belonging to earth, springing from the under-ground, 'chthonic.'

[5] p. 159.

perched on a sacred oak gave oracles, among the Aborigines the oracles were given in like fashion by a god-sent bird called by them Picus (the Greeks name it Dryokolaptes) which appears on a wooden pillar[1].

Denys of Halicarnassos, a Greek by birth, and one to whom Latin was an acquired language, saw the Roman Antiquities, to the study of which he devoted so much of his life, through Greek eyes, and again and again in dealing with things primitive he divines the substantial identity behind the superficial difference[2]. Dodona, her sacred oak, her sacred doves, her human god-king Zeus; Tiora, her tree-pillar, her woodpecker, her human god-king Mars.

So far Picus is just a pie, an oracular bird. The term *picus* or pie, covered, it would seem, in Latin the genus woodpecker, called by the Greeks the wood-tapper (δρυοκολάπτης), and also from his carpentering habits the axe-bird (πελεκᾶς). The modern mag-*pie* has fallen on evil days. Mag is Meg, a common woman's name and one that stands for woman. Women from Hesiod's days downwards have always chattered; the social silences of man are, in truth, compared to those of woman, more spacious and monumental. The magpie is now a thief, and worse, she is a spotted she-chatter-box. But the old folk-rhyme remembers when man listened reverently to the magpie's uncouth chatter and marked her ominous coming and knew that for him the more magpies the merrier.

> One for sorrow,
> Two for mirth,
> Three for a wedding,
> And four for a birth.

We have seen the woodpecker Picus perched upon the tree-post, and when we meet him next he is not only associated with a tree but closely bound up with its life. The Latins, Plutarch[3] tells us, gave special honour and worship to the woodpecker, the bird of Mars. And well they might. Twice did the woodpecker

---

[1] Dion. Hal. *Antiq.* ι. 14 Τιώρα δὲ ἀπὸ τριακοσίων, ἡ καλουμένη Ματιήνη. ἐν ταύτῃ λέγεται χρηστήριον Ἄρεος γενέσθαι πάνυ ἀρχαῖον· ὁ δὲ τρόπος αὐτοῦ παραπλήσιος ἦν ὣς φασι τῷ παρὰ Δωδωναίοις μυθολογουμένῳ ποτὲ γενέσθαι· πλὴν ὅσον ἐκει μὲν ἐπὶ δρυὸς ἱερᾶς ⟨πελεία⟩ καθεζομένη θεσπιῳδεῖν ἐλέγετο, παρὰ δὲ τοῖς Ἀβοριγῖσι θεόπεμπτος ὄρνις ὃν αὐτοὶ μὲν πῖκον, Ἕλληνες δὲ δρυοκολάπτην καλοῦσιν, ἐπὶ κίονος ξυλίνου φαινό-μενος τὸ αὐτὸ ἕδρα.

[2] As will later (p. 194) be seen, he was the first to see the substantial identity of the Roman Salii and the Greek Kouretes.

[3] *Vit. Rom.* IV. τὸν δὲ δρυοκολάπτην καὶ διαφερόντως Λατῖνοι σέβονται καὶ τιμῶσιν.

interfere to save the divine twins Romulus and Remus; once to save the holy trees with which their life was bound up, once to feed and protect them when they were exposed by the wicked uncle. It is obvious, I think, that the two versions are substantially the same; the life of the two trees and of the two royal children is really one.

Before the birth of the royal twins, Silvia their mother dreamt a well-omened dream. She saw, wondrous to behold, two palm-trees shoot up together, the one taller than the other. The tall one with its heavy branches overshadowed the whole earth and with its topmost tresses touched the uttermost stars. She saw too her father's brother, the wicked uncle, brandish an axe against the trees, and her heart trembled within her. But a woodpecker,

Fig. 18.

bird of Mars, and a she-wolf, delightful companions in arms, fought for the trees and by their aid both palm-trees were unharmed.

> Martia picus avis gemino pro stipite pugnant
> Et lupa. Tuta per hos utraque palma fuit[1].

In her dream Silvia sees her children in tree-shape; so Althaea dreamed of the blazing log that held Meleager's life; so Clytemnaestra dreamed of the snake that was her fatal son. Then we have the humanized form of the story. The wicked uncle is routed by the comrades in arms, the wolf and woodpecker of Mars. The twins are born, and in canonical fashion the order is given

---

[1] Ovid, *Fasti*, III. 37.

that they should be drowned. The Tiber shrinks back from contact with so much royal *mana* and leaves the twins on dry ground. There they are suckled by—a she-wolf.

Ovid in his polite way assumes that we shall know a little more elementary mythology; that we shall not forget that the woodpecker too was their foster-nurse, who, though he might not suckle them, yet raven-like brought them their daily bread.

> Lacte quis infantes nescit crevisse ferino,
> Et picum expositis saepe tulisse cibos[1].

On a denarius[2] of Sextus Pompeius Faustulus (Fig. 18) the scene is depicted in full. The she-wolf and the twins; above them the sacred fig-tree (*Ficus ruminalis*), and perched upon it the sacred birds.

In Rome to-day an old she-wolf still howls in desolation on the Capitoline hill; but there is no woodpecker to make lamentation.

Picus was an oracular bird, a tree-guardian, a guardian of kings; he was also himself a king, king over a kingdom ancient and august. Vergil[3] tells how when Æneas sent his messengers to interview the aged Latinus they found him in his house 'stately and vast, upreared on an hundred columns, once the palace of Laurentian Picus, amid awful groves of ancestral sanctity.' It was a place at once palace and temple, befitting the old divine king. There each successive king received the inaugural sceptre. There was the sacred banqueting hall, where after the sacrifice of rams the elders were wont to sit at the long tables. 'There stood around in the entry the images of the forefathers of old in ancient cedar'—figures some of them faint and impersonal, Italus and Sabinus, mere eponyms, but among them figures of flesh and blood, primal god-kings, 'gray Saturn and the likeness of Janus double-facing,' and—for us most important of all—holding the divining rod of Quirinus, girt in the short augural gown, carrying on his left arm the sacred shield, Picus the tamer of horses. *Picus equum domitor*, a splendid climax; but Picus, the poet

---

[1] Ovid, *Fasti*, iii. 53.

[2] Babelon, ii. 336. The same scene—except that the tree is, oddly, a vine—occurs on an antique violet paste at Berlin, published by Imhoof Blumner and Otto Keller, *Tier- und Pflanzen-bilder*, Pl. 21, 15, cf. Furtwängler, *Geschnittene Steine im Antiq.* No. 4379. My attention was drawn to these monuments by the kindness of Mr A. B. Cook.

[3] *Æn.* vii. 170 ff.

knows, is also a spotted pie, a woodpecker.   Vergil is past-master
in the art of gliding over these preposterous orthodoxies.   He
sails serenely on through the story's absurd sequel, the love of
Circe, her potions, the metamorphosis[1] of the tamer of horses into
a spotted pie,

> Picus equum domitor, quem capta cupidine conjunx
> Aurea percussum virga, versumque venenis
> Fecit avem Circe, sparsitque coloribus alas,

and in the solemn splendour of the verbiage one forgets how
childish is the content.

Picus holds the *lituus*, the augur's curved staff; he is girt with
the short *trabea*, the augur's robe of purple and scarlet, and he
carries on his left arm the *ancile*, the sacred shield borne by the
Salii.   He is a bird, an augur and a king.   In Vergil, spite of
the inevitable bird-end and the augur's dress, Picus is more king
than bird or even augur; he remains remote and splendid.   Ovid
however tells us more of what manner of king he was, and the
revelation is a strange one. ·In the third book of the *Fasti*[2] he
tells us an odd story about Picus, and tells it with his usual output
of detailed trivialities, significant and insignificant, which must
here be briefly resumed.

Numa, Numa Pompilius be it noted (to the importance of
the name we shall return later), with the help of Egeria has
been carrying out his admirable religious reforms.   In the grove
of Aricia, he has been teaching his people the fear of the gods,
and the rites of sacrifice and libation, and in general he has
been softening their rude manners.   In the midst of all this
very satisfactory piety down came a fearful thunderstorm, the
lightning flashed, the rain fell in torrents, fear took possession
of the hearts of the multitude.   Numa consulted Egeria.   She
was no good on her own account, she could not stop the storm,
but being a wood nymph, and of the old order of things, she knew

---

[1] The story of how Picus spurned the love of Circe and was turned into a
woodpecker is told with his customary detail by Ovid, *Met.* XIV. 6.

[2] *vv.* 285—348.   The story forms part of the whole account of the ceremonies of
the Salii in March and especially of the origin of the *ancilia*, the original of which,
worn by Picus on his left arm, had descended from the sky at sunrise in a thunderstorm.   The *ancilia* will be discussed later, p. 196.

it could be stopped, and better still who could do it—Picus and Faunus, ancient divinities of the soil.

piabile fulmen
Est ait et saevi flectitur ira Jovis.
Sed poterunt ritum Picus Faunusque piandi
Prodere, Romani numen uterque soli[1].

Ovid swings neatly balanced between two orders, the old and the new. The old story is of the thunder (*fulmen*), a sanctity in itself, *the* vehicle of *mana*. This *fulmen* is *piabile*, you can manipulate it magically for your own ends. The new order tells of a human-shaped Jove whose weapon is the thunder which he hurls in his anger. Clearly he is not wanted here. Numa has just been teaching his people those rites of fire-sacrifice and libation dear to the full-blown anthropomorphic god. The most unreasonable and ungovernable of the Olympians could scarcely have chosen such a moment to manifest his ire. Ovid is caught in the trap set by his own up-to-date orthodoxy.

The necessity of dragging in the Olympian Jupiter constantly complicates and encumbers the story. Picus and Faunus really make the weather, but by Ovid's time Jupiter has got full possession of the thunderbolt as his 'attribute.' Old Faunus was embarrassed and shook his horns in perplexity as to the etiquette of the matter; he and Picus had their own province, they were gods of the fields and the high mountains, but *Jupiter must decide about his own weapons*:

Di sumus agrestes, et qui dominemur in altis
Montibus. Arbitrium est in sua tela Jovi[2].

Finally they arrive at a sort of pious, obscurantist compromise: they must not meddle with the thunder, but by their spells they will induce Jupiter himself to allow himself to be dragged down from the sky. He is worshipped as *Elicius*, he will allow himself to be *elicited*:

Eliciunt caelo te, Jupiter; unde minores
Nunc quoque te celebrant, Eliciumque vocant[3].

Picus and Faunus are not regular *dei* like Jove, they are *numina*, spirits, genii, a bird-spirit and a wood-spirit; like the

---

[1] *Fasti*, III. 289.   [2] *Fasti*, III. 315.
[3] *Fasti*, III. 327. In all probability as Mr A. B. Cook suggests (*Class. Rev.* XVII. 1904, p. 270) Jupiter Elicius is really Jupiter of the ilex-tree: but this question does not here concern us.

Tree-King who watched over the Golden Bough, they haunt the dark groves.   At the foot of the Aventine was a grove so dim it seemed a spirit must dwell there.

> Lucus Aventino suberat niger ilicis umbra
> Quo posses viso dicere, Numen inest[1].

Here Picus and Faunus were run to earth, but like the genuine old bogey-magicians they were, like Proteus himself, they had to be caught and manacled before they would speak.   In the best accredited fashion, they changed themselves, Plutarch tells us, into all manner of monstrous shapes[2].   But caught and bound at last they were, and they handed over to Numa the whole magician's bag of tricks; they taught him to foretell the future, and most important of all, they taught him the charm, a purification (καθαρμόν), against thunderbolts.   The charm was in use in Plutarch's days; it was pleasantly compounded of onions, hairs, and pilchards.

Picus and Faunus are magicians, medicine-men, and medicine-men of a class with which we are already familiar.   On this point Plutarch[3] is explicit.   'The daemons, Picus and Faunus,' he says, 'were in some respects (i.e. in appearance) like Satyrs and Panes, but in their skill in spells and their magical potency in matters divine they are said to have gone about Italy *practising the same arts as those who in Greece bore the name of Idaean Daktyls.'*

Now at last we are on firm familiar ground.   The Daktyls of Crete, the initiates of Idaean Zeus we know, they were the men who purified Pythagoras with the thunder-stone[4] and initiated him into the thunder-rites of the Idaean cave.   If Picus the Bird-King was of their company, small wonder that he could make and unmake the thunder.   As we have already seen they were, compared to the Kouretes, a specialized society of sorcerers.   Of like nature were the Telchines in Rhodes, of whom Diodorus[5] says in an instructive passage, 'they are also said to have been

---

[1] *Fasti*, III. 295.

[2] *Vit. Num.* xv. ...ἀλλόκοτα φάσματα καὶ φοβερὰ τῆς ὄψεως προβαλλομένους...ἀλλὰ τε προσθεσπίσαι πολλὰ τῶν μελλόντων καὶ τὸν ἐπὶ τοῖς κεραυνοῖς ἐκδιδάξαι καθαρμὸν ὃς ποιεῖται μεχρὶ νῦν διὰ κρομμύων καὶ τριχῶν καὶ μαινάδων.

[3] *Vit. Num.* xv. ...φοιτᾶν δύο δαίμονας Πῖκον καὶ Φαῦνον· οὓς τὰ μὲν ἄλλα Σατύρων ἄν τις ἢ Πανῶν γένει προσεικάσειε, δυνάμει δὲ φαρμάκων καὶ δεινότητι τῆς περὶ τὰ θεῖα γοητείας λέγονται ταὐτὰ τοῖς ὑφ' Ἑλλήνων προσαγορευθεῖσιν Ἰδαίοις Δακτύλοις σοφιζό-μενοι περιϊέναι τὴν Ἰταλίαν.

[4] See *supra*, p. 56.   [5] v. 55. 3.

magicians (γόητες), and to have had the power of inducing at their
will clouds and rain-showers and hail, and they could also draw
down snow, and it is said that they could do these things just like
the magi. And they could change their shapes and they were
jealous in the matter of teaching their arts.' In this 'jealousy'
we see the note of a secret society.

In the story of Numa's dealings with Picus and Faunus we
have the clearest possible reflection and expression of the conflict
of new and old, and further of the inextricable confusion caused
by obscurantist attempts at reconciling the irreconcilable. In
the old order you, or rather your medicine-king, made the weather
magically by spells; in the new order you prayed or offered gift-
sacrifice to an anthropoid god, a sky-god, Zeus or Jupiter, and left
the issue confidently in his hands. Plutarch[1] is loud in his praises
of the way that Numa hung all his hopes on 'the divine.' When
news was brought that the enemy was upon him, Numa smiled
and said, 'But I am offering burnt sacrifice.' Plutarch is no
exception. For some reason not easy to divine, mankind has
always been apt to regard this attitude of serene and helpless
dependence as peculiarly commendable.

Numa is Numa Pompilius and his gentile name tells us that
he was not only an innovator, but an interloper, a conqueror.
Umbrians, Sabellians and Oscans, tribes who came in upon the
indigenous people of Italy from the north are labializers[2]; their
king is not Numa Quinquilius, but Numa *Pompilius*. The worshippers of Picus, the Woodpecker medicine-king, were, as Denys
tells us, aborigines. These northerners, though originally of the
same stock, had passed into a different and it may be a higher
phase of development, they had passed from spell to prayer, from
sacrament to gift-sacrifice. They came back again into the plains
of Italy as the Achaeans came into Ægean Greece, bringing a full-
blown anthropoid sky-god, Jupiter. They found a people still in
the magical stage ruled over by a medicine-king[3], Picus.

---

[1] *Vit. Num.* xv. αὐτὸν δὲ τὸν Νομᾶν οὕτω φασὶν εἰς τὸ θεῖον ἀνηρτῆσθαι ταῖς ἐλπίσιν,
ὥστε καὶ προσαγγελίας αὐτῷ ποτε γενομένης ὡς ἐπέρχονται πολέμιοι μειδιᾶσαι καὶ εἰπεῖν,
'Εγὼ δὲ θύω.

[2] I follow Prof. Ridgeway, *Who were the Romans?* Proceedings of the British
Academy, vol. iii. 1907.

[3] I borrow the term from Professor Gilbert Murray. The expression 'divine-
king' is as he has clearly shown (*Anthropology and the Classics*, p. 77) misleading.

The indigenous weather-daemon Picus and the incoming thunderer Jupiter have similar and therefore somewhat incompatible functions; it is inevitable that their relations will be somewhat strained, a *modus vivendi* has to be found.   One of two things will happen. If you are a mild, peace-loving Pelasgian with a somewhat obscurantist mind, you will say, 'Ah! here are two great powers, Picus and Jupiter or Zeus, doing the same great work, making the rain to fall, the sun to shine, commanding the thunder; Picus has 'entered the service of Zeus,' Picus is 'the son of Zeus,' Picus is 'a title of Zeus[1],' or best of all, are they not both one and the same?'   Picus himself, according to the Byzantine syncretizers, knew that he was really Zeus. 'When he had handed over the western part of his kingdom he died at the age of 120, and when he was dying he gave orders that his body should be deposited in the island of Crete, and that there should be an inscription :

Here lies dead the Woodpecker who also is Zeus[2].'

But it may be that you are of sterner mould and of conquering race, that you are an incoming intransigent Achaean ; you come down into Thessaly and find the indigenous Salmoneus or it may be Kapaneus at Thebes making thunder and lightning with his rain-birds and water-pails and torches. What! An earthly king, a mortal man, presume to mock Zeus' thunder! Impious wretch, let him perish, blasted by the divine inimitable bolt :

Demens ! qui nimbos et non imitabile fulmen
Aere et cornipedum pulsu simularet equorum[3].

The racial clash and conflict is interesting, and in dealing with the story of Picus as told by Ovid some mention of it was inevitable, but our business for the present lies solely with the development of the lower indigenous stratum.   In the figure of Picus are united, or rather as yet undifferentiated, notions, to us incompatible, of bird, seer-magician, king and *daimon*, if not god. The *daimon* as we have already seen with respect to the Kouros

Kings were not deified because there were as yet no *dei*. The medicine-king is predeistic, but possessed of those powers which later and more cultured ages have relegated to the 'gods.'

[1] Cf. such titles as Zeus Amphiaraos.

[2] Suidas, *s.v.* Πῆκος·
                     ἐνθάδε κεῖται θανὼν...Πῆκος ὁ καὶ Ζεύς

[3] Verg. Æn. vi. 590.

and the Bacchos is but the reflection, the collective emphasis, of a social emotion. The Kouretes utter themselves in their Greatest Kouros, the Woodpecker-Magicians in the Woodpecker, Picus. When the group dissolves and the links that bound leader and group together are severed, then Picus will become a god, unless his figure be effaced by some conquering divinity.

Finally Picus enshrines a beautiful lost faith, the faith that birds and beasts had *mana* other and sometimes stronger than the *mana* of man. The notion that by watching a bird you can divine the weather is preceded by the far more primitive notion that the bird by his *mana* actually makes the weather, makes and brings the rain, the thunder, the sunshine and the spring. Beasts and birds in their silent, aloof, goings, in the perfection of their limited doings are mysterious still and wonderful. We speak of zoomorphic or theriomorphic or ornithomorphic *gods*, but again we misuse language. Birds are not, never were, gods; there is no definite bird-cult, but there are an infinite number of bird-sanctities. Man in early days tries to bring himself into touch with bird-*mana*, he handles reverently bird-sanctities.

There are many ways in which man could participate in bird-*mana*. He could, and also ruthlessly did, eat the bird. Porphyry[1] says those who wish to take unto themselves the spirits of prophetic animals swallow the most effective parts of them, such as the hearts of crows and moles and hawks. It is not that you eat a god-bird, it is that you participate in a substance full of a special quality or *mana*.

Scarcely less efficacious, you can wear the skin of the animal whose *mana* you want, and notably the feathers of a bird. The Carthaginian priestess[2], whose image sculptured on a sarcophagos is reproduced in Fig. 19, wore a bird-robe, the robe of the Egyptian goddess Isis-Nephthys. The goddess was but the humanized, deified form of the holy bird. The body of the priestess is enfolded by the bird's two wings. The bird-head appears above the headdress, and in her right hand she holds

---

[1] *de Abst.* II. 48. See my *Prolegomena*, p. 487.
[2] First published by Miss M. Moore, *Carthage of the Phenicians*, 1905, frontispiece in colour, and reproduced here by kind permission of Mr W. Heinemann.

a bird. She is all bird. The colouring of the feathers is a dark vivid blue and the colourless reproduction gives but a slight idea of the beauty of the bluebird-priestess.

The wearing of bird-robes and bird-headdresses with magical intent goes on to-day among primitive peoples. Among the Tara-humares now-a-days a sha-man may be seen at feasts wearing the plumes of birds, and through these plumes it is thought the wise birds impart all they know[1]. Like Teiresias, like Mopsos, like Melampos, like Kassandra, these shamans understand the speech of birds. A little bird tells them.

Further you can secure much bird-*mana* by a bird-dance. These same Tarahu-mares assert that their dances have been taught them by animals. Animals they hold are not inferior creatures ; they practise magic. The deer and the turkey dance in spring, the birds sing and the frogs croak to induce the gods to let it rain. Here it is evident we are in a transi-tion stage ; gods are already

Fig. 19.

[1] C. Lumholtz, *Unknown Mexico*, vol. i. p. 313. For the general attitude of primitive man towards birds, see E. J. Payne, *History of America*, ii. p. 161, and especially McDougall, *Journ. Anthrop. Inst.* 1901, xxxi. pp. 173—213.

developed, but it is the turkey and the deer who do the real
work, the dancing, for, among the Tarahumares, dancing, *noldova*,
means literally to 'work.' Their two principal dances are the
Yumari and the Rutuburi. The Yumari, which was older, was
taught to the people by the deer. The words sung at the
Rutuburi dance show clearly the magical intent[1]. After a short
prelude the song begins[2]:

> The water is near;
> Fog is resting on the mountain and on the *mesa*,
> The Blue bird sings and whirs in the trees, and
> The Male Woodpecker is calling on the Uano;
> Where the fog is rising.
> The large Swift is making his dashes through the evening air;
> The rains are close at hand.
> When the Swift is darting through the air he makes his whizzing
>   humming noise.
> The Blue Squirrel ascends the tree and whistles.
> The plants will be growing and the fruit will be ripening,
> And when it is ripe it falls to the ground.
> It falls because it is so ripe.
> The flowers are standing up, waving in the wind.
> The Turkey is playing, and the Eagle is calling;
> Therefore, the time of rains will soon set in.

The dance goes on for hours. It is danced on one of the *patios*
or level dancing-places where the Tarahumare performs all his
religious exercises. The dance is performed in the open air
ostensibly that the principal divinities of the people, Father-Sun
and Mother-Moon, may see it and be induced to send rain; but, as
there is no mention whatever of either Father-Sun or Mother-
Moon, it is probable that the service of the magical birds preceded
that of these Tarahumaran Olympians.

It is of course not only birds who teach man to dance, there
are sterner potencies whose gait and gestures it is well to imitate.
The Grizzly Bear dance of the North American Indians is thus
described[3]. The drummers assemble and chant 'I begin to grow
restless in the spring,' and they represent the bear making ready
to come from his winter den. Then 'Lone Chief' drew his robe

[1] Carl Lumholtz, *Unknown Mexico*, vol. i. p. 330.
[2] It is probable that the various bird-dances of the ancients had the like magical intent, e.g. the dances called γλαῦξ (Athen. xiv. 629) and σκώψ (Athen. ix. 391) and the famous γέρανος (Plut. *Thes.* xxi.). Mr D'Arcy Thompson says (*s.v.*) that the dancing of cranes may be seen in the opening of the year in any zoological garden.
[3] W. McClintock, *The Old North Trail*, p. 264.

about him and arose to dance imitating the bear going from his
den and chanting :

> I take my robe,
> My robe is sacred,
> I wander in the summer.

'Lone Chief' imitated with his hands a bear holding up its paws
and placing his feet together he moved backward and forward
with short jumps, making the lumbering movements of a bear,
running, breathing heavily and imitating his digging and turning
over stones for insects.

Any bird or beast or fish, if he be good for food, or if in any
way he arrest man's attention as fearful or wonderful, may become
sacred, that is, may be held to be charged with special *mana*; but,
of all living creatures, birds longest keep their sanctity.   They
come and go where man and beast cannot go, up to the sun, high
among the rain clouds; their flight is swift, their cries are strange
and ominous, yet they are near to man; they perch on trees, yet
they feed on earth-worms; they are creatures half of Gaia, half of
Ouranos.   Long after men thought of and worshipped the gods
in human shape they still remembered the ancient Kingdom of
the Birds.   On the archaic patera[1] in Fig. 53, p. 207, is depicted the
sacrifice of a bull—it may be at the Bouphonia.   Athena is present
as Promachos with shield and uplifted spear.   Behind her is the
great snake of Mother Earth which she took over, in front on a
stepped altar where the fire blazes is a holy bird.   What bird is
intended is uncertain; assuredly no owl, but perhaps a crow,
though Aristotle[2] says no crow ever entered the Acropolis at
Athens.   At Korone, Crow Town, there was a bronze statue of
Athena holding a crow in her hand[3].

We do not associate Artemis with any special bird, still less
do we imagine her in bird-form; she is altogether to us the human
maiden.   Yet we know of the winged, or, as she used to be called,
the 'Persian' Artemis, with her high curved wings.   The recent
excavations of the British School at Sparta have taught us that

---

[1] *Brit. Mus. Cat.* B 405, C. Smith, *J.H.S.* I. p. 202, Pl. III., and see my *Ancient Athens*, p. 289, Fig. 30.

[2] *Frg.* 324.

[3] Paus. IV. 34. 6; for the relation of Athens to the crow and the enmity of crow and owl see Dr Frazer's note on Paus. II. 11. 7, and for crow superstitions, κορωνίσ-ματα, etc., see D'Arcy Thompson, *op. cit., s.v.* Κορώνη.

these wings are not oriental, and not even mere attributes of swiftness, they are just survivals of an old bird-form. On the carved ivory *fibula* in Fig. 20[1], from the sanctuary of Orthia, we see the primitive goddess who went to the making of Artemis. She has high curved wings, and she grasps by the neck two water-birds who dwelt in her *Limnae*. On one of the *fibulae* two birds are also perched on her shoulders; she is all bird.

Fig. 20.

The Greeks early shrank from monstrosities, and our hand-books tell us it is because of the sureness and delicacy of their instinctive taste. But a hybrid form is not necessarily ugly; it may be of great imaginative beauty. There are Egyptian statues of the ram-headed Knum, more solemn, more religious than any human Zeus the Greeks have left us. In Fig. 21[2] we have the Chinese Thunder-God Zin-Shin, half bird half man as the Greeks

[1] Reproduced by kind permission from R. M. Dawkins' *Laconia, Sparta* in B.S.A. xiii. 1906–7, p. 78, Fig. 17 b.
[2] Reproduced by kind permission of Messrs Macmillan from W. Simpson, *The Buddhist Praying Wheel*, 1896, Fig. 41.

themselves imagined but feared to picture Zeus. He is fantastic and beautiful with his wings and eagle beak and claws, riding the clouds in his circle of heavenly thunder-drums. The Greeks had just the same picture in their minds—a bird-god, a cloud-god,

Fig. 21.

a thunder-god—but they dare not adventure it all together, so they separate off the 'attributes'; rationalists as they are they divide and distinguish, and give us pictures like the lovely coins of Elis (Fig. 22). But there is loss as well as gain.

Fig. 22.

With this primitive sanctity of birds rather than their definite divinity in our minds, much that is otherwise grotesque becomes simple and beautiful—Bird-bridegrooms, Bird-parentages, Egg-cosmogonies, Bird-metamorphoses. We no longer wonder that

Trochilos the Wren is father of Triptolemos, that Ion is son of Xouthos the twitterer, himself the son of Aiolos the Lightning, nor that the Kouretes have for their mother Kombe the Crow. Bird-metamorphoses cease to be grotesque because they are seen not to be metamorphoses at all—only survivals misunderstood of the old Bird-sanctities.

The heavenly swan woos Leda, and Nemesis in the form of a swan flies before the swan-god[1]. When Aidos and Nemesis leave miserable mortals to their sins and sorrows, they do on their swan bodies[2] once again and fly up to Olympus, their fair flesh hidden in white and feathery raiment, to the kingdom of the deathless ones—the birds. To that same quiet kingdom the chorus of the *Hippolytus*[3], strained to breaking-point by the passion of Phaedra, will escape.

> Could I take me to some cavern for mine hiding
>   In the hill-tops where the Sun scarce hath trod,
> Or a cloud make the home of mine abiding
>   As a bird among the bird-droves of God!

In far-off savage Tauri the leader of the chorus of Greek maidens, bird-haunted, remembers the bird and tree-sanctuary at Delos, where dwells the sacred swan-bird of the sun-god, and, halcyon-like, she sings[4]:

> Sister, I too beside the sea complain,
>   A bird that hath no wing.
> Oh for a kind Greek market-place again,
> For Artemis that healeth woman's pain;
>   Here I stand hungering.
> Give me the little hill above the sea,
> The palm of Delos fringèd delicately,
> The young sweet laurel and the olive-tree
>   Grey-leaved and glimmering;
> O Isle of Leto, Isle of pain and love,
> The Orbèd Water and the spell thereof,
> Where still the Swan, minstrel of things to be,
>   Doth serve the Muse and sing.

---

[1] See Roscher, *s.v.* Nemesis.

[2] This, considering the swan-form of Nemesis, must, I think, be the meaning of Hesiod, *Op.* 200

λευκοῖσιν φαρέεσσι καλυψαμένω χρόα καλόν.

For these 'femmes cygnes' and the way they doff and do on their 'chemises de cygne' see S. Reinach, 'Les Theoxenies et le vol des Dioscures,' in *Cultes, Mythes et Religions*, II. p. 55, though M. Reinach is not responsible for my interpretation of Hesiod.

[3] Eur. *Hipp.* 732.

[4] Eur. *Iph. in T.* 1095.

In the last two chapters we have seen that magic takes its rise, not only or chiefly in any mistaken theory, but in a thing done, a δρώμενον, predone.   We have further passed in review, in unavoidable fusion and confusion, three stages of magical development ; we have seen magic as open and public, an affair of the tribe, we have seen it as the work of a specialized group, and last, as the work of an individual medicine-man or medicine-king. Further, we have seen the magical efficacy of birds, as first making, and then foretelling, the weather.   Finally we have seen, in the figure of Picus, the strange blend of bird-magician and human king.   The cause of these various stages of magic, and the social conditions underlying the fusion of man and bird or beast will be examined in the next chapter, when we come to the question of sacrifice and the social, totemistic conditions that underlay it.

This brings us to the second rite in the Kouretic initiation of a Bacchos, the *omophagia.*

Picus Martius.

Note to p. 89. For the thunderbolt see Blinkenberg, *The Thunder-weapon in Religion and Folklore,* 1911.

Note to p. 101. For the woodpecker see Rendel Harris, *Picus who is also Zeus,* 1916, and for a counter-theory see W. R. Halliday, *Classical Review,* 1922, p. 110.

CHAPTER V.

TOTEMISM, SACRAMENT AND SACRIFICE.

'WHAT MEANEST THOU BY THIS WORD SACRAMENT?

WE have seen how the mystic, at his initiation by the Kouretes, 'accomplished the Thunders.' Another rite remains, more dread and, to our modern thinking[1], utterly repugnant. Before he can become a Bacchos, the candidate must have

> Fulfilled his red and bleeding feasts[2]

The *omophagia* or *Eating of Raw Flesh* was a rite not confined to the Kouretic initiation of a Bacchos. We meet it again in the Thracian worship of Dionysos. The Bacchae when they recount τὰ νομισθέντα, their accustomed rites, sing the glory and

> joy of the quick red fountains,
> The blood of the hill-goat torn[3].

The Bacchoi in Crete eat of a bull, the Bacchae in Thrace and Macedon of a hill-goat; the particular animal matters little, the essential is that there should be a communal feast of Raw Flesh, a δαὶς ὠμοφάγος.

Physically repugnant the rite must always be to our modern taste, which prefers to cook its goats and bulls before eating them; but our moral repugnance disappears, or at least suffers profound modification, when the gist of the rite is understood. What specially revolts us is that the tearing and eating of bulls and

---

[1] Plutarch in his *de defect. oracul.* raises a horrified protest. See my *Prolegomena*, p. 484.

[2] τάς τ' ὠμοφάγους δαῖτας τελέσας.

[3] Eur. *Bacch.* 135

> ἡδὺς ἐν ὄρεσιν...
> ...ἀγρεύων
> αἷμα τραγοκτόνον, ὠμοφάγον χάριν.

goats should be supposed to be a sacrifice pleasing to a god.   We naturally feel that from the point of view of edification the less said about the worship of such gods the better.   Nor is our moral sense appeased if we are told that the sacrifice is a sacrament, that the bull or goat torn and eaten is the god himself, of whose life the worshippers partake in sacramental communion.   In thus interpreting ancient rites we bring our own revolting horrors with us.   The *omophagia* was part of a religion, that is a system of sanctities, that knew no gods; it belongs to a social organization that preceded theology.   The origin of sacrifice and sacrament alike can only be understood in relation to the social structure and its attendant mode of thinking from whence it sprang— totemism.   Only in the light of totemistic thinking can it be made clear why, to become a Bacchos, the candidate must partake of a sacrament of Raw Flesh.

'Totemism,' Dr Frazer[1] says—and we cannot do better than adopt his definition—'is an intimate relation which is supposed to exist between a group of kindred people on the one side and a species of natural or artificial objects on the other side, which objects are called the totems of the human group.'

We observe at the outset that totemism has two notes or characteristics: it has to do with a group not an individual, and that *group* is in a peculiar relation to another *group* of natural and occasionally of artificial objects.

It is of the utmost importance that we should be clear as to the first note or characteristic, i.e. that totemism has to do with a *group*.   In Dr Frazer's earlier work on totemism, published in 1887, his definition ignored the human group.   It reads as follows[2]:

A totem is a class of material objects which *a* savage regards with super- stitious respect, believing that there exists between *him* and every member of the class an intimate and altogether special relation.

In this earlier definition, it will be noted, a class of objects is regarded as in relation to an individual savage: in the later to a *group* of men.

As to the importance of the group, the word *totem*, it would seem, speaks for itself.   It means, not plant or animal, but simply

---

[1] *Totemism and Exogamy*, 1910, vol. IV. p. 3.
[2] J. G. Frazer, *Totemism*, 1887, p. 1.   The italics are our own.   This mono- graph is reprinted without alteration in vol. I. of Dr Frazer's great work *Totemism and Exogamy*.

tribe. Various forms of the word are given by various authorities. The Rev. Peter Jones, himself an Ojibway, gives *toodaim.* Francis Assikinack, an Ottawa Indian, gives *ododam.* The Abbé Thavenal says the word is properly *ote* in the sense of 'family or tribe,' the possessive of which is *otem.* He adds that the Indians use *ote* in the sense of 'mark' (limited, Dr Frazer[1] says, apparently to family mark), but he argues that the word must mean 'family or tribe,' in some sense 'group.'

This simple, familiar and, we believe, undisputed fact that totem means 'tribe or group' has not we think been sufficiently emphasized. The totem-animal, it has long been admitted, is not an individual animal, it is the whole species. This at once delimits the totem, even when it is an artificial object, from the fetich. The fetich is never a class. But, though the group-character of the totem-animal is admitted, the correlative truth, that it is the human *group*, not the human individual that is related to the totem, has been left vague. Hence all the controversy as to whether the individual totem is prior to the group-totem or *vice versâ,* whether or not the guardian animal or spirit of the individual precedes the totem-animal. Hence also the significance of Dr Frazer's[2] modification of his original definition, his substitution of the words 'group of kindred people' for 'a savage.'

First and foremost then in totemism is the idea of the unity of a group. Next comes the second note or characteristic; this human group is in a special relation to another group—this time of non-human objects. In far the greater number of cases these non-human objects are animals and plants, occasionally meteoric objects, sun, moon, rain, stars, and still more rarely artificial objects, nets or spears[3]. This relation between the human and the non-human group is so close as to be best figured by kinship, unity of blood, and is

[1] *Totemism,* 1887, p. 1, note 6.
[2] Facts have forced upon Dr Frazer this modification—and to facts he always yields ungrudging obedience—but I cannot help thinking that, as he nowhere calls attention to this modification, the full significance of these facts escapes him, otherwise he would not base his new theory of totemism on the chance error of individual women. See *Totemism and Exogamy,* IV. p. 57.
[3] Frazer, *Totemism and Exogamy,* I. p. 4.

expressed in terms of actual identity[1]. A Central Australian pointing to a photograph of himself will say, 'That one is just the same as me,' so is a kangaroo (his totem). We say the Central Australian 'belongs to the kangaroo tribe'; he knows better, he *is* kangaroo. Now it is this persistent affirmation of primitive man in the totemistic stage that he *is* an animal or a plant, that he *is* a kangaroo or an opossum or a witchetty grub or a plum tree, that instantly arrests our attention, and that has in fact obscured the other and main factor in totemism, the unity of the human group. The human group we understand and realize to a certain extent. Man, we know, is gregarious, he thinks and feels as a group. So much our latter-day parochialism or patriotism or socialism may help us to imagine. It is the extension of the group to include those strange tribesmen, plants, animals and stones, that staggers us[2]. 'What,' we ask, 'does the savage mean by being one, identical with them? Why does he persistently affirm and reaffirm that he *is* a bear, an opossum, a witchetty grub, when he quite well knows that he is not?'

Because to know is one thing, to feel is another. Because to know is first and foremost to distinguish, to note differences, to discern qualities, and thereby to classify. Above all things it is to realize the distinction between *me* and *not-me*. We all remember Tennyson's 'Baby new to earth and sky.' He and the savage have never clearly said that 'this is I.' Man in the totemistic stage rarely sets himself as individual over against his tribe; he rarely sets himself as man over against the world around him[3]. He has not yet fully captured his individual or his human soul, not yet drawn a circle round his separate self. It is not that he confuses between himself and a kangaroo; it is that he has not yet drawn the clear-cut outline that defines the conception kangaroo from that of man and eternally separates them. His mental life is as yet mainly emotional, one of felt *relations*.

[1] See Lévy-Bruhl, *Les Fonctions Mentales dans les Sociétés Inférieures*, 1910, p. 25.

[2] But not if we become 'as little children.' Mr S. Reinach in his delightful *Orpheus* says of totemism (p. 22), 'Ce respect de la vie d'un animal, d'un végétal, n'est autre chose qu'une exagération, une hypertrophie de l'instinct social. Il suffit de mener un jeune enfant dans un jardin zoologique pour s'assurer que cette hypertrophie est très naturelle à l'homme.'

[3] For an illuminating account of the psychology of this process see the chapter on 'Wahrnehmung' (Perception) in Dr P. Beck's *Die Nachahmung*, 1904.

If we can once think ourselves back into totemistic days we shall be rid for ever of an ancient and most pernicious orthodoxy, the old doctrine that the religion of primitive man was anthropomorphic. Facts tell us that it was *not*; that theriomorphism and phytomorphism came first. Yet the ancient dogma flourishes. Again and again we find the unqualified statement that man projects his own image on the universe, sees in it his own human will, peoples all nature with human souls. Totemism teaches us just the contrary; it is as it were the fossil form of quite another creed. It stands for fusion, for *non*-differentiation. Man cannot project his individual self, because that individual self is as yet in part undivided; he cannot project his individual human will, because that human will is felt chiefly as one with the undifferentiated *mana* of the world; he cannot project his individual soul because that complex thing is as yet not completely compounded[1].

Totemism, then, is not so much a special social structure as a stage in epistemology. It is the reflexion of a very primitive fashion in thinking, or rather feeling, the universe, a feeling the realization of which is essential to any understanding of primitive religion. It is not a particular blunder and confusion made by certain ignorant savages, but a phase or stage of collective thinking through which the human mind is bound to pass. Its basis is group-unity, aggregation, similarity, sympathy, a sense of common group life, and this sense of common life, this *participation*[2], this unity, is extended to the non-human world in a way which our modern, individualistic reason, based on observed distinctions, finds almost unthinkable.

We find totemism unthinkable because it is non-rational. We are inclined to make the quite unauthorized assumption that true judgments, i.e. judgments which correspond to observed fact, are natural to man. False judgments like totemism we feel are anomalous and need explanation. Man's opinions, his judgments, we fondly imagine, are based on observation and reason. Just the contrary is the case; beliefs of every kind, at least in man's early

---

[1] The late character of the individual 'soul' will be discussed when we come to the question of Hero-Worship in chapter VIII.

[2] For a full analysis of the primitive idea of *participation* see Lévy-Bruhl, *op. cit.* chapter II. La loi de participation.

stages of development are prior to experience and observation, they are due to suggestion. Anything suggested is received unless there is strong reason, or rather emotion, to the contrary[1]. It is not the acceptance of an opinion, however absurd, that needs explanation; it is its criticism and rejection[2]. Suggest to a savage that he has eaten tabooed food, he accepts the suggestion and— dies. The strongest form of suggestion is of course the collective suggestion of his whole universe, his group, his public opinion. Such suggestion will certainly be accepted without question, if it appeal to a powerful or pleasing emotion.

That outlook on the universe, that stage in epistemology which we call totemism has its source then not in any mere blunder of the individual intellect, but in a strong collective emotion. The next question that lies before us is naturally—What is the emotion that finds its utterance, its expression, its representation, in totemism? To answer this question we must look at the relations of primitive man to his totem. These relations are most clearly marked and will be best understood in that large majority of cases where the totem is an edible plant or animal.

As a rule a savage abstains from eating his totem, whether plant or animal: his totem is *tabu* to him; to eat it would be disrespectful, even dangerous. An Ojibway who had unwittingly killed a bear (his totem) described how, on his way home after the accident, he was attacked by a large bear who asked him why he had killed his totem. The man explained, apologised, and was dismissed with a caution[3]. This *tabu* on the eating of a totem is natural enough. The man is spiritually, mystically, akin to his totem, and as a rule you do not eat your relations. But this *tabu* is in some parts of the world qualified by a particular and very interesting injunction. A man may not as a rule eat of his totem, but at certain times and under certain restrictions a man not only

---

[1] W. James, *Principles of Psychology*, II. p. 319, 'the primitive impulse is to affirm immediately the reality of all that is conceived,' 'we acquire disbelief,' and p. 299, 'we believe as much as we can.'

[2] This important point has been well brought out in an article in the Edinburgh Review (vol. ccx. p. 106) on *Fallacies and Superstitions*. The anonymous writer reminds us that the writer of the *Problems* attributed to Aristotle (Θ, p. 891, a. 7), raised the question 'why do men cough and cows do not?' a difficulty he might have spared himself had his judgments been based on observation.

[3] Frazer, *Totemism and Exogamy*, I. p. 10.

may, but must, eat of his totem, though only sparingly[1], as of a thing sacro-sanct. This eating of the totem is closely connected with its ceremonial multiplication. You abstain from your totem as a rule because of its sanctity, i.e. because it is a great focus of *mana*; you eat a little with infinite precautions because you want that *mana* and seek its multiplication. This double-edged attitude towards things sacred lies, as we shall later see, at the very foundation of the ideas both of sacrament and sacrifice.

The totem-animal is in general the guardian and protector of its human counterpart, but the relation is strictly mutual; the animal depends on the man as the man on the animal. This comes out very clearly in the *Intichiuma* ceremonies performed by the Central Australian tribes[2]. By *Intichiuma* are meant magical ceremonies performed by members of a totem-group to induce the multiplication of the totem. As a typical instance we may take the ceremonies of the Emu totem.

When men of the Emu totem desire to multiply emus they set about it as follows. Several of the men open veins in their arms and allow the blood to stream on the ground till a patch about three yards square is saturated with it. When the blood is dry it forms a hard surface on which the men of the totem paint in white, red, yellow and black a design intended to represent various parts of the emu, such as the fat, of which the natives are very fond, the eggs in various stages of development, the intestines, and the feathers. Further, several men of the totem, acting the part of ancestors of the Emu clan, dress themselves up to resemble emus and imitate the movements and aimless gazing about of the bird; on their heads are fastened sacred sticks (*churinga*) about four feet long, and tipped with emu feathers, to represent the long neck and small head of the emu[3].

The ceremony has really, like all *Intichiuma* ceremonies, two main elements: (1) the shedding of the blood of the human Emu, and (2) his counterfeit presentment of the bird-Emu. The human blood helps out the animal life, renews, invigorates it; the man, by dressing up as the Emu and making pictures of it, increases his mystic sympathy and communion. In the ceremony for promoting the Witchetty Grub a long narrow structure of boughs is got ready. It represents the chrysalis from which the full-grown insect emerges. Into this structure the men of the Witchetty Grub totem, painted over with the device of the totem in red ochre and pipe clay, each in turn enter and sing of the grub in its

---

[1] Frazer, *op. cit.* IV. p. 6.
[2] Spencer and Gillen, *Native Tribes of Central Australia*, chapter VI., Intichiuma ceremonies.
[3] Frazer, *op. cit.* I. p. 106.

various stages of development.   They then shuffle out one by one
with a gliding motion to indicate the emergence of the insect[1].
They enact, they represent their own union and communion, their
identity with their totem, and thereby somehow intensify its life
and productiveness.   At the back of the whole grotesque performance lies, not so much a mistaken ratiocination, but an intense
desire for food, issuing in a vivid representation.

Totemism and totemistic ceremonies and ways of thinking are
based, we have seen, on group-emotion, on a sense of solidarity, of
oneness.   No distinction is felt between the human and non-
human members of the totem-group, or rather, to be more exact,
the beginning of a distinction is just dawning.   The magical
ceremonies, the shedding of the human blood, the counterfeiting
of the animal, have for their object to bridge the gulf that is just
opening, to restore by communion that complete unity which is
just becoming conscious of possible division.   The ceremonies are
however still intensely sympathetic and cooperative; they are, as
the Greeks would say, rather *methektic* than *mimetic*, the expression, the utterance, of a common nature participated in, rather
than the imitation of alien characteristics.   The Emu man still
feels he *is* an Emu; the feathers he puts on, the gait he emulates,
are his own, not another's.

But, strong though the sense of group-unity is in Totemism,
the rift has begun.   Totemism means not only unity of one group,
but also disparity from other groups.   The Emu men are one
among themselves, and one with the Emu birds, but they are
alien to the Witchetty Grub men, and have no power to multiply
Witchetty Grubs—or Kangaroos.   Behind the totemistic system
may lie a pre-totemistic social state[2], when the tribe was all one, not
yet broken into totemistic groups.   The cause of the severance we
can only conjecture.   Probably it was due to the merely mechanical
cause of pressure of population.   The tribe growing over-populous
loses coherence and falls asunder by simple segmentation.   Once
that segmentation occurs each half gathers round a nucleus.

[1] Frazer, *op. cit.* I. p. 106, of how food comes to be.
[2] I am indebted for this idea to views expressed by Mr A. R. Brown in a course
of lectures delivered in 1909 at Trinity College, Cambridge.   Mr Brown suggested
that the Andaman Islanders and the Esquimaux were perhaps instances of *pre-
totemistic* peoples.

We then have forces at work not only of attraction, but of repulsion; union is intensified through disunion. This double force which makes and remakes society Empedocles[1] saw reflected in his cosmos:

A two-fold tale I tell thee. At one time
The One grew from the many. Yet again
Division was—the many from the one.

And these things never cease, but change for ever.
At one time all are joined and all is Love,
And next they fly asunder, all is Strife.

Now that we realize a little what totemism is, we are able to understand much better the various stages and developments of magic and also something of the relation of magic to religion. The totem-group when it performs its rites of multiplication has indeed some dawning sense of differentiation, but its main emotion and conviction is of unity, emotional unity with its totem, a unity which it emphasizes and enhances and reintegrates by its ceremonies of sympathy. The whole human group acts and reacts on the whole plant or animal group, the *mana* of the human and the animal group is *felt* as continuous. This is the first stage. But as intelligence advances and as actual individual observation tends to take the place of collective suggestion, the sense of unity is obscured. Little by little the attention is focused on distinctions. Man, though he is dressed up as an emu, becomes more and more conscious that he *is not* an emu, but that he is *imitating* an emu, a thing in some respects alien to himself, a thing possessed of much *mana*, but whose *mana* is separate, a thing to be acted on, controlled, rather than sympathetically reinforced. Then, as the Greek would say, μέθεξις gives place to μίμησις, participation to imitation[2].

Any dawning sense of distinction between the human and the animal member of the group is like a traitor in the very heart of the citadel. But custom is strong, and totemistic rites go on long

---

[1] Diels, *Frg.* 17, p. 177

διπλ' ἐρέω· τοτὲ μὲν γὰρ ἓν ηὐξήθη μόνον εἶναι
ἐκ πλεόνων, τοτὲ δ' αὖ διέφυ πλέον' ἐξ ἑνὸς εἶναι

καὶ ταῦτ' ἀλλάσσοντα διαμπερὲς οὐδαμὰ λήγει,
ἄλλοτε μὲν Φιλότητι συνερχόμεν' εἰς ἓν ἅπαντα,
ἄλλοτε δ' αὖ δίχ' ἕκαστα φορεύμενα Νείκεος ἔχθει.

The analogy of the Greek μέθεξις was pointed out to me by Mr F. M. Cornford.

after that faith in unity, in consubstantiality, which is of its essence, is dying or even dead. The stages of its death are gradual. The whole group ceases to carry on the magical rite, which becomes the province of a class of medicine-men; the specialized Kouretes, as we have seen, supplant the whole body of Kouroi. Finally the power is lodged in an individual, a head medicine-man, a king whose functions are at first rather magical than political.

As the wielder of the power becomes specialized and individualized, his power becomes generalized. In primitive totemistic conditions the Emu man, by virtue of his common life, his common *mana*, controlled, or rather sympathetically invigorated, Emus; but his power was limited to Emus. Once the totemistic system begins to break down, this rigid departmentalism cannot be kept up. The band of magicians, and later the individual medicine-man or medicine-king began to claim control over the food supply and over fertility in general, and also over the weather, on which, bit by bit, it is seen that the food supply depends. The medicine-king tends towards, though he never attains, complete omnipotence.

One other point remains to be observed.

'It is a serious though apparently a common mistake,' says Dr Frazer[1], 'to speak of a totem as a god and say that it is worshipped by the clan. In pure totemism, such as we find it among the Australian aborigines, the totem is never a god, and is never worshipped. A man no more worships his totem and regards it as his god than he worships his father and mother, his brother and his sister, and regards them as gods.'

The reason why pure totemism cannot be a system of worship is now abundantly clear. Worship involves conscious segregation of god and worshipper. The very idea of a god, as we have seen in the case of the Kouros and the Bacchos, belongs to a later stage of epistemology, a stage in which a man stands off from his own imagination, looks at it, takes an attitude towards it, sees it as *object*. Worship connotes an object of worship. Between totemism and worship stands the midway stage of magic. Magic in its more elementary forms we have already seen in considering the Thunder-Rites. Two later developments have now to be examined, developments closely analogous, Sacramental Communion and Sacrifice.

---

[1] *Totemism and Exogamy*, 1910, vol. IV. p. 5.

Before entering on this enquiry we must however pause for a moment. We have assumed so far that totemism lies behind Greek religion, and that Greek religion can only be rightly understood on this assumption. The assumption is not so bold as it may seem. We do not claim for Greece a fully developed totemistic social system, but rather that totemistic habit of thought, which is, we believe, common to all peoples in an early phase of their epistemology[1]. Totemism, we have tried to show, is to our mind a habit of collective thinking based on collective emotion. The main characteristic of such thinking is union, or rather lack of differentiation, of subject and object. This lack of differentiation, this felt union, shows itself in many ways, and chiefly in one salient example, the belief in the identity of groups of human beings with groups of animals or plants In practice, that is in ritual, totemism finds its natural development in the manipulation of the spiritual *continuum*, in magic.

This habit of collective thinking, this lack of differentiation[2] is, we believe, characteristic not of one race, but of all races at a given stage of their mental development. It is further, I believe, *the* characteristic of Greek religion that it emerged early from the totemistic magical stage. The Greeks were a people who drew clear-cut outlines and sharp distinctions. But we cannot understand this rapid emergence unless we understand from what they emerged. Very early the Greeks shed their phytomorphic and theriomorphic gods. With strong emphasis by the mouth of Pindar[3] they insist that a god be clearly and impassably delimited from man. Have we any evidence of the earlier stage of thought against which the protest is raised? Are there in Greek mythology or Greek cultus definite traces of totemistic unification?

---

[1] Such a system probably only occurs sporadically where man's progress in epistemology has been arrested and the social structure crystallizes. Since writing the above I am delighted to find that my conjecture, which might appear hazardous, has been anticipated by Mr A. B. Cook. He writes (*J.H.S.* xiv. 1894, 157) 'On the whole I gather that the Mycenaean worshippers were not totemists pure and simple but that the mode of their worship points to its having been developed out of still earlier totemism.'

[2] For an analysis of primitive mentality, see Lévy-Bruhl, *Les Fonctions Mentales dans les Sociétés Inférieures*, 1910.

[3] *Ol.* v. 58   μὴ ματεύ-
                        ση θεὸς γενέσθαι,

and *Isth.* v. 20

                        θνατὰ θνατοῖσι πρέπει.

See my *Prolegomena*, p. 477.

The people of the island of Seriphos would not for the most part use lobsters for food, accounting them sacred. Ælian[1] was told that if they found one dead they would bury it and lament for it. If they took one alive in their nets they cast it back into the sea. The dead totem is often mourned for as a clansman. In Samoa, if an Owl man finds a dead owl, he will sit down by it and weep over it and beat his forehead with stones till the blood flows[2]. In Phrygia there was a clan called the Snake-born ('Οφιογενεῖς), reputed to be descended from a sacred snake of great size who had once lived in a grove[3]. At Parium was another group of Snake-born men. The males of the group had the power, Strabo[4] tells us, of curing the bite of serpents by touching the patient. The Psylli, a Snake clan of Africa, exposed their new-born children to the bite of snakes. If bitten they were bastards, if left untouched legitimate[5]. If stories such as these are not survivals of totemistic thinking, it is hard to know what is.

In poetry more even than in prose or than in the practice of actual rites, primitive ways of thinking, totemistic unifications of man and animal are sure to survive. In the *Bacchae* of Euripides, in that very religion of the Kouros which we have seen to be so elemental, we have an instance of strange beauty and significance.

One secret of the thrill of the *Bacchae* is that the god is always shifting his shape. Dionysos is a human youth, lovely, with curled hair, but in a moment he is a Snake, a Lion, a Wild Bull, a Burning Flame. The leader of the chorus cries[6]

> Appear, appear whatso thy shape or name,
> O Mountain Bull, Snake of the Hundred Heads,
>   Lion of Burning Flame,
> O God, Beast, Mystery, come!

When Pentheus comes out from the palace, hypnotised, intoxicated, seeing two suns, two walls with seven gates, the most

---

[1] Æl. *N.A.* XIII. 26 on the τέττιξ ἐνάλιος. Οὐ σιτοῦνται δὲ αὐτὸν οἱ πολλοί, νομίζοντες ἱερόν. Σεριφίους δὲ ἀκούω καὶ θάπτειν νεκρὸν ἑαλωκότα· ζῶντα δὲ εἰς δίκτυον ἐμπεσόντα οὐ κατέχουσιν, ἀλλὰ ἀποδιδόασι τῇ θαλάττῃ αὖθις. Θρηνοῦσι δὲ ἄρα τοὺς ἀποθανόντας.
[2] Dr Frazer, *Totemism and Exogamy*, 1910, IV. p. 15.
[3] Æl. *N.A.* XII. 39.   [4] XIII. 1. 14.
[5] Varro, *ad Prisc.* X. 82.   [6] *v.* 1017.

frightening thing of all is that he sees the Bacchos not as man, but bull[1]:

> And is it a Wild Bull this, that walks and waits
> Before me? There are horns upon thy brow!
> What art thou, man or beast? For surely now
> The Bull is on thee!

Now all this is usually[2] explained as a 'late' mysticism, a sort of pantheism, the god in all nature. In reality it goes back to things simpler and deeper. It is important to note that this shift to animal shape is *not* a power of transformation due to the mature omnipotence of the god; it is with the Dithyrambos *from his birth*; it is part of his essence as the Twice-Born. The first chorus[3], as well as the third already analysed, is in part a Birth-song, a Dithyramb. The chorus sing of the coming of Bromios from Phrygia, of the Thunder Epiphany, the smiting of Semele the Mother, and the second birth from the Father:

> And the Queen knew not beside him
> Till the perfect hour was there.
> Then a hornèd God was found.

The Dithyramb is a bull-god, reborn into his tribe not only as a full-grown male but as a sacred beast[4].

Thus, in the very kernel of our subject, in the Rite of the New Birth, we find the totemistic way of thinking. The boy to be initiated is reborn as his totem-animal.

In describing the ceremony of the Second Birth among the Kikúyus we have seen[5] that the rite was called either *To be born again* or *To be born of a goat*. As the Kikúyu have no goat totem we cannot certainly connect the ceremony with totemism, but among other peoples the connection is clear. Thus, when a South Slavonian[6] woman has given birth to a child, an old woman runs out of the house and calls out, 'A she-wolf has littered a he-wolf.' To make assurance doubly sure, the child is drawn through a

---

[1] *v.* 920.

[2] Again I find that what I believe to be the right explanation is given by Mr A. B. Cook (*J.H.S.* xiv. 108).

[3] *Bacch.* 99.

[4] It is scarcely necessary to say that Euripides was all unconscious of that sub-stratum of totemism of which he makes such splendid poetical use.

[5] p. 21.

[6] J. G. Frazer, *Totemism*, 1887, pp. 32 and 33.

wolf-skin so as to simulate actual birth from a wolf. The reason now *assigned* for these customs is that by making a wolf of the child you cheat the witches of their prey, for they will not attack a wolf. But the origin of the custom must surely be the simpler notion that you mean what you do to the child—you make a wolf of him.

Very instructive in this respect is a Hindu custom[1]. When a Hindu child's horoscope looks bad, he has to be born again of a cow. He is dressed in scarlet, tied on a new sieve and passed between the hind legs of a cow forward through the forelegs to the mouth and again in the reverse direction to simulate birth; the ordinary birth-ceremonies, aspersion and the like are then gone through. The child is new born as a holy calf. This is certain, for the father sniffs at his son as a cow smells her calf. A like ceremony of new birth as a beast may be gone through merely with a view to purification. If in India a grown person has polluted himself by contact with unbelievers, he can be purified by being passed through a golden cow. This brings out very clearly the sense in which new birth and purification are substantially the same: both are *rites de passage,* the spirit of both is expressed by the initiation formulary, ἔφυγον κακὸν εὗρον ἄμεινον.

The second birth then of the infant Dionysos as a 'horned child' is best explained by totemistic ways of thinking. If the view[2] here taken be correct, totemism arises, not from any intellectual blunder of the individual savage, but rather from a certain mental state common to all primitive peoples, a state in which the group dominates the individual and in which the group seeks to utter its unity, to emphasize its emotion about that unity by the avowal of a common kinship with animal or plant. If this be so, the Greeks will be no exception to the general rule. They must have passed through the stage of undifferentiated thinking and group-emotion from which totemism, magic and the notion of *mana* sprang[3], and we may safely look for survivals of a totemistic

[1] Frazer, *op. cit.* p. 33.
[2] The view taken is substantially that of Prof. Durkheim or at least arises out of it. See E. Durkheim, *Sur le totémisme,* in L'Année Sociologique, 1902 (v.), p. 82.
[3] Dr Frazer in his great work, *Totemism and Exogamy,* vol. IV. p. 13, says that the evidence adduced in support of the existence of totemism among the Semites and among the Aryans, notably among the ancient Greeks and Celts, leaves him

habit of thought. That these survivals abound among primitive red-skins and black-skins rather than among Semites and Aryans need surprise no one.

Another totemistic relic remains to be considered; it is again enshrined with singular beauty in the *Bacchae*. Among totemistic peoples it is frequently the custom to tattoo the member of the totem-group with the figure of the sacred plant or animal. That

FIG. 23.

this custom was in use among the Thracian worshippers of Dionysos we have clear evidence in Fig. 23. The design is from a beautiful cylix with white ground in the National Museum at Athens[1]. The scene is the slaying of Orpheus by a Maenad. Only the Maenad is figured here. On her right arm is distinctly tattooed a fawn, on her left some object not yet explained.

'doubtful or unconvinced. To a great extent it consists of myths, legends and superstitions about plants and animals which, though they bear a certain resemblance to totemism, may have originated quite independently of it.'

[1] See my paper on *Some Fragments of a Vase presumably by Euphronios*, in J.H.S. IX. 1888, p. 143.

The female worshippers of Dionysos were it would seem
tattooed with the figure of a fawn; the male worshippers were
stamped with an ivy leaf[1]. The ivy, rather than the vine, was in
early days the sacred plant of Dionysos. The Bacchic women
chewed ivy in their ecstasy, possibly as a sort of sacrament[2].
Pliny[3] was surprised at the veneration paid to ivy because it is
hurtful to trees and buildings. The reason of its sanctity is
simple if mystical. Ivy lives on when other plants die down. It
is the vehicle of the external, undying, totem-soul, the vehicle of
Dionysos, god of the perennial new birth. When Ptolemy Philo-
pator converted the Egyptian Jews to the religion of Dionysos he
had them branded with the ivy leaf[4].

The ivy then was the primitive phytomorph, the fawn the
theriomorph. You want to identify yourself with your totem,
who by now has developed into your god. To effect this union,
this consubstantiality, it is well to carry his symbols and to dance
his dances, on occasion it is well to eat him; but, best and
simplest, be stamped indelibly with his image. The Bacchant
wore the nebris, the fawn-skin, on her feet were sandals of
fawn-skin; stamped with the figure of a fawn, she *is* a fawn
and fleeing from the human hounds to the shelter of the
woodland she sings:

> O feet of a fawn to the greenwood fled,
>   Alone in the grass and the loveliness[5]

We have then in Greek and especially in Bacchic religion
traces slight but sufficient, not of a regular totemistic social
system, but of totemistic ways of thinking. We pass on now to
show how these totemistic ways of thinking explain the gist of
the *Feast of Raw Flesh* (δαὶς ὠμοφάγος) which was part of the
rite of Bacchic initiation. We shall find that this Feast is as it
were the prototype of all sacrament and sacrifice.

---

[1] P. Perdrizet, *Le Fragment de Satyros*, in Revue des Études Anciennes, xii.
1910, p. 235.

[2] Plut. *Q. R.* 112 αἱ ἔνοχοι τοῖς βακχικοῖς πάθεσι γυναῖκες εὐθὺς ἐπὶ τὸν κιττὸν
φέρονται, καὶ σπαράττουσι δραττόμεναι ταῖς χερσὶ καὶ διέσθουσαι τοῖς στόμασιν.

[3] *H. N.* xvi. 144.

[4] Perdrizet, *op. cit.* p. 235.

[5] Eur. *Bacch.* 866

> ὡς νεβρὸς χλοεραῖς ἐμπαί-
>   ζουσα λείμακος ἡδοναῖς.

That sacrifice and sacrament are near akin the similarity of the two words would lead us to suspect. One obvious distinction is, however, worth noting at the outset. Sacrifice, as part of our normal religious ritual, is now-a-days dead and gone. Sacraments show no sign of dying, but rather of renewed life and vigour. This need not surprise us. It will shortly appear that sacrifice is but a specialized form of sacrament, both sacrament and sacrifice being themselves only special forms of that manipulation of *mana* which we have agreed to call magic. Of the two, sacrifice and sacrament, sacrament is the more primitive; sacrifice contains elements that are plainly of late development. The oldest things lie deepest and live longest; it is the specializations, the differentiations, that dwindle and die. We begin then by asking—What is sacrifice? What is the late element in it as compared with sacrament? And, incidentally, why was it doomed to a relatively early death?

The current common-sense view of sacrifice is the gift-theory[1], *do ut des*, I give, at some personal 'sacrifice,' to you, the god, in order that you may give me a *quid pro quo*. I bring a gift to a god as I might to an oriental potentate to 'smooth his face.' This theory presupposes a personality, not to say a personage, to whom the gift may be offered. It further supposes that the personality is fairly benevolent and open to a bribe. An important modification of the *do ut des* theory of sacrifice is the *do ut abeas* variety, 'I give that you may keep away.' It only differs in supposing malevolence in the person approached. When we come to consider animism it will be seen that *do ut abeas* probably precedes *do ut des*.

The gift-theory of sacrifice was unquestionably held by the Greeks of classical times, though with an increasing sense of its inadequacy. 'Holiness,' says Socrates[2] to Euthyphron, 'is a sort of science of praying and sacrificing'; further he adds, 'sacrifice is giving to the gods, prayer is asking of them; holiness then is a science of asking and giving.' If we give to the gods they also want to 'do business with us.' Euthyphron, with his orthodox mind, is made very uncomfortable by this plainness of speech, but has nothing he can urge against it.

[1] See my *Prolegomena*, pp. 3—7, where I accept this theory which I now see to be, as regards primitive sacrifice, wholly inadequate.
[2] Plat. *Euthyphro*, 15 D.

The gift-element in sacrifice is real, though as we shall immediately see it is a late accretion, and it is this gift-element that has killed sacrifice as distinct from sacrament. The gift-element was bound to die with the advance of civilization. We have ceased to tremble before those stronger and older than ourselves, we therefore no longer try to placate our god, we have ceased to say to him, *do ut abeas*. We have come to see that to bribe a ruler does not conduce to good government; so to the giver of all good things we no longer say, *do ut des*. To this cause of the decay of sacrifice is added, in the matter of animal sacrifice, the increase of physical sensitiveness. Physically the slaying of innocent animals is beginning to be repulsive to us. Some of us still do it for sport; many of us allow others to do it for us to procure flesh food; but we no longer associate slaughter with our highest moral and religious values[1].

Sacrifice then in the sense of *gift-sacrifice* is dead. It is worth noting that an element which has been essential and universal in religion can drop out and leave religion integral. Instead of *quod semper quod ubique*, we must now adopt as our motto, *tout passe, tout lasse, tout casse*.

The lateness of this somewhat ephemeral gift-element in sacrifice is apparent. It presupposes the existence of a well-defined personality with whom man can 'carry on business.' In a word the gift-theory of sacrifice is closely bound up with the mistaken psychology that assumes the primitiveness of animism and anthropomorphism. As Dr Tylor[2] says with his wonted trenchancy:

Sacrifice has its apparent origin in the same early period of culture and its place in the same animistic scheme as prayer, with which through so long a range of history it has been carried on in the closest connection. As prayer is a request made to a deity as if he were a man, so a sacrifice is a gift made to a deity as if he were a man.

Dr Tylor, the great exponent of the 'gift-theory,' operates, it is clear, from the beginning with a full-blown anthropomorphic god. But the totemistic stage of thinking, we have seen, knew no god, only a consciousness felt collectively of common *mana*. Was there sacrifice in days of totemistic thinking before a god had been fashioned in man's image, and if so, what was its nature?

[1] It will later be seen that killing is not an essential part of sacrifice.
[2] *Primitive Culture*[2], 1873, p. 375.

Robertson Smith[1] was the first to see that Dr Tylor's gift-theory, apparently so simple and satisfactory, did not cover the whole of the facts.   He noted that, when you sacrificed, when you gave, as it was thought, a gift to your god, you seldom gave him all of it.   You ate some of it, most of it yourself, and gave the god bones and specimen bits.   Now with a jealous god—and the god of the Hebrews with whom Robertson Smith was chiefly concerned *was* a jealous god—this method of carrying out your sacrifice would clearly, if the gift-theory were true, not work.   A 'jealous god' must be either a fool or a saint to stand it.   The sacrificer would surely share the just fate of Ananias and Sapphira who 'kept back part.'   In a word Robertson Smith, fired by the recent discoveries of totemism, saw what had necessarily escaped Dr Tylor, that the basis of primitive sacrifice was, not the giving a gift, but the eating of a tribal communal meal.   In a splendid blaze of imagination his mind flashed down the ages from the Arabian communal camel to the sacrifice of the Roman mass.

Even Robertson Smith, great genius though he was, could not rid himself wholly of animism and anthropomorphism.   To him primitive sacrifice was a commensal meal, but *shared with the god*; by the common meal the common life of god and group was alike renewed.   Still hampered as he was with full-fledged divinity as contrasted with sanctity, he could not quite see that in sacrifice the factors were only two, the eater and the eaten, the 'worshipper,' that is the eater, and the sacred animal consumed.   Once the sacred animal consumed, his *mana* passes to the eater, the worshipper, and the circuit is complete.   There is no third factor, no god mysteriously present at the banquet and conferring his sanctity on the sacred animal.   As will later be seen this third factor, this god, arose partly out of the sacrifice itself.   From Robertson Smith's famous camel[2], devoured raw, body and bones, before the rising of the sun, no god developed; from the ὠμοφαγία of the more imaginative Greek arose, we shall presently see, the bull-Dionysos.

The word *sacrifice*, like *sacrament*, tells the same tale.   Etymologically there is nothing in either word that tells of a gift, nor

[1] *Religion of the Semites*, 1889.
[2] Robertson Smith, *Religion of the Semites*, p. 320.   I have previously, *Prolegomena*, pp. 486 ff., discussed in full this important instance of ὠμοφαγία.

yet of a god, no notion of renouncing, giving up to another and a greater. Sacrifice is simply either 'holy doing' or 'holy making,' ἱερὰ ῥέζειν, just *sanctification*, or, to put it in primitive language, it is handling, manipulating *mana*. When you sacrifice you build as it were a bridge[1] between your *mana*, your will, your desire, which is weak and impotent, and that unseen outside *mana* which you believe to be strong and efficacious. In the fruits of the earth which grow by some unseen power there is much *mana*; you want that *mana*. In the loud-roaring bull and the thunder is much *mana*; you want that *mana*. It would be well to get some, to eat a piece of that bull raw, but it is dangerous, not a thing to do unawares alone; so you consecrate the first-fruits, you sacrifice the bull, and then in safety you—communicate.

We are accustomed to the very human gift-theory of sacrifice, it appeals to us by its rather misleading common-sense. Compared with it this theory of sacrifice as a medium, a bridge built, a lightning-conductor interposed, may seem vague and abstract. It is not really abstract; it belongs to a way of thinking that was inchoate rather than abstract. When they began to theorize about sacrifice, it was familiar to the ancients themselves. Sallust[2] the Neo-Platonist, the intimate friend of Julian, wrote, at Julian's request, a tract *About the Gods and the World*. He devotes two chapters to Sacrifice. Why does man give gifts to the gods who do not need them? Sacrifice is for the profit of man not the gods. Man needs to be in contact (συναφθῆναι) with the gods. For this he needs a medium (μεσότης) between his life and the divine life. That medium is the life of the sacrificed animal. Sallust is as much—and more—obsessed by full-blown gods as Dr Tylor, but he comes very near to the notion of *mana*-communion.

It should be noted at this point that eating is not the only means of communicating, though perhaps it is among the most effective. What you want is contact, in order that *mana* may work unimpeded. When you hang a garment on a holy tree or

[1] This idea has been very fully developed by MM. Hubert et Mauss in their illuminating *Essai sur la Nature et la Fonction du Sacrifice* which first appeared in the Année Sociologique, II. 1897-8, and has since been republished by them in the Mélanges d'Histoire des Religions, 1909.

[2] I owe my knowledge of Sallust's Περὶ θεῶν καὶ κόσμου to Professor Gilbert Murray. See his article *A Pagan Creed—Sallustius's 'De Diis et Mundo'* in the English Review, December, 1909, p. 7.

drop a pin into a holy well, you are not making an offering. Such an offering would be senseless; a well has no use for pins, nor a tree for raiment. What you do is to establish connection, build a sacramental bridge, a lightning-conductor. So Kylon[1], by way of safeguard, tied himself by a thread to the holy xoanon of Athens, thereby establishing sacramental communion. Sometimes you need no bridge, you have only to lie open to spiritual influences. Thus among the Algonkins in North America, a Fox man in telling a missionary of his experiences in the sweat lodge said:

Often one will cut oneself over the arms and legs, slitting oneself through the skin. This is done to open up many passages that the *manitou* (the Algonkin equivalent of *mana*) may get through. The *manitou* comes out of its place of abode in the stone. It becomes raised by the heat of the fire and proceeds out of the stone when the water is sprinkled on it. It comes out in the steam, and in the steam it enters the body wherever it can find entrance. It moves up and down and all over inside the body, driving out everything that inflicts pain. Before the *manitou* returns to the stone, it imparts some of its nature to the body. That is why one feels so well after having been in the sweat lodge[2].

Magic, sacrament and sacrifice are fundamentally all one; they are all the handling of the sacred, the manipulation of *mana*, but usage has differentiated the three terms. Magic is the more general term. Sacrament is usually confined to cases where the ceremonial contact is by eating; sacrifice has come to be associated with the killing of an animal or the making over of any object by a gift. Sacrament is concerned rather with the absorbing of *mana* into oneself, magic deals rather with the using of that *mana* for an outside end. Moreover sacrifice and sacrament tend to go over to the public, ceremonial, recurrent contacts effected collectively; whereas individual, private, isolated efforts after contact tend to be classed as magic.

It is sometimes felt that whereas the gift-theory of sacrifice is simple, straight-forward, common-sensical, the medium, or contact or communion theory is 'mystical,' and therefore to be regarded with suspicion by the plain man. 'Mystical' assuredly it is in the sense that it deals with the unseen, unknown *mana*;

---

[1] Plut. *Vit. Sol.* XII. ἐξάψαντας δὲ τοῦ ἔδους κρόκην κλωστὴν καὶ ταύτης ἐχομένους κ.τ.λ.

[2] William Jones, *The Algonkin Manitou* from the Journal of American Folklore, XVIII. p. 190, quoted by I. King, *The Development of Religion*, 1910, p. 137.

but, once the primitive mind is realized, it is more and not less common-sensical. Religion focuses round the needs and circumstances of life. Religion is indeed but a representation, an emphasis of these needs and circumstances collectively and repeatedly felt. The primary need, more primary, more pressing than any other, is Food[1]. Man focuses attention on it, feels acutely about it, organizes his social life in relation to it; it is his primary value, it and its pursuit necessarily become the subject-matter of his simplest religion, his δρώμενα, his rites.

When Elohim beheld the world he had created he 'saw that it was very good.' The Hebrew word for 'good' (טוֹב) seems primarily to have been applied to ripe fruits; it means 'luscious, succulent, good to eat[2].' The same odd bit of human history comes out in the Mexican word *gualli*, which though it means 'good' in general is undoubtedly formed from *gua* 'to eat'—the form *gualoni*, 'eatable,' keeps its original limited sense. 'Evil' in Mexican is *am ogualli* or *a gualli*, i.e. 'not good to eat'; *gua gualli*, 'good, good,' 'extremely good,' is really 'superlatively eatable.' The word *xochill* means 'flower'; the word for 'fruit' is 'good, i.e. eatable flower,' *xochigualli*. Most instructive of all, the act of making a meal is 'I do myself good,' *Nigualtia*[3].

Food then, what is good to eat, may well have been the initial, and was for long the supreme, good. For primitive man it was a constant focus of attention, and hence it was what psychologists call a 'value centre.' The individual who ate a meal, especially a flesh meal, felt the better for it, he was conscious of increased *mana*, of general elation and well being. Meat to those who eat it rarely has the effect of a mild intoxicant. This stimulus felt by the individual would constitute in itself a vague sanctity. It needed however reinforcement from collective emotion. This brings us to the communal meal, the δαίς, a meal normally of flesh-food.

---

[1] See Professor E. S. Ames, *The Psychology of Religious Experience*, 1910, chapter III., On Impulses in Primitive Religion. The social values that centre round sex and that find representation in the system of exogamy do not immediately concern us. Dr Frazer's view that totemism and exogamy are not necessarily related will be found in his *Totemism and Exogamy*, 1910, IV. p. 120. Professor Durkheim's view that the two are necessarily related is stated in his *Prohibition de l'Inceste et ses Origines* in L'Année Sociologique, 1898, pp. 1—70.

[2] Schultens *ad Prov. Sal.* XIII. 2 tôb: succosum, uber, uberi succo vigens.

[3] E. J. Payne, *History of the New World called America*, 1892, I. p. 546 note.

THE COMMUNAL MEAL ($\delta\alpha\acute{\iota}\varsigma$).

In the light of totemistic ways of thinking we see plainly enough the relation of man to food-animals, a relation strangely compounded of *mana* and *tabu*. You need or at least desire flesh food, yet you shrink from slaughtering 'your brother the ox[1]'; you desire his *mana*, yet you respect his *tabu*, for in you and him alike runs the common life-blood. On your own individual responsibility you would never kill him; but for the common weal, on great occasions, and in a fashion conducted with scrupulous care, it is expedient that he die for his people, and that they feast upon his flesh.

Among many primitive peoples the eating of meat is always communal. Among the Zulus, when a man kills a cow, which is done rarely, with reluctance, the whole hamlet assembles, uninvited but expected as a matter of course, to eat it. The Damaras of South Africa look upon meat as common property. They have great reverence for the ox, only slaughter it on great occasions, and every slaughter is regarded as a common festival. When the Patagonians sacrifice a mare, the feast on her flesh is open to all the tribe[2].

This sanctity of the food-animal and the ordinance that the meal should be communal is not confined to domestic animals, in whose case it might be thought that such sanctity arose from daily contact and usage. Among the Ottawas the Bear clan ascribe their origin to a bear's paw and call themselves Big Feet. Whenever they killed a bear they used to offer the animal a part of his own flesh and spoke to him thus:

Do not bear us a grudge because we have killed you. You are sensible, you see that our children are hungry. They love you, they wish to put you into their body. Is it not glorious to be eaten by the sons of a chief[3]?

This strange and thoroughly mystical attitude towards the sacrificed food-animal comes out very beautifully in the Finnish *Kalevala*[4], where a whole canto is devoted to recounting the

[1] See Professor Murray's beautiful account of the relation between man and beast in the normal condition of Greece and the contrast of this with the Homeric scenes of animal slaughter, *Rise of the Epic*, pp. 59 ff.

[2] These instances are taken from the collection in Dr Jevons's *Introduction to the History of Religion*, p. 158.

[3] Frazer, *Totemism and Exogamy*, iii. p. 67, and see also the pathetic account of the bear-festival among the Ainos, too long for quotation here, in Dr Frazer's *Golden Bough*[2], ii. pp. 375 ff.

[4] Kalevala, translated by W. F. Kirby, Rune xlvi., Väinonämöinen and the Bear.

sacrificial feast to and of Otso the mountain bear. They chant
the praises of the Holy Bear, they tell of his great strength and
majesty, the splendour of his rich fur, the glory and the beauty of
his 'honey-soft' paws. They lead him in festal procession, slay
and cook and eat him and then, as though he were not dead, they
dismiss him with valedictions to go back and live for ever, the
glory of the forest[1]. In the litany addressed to him the sacramental use of his flesh comes out very clearly. Limb by limb he
is addressed:

> Now I take the nose from Otso
> That my own nose may be lengthened,
> But I take it not completely,
> And I do not take it only.
> Now I take the ears of Otso
> That my own ears I may lengthen.

The notion that the slaying of a food-animal involves a
communal δαίς, a distribution, comes out very clearly among
the Kurnai, a tribe of South-East Australia[2]. The 'native bear'
when slain is thus divided. The slayer has the left ribs: the
father the right hind leg, the mother the left hind leg, the elder
brother the right fore-arm, the younger brother the left fore-arm,
the elder sister the backbone, the younger the liver, the father's
brother the right ribs, the mother's brother of the hunter a piece
of the flank. Most honourable of all, the head goes to the camp
of the young men, the κοῦροι.

A somewhat detailed account of savage ceremonial has been
necessary in order that the gist of sacramental sacrifice should be
made clear. We have now to ask—Had Greece herself, besides her
burnt-offerings to Olympian gods, any survival of the communal
feast?

On the 14th day of Skirophorion (June—July), the day of the
full moon of the last month of the Athenian year, when the
threshing was ended and the new corn gathered in, on the
Acropolis at Athens, a strange ritual was accomplished. Cakes
of barley mixed with wheat were laid on the bronze altar of Zeus
Polieus. Oxen were driven round it, and the ox which went up
to the altar and ate of the cakes, was by that token chosen as

[1] In the bear-sacrifice of the Ainos the bear is thus addressed: 'We kill you
O bear! come back soon into an Aino'; Frazer, *Golden Bough*[2], II. p. 379.
[2] A. W. Howitt, *Native Tribes of South-East Australia*, p. 759.

victim for the sacrifice. Two men performed the sacrifice; the one, the Boutypos, felled the ox with an axe, another, presumably the Bouphonos, cut its throat with a knife. Both the murderers threw down their weapons and fled. The weapons were subsequently brought to trial. The celebrants feasted on the flesh, and the ox itself was restored to life in mimic pantomime[1].

The uncouth ritual of the Bouphonia went on as late as the days of Theophrastos, but, by the time of Aristophanes[2], it stood for all that was archaic and well-nigh obsolete. The Unjust Logos when told about the old educational system at Athens says:

> Bless me, that's quite the ancient lot, so Diipolia-like,
> Of crickets and Bouphonia full.

What struck Pausanias[3] when he was told about the ritual, was that when the ox-striker had flung away the axe and himself had fled, 'as though in ignorance of the man who did the deed' they bring the axe to judgment. It is just this one detail and all the elaborate House-that-Jack-built shifting of the blame from one celebrant to another till it rested on the lifeless axe which has diverted the attention of modern commentators from what is, I now[4] feel, *the* all-important factor or rather factors. The Bouphonia was (1) a communal feast, (2) the death of the ox was only incidental to the feast, and it was followed by a mimic Resurrection.

(1) *The Bouphonia was a communal feast.* Our fullest account is given by Porphyry[5] who borrows it from Theophrastos. Porphyry is explicit. The Bouphonia is a communal sacrifice (κοινὴ θυσία). In the aetiological myth it is related that the ox was first smitten by a stranger, either Sopatros[6] or Dromos,

---

[1] I have elsewhere, *Ancient Athens*, pp. 424–6, and *Prolegomena*, p. 111, discussed the Bouphonia in detail. I can here only examine such elements as are important for my immediate argument. Attention was, I believe, first drawn to the great significance of the Bouphonia by Professor Robertson Smith, *Religion of the Semites*, pp. 286 ff. The literary sources are collected and discussed by Dr Frazer, *Golden Bough*[2], II. pp. 294 ff. See also H. v. Gaertringen, *Zeus Thaulios* in Hermes, 1911, Miscellen, p. 154.

[2] *Nub.* 984

ἀρχαῖά γε καὶ Διπολιώδη καὶ τεττίγων ἀνάμεστα
καὶ Κηκείδου καὶ Βουφονίων.

[3] I. 24. 4. As Professor Robertson Smith observes, *ad loc.*, in Pausanias' time the rite had undergone some simplification, otherwise his account is inadequate.

[4] In my previous discussions of the Bouphonia, through ignorance of the magical character of sacrifice, I fell into the usual error of emphasis.

[5] *de Abst.* II. 28 ff.

[6] So-patros may be the *Saviour of the* πάτρα as Sosi-polis is *Saviour of the state.*

a Cretan. He happened to be present at the 'communal sacrifice' at Athens, and seeing the ox touch the sacred cakes, was seized with indignation and slew it. He then fled to Crete. The usual pestilence followed. Sopatros was discovered and then thought he could escape the pollution he had incurred 'if they would all do the deed in common' and if the ox was smitten 'by the city.' In order to effect this the Athenians were to make him a citizen, and thus make themselves sharers in the murder[1]. That the Bouphonia was not merely a 'common sacrifice' but also a communal feast is certain from the name given to a family who shared it. Theophrastos mentions in this connection, not only families of Ox-smiters (Βουτύποι) and Goaders (Κεντριάδαι), but also a family of Dividers (Δαιτροί), so called, he says, from the 'divided feast' (Δαίς) which followed the partition of the flesh[2]. Moreover we have the actual ritual prescription. After the axe and the knife had been sharpened, one celebrant struck the ox, another slew him, and *of those who afterwards flayed the ox, all tasted his flesh*[3].

(2) *The death of the ox was followed by a mimic Resurrection.* When the ox had been flayed and all the flayers had tasted his flesh, Porphyry[4] tells us 'they sewed up the hide and stuffed it out with hay and set it up just as it was when it was alive, and they yoked a plough to it as though it were ploughing.' Such a ritual in the heart of civilized Athens was more surprising than any trial of a double axe. The scholiast on the *Peace*[5] tells us that the Diipolia was a 'mimetic representation' (ἀπομίμημα). He exactly hits the mark, though he certainly does not know it. The ox is brought to life again, not because they want to pretend that he has never died and so to escape the guilt of his murder (though later that element may have entered), but because his resurrection is the *mimetic representation* of the new life of the new year[6] and

---

[1] *op. cit.* II. 29 Σώπατρος νομίσας τῆς περὶ αὐτὸν δυσκολίας ἀπαλλαγήσεσθαι ὡς ἐναγοῦς ὄντος, εἰ κοινῇ τοῦτο πράξειαν πάντες ἔφη...δεῖν κατακοπῆναι βοῦν ὑπὸ τῆς πόλεως, ἀπορούντων δὲ τίς ὁ πατάξων ἔσται, παρασχεῖν αὐτοῖς τοῦτο εἰ πολίτην αὐτὸν ποιησάμενοι κοινωνήσουσι τοῦ φόνου.

[2] *op. cit.* II. 30 τοὺς δ' ἀπὸ τοῦ ἐπισφάξαντος δαιτροὺς ὀνομάζουσιν διὰ τὴν ἐκ τῆς κρεονομίας γιγνομένην δαῖτα.

[3] *op. cit.* II. 30 τῶν δὲ μετὰ ταῦτα δειράντων, ἐγεύσαντο τοῦ βοὸς πάντες.

[4] *op. cit.* II. 30 τῶν δὲ μετὰ ταῦτα δειράντων ἐγεύσαντο τοῦ βοὸς πάντες, τούτων δὲ πραχθέντων τὴν μὲν δορὰν τοῦ βοὸς ῥάψαντες καὶ χορτῷ ἐπογκώσαντες ἐξανέστησαν, ἔχοντα ταὐτὸν ὅπερ καὶ ζῶν ἔσχεν σχῆμα, καὶ προσέξευξαν ἄροτρον ὡς ἐργαζομένῳ.

[5] *ad v.* 50 ἐστι δὲ ἀπομίμημα τῶν περὶ τῶν πελάνων καὶ τὰς βοῦς συμβάντων.

[6] The New Birth in the spring will be discussed in the next chapter.

this resurrection is meant to act magically. The worshippers taste the flesh to get the *mana* of the ox, and to do that they must slay him. To taste the flesh is good, but best of all is it that the ox himself should on his resurrection renew his life and strength.

It is not a little remarkable that in the detailed accounts we have of the Bouphonia, all mention of Zeus, to whom it is supposed the sacrifice is made, is conspicuously absent. The ox is indeed said to have been driven up to the table of Zeus Polieus, but on that table the offering of cakes and the like is already complete. It is clear that the Bouphonia is just what its name says, an *ox-murder* that might be connected with any and every god. It is the sacrifice itself, not the service of the god, that is significant, the ox bulks larger than Zeus.

Fig. 24.

In this connection it is worth noting that in the calendar-frieze[1], now built into the small Metropolitan Church at Athens, the month Skirophorion is marked, not by any image of Zeus Polieus, but by the figure of the Boutypos, the Ox-smiter and his ox (Fig. 24). Above the diminutive ox is the sign of the Crab. To the right of the Boutypos is seen the Panathenaic ship, effaced and sanctified by the Christian symbol of the wheel and cross. The next great festival after the Bouphonia, which closed the old year, was the Panathenaia in Hecatombaion, which opened the new. The Panathenaia itself was superimposed upon the ancient Kronia[2].

[1] See my *Ancient Athens*, p. 153. For full discussion of this calendar-frieze see J. N. Svoronos, *Der athenische Volkskalendar* in Journal Internationale d'Archéologie numismatique, 1899, ii. 1.

[2] A. Mommsen, *Heortologie*, p. 108.

This point—the supremacy of the ox and the nullity of the god—is well illustrated by the design in Fig. 25 from a black-figured hydria[1] in Berlin. In a small Doric shrine stands an ox; in front of him a blazing altar. To the left is Athena seated, her sacred snake by her side. She extends her right hand holding a phiale; she is waiting for libation. She may wait, it would seem, for the priestess raises her hand in adoration or consecration of—the ox. The ox is within the sanctuary, the goddess outside. Now it is of course impossible to be certain that we have here the ox of the Bouphonia. What *is* certain is that we have a holy ox, holy on his own account with a sanctuary of his own, and that this holy

Fig. 25

ox is associated with not Zeus, but Athena. Whatever Olympian was dominant at the moment would take over the intrinsically holy beast.

The simple fact is that the holy ox is before the anthropomorphic god, the communal feast (δαίς) before the gift-burnt sacrifice (θυσία). The Bouphonia belongs to the stage of the communal feast followed by the resurrection. Of this its name bears witness. The word to 'ox-slay,' βουφονέω, occurs in Homer[2]

[1] See my *Myth. and Mon. Ancient Athens*, p. 428, Fig. 37.
[2] *Il.* vii. 465   δύσετο δ' ἠέλιος, τετέλεστο δὲ ἔργον Ἀχαιῶν
                         βουφόνεον δὲ κατὰ κλισίας καὶ δόρπον ἕλοντο.
Schol. ad loc. βουφονεῖν ἐστὶν οὐ τὸ θύειν θεοῖς (ἄτοπον γὰρ ἐπὶ θυσίας φόνον λέγειν) ἀλλὰ τὸ φονεύειν βοῦς εἰς δείπνου κατασκευήν.

with the simple meaning to kill an ox for eating purposes. 'The sun went down and the work of the Achaeans was finished'—they had been burning their dead—'and they slaughtered oxen amid the huts and took their supper.' The scholiast on the passage, with probably the Bouphonia in his mind, says explicitly, '*βουφονεῖν*, to slay or murder oxen, is not sacrificing to the gods (for it would be absurd to apply the term of murder to a sacrifice) but it is slaying oxen as a preparation for a meal.'

The scholiast rightly notes that the 'ox-slaying' concerned the ox as food, not the god as eater. What he could not know was that a *Bouphonia*, a slaying for a Banquet, though it need have nothing to do with gods, could yet be of supreme sanctity—a sanctity preceding the gods and even begetting them. The speaker in a fragment of the *Triptolemos* of Sophocles says more truly than he knows,

'Then came fair *Dais, the eldest of the Gods*[1].'

You eat your sacred animal to get his *mana*; you then personify that *mana*, informing it with the life-blood of your own desire, provide him with your own life-history, and then, if you are an orthodox ritualist, you land yourself in the uncouth predicament that you must eat your personal god. From such relentless logic all but the most convicted of conservatives are apt to shrink. There are side ways, down which you may go, softenings and obscurantist confusions by which you may blunt the horns of your dilemma. Ritual says you must eat the holy ox; imagination has conceived for you a personal Zeus, Father of Gods and men. You slay your ox, partake of his flesh, sew up his skin and yoke it to a plough. Yet all is well, for the whole holy and incompatible hocus-pocus is a 'sacrifice to Zeus Polieus.'

Such strange blendings of new and old, such snowball-like accumulations, are sometimes caused, or rather precipitated, by definite political action. Peisistratos, feeling no doubt that Olympia might be a dangerous religious and social rival to Athens, conscious too that, at a time when the Homeric pantheon was rapidly being domesticated in Greece, the fact that Athens should have no important local worship of Zeus stamped Athens as

---

[1] Hesych. *s.v.* δαίς· Σοφοκλῆς
        ἦλθεν δὲ Δαὶς θάλεια πρεσβίστη θεῶν,
ἡ δι' ἐράνων εὐωχία.

provincial, introduced in the lower town near the Ilissos the worship of Zeus Olympios, and with it he wisely transplanted a whole complex of primitive Olympian cults, making a sanctuary for Kronos and Rhea, and a precinct containing a chasm and dedicated to Gaia, with the title Olympian. It may be suspected, though it cannot be proved, that at the same time, though Zeus never got any substantial footing on the Acropolis, it was arranged that he should take under his patronage the ancient festival of the Ox-slaying[1].

Some such arrangement is reflected in the story told by Hesychius[2] in his explanation of the proverbial saying 'Zeus' seats and voting pebbles' (Διὸς θᾶκοι καὶ πεσ(σ)οί). 'They say that, in the ballot of the Athenians, when Athena and Poseidon were contending, Athena entreated Zeus to give his vote for her and she promised in return that she would have the sacrificial victim of Polieus sacrificed for the first time on an altar.' The victim, that is the bull, was called, according to Hesychius, the victim of Polieus (τὸ τοῦ Πολιέως ἱερεῖον). I suspect that an ι has been interpolated and that the earlier term was τὸ τοῦ πόλεως ἱερεῖον, the communal victim (cf. κοινὴ θυσία) which preceded the personal god. Anyhow, though Hesychius probably means by his statement πρῶτον θύεσθαι ἐπὶ βωμοῦ, that Athena promised she would first sacrifice on *the* altar of Zeus, what he really says is that she promised first to sacrifice on *an* altar, that in a word the slaying of the ox for a feast should become the offering of an ox on an altar, the δαίς should be a θυσία, a burnt sacrifice offered on the altar of an Olympian.

A sacrifice brings to our modern minds an altar as inevitably as it brings a god; both, in the sense we understand them, are late and superfluous. To sacrifice is, as the word implies, and as has been previously shown, to sanctify, to make sacred; and to make sacred is to bring into contact with any source of force and fear, with any vehicle of *mana*. In one version of the story the slain

---

[1] See my *Ancient Athens*, p. 192. That the Bouphonia was primarily associated with the cult of Erechtheus in the Erechtheion rather than with that of Zeus, will appear in the next chapter.

[2] s.v. Διὸς Θᾶκοι...φασὶ δὲ τὴν Ἀθηνᾶν Διὸς δεηθῆναι ὑπὲρ αὐτῆς τὴν ψῆφον ἐνεγκεῖν καὶ ὑποσχέσθαι ἀντὶ τούτου τὸ τοῦ Πολιέως ἱερεῖον πρῶτον θύεσθαι ἐπὶ βωμοῦ. Cf. Pausanias i. 28. 10.

bull of the Bouphonia is buried[1]. If this statement be correct, the *mana* of the bull is put into direct contact with the earth it is to fertilize[2], a practice known in sacrifice among many primitive peoples.

We have seen in a previous chapter how the god, the Kouros, arose out of the collective emotion of his worshippers; we now realize another source of divinity, none other than the sacrifice itself. The victim is first sanctified, sacrificed, then divinized. *Le dieu, c'est le sacré personnifié.*

Fig. 26.

On the votive relief[3] in Fig. 26 we see the process of divinization go on as it were under our very eyes. The relief falls into

[1] Theophrastus in Porph. *de Abst.* II. 29 ...τὸν μὲν βοῦν θάπτει (Σώπατρος). The motive given by Theophrastus is fear, but burial of the remainder of the ox after all had tasted may well have been part of the ritual, either for the purpose of fertilizing the earth by contact with the bull's *mana*, or to secure the unwary from chance contact with a sanctity so terrific.

[2] Compare the well known custom of the Khonds who scatter the flesh of human victims over their fields to ensure fertility. In civilized Europe to-day the bones of animals killed at Easter and other festivals are sometimes scattered on the fields 'for luck.' See Hubert et Mauss, *Essai sur le Sacrifice*, Année Sociologique 1898, p. 112.

[3] Imperial Museum, Constantinople, Inv. 1909. See Edhem Bey, *Relief votif du Musée Impérial Ottoman* in Bull. de Corr. Hell. XXXII. (1908). Pl. v. reproduced by kind permission of the Director of the École Française à Athènes.

three portions. In the gable at the top is a bull's head. In the centre is the figure of the god to whom the relief is. dedicated, Zeus Olbios[1], Zeus of Wealth or Prosperity: he pours libation on an altar, near him is his eagle. Below, the scene represented is a Bouphonia. An ox is tethered by a ring to the ground near the blazing altar. Behind him is an Ox-Smiter (Boutypos) with axe uplifted ready to strike. To the left behind the ox a girl approaches, holding in her left hand a plate of fruit and flowers. The woman behind holds *infulae* in her left hand. To the right are a man and boy holding objects that cannot certainly be made out.

So far all seems well in order. The bull is sacrificed to the Olympian Zeus, who stands there dominant with his attribute, the

Fig. 27.

eagle, by his side. But if we look at the god's figure more closely we see that, if Zeus he be, it is in strange form[2]. On his head are horns: he is ταυροκέρως, bull-horned, like Iacchos; he is bull-faced, βούπρωρος, like the infant Dithyrambos. Now, when these animal gods come to light, it is usual to say the god assumes the shape of a bull, or is incarnate in the form of a bull. The reverse is

---

[1] The dedication is as follows:

Εὐοδίων ἱερεὺς Διὸς ᾽Ολβίου
ὑπὲρ τῶν ἰδίων πάντων καθὼς ἐκέλευ-
σεν ἀνέθηκα εὐχαριστήριον.

[2] Miss M. Hardie, of Newnham College, kindly examined the original of the relief and writes to me that, so far as it can be made out, there is all the appearance of a bull-mask worn by a human head. If this were certain we should have the figure of a priest impersonating a bull-god, which would be of singular interest.

manifestly the case. The lower end of the ladder is on earth, planted in the reality of sacrifice. The sanctified, sacrificed animal becomes a god. He then sheds his animal form, or keeps it as an attribute or a beast of burden, or, as in the case of Jupiter Dolichenus[1] in Fig. 27, he stands upon the animal he once was, stands in all the glory of a deified Roman Emperor with double axe and thunderbolt. Any animal in close relation to man, whether as food or foe, may rise to be a god, but he must first become sacred, sanctified, must first be *sacrificed*. The fact that the sacrifice is, for reasons to be discussed later, renewed year by year, makes the personality of the god durable.

The Bouphonia, it was acknowledged on all hands, was a ceremonial primitive and tending to be obsolete. It may be instructive to examine another instance of bull-sacrifice, where some of the more archaic and uncouth details have dropped away, yet where the intent remains the same, and where even more clearly than in the case of the Bouphonia we have gift-sacrifice to an Olympian appearing as an idea clearly superimposed on a primitive communal feast, a sacrament or sanctification of intent purely magical. Such an instance we have in the yearly sacrifice of a bull to Zeus Sosipolis[2], of Magnesia on the Maeander. The full details of this sacrifice are happily known to us from an inscription found on one of the *antae* of the temple of Zeus in the agora at Magnesia, and dating about the middle of the third century B.C.[3]

At the annual fair (πανήγυρις) held in the month Heraion, a bull, the finest that could be got, was to be bought each year by the city stewards, and at the new moon of the month Kronion, *at the beginning of seed-time*, they were to 'dedicate' it to Zeus[4]. Uncertain as the dating of months in local calendars

---

[1] Seidl, *Dolichenuskult*, Taf. III. 1.

[2] For the (Zeus) Sosipolis of Olympia in his snake form and his analogies with the Cretan infant Zeus see C. Robert, *Mitt. Arch. Inst. Athen* XVIII. 1893, p. 37, and Frazer *ad* Pausanias VI. 20. 2—5, and *infra*, p. 241.

[3] O. Kern, *Inschriften v. Magnesia*, No. 98, discussed by O. Kern, *Arch. Anz.* 1894, p. 78, and Nilsson, *Griechische Feste*, 1906, p. 23.

[4] ...ταῦρον ὡς κάλλιστον τοῦ μηνὸς Ἡραιῶνος ἐν τῆι πανηγύρει ἑκάστου ἔτους καὶ ἀναδεικνύωσι τῶι Διὶ ἀρχομένου σπόρου μηνὸς Κρονιῶνος ἐν τῆι νουμηνίαι.

sometimes is, it is a relief to find ourselves here on safe ground, the dedication (ἀνάδειξις) of the bull takes place at the beginning of the agricultural year; the bull's sanctified, though not his actual, life and that of the new year begin together.

The dedication, or rather *indication*, of the bull was an affair to be conducted with the utmost official solemnity. The bull was led in procession, at the head of which were the priest and priestess of the chief and eponymous goddess of the place, Artemis Leucophryne, and the Stephanephoros. With them also went the Hierokeryx, the Sacrificer and two bands of youths and of maidens whose parents were still alive (ἀμφιθαλεῖς). The Hierokeryx, together with the rest of the officials named, pronounces a prayer on behalf of the 'safety of the city, and the land, and the citizens, and the women and children, for peace and wealth, and for the bringing forth of grain, and of all the other fruits, and of cattle[1].'

We are back with the Kouretes at Palaikastro, before the altar of Diktaean Zeus[2]. The sober citizens of Magnesia in the second century B.C. do not bid their Sosipolis 'leap,' but their prayer is of the same intent—for peace and wealth, for flocks and fruits, for women, for children, and first and foremost it is, like the invocation of the Kouros, εἰς ἐνιαυτόν—for the Year-Feast. The Kouretes, the young men, leap alone to their Kouros; in the Magnesian procession nine maidens also walked and sang. Both youths and maidens alike must have both parents alive[3], because where fertility is magically invoked there must be no contagion of death.

On the reverse of the coins of Magnesia a frequent device is the figure of a 'butting bull.' A good instance is given in Fig. 28 *a*[4]. The bull stands, or rather kneels, on a *Maeander* pattern, behind him is a constant symbol, an ear of grain, which characterises significantly enough the bull's function as a fertility *daemon*. The bull is, I think, kneeling, not butting. This is

---

[1] καὶ ἐν τῶι ἀναδείκνυσθαι τὸν ταῦρον κατευχέσθω ὁ ἱεροκῆρυξ...ὑπέρ τε σωτηρίας τῆς τε πόλεως καὶ τῆς χώρας καὶ τῶν πολιτῶν καὶ γυναικῶν καὶ τέκνων καὶ ὑπὲρ εἰρήνης καὶ πλούτου καὶ σίτου φορᾶς καὶ τῶν ἄλλων καρπῶν καὶ τῶν κτηνῶν.

[2] p. 9. The full force of the words εἰς ἐνιαυτόν will be considered in the next chapter.

[3] For the ἀμφιθαλὴς παῖς who carried the Eiresione see Eustath. *ad Il.* xxii. 496, p. 1283, and my *Prolegomena*, p. 79. The ritual prescription that a young celebrant should be ἀμφιθαλής occurs frequently.

[4] *Brit. Mus. Cat.* Ionia xviii. 4 enlarged.

certainly clear in the second coin figured *b*[1]. Here the bull is being driven by a youth to the mouth of what seems to be a cave. In front of it he kneels down as though in willing acceptance of his fate.

The sacred animal, already half divinized, had to be free, had to choose, designate itself. We are not told that the bull of Magnesia designated itself either by kneeling or bowing its head, though the coins figured make it probable. But, in the sacrifice of a bull to Zeus Polieus at Kos[2]—a sacrifice which has many analogies to the Bouphonia—the ritual prescription is clear. Each ninth part of the three Dorian tribes drove up a bull to the sacrificial table of Zeus Polieus, at which the officials were seated,

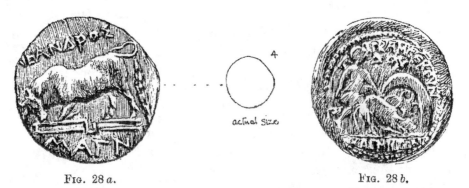

FIG. 28 *a*.   FIG. 28 *b*.

and that bull was chosen 'who bent himself[3].' Possibly he bent down to taste corn on the sacred table like the ox at the Bouphonia, possibly he was induced to kneel. Anyhow he gave some sign that he was a freewill offering.

The bull has been solemnly designated, set apart. He is sacred now, charged with the *mana* of the coming year, and his nurture is matter of scrupulous religion. The feeding of the holy

[1] *Brit. Mus. Cat.* xix. 9. For the Bull-God and the cave and the periodical sacrifice in relation to Minos and the period of nine *horai* (ἐννέωρος βασίλευε, τ 179) see Prof. Murray, *Rise of the Greek Epic*[2], p. 156[1].

[2] Paton and Hicks, *Inscriptions of Kos*, No. 37, *S.I.G.*[2] 616. See Nilsson, *Griechische Feste*, p. 17. Similarly at Halicarnassos, the goat chosen for sacrifice issued from the herd of his own free will and went up to the altar. See Apollonios, *Paradoxogr.* c. 13, p. 107, and at Pedasa in Karia a goat led the procession for seventy stadia. Hence the notion of Βοῦς ἡγεμὼν and Καθηγεμών.

[3] There is unfortunately a lacuna at the exact word describing the action αἰ μέγ κα ΤΠΟ...ΕΙ, but the ὑπο is certain and the restoration ὑποκύψει almost certain. V. Prott, *Leges Graecorum Sacrae*, p. 19, note 3 ad v. 20, says of Hicks, postea ipse in ectypo ΤΠΟΚΤΨΕΙ legere sibi visus est: ὑποκύπτειν is said of an animal drinking.

bull is in the inscription given over to a contractor (ὁ ἐργολαβήσας).
This is probably a late arrangement; anyhow, though this official
buys food, he has to drive the bull to the market, and 'it is good'
for those corn-merchants who give the bull grain as a gift[1]. This
probably looks back to the time when the bull was maintained
by free contributions from each member of
the tribe. The communal character of
these bull-sacrifices comes out very vividly
in the coin of Kolophon in Fig. 29[2]. In
the background is the temple of Apollo
Klarios with its seated god. But in the
foreground is the real focus of attention, a
bull and an altar. Around it stand the
thirteen representatives of the thirteen
cities of the Ionian league.

FIG. 29.

On the 12th of Artemision, the month of Artemis—who is, at
least in Asia Minor, but a form of the Great Mother—the bull
was sacrificed. The month Artemision is in Sparta equated by
Thucydides[3] (quoting a decree) with the Attic Elaphebolion—
i.e. *circ.* March 24 to April 23—so that we may fix the festival as
about the 6th of April, i.e. for Greece the time of the late spring
or early summer.

On the day of the sacrifice there was again a great procession,
again led by the priest and priestess of Artemis Leucophryne.
Behind them came the senate, priests and various officials, and also
certain chosen *epheboi*, youths (νέοι) and children (παῖδες), also
the victors in the games of the goddess, and other victorious
competitors[4]. The Stephanephorus, who with the priest and
priestess led the procession, had to bring with him the images of
the twelve gods in their best clothes. A circular hut was to be
set up, evidently to shelter the images, and three couches were to
be strewn. This hut or tholos was to be near the altar of the
twelve gods in the agora.

---

[1] l. 60 ff. This enactment comes at the end of the inscription as a sort of codicil
after the account of the sacrifice.

[2] *Brit. Mus. Cat.* Ionia VIII. 15. The coin, of imperial date, bears the inscription
under the god's temple TO KOINON IΩNΩN.

[3] v. 19. 1 quoting a decree of 42 B.C. Ἀρτεμισίου μηνὸς τετάρτῃ φθίνοντος, ἐν δὲ
Ἀθήναις...Ἐλαφηβολιῶνος μηνὸς ἕκτῃ φθίνοντος. See Pauly-Wissowa, *s.v.* Artemisia.

[4] συμπομπεύειν...καὶ τοὺς ἐφήβους καὶ τοὺς νέους καὶ τοὺς παῖδας καὶ τοὺς τὰ
Λευκοφρύηνα νικῶντας καὶ τοὺς ἄλλους τοὺς νικῶντας τοὺς στεφανίτας ἀγῶνας.

Here we find ourselves in full Olympianism. The twelve gods, primitive wooden images though they be, and decked in fine raiment, are to be present at the festival. Themistocles, we remember, was the founder of Magnesia, and these twelve ancient xoana are the counterpart of the twelve Olympians of the east Parthenon frieze. But again it is clear that, honoured though they are as guests, they are *not* integral to the ceremony. It is expressly ordered indeed that Zeus Sosipolis should have a ram sacrificed to him, Artemis a she-goat, and Apollo a young he-goat (ἄττηγος), but for the rest of the twelve no manner of provision is made.

The added sacrifice of a ram to Zeus is, I think, highly significant. The bull, one would have thought, might have sufficed. But the reason is clear. The bull-sacrifice was at first no gift-sacrifice to Zeus or to any Olympian: it was, as immediately appears, a *dais*—a communal meal. *When they shall have sacrificed the bull let them divide it up among those who took part in the procession*[1]. The mandate is clear. The bull is not a gift to Zeus, but a vehicle of *mana* for distribution among the people. In him is concentrated as it were the life of the year: he is the incarnate ideal of the year; his life begins with the sowing, is cherished through the winter, and when it comes to full maturity in the early summer dies to live again in the people through the medium of the sacrificial banquet. He is sacred rather than divine; but divinity is, we have seen, born of sanctification, and sacrifice is but a sanctification to the uttermost. The bull is Sosipolis, Saviour of the city, in the making[2].

The bull-ceremony then had two acts, the ἀνάδειξις or indication, and the δαίς or communal, magical feast. As regards the first, one point remains to be noted. Commentators in explaining the festival have usually translated ἀνάδειξις as *dedication*, and held that the ceremony meant a solemn consecration of the bull

---

[1] τὸν δὲ βοῦν ὅταν θύσωσιν [δ]ιανεμέτωσαν τοῖς συμπομπεύσασιν.

[2] Sosipolis at Olympia was a chthonic δαίμων rather than a θεός; he was a snake-child like Erichthonios. At Magnesia he is a bull and, as Mr Cook suggests to me, when Themistocles (Plut. *Vit. Them.* XXXI. sub fin.) drank bull's blood, he identified himself with Sosipolis in his bull-form. A coin of Magnesia shows him with *phiale* in hand, standing beside a lighted altar with a slain bull at his feet (*Ath. Mitt.* XXI. 1896, p. 22; P. Gardner, *Corolla Numismatica*, 1906, p. 109). This coin represents the μνημεῖον in the market-place at Magnesia (Thuc. I. 138). At the Peiraeos Themistocles had a βωμοειδὴς τάφος (Plut. *Vit. Them.* XXXII.).

to the service of Zeus. As such undoubtedly it would have been, at least in part, understood in the time, say, of Themistocles. The bull would have been supposed to get his sanctity from Zeus rather than Zeus his divinity from the bull. This was, I am sure, not the original sense of ἀνάδειξις. Another holy bull makes this certain.

Plutarch in his ixth Greek Question[1] asks 'Who is the *Hosioter* among the Delphians?' The answer is, 'They call *Hosioter* the animal sacrificed when a *Hosios* is designated.' It is at first sight astonishing to find the name *Hosioter*—*He who consecrates*, the Consecrator—applied to the victim rather than the priest. But in the light of the primitive notion of sacrifice explained above (p. 137 ff.) all is clear—the Holy Bull is the source of *mana*. In him *mana* is as it were incarnate. He it is who consecrates. At Delphi he became and *was* a god—the Bull-Dionysos. Lycophron[2] tells us that at Delphi Agamemnon before he sailed

> Secret lustrations to *the Bull* did make,
> Beside the caves of him, the God of Gain
> Delphinian.

Plutarch adds to his enquiry, 'Who is the *Hosioter*?' a second question, 'and why do they call one of their months Bysios?' Evidently the two are connected. The month Bysios was, Plutarch tells us, at the beginning of spring, the time of the blossoming of many plants. The 8th of Bysios was the birthday of the god, and in olden times on this day only did the oracle give answers. At Magnesia the new daimon comes in at the time of sowing; at Delphi the *Thyiades* 'wake up the infant god Liknites at the time when the Hosioi offer their secret sacrifice, presumably first *of* and then *to* the Hosioter, the Bull. The death of the old-year daimon may be followed immediately by his resurrection as the spirit of the new year. The death of the Old Year and the New Birth or Resurrection of the New, will form the subject of the next chapter.

The ἀνάδειξις of the Magnesian bull is not then its consecration to Zeus, but simply its indication, its exhibition, its designation

---

[1] For full discussion of this passage see my *Prolegomena*, p. 501. Plutarch says Ὁσιωτῆρα μὲν καλοῦσι τὸ θυόμενον ἱερεῖον, where τὸ θυόμενον must be passive.

[2] *Al.* 207   Δελφινίων παρ᾽ ἄντρα Κερδῴου θεοῦ
             Ταύρῳ κρυφαίας χέρνιβας κατάρξεται,

and the scholiast *ad loc.* says ταῦρος δὲ ὁ Διόνυσος...ὅτι ἐν παραβύστῳ τὰ μυστήρια ἐτελεῖτο τῷ Διονύσῳ.

as best and fairest of the year, fittest vehicle of the life and *mana* of the people and the crops, like to a corn spirit, but of wider content. This holy vehicle of the year's *mana*, this ἐνιαυτός-daimon who died for the people, became at Delphi and in many other places a bull-god, a divinity born of his own sacrifice, i.e. of his own sanctification. At Magnesia he remains supremely sanctified indeed, but mainly the material of a *dais*, a sacramental Feast. To us the sacrifice of a god seems a miracle or a blasphemy, but when the god is seen to be begotten of the sacrifice the anomaly is softened.

It remains to resume our argument as to the sacrifice of the bull.

The bull is slain, not because his death has value to bribe or to appease, but in order that he may be eaten. He is eaten because he is holy; he is holy because of the magical *mana* within him, what Homer would call his ἱερὸν μένος. You would eat the bull alive if you could, but eating a bull alive is beset with difficulties. So you kill him first and have a *feast of raw flesh*, an ὠμοφάγος δαίς. If you become a Bacchos you will partake of that feast but once in your life, and henceforth will observe the *tabu* on flesh food—the flesh of 'your brother the ox.'

And because you belong to a group, a *thiasos*, you do not sit alone eating raw bull; you have a communal feast, a δαίς.

You have at first no thought of worshipping or even holding communion with any god. All you desire is to absorb the *mana* of the holy bull's raw flesh. But bit by bit out of your sacrifice of that bull grew up a divine figure of the Feast, imagined, incarnate. You may call the figure by many names, Zeus Olbios, or the 'horned Iacchos,' or Zagreus, or Dionysos Tauromorphos.

One name the Initiated gave him, which reveals his origin and shows how the ancient mind naturally focused on sacramental communion. In his account of the contrast between Apollo and Dionysos, Plutarch[1] tells of the 'manifold changes' that Dionysos

---

[1] *de Ei ap. Delph.* IX. Διόνυσον δὲ καὶ Ζαγρέα καὶ Νυκτέλιον καὶ Ἰσοδαίτην αὐτὸν ὀνομάζουσι καὶ φθορὰς τινας καὶ ἀφανισμοὺς καὶ τὰς ἀναβιώσεις καὶ παλιγγενεσίας οἰκεῖα ταῖς εἰρημέναις μεταβολαῖς αἰνίγματα καὶ μυθεύματα περαίνουσι. I have elsewhere (*Prolegomena*, p. 482, note 1) conjectured that the curious and hitherto unexplained title Ἰσοδαίτης was connected with the ὠμοφάγοι δαῖτες, but I did not then understand the importance of the communal meal.

suffers into winds and water, and earth and stars, and how the births of plants and animals are enigmatically termed 'rending asunder' and 'tearing limb from limb'; and he adds, 'when they tell of certain Destructions and Disappearances, and Resurrections and New Births, which are fables and riddles appertaining to the aforesaid changes—then they call the god Dionysos and Zagreus, and Nuktelios and Isodaites'—*Him of the equal Feast.*

So far our attention has been focused on sacrifice considered as a sacramental communion, as a means by which the communicant might secure for himself and manipulate for his own ends the *mana* of the sacrificed animal. We have now to consider more in detail these ends to which the *mana* is applied. They will be found to be very simple and rather what we should call material than spiritual. In the Magnesian sacrifice, it will be remembered (p. 151), the Hierokeryx prayed year by year for the land and the citizens and the women, for peace and wealth, and for the bringing forth of the other 'fruits and of cattle.' We shall see this annual prayer embodied, represented as it were, on a monument of great importance to be considered in the next chapter, the famous Hagia Triada sarcophagos.

Note to p. 119. For a more recent view of the origin and significance of totemism and its relation to exogamy, etc. see S. Freud, *Totem and Tabu*, 1913, the main thesis of which I have resumed and adopted in my *Epilegomena*, pp. 7—14. For a quite different theory on this difficult subject see also W. J. Perry, *Children of the Sun*, 1923, chapter xxi. Both books should be read but neither invalidates my main contention as to the nature of totemistic ways of thought.

Note to p. 121. For the psychology of Totemism, Sacrifice and Sacrament see S. Freud, *Totem and Tabu*, 1913, and J. E. Harrison, *Epilegomena*, pp. 7—14.

CHAPTER VI.

THE DITHYRAMB, THE SPRING-FESTIVAL AND THE
HAGIA TRIADA SARCOPHAGOS.

ἦλθ' ἦλθε χελιδών,
καλὰϲ ὥραϲ ἄγογϲα,
καλοὺϲ ἐνιαγτούϲ.

Vere concordant amores, vere nubunt alites,
Et nemus comam resolvit de maritis imbribus.

THE painted stone sarcophagos[1] which forms in a sense the
text of the present chapter is now in the museum of Candia,
but it was found, in 1903, not at Knossos but close to the palace
of Hagia Triada at Phaistos, on the southern coast of Crete.
Immediately on its discovery its great importance was recognized,
and, as there was fear of the frescoes fading, it was promptly
carried, on the shoulders of men, a three days' journey across the
island to the museum at Candia, where it could be safely housed.

The tomb in which the sarcophagos was found is of a type
familiar in Lycia but not in Crete[2]. It consisted of a walled,
square chamber with a door at the north-west corner, somewhat
after the fashion of the Harpy-Tomb now in the British Museum.
This analogy is not without its importance, as the scenes represented, if we rightly interpret them, embody conceptions familiar

---

[1] First published with full commentary and illustration by R. Paribeni, *Il
Sarcofago dipinto di Hagia Triada* in Monumenti Antichi della R. Accademia dei
Lincei, XIX. 1908, p. 6, T. I—III. and reproduced here by kind permission of the
Accademia. See also F. von Duhn, *Der Sarkophag aus Hagia Triada* in Archiv
f. Religionswissenschaft, XII. 1909, 161, and E. Petersen, *Der Kretische Bildersarg*
in Jahrbuch Arch. Inst. XXIV. 1909, p. 162, and René Dussaud, *Les Civilisations
Pré-Helléniques dans le bassin de la mer Égée*, 1910, p. 261. I follow in the
main Dr Petersen's interpretation, though, in the matter of the bull-sacrifice, my
view is independent.

[2] Paribeni, *op. cit.* p. 9; for the Lycian tombs see Perrot-Chipiez, *Hist. de l'Art*,
v. p. 361 ff.

in Asia Minor. Inside the tomb-enclosure were found two sarcophagoi, the large painted stone sarcophagos now before us, and a smaller one in terra-cotta. The discoverer, Dr Halbherr, dates the tomb and its contents at from 1500—1300 B.C.

We begin with the principal scenes depicted on the two long sides of the sarcophagos, and first with the scene in Fig. 30. In the centre we have the sacrifice of a bull, of the kind, with large, curved horns, once common in the Aegean, now extinct.

Fig. 30.

He is dying, not dead; his tail is still alive and his pathetic eyes wide open, but the flute-player is playing and the blood flows from the bull's neck into the situla below. Two Cretan goats with twisted horns lie beneath the sacrificial table on which the bull is bound. They will come next. A procession of five women comes up to the table; the foremost places her hands on or towards the bull, as though she would be in touch with him and his *mana*. She will consecrate, I think, not him but herself, put herself in touch with his great life which ebbs with the flowing blood.

Why does he die? In the light of the last chapter we might safely assume that he died because his sacrificers desired his *mana*. But on the sarcophagos we have no communal feast; nor is there present the figure of any Olympian to receive the bull's blood as a gift-offering. How then is it to be made effective? A clue will be found in the scene immediately to the right of the bull, a scene not a little surprising. But before we pass to this scene some details of the bull-sacrifice must be noted.

After what has been said about sacrifice we understand the pathetic figure of the slain bull, huddled up with sad despairing face. Very literally he dies for the people, that they may have new life, new *mana*, new μένος, his life and his life-blood. We are reminded of the scene in the *Odyssey*[1] where the heifer is sacrificed to Athene,

> Then, straightway, Nestor's son
> Stood near and struck. The tendons of the neck
> The axe cut through, and loosed the heifer's might.

And, as the life is let loose, the women raise their cry of apotropaic lamentation, their ὀλολυγή. It is a moment of high tension, for the life with all its might and sanctity is abroad. Then, to make assurance doubly sure and to get the actual vehicle of the life, the blood, they cut the victim's throat:

> The black blood gushed, the life had left the bones[2].

We come now to the object of the sacrifice. On the extreme right of the design is a 'Mycenaean' shrine with 'horns of consecration.' Growing out from the middle of it, probably actually

---

[1] *Od.* III. 448

> αὐτίκα Νέστορος υἱός, ὑπέρθυμος Θρασυμήδης,
> ἤλασεν ἄγχι στάς· πέλεκυς δ' ἀπέκοψε τένοντας
> αὐχενίους, λῦσεν δὲ βοὸς μένος· αἱ δ' ὀλόλυξαν
> θυγατέρες τε νυοί τε καὶ αἰδοίη παράκοιτις
> Νέστορος.

Here undoubtedly λῦσεν δὲ βοὸς μένος means that the strength of the heifer collapsed, she fell in a heap on the ground. But the idea was originally that something holy and perilous escaped; this is clear from the instant raising of the ὀλολυγμός. That the ὀλολυγμός was a γυναικεῖος νόμος is plain from Aesch. *Ag.* 572. I believe its primary use to have been apotropaic. For the ὀλολυγμός see Stengel, *Hermes*, 1903, pp. 43—44, and *Kultusalterthümer*, p. 101.

[2] *v.* 455 τῆς δ' ἐπεὶ ἐκ μέλαν αἷμα ῥύη, λίπε δ' ὀστέα θυμός.

surrounded by it, is an unmistakable olive-tree. On a step in front of the shrine is a slender obelisk, and on, or rather hafted into, the obelisk, to our delight and amazement, a sacred object now thrice familiar, a double axe, and, perched on the double axe, a great black mottled bird. The conjunction rather takes our breath away. Sacred obelisks we know, of double axes as thunder-symbols we have lately heard perhaps enough[1]; birds are the familiar 'attributes' of many an Olympian; but an obelisk and a battle-axe and a bird with a sacrificial bull and a

Fig. 31.

'Mycenaean' tree-shrine—who would have dared to forecast it, and what does it all mean?

Before this question can be answered we must turn to the other side of the sarcophagos in Fig. 31 and learn what is the

[1] The most illuminating study on the double-axe, its cult and significance, is a paper by Mr A. B. Cook, *The Cretan Axe-Cult outside Crete*, published in the Transactions of the Third International Congress for the History of Religions. Oxford, 1908, II. p. 184. A further discussion by Mr Cook may be looked for in his forthcoming book *Zeus*, chapter II., section 3, paragraph (c), division i, 'The double axe in Minoan cult.' For the bird and the axe see also *A Bird Cult of the Old Kingdom* by P. E. Newbery in the Liverpool Annals of Archaeology and Anthropology, II. p. 49, and *Two Cults of the Old Kingdom, op. cit.* I. p. 24, and O. Montelius, *The Sun-God's Axe and Thor's Hammer*, in Folk-Lore, 1910, p. 60.

sequel of the sacrifice. There is, as before said, no hint of a sacramental banquet; but there are other means of contact, of sacramental communion, besides eating and drinking. The blood of the bull is not drunk by the worshippers; it is brought and poured—the liquid is red—by a woman dressed in sacramental raiment, from a situla into a great two-handled krater which stands between two obelisks again surmounted by double axe and bird. The woman celebrant is followed by another woman bearing two situlae on a pole over her shoulders, and by a man playing on a lyre. At this point the scene clearly ends. The next figure, carrying a calf, turns his back and walks in the contrary direction. The distinction between the two scenes is, in the original, made clearer by the differing colours of the background[1].

As to the double cultus-objects, two points must be carefully noted. The two sets of double axes, or rather double-double axes, are not quite the same. The one to the right is decorated with cross stripes, that to the left is plain. The double axe on the red obelisk on the other side of the sarcophagos has similar cross markings. Further the obelisk to the right is considerably taller than the obelisk to the left. This is I think intentional, not due to either accident or perspective, but to the fact that they stand for male and female potencies. The most surprising and significant difference in the cultus-objects of the two sides yet remains. The obelisk in Fig. 30 is merely an obelisk painted red; the two obelisks in Fig. 31 are burgeoning out into leaves, and they are painted green; they are trees alive and blossoming. They are not indeed actual trees[2], but mimic trees, obelisks decked for ritual purposes with cypress leaves.

The blood, the μένος of the bull, is brought to the two obelisks. It is abundantly clear that we have no gift-offering to a divinity. Birds and thunder-axes and trees have no normal, natural use for warm blood. The blood, the *mana*, must be brought with magical intent. Contact is to be effected between the unseen mystical *mana* of the bull and the *mana* of the tree. But, on the sarcophagos, we do not see the actual contact, the actual communion effected. The priestess does not apply the blood, does not asperge the obelisks. The evidence of the sarcophagos

---

[1] The significance of the scene to the right will be considered later, p. 209.
[2] This was, I think, first pointed out by Professor von Duhn, *op. cit.* p. 173.

can here be supplemented by other sacrifices in which bulls and trees and tree-posts are involved.

In the island of Atlantis Plato[1] describes a strange bull-sacrifice, evidently founded on some actual primitive ritual. The essential feature of this sacrifice was the actual contact of the victim's blood with a pillar or post on which laws were engraved. Here we have direct contact with the object to be sanctified; no altar or even table intervenes. It is sacrifice, i.e. magical contact, in its most primitive form. Kritias in his description of the sunk island says that in the centre of it was a sanctuary to Poseidon within which certain sacred bulls ranged freely. Poseidon it may be noted in passing is one of the gods who grew out of a bull; his wine-bearers at Ephesus[2] were *Bulls*, and, in answer to the imprecation of Theseus, as a Bull he appears out of his own flood to wreck the chariot of Hippolytus[3]. It is to the Cretan Poseidon not to Zeus that Minos[4] promised the sacrifice of his finest bull.

In this sanctuary of Poseidon was a column of orichalcum on which were inscribed the injunctions of Poseidon, which seem to have constituted the laws of the country. On the column, beside the law, was a Curse (Ὅρκος) invoking great maledictions on the disobedient. Now there were bulls who ranged free (ἔφετοι) in the sanctuary of Poseidon, and the ten kings who were alone in the sanctuary prayed to the god that they might take for victim the bull that was pleasing to him, and they hunted the bull without iron, with staves or snares. The bull, be it noted, is free because divine; he is not smitten with a weapon lest his μένος should prematurely escape. They then led the bull to the column and slew him *against the top of the column over the writing*[5]. The whole strength and *mana* of the bull is thus actually applied to, tied up with, the ὅρκος. To make assurance

---

[1] *Krit.* 119 D and E.

[2] Hesych. *s.v.* Ταῦροι· οἱ παρὰ Ἐφεσίοις οἰνοχόοι and *s.v.* Ταυρία· ἑορτή τις ἀγομένη Ποσειδῶνος. Athen. x. 25 παρὰ Ἐφεσίοις οἱ οἰνοχοοῦντες ἤθεοι τῇ τοῦ Ποσειδῶνος ἑορτῇ ταῦροι ἐκαλοῦντο.

[3] Eur. *Hipp.* 1214 κῦμ᾽ ἐξέθηκε ταῦρον, ἄγριον τέρας. Cf. Hesiod, *Scut.* 104 ταύρεος ἐννοσίγαιος.

[4] Apollod. 2. 5. 7.

[5] Plat. *Krit.* 119E ...ὃν δὲ ἕλοιεν τῶν ταύρων, πρὸς τὴν στήλην προσαγαγόντες κατὰ κορυφὴν αὐτῆς ἔσφαττον κατὰ τῶν γραμμάτων.

doubly sure they afterwards filled a bowl with wine, dropped into it a clot of blood for each of the kings, and then drank, swearing that they would judge according to the laws on the column. Such a sacrifice is pure magic; it has primarily nothing to do with a god, everything to do with the magical conjunction of the *mana* of victim and sacrificer.

It has been happily suggested that the lost island of Atlantis

FIG. 32.

reflects the manners and customs, the civilization generally, of Crete[1], which after its great Minoan supremacy sank, for the rest of Greece, into a long oblivion. It is also very unlikely that Plato would *invent* ritual details which in his day would have but little significance. But we have definite evidence that the ritual described is actual, not imaginary, though this evidence comes not from Crete but from another region of the 'Mycenaean' world. The coin of Ilium[2] reproduced in Fig. 32 shows, I think, very clearly, how the bull was sacrificed. The human-shaped goddess Athena Ilias is there with her fillet-twined spear and her owl; but to the right is an older sanctity, a pillar *on to which is hung a bull.* He will be sacrificed, not *on* the pillar's top, which would be extremely awkward, but with his head and his throat to be cut against the top, alongside of it, down over it (κατὰ κορυφὴν).

That the divine or rather the chief sanctity of Ilium was a pillar is clear, I think, from the representation in Fig. 33 *a.* The ox, or rather cow[3], is still free and stands before the goddess. She has human shape, but she is standing on the pillar she once was. On the obverse of another coin (*b*) she has left her pillar. Most remarkable and to us instructive of all, is the design on a third coin of Ilium in Fig. 33 *c.* The goddess is present, as

---

[1] See an interesting article *The Lost Continent* in the Times for Feb. 19, 1911.

[2] The four coins reproduced in Figs. 32 and 33 are published and discussed by Dr H. v. Fritze in the section *Die Münzen von Ilion* of Prof. Dörpfeld's *Troja und Ilion,* II. p. 514, Beilage, Pl. 61, No. 19, Pl. 63, Nos. 67, 68 and 69, and are here represented by Prof. Dörpfeld's kind permission. Dr Fritze in his interesting commentary does not note the Atlantis parallel, but he draws attention to the fact that the suspended bull explains the formulary that often occurs in ephebic inscriptions αἴρεσθαι τοὺς βοῦς. Thus CIA II¹. 467 ἤραντο δὲ καὶ τοῖς Μυστηρίοις τοὺς βοῦς ἐν Ἐλευσῖνι τῇ θυσίᾳ and CIA II¹. 471, 78 f. ἐπο[ιήσ]ατο δὲ καὶ τὰς ἄρσεις τῶν βοῶν ἐπάνδρως ἐν τῇ Ἐλευ[σῖνι τῇ θυ]σίᾳ καὶ τοῖς πρ[οηροσίοις].

[3] That the animal sacrificed before the Palladion is female is certain from the ἡ βοῦς of the inscription of Ilium.

before, mounted on her pillar.   Before her is the cow suspended
head uppermost on a tree.   Behind the cow and apparently
seated on the tree is the sacrificer, known by his short sleeveless
chiton. He has seized the horn of the cow in his left hand and
with his right he is about to cut her throat.   The goddess may
be present as much as she likes, but she was not the original
object of the cow-slaying.   The intent is clear, the blood of the
cow is to fall on the sacred tree and will bring it new *mana*.   No
other explanation can account for a method of sacrifice at once
so difficult and so dangerous.

The gist of bringing the bull's blood to the obelisks on the
sarcophagos is then, in the light of the coins of Ilium, clear.   It
is to bring the *mana* of the bull in contact with the mimic trees.
Tree and pillar and obelisk are all substantially one; the living

(a)   (b)   (c)

Fɪɢ. 33.

tree once cut down becomes a pillar or an obelisk at will,
and, dead though it may be, does not lose its sanctity.   All trees
tend to be sacred or possessed by an unseen life, but above all
fruit-trees are sacred[1], they are foci of eager collective attention.
Long before agricultural days and the sanctity of grain came the
sanctity of natural fruit-trees.   On the sarcophagos it is clear
that we have, not as in the Bouphonia an agricultural, but what
we might call a vegetation, a tree and fruit ceremony.

The importance of the fruit-tree and the religious reverence
paid it come out very clearly in Mycenaean gems[2].   Not only are
the shrine and the sacred Tree constantly and closely associated,
but we have scenes of fruit-gathering accompanied by ritual

---

[1] Prof. **Myres** (*Proceedings of Class. Assoc.* 1910) remarks that Greeks have no
word for *tree* in general. δένδρον = *fruit* tree.

[2] A. J. Evans, *Mycenaean Tree and Pillar Cult*, J.H.S. xxɪ. (1901), Fig. 53.

dances and gestures.   Such a scene is depicted on the gold signet-
ring from Mycenae in Fig. 34.   To the right we have a shrine
with a pillar and a sacred Tree.   A male worshipper pulls the
fruit-laden tree downwards, as though to shake off its fruit or
possibly to uproot it for ritual purposes.   A woman figure, perhaps
a goddess, more likely a priestess, makes ritual gestures with her
hands, it may be to indicate hunger[1]; a second woman leans over
an altar table beneath which is a betyl.   A similar scene is
represented on a gold signet-ring from Vapheio[2].   Here the tree is
planted in a pithos, and the so-called priestess is evidently dancing.

Fig. 34.

Primitive man then in general, and assuredly the ancient
Cretan, is intensely concerned with the fruits of the Earth—not
at first with the worship of Earth in the abstract, but with the
food[3] that comes to him out of the Earth.   It is mainly because
she feeds him that he learns to think of Earth as the Mother.
Rightly did the ancient Dove-Priestesses of Dodona sing[4]:

Earth sends up fruits—call ye on Earth the Mother.

[1] Dr Evans in commenting on the ring, *op. cit.* p. 177, says, 'a gesture for
hunger common among the American Indians may supply a useful parallel.   It is
made by passing the hands towards and backward from the sides of the body,
denoting a gnawing sensation.'   See Garrick Mallery, *Pictographs of the North
American Indians*, in Fourth Annual Report of Bureau of Ethnology, 1886, p. 236,
and Fig. 155, p. 235.

[2] Evans, *op. cit.*, Fig. 52.

[3] The importance of food as a factor in civilization and the successive quest of
roots, fruits, cereals, etc., has been well discussed by Mr E. J. Payne in his *History
of the New World called America*, vol. I. pp. 276 ff.

[4] Paus. x. 12. 10

Γᾶ καρποὺς ἀνίει, διὸ κλῄζετε μητέρα γαῖαν.

And of these fruits, before cereals came in with settled agriculture, most conspicuous and arresting would be the fruits of wild trees. The fruit-growing tree would be sacred, and its sanctity would quickly pass to other trees. There was the like sanctity, the like *mana* in all edible plants and roots, but the tree would stand foremost.

Earth as the Mother *because* the fruit-bearer is very clearly shown in Fig. 35, a design from a hydria in the Museum at Constantinople[1]. The scene is at Eleusis, marked by the presence of Triptolemos in his winged car. From the earth rises Ge. In

FIG. 35.

her hand she bears a cornucopia, full of the fruits of the earth *From the cornucopia rises a child.* Art could not speak more plainly. Ge is mother because fruit-bearer. Earth then is fitly embodied by the primaeval fruit-bearer, the tree.

Earth sent up fruits, but not without help from heaven. In the scenes of fruit-gathering this is not forgotten. On the signet-ring in Fig. 34 above the tree and the priestess is a rather rudimentary indication of the sky, a dotted line and what is probably

[1] S. Reinach, *Rev. Arch.* 1900, p. 87; and see also Dr Svoronos, *Journal d'Archéologie et Numismatique*, 1901, p. 387.

a crescent moon. If there is any doubt what is meant we have only to turn to the gold signet-ring from the Acropolis treasure of Mycenae in Fig. 36[1]. Here we have the Earth-goddess or her priestess under her great fruit-bearing tree; she holds poppies in her hand; worshippers approach her bearing flowers and leaf-sprays; behind her a woman gathers fruit, while above her is all the glory of Ouranos, Sun and Moon and Milky Way, and down from the sky come the powers of the sky, the thunder in its

Fig. 36.

double manifestation of shield-demon and battle-axe. The Earth is barren till the Thunder and the Rainstorm smite her in the springtime—till in his Epiphany of Thunder and Lightning Keraunos comes to Keraunia, the Sky-god weds Semele the Earth, the

> Bride of the bladed Thunder[2].

In the light of the scene on the signet-ring we do not need to ask the significance of the axe hafted into the obelisk[3]. It is the

---

[1] *J.H.S.* 1901.

[2] Eur. *Hipp.* 559 βροντῇ ἀμφιπύρῳ τοκάδα. Cf. Eur. *Bacch.* 3 Σεμέλη λοχευθεῖσ' ἀστραπηφόρῳ πυρί. Other instances of thunder-Brides are Alkmene, wife of Amphitryon, the *double-borer*, the *bidens*, Dido wedded to Aeneas in a thunderstorm.

[3] First rightly explained by Mr A. B. Cook, *Cretan Axe-Cult outside Crete*, Transactions of the Third International Congress for the History of Religions, Oxford, 1908, II. 193.

symbol, or rather I should prefer to say the representation, the
emphasis of the union of the *mana* of Earth and Sky, of what a
more formal, anthropoid theology would call the Sacred Marriage
(ἱερὸς γάμος) of Ouranos and Gaia. This union, this marriage is
further symbolized by the bird. But before we pass to the bird,
it remains to note a curious and instructive parallel to this cult of
axe and tree and bull, a parallel which takes us back for a moment
to the ritual of the Bouphonia. We shall find this parallel in a
place where we little expect it, in the Erechtheion on the Athenian
Acropolis.

Pausanias[1], when he is discussing the Court of the Prytaneum
where iron and all lifeless things were brought to trial, naturally
thinks of the classical instance of the axe at the Bouphonia. He
makes incidentally a statement that has not, I think, received the
attention it deserves. '*When Erechtheus was king of the Athenians,*
the Ox-Slayer slew an ox for the first time on the altar of Zeus
Polieus.' The Bouphonia was then traditionally connected, not
only, nor I think primarily, with Zeus, but with Erechtheus.

This connection of Erechtheus with the bull-sacrifice is confirmed by a famous passage in the *Iliad*. In the *Catalogue of the
Ships*[2] the contingent of the Athenians is thus described:

> Athens they held, her goodly citadel,
> Realm of Erechtheus, high of heart, whom erst
> Athene reared, daughter of Zeus, what time
> The grain-giver did bear him, and she set
> Erechtheus there in Athens, in her own
> Rich temple. There, as each Year's Feast goes round,
> The young men worship him with bulls and lambs.

Earth is his mother, or rather the ploughed field, the tilth, the
grain-land (ἄρουρα). Athena, the humanized form of this earth-
daimon, is but his foster-mother. The young men (κοῦροι), like
the *kouroi* on the sarcophagos, worship him with bulls and lambs

---

[1] I. 28. 10.
[2] *Il.* II. 546 οἱ δ' ἄρ' Ἀθήνας εἶχον, εὐκτίμενον πτολίεθρον,
δῆμον Ἐρεχθῆος μεγαλήτορος, ὅν ποτ' Ἀθήνη
θρέψε Διὸς θυγάτηρ, τέκε δὲ ζείδωρος ἄρουρα·
κὰδ δ' ἐν Ἀθήνῃς εἷσεν, ἑῷ ἐνὶ πίονι νηῷ·
ἔνθα δέ μιν ταύροισι καὶ ἀρνειοῖς ἱλάονται
κοῦροι Ἀθηναίων περιτελλομένων ἐνιαυτῶν.
For the present purpose it is of no consequence whether the passage is interpolated or not, nor does the archaeological question of the various νηοί concern us.

'as each Year's Feast goes round.' It is a yearly sacrifice, a year-sacrifice. For Athenian κοῦροι, he, Erechtheus, is their μέγιστος κοῦρος.

The whole atmosphere of the passage is agricultural; but, when we ask what natural and social facts lie behind the figure of Erechtheus, we find ourselves surrounded by sanctities more primitive. The cult and character of Erechtheus must be sought, if anywhere, in the Erechtheion, the sanctuary which stands on the site of the old kings' palace of the Acropolis and which still bears his name. The present temple is of course a building of the end of the fifth century B.C. All we know certainly of its date is that

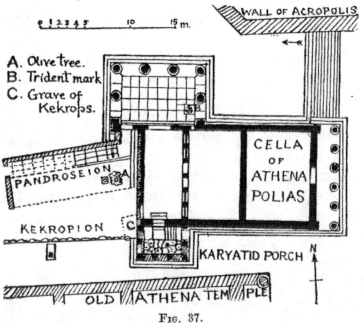

A. Olive tree.
B. Trident mark.
C. Grave of Kekrops.

FIG. 37.

it was unfinished in B.C. 408. What concerns us are the ancient sanctities that the comparatively modern structure was built to enshrine and safeguard[1]. Of these for our purpose we need only consider three, the famous σημεῖα or tokens:

A sacred olive tree,
A 'sea' or well called after Erechtheus ('Ερεχθηΐς),
A 'trident' mark.

The disposition of trident-mark and olive tree is seen in Fig. 37. The well must have been close to the holy tree.

[1] A discussion of the topography of the Erechtheion will be found in my *Ancient Athens*, 1890, p. 481, and my more recent views as to the disposition of the σημεια

When we hear of the trident-mark, the salt sea-well and the olive tree, we think instinctively of the west pediment of the Parthenon, of the great strife between Athena and Poseidon for the land of Attica. The salt sea-well and the trident-mark are 'tokens,' we are told, of the defeat of Poseidon; the olive is the 'token' of the triumph of Athena. An awkward story for theology and one that required much adjustment and subsequent peace-making, as the rivals Athena and Poseidon had to share a sanctuary. The story is as untrue as it is awkward. If we would understand the 'tokens,' we must get back behind these intrusive, grasping Olympians and see what the sanctities themselves signify before they were anyone's 'tokens.'

The olive grew in the Pandroseion[1]; it also grew in the older Erechtheion, in its precinct at least, if not in the actual building. Herodotus[2] says, 'There is on this Acropolis a temple of Erechtheus who is called Earth-born, and in it are an olive tree and a sea which according to current tradition among the Athenians Poseidon and Athena planted as tokens when they contended for the country.' What has the olive to do with Erechtheus? Again the Hagia Triada sarcophagos explains. In the obelisks, the artificial tree-posts, are planted the thunder-axes that bring the rain-storm to fertilize the earth. From that marriage springs the tree. The trident-mark, we have already seen (p. 92), was no symbol of the sea-god, but, as was shown by the hole in the roof, it was the token of Kataibates, the *Descender* from the sky. According to Hyginus[3] Erechtheus was smitten not by the trident of Poseidon, but by the lightning of Zeus, at the request of Poseidon. The well too we may conjecture only became brackish when Erechtheus the Earth-shaker, Phytalmios, Nurturer of plants, took on a sea-god's attributes.

in *Primitive Athens*, 1906, p. 39, from which Fig. 37 is taken. The view here taken of Erechtheus as Thunder-god was first proposed by O. Gilbert, *Gr. Götterlehre*, 1898, p. 170, and is adopted by Dr E. Petersen in *Die Burgtempel der Athenaia*, 1907, p. 73.

[1] A close analogy to the Pandroseion at Athens is offered by the Pantheion at Olympia, in which grew the sacred olive-tree (Aristotle, Θαυμάσια ἀκούσματα, 51, and Schol. *ad Ar. Plut.* 586). This Pantheion had obviously nothing to do with 'all the gods.' It was simply the 'altogether holy place.' Cf. the πάνθειος τελετή of the Orphic Hymns. For the *Pantheion* see L. Weniger, *Der heilige Oelbaum in Olympia*, Weimar Programm No. 701, 1895, but unhappily Dr Weniger, spite of the evidence he brings together, clings to the old view that the *Pantheion* was in our modern sense a Pantheon.

[2] VIII. 55. [3] *Fab.* 46 ab Iove. Neptuni rogatu, fulmine est ictus.

In the light of the Hagia Triada sarcophagos it is all quite
simple and clear.   As there, so here, we have an olive tree:

> The holy bloom of the olive, whose hoar leaf
> High on the shadowy shrine of Pandrosos
> Hath honour of us all.

Apollodorus[1] says that Athena came after Poseidon and having
made Kekrops witness of her seizure (καταλήψεως), planted the
olive which now is shown in the Pandroseion.   Athena is manifestly a superfluous interloper.   There is a holy tree whose name
we may conjecture was the 'All Dewy One.'   It was tended by
maidens who did the service of the Hersephoria; the Dew-carrying
Maidens to this day go out before the dawn to catch the dew of
May Day which is magical for bloom and health.   The Hersephoria,
the Dew Service, took place on the 13th of Skirophorion, the night
before the Bouphonia[2].   It is natural to ask, Was there any
possible connection between the two?

Not far from the statue and altar of Zeus Polieus on the Acropolis, where the Bouphonia was enacted, there was, Pausanias tells
us, an image of Ge praying to Zeus for rain[3].   Cut in the living rock
about a dozen yards north of the Parthenon is an inscription near
to a basis that once held a votive statue 'Of Ge the Fruit-bearer
according to the oracle[4].'   Possibly the lost statue was the very
image seen by Pausanias.   Ge prayed to Zeus in his capacity of
Hyetios, the Rainy.   A contemporary of Lucian, Alciphron by
name, has left us in his imaginary letters[5] some details of the
cult of Zeus Hyetios.   A certain Thalliskos writes as follows to
Petraios:

> A drought is upon us.   Not a cloud is to be seen in the sky, and we
> want a regular downpour.   You have only to look at the ploughed land to
> see how dreadfully parched the soil is.   I am afraid all our sacrifices to

---

[1] III. 14. 2.

[2] For the evidence see Mommsen, *Heortologie*, p. 44.   The month Skirophorion
is certain, for the Etymologicum Magnum says of the ἀρρηφορία· ἑορτὴ ἐπιτελουμένη
τῇ Ἀθηνᾷ ἐν τῷ Σκιροφοριῶνι μηνί.   The exact day, the 13th, is not certain, but
highly probable.   Suidas says of the Bouphonia, ἑορτὴ παλαιὰ ἣν φασιν ἄγεσθαι
μετὰ τὰ μυστήρια.   The μυστήρια cannot be the Eleusinian mysteries which were
celebrated in Boedromion (September), they may well be the Arrephoria, which
were certainly mysterious.   The Etym. Mag. explains the word as applied παρὰ τὸ
ἄρρητα καὶ μυστήρια φέρειν.

[3] P. I. 24. 3.

[4] For facsimile of inscription see my *Mythology and Monuments of Ancient
Athens*, p. 415.

[5] Alk. *Epist.* III. 35.   For the βοηγία of Zeus Hyetios at Didymoi see
B. Haussoullier, *Le Culte de Zeus à Didymes* in Mélanges Weil, 1898, p. 147.

Jupiter Pluvius have gone for nothing, and yet all we villagers outdid each other to make a good sacrificial show. Each man brought what he could according to his means and ability. One brought a ram, another a goat, another some fruit, the poor man brought a cake, and the positive pauper some lumps of decidedly mouldy incense. No one could run to a bull, for our Attic soil is thin and cattle are scarce. But we might have saved our expense. Zeus it would seem is 'on a journey' and cannot attend to us.

We begin to suspect that the sacrifice of the bull in the Bouphonia was a rain 'charm,' later a 'sacrifice to Zeus Hyetios,' and this, it may be, explains a strange detail in the ritual. Among the attendants at the sacrifice were certain maidens called Water-Carriers (ὑδροφόροι). They brought the water, Porphyry[1] says, to sharpen the knife and the axe. But for such a function was it necessary that maidens should be carefully selected? Is it not at least possible that the water poured on the holy axe was to act as a rain 'charm'? The axe was the symbol, the presentation of the Sky-Zeus; what acted prayer could be more potent, more magical, than to sprinkle the axe with water[2]?

Be this as it may, we can scarcely avoid the conclusion that the Bouphonia and the Hersephoria, widely different in character though they were, had the same intent, to induce the sky to let fall upon the parched earth its rain or dew, that so the sacred olive, and with it all other plants and crops, might blossom and bear fruit. The Hersephoria was to induce the fall of fertilizing dew[3]. According to a wide-spread belief, the dew gathered on Midsummer Night had special potency to beautify and bless[4]. Dew, according to common credence, falls thickest on the night of the full moon, and the Hersephoria took place on the night of the

---

[1] *de Abst.* II. 30 ὑδροφόρους παρθένους κατέλεξαν· αἰ δ' ὕδωρ κομίζουσιν, ὅπως τὸν πέλεκυν καὶ τὴν μάχαιραν ἀκονήσωσιν.

[2] This delightful suggestion is entirely due to Mr A. B. Cook, by whose permission I mention it.

[3] See my *Prolegomena*, p. 122, note 2. The dew was unquestionably regarded as the fertilizing seed of the Sky-God. Mr A. B. Cook draws my attention to a passage in the *Dionysiaka* of Nonnus (VII. 144 ff.), where Semele in a dream sees the fate to come upon her (her bridal with Zeus), in the vision of a tree, watered by the eternal dew of the son of Kronos:

ἔλπετο καλλιπέτηλον ἰδεῖν φυτὸν ἔνδοθι κήπου
ἔγχλοον, οἰδαλέῳ βεβαρημένον ὄμφακι καρπῷ
. . . .
καὶ Σεμέλη φυτὸν ἦεν.

A *bird* carries the fruit of the tree to the lap of Zeus, and from him a full-grown *bull-man* is born.

[4] Brand H. Ellis, *Popular Antiquities of Great Britain*, 1849, I. 218; P. Sebillot, *Folk-Lore de France*, 1904, I. 94.

last full moon of the Attic year[1]. The maidens gathered their dew in the precinct of Ourania in the Gardens. The Bouphonia was an appeal to the sterner powers of the sky, to thunder, and lightning, and the rain-storm.

It is worth noting that an invocation of dew for the fertilization of man and plants and cattle forms part of an Epiphany δρώμενον that goes on in the island of Imbros[2] to-day. A sort of 'aetiological myth' is chanted, telling of the 'Baptism of Christ.' Our Lady goes down to Jordan, takes water, washes and then entreats S. John Baptist to baptize the Holy Child. S. John makes answer:

> Let him wait till the morn
> That I may ascend into heaven,
> To send down dew upon earth,
> That the master and his lady may be bedewed,
> That the mothers and their children be bedewed,
> That the plains with the trees be bedewed,
> That the springs and the waters be bedewed,
> That the cattle may be tame,
> And the idols may fall down.

We find ourselves in full magic, S. John the Baptist and the Baptism of life-giving dew—the New Birth. S. John must ascend, must become a 'sky-god,' before he can descend.

If, spite of the conjunction of thunder-axe and tree on the sarcophagos, the thunder-god Erechtheus and the olive tree strike us still as dissonant, we may find conviction when it appears that the same strange marriage is found in the lower city. In the Academy Pausanias[3] saw an olive plant, said to have been the second to appear. It was doubtless fabled to have been a graft from the sacred olive of the Acropolis. All olive trees throughout Attica which could claim this high descent were called *Moriae* (propagated, μεμορημέναι) and were protected by special sanctions under the immediate care of the Areopagos[4]. They were also

---

[1] Gruppe, *Gr. Mythologie und Religion*, p. 34. The whole question of the dew and rain aspects of the Sky-god will be fully discussed by Mr A. B. Cook in his forthcoming work '*Zeus*,' chapter II. § 8, 'Zeus and the Dew,' § *g* 'Zeus and the Rain,' § *h* Zeus Hyetios II. Diipoleia. Since the above was written it has been shown by Dr E. Maass (*A. Mitt.* xxxv. 3, p. 337, *Aglaurion*) that Aglauros is a well-nymph, goddess of the clear shining water, of ἀγλαὸν ὕδωρ. She and her sisters are therefore a trinity of water and dew.

[2] I owe my knowledge of this interesting song to the kindness of Mr A. Wace, who allowed me to see a proof of his forthcoming article on *North Greek Festivals*.

[3] I. 30. 2 καὶ φυτόν ἐστιν ἐλαίας, δεύτερον τοῦτο λεγόμενον φανῆναι.

[4] See Lysias, *Orat.* 7.

under the special charge of Zeus Morios. His altar was in the Academy and he was worshipped, we learn to our delight, not only as Morios but as Kataibates[1]. Later moralists would explain that this was because he avenged sacrilege by lightning; the real truth lies deeper and is benignant; he, the rain and thunder-god, fertilized the earth and brought forth the sacred olives.

The scholiast who gives us this welcome information about Zeus, who is both Morios and Kataibates, is commenting on the famous chorus in praise of Athens in the *Oedipus Coloneus*[2]:

And this country for her own has what no Asian land has known,
Nor ever yet in the great Dorian Pelops' island has it grown,
The untended, the self-planted, self-defended from the foe,
Sea-gray children-nurturing olive tree that here delights to grow.
None may take nor touch nor harm it, headstrong youth nor age grown
    bold,
For the round of heaven of Morian Zeus has been its watcher from of
    old.
He beholds it and, Athene, thy own sea-gray eyes behold.

Athena with her sea-gray eyes we expect: watching her olive tree she is canonical; but, to most readers, the round eye of Morian Zeus comes as something of a surprise. If we remember the ἄβατον on the Acropolis, with the lightning trident-mark and the hole in the roof, we wonder no longer that the old sky-god, with his round eye, should be looking down on his own olive tree. What was a mere poetical image becomes a ritual reality and gathers the fresh bloom of a new if somewhat homely beauty.

Nor is it only a poet praising his own city who remembers such local sanctities. Aeschylus in the *Danaides*[3] told of the sacred

---

[1] Apollodorus, *ap.* Schol. ad Soph. *Oed. Col.* 705 περὶ ᾽Ακαδημίαν ἐστὶν ὅ τε τοῦ Καταιβάτου Διὸς βωμὸς ὃν καὶ Μόριον καλοῦσι [ἀπὸ] τῶν ἐκεῖ μοριῶν.

[2] Soph. *Oed. Col.* 704

ὁ γὰρ αἰὲν ὁρῶν κύκλος
λεύσσει νιν Μορίου Διὸς
χἀ γλαυκῶπις ᾽Αθάνα.

The translation in the text is by Mr D. S. MacColl.

[3] Nauck, *frg.* 44, *ap.* Athen. xiii. 600 καὶ ὁ σεμνότατος δ᾽ Αἰσχύλος ἐν ταῖς Δαναῖσιν αὐτὴν παράγει τὴν ᾽Αφροδίτην λέγουσαν

ἐρᾷ μὲν ἁγνὸς οὐρανὸς τρῶσαι χθόνα,
ἔρως δὲ γαῖαν λαμβάνει γάμου τυχεῖν·
ὄμβρος δ᾽ ἀπ᾽ εὐνατῆρος οὐρανοῦ πεσὼν
ἔδυσε γαῖαν· ἡ δὲ τίκτεται βροτοῖς
μήλων τε βοσκὰς καὶ βίον Δημήτριον
δένδρων τις ὥρα δ᾽ ἐκ νοτίζοντος γάνους
τέλειός ἐστι· τῶνδ᾽ ἐγὼ παραίτιος.

Trans. Murray. The γάνος of the fragment recalls the παγκρατὴς γάνους of the Hymn of the Kouretes, see p. 7.

marriage of Earth and Sky. He puts the words into the mouth
of Aphrodite, goddess in later days of human passion, but we seem
to stand in the ancient Cretan shrine, with about us the symbols
of Ouranos, the lightning-axe and the bird, and Gaia, the upspringing tree dew-watered, and we hear words august and
venerable which tell of things that were before man and may
outlast him:

> Lo, there is hunger in the holy Sky
> To pierce the body of Earth, and in Earth too
> Hunger to meet his arms. So falls the rain
> From Heaven that is her lover, making moist
> The bosom of Earth; and she brings forth to man
> The flocks he feeds, the corn that is his life.
> To trees no less there cometh their own hour
> Of marriage which the gleam of watery things
> Makes fruitful—Of all these the cause am I.

By the time of Aeschylus most men had probably forgotten
that the Danaides, the heroines of the play, were the water-
bearers, the well-nymphs who watered thirsty Argos[1]; but,
when Aphrodite made her great speech, there was not an
initiated man in the theatre but would remember the final
ceremonial of the Eleusinian mysteries—how, looking up to
heaven, they cried aloud, ὕε, 'rain,' and looking down to earth,
κύε, 'be fruitful.'

We return now to the other side of the sarcophagos, on which
the sacrifice of the bull is depicted. The remainder of the scene
towards the right is given somewhat enlarged in Fig. 38. Here
we have what, with the Acropolis of Athens in our minds[2],
we might call a Pandroseion: an olive tree in a sanctuary,
surmounted by bulls' horns, and the thunder-axe on the bare
obelisk standing for Erechtheus. Upon the thunder-axe is
perched a bird[3].

---

[1] *Prolegomena*, p. 620.
[2] *Prolegomena*, p. 161.
[3] I conjecture that the Bouphonia on the Acropolis and its relation to the
Erechtheion and the olive tree date back to the days when Athens was but
a tributary of the great Minoan thalassocracy. Sopatros, we remember (p. 142),
was a native of Crete. The religious dependence of Athens on Crete outlasted the
political strife, as Solon witnessed when he sent for Epimenides to purify Athens,
see p. 52. For the Cretan origin of the Bouphonia see Mr Cook, *J.H.S.* XIV. 131.

Upon the thunder-axe we expect to see the thunder-bird of Zeus, the eagle, but this is assuredly no eagle, however 'conventionally treated.' It is the bird of spring, with heavy flight and mottled plumage, the cuckoo[1].

> *When first the cuckoo cuckoos in the oak,*
> Gladdening men's hearts over the boundless earth,
> *Then may Zeus rain[2].*

FIG. 38

[1] Many birds have been suggested. The raven has the high authority of Mr Warde Fowler; Dr Hans Gadow suggested to me the magpie. The woodpecker was tempting, because of the analogy between πέλεκυς and πελεκάν, but as Dr Petersen (*op. cit.* p. 163) points out, the pose of the bird, with wings open, not closed, when perching, is characteristic of the cuckoo, though here it may be depicted to show the bird has just alighted. The particular bird intended is not of great moment. The idea, the coming of a life-spirit from the sky, is the same whatever bird be the vehicle. I have elsewhere (*Bird and Pillar-Worship in connexion with Ouranian divinities*, in Transactions of the Third International Congress for the History of Religions, Oxford, 1908, II. p. 154) hazarded the conjecture, suggested by Mr Cook, that the ritual robe of the celebrant and other worshippers on the sarcophagos is a feather dress ending in a bird-tail—but Sig. Paribeni has brought evidence, *op. cit.* p. 17, to show that the feather-like drawing on the robe is used to indicate a bull's skin.

[2] Hesiod *Op.* 486; see p. 97.

That is the prayer in the heart of the priestess, and she utters it, emphasizes it, by her offering of water which she has poured out of the high jug into the basin before her, over which she lays her hands, perhaps in token that the water is the rain-bath (λουτρά) of the earth's bridal. Above are the fruit-shaped cakes (μάζαι), for it is food that the cuckoo of spring is to bring her.

The picture speaks for itself; it is the passing of winter and the coming of spring, the passing of the Old Year, the incoming of the New, it is the Death and Resurrection of Nature, her New Birth. Clearly though this is represented, it confuses us a little at first by its fulness and by its blend of animal and vegetable and atmospheric life, of tree and bull and bird and thunder-axe[1]. All this, so natural, so inevitable to the primitive mind, to us, who have lost the sense of common kinship and common *mana*, seems artificial, metaphorical. We need first to meditate over it, to disentangle its various strands, before, by an effort of imagination, we can do what, if we would understand aright, is supremely necessary, think ourselves back into the primaeval fusion of things, a fusion always unconsciously present in the mind of poet and primitive.

It is the springtime of man and bird and flower:

> Rise up, my love, my fair one, and come away.
> For, lo, the winter is past, the rain is over and gone;
> The flowers appear on the earth;
> The time of the singing of birds is come,
> And the voice of the turtle is heard in our land.
> The fig tree putteth forth her green figs,
> And the vines with the tender grape give a good smell
> Arise, my love, my fair one, and come away[2].

Again in the thirteenth-century roundel[3]:

> Sumer is icumen in,
>   Lhude sing cuccu!
> Groweth sed and bloweth med,
>   And springth the wdë nu,
>   Sing cuccu!
> Awë bleteth after lomb,
>   Lhouth after calvë cu,
> Bulloc sterteth, buckë verteth,
>   Murie sing cuccu!

---

[1] Just such a blend of tree, bird, bull, thunder, dew and humanity, is found in Semele's tree, see p. 173, note 3.

[2] Song of Solomon, ii. 10.

[3] See E. K. Chambers, *Mediaeval Stage*, 1903, i. 168.

It is the bridal of the Earth and Sky, the New Birth of the
World:

> Cras amet qui nunquam amavit, quique amavit cras amet,
> Ver novum, ver jam canorum ver renatus orbis est,
> Vere concordant amores, vere nubunt alites,
> Et nemus comam resolvit de maritis imbribus[1].

So the poet, but the common man who has no words with
which to speak is yet a poet in his own way, and the drama of
winter and spring, death and life, he feels, and makes of it
a δρώμενον, a ritual.   Theopompos, according to Plutarch[2], relates
that

Those who dwell in the west account and call the Winter Kronos and
the Summer Aphrodite, the Spring Persephone, and from Kronos and
Aphrodite all things take their birth.   And the Phrygians think that in the
Winter the god is asleep, and that in the Summer he is awake, and *they
celebrate to him Bacchic revels, which in winter are Goings to Sleep, and in
summer Wakings-up.*   And the Paphlagonians allege that in winter the god is
bound down and imprisoned, and in spring aroused and set free again.

Such rites are not only for the outlet of man's emotion, not
only for the emphasis of that emotion by representation, they are,
as we have seen all rites tend to be, the utterance of his desire
and will, they are pre-presentations of practical magical intent
And this in very definite fashion; for, though man does not live
by bread alone, without his daily bread he cannot live.

The cuckoo is summoned to bring new life to the tree, dead in
the winter, to bring the rain that will bring the food-fruits.   The
water and cakes are as it were a visualized prayer, they are εὐχαί.
But when the gods are formulated and become men and women,
when Zeus and Hera have supplanted Ouranos and Gaia, then the
coming of the cuckoo takes on the shape of human wedlock.
'Women,' says Praxinoë to Gorgo, in the famous Syracusan Idyll
of Theocritus[3], 'Women know everything,

> Yes, and how Zeus married Hera,'

---

[1] *Pervigilium Veneris.*

[2] *de Isid. et Osir.* LXIX. Φρύγες δὲ τὸν θεὸν οἰόμενοι χειμῶνος καθεύδειν θέρους
δ' ἐγρηγορέναι, τότε μὲν κατευνασμούς, τότε δ' ἀνεγέρσεις βακχεύοντες αὐτῷ τελοῦσι.
Παφλαγόνες δὲ καταδεῖσθαι καὶ καθείργνυσθαι χειμῶνος, ἦρος δὲ κινεῖσθαι καὶ ἀναλύεσθαι
φάσκουσι.   See my *Prolegomena*, p. 128.

[3] xv. 64

> πάντα γυναῖκες ἴσαντι, καὶ ὡς Ζεὺς ἀγάγεθ' Ἥραν.

The expression is clearly proverbial, and no doubt arose not from the secrecy of the
marriage, but—when the meaning of the cuckoo myth was forgotten—from its
strangeness.   It is one of the stories which Pausanias (II. 17. 5) says he (fortunately
for us) 'records but does not accept.'

and the scholiast on the passage, quoting, he says, from Aristotle's treatise on the sanctuary of Hermione, thus tells the tale:

Zeus planned to marry Hera and wishing to be invisible and not to be seen by her he changed his shape into that of a cuckoo and perched on a mountain, which, to begin with, was called Thronax, but now is called Cuckoo. And on that day *Zeus made a mighty storm.* Now Hera was walking alone and she came to the mountain and sat down on it, where now there is the sanctuary of Hera Teleia. And the cuckoo was frozen and shivering from the storm, so it flew down and settled on her knees. And Hera, seeing it, had pity and covered it with her cloak. And Zeus straightway changed his shape and caught hold of Hera....The image of Hera in the temple (at Argos) is seated on a throne, and she holds in her hand a sceptre, and on the sceptre is a cuckoo.

Pausanias confirms or perhaps quotes Aristotle. In one detail he corrects him. Aristotle mentions a statue of Full-grown or Married[1] (τελεία) Hera on the Cuckoo-Mountain, but Pausanias in describing the site says, 'there are two mountains, and on the top of each is a sanctuary, on Cuckoo-mountain is a sanctuary of Zeus and on the other mountain called Pron there is a sanctuary of Hera.' Be that as it may, behind the figure of Father Zeus we have the Bridegroom-Bird and the wedding that is a rain-storm[2].

Fig. 39 *a*.   Fig. 39 *b*.

The Bird-Lover lives on in a beautiful series of coin-types from Gortyna in Crete[3]. In the first of these (Fig. 39 *a*), we have a

---

[1] That the surname *Teleia,* 'complete,' practically means 'married' is certain from another passage in Pausanias (VIII. 22. 2). Temenos, the son of Pelasgos, he says, who dwelt in old Stymphalos, founded three sanctuaries in honour of the goddess and gave her three surnames: while she was yet a girl he called her *Child* (παῖς), *when she married Zeus* he called her *Teleia,* when she quarrelled with Zeus he called her Widow (χήρα).

[2] Cf. the wedding of Dido and Aeneas in the thunderstorm (Verg. Æn. IV. 160), where the background of the elemental wedding of earth and sky is manifest.

[3] Svoronos, *Numismatique de la Crète,* vol. I. XIII. 2219, XIV. 16 and 18, XV. 7. Mr Cook, to whom I owe my knowledge of these coins, favours M. Svoronos's explanation, that the nymph is Britomartis. The evidence scarcely seems to me sufficient; see *Zeus, Jupiter and the Oak,* Class. Rev. 1903, p. 405.

maiden seated disconsolate in a barren, leafless tree. In the second
(Fig. 39 b), the same maiden is seated, but the pose is less desolate;
she lifts her head and the tree is breaking out into leaf. In the
third (Fig. 40 a) a bird comes, perching timidly, the tree blossoms
and fruits. In the fourth (Fig. 40 b) the maiden is a bride, a

Fig. 40 a.   Fig. 40 b.

nymph; she raises her head with the gesture characteristic of Hera.
In the fifth (Fig. 41 a) the maiden cherishes the bird, as Hera, in
the myth, cherished the Bridegroom-Cuckoo in the rainstorm.
She is a royal bride with a sceptre, and on the sceptre is a bird.

Fig. 41 a.   Fig. 41 b.

In the sixth (Fig. 41 b) the bird is a royal bird, an eagle, and
with his great sanctity he overshadows both tree and maid. And,
delightful thing, amid all this beauty of bird and spring and maid
and tree, the old bull is not forgotten. His irrelevant head is
seen peering through the branches.

Fig. 42 a.   Fig. 42 b.

The seventh coin (Fig. 42 a) offers us a riddle as yet unread.
We have the nymph seated on the tree as usual, but between the

upper branches of the tree, and continuing down actually *on* the leftmost branch, is an inscription[1] in early Corinthian letters, TSMVPOS, Τισυροι. The word is in the nominative plural, not the ordinary genitive of place. Does 'Τισυροι' stand for 'Tityroi'? And does Tityroi stand for 'play of the Tityroi,' as *Satyroi* stands for 'play of the Satyrs'? Can the inscription refer to a δρώμενον, a Satyr-play of the return of spring, the blossoming of the tree, and the marriage of the maiden? On the reverse of all these coins the type is a bull (Fig. 42 *b*). Was the δρώμενον accompanied, as on the sarcophagos, by a bull-sacrifice?

In Athens, then, we have the uncouth δρώμενον of the Bouphonia with its mimic resurrection of the ox; in Crete, on the sarcophagos, we have the new life of spring represented and induced by a δρώμενον of obelisks leaf-covered, with thunder-axes and spring birds. Now the Bouphonia was celebrated, as has been seen, at the last full moon of the Attic year, in midsummer, when the land was parched. Its object was to induce dew; the Cretan δρώμενον was manifestly, like the sacrifice of the bull at Magnesia, celebrated in spring. This brings us straight to the question of seasonal festivals, and takes us back to the Hymn of the Kouretes.

In the refrain, it will be remembered (p. 8), the Kouros is bidden to come to Dikte 'for the Year' (ἐς ἐνιαυτόν), and, when the aetiological myth has been recounted, it is said 'the Horae began to be fruitful year by year,' ['Ὧραι δὲ βρ]ύον κατῆτος. Not only was the Kouros bidden to come for the Year, but if we may credit Aratus[2], the Kouretes of Dikte, when they deceived Kronos, hid Zeus in the cave and reared him *for the Year* (εἰς ἐνιαυτόν).

---

[1] The inscription was read as Τίσυροι by Dr von Sallet, who first published the coin in the Zeitschrift f. Numismatik, VI. p. 263. See also W. W. Wroth, *Cretan Coins* in Numismatic Chronicle, IV. 1884, p. 35. The suggestion that Τίσυροι may indicate a δρώμενον of *Tityroi* is due to Mr A. B. Cook. For Tityros as goat-daemon see Paul Baur, *Tityros* in American Journal of Archaeology, IX. 1905, Pl. v. p. 157. The goat-daemon here published holds a cornucopia.

[2] *Phaen.* 163, 164

ὅ μιν τότε κουρίζοντα,

Δίκτωι ἐν εὐώδει, ὄρεος σχεδὸν Ἰδαίοιο,
ἄντρωι ἐγκατέθεντο καὶ ἔτρεφον εἰς ἐνιαυτόν,
Δικταῖοι Κούρητες ὅτε Κρόνον ἐψεύδοντο.

For Δίκτωι should probably be read Λύκτωι. Diels, *Frg. d. Vors.* II. p. 497, attributes this legend to the *Kretika* of Epimenides.

The expression 'for the Year' is somewhat enigmatic. It should be carefully noted that the 'Year' for which the Kouros is 'summoned' and 'reared' is not an ἔτος but an ἐνιαυτός[1]. The two words are in Homer frequently juxtaposed[2], and the mere fact of the juxtaposition shows that they are distinguished. What then exactly is an ἐνιαυτός[3], how does it differ from an ἔτος, and why is the Kouros summoned for an ἐνιαυτός rather than an ἔτος?

The gist of the ἐνιαυτός as distinguished from the ἔτος comes out in the epithet τελεσφόρος 'end bringing,' which is frequently applied to ἐνιαυτός[4]. The ἔτος or year proper is conceived of as a circle or period that turns round[5]. This ἔτος varies, as will presently be seen, from a month to nine years or even longer. The ἐνιαυτός is not a whole circle or period but just the point at which the revolution is completed, the end of the old ἔτος[6], the beginning of the new. It is easy to see that this significant point might later be confused with the whole revolution[7].

[1] The distinction is marked in the translation (p. 9) by a capital letter, and throughout, whenever Year is a rendering of ἐνιαυτός.

[2] E.g. *Od.* XIV. 292

> ἔνθα παρ' αὐτῷ μεῖνα τελεσφόρον εἰς ἐνιαυτόν.
> ἀλλ' ὅτε δὴ μῆνές τε καὶ ἡμέραι ἐξετελεῦντο,
> ἂψ περιτελλομένου ἔτεος καὶ ἐπήλυθον ὧραι.

[3] The view of the ἐνιαυτός given here is entirely due to Dr Prellwitz, *Eine griechische Etymologie*, in Festschrift für Friedländer (1895), p. 382. Dr Prellwitz is concerned only with the etymology and literary interpretation of ἐνιαυτός and is of course in no way responsible for the conclusions I draw as to ritual.

[4] See *Od.* XIV. 240.

[5] The participle naturally associated with ἔτος as well as with ἐνιαυτός is περιτελλόμενος, of which the aorist, in *form* as well as in use, has been shown by Dr Prellwitz (*op. cit.*) to be περιπλόμενος. The word πόλος means axis, point round which you turn, and its root πολ, reduplicated and in guttural form, appears in κύκλος. The original *q*-sound appears in Greek before *e* as a dental, before a liquid followed by weak *o* as π.

[6] ἔτος is of course a cognate of the Latin *vetus* and means the completed revolution of the old year, cf. also ai *vatsa* 'year,' ksl *vĕtŭchŭ* 'old,' and Albanian *viet* 'year.' Though ἔτος has many cognates, ἐνιαυτός has none. All attempts to connect it with ἔτος fail because the *a* remains unexplained. This inclines us to accept Dr Prellwitz's derivation, which at first sight—perhaps because Plato makes an analogous guess—seems grotesque. Dr Prellwitz makes ἐνιαυτός a nominative formed from a prepositional clause ἐνι-αὐτῷ, originally ἐνί-αὖ τῷ 'at-again-the point.' This admirably suits the new meaning. Ἐνιαυτός on this showing is '*Here we are again*' incarnate.

[7] The scholiast on Ar. *Ran.* 347

> ἀποσείονται δὲ λύπας
> χρονίους [ἐτῶν] παλαιούς τ' ἐνιαυτούς

says: ζητεῖται πῶς εἶπεν ἐνιαυτοὺς ἐτῶν, ἐπεὶ ἔτος καὶ ἐνιαυτὸς ταὐτόν; but the Etymologicum Magnum carefully defines ἐνιαυτός thus: ἀπὸ τοῦ ἐν ἑαυτῷ ἰέναι· ἀπὸ γὰρ τοῦ κέντρου καὶ τοῦ ὁρίζοντος οὗ ἦν ὁ ἥλιος κατὰ τὸν Μάρτιον μῆνα, δι' ὅλου κινούμενος τοῦ χρόνου ἐν ἐκείνῳ πάλιν ἔρχεται ὡς καὶ ὁ Χριστὸς ἀπὸ τοῦ πατρός.

The ἐνιαυτός then was the cardinal turning-point of the year, it was ἔνη καὶ νέα in one. Such a day to ancient thinking must be marked out by *rites de passage*, for the issues were perilous. Such *rites de passage* are those of Closing and Opening, of Going to sleep and Waking up again, of Death and Resurrection, of killing or carrying out the Old Year and bringing in the New. To such rites it was natural, nay, it was necessary, to summon the Kouros.

We have now briefly to consider the ἔτος or period of revolution with its varying lengths and various seasons.

We think of the 'year' as a period of twelve months, beginning in January and ending in December, and we think of the *Horae* or Seasons as four in number—Spring, Summer, Autumn, Winter. Clearly the year for which the Kouros is bidden to come begins, not in Hecatombaion, at Midsummer, as at Athens, nor in midwinter as with us, but in the springtime. Our year with its four seasons is a sun-year, beginning about the winter solstice. It has four seasons because the four cardinal sun-periods are the two solstices, winter and summer, the two equinoxes, spring and autumn.

The important point about a year proper or ἔτος is that it is a recurrent period of a length that varies with man's particular methods of counting time. It is, in fact, a recurrence or cycle of times of special tension and interest, a calendar of festivals[1] connected mainly with man's food-supply. Broadly speaking, the distinction between a *cult* and a *rite* is that a rite is occasional, a cult is recurrent. Seasonal recurrence has been one great, if not the principal, factor in religious stability.

It is obvious that primitive man would not base his calendar on solstices and equinoxes which are only observed late; his year would be based not on astronomy, but on the seasons of his food-supply. Among the early inhabitants of Europe[2] there were two seasons only—winter and summer. The people being mainly pastoral, winter began in November with the driving home of

[1] Hubert et Mauss, *La Représentation du Temps dans la Religion et la Magie* in Mélanges d'Histoire des Religions, 1909, p. 189; see also the interesting chapter on 'Periodicity in Nature' in Dr Whitehead's *Introduction to Mathematics* in the Home University Library.
[2] E. K. Chambers, *Mediaeval Stage*, I. pp. 110 ff.

cattle from the pastures, and summer when they were driven up again to the hills somewhere about March. When and where agriculture is important, the year opens with the season of ploughing and sowing. The Greeks themselves had at first two, not three, Horae. In early days it is not realized that the Seasons, and with them the food-supply, depend on the Sun. The Seasons, the Horae, are potencies, divinities in themselves, and there are but two Seasons, the fruitful and the fruitless.

The year and the seasons derive then their value, as was natural, from the food they bring. They are not abstractions, divisions of time; they are the substance, the content of time. To make of ἐνιαυτός a god, or even a *daimon*, seems to us, even when he is seen to be not a year but a Year-Feast, a chilly abstraction, and even the Horae as goddesses seem a little remote. But to the Greeks, as we see abundantly on vase-paintings, their virtue, their very being, was in the flowers and fruits they always carry in their hands; they are indistinguishable from the Charites, the Gift- and Grace-Givers. The word *Hora*, it is interesting to note[1], seems at first to have been almost equivalent to Weather. In a drought the Athenians, Philochoros[2] tells us, sacrificed to the Horae, and on this occasion they boiled their meat and did not roast it, thereby inducing the goddesses to give increase to their crops by means of moderate warmth and seasonable rains. As warders of Olympos it is theirs to 'throw open the thick cloud or set it to[3].'

Athenaeus[4] has preserved for us a fragment of the fourth book of the *History of Alexandria* by Kallixenos the Rhodian. In it is described a great spectacle and procession exhibited by Ptolemy Philadelphos in honour of Dionysos[5]. One group in the procession is of interest to us. The procession was headed by Silenoi clad,

---

[1] O. Gruppe, *Gr. Myth.* II. 1063, note 3. Dr Gruppe compares the Latin *tempus*, *tempestas*, which again shows clearly the focus of the primitive mind on the *practical* side of times and seasons.

[2] *Ap.* Athen. XIV. 73 Ἀθηναῖοι δ', ὥς φησι Φιλόχορος, ταῖς Ὥραις θύοντες οὐκ ὀπτῶσιν, ἀλλ' ἕψουσι τὰ κρέα.

[3] Hom. *Il.* V. 751

ἠμὲν ἀνακλῖναι πυκινὸν νέφος ἠδ' ἐπιθεῖναι.

[4] V. 27. 198.

[5] As Macedonians all the Ptolemies were addicted to the worship of Dionysos. The ceremonies to which they were addicted probably enshrined and revived many primitive traits. See the interesting monograph by M. Paul Perdrizet, *Le Fragment de Satyros* in Rev. des Études Anciennes, 1910.

some in purple, some in scarlet, to keep off the multitude; next followed twenty Satyrs bearing lamps; next figures of Nike with golden wings; then Satyrs again, forty of them, ivy-crowned, their bodies painted, some purple, some vermilion. So far it is clear we have only the ministrants, the heralds of the god to come. After these heralds comes the first real *personage* of the procession, escorted by two attendants. His figure will not now surprise us.

After the Satyrs came two Sileni, the one with petasos and caduceus as herald, the other with trumpet to make proclamation. *And between them walked a man great of stature, four cubits tall, in the dress and mask of a tragic actor and carrying the gold horn of Amaltheia. His name was Eniautos.* A woman followed him, of great beauty and stature, decked out with much and goodly gold; in one of her hands she held a wreath of peach-blossom, in the other a palm-staff, and she was called Penteteris. She was followed by four Horai dressed in character and each carrying her own fruits.

The human Dionysos came later, but surely the procession is for the Year-Feast, εἰς Ἐνιαυτόν.

Eniautos held in his hands the horn of Amaltheia, the cornu-copia of the Year's fruits. He is his own content. Athenaeus[1] in his discussion of the various shapes and uses of cups, makes a statement that, but for this processional figure, would be some-what startling. 'There is a cup,' he says, 'called *The Horn of Amaltheia* and *Eniautos*.' The Horae too carry each her own fruits. This notion that the year is its own content, or rather perhaps we should say that the figure of the divine Year arises out of the food-content, haunted the Greek imagination. Plato[2], following the Herakleiteans, derives ἐνιαυτός from ἐν ἑαυτῷ, *he who has all things in himself*, and the doctrine was popular among Orphics. Kronos was identified with Chronos, Time, and hence with Eniautos; for Time, with the recurrent circling Seasons, has all things *in Himself*.

The Seasons, the Horae, in late Roman art are four in number. As such they are shown in the two medallions of Commodus[3] in Fig. 43. In the first (*a*) Earth herself reclines beneath her tree.

---

[1] xi. 25, p. 783.

[2] *Kratyl.* 410 D τὸ γὰρ τὰ φυόμενα καὶ τὰ γιγνόμενα προάγον εἰς φῶς καὶ αὐτὸ ἐν ἑαυτῷ ἐξετάζον...οἱ μὲν ἐνιαυτόν, ὅτι ἐν ἑαυτῷ κ.τ.λ. See Mr F. M. Cornford, *Hermes, Pan, Logos* in Classical Quarterly, iii. 1909, p. 282. For the connection of Kronos and Ἐνιαυτός see W. Schulz, Αὐτός in Memnon iv. 1910. The identity of Kronos with Chronos is as old as *Pherekydes*.

[3] *Cat. of Roman Medallions in British Museum*, Pl. xxx. 1 (a), 2 (b).

Under her hand is the globe of heaven studded with stars. Over
it in procession pass the four seasons. On the second medallion (*b*)
the four seasons are issuing from an arch. The figure of a boy
bearing a cornucopia comes to meet them. He is the Young Year
bearing the year's fruits. In late art four seasons are the rule,
but the notion of fourness had crept in as early as Alkman[1]. He,
it would seem, had not quite made up his mind whether they were
three or four.

> Three Seasons set he; summer is the first,
> And winter next, and then comes autumn third,
> And fourth is spring, when the trees blossom, but
> Man may not eat his fill.

Possibly in Alkman we have a mixture of two systems (1) two
parts of the year: χειμών and θέρος; (2) two or three *Horae* (Spring

Fig. 43 *a*.

Fig. 43 *b*.

and Summer (and Autumn)). The two-part system may have
belonged to the North, where winter is emphatic and important,
the two or three Horae may have been the fruitful seasons of the
indigenous southerners, where winter is but negative. Auxo,
Thallo and Karpo obviously do not cover the whole year. Winter
is no true Hora. Theognis[2] knew that

'*Love comes at his Hour*, comes with the flowers in spring.'

[1] *Frg.* Bergk 76

> Ὧρας δ' ἔσηκε τρεῖς, θέρος
> καὶ χεῖμα κὠπώραν τρίταν,
> καὶ τέτρατον τὸ ϝῆρ, ὄκα
> σάλλει μέν, ἐσθίεν δ' ἄδαν
> οὐκ ἔστιν.

[2] 1275 Ὡραῖος καὶ Ἔρως ἐπιτέλλεται. See my *Prolegomena*, p. 634. The blend
of the two systems in Alkman was suggested to me by Mr Cornford.

But when we come to early works of art where tradition rules, we find the Horae are steadfastly three.   On the archaic relief in Fig. 44[1], found on the Acropolis at Athens, they dance hand in hand to the sound of the pipe played by Hermes, and with them comes joyfully a smaller, human dancer.   This human figure has been usually explained as a worshipper, perhaps the dedicator of

Fig. 44.

the relief; but surely in the light of the medallion of Commodus a simpler and more significant explanation lies to hand.   He is the young *Eniautos*, the happy New Year.

The four Horae are sufficiently explained by the two solstices and the two equinoxes.   We have now to consider why in earlier days the Horae were three.

[1] From a photograph. For other interpretations see Lechat, *Bulletin de Corr. Hell.* 1889, XIII. pl. XIV. pp. 467—476; see also Lechat, *Au Musée de l'Acropole d'Athènes*, p. 443, and G. C. Richards, *J. H. S.* XI. 1890, p. 285.

In Athens, in the days of Porphyry, and it may be long before, the Horae and Helios had a procession together in which was carried the Eiresione, the branch decked with wool and hung with cakes and fruits.   By that time men knew that the Sun had power over the Seasons; but at first the Horae were linked with an earlier potency, and it is to this earlier potency that they owe their three-ness.   The three Horae are the three phases of the Moon, the Moon waxing, full and waning.   After the simple seasonal year with its two divisions came the Moon-Year with three, and last the Sun-Year with four Horae[1].

In the third *Æneid*, when Æneas and his men are weather-bound at Actium, they have as usual athletic contests to pass the time.   Vergil[2] says

Interea magnum sol circumvolvitur annum.

Scholars translate the passage 'meantime the sun rounds the great circle of the year'; but if we take the words literally it is the year that is qualified as great, and we are justified in supposing that if there is a *great* year there is also a small one, a *parvus annus*.   Such in fact there is, and so Servius in commenting understands the passage.   'He (i.e. Vergil) says *magnus* in addition lest we should think he means a lunar year.   For the ancients computed their times by the heavenly bodies, and *at first they called a period of* 30 *days a lunar year*.'   'Year,' *annus*, is of course only a ring, a revolution.   'Later,' Servius goes on, 'the year of the solstices was discovered, which contains twelve months.'

The great calendar crux of antiquity was the fitting together of this old Moon-Year with the new Sun-Year.   Into this problem and the various solutions of trieteric and pentaeteric 'years' we need not enter[3].   It is enough for our purpose to realize that the Moon is the true mother of the triple Horae, who are themselves Moirae, and the Moirae, as Orpheus[4] tells us, are but the three

---

[1] See *Abst.* II. 7 οἶς μαρτυρεῖν ἔοικεν καὶ ἡ Ἀθήνησιν ἔτι καὶ νῦν δρωμένη πομπὴ Ἡλίου τε καὶ Ὡρῶν.

[2] v. 284 Servius, *ad loc. Magnum,* ne putemus lunarem esse, propterea dixit : antiqui enim tempora sideribus computabant, et dixerunt primo lunarem annum triginta dierum...Postea solstitialis annus repertus est qui XII. continet menses.

[3] For further discussion of this interesting point see Mr F. M. Cornford in chapter VII.

[4] Clement of Alexandria in the *Stromata* quotes a book in which Epigenes noted a number of peculiarities (τὰ ἰδιάζοντα) of Orpheus, φησὶ...Μοίρας τε αὖ μέρη τῆς σελήνης τριακάδα καὶ πεντεκαιδεκάτην καὶ νουμηνίαν (Abel, *frg.* 253).

moirae or divisions (μέρη) of the Moon herself, the three divisions of the old Year. And these three Moirae or Horae are also Charites[1].

The cult of the Moon in Crete, in Minoan days, is a fact clearly established. On the lentoid gem[2] in Fig. 45 a worshipper approaches a sanctuary of the usual Mycenaean type, a walled enclosure within which grows an olive tree. Actually *within* the sanctuary is a large crescent moon. The conjunction of moon and olive tree takes us back to the Pandroseion (p. 170), itself in all

FIG. 45.

probability a moon-shrine, with its Dew-Service, its Hersephoria. Minoan mythology knows of the Moon-Queen, Pasiphaë, *She who shines for all*, mother of the holy, horned Bull-Child.

With respect to the Pandroseion it may be felt that, though we have the Dew-Service at the full moon in the shrine of the

[1] *Hymn. Magic.* v. Πρὸς Σελήνην, 6
ἢ Χαρίτων τρισσῶν τρίσσαις μορφαῖσι χορεύεις,
and cf. the triple Charites who dance round Hekate the Moon. See my *Myth. and Mon. Ancient Athens*, p. 378, Figs. 15 and 16.
[2] A. Evans, *Tree and Pillar Cult*, 1901, p. 185, Fig. 59. This lentoid gem does not stand alone. The same scene, a Mycenean shrine with tree and crescent moon, before it a female worshipper, appears on a steatite gem found at Ligortyno in Crete. See René Dussaud, *Les Civilisations préhelléniques*, p. 273, Fig. 196.

All-dewy-One, we have no direct evidence of a moon-cult[1] in the Erechtheion, no Athenian gem with a crescent moon, shining in a sanctuary. This is true, but the coinage of Athens reminds us that the olive is clearly associated with the moon. On the reverse of an Athenian tetradrachm in Fig. 46 is the owl of Athena, the owl she once was, and in the field is not only an olive spray, but a crescent moon. Athena and the moon shared a name in common—*Glaukopis*[2]. The ancient statues of Athena's 'maidens' carry moon-haloes (μηνίσκοι)[3]. She herself on her shield carries for blazon the full moon[4].

FIG. 46.

Yet another shrine not far from Crete, of early sanctity, with holy olive tree and moon-goddess, cannot in this connection be forgotten.

> Give me the little hill above the sea,
> The palm of Delos fringèd delicately,
> The young sweet laurel and the olive tree,
>   Grey-leaved and glimmering[5].

Here we have a succession of holy trees brought one by one by successive advances in civilization, but over them watched always one goddess, though she had many names, Artemis, Oupis, Hekaerge, Loxo. Behind her humanized figure shines the old moon-goddess,

> Oupis the Queen, fair-faced, the Light-Bearer[6].

[1] In the *Clouds* of Aristophanes (610) the Moon complains bitterly of the neglect into which she has fallen, δεῖνα γὰρ πεπονθέναι.

[2] Eur. *frg.* (Nauck 997)

γλαυκῶπίς τε στρέφεται μήνη.

In the old days the Acropolis of Athens was called the *Glaukopion*. E. Maass, *Der alte Name der Akropolis* in Jahrb. d. Inst. 1907, p. 143.

[3] Ar. *Av.* 1114, and schol. *ad loc.*, but see H. Lechat, *Au Musée de l'Acropole d'Athènes*, 1903, p. 215, Le 'Meniscos.'

[4] On a vase, see *Mon. d. Inst.*, XXII. 6ª.

[5] Eur. *Iph. in T.* 1098, trans. Prof. Murray.

[6] Callim. *Hymn. ad Dianam*, 204

Οὖπι ἄνασσ' εὐῶπι, φαεσφόρε.

When the Delians, fearing the Persian onset, fled to Tenos, Datis, the Persian general, would not so much as anchor off the holy island, but sent a herald to bid the Delians return and fear nothing, for 'in the island where were born the two gods no harm should be done[1].' The Persians saw in Artemis and Apollo, though the Greeks had in part forgotten it, the ancient divinities they themselves worshipped, the Moon and the Sun[2].

That the moon was worshipped in Crete in her triple phases is at least probable. Minos, Apollodorus[3] tells us, sacrificed in Paros to the Charites, and the Charites are in function indistinguishable from the Horae. Like the Horae they are at first

Fig. 47.

two, then three[4]. In Athens two Charites were worshipped under the names Auxo (Increaser) and Hegemone (Leader), and these were invoked, Pausanias says, together with the Horae of Athens, Thallo (Sprouting) and Karpo (Fruit), and the Dew-Goddess, Pandrosos. Among many primitive peoples the waxing and waning of the moon is supposed to bring increase and decrease to all living things. Only the lawless onion sprouts in the wane and withers in the waxing of the moon[5].

[1] Herod. vi. 97.   [2] Herod. i. 131.   [3] 3. 15. 7.
[4] For the whole question of the double and triple Charites at Athens and elsewhere, and for their connection with the Horae, see my *Myth. and Mon. of Ancient Athens*, 1890, p. 382, and my *Prolegomena*, p. 286, The Maiden Trinities. I did not then see that the triple form had any relation to the Moon.
[5] Aulus Gellius, xx. 8. See Frazer, *Adonis Attis Osiris*[2], 1907, p. 362.

The Charites at Orchomenos[1] were unhewn stones which had
fallen from heaven. Small wonder, if they were phases of the
moon. On the Phoenician stelae in Fig. 48[2] we see the moon
figured as three pillars, a taller between two shorter ones,
indicating no doubt the waxing, full and waning moon. The cult
of the triple pillars is familiar in Crete. In Fig. 48[3] we have the
well-known triple columns surmounted by the life-spirit, the dove.
It is probable, though by no means certain, that we have in them
primitive pillar-forms of the Charites.

FIG. 48.

The Kouretes, we have noted (p. 182), according to Cretan
tradition nourished the infant Zeus 'for the year.' The Kouretes
bid the Kouros leap 'for the year.' Did they ever leap and dance
for the old Moon-Year? When we remember the Moon-cult of
Crete, it seems probable; we have, however, no definite evidence.
But, when we come to the Roman brothers of the Kouretes, the
Leapers or Salii, we can speak with certainty. It often happens
that Roman ritual and Roman mythology, from its more conservative and less imaginative character, makes clear what the
poetry of the Greeks obscures. The Salii will help us to understand more intimately the nature of the Kouretes, and may even
throw light on the nature and name of the Dithyramb. They must
therefore be considered at this point in some detail.

[1] Paus. IX. 35. 1.
[2] *Monimenti Ant. dei Lincei*, XIV. 1905; Taf. XXI. 2ª and XXV. 2.
[3] A. Evans, *B.S.A.* VIII. 1901–2, p. 29, Fig. 14. I owe the suggestion that in
these triple pillars we may have the Cretan Charites worshipped by Minos to
Mr Cook's kindness.

THE SALII.

Denys of Halicarnassos[1] in his full and interesting account of the Salii saw that Kouretes and Salii were substantially the same: 'In my opinion,' he says, 'the Salii are what in the Greek language are called Kouretes. We (i.e. the Greeks) give them their name from their age, from the word κοῦροι, the Romans from their strenuous movements, for jumping and leaping is called by the Romans *salire*.' Denys exactly hits the mark: the term *Kouretes* expresses the essential fact common to Salii, Korybantes, etc., that all are youths; the various special names, the meanings of some of which are lost, emphasize particular functions.

Fig. 49.

Denys[2] describes in detail the accoutrement of the Salii, which reminds us rather of priest than warrior. He notes the purple chitons and bronze girdles, the short cloaks and the conical caps[3] (apices) called, he says, by the Greeks κυρβασίαι, a name with which very possibly the word Kurbas, a by-form of Korybas, was connected. One point in his description is of special interest:

---

[1] *Ant. Rom.* II. 70, 71 καὶ εἰσὶν οἱ Σάλιοι κατὰ γοῦν τὴν ἐμὴν γνώμην Ἑλληνικῷ μεθερμηνευθέντες ὀνόματι Κουρῆτες, ὑφ' ἡμῶν μὲν ἐπὶ τῆς ἡλικίας οὕτως ὠνομασμένοι παρὰ τοὺς κούρους, ὑπὸ δὲ Ῥωμαίων ἐπὶ τῆς συντόνου κινήσεως. τὸ γὰρ ἐξάλλεσθαί τε καὶ πηδᾶν σαλίρε ὑπ' αὐτῶν λέγεται.

[2] *Loc. cit.* καὶ τὰς καλουμένας ἀπίκας ἐπικείμενοι ταῖς κεφαλαῖς, πίλους ὑψηλοὺς εἰς σχῆμα συναγομένους κωνοειδές, ἃς Ἕλληνες προσαγορεύουσι κυρβασίας.

[3] Among savages a conical cap of striking appearance is a frequent element in the disguise of the initiator or medicine-man. See Schurtz, *Altersklassen und Mannerbünde*, 1902, pp. 336, 370, 384, and L. v. Schroeder, *Mimus und Mysterium*, p. 476, and Codrington, *The Melanesians*, p. 78.

each man, he says, is girt with a sword, and in his right hand wields 'a spear or a staff or something of that sort[1],' in his left is a Thracian shield.   We think of the Salii as clashing their swords on their shields, but the Salii seen by Denys seem to have had some implement as to the exact nature of which Denys is uncertain.

The design in Fig. 49 from a relief found at Anagni[2] may throw some light on this uncertainty.   The Salii are shown in long priestly robes with shields in their left hands.   In their right is not, as we should expect, a spear or a sword, but an unmistakable drumstick.   Some such implements Denys must have seen.   It looks back to the old days when the shield was not of metal but of skin.   Euripides[3], speaking of Crete, says that there the triple-crested Korybantes found for Dionysos and his Bacchants their 'skin-stretched orb.'   In a word timbrel and shield were one and the same, a skin stretched on a circular or oval frame and played on with a drumstick; the gear of Salii and Korybantes alike was, to begin with, musical as well as military.

The helmets worn by the Salii on the relief may also be noted. They are not of the form we should expect as representing the canonical *apex*.   They have three projections, and in this respect recall the 'triple-crested' Korybants of Euripides.   Possibly the central knob may have been originally of greater length and prominence and may have given its name to the apex.   The shields carried on the Anagni relief are slightly oblong but not indented.

---

[1] *Loc. cit.* παρέζωσται δ' ἕκαστος αὐτῶν ξίφος καὶ τῇ μὲν δεξιᾷ χειρὶ λόγχην ἢ ῥάβδον ἤ τι τοιοῦθ' ἕτερον κρατεῖ, τῇ δ' εὐωνύμῳ κατέχει πέλτην Θρᾳκίαν.

[2] *Annali d. Inst.* 1869, Tav. d' agg. E.   Benndorf, who publishes the relief, does not say where it now is.   That the relief should have been found at Anagni (the ancient Anagnia) is a fact of singular interest.   Marcus Aurelius, in going through Anagnia on his way to his Signian villa writes thus to Fronto (*Frontonis et Aurelii Epistulae*, Naber 1867, pp. 66, 67):

Priusquam ad villam venimus Anagniam devertimus mille fere passus a via. Deinde id oppidum anticum vidimus, minutulum quidem sed multas res in se antiquas habet, aedes sanctasque caerimonias supra modum.   Nullus angulus fuit, ubi delubrum aut fanum aut templum non sit.   Praeterea multi libri linitei, quod ad sacra adtinet.   Deinde in porta cum eximus ibi scriptum erat bifariam sic: flamen sume samentum.   Rogavi aliquem ex popularibus quid illum verbum esset? Ait lingua hernica pelliculam de hostia quam in apicem suum flamen cum in urbem introeat inponit.

I owe this interesting reference to the kindness of Mr Spenser Farquharson.

[3] *Bacch.* 123

ἔνθα τρικόρυθες ἄντροις
βυρσότονον κύκλωμα τόδε
μοι Κορύβαντες ηὗρον.

The regular indented 'Mycenaean' shape is well seen on an Etruscan gem in the Museum at Florence[1].

The first month of the old Roman year, March, the month of Mars, was given up to the activities of the Salii. We have no evidence that they took any part in initiation ceremonies, but it is worth noting that it was in the month of March (17th) at the Liberalia, that, according to Ovid[2], the Roman boy assumed the toga. This assumption qualified him for military service and may have been the last survival of a tribal initiation-ceremony. On the first day of the year, the birthday of Mars, it was fabled, the original ancile fell from heaven[3], and through the greater part of the month the holy shields were kept 'moving.' Of the various and complex ceremonials conducted by the Salii we need only examine two[4] which throw light, I think, on the Palaikastro hymn :—

    (a) the Mamuralia (March 14).

    (b) the festival of Anna Perenna (March 15).

Both have substantially the same content.

    (a) Ovid[5] asks

> Quis mihi nunc dicat, quare caelestia Martis
> Arma ferant Salii, Mamuriumque canant?

The question has been long ago answered by Mannhardt, Usener, and Dr Frazer[6]. Ovid will have it that Mamurius is

---

[1] See Ridgeway, *Early Age of Greece*, p. 455, Fig. 83. Denys states that the shield carried on the left arm was a Thracian *pelta*. Prof. Ridgeway concludes (*op. cit.* p. 465) that it was the shield of the true Thracians, the kindred of the Mycenaean people, and that it survived in the rites of the Kouretes. According to Clement (*Strom.* I. 16 *sub init.*) the *pelta* was invented by the Illyrians, who, if Prof. Ridgeway is right, belong to the primitive Aegean stock. A curious double *ancile* appears on a denarius of P. Licinius Stolo, figured by Mr W. Warde Fowler, *Roman Festivals*, p. 350. On the same coin the *apex* is very clearly shown.

[2] Ovid, *Fasti*, III. 771
> Restat ut inveniam quare toga libera detur
> Lucifero pueris, candide Bacche, tuo.

We should like of course to have definite evidence that rites of tribal initiation were practised among the Greeks and Romans *in the spring*, but such evidence is not forthcoming. As regards the Mithraic mysteries we are better informed. F. Cumont, *Monuments figurés relatifs aux mystères de Mithras*, I. p. 336, writes: 'Les initiations avaient lieu de préférence vers le début du printemps en mars et en avril.'

[3] Ovid, *Fasti*, III. 259—273.

[4] The sources for both festivals are fully given in Roscher's *Lexicon*, s.v. *Mars*, and in Mr Warde Fowler's *Roman Festivals*, pp. 44—54.

[5] *Fasti*, III. 259.

[6] Mannhardt, *Baumkultus*, 266, 297; Usener, *Italische Mythen* in Rhein. Mus. 1875, p. 183; Frazer, *Golden Bough*[2], vol. III. pp. 122 ff.

commemorated because he was the skilful smith who made the eleven counterfeit ancilia, but Lydus[1] lets out the truth. On March 14, the day before the first full moon of the new year, a man dressed in goat-skins was led in procession through the streets of Rome, beaten with long white rods, and driven out of the city. His name was, Lydus says, Mamurius, and Mamurius we know was also called Veturius[2]. He is the old Year, the Old Mars, the Death, Winter, driven out before the incoming of the New Mars, the spring[3].

(b) Not less transparent as a year-god is Anna Perenna, 'year-in year-out.' The details of her festival have no special significance. Ovid[4] describes it as a rude drinking bout of the plebs; men and women revelled together, some in the open Campus Martius, others in rough huts made of stakes and branches; they sang and danced and prayed for as many years of life as they could drink cups of wine. It was just an ordinary New Year's festival. Lydus[5] gives us the gist of it, though he does not mention Anna Perenna. On the Ides of March he says there were public prayers that the coming year might be healthy. The name Anna Perenna speaks for itself. Obviously Anna is the year, presumably the New Year. *Perenna*[6], *Peranna* is the year just passed through, the Old Year— *perannare* is 'to live the year through.' Anna Perenna was not two divinities, but as it were a Janus with two faces, one looking back, one forward, Prorsa, Postverta. This comes out very clearly in a story told by Ovid[7], a story that may reflect a bit of rustic ritual. Mars is about to marry; the wedding-day is come, he seeks his bride. Instead he finds old Anna (Anna Perenna) who has veiled her face and counterfeits the bride[8]. The young Year-god will wed

---

[1] *De Mens.* IV. 49 ἤγετο δὲ καὶ ἄνθρωπος περιβεβλημένος δοραῖς, καὶ τοῦτον ἔπαιον ῥάβδοις λεπταῖς ἐπιμήκεσι Μαμούριον αὐτὸν καλοῦντες.

[2] The reduplicated form Marmar occurs in the *Carmen Arvale* and from it Mamurius is probably formed, see Wald, *Lat. Etym. Wörterbuch*, s.v. For Veturius as the old year cf. Gk. ϝέτος.

[3] Roscher, *Lexicon*, s.v. *Mars*, pp. 23—99.

[4] *Fasti*, III. 523 ff.

[5] *De Mens.* IV. 49 καὶ εὐχαὶ δημόσιαι ὑπὲρ τοῦ ὑγιεινὸν γενέσθαι τὸν ἐνιαυτόν.

[6] Varro, *Sat. Menipp.* p. 506 te Anna ac Peranna, and Macrob. I. 12. 6 publice et privatim ad Annam Perennam sacrificatum itur ut annare et perannare commode liceat.

[7] *Fasti*, III. 695. Ovid recounts the story as aetiological,
Inde ioci veteres obscenaque dicta canuntur.

[8] For the whole subject of May Brides and the False Bride see Miss G. M. Godden, *Folk-Lore*, IV. 1893, pp. 142 ff.

the young Year-goddess, Anna; the old Year-goddess he cannot and will not wed. Anna Perenna is the feminine equivalent of Mamurius Veturius.

Ovid[1] piles up conjectures as to who and what Anna was. Out of his rubbish heap we may pick up one priceless jewel.

> Sunt quibus haec Luna est, quia mensibus impleat annum:
>   Pars Themin, Inachiam pars putat esse bovem.

Luna, Themis (order), and the Inachian cow are of course all one and the same, the Moon as the Measurer and as the Hornèd Wanderer through the sky. Man measures time, we have seen,

Fig. 50.

first by recurrent days and nights, then by recurrent Moons, then by the circle of the Sun's year and its seasons; finally he tries to adjust his Sun Year to twelve Moon-months[2]. The original *ancile* or moon-shield fell from heaven into the palace of Numa; that was the one sacred month in the spring in which so many ancient festivals were concentrated. When the solar year came in, eleven Moon-shields are made by the smith Mamurius to counterfeit the

---

[1] Ovid, *Fasti*, III. 657.
[2] The development among primitive peoples from weather gods (e.g. thunder) to moon and sun gods, a sequence which appears to be regular, is well explained by E. J. Payne, *History of the New World called America*, vol. I. pp. 491 ff., and see *infra*, chapter IX.

one actual Moon-month. Broadly speaking, Anna, though she
cannot be said to *be* the Moon, stands for the Moon-Year, Mamurius
for the Sun-Year, and Anna is the earlier figure of the two.

This idea of Anna and Mamurius as Moon-Year and Sun-Year
throws light on a curious Etruscan monument that has hitherto
baffled explanation. In Fig. 50 we have a portion of the design
from a Praenestine cista[1] now in the Berlin Museum. *Menerva*
holds a young boy over a vessel full of flaming fire; she seems to
be anointing his lips. The boy is armed with spear and shield,
and his name is inscribed *Mars*: the scene is one of triumph, for
over *Menerva* floats a small winged Victory holding a taenia. The
scene is one of great solemnity and significance, for on the
rest of the design, not figured here, we have an influential assembly
of gods, *Juno, Jovos, Mercuris, Hercle, Apolo, Leiber.*

Mars is, of course, the new *fighting-season* which opens in
spring, as well as the new agricultural season. But if Mars were
only the War-God, what sense is there in this baptism of fire?
For the young Sun what could be more significant? At the
Sun-festivals of the solstice[2] to-day, to feed the sun and kindle
him anew and speed his going, the *Johannisfeuer* is lighted year
by year and the blazing wheel rolled down the hill.

The band of honeysuckle ornament that runs round the cista
is oddly broken: just at the point above the young Sun-god's head
is the figure of the triple Cerberus. A strange apparition; but he
ceases to be irrelevant when we remember that Hecate the Moon,
to whom dogs were offered[3] at the crossways, was once a three-
headed dog herself.

From the Salii we have learnt that the function of the armed
dancers of Rome was to drive out the Old Year, the Old Mars,
and bring in the New. Mars as a Year-God, like the Greek Ares,
and indeed like almost every other male God, took on aspects
of the Sun, Anna Perenna of the Moon. Can we trace in the
Kouretes any like function?

---

[1] *Mon. dell' Inst.* ix. Tav. 58. See Marx, *Ein neuer Ares Mythus*, A.Z. xliii.
1885, p. 169.

[2] H. Gaidoz, *Le Dieu Gaulois du Soleil et le Symbolisme de la Roue*, Rev. Arch.
1884, 32 ff.

[3] Maurice Blomfield, *Cerberus the Dog of Hades*, 1905. Cerberus, çabalas, the
heavenly dog of the Veda, was later translated to Hades. Cf. the fate of Ixion. For
Hekate as dog cf. Porph. *de Abstin.* iii. 17 ἡ δ' Ἑκάτη ταῦρος, κύων, λέαινα.

The design in Fig. 51[1] is from a red-figured krater in the Louvre: Helios is rising from the sea. By an odd conjunction he has, to bear him on his way, both boat and quadriga. His horses are guided by Pan holding a quadruple torch. To the right hand stands a dancing Korybant or Koures, with shield and uplifted sword. In the chariot with Helios, stands the horned Selene: clearly the vase-painter recognised that one function of the Koures was to clash his shield at the rising of the Sun, and, it would seem, at the marriage of the Sun and Moon.

The Moon was married to the Sun[2] and in patriarchal fashion sank into wifely subjection. As soon as it was understood that

FIG. 51.

the Sun was the source of the Seasons, the Food-bringers, and that increase came from his light and heat, not from the waxing and waning of the Moon, he rose to complete and permanent supremacy. In the vase-painting[3] in Fig. 52 we see the Sun figured as greatest Kouros; the laurel spray reminds us that Helios is Apollo in the making. His uprising is greeted by a dance of Satyrs, those *daimones* of fertility who were, as Strabo[4] reminds us, own brothers to the Kouretes.

---

[1] *Annali d. Inst.* 1852, Pl. F. 3. Nonnus also makes the Korybantes dance at Knossos at dawn, *Dionysiaka*, 361

ἤδη δ' ἔκλαγεν ὄρνις ἑῷος ἠέρα τέμνων,
καὶ στίχες εὐπήληκες ἐρημονόμων Κορυβάντων
Κνώσσιον ἐκρούσαντο σακέσπαλον ἄλμα χορείης
ἴχνεσι μετρητοῖσιν.

[2] The marriage of Sun and Moon and its religious content in relation to the Eniautos will be discussed in the next chapter, p. 227.

[3] E. Gerhard *Ueber die Lichtgottheiten auf Kunstdenkmälern* 1840. The vase, a krater, is now in the Louvre Museum.

[4] *Supra*, p. 25.

The custom of greeting the rising sun with dances and the clash of instruments is world-wide. Lucian[1] says that the Indians, when they rise at dawn, worship Helios, and he adds that they do not, like the Greeks, account their devotion complete when they have kissed their hands, but they stand facing the east and greet Helios by dancing, assuming certain attitudes in silence and imitating the dance of the god. The intent is obviously magical; man dances to reinforce his own emotion and activity; so does the sun; and man's dance has power to reinforce the strength of the rising sun. In Germany, Scandinavia, and England the belief is still current that on Easter Morning the sun dances and leaps three times for joy[2]. The Dawn with the Greeks had her dancing places[3]. In the light of such representations it is not

Fig. 52.

surprising that the Korybantes should be called the children of Helios[4], and we understand why Julian[5] says 'Great Helios who is enthroned with the Mother is Korybas,' and again, 'the Mother of the gods allowed this minion of hers to leap about, that he might resemble the sunbeams.' Rites often die down into children's

---

[1] *De Salt.* 17 ...ἀλλ' ἐκεῖνοι πρὸς τὴν ἀνατολὴν στάντες ὀρχήσει τὸν Ἥλιον ἀσπάζονται σχηματίζοντες ἑαυτοὺς σιωπῇ καὶ μιμούμενοι τὴν χορείαν τοῦ θεοῦ.

[2] See L. v. Schroeder, *Mimus und Mysterium*, p. 45, and Usener, *Pasparios* in Rhein. Mus. 1894, p. 464.

[3] *Od.* XII. 4
ὅθι τ' Ἠοῦς ἠριγενείης
οἰκία καὶ χοροί εἰσι καὶ ἀντολαὶ Ἠελίοιο.

[4] Strabo, 202 ...ὡς εἶεν Κορύβαντες δαίμονές τινες Ἀθηνᾶς καὶ Ἡλίου παῖδες.

[5] *Or.* v. 167 Κορύβας ὁ μέγας ἥλιος ὁ σύνθρονος τῇ Μητρί, and 168.

games, and Pollux[1] tells us that there was a game called 'Shine out, Sun,' in which children made a din when a cloud covered the sun.

With the Salii in our minds leaping in March, the first month of the New Year, with the Kouretes clashing their shields and dancing over the child they had reared to be a Kouros for the Year-Feast (εἰς ἐνιαυτόν), we come back to a clearer understanding of the Dithyramb; we may even hazard a conjecture as to the etymology of the word. But first, one point remains to be established. The Dithyramb, like the Hymn of the Kouretes, is not only a song of human rebirth, it is the song of the rebirth of all nature, all living things[2]; it is a Spring Song 'for the Year-Feast[3].'

This is definitely stated in the dithyrambic Paean[4] to Dionysos

---

[1] IX. 123 Ἡ δὲ ἔξεχ' ὦ φίλ' ἤλιε παιδιά, κρότον ἔχει τῶν παιδίων σὺν τῷ ἐπιβοή- ματι τούτῳ, ὁπόταν νέφος ἐπιδράμῃ τὸν θεόν· ὅθεν καὶ Στράττις ἐν Φοινίσσαις,

εἶθ' ἥλιος μὲν πείθεται τοῖς παιδίοις,
ὅταν λέγωσιν, ἔξεχ', ὦ φίλ' ἤλιε.

[2] It is curious how this notion, that on the resurrection or Epiphany of a god depends the fertility of the year, lasts on in the mind of the peasant to-day. Mr Lawson in his interesting book on *Modern Greek Folklore* (p. 573) tells us that a stranger, happening to be in a village in Euboea during Holy Week, noticed the general depression of the villagers. On Easter Eve he asked an old woman why she was so gloomy, and she at once answered, 'Of course I am anxious, for *if Christ does not rise to-morrow, we shall have no corn this year.*' Her words come to us with a shock as of profanity, but a worshipper of the μέγιστος Κοῦρος would have felt them to be deeply, integrally religious.

[3] It is worth noting that even now to the farmer a good *year* means a good *harvest*; Time's content is set for a period of time, with which may be compared the popular use of the German *Jahr*. Either spring or autumn as season of fruits often stands for the whole year; thus in the *Lex Bajuvariorum* dates are reckoned by *autumni*. Our word 'year' is etymologically the same as the Greek ὥρα the spring. Much interesting material on this question is collected by Schrader *Reallexicon* s.v. 'Jahr und Jahreszeiten.'

[4] H. Weil, *Bull. de Corr. Hell.* XIX. p. 401. Dr Weil reads

[Δεῦρ' ἄνα Διθ]ύραμβε, Βάκχ',
ε[ὔιε θυρσῆ]ρες, Βραΐ-
τά, Βρόμι(ε), ἠρινα[ῖς ἱκοῦ
ταῖσδ(ε) ἱεραῖς ἐν ὥραις.
Εὐοῖ ὦ ἰὸ [Βάκχ' ὦ ἱὲ Παιὰ]ν
[ὃ]ν Θήβαις ποτ' ἐν εὐίαις
Ζη[νὶ γείνατο] καλλίπαις Θυώνα.
πάντες δ' [ἀστέρες ἀγχ]όρευ-
σαν πάντες δὲ βροτοὶ χ[αρή-
σαν σαῖς] Βάκχιε γένναις.

In my *Prolegomena* pp. 417 and 439 I followed Dr Weil, but Dr Vollgraff (*Mnemosyne*, 905, p. 379) has shown that in the second line ΒΡΑΙΤΑ has been misread for ΧΑΙΤΑ; he proposes to restore ε[ὔιε, ταῦρε κισσο]χαί-, but as the reading is problematical—though I should welcome 'ταῦρε'—I leave the 3rd line un-translated.

recently discovered at Delphi.   Like the Hymn of the Kouretes it
is an Invocation Hymn.   It opens thus:

> *Come, O Dithyrambos, Bacchos, come*
> *   *   *   *   *   *
> Bromios come, and coming with thee bring
> Holy hours of thine own holy spring.
> *Evoë, Bacchus hail, Paean hail,*
> Whom, in sacred Thebes, the Mother fair
> She, Thyone, once to Zeus did bear.
> All the stars danced for joy.   Mirth
> Of mortals hailed thee, Bacchos, at thy birth.

The new-born god is Dithyrambos, born at the resurrection of
earth in the springtime.

The Delphic Paean is later in sentiment than the Hymn of
the Kouretes.   We have the old matriarchal divine pair, the
Mother and the Child, but Thyone the mother is married to Zeus.
Next and most beautiful of the Spring Dithyrambs left us is
Pindar's fragment, written to be sung at Athens, in the agora in
or near to the most ancient sanctuary of Dionysos-in-the-Marshes
and like the Delphic Paean it celebrates, as though they were
one and the same, the coming of spring, the birth of the child
Bromios.

> Look upon the dance, Olympians, send us the grace of Victory, ye gods,
> who come to the heart of our city where many feet are treading and incense
> steams : in sacred Athens come to the Market-place, by every art enriched
> and of blessèd name.   Take your portion of garlands pansy-twined, libations
> poured from the culling of spring, and look upon me as, starting from Zeus,
> I set forth upon my song with rejoicing.
> Come hither to the god with ivy bound ; Bromios we mortals name Him
> and Him of the mighty Voice.   I come to dance and sing, the child of a father
> most high and a woman of Cadmus' race.   The clear signs of his Fulfilment
> are not hidden, whensoever the chamber of the purple-robed Hours is opened
> and nectarous flowers lead in the fragrant Spring.   Then, then, are flung over
> the immortal Earth lovely petals of pansies, and roses are amid our hair ; and
> voices of song are loud among the pipes, the dancing-floors are loud with the
> calling of crownèd Semele[1].

To resume: the Dithyramb, we have seen, is a Birth-Song, a
δρώμενον giving rise to the divine figures of Mother, Full-grown
Son and Child; it is a spring-song of magical fertility for the
new year; it is a group-song, a κύκλιος χόρος, later sung by a
thiasos, a song of those who leap and dance rhythmically
together.

---

[1] Pindar, Dithyramb 75.   The 'calling of crownèd Semele' will be further discussed in chapter IX.

The word *Dithyramb* now speaks for itself. The first syllable
Διˉ for Διˉ is from the root that gives us Ζεύς and Διός. The
termination αμβος is probably the same as that in ἴαμβος,
σήραμβος. We are left with the syllable θυρ, which has always
been the crux. But the difficulty disappears if we remember
that, as Hoffmann has pointed out, the northern peoples of Greece
tend, under certain conditions, to substitute ῠ for ŏ, which gives
us for Διˉ-θῠρ-αμβος Διˉ-θορ-αμβος—Zeus-leap-song, the song
that makes Zeus leap or beget[1]. Our Hymn of the Kouretes
is *the Di-thor-amb*[2].

We seem to have left the Bull far behind, for the Delphic
Paean and Pindar's Dithyramb and even our *Hymn of the
Kouretes* know nothing of the bull-sacrifice; they tell only of the
human child, not the theriomorph. Only on the sarcophagos do
we get the bull-sacrifice and the Spring δρώμενον together. But
Pindar knew that the Dithyramb was the song of the Bull as well
as of the Child and the Spring. In the XIIIth Olympian[3] he is
chanting the praises of Corinth, home of the Dithyramb, Corinth,
the home of splendid youths (ἀγλαόκουρον), Corinth, where dwelt
as in ancient Crete, the Horae, Eunomia and Dike and Eirene,
givers of Wealth, golden daughters of Themis. These golden
Horae had brought to Corinth from of old subtleties of invention;
for 'whence,' asks Pindar, in words that are all but untranslatable,

'Whence did appear the Charites of Dionysos
With the Bull-driving Dithyramb?'

[1] I owe this brilliant suggestion to Mr A. B. Cook and publish it by his kind
permission. Previous attempted derivations will be found in Pauly-Wissowa, s. v.
Dithyramb. To these may be added the recent *Studies in Greek Noun-Formation*
by E. H. Sturtevant in Classical Philology, Chicago, 1910, v. p. 329. For the
interchange of ῠ and ŏ see Hoffmann, *Die Makedonen*, p. 242.

[2] Mr Cook also kindly draws my attention to a gloss of Hesychius which presents a
very instructive parallel: Δειπάτυρος· Θεὸς παρὰ [Σ]τυμφαίοις. This important note
preserves the name of 'Zeus the Father' as used in the district of Mt Stymphe, not
far from Dodona on the frontier of Epirus, Macedonia and Thessaly. It furnishes
a precise parallel both for the compound Διˉ and for the weakening of ŏ into ῠ, in
short for both the disputable elements in Διθύραμβος. Moreover—a still more
interesting point—the meaning as well as the form is parallel: Zeus the Father,
Zeus the begetter, cf. Æsch. *Eum.* 663 τίκτει δ' ὁ θρῴσκων. As initiated Kouros the
young god has come to maturity of his functions.

[3] *v.* 16   πολλὰ δ' ἐν καρδίαις ἀνδρῶν ἔβαλον
Ὧραι πολυάνθεμοι ἀρ-
χαιˉ σοφίσματα· πᾶν δ' εὑρόντος ἔργον.
ταὶ Διωνύσου πόθεν ἐξέφανεν
σὺν βοηλάτᾳ Χάριτες διθυράμβῳ;

Why is the Dithyramb Bull-driving? Why does the Bull-driving Dithyramb come with the Charites?

Pindar no doubt was thinking of the new Graces of tragedy; but behind them come the figures of the older Charites, the Givers of all Increase, the Horae who bring back the god in the Spring, be he Bull or human Kouros. In our oldest Dithyramb they bring him as a Bull.

In his XXXVIth Greek Question Plutarch asks, 'Why do the women of Elis summon Dionysos in their hymns to be present with them with his bull-foot?' Happily Plutarch preserves for us the very words of the little early ritual hymn—

> In Springtime, O Dionysos,
> To thy holy temple come,
> To Elis with thy Graces,
> Rushing with thy bull-foot, come,
>   Noble Bull, Noble Bull[1].

Fig. 53.

Plutarch[2] tries as usual to answer his own question and at last half succeeds. 'Is it,' he suggests, 'that some entitle the god as born of a bull and as a bull himself,......or is it that many hold that the god is the beginner of sowing and ploughing?' We have seen how at Magnesia the holy Bull was the beginner (ἀρχηγός) of ploughing and sowing.

> Ἐλθεῖν ἥρ᾽ ὦ Διόνυσε
> Ἀλείων ἐς ναὸν
> ἁγνὸν σὺν χαρίτεσσιν,
> ἐς ναὸν τῷ βοέῳ ποδὶ θύων.
> Ἄξιε ταῦρε, ἄξιε ταῦρε.

I adopt in the first line Mr A. B. Cook's simple and convincing emendation ἥρ᾽ ὦ for ἥρω. The vocative ἥρω does not exist. Schneidewin emends ἥρως. Bergk (ed. 4) keeps ἥρω, observing 'non ausus sum ἥρως substituere.' For elision of the dative see Monro, *Homeric Grammar*, ed. 2, §§ 376.

[2] op. cit. note 1 πότερον ὅτι καὶ βουγενῆ προσαγορεύουσι καὶ ταῦρον ἔνιοι τὸν θεόν; ...ἢ ὅτι καὶ ἀρότρου καὶ σπόρου πολλοὶ τὸν θεὸν ἀρχηγὸν γεγονέναι νομίζουσι.

On a cameo in the Hermitage at St Petersburg in Fig. 53[1] we see the 'noble Bull' rushing 'with his bull-foot' and he is coming 'with the Charites': they are perched, a group of three, oddly enough between his horns. Above the holy Bull are the Pleiades[2]; their rising twenty-seven days after the vernal equinox was the signal in Greece for the early harvest. The women of Elis 'summon' the Bull, sing to him, praise him; but after all if you want a Bull to come to his holy temple, it is no use standing and 'summoning' him, you must drive him, drive him with a 'Bull-driving Dithyramb.'

From the leaders of the Dithyramb Aristotle has told us arose tragedy, the Goat-Song. Yet the Dithyramb is a song of Bull-driving. The difficulty is not so great as it seems. Any young full-grown creature can be the animal form of the Kouros, can be sacrificed, sanctified, divinized, and become the *Agathos Daimon*, the 'vegetation spirit,' the luck of the year. All over Europe we find, as Dr Frazer[3] has abundantly shown, goats, pigs, horses, even cats can play the part. Best of all perhaps is a bear, because he is strongest; this the Athenian maidens remembered in their Bear-Service (ἀρκτεία). But bears, alas! retreat before advancing civilization. Almost equally good is a bull, if you can afford him. But in Attica, as Alciphron has told us (p. 173), a bull was too expensive. A goat is not a bad life-spirit, as anyone will quickly discover who tries to turn him back against his will. Crete, the coast-land of Asia Minor, and Thrace, as we know from their coins, were bull-lands with abundant pastures. Attica, stony Attica, is a goat-land. If you go to Athens to-day, your morning coffee is ruined because, even in the capital, it is hard to get a drop of cow's milk. Instead you have, as an abundant and delicious food, sour goat's milk, γιαοῦρτι.

On the archaic *patera* in Fig. 54[4] in the British Museum[5] we

---

[1] Baumeister, *Denkmäler*, Fig. 413, p. 377.

[2] For the Pleiades and their importance in the farmer's year cf. Hesiod 615 and 619. See A. W. Mair's *Hesiod, Poems and Fragments*, 1908, Addenda, p. 136. Prof. Mair quotes the scholiast on the *Phaenomena* of Aratos, 264 ff., who says the Pleiades rise with the sun at dawn when he is in Taurus, which with the Romans is in April. The bull on the gem may have some reference to the constellation Taurus.

[3] *The Golden Bough*[2], ii. 261—269. For the Bear-Service see my *Myth. and Mon. of Ancient Athens*, p. 410.

[4] *Myth. and Mon. of Ancient Athens*, p. 289, Fig. 30.

[5] Cat. B, 80, published by C. H. Smith, *J.H.S.* i. Pl. 7, p. 202. See also *Class. Rev.* i. (1887), p. 315.

see depicted two scenes: one to the left the sacrifice of an ox, a
Bouphonia, the other to the right a festival that centres round
a goat, which perhaps we may venture to associate with a *tragoedia*.
Some of the figures round the goat hold wreaths, and it may be
that the splendid animal in the midst of them is the tragic prize.
Behind the goat-scene, and evidently part of it, is a primitive
mule-car. This recalls Thespis and his cart, and the canonical
jests 'from the cart.' The scene to the left is in honour of
Athena. She and her great snake and her holy bird await the

FIG. 54.

sacrificial procession. A flute-player leads the Bull-driving Dithyramb. The Bull is led or rather driven by a cord attached to one of
his hind legs; the other men hold wreaths, a staff, and an oinochoë.

On another and much later red-figured vase, in the Naples
Museum[1], reproduced in Fig. 55[2], we have another scene of
goat-sacrifice. This time the god Dionysos himself is present.
His stiff xoanon stands close to the altar and table at which

[1] Heydemann, Cat. 2411.
[2] *Mon. dell' Inst.* VI. 37. See also Farnell, *Cults of the Greek States*, v. p. 256.

the offerings are to be made.   A priestess is about to slay a very lively looking goat.   About are dancing Maenads with their timbrels.   But though a goat is sacrificed, the old bull-service is not forgotten.   The altar is decorated with a *boukranion*, the holy filleted head of a bull.

To resume.   In Crete we have the worship of the Mother and the Child the Kouros; without the Child the worship of the Mother is not; we have also the theriomorph, the holy Bull, the 'horns of consecration'; we cease to wonder that the Cretan

Fig. 55.

palace is full of bulls and horns, we cease to wonder at the story of Pasiphae and the Minotaur.   In Asia Minor, in Phrygia, the same conjunction, the Mother and the Child and the Bull; in Thrace, in Macedon, in Delphi, in Thracianized Thebes again the same.   It was this religion of the Mother and the holy Bull-Child and the spring δρώμενον that came down afresh, resurging from Macedon to startle and enthrall civilized, Olympianized, patriarchalized, intellectualized Athens, that Athens which, centuries before, under the sea-supremacy of Minos, had had her legend of the Cretan Bull, her Cretan ritual of the Bouphonia.

Matriarchy died out; Athena was 'all for the father'; hence the scandal caused by the Bacchants.   But the Bull and the spring δρώμενον went on, to be the seed of the drama.

The most ancient Dionysia at Athens were, Thucydides[1] tells us, in the month Anthesterion, the month of the rising of the dead and the blossoming of flowers. At the Anthesteria were dramatic contests known as Pot Contests[2], but we know of no Dithyramb, and no Bull-sacrifice. On the eve of the great Dionysiac festival, the Epheboi of Athens, the Kouroi, brought the image of Dionysos by torch-light into the theatre. They brought him by night—for was he not νυκτέλιος, νυκτίπολος? They brought their Greatest Kouros in human shape, an image such as we have seen on the vase, but, in the same procession, they brought their god, their Kouros, in animal shape—a splendid bull. Surely as they went they sang their Bull-driving Dithyramb.

It was expressly ordained, an inscription[3] testifies to it, that this bull should be 'worthy of the god.' Worthy of the god forsooth! Why, he *was* the god.

ἄξιε ταῦρε, ἄξιε ταῦρε.

It will not have escaped the reader's attention that one, and perhaps the most important, portion of the scene on the sarcophagos has been left undescribed. To the extreme right (Fig. 31, p. 161) is a small building variously interpreted as tomb or sanctuary; it is richly decorated. In front of it stands the closely draped figure of a youth, by his side a tree, and in front of him a stepped altar. To him approach three youths bearing offerings. The foremost brings a moon-shaped boat, the two last bring, not the blood of the dead bull, but young bull-calves, leaping and prancing; the somewhat irrelevant pose of the calves reminds us of the bull on the fresco of Tiryns. All three youths wear strange beast-skin robes[4]

---

[1] II. 15 καὶ τὸ ἐν Λίμναις Διονύσου (ᾧ τὰ ἀρχαιότερα Διονύσια τῇ δωδεκάτῃ ποιεῖται ἐν μηνὶ Ἀνθεστηριῶνι). For the whole question of the various Dionysia see my *Primitive Athens*, p. 85. The significance of the Anthesteria in relation to the Dithyramb and the drama will be further discussed in chapter VIII.

[2] Schol. *ad Ar. Ran.* 218 ἤγοντο ἀγῶνες αὐτόθι οἱ χυτρινοὶ καλούμενοι. See *Primitive Athens*, p. 87, note 6.

[3] Ἐφημ. 4098, l. 11 εἰσήγαγον δὲ καὶ τὸν Διόνυσον ἀπὸ τῆς ἐσχάρας εἰς τὸ θέατρον μετὰ φωτὸς καὶ ἔπεμψαν τοῖς Διονυσίοις ταῦρον ἄξιον τοῦ θεοῦ, ὃν καὶ ἔθυσαν ἐν τῷ ἱερῷ τῇ πομπῇ.

[4] Signor Paribeni has shown (*op. cit.*) that these celebrants, male and female, wearing beast robes, are 'girded with sackcloth.' Our word 'sackcloth' is the Hebrew שׂק, Assyrian *sakku*, Coptic *sok*, which gave the Greeks their σάκκος. It means simply rough, hairy beast-skin. In the familiar Bible passages, it will be noted that when sackcloth is worn it is not a complete dress, it is an extended

like that of the woman celebrant, but their procession seems to have nothing to do with hers, for they are turned back to back.

Two interpretations of the scene have been offered. Dr Petersen[1], whose theory as to the meaning I have, in the main, followed, holds that the building to the right is a sanctuary, the figure in front of it a god, Dionysos, closely draped because phallic. Dionysos is here as god of fertility, worshipped in spring; the tree beside him marks one of his aspects, as *Dendrites*. A more widely current interpretation, offered by the first publisher of the sarcophagos, Sig. Paribeni[2], is that the building is a tomb, the figure in front a dead man, a hero. The boat and calves are offerings to the dead man, the boat in Egyptian fashion provided for his journey, the young bulls to revive his life and strength.

We are now brought face to face with an all-important question, Is the spring δρώμενον on the sarcophagos conceived as celebrated in honour of, in relation to, a god or a mortal, Dionysos or a dead hero? Further, since, as we have seen, drama and δρώμενον are closely connected, this question leads straight on to another problem, 'Does Greek drama arise from the worship of Dionysos, or, as has been recently maintained, from the worship of the dead?' This question is not a mere curiosity of literary history, still less is its importance to be measured by the heat of a passing controversy. The answer lies, I believe, deep down in the very nature of religion, and in that peculiar quality of the Greek mind on which the differentiation of their religion from that of other peoples depended. The solution can only be attempted after a very careful analysis of the meaning of the terms employed and especially the term *hero.*

loin-cloth, girt on as in the case of the celebrants on the sarcophagos, e.g. Isaiah iii. 24, describing the mourning of Zion, says, 'Instead of well set hair there shall be baldness, and instead of a stomacher a *girding of sackcloth*,' and again in Psalm xxx. 12:

'Thou hast turned my heaviness into joy:
Thou hast *put off my sackcloth, and girded me* with gladness.'

The wearing of sackcloth was in all likelihood originally not merely a sign of mourning, but a means of magical identification with the holy, sacrificed beast.

[1] *Jahrb. d. Arch. Inst.* 1909, p. 162.
[2] *Supra*, p. 158, note 1.

But, before that analysis is attempted, we have to consider another series of δρώμενα, which present interesting analogies to the δρώμενα of the Dithyramb. Like these they are magical and recurrent, having for their object to influence and induce a good year. Like them, they became closely intertwined with the worship of heroes. We mean the contests (ἀγῶνες) celebrated widely and periodically in Greece, and first and foremost those contests which set the clock for Hellas—the great Olympic Games.

Note to p. 158. For the Hagia Triada Sarcophagos see Arthur Evans, *Palace of Minos*, I. pp. 438 ff.

Note to p. 169. For my present views on Poseidon's connection with the Minos-bull of Crete see my 'Mythology' in *Our Debt to Greece and Rome*, p. 26.

Note to p. 204. For an entirely new derivation of the Dithyramb see W. M. Calder, 'The Dithyramb an Anatolian Dirge,' in *Classical Review*, Feb.-March, 1922, p. 11.

Note to p. 205. On the question of the Bull-driving Dithyramb and the Bouphonia I should like to draw attention to the close analogy observable between the Cretan Taurokathapsia and the modern bull-fights of Spain. At Seville the bull was clearly regarded as in a sense sacred. It had, as always, necessarily to be slain, it was a sacrifice. Its flesh was sold in the Seville market on the Monday following the Sunday bull-fight. The tail especially brought luck to the eater. I tried to obtain a portion, but all was too quickly sold. In the market-place were also exposed small figures of bulls in rude pottery, one of which I secured. For the Taurokathapsia of which I believe the bull-fight to be a survival, and the connection between Βοηγία and Ταυροκαθάψια see Sir Arthur Evans, 'The Ring of Nestor' in *J.H.S.* 1925, p. 8.

CHAPTER VII.

THE ORIGIN OF THE OLYMPIC GAMES.

By F. M. Cornford.

More than one theory has recently been put forward by English scholars, to account for the origin of the Olympic Games. It has been felt that the naive view[1] which sees in these athletic contests no more than the survival of an expedient, comparable to the whisky-drinking àt an Irish wake, for cheering up the mourners after the funeral of a chieftain, clearly leaves something to be desired; for it entails the rejection of the whole ancient tradition recorded by Pindar, Pausanias, and others. Some part of this tradition is, indeed, undoubtedly fictitious—the deliberate invention of incoming peoples who wished to derive their claims from a spurious antiquity. Nothing is easier than to detect these genealogical forgeries; but when we have put them aside, there remains much that is of a totally different character—the myths, for instance, used by Pindar in his first *Olympian*. This residuum calls for some explanation; and no theory which dismisses it bodily as so much motiveless 'poetic fiction' can be accepted as satisfactory.

The first hypothesis that claims serious consideration is the current view, lately defended by Professor Ridgeway[2]. Games were held, he says, in honour of heroes, beside the tomb, 'in order doubtless to please the spirit of the dead man within.' 'Athletic feats, contests of horsemanship, and tragic dances are all part of the same principle—the honouring and appeasing of the dead.'

[1] Stated, e.g., by Christ (*Pindari Carmina*, 1896, p. lxii ff.): ludos instituebant *ad animos recreandos atque post luctum exhilarandos*...Aliam opportunitatem ludos faciendi faustus eventus belli obtulit. Namque et *hominum animi libenter* post atroces belli casus laboresque *reficiebantur*, etc.

[2] *Origin of Tragedy*, pp. 36, 38.

It will be noted that this hypothesis marks an advance upon what we call the naive view, in that it recognises the religious character of the games. Athletic feats were performed, not solely to cheer the spirits of the performers, but as an act of worship, to 'honour and appease' the spirit of a hero. The theory holds that the performance originates in funeral games at the barrow of a dead chief—in the case of Olympia, at the Pelopium—and is perpetuated because dead warriors like to be remembered by their survivors and can visit neglect with unpleasant consequences. Hence it is prudent to honour and appease them.

Dr Frazer[1] brings forward evidence in support of this theory of the funeral origin. It consists chiefly[2] of instances of games celebrated at funerals or founded in historic times, either in Greece or elsewhere, to do honour to famous men, such as Miltiades, Brasidas, Timoleon, who were worshipped as heroes with annual sacrifices and games. Dr Frazer concludes that 'we cannot dismiss as improbable the tradition that the Olympic Games and perhaps other great Greek games were instituted to commemorate real men who once lived, died, and were buried on the spot where the festivals were afterwards held.'

The objection to this apparently simple theory is stated by Dr Frazer himself, and he feels its force so strongly that he propounds another hypothesis of his own, which, as we shall later see (p. 259), is actually inconsistent with the funeral origin. He remarks that the funeral theory does not explain all the legends connected with the origin of the Olympic Games. We might almost go so far as to say that it does not explain any of the more ancient legends. The earliest, indeed the only, authority cited by Dr Frazer for the statement that the games were founded 'in honour of Pelops' is Clement of Alexandria[3]. Our older authorities, Pindar, for instance, and the sources used by Pausanias, tell a quite different story. About the death and obsequies of Pelops,

---

[1] Part III. of the *Golden Bough*, ed. 3, p. 92 ff.

[2] The lashing of all the youths in the Peloponnese on the grave of Pelops till the blood streamed down as a libation to the departed hero, to which Dr Frazer adduces parallels from savage mourning customs, may perhaps be dismissed as an unfortunate attempt of the Scholiast on Pindar *Ol.* I. 146 to derive αἱμακουρίαι from αἷμα κούρων.

[3] *Protrept.* II. 34, p. 29, ed. Potter. It should be noted that Clement is advocating a theory of his own, that Games held for the dead, like oracles, were 'mysteries.'

which ought to be the centre and core of the Olympian tradition, that tradition is absolutely silent. Pindar[1] dates the Games from the victory of Pelops over Oinomaos in the chariot-race, which ended in the death of Oinomaos, not of Pelops. The Elean informants of Pausanias[2] had no tradition of any funeral games in honour of that hero; they traced the origin of the festival to a higher antiquity, and said that 'Pelops celebrated the Games in honour of Olympian Zeus in a grander way than all who had gone before him.'

It is true that Pausanias says, 'the Eleans honour Pelops as much above all the heroes of Olympia as they honour Zeus above the rest of the gods'; and that a black ram was annually sacrificed at his precinct[3]. Pausanias calls the enclosure a 'precinct' ($\tau\acute{\epsilon}\mu\epsilon$-$\nu o\varsigma$), not a grave[4]. The German excavators have dug down to the neolithic stratum, and no trace of any real interment, except a neolithic baby, has been found[5]. Thus, although the mound in this precinct was, as early as Pindar's time, regarded as the barrow of Pelops, there is no material evidence that any real chieftain was ever buried there at all. The case of Pelops at Olympia is, moreover, exceptionally favourable to the funeral theory. The 'dead' who were connected with the festivals at the other three centres of panhellenic games[6] were not chieftains whose warlike deeds could be commemorated. At Nemea the 'dead' who was honoured was Archemoros, an infant; at the Isthmus, Glaukos, a sea-daemon; at Pytho, a snake.

Further, whereas the games were held once in every four years, the hero-sacrifices at the supposed tomb of Pelops were annual, and we have no reason to believe that they were even held at the same time of year.

It thus appears that the funeral theory, which would have the whole Olympic festival originate in the obsequies of an actual man called Pelops, is contradicted by the more ancient traditions of Elis and unsupported by any monumental evidence. The field is clear for an alternative theory which will take account of the fact that the Games were believed to be older than the time of

---

[1] *Ol.* I.　　　　　　　　　　　　　　[2] Paus. v. 8. 2.
[3] Paus. v. 13. 1.
[4] Cf. Schol. ad Pind. *Ol.* I. 149, $\tau\iota\nu\acute{\epsilon}\varsigma$ $\phi\alpha\sigma\iota$ $\mu\grave{\eta}$ $\mu\nu\hat{\eta}\mu\alpha$ $\dot{\alpha}\lambda\lambda'$ $\iota\epsilon\rho\grave{o}\nu$ $\tau o\hat{\upsilon}$ $\Pi\acute{\epsilon}\lambda o\pi o\varsigma$.
[5] Dörpfeld, *Olympia in prähistorischer Zeit*, Mitth. Ath. xxxiii. (1908) p. 185 ff.
[6] The four Great Games—Olympian, Pythian, Nemean, and Isthmian, seem to be distinguished from others more than once in Pindar by the epithet $\iota\epsilon\rho o\acute{\iota}$.

Pelops, who was associated with a reconstitution of them on a grander scale, and will also interpret, instead of rejecting, the legends about their origin.

The point of general and fundamental interest involved in this controversy is the significance of hero-worship and its place in the development of Greek religion—a question which, as has been remarked already (p. 210), is vital also for the history of the drama. For the drama and for the games alike the modern Euhemerist like Professor Ridgeway supposes a funeral origin. In other words, wherever we find hero-worship or ceremonies more or less connected with the commemoration of 'heroes,' we are to suppose that they originated in memorial rites dating from the actual obsequies of some man or men who died and were buried (or at least had a cenotaph) on the spot. This view has led Professor Ridgeway to take up an extreme position with regard to the whole order of religious development.

'A great principle,' he says[1], 'is involved in this discussion, since the evidence shows that whereas it is commonly held that the phenomena of vegetation spirits and totemism are primary, they are rather to be regarded as secondary phenomena arising from the great primary principle of the belief in the existence of the soul after death, and the desirability of honouring it.

'Scholars had begun at the wrong end, taking as primary the phenomena of vegetation spirits, totemism etc., which really were but secondary, arising almost wholly from the primary element, the belief in the existence of the soul after the death of the body. As prayer, religion proper, was made to the dead, religion must be considered antecedent to magic, which is especially connected with the secondary elements[2].'

Of the extreme view stated in the last sentence the whole of this book may be taken as a refutation. Prof. Ridgeway's view was instantly challenged by Dr Frazer[3], who 'contended that totemism, the worship of the dead, and the phenomena of vegetation spirits should be considered as independent factors, and that none of the three should be held to be the origin of the others.' With this denial that 'religion proper,' identified with prayers to the dead, is prior to magic—the immediate manipulation of *mana*—our whole argument is, of course, in agreement. Where

---

[1] Summary of a paper on *The Origin of the Great Games of Greece*, delivered before the Society for the Promotion of Hellenic Studies, May 9, 1911.

[2] Report of the same paper in the *Athenaeum*, May 20, 1911.

[3] *Athenaeum*, loc. cit.

we go beyond Dr Frazer's pronouncement is in attempting to show how the three factors he calls 'independent' are related to one another.

What is now clear is that behind the theory of the funeral origin of the Games and of the drama, as advocated by Professor Ridgeway, lies the view that the primary religious phenomenon is prayer, or other rites, addressed to one or more individuals, whether dead men or gods, with the purpose of 'honouring and appeasing' them, and thereby securing the benefits, especially the food-supply, which they can give or withold. The *do ut des* principle is taken as primary and ultimate. Further, since dead men are most suitably appeased by commemoration of their exploits, the primitive rite is essentially commemorative, only secondarily designed to secure tangible benefits.

Against this general view of religious development it has already been argued (p. 134) that the *do ut des* principle is not early, but late; and that magic—the magic which immediately controls the food-supply and the natural phenomena on which it depends—was carried on before there were any gods at all, and can be carried on by direct mimetic methods, without any prayerful appeals to dead ancestors. The special topic of hero-worship and the detailed analysis of the term 'hero' are reserved for the next chapter. Our object here is to state a theory of the origin of the Great Games which will not rest on the foundations, in our opinion false, which support Professor Ridgeway's funeral hypothesis.

According to the view which we shall put forward, the Games are to be regarded as originally and essentially a New Year's festival—the inauguration of a 'Year.' If it can be shown that the legends can be interpreted as reflecting rites appropriate to such a festival, the hypothesis will have some claim to acceptance.

Our simplest course will be to examine the myths about the origin of the Games, contained in Pindar's first *Olympian*, and to disentangle the separable factors in this complex legend. We shall begin with the story of the so-called chariot-race, in which Pelops defeated the wicked king Oinomaos, and won the hand of his daughter Hippodameia and with it the succession to the kingdom. We shall then examine the dark and disreputable story (as it seemed to Pindar) of the Feast of Tantalus and offer an explanation which will connect it with the institution of the Games in their earliest form.

Our enquiry will proceed on the assumption that these myths are not saga-episodes, but belong to the class of ritual myths. In other words, they are not poeticised versions of unique historical events in the life of any individual 'hero'; but reflect recurrent ritual practices, or δρώμενα[1]. The failure to distinguish these two classes of myths leads the Euhemerist into his worst errors; and in this particular case it puts the advocate of the funeral theory into a serious difficulty. For on that theory these stories must represent those exploits of the dead chieftain, of which his ghost will most like to be reminded; and it is difficult to understand what satisfaction the departed Pelops could find in having his attention periodically drawn to the fact that his father had been damned in Hell for cooking him and trying to make the gods eat him at dinner. If, on the other hand, we recognise that all these myths are of the ritual type, it must be observed that 'Pelops' is stripped of every vestige of historic personality. He becomes an empty name, an eponym. The only semblance of historic fact that remains about him is the statement that he came from Lydia to his own island, the Peloponnese; and, as Gruppe[2] shows, it is probable that this is the reverse of the truth, and that his legend was first carried to Asia Minor at a comparatively late date by settlers from central Greece. The funeral theory is thus reduced to deriving the most important of Hellenic festivals from the unrecorded obsequies of a person of whom nothing whatever is known, and who, in all probability, never existed.

But it is time to put controversy aside and reconstruct the meaning of Pindar's myths.

---

[1] For the relation of myth to ritual see *infra*, p. 327.
[2] *Griech. Myth. und Rel.* I. 653. Gruppe holds that the ancestors of the Atreidae, Tantalus and Pelops, were transplanted to Lydia with the rest of the Ionian Saga early in the sixth century, especially in the reigns of Alyattes and Croesus.

THE CONTEST WITH OINOMAOS.

Pindar[1] thus describes the contest:

When, towards the fair flowering of his growing age, the down began to shade his darkening cheek, Pelops turned his thoughts to a marriage that lay ready for him—to win from her father of Pisa famed Hippodameia.

He came near to the hoary sea, alone in the darkness, and cried aloud to the Lord of the Trident in the low-thundering waves. And he appeared to him, close at his foot. And Pelops spoke to him: Come now, O Poseidon, if the kindly gifts of the Cyprian in any wise find favour with thee, do thou trammel the bronze spear of Oinomaos, speed me on swiftest chariot to Elis, and bring victory to my embrace. For thirteen men that sued for her he hath overthrown, in putting off the marriage of his daughter....

So he said, and he attained his prayer, which went not unfulfilled. The God glorified him with the gift of a golden car and horses with wings unwearied. And he overcame mighty Oinomaos, and won the maiden to share his bed; and she bore him six sons, chieftains eager in prowess.

Thus indirectly and allusively Pindar tells the story which forms the subject of the Eastern pediment of the temple of Zeus at Olympia. Probably most readers of the *First Olympian* think of the contest between Pelops and Oinomaos as a chariot-race— the mythical prototype of the chariot-races of the historic Games.

FIG. 56.

So too it may have been regarded by Pindar. But if we examine the story as known to us from other sources, it becomes plain that this was not its original meaning.

The scene is represented in the design (Fig. 56) on a polychrome bell-shaped krater in the Naples Museum[2]. In the right fore-ground Pelops and the bride Hippodameia are driving off in the same chariot; for it was Oinomaos' custom to make the suitors

---

[1] *Ol.* i. 69 ff.
[2] *Arch. Zeit.* 1853, Taf. LV.

drive with her from Elis to the altar of Poseidon at the Corinthian Isthmus[1]. Meanwhile the king himself, who is armed with spear and helmet, stays behind to sacrifice, before a column surmounted by a female divinity[2], the ram which an attendant is bringing up on the left. Then Oinomaos will mount the chariot held in readiness by his charioteer Myrtilus, and drive in pursuit of the flying pair. On overtaking them, he intends to stab Pelops in the back with his bronze spear. He has already disposed of thirteen suitors in this questionable way. But Pelops will escape; for Hippodameia has persuaded Myrtilus to remove the linchpins of the king's chariot. Oinomaos will be tumbled out and killed by Pelops with his own spear. His grave—a mound of earth enclosed by a retaining wall of stones—was shown on the far side of the Kladeos. Above it stood the remains of buildings where he was said to have stabled his mares[3].

It is obvious that this story does not describe a primitive form of mere sport. It is made up of at least two distinct factors. (a) There is, first, the contest between the young and the old king, ending in the death of the elder and the succession of the younger to the kingdom. (b) Second, there is the carrying off (ἁρπαγή) of the bride; for Pelops and Hippodameia drive off in the same chariot, with the chance of altogether escaping the pursuing father. This is not a chariot-race, but a flight, such as often occurs in marriage by capture[4].

These two factors must be briefly examined. We shall see that both can be interpreted on the hypothesis that the rites reflected in these myths are appropriate to a New Year's festival.

(a) *The Contest between the Young and the Old King.* This feature of the story is taken by Mr A. B. Cook[5] as the basis of his theory of the origin of the Great Games. The parallel story of

---

[1] Weizsäcker in Roscher's *Lex.*, s.v. *Oinomaos*, col. 768, holds that this trait must belong to a Phliasian legend of Oinomaos, and that Oinomaos was transferred from Phlius to Olympia.

[2] The sacrifice is said to have been made to Zeus Areios (Paus. v. 14. 6) or to Ares (Philostr. *Imag.* 10). Earlier vases show Oinomaos and Pelops taking the oath before a pillar, in one case inscribed ΔΙΟΣ, in another surmounted by a male divinity. See A. B. Cook, *Class. Rev.* xvii. p. 271.

[3] Apollod. ii. 4; Paus. v. 17. 7; Diod. iv. 73; Paus. vi. 21. 3.

[4] See Weizsäcker in Roscher's *Lex.*, s.v. *Oinomaos*.

[5] *Zeus, Jupiter, and the Oak*, Class. Rev. xvii. 268 ff., and *The European Sky-God*, Folk-Lore 1904. To the learning and ingenuity displayed in these articles, as well as to other help from Mr Cook, I am deeply indebted.

Phorbas, king of the Phlegyae, shows that we are justified in regarding the contest for the kingship as a separable factor; for in that story we have the contest alone, without either the chariot-driving or the flight with the bride. Phorbas dwelt under an oak, called his 'palace,' on the road to Delphi, and challenged the pilgrims to various athletic feats. When he had defeated them, he cut off their heads and hung them on his oak. Apollo came as a boxer and overthrew Phorbas, while his oak was blasted by a thunderbolt from the sky.

The sacred tree and the thunderbolt reappear in the case of Oinomaos. Between the Great Altar and the sanctuary of Zeus in the Altis stood a wooden pillar or post, decayed by time and held together by metal bands. It was further protected by a roof supported on four columns. This pillar, it was said, alone escaped when the house of Oinomaos was blasted by lightning[1]. Near it stood an altar of Zeus Keraunios, said to have been erected when Zeus smote the house[2]. The place was, in fact, sanctified by being struck by lightning. Oinomaos, whom legend made both husband and son of Sterope, the lightning-flash, was one of those weather-kings with whom we are already familiar (p. 105), who claimed to control the thunder and the rain, and like Salmoneus who, as we have seen (p. 81), migrated from Thessaly to Elis, were liable to be blasted by the later thunder-god of Olympus. Oinomaos with his bronze spear was ἐγχεικέραυνος[3]. He too, like Phorbas, hung up the heads of the defeated suitors on his house. Again we encounter the same complex as we found in the Erechtheion (pp. 92 and 171)—a sacred tree or pillar, and the token of the thunderer. The Pandroseion of the Athenian Acropolis has its analogue in the Pantheion—the all-holy or all-magical place—which contained the sacred olive tree at Olympia[4].

On the basis of this conjunction of weather king and sacred tree, Mr Cook suggests that 'in mythical times the Olympic contest was a means of determining who should be king of the district and champion of the local tree-Zeus.' The holder of the office for the time being was analogous to the Rex Nemorensis of the Golden Bough—an incarnation of the Tree and Sky God,

---

[1] Paus. v. 20. 6.   [2] Paus. v. 14. 6.
[3] An epithet applied by Pindar to Zeus (*Pyth.* iv. 194; *Ol.* xiii. 77). Athena is ἐγχειβρόμος, *Ol.* vii. 43.
[4] *Supra*, p. 171, note 1.

and, like his Italian parallel, defended his office against all comers, until he was finally defeated and superseded by the successful combatant.

The Olympic victor, he points out, was treated with honours both regal and divine; feasted in the prytaneum; crowned with a spray of olive like the wreath of Zeus himself; pelted, like a tree-spirit or Jack-in-the-Green, with leaves[1]. As such he is represented in the vase-painting in Fig. 57[2].

Finally, on his return to his native city, the victor was dressed in royal purple and drawn by white horses through a breach in the walls. In many cases he was worshipped after death, as a hero; not because he was a successful athlete, but because he had once been an incarnate god.

Fig. 57.

This hypothesis of Mr Cook's we believe to be fundamentally correct. Plutarch in his *Symposiac Questions*[3], after remarking that the foot-race was the sole original contest at Olympia, all the other competitions having been added later, proceeds:

---

[1] Porphyry, *Vit. Pyth.* 15, says that Pythagoras advised men to compete, but not to win, at Olympia, συμβαίνει γὰρ καὶ ἄλλως μηδ' εὐαγεῖς εἶναι τοὺς νικῶντας καὶ φυλλοβολουμένους. Why had the φυλλοβολία this effect?

[2] A kylix from Vulci now in the Bibl. Nat. Paris; *Arch. Zeit.* 1853, Taf. LII., LIII.; figured and discussed by Mr Cook, *C.R.* XVII. p. 274.

[3] v. 2, p. 675 c τοῖς δ' Ὀλυμπίοις πάντα προσθήκη πλὴν τοῦ δρόμου γέγονε...δέδια δ' εἰπεῖν ὅτι πάλαι καὶ μονομαχίας ἀγὼν περὶ Πίσαν ἤγετο μέχρι φόνου καὶ σφαγῆς τῶν ἡττωμένων καὶ ὑποπιπτόντων.

> I hesitate to mention that in ancient times there was also held at Pisa a contest consisting of a single combat, which *ended only with the slaughter and death of the vanquished.*

Plutarch rightly feels that this was not a form of athletic sport. This single combat is again reflected in myth as a wrestling match between Zeus and Kronos for the kingdom, from which some dated the institution of the games[1].

. But although we accept the essence of Mr Cook's theory of this single combat, we prefer to avoid some of the terms in which he describes its significance. The words 'king,' 'god,' 'incarnation of the tree-Zeus' may all be somewhat misleading[2]. In the light of the preceding chapters, we see that a weather-magician like Oinomaos, though a late theology may see in him the temporary incarnation of a god, goes back to a time when there was no god to be incarnated: on the contrary the sky god is only a projected reflex of this human figure of the magician, who claims to command the powers of the sky and to call down its rain and thunder by virtue of his own *mana*. We shall be on safer ground if we restrict ourselves to the simple primitive group, consisting of the weather-magician who wields the fertilising influences of Heaven, and the tree which embodies the powers of the Earth—the vegetation which springs up when the thunder shower has burst, and Heaven and Earth are married in the life-giving rain[3].

To this we must add the conception, with which Dr Frazer has made us familiar[4], of the limited period of office enjoyed by such a personage. The individual on whose vigour and exceptional powers the fertility of earth depends, cannot be allowed to continue in office when his natural forces fall into decay. Hence the single combat, in which he has to make good his right to a renewed period or else to die at the hands of his more vigorous antagonist.

Now, in some cases at least, this period of office was not limited merely by the duration of its holders' natural strength:

---

[1] Paus. v. 7 Δία δὴ οἱ μὲν ἐνταῦθα παλαῖσαι καὶ αὐτῷ τῷ Κρόνῳ περὶ τῆς ἀρχῆς, οἱ δὲ ἐπὶ κατειργασμένοις ἀγωνοθετῆσαί φασιν αὐτόν.

[2] See *supra*, p. 149. Mr Cook has since restated his view in *Zeus*, vol. ι. (1914).

[3] See *supra*, p. 176.

[4] *Lectures on the Early History of the Kingship*, p. 264. See also for the periodicity of the rule of Minos (τ 179 ἐννέωρος βασίλευε) Prof. Murray, *Rise of the Greek Epic*[2], 127 note.

it bore some fixed relation to the year, and to the seasonal cycle of vegetable life in nature. In other words the term of office was a 'year'—a term which, as we have seen (p. 189), may denote a lunar or solar year or a longer period of two, four, or eight solar years—a *trieteris, penteteris,* or *ennaeteris.* During this period, long or short as it might be, the tenant of the office represented, or rather *was,* the power which governed the rains of heaven and the fruits of earth; at the end of it he was either continued for a new *eniautos,* or violently dispossessed by a successor. Further, since the *eniautos* itself could be concretely conceived as a *daimon* carrying the horn of plenty[1]—the contents and fruits of the 'year' in the more abstract sense—we may think of the temporary 'king' as actually being the *eniautos-daimon* or fertility spirit of his 'year.' When the year is fixed by the solar period, we get festivals of the type of the Roman Saturnalia or the Greek Κρόνια (with which the Saturnalia were regularly equated in ancient times), and the single combat appears as the driving out of winter or of the dying year by the vigorous young spirit of the New Year that is to come. It is as *eniautos-daimon,* not at first as 'incarnate god' or as king in the later political sense, that the representative of the fertility powers of nature dies at the hands of the New Year. In this combat we may see, in a word, the essential feature of a Saturnalian or Kronian festival.

This view is supported by a curious feature, to which Mr Cook calls attention, in the vase-painting of Salmoneus figured above on p. 80. Salmoneus, the weather-king, arrayed, as we have seen, with the attributes of the Olympic victor, wears on his left ankle an unmistakable fetter. We may suspect, as Mr Cook remarks, that this is part of his disguise as a would-be god, and it shows that the god imitated is not Zeus, but the fettered Kronos, Κρόνος πεδήτης. Once a year, at the Saturnalia, the statue of Saturn slipped the woollen fetter with which it was bound throughout the rest of the year[2].

Hesiod[3] tells us that, after Kronos had vomited forth the stone which he swallowed instead of his son, Zeus entering on his

[1] See *supra,* p. 186, and *infra,* p. 285.

[2] Macrob. *Sat.* 1. viii. 5, Saturnum Apollodorus alligari ait per annum laneo vinculo et solvi ad diem sibi festum, id est mense hoc Decembri. For the fettered Kronos see Roscher, *Lex.,* s.v. *Kronos,* col. 1467.

[3] *Theog.* 501. The lines are regarded by some editors as interpolated. For the release of Kronos see Hesiod, *Erga,* 169[b] (ed. Rz. 1902).

reign, released from their bonds the brothers of Kronos, the Titans, who then gave Zeus the thunder and lightning. The unfettering of Kronos or Saturn appears to be a reflection of the custom at Saturnalian festivals of releasing prisoners and slaves—the mock subjects of the mock king of the feast, himself a prisoner or a slave. It may have symbolised a brief return of the older reign of Kronos, or the Golden Age, lasting over the intercalary days between two years of the reign of Zeus. At any rate in this design are united the attributes of the old Thunderer and Vegetation Spirit, of the Olympic victor, and of the unfettered Kronos—a combination which strongly confirms our suggestion that the Games were connected with a Saturnalian feast.

Against the view here suggested an objection might be urged on the score of the date of the Olympic Festival. Saturnalian feasts fall usually in the neighbourhood of Christmas (the winter solstice) or of Easter (the vernal equinox) or at some season of carnival between these two dates. The Olympic Games, on the other hand, were held in the late summer. The earliest date on which they could fall was August 6; the latest, September 29. Moreover they were not annual, but penteteric; that is to say they were celebrated once in every four years. How then can they be connected with Saturnalian rites?

The answer to this objection will throw light on the second factor in the myth of Pelops and Oinomaos—the capture of the bride, Hippodameia.

(b) *The Marriage of Pelops and Hippodameia.* The date at which a celebration of the Games fell due was reckoned by a singularly complicated process, comparable with the mysterious method laid down by the Christian churches for the calculation of Easter; for, like Easter, the Games were a moveable feast, determined by astronomical considerations. The Scholiast on Pindar[1] quotes from Comarchos what appears to be the official prescription for fixing the dates, copied possibly from some inscription in the Prytaneum at Olympia.

[1] Ad *Ol.* III. 33 restored as follows by Weniger, *Das Hochfest des Zeus in Olympia*, Klio, 1905, p. 1 ff.: Κώμαρχος ὁ τὰ περὶ Ἠλείων συντάξας φησὶν οὕτως· πρῶτον μὲν οὖν παντὸς περίοδον συνέθηκε πεντετηρίδα· ἄρχειν (note the official jussive

The Games were held alternately in the Elean months Apollonios and Parthenios—probably the second and third months of the Elean year, if we may suppose that this, like the Delphic and Attic years, began about midsummer. The interval between two celebrations was alternately 49 and 50 months. This fact shows that the festival cycle is really an octennial period (ennaeteris) divided into two halves—a period which reconciles the Hellenic moon year of 354 days with the solar year of $365\frac{1}{4}$[1]. According to the document preserved by Comarchos, the reckoning is made in a peculiar way, which seems to call for explanation. It starts from the winter solstice. Take the first full moon after the solstice—this will fall on January (Thosuthias) 13[2]—and count 8 months. This will give the full moon (Aug. 22, 776 = OL. I.) of Apollonios (Aug. 8—Sept. 5) as the central day for the first celebration. The next will fall four years later, after fifty months, at the full moon (Sept. 6, 772 = OL. II.) of the month Parthenios (Aug. 23—Sept. 21). Forty-nine months later we shall be again at the full moon of Apollonios (Aug. 23, 768 = OL. III.), and so the cycle recurs.

The singular plan of starting the whole reckoning from the winter solstice seems to indicate that the year at Elis, as at Delos and in Boeotia and probably also at Delphi and Athens, formerly began in winter; and this circumstance at once suggests that the single combat of the young and old *eniautos-daimons* may have originally belonged to the season of midwinter—the season at which the Roman Saturnalia were ultimately fixed[3].

infinitive) νουμηνίαν μηνὸς ὃς Θωσυθιὰς (?) ἐν Ἤλιδι ὀνομάζεται, περὶ ὃν τροπαὶ ἡλίου γίνονται χειμεριναί· καὶ πρῶτα Ὀλύμπια ἄγεται ἡ' μηνί· ἑνὸς δέοντος διαφερόντων τῇ ὥρᾳ, τὰ μὲν ἀρχομένης τῆς ὀπώρας, τὰ δὲ ὑπ' αὐτὸν τὸν ἀρκτοῦρον. ὅτι δὲ κατὰ πεντετηρίδα ἄγεται ὁ ἀγών, καὶ αὐτὸς ὁ Πίνδαρος μαρτυρεῖ. Schol. ad *Ol.* v. 35 γίνεται δὲ ὁ ἀγὼν ποτὲ μὲν διὰ μθ' μηνῶν, ποτὲ δὲ διὰ ν', ὅθεν καὶ ποτὲ μὲν τῷ Ἀπολλωνίῳ μηνί, ποτὲ δὲ τῷ Παρθενίῳ ἐπιτελεῖται. The account in the text is based on Weniger's admirable analysis in the above-mentioned article.

[1] The $11\frac{1}{4}$ days by which the lunar falls short of the solar year amount in 8 years to 90 days, which were distributed over the period in 3 months intercalated in winter. The 8-year period thus = 96 + 3 months = 99 = 49 + 50.

[2] The dates given *exempli gratia* are those for the first Olympiad, starting from Decr. 25, 777. See Weniger, *loc. cit.*

[3] This may also throw light on an unexplained obscurity in Pindar, who, describing the institution of the Games by Herakles, says (*Ol.* x. 49) that Herakles first gave its name to the Hill of Kronos, 'which before was nameless, while Oinomaos ruled, and was *wetted with much snow*'—πρόσθε γὰρ νώνυμος, ἇς Οἰνόμαος ἆρχε, βρέχετο πολλᾷ νιφάδι. What can this possibly mean, if not that a tradition survived connecting the hill with some mid-winter festival? It suggests that the defeat of 'Oinomaos' and the termination of his 'rule' coincided with the introduction of the new octennial *eniautos* and the shift to August.

A cycle such as this is obviously a late and very artificial invention, implying fairly exact astronomical knowledge. It is independent of the seasons and concerned solely with the motions of the sun and moon. There is no reason why it should begin at the same season as the pastoral or the agricultural year. The most propitious moment would be the summer, as near as can conveniently be managed[1] to the summer solstice, when the sun is at the height of his power. The moon too is taken at the full. The union of the full moon and the full-grown Sun is one form—the astronomical—of that sacred marriage which in many parts of the ancient world was celebrated at midsummer. This union, we suggest, is symbolised by the marriage of Pelops and Hippodameia. The suggestion has the support of Dr Frazer's high authority. He gives reason for holding that 'under the names of Zeus and Hera the pair of Olympic victors' (that is, the victor in the chariot-race and the girl who won the virgin's race at the Heraea, which we shall discuss later) 'would seem to have really personated the sun and moon, who were the true heavenly bridegroom and bride of the ancient octennial festival[2].'

Thus the second factor under consideration—the marriage of Pelops and Hippodameia—is explained. It was symbolised, as we saw, by the flight of bride and bridegroom in the same chariot. As such it appears in the design (Fig. 58) of a red-figured amphora[3] with twisted handles. Hippodameia stands erect,

[1] Some mention will be made later (p. 230) of the difficulties which seem to have forced the founders of the cycle to choose just this part of the summer. The month Apollonios corresponded with the Delphic Bukatios (Pythian Games) and the Laconian Karneios (festival of the Karneia). It was clearly convenient to fix these greater festivals at a time when the labours of harvest were well over and agricultural work was at a standstill. Earlier writers, for instance Boeckh and Ideler, believed that the Games were held at the *first* full moon after the summer solstice.

[2] See Part III. of the *Golden Bough*, ed. 3, p. 91. Dr Frazer arrived at this conclusion some years ago, and, after hearing that I had reached it also, kindly allowed me to see the proofs from which the above sentence is quoted. I believe the explanation was first suggested to me by one of Mr A. B. Cook's articles on *The European Sky-God* in Folk-Lore xv. p. 377 ff.

[3] Now in the Museo Pubblico at Arezzo. First published in the *Monimenti* (VIII. 3) of the German Archaeological Institute. I am glad to find that Prof. Furtwängler in commenting on this vase has pointed out that the scene here and on the other Oinomaos vases is a rape rather than a race. He writes (*Griechische Vasenmalerei*, Serie II. Taf. 67, Text p. 34) 'Dass die Fahrten der Freier der Hippodameia und damit die des Pelops ursprünglich nicht als Wettrennen sondern als Entführung, als Brautraub gemeint und Oinomaos der Verfolger war, dies ist in den verschiedenen Sagenvarianten, und in den Kunstdenkmälern immer deutlich geblieben.' Prof. Furtwängler makes the interesting suggestion that this vase is from the hand of the same master as the famous Talos vase in Ruvo.

looking much more like a goddess than a ravished bride. The olive trees and the two doves flying close together to perch on one of them seem to take us back to the trees and birds of the marriage of Sky and Earth on the Hagia Triada sarcophagos[1].

The chariot of Pelops is the four-horsed chariot of the sun, which Erichthonios the mythical founder of the Panathenaea also imitated[2]. That the Sun and Moon should drive in the same chariot may seem strange, since of course they never rise together in the same quarter of the sky. But we have already seen them

Fig. 58.

so represented on the Louvre krater (Fig. 51)[3]; and the same conjunction appears in literature. At the marriage of Kapaneus, Helios and Selene drove their chariot together over the sky[4]. At the two ends of the pedestal of the great statue of Zeus at

[1] *Supra*, p. 176.

[2] Verg. *Georg.* III. 113 Primus Erichthonius currus et *quatuor* ausus | iungere equos. Eratosth. *catast.* 13 τῇ τοῦ Ἡλίου ἀντίμιμον ἐποιήσατο διφρείαν. Hyg. *Astr.* II. 13 *Heniochus*, Erichthonium...quem Jupiter, cum vidisset primum inter homines equos *quadrigis* iunxisse, admiratus est ingenium hominis ad *Solis inventa* accessisse, quod is princeps quadrigis inter deos est usus. Others identified the celestial Charioteer with Myrtilus, Hyg. *ibid.*

[3] Compare also the coin of Gellia, figured in Roscher, *Lex.*, s.v. *Mars*, col. 2410, which shows Mars as a warrior and Nerine—the Roman Sun or Year God with his bride—standing in a quadriga.

[4] Eur. *Suppl.* 990   τί φέγγος, τίν' αἴγλαν
                          ἐδιφρεύετον Ἅλιος
                          Σελάνα τε κατ' αἰθέρα
                          †λαμπάδ' ἵν' ὠκυθόαι νύμφαι†...
My attention was drawn to this passage by Prof. Murray.

Olympia, the sun drove in his chariot and the moon rode her horse: she is Hippodameia, the horse-rider[1].

The chariot-drive of Pelops and Hippodameia, itself a flight rather than a race, was however connected by tradition with the historic chariot-races at Olympia. We have evidence too that the chariot-races of the Roman circus were associated with the courses of the heavenly bodies.

Cassiodorus[2], a sixth century writer, tells us that the Roman Circus represented the change of seasons, and the courses of the Sun and Moon. The two-horse chariot-race represented the course of the moon, the four-horse chariot-race that of the sun.

Lydus[3] mentions that the Circus Maximus at Rome contained altars of the planet gods. Below the pyramid of the Sun stood altars of the Moon, Mercury and Venus; above it, altars of Saturn, Jupiter, and Mars. Tertullian[4] says that the whole circus was dedicated to the Sun.

So, at Olympia itself, the twelve rounds of the chariot-race —δωδεκάγναμπτος as Pindar[5] calls it—may well have represented the course of the Sun through the twelve signs. In the hippodrome the pillar which marked the starting-point had beside it an altar of the Heavenly Twins[6]. At the starting-point of the foot-races in the Stadium stood the tomb of Endymion, the sinking Sun who married Selene the Moon[7]. The most cautious scholars accept Boeckh's view that the fifty daughters of this marriage are the fifty moon months of the Olympiad.

We have thus disentangled two elements in the complex story of Pelops and Oinomaos, as told by Pindar. The marriage of the sun and moon must clearly be coeval with the reconstitution of the Games 'on a grander scale' associated with 'Pelops'; and presumably this reconstitution meant the reform of the calendar by

---

[1] Paus. v. 11. 8. Stone images of the Sun with rays and the Moon with horns stood in the market-place of Elis, Paus. vi. 24. 6.

[2] *Var. Ep.* iii. 51 Biga quasi lunae, quadriga solis imitatione reperta est... Obeliscorum quoque prolixitates ad caeli altitudinem sublevantur; sed potior soli, inferior lunae dicatus est.

[3] *De mensibus* 1, pp. 4 and 12.

[4] *De spect.* 8 Circus Soli principaliter consecratur, cuius aedes in medio spatio et effigies de fastigio aedis emicat...quadrigas Soli, bigas Lunae sanxerunt. See Roscher, *Lex.*, s.v. *Mondgöttin*, col. 3182.

[5] *Ol.* ii. 50.

[6] Pind. *Ol.* iii. 36. Paus. v. 15.   [7] Paus. vi. 20. 9.

the introduction of the octennial period which is symbolised by
this particular form of the sacred marriage. The case of the
Panathenaea, deliberately modelled on the Olympic Festival, is
precisely similar. The Great Panathenaea of Peisistratos were
penteteric; but they were only an enlargement of the ancient
Lesser Panathenaea, founded by Erichthonios, which were annual.
In the same way at Olympia itself, as we shall see (p. 231), the
Heraea were probably at first annual, and later came to be
celebrated with especial grandeur and additional rites in every
fourth year. We may be fairly sure that the Olympic Games
themselves had similarly been at first an annual feast; and there
is no reason to suppose that this annual feast was held in the late
summer, since that date is due solely to the conjunction of sun
and moon.

Before we pass on to the Elean tradition of the origin of the
Games, we must discuss the, probably older, Women's Games,
which seem to date from the earlier system of time-reckoning by
the moon.

THE HERAEA.

We have seen that the Olympic festival was a moveable feast,
and occurred alternately in Apollonios and Parthenios, which were
probably the second and third months of the Elean year. This
variation of the month is a strange and inconvenient arrangement[1].
Moreover it is unique. The Pythia also were held at intervals of
50 and 49 months, but the incidence of the intercalated months of
the octennial period was so arranged that the festival itself always
fell in the same month (Bukatios) of the Delphic year. In the
same way the Panathenaea, though penteteric, always fell in
Hekatombaion. There must have been some very strong reason
for the troublesome variation of months in the sole case of the
most important of panhellenic gatherings.

Weniger finds the reason in the existence of an older im-
movable festival at the very season at which the reconstituted
Games were to be fixed. Every fourth year a college called the
Sixteen Women wove a robe for Hera and held games called the

---

[1] The following argument as to the month of the festival and its relation to the
Heraea is taken from the penetrating analysis of Weniger, *loc. cit.*, *supra*, p. 224.

Heraea[1]. The games consisted of a race between virgins[2], who ran in order of age, the youngest first, and the eldest last. The course was the Olympic stadium, less about one-sixth of its length (i.e. 500 instead of 600 Olympic feet). The winners received crowns of olive and a share of the cow sacrificed to Hera. 'They trace the origin of the games of the virgins, like those of the men, to antiquity, saying that Hippodameia, out of gratitude to Hera for her marriage with Pelops, assembled the Sixteen Women, and along with them arranged the Heraean games for the first time.'

It is highly probable that these games of virgins (Parthenia) gave its name to the month Parthenios, and were in honour of Hera Parthenos—Hera, whose virginity was perpetually renewed after her sacred marriage with Zeus. It is also probable that they were held at the new moon, that is, on the first day of Parthenios[3]. Further, if these games gave the month its name, in that month they must always have fallen. Thus the octennial period of the Heraea is of the usual straightforward type, which keeps always to the same month. The natural inference is that the Heraea were first in the field. and that. when the men's games were fixed at the same season, it was necessary to avoid this older fixed festival. At the same time, if the games of Zeus were allowed to be established regularly in the middle of the previous month Apollonios, it was obvious that the Heraea would sink into a mere appendage. Zeus, on the other hand, was not inclined to yield permanent precedence to Hera. The deadlock was solved by a characteristic compromise. The octennial period for the Games of Zeus was so arranged that in alternate Olympiads they should fall fourteen days before, and fourteen days after, the Heraea (on Apollonios 14/15 and Parthenios 14/15). By this device of priestly ingenuity the honour of both divinities was satisfied, and so the inconvenient variation of months for the Olympic festival is explained.

---

[1] Paus. v. 16. 2.

[2] The winners were allowed to dedicate statues of themselves (Paus. v. 16. 3). The girl-runner in the Vatican is probably one of these votive statues. Beside the girl, in this marble copy of the bronze original, is a palm branch on a stump as symbol of victory.

[3] Cf. Lydus, *de mens.* III. 10 αἱ Καλένδαι Ἥρας ἑορτὴ ἐτύγχανον, τουτέστι Σελήνης. The Heraea cannot in any case have fallen between the 10th and 16th of Parthenios, when the men's games were held in alternate Olympiads.

The Heraea, then, were probably older than the reconstituted Olympia; and if they gave its name to the month Parthenios, they must have been annual before they were octennial or penteteric. They carry us back to the old lunar year, which preceded the combined sun-and-moon penteteris. Here again, as at Athens (p. 191), we find the moon associated with the olive tree; she has also her horned cow, a portion of whose flesh fell to the victor in the virgin's race. The eating of this portion and the wearing of the olive crown symbolised that the victorious virgin was, in an especial sense, identified with the moon. She became the Hippodameia of her year[1], and the chosen bride of the sacred marriage. It was not, at first, that she impersonated Hera Parthenos[2]: on the contrary, Hera Parthenos is the divinised projection and reflex of the Moon-maiden, the queen of the virgins that bore her company and, in all probability, went down to the river Parthenias, a tributary of the Alpheus, to draw the water for her nuptial bath[3].

THE FOOT-RACE FOR THE BRIDE.

If the moon-bride was chosen by a foot-race, so also, it would seem, was the sun-bridegroom. We have already seen that the fifty daughters whom the moon bore to Endymion were the fifty

---

[1] The accusation against Oinomaos of incest with his daughter Hippodameia simply means that Hippodameia was the title of his 'wife' and also of her successor, the wife of *his* successor, represented in myth as his 'daughter.'

The Sixteen Women 'get up two choruses' (χόρους δύο ἱστᾶσι), one for Physcoa, and one for Hippodameia. Weniger, *loc. cit.*, holds that this marks the union of two colleges—the Thyiads of Elis who honoured Physcoa and Dionysus, and a college in Pisatis who worshipped Hera and Hippodameia. It looks as if Oinomaos and Hippodameia were the Olympian doubles of Dionysus and Physcoa. For the equation Oinomaos = Dionysus cf. Athenaeus x. 426 F who cites Nicochares, *Amymone* (Kock I. 770) Οἰνόμαος οὗτος χαῖρε πέντε καὶ δύο (the mixture of two parts wine with five water) and Eupolis, *Αἶξ* (Kock I. 260), Διόνυσε χαῖρε· μή τι πέντε καὶ δύο. Gruppe, *Gr. Myth. u. Rel.* I. 150, notes that Physcoa and Dionysus were worshipped at Oinoe (north of Olympia) and connects the name Oinomaos with Oinoe.

[2] Dr Frazer, *G. B.*³, Part III. p. 91, writes: 'If the olive-crowned victor in the men's race at Olympia represented Zeus, it becomes probable that the olive-crowned victor in the girls' race, which was held every fourth year in honour of Hera represented in like manner the god's wife....But under the names of Zeus and Hera the pair of Olympic victors would seem to have really personated the Sun and Moon, who were the true heavenly bridegroom and bride of the ancient octennial festival.'

[3] Parthenias (Strabo VIII. 357) or Parthenia, beside which was the grave of the mares (Parthenia and Eripha) of Marmax, first of Hippodameia's suitors (Paus. VI. 21. 7). Hesych. Ἡρεσίδες· κόραι αἱ λουτρὰ κομίζουσαι τῇ Ἥρᾳ. *Etym. Mag.* p. 436 Ἡρεσίδες· αἱ ἱέρειαι τῆς ἐν Ἄργει Ἥρας· ἀπὸ τῆς Ἥρας· ἢ παρὰ τὸν ἀρύσω μέλλοντα, ἀρυσίτιδες, αἱ ἀρυόμεναι τὰ λουτρά. Cf. Paus. II. 17. 1; Weniger, *loc. cit.*

moon months of the penteteris, and we are also told of Endymion, that he set his sons to race at Olympia for the kingdom[1]. This is a variant of the race of suitors for the hand of the princess, which in other similar stories carries the kingdom with it.

Now we know of another family of fifty daughters whose hands were disposed of by competition in a foot-race—the Danaids. In the Ninth *Pythian* Pindar tells how the Libyan king Antaeus, desiring to compass a famous marriage for his daughter, followed the example of Danaus in Argos, who

contrived for the *forty and eight* maidens a wedding most swift, before midday should be upon them. He presently made the whole company stand at the goal of the race-course and bade determine by a foot-race which maiden each hero should have, of all that came to be his sons-in-law.

But, whereas Antaeus offered only one daughter as the prize for one out of many suitors, Danaus offered a bunch of forty-eight; and another authority lets out the truth that some, if not all, of these eight and forty got no husbands.

Pausanias[2] telling how Icarius set the wooers of Penelope to run the race in which of course Odysseus was successful, adds that Icarius (like Antaeus) imitated Danaus, who set the suitors to run for his daughters. The first man home had first choice of a Danaid, the second, the second choice, and so on. '*The daughters that were left had to wait till other wooers came and had run another race.*' Now in Pindar's version forty-eight Danaids are offered. Why this number? Because, we are told, two were already married—Hypermnestra and Amymone. Who are the forty-eight who cannot get husbands?

If the fifty daughters of Danaus are doubles of the fifty daughters of Endymion and the Moon, the answer is clear. The two who are married must be the first and last months of the penteteric cycle—the moons who are paired in sacred marriage with the midsummer sun[3].

The Danaids are also well-maidens, with functions, perhaps, like those of the Athenian Dew-Carriers (p. 173). To the moon-bride may have fallen the duty of bringing water for rain-charms,

---

[1] Paus. v. 1. 3.   [2] III. 12. 1.

[3] Note that Pindar says (*v.* 113) the race was to be run 'before midday should overtake them' (πρὶν μέσον ἆμαρ ἐλεῖν); before, that is to say, the sun at his height of noon or of midsummer carries off the one who *is* married. It may be observed that $48 = 16 + 16 + 16$; does this account for the number of the *Sixteen* Women—sixteen for each of the remaining three years of the penteteris?

while the sun-bridegroom was charged with the maintenance of the solar fire[1].

Now, the Elean antiquaries said that for the first thirteen Olympiads from the beginning of the unbroken tradition, the only competition was the foot-race[2]. This is the race which we have seen reflected in myth as the race for the kingdom and the hand of the princess. In literal fact it seems to have been a contest to determine who should represent the male partner in the sacred marriage with the victor of the virgin's race. It has already been suggested that this personage could be regarded as, in a certain sense, the *daimon* of his 'year,' the 'king' for a limited period, on whom the rains of heaven and the fruits of earth would depend.

Modern analogies support this view of the significance of the foot-race. 'Games,' says Mr Chambers[3], 'were a feature of seasonal, no less than of funeral feasts....A bit of wrestling or a bout of quarter-staff is still *de rigueur* at many a wake or rush-bearing, while in parts of Germany the winner of a race or of a shooting-match at the ·popinjay is entitled to light the festival fire, or to hold the desired office of May-King.'

The suggestion is further confirmed by an interesting ancient analogy. The Laconian Karneia were celebrated in the month Karneios, which corresponds to the Elean Apollonios. Their date, moreover, like that of the Olympian festival, with which they sometimes coincided[4], seems to have been fixed with reference

---

[1] Cf. Chambers, *The Mediaeval Stage*, i. 122. In modern agricultural festivals 'water is thrown on the fields and on the plough, while the worshippers themselves, or a representative chosen from among them, are sprinkled or immersed. To this practice many survivals bear evidence; the virtues persistently ascribed to dew gathered on May morning, the ceremonial bathing of women annually or in times of drought with the expressed purpose of bringing fruitfulness on man or beast or crop, the "ducking" customs...,' etc. The interpretation of the Danaids is due to Mr A. B. Cook. See further his *Zeus*, vol. i. Index i. *s.v.* Danaides.

[2] Paus. v. 8. 6. Cf. Plut. *Symp. Qu.* v. 2. 675 c (above, p. 221).

[3] *The Mediaeval Stage*, i. 148. Mr Chambers refers to Frazer, *G. B.*[2] i. 217; iii. 258. Cf. Mannhardt, *Ant. Wald- und Feldkulte*, p. 254, 'Jene deutschen Maitags- und Ernteumgänge nehmen mehrfach auch die Form eines *Wettlaufs* an, bei welchem entweder die letzte, den Korndämon darstellende Garbe oder der Maibaum das Ziel ist, oder durch welchen *die Rollen bei dem Umgange mit dem Laubmann, Pfingstbutz u.s.w. entschieden werden.* Der Wettlauf bildet den ersten Akt, die Prozession mit dem durch den Sieger in demselben dargestellten Vegetationsdämon den zweiten Akt der Festbegehungen.'

[4] For instance in the year 480 B.C., Herod. vii. 206; viii. 72.

to the full moon[1]. The festival was conducted by a college of Karneatai, young, unmarried men, who were chosen, five from each tribe (?), and held office for four years[2]—a period which seems to indicate that this annual festival was held with especial splendour once in each penteteris.

The rite which specially concerns us is the race of the Staphylodromoi[3]. These were young men, chosen from among the Karneatai; their title was derived from the clustered vine-branches which they carried in their hands. One of their number decked himself with garlands and ran, 'praying for a blessing on the city'; the rest pursued him. If he was overtaken, it was supposed to bring good luck; if not, the reverse.

The race here takes a different form from those we have been concerned with—probably an older form[4], which did not degenerate into a mere athletic competition. The young man, decked with garlands and perhaps also disguised with the skin of a beast so as to be the 'mumming representative of a *daimon*[5],' embodies the luck of the year, which will be captured or lost, according as the youth is overtaken or escapes. His connection with the fruits of the year is marked by the vine-clusters; and it does not surprise us to find that at Cyrene the festival of Apollo Karneios was celebrated with the slaughter of many bulls, and that his altars were decorated 'in spring with all the flowers the Horae bring when the west wind blows laden with dew, and in winter

---

[1] Eur. *Alk.* 448,

Σπάρτᾳ κύκλος ἀνίκα Καρνείου περινίσσεται ὥρας
μηνός, ἀειρομένας παννύχου σελάνας.

For the Karneia see S. Wide, *Lakonische Kulte*, p. 73 ff., Nilsson, *Gr. Feste*, p. 118 ff.

[2] Hesych. καρνεᾶται· οἱ ἄγαμοι· κεκληρωμένοι δὲ ἐπὶ τὴν τοῦ Καρνείου λειτουργίαν· πέντε δὲ ἀφ' ἑκάστης <φυλῆς Castellanus> ἐπὶ τετραετίαν ἐλειτούργουν.

[3] Bekk. *Anecd.* I. p. 305 σταφυλοδρόμοι· κατὰ τὴν τῶν Καρνείων ἑορτὴν στέμματά τις περιθέμενος τρέχει ἐπευχόμενός τι τῇ πόλει χρηστόν, ἐπιδιώκουσι δὲ αὐτὸν νέοι, σταφυλοδρόμοι καλούμενοι. καὶ ἐὰν μὲν καταλάβωσι αὐτόν, ἀγαθόν τι προσδοκῶσιν κατὰ τὰ ἐπιχώρια τῇ πόλει, εἰ δὲ μή, τοὐναντίον. The *Oschophoria* at Athens was a similar festival, see Athenaeus XI. 62, p. 496. It began with a race of epheboi carrying ὄσχοι and they διημιλλῶντο πρὸς ἀλλήλους δρόμῳ. The victor (ὁ πρότερος) went in procession with his band, κωμάζει μετὰ χοροῦ. For the Oschophoria see *infra*, p. 320.

[4] Compare the Regifugium on Feb. 24, four days from the end of the old Roman year, discussed by Dr Frazer (*G.B.*[3] Part I. vol. ii. pp. 308—312), who compares this 'flight' to races for the kingdom.

[5] Hesych. στεμματιαῖον· δίκηλόν τι ἐν ἑορτῇ πομπεῦον (codd. πομπέων) δαίμονος. Δίκηλον is glossed as φάσμα, μίμημα, εἴδωλον, ξῴδιον, etc.; δικηλικταί are mummers. See S. Wide, *loc. cit.*

with the sweet crocus[1].' The slain bulls were eaten at a *dais* or *eranos*[2]. The Karneia are an instructive instance, because they show us the complete series: first the animal—κάρνος means a ram; next the human youth with animal disguise; then the daimon Karneios, or Kranios Stemmatios[3]; finally the Olympian Apollo, surnamed Karneios and Dromaios to remind him that he had taken the place of a ram-racer.

The Foot-race of the Kouretes.

We are now in a position to interpret the Elean legend of the origin of the Games—a legend which has been persistently rejected, merely because the facts which have been thrown into relief in the preceding chapters of this book were unknown or not understood[4].

With regard to the Olympic games, the Elean antiquaries say that Kronos first reigned in Heaven, and that a temple was made for him by the men of that age, who were named the Golden Race; that when Zeus was born, Rhea committed the safe-keeping of the child to the Idaean Daktyls or Kouretes, as they are also called; that the Daktyls came from Ida in Crete, and their names were Herakles, Paeonaeus, Epimedes, Jasios, and Idas; and that in sport Herakles, the eldest, set his brethren to run a race, and crowned the victor with a branch of wild olive, of which they had such an abundance that they slept on heaps of its fresh green leaves[5].

After what has gone before, no lengthy comment is needed. The Games are traced back to an original foot-race, held by young men, Kouretes, from Crete[6], presumably analogous to the young, unmarried Karneatai of Sparta. The race, we may suppose, determined who should be *the* Kouros—the Greatest Kouros—of his year. The winner received, not a prize of commercial value such

---

[1] Kallim. *in Apoll.* 77 ff.

[2] Pind. *Pyth.* v. 77 πολύθυτον ἔρανον ἔνθεν ἀναδεξαμέναν, Ἄπολλον, τεᾷ, Καρνήι᾽, ἐν δαιτὶ σεβίζομεν Κυράνας ἀγακτιμέναν πόλιν.

[3] Paus. III. 20. 9, Kranios Stemmatios had a temenos on the road from Arcadia to Sparta.

[4] The Elean tradition reported by Pausanias is not to be despised; for it must be remembered that its natural custodians, the two priestly houses of the Iamidae and Klytiadae, held office at Olympia with unbroken continuity down to the third century A.D. (cf. Weniger, *Der heilige Ölbaum in Olympia*, Weimar, 1895, p. 2).

[5] Paus. v. 7. 6.

[6] Plato, *Laws*, 625 D: Crete is uneven and specially suited to foot-racing. The social importance of foot-races is marked at Gortyn, where the ephebi not yet admitted to full rights were called ἀπόδρομοι, διὰ τὸ μηδέπω τῶν κοινῶν δρόμων μετέχειν (Ar. Byz.); whereas δρομεῖς possessed rights of mature years, see Busolt, *Gr. Gesch.* I. 344. At the Panathenaea there was a 'long foot-race' (μακρὸς δρόμος) of the ephebi from the altar of Eros, where they lighted torches; the πυρά of the Goddess' victims was lighted with the victor's torch, Schol. ad Plat. *Phaedr.* 231 E. Philostratus, π. γυμν. 5, describes the stadion race at Olympia as a race for the honour of lighting the fire on the altar.

as were usual in funeral games, but a symbol of his office as
vegetation-*daimon*—the branch of the sacred tree. This branch
reminds us of the golden bough, and perhaps, links the foot-race
of the young men to the contest between the young and the old
king. For in the famous wood at Nemi, it was he who succeeded
in tearing a bough from the sacred tree, who had a right to contend in single combat with the King of the Wood for succession
to his office[1].

It is possible that the sacred tree from which the victor's
wreath or branch was plucked was not at first the olive-tree, which
may have belonged rather to the moon and the virgin victor of
the Heraea. One curious tradition points to another fruit-tree—
the apple. Phlegon of Tralles[2], a contemporary of Pausanias, tells
how in the sixth Olympiad, Iphitus consulted the Delphic oracle
as to how the victors should be crowned. The God told him *not
to make the fruit of the apple the prize of victory*, but to take the
wild olive, 'now wreathed in the light web of the spider.' Iphitus
found among the many wild olives of the temenos one which was
covered with spider's webs, and he built a wall round it. The first
victor to be crowned with olive was Daïkles of Messene, who won
the footrace in the seventh Olympiad. If this tradition has any
truth in it, we may suppose that the original apple-bough was
superseded by the olive borrowed from the moon-goddess[3], possibly
when the race of the young men was combined with that of the
virgins, at the introduction of the sun-and-moon calendar, and
the men's games were assimilated as closely as possible to the
women's.

Even before it became the moon-tree, the holy olive probably
belonged to Earth. We have seen how the Kouretes 'slept on
heaps of its fresh green leaves.' They were like the Selloi of
Dodona who slept upon the ground (χαμαιεῦναι), in order that

---

[1] Servius ad *Æn.* vi. 136 Dabatur autem fugitivis potestas ut si quis exinde
ramum potuisset auferre, monomachia cum fugitivo templi sacerdote dimicaret.

[2] *F.H.G.* iii. p. 604

Ἴφιτε, μήλειον καρπὸν μὴ θῇς ἐπὶ νίκῃ,
ἀλλὰ τὸν ἄγριον ἀμφιτίθει καρπώδη ἔλαιον,
ὃς νῦν ἀμφέχεται λεπτοῖσιν ὑφάσμασ' ἀράχνης.

[3] According to the legend told in Pind. *Ol.* iii. Herakles went to the land of the
Hyperboreans to fetch the wild olive. On his former visit, in quest of the golden-
horned hind, he was welcomed there, not by Apollo, but by Artemis, the horse-
rider (ἱππόσοα, cf. Hippodameia), and then it was that he 'stood and marvelled at
the trees.'

in their dreams they might draw oracular wisdom from the Earth[1]. Olympia also had its Earth oracle and its cult of Demeter Chamyne[2], whose priestess sat enthroned in a place of honour and witnessed the Games of Zeus.

The theory, of course, presupposes that the Olympic Games, like the Karneia, the Panathenaea, the Heraea, and others, were annual before they were penteteric; for the penteteris, as we have remarked, is an astronomical cycle independent of the yearly upspringing and decay of vegetation[3]. The supposition is very probable, when we consider the late and artificial character of periods which combine the sun calendar with the older reckoning by the moon. In discussing that combination we agreed with Dr Frazer that from its introduction the Olympic victor represented the Sun united in marriage with the Moon. Even if there were no further evidence, it would still be a reasonable conjecture that in earlier days, the sacred marriage, here as elsewhere, had been an annual feast, and its protagonists instead of being related to the celestial bridegroom and bride, had embodied the powers of fertility in a more primitive form directly associated with the seasonal life of nature. If that is so, the new penteteric festival in the late summer may have attracted to itself features, such as the single combat and the foot-race for the olive branch, from feasts which under the older systems of time-reckoning would naturally belong to winter or to spring. We are therefore untouched by objections based on the time of year of the historic Games—a time fixed solely with reference to the Sun and Moon. We are at liberty to suppose that the winner of the foot-race represented the fertility-*daimon*, before he represented the Sun. As one mode of time-reckoning supersedes another, so in the sphere of religion emphasis is successively laid on Earth, with her changing seasons and meteoric phenomena, on the Moon, and on the Sun. This line of enquiry may set at rest many old-standing controversies.

[1] Hom. *Il.* xvi. 234. This analogy is pointed out by Weniger, *Der heilige Ölbaum*, p. 19.

[2] Gruppe, *Gr. Myth. u. Rel.* i. 142, calls attention to the probable identity of Iasios, one of the Idaean Daktyls called the brothers of Herakles in the Elean legend, with Iasion who lay with Demeter on the ground (Hes. *Theog.* 969, *Od.* v. 125).

[3] We here welcome the support of Professor Ridgeway, who, as reported in the *Athenaeum*, May 20, 1911, 'pointed out that the astronomical cycles, such as the Metonic, were late, and may have come in with the remaking of the games, which must have existed long before B.C. 776 at Olympia.'

Take such a divinity as Osiris, who began life as a vegetation-spirit, manifest in trees or in the corn.   Ancient theologians and modern students have again and again upheld or refuted the propositions that 'Osiris is the Moon,' 'Osiris is the Sun,' or that he is neither.   The truth will, we believe, prove to be more complex.   These vegetation-spirits or Year Gods successively take on moon and sun attributes, when the lunar calendar supersedes the agricultural, and again when the lunar calendar is first combined with, then superseded by, the solar.   There is no simple answer to the question: 'Is Osiris the Moon, or is he the Sun?' He began as neither, and has passed through both phases.

As each new stage succeeds, the older festivals are not abolished. Some are adapted, with necessary shifts to a different season of the year.   Others survive in a degenerate form, as holidays.   So, and so only, can we account for the extraordinary duplication of festivals in ancient calendars, and for the occurrence, at different times of the year and attached to different divinities, of rites which are obviously identical in content.

If we may assume the same succession of calendars at Olympia, the several stages would correspond to the succession we have made out for the sacred Tree.   In the earliest, seasonal or agricultural, stage the olive belonged to Earth, to Demeter Chamyne. Then it passed to Hera the moon-goddess and became the prize of the moon-virgin's race.   Finally, when sun and moon were united in the ennaeteris, the olive-branch supplanted the original apple-bough, and became the prize also for the foot-race of the Sun-bridegroom.

THE MOTHER AND CHILD AND KOURETES AT OLYMPIA.

Further evidence is not wanting in support of the tradition at Olympia of the Idaean Daktyls or Kouretes, to whose foot-race for the olive-branch the Games were traced back.   This tradition is firmly rooted in the monuments and cults of Olympia.   The legend, as we have seen, says that 'when Zeus was born, Rhea committed the safe-keeping of the child to the Idaean Daktyls or Kouretes, who came from Ida in Crete.'   Pindar[1] himself is

---

[1] *Ol.* v. 17   Σωτὴρ ὑψινεφὲς Ζεῦ, Κρόνιόν τε ναίων λόφον
τιμῶν τ' Ἀλφεὸν εὐρὺ ῥέοντα Ἰδαῖόν τε σεμνὸν ἄντρον.
Schol. ad v. 42 Ἰδαῖον ἄντρον ἐν Ἤλιδι Δημήτριος ὁ Σκήψιος...ἱερὸν Διός. ἔνιοι δὲ νομίζοντες μὴ τῶν ἐν Ἤλιδι χωρίων αὐτὸν μεμνῆσθαι ὑπέλαβον μνημονεύειν Ἴδης τῆς ἐν Κρήτῃ....

our witness that on the hill of Kronos Olympia had a Cave which
was called Idaean, manifestly because it was a counterpart of the
Cave of the Birthplace on Cretan Ida. To this Cave the legend
of the κουροτροφία belongs. We must look for it among a small
group of sanctuaries, whose high antiquity is marked, among other
things, by their close neighbourhood to the foot of the sacred hill
of Kronos. The later shrines and precincts of Pelops and the
Olympian Father Zeus had to find room further out towards
the river.

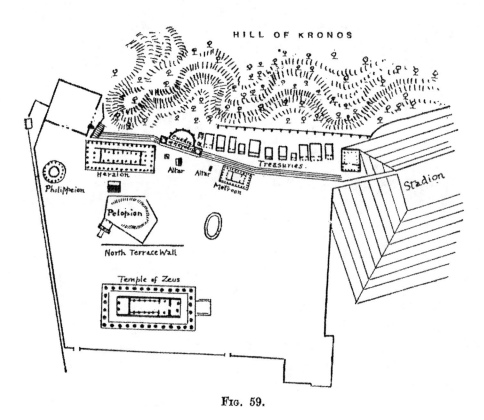

Fig. 59.

In this group (Figs. 59 and 60) we find, first, the Metroon,
marking the site of a very ancient cult of the Mother Goddess;
and close by it an altar of the Kouretes[1]. Right on the skirts of
the hill, behind the line of the later treasuries, stood a small
shrine of the Mother and Infant—Eileithyia and Sosipolis[2]. This
little temple moreover did not stand clear of the hillside; the
back wall appears to have been actually engaged in it. This
circumstance, observed by Dörpfeld, has led to the identification

[1] Paus. v. 8. 1.   [2] Paus. vi. 20. 2.

of the shrine with the Idaean Cave, and of 'Zeus the Saviour, who as Pindar says honoured it, with the Saviour of the City, Sosipolis[1].

So we find among the most ancient monuments of the Altis a complex of shrines dedicated to the Mother and Child, and the attendant Kouretes—a group whose significance has already been made clear[2]. It represents the three essential factors of a matrilinear society[3].

The ritual of this shrine of Eileithyia and Sosipolis was simple[4]. The priestess, an old woman annually chosen, brought water to wash the infant god, and set out barley cakes kneaded with honey. These honey-cakes were food for the serpent—the animal form

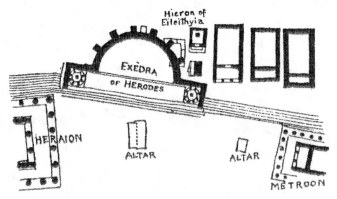

Fig. 60.

of the god. For legend said that once, when the Arcadians in-vaded Elis, the baby Sosipolis was set naked before the Elean army; and he changed into a snake and the Arcadians ran away. Then the snake vanished into the earth, no doubt at the very spot where this cave-shrine was afterwards built.

Only the aged priestess might enter the inner shrine. Outside, the maids and matrons waited, singing a hymn, and offering incense of all sorts, but with no libations of wine. These offerings—incense and wineless libations—are, as we know, characteristic of

[1] See Carl Robert, *Sosipolis in Olympia*, Mitth. d. Arch. Inst. Athen, Abth. XVIII. 1893, p. 37 ff.
[2] It may be observed that the next stage of the Elean tradition is the arrival from Crete of Klymenos. a descendant of the Idaean Herakles, who erects an altar of ashes to Olympian Hera, and an altar to Herakles surnamed Parastates, and the other Kouretes (Paus. v. 8. 1 and 14. 8).
[3] See *supra*, p. 39, and *infra*, chapter XI.
[4] Paus. VI. 20. 2.

pre-Olympian divinities—the elder gods of the Earth or of the Sky[1]. Sosipolis, the snake-child, like Erichthonios, was of the Earth[2]. The Earth was his mother; for 'Eileithyia' is only one name of the Mother Goddess, Rhea, Demeter, Gaia.

In Magnesia, as we have seen (p. 154), Sosipolis has become Zeus Sosipolis. Nevertheless, right down into Imperial times the tradition survived of his infant form and of his theriomorph, the snake. Fig. 61 shows one of a series of bronze coins of Magnesia of the time of Caracalla[3]. On it appears the infant Saviour seated on a table or throne with legs of thunderbolt pattern. Round him are his

FIG. 61.

Kouretes, clashing their shields; and, underneath, the snake emerges from a cista.

Who was the child Sosipolis? Not far from Olympia, at Elis itself, Sosipolis had a sanctuary in common with Tyche. There he was represented not as an infant, but as a boy, clad in a star-spangled robe and holding the horn of Amaltheia, the goat who suckled the infant Zeus in Crete[4]—the cornucopia with the fruits of the year[5]. Tyche and Sosipolis are the same as Eirene and the child Ploutos—the Hora[6] carrying the Wealth of the year.

The festival of Magnesian Sosipolis has already been discussed (p. 150); and it has been argued that the bull, who was designated at the full moon of the month Kronion—the month of seed-time—fed up all through the winter, and eaten at a communal meal in spring or early summer, embodied the life of the year, was the

---

[1] See J. E. Harrison, *Prolegomena*, p. 89.

[2] Compare the snake-child Opheltes-Archemoros associated with the founding of the Nemean Games (Apollod. III. 6. 4; Bacchyl. VIII. 10) and the child Aix which tended its father the Python slain by Apollo, connected with the origin of the Pythia (Plut. *Qu. Gr.* p. 293 c; see Nilsson, *Gr. Feste*, p. 151). Another Olympian hero, Iamos, is nursed by snakes, Pind. *Ol.* VI. 45.

[3] From Rayet, *Milet et le golfe Latinique*, Fig. 36, p. 139. The obverse has the laurel-crowned head of Caracalla. See also Imhoof-Blumer, *Gr. Münzen*, 1890, pl. 8. 33.

[4] The Cretan Zeus also has his snake form, Schol. *Arat.* 46; Eratosth. *catast.* 25. 62; cf. C. Robert, *loc. cit. supra.*

[5] Compare also the *Eniautos* with Amaltheia's horn in Ptolemy's procession, p. 186, *supra.*

[6] Hesiod, *Theog.* 903; Pind. *Ol.* XIII. 6 Εὐνομία...Δίκα...Εἰρήνα, ταμίαι ἀνδράσι πλούτου.

daimon of the *eniautos*. He is identical with the Kouros of the Cretan hymn, who comes 'for the Year,' and brings with him the blossoming of the Seasons[1].

Before we leave the Kouretes and their foot-race, we must mention a curious parallel from Hebrew tradition[2], which gives us a combination of moon and sun races, and also seems to confirm the identification, already mentioned (p. 193), of the Kouretes with the Roman Salii.

The Jewish Agada contains a dialogue between certain Rabbis and their disciples concerning the hippodrome of Solomon. Solomon held twelve horse-races in each year, one in every month. 'Why not thirteen?' says a disciple, for there were thirteen months. One race, replies the Rabbi, was not a horse-race, but a foot-race of young men of the tribe of Gad, as it is written[3]: 'And of the Gadites there separated themselves unto David into the hold to the wilderness, mighty men of valour, men trained for war, that could handle shield and spear; whose faces were like the faces of lions, and they were swift as the roes upon the mountains.' This race of youths was run in the intercalary month Tebeth which contains the winter solstice. They also carried golden shields. It is written of them[4]: 'As oft as the king went into the House of the Lord, the Runners bare them (the golden shields), and brought them back to their chamber.'

These young men called 'Runners' (הָרָצִים) seem strangely analogous to the Roman 'Leapers' (the Salii), who also kept shields (*ancilia*) in a chamber and brought them out in solemn procession in the month of Mars—the first month of the old Roman year. The interesting point about Solomon's Kouretes-Salii is that their race, falling in the intercalary month, seems to be a moon-race on foot, as contrasted with the horse-races of the sun in the other twelve months. Such may originally have been the foot-race of the Idaean Kouretes at Olympia, becoming a sun-race when the Kouros was identified with the sun.

[1] Does this conception throw light on the obscure figure of the 'Saviour Year' (Λυκάβας Σώζων) in Asia Minor? Cf. Roscher, *Lex.*, s.v. *Orthopolis*. Λυκάβας, according to Stengel (*Hermes*, XVIII., p. 304) is the moon.

[2] See Wünsche, *Salomos Hippodrom als Abbild des babylonischen Himmelsbildes*, Leipzig, 1906. Cf. Eisler, *Arch. f. Religionswiss.* XI. (1907) 150.

[3] 1 Chron. xii. 8.

[4] 1 Kings xiv. 28. The Authorised Version not understanding the Runners translates הָרָצִים by 'the guard.'

The Saviour of the City may, then, be represented either as an animal—a bull among a pastoral people, or a snake when he is a 'local daimon[1]' or hero—or as a human infant, boy, or youth. We need not be disturbed by the differences of age[2]. The change from the old year to the new may be symbolised in various ways. We are familiar with the venerable Father Christmas on the verge of the grave, and with the New Year as an infant.

At Olympia Sosipolis became fixed in his infant shape beside his mother Eileithyia. Every year he must be born anew and washed with the holy water by his venerable nursing-mother. But another type is well-known—the youth (Adonis, Attis, Osiris), who dies and rises again in spring.

This Easter death and resurrection of the same individual is evidently at first distinct from the death of the Old Year at the hands of the New, where the two individuals are necessarily different and the death might be a real death. The death, on the other hand, which is followed by a resurrection, cannot be real; it must always have been a mimetic rite. Does the Olympian legend of Pelops preserve traces of a δρώμενον of this type? We shall attempt to show that it does.

THE FEAST OF TANTALUS.

One element in the legend of Pelops, as told by Pindar in the first *Olympian*, still waits to be explained—the banquet of Tantalus. We have remarked that it constitutes a crux for the theory of the funeral origin of the Games. If the Games merely commemorated the achievements of Pelops, why had this dark and monstrous story lasted down to Pindar's time as part of the Olympian legend of the hero? To ignore or to suppress it would have been simpler than to keep it and explain it away.

---

[1] Paus. v. 20. 2 Σωσίπολις Ἠλείοις ἐπιχώριος δαίμων.

[2] Cf. the various ages of Dionysos, p. 41, and Macrob. *Sat.* I. xviii. 9 on the various ages of the Sun: item Liberi Patris (=Solis in inferno hemisphaerio) simulacra partim puerili aetate, partim iuvenis fingunt. Praeterea barbata specie, senili quoque...hae autem aetatum diversitates ad solem referuntur, ut parvulus videatur hiemali solstitio, qualem Aegyptii proferunt ex adyto die certa, quod tunc brevissimo die veluti *parvus et infans* videatur. Exinde autem procedentibus augmentis aequinoctio vernali similiter atque *adulescentis adipiscitur vires* figuraque iuvenis ornatur. Postea statuitur eius aetas plenissima effigie barbae solstitio aestivo, quo tempore summum sui consequitur augmentum. Exinde per diminutiones veluti senescenti quarta forma deus figuratur.

We shall proceed, as before, on the supposition that this incident, like the other factors in the myth already explained, is not an event in the real history of an individual called Pelops, but reflects a rite or δρώμενον. It may have escaped suppression because the ritual was more important than the reputation of the hero and his father. We hope to show further that this rite was of a nature which enables us to relate it to the New Year rites we have already found embedded in other parts of the legend.

The story of the Feast of Tantalus, with the primitive and horrible features which so shocked the conventional piety of Pindar, is as follows. Invited by the gods to eat nectar and ambrosia at their table, Tantalus asked them in return to a banquet on the summit of Mount Sipylos. The feast was an *eranos*; that is to say, each guest brought a contribution. Tantalus, at the last course, served the flesh of his son Pelops, whom he had cut in pieces and boiled in a cauldron. The deities were taken at unawares, and one of them, Demeter, ate of the horrible dish. Then Zeus, seeing what had been done, ordered that the flesh should be put back into the cauldron and the child restored whole and sound. According to Bacchylides[1], it was Rhea, the mother goddess, who revived Pelops by passing him through the cauldron. In Pindar's revised and expurgated version, the infant is taken out of a 'pure cauldron' by Klotho, the Birth Fate—καθαροῦ λέβητος ἔξελε Κλώθω. Finally, Zeus blasted Mount Sipylos with thunder and earthquake, to punish Tantalus for his impiety, or else (as some have held) for carrying piety to an indiscreet excess. One reason why it is so hard to please the gods is that it is so hard to know beforehand at what moment they will have outgrown the sort of things which used to please them.

Now, what was the essential purport of the ritual described in this myth? What was actually done to the infant, and with what intent? In the right answer to this question lies our hope of connecting the Feast of Tantalus with the institution of the Games.

Is it a human sacrifice, counteracted by a miracle? Such is the common view[2], which sees a parallel to the more famous

---

[1] Bacch. frag. 54 (Jebb) ap. Schol. Pind. *Ol.* i. 40 ὁ δὲ Βακχυλίδης τὸν Πέλοπα τὴν Ῥέαν λέγει ὑγιάσαι καθεῖσαν διὰ λέβητος. I suspect that Bacchylides is meant by the πρότεροι whom Pindar controverts, *Ol.* i. 37.

[2] See Roscher, *Lex.*, s.v. *Pelops*.

sacrifice of Isaac on the mountain top.   But in such stories do we not always find a vicarious victim?   Something at least is really made over to the gods—if not Isaac, then a ram caught in a thicket; and the original human victim escapes.   Here, on the contrary, there is no substitute; the gods get no equivalent for the victim. A sacrifice in which nothing is really made over to the gods is not a sacrifice in the usual sense.

If we put aside this explanation, what remains?   Nothing is more certain than that if you cut a child to pieces and boil it, you cannot afterwards restore it to life by boiling it a second time.   If the child was really killed, the restoration to life was miraculous; in other words, it did not happen.   But suppose that the restoration to life' was, not a miraculous interruption of the rite, but the central core of the rite itself.   Suppose, in fact, that it was a ritual, not of sacrifice, but of regeneration, of New Birth? Then, as in countless other such ceremonies, the symbolic resurrection is preceded by a symbolic and counterfeit death.   A pretence is made of killing the child in order that it may be born again to a new life.   Pindar writes more wisely than he knows when he says the child Pelops was taken out of a 'pure' or 'purifying' cauldron by Klotho, a *Birth*-Fate.   The ritual was of Birth—of that Second Birth which, sooner or later, comes to be conceived as 'purification[1].'

To prove that it is so, the other features of the narrative must be explained.   Why does this rite of new birth take place at the conclusion of a feast on a mountain-top?   Why does the mimic death of the child take the form of his being dismembered, cooked, and eaten?   Why is the mountain riven with thunder at the close?

First, what mountain was the scene of this banquet of the gods?

Pindar accepts the tradition that Pelops came from Lydia, and that the mountain was Sipylos in Magnesia.   There, on the very summit of an isolated crag is still to be seen the rock-cut seat

[1] Rejuvenation by cooking occurs in the legend of Medea, who persuaded the daughters of Pelias (whom Gruppe, *Gr. Rel. u. Myth.* i. 145, regards as a double of Pelops) to dismember and boil him.   To convince them, Medea made a ram into a lamb by the same process (Apollod. i. 9. 27).   This, I suspect, was the Golden Ram or Lamb, that is the Sun, whose daughter Medea was.   Compare Menerva cooking the young Mars on the Praenestine cista in Fig. 50, p. 198.   Cf. Roscher, *Lex.*, s.v. *Mars*.   See A. B. Cook. *Zeus*, i. (1914), 419[10].

called the Throne of Pelops; and, lower down on the face of the cliff, the sanctuary of the Mountain Mother, here worshipped under the name of Mother Plastene[1]. But this was not the only home of the legend of Tantalus. There is also a Mount Tantalus in Lesbos, where some traits of the story reappear[2]. And not only so; but no less an authority than Aeschylus makes King Tantalus reign on Mount Ida in Phrygia. The poet even transfers Sipylos to the neighbourhood of Ida[3].

Strabo complains of Aeschylus for making (as he says) this 'confusion'; but in another passage[4] Strabo himself tells us how the confusion came about. It was due to identity of cults in the two places. The Great Mother of Mount Sipylos was also the Lady of Ida. 'The Berekyntes,' he says, 'and the Phrygians in general, and the Trojans living at *Ida* worship Rhea with mystical rites...and after the various places of her cult, they call her *Idaea*, Dindymene, *Sipylene*, Pessinuntis, Kybele.' 'The Greeks,' he adds, 'call her attendants *Kouretes*.'

This gives us a clue. It suggests a form of cult to which we can refer the ritual of Tantalus' Feast—the cult, namely, which prevailed all down the coast of Asia Minor, of the Great Mother and her Child, with her attendant Kouretes or Korybantes—the very cult which we have found established at the foot of the hill of Kronos at Olympia.

Following this clue let us move southward again from Mount Ida to Ephesus. Here we shall find an Olympianised form of this same cult of the Mother and Child, flourishing throughout historical antiquity[5]. This instance is specially important for us, because here, at Ephesus, we have as a constituent part of the cult, a banquet, a *eranos* feast, on the top of a mountain. Strabo's account[6] is as follows:

On the coast near Ephesus, a little above the sea, lies Ortygia, a splendid grove (ἄλσος) of trees of all sorts, mostly cypress. Through it flows the river Kenchrios where they say Leto washed after her travail. For here legend tells of the Birth, of the nurse Ortygia, of the Birth-place, where no one may enter, and of the olive-tree close by where the goddess is said to have rested after her travail.

---

[1] Paus. v. 13. 7, and Frazer, *ad loc.*
[2] In Lesbos we hear also of Thyestes (whose homonym in Argive legend was, like Tantalus, concerned in a τεκνοφαγία) and Daito, who must be connected with some ritual *dais*. See schol. and Tzetzes ad Lyk. *Al.* 212.
[3] Strabo XII. 580, Aesch. frag. 156.
[4] Strabo x. 469.
[5] See Tac. *Ann.* III. 61.
[6] XIV. 639.

Above this grove is a mountain, Solmissos, where they say the Kouretes took their stand and with the clash of their arms frightened the jealous Hera who was lying in wait, and helped Leto to conceal the birth. (There are ancient temples with ancient images of wood, as well as later temples with statues by Scopas and others.)

Here, every year, the people assemble to celebrate a festival, at which it is the custom for the young men to vie with one another in the magnificence of their contributions to the entertainment. At the same season a college of the Kouretes holds banquets and performs certain mystical sacrifices.

There is little doubt that the ancient wooden images in these mountain shrines had represented a Mother and Infant of an older type than Leto and her children. The presence of the Kouretes, the attendant ministers of Rhea, is proof enough. Leto has superseded Rhea, just as in later times Leto's daughter, 'Great Artemis of the Ephesians, whom all Asia and the world worshippeth,' gave place in her turn to yet another Asiatic mother with her divine child.

On Mount Solmissos, above the cypress grove of the Birth-place, the tradition at least, if not the practice, survived, of a dance of young men in arms to conceal the divine birth. Certainly, the young men played a prominent part in the banquet on the mountain top, held by the college of Kouretes and their president, the Protokoures[1], with certain sacrifices called 'mystical' ($\mu\nu\sigma\tau\iota\kappa\alpha\grave{\iota}$ $\theta\nu\sigma\acute{\iota}\alpha\iota$), to mark that they were not ordinary Olympian sacrifices, such as would naturally belong to the cult of Leto and her twins. Of what nature were the mystical rites of this mountain-banquet? To answer that question we must go southward again to a still more famous seat of the same cult, where we shall find the remaining features of the Feast of Tantalus, and an explanation of their significance.

In Crete[2], as we have already seen (p. 13), the birth of a divine child, called Zeus, was concealed from his father Kronos, who had eaten his other children immediately after their birth. Here too the concealment was aided by a dance of young men in arms, called Kouretes.

The myth and ritual of Zagreus have already (p. 14) been examined. It has been shown that the ceremonies, in a comparatively late and civilised form, including a banquet, a procession with

---

[1] See Pauly-Wiss. s.v. *Ephesia*, col. 2756, and *supra*, p. 46, and R. Heberdey, *Jahreshefte Oestr. Inst.* VIII. 1905, Beiblatt, p. 77, for recent discoveries of inscribed drums with names of Kouretic officials.

[2] Strabo x. 468.

torches of the mountain mother, and certain thunder-rites, formed
a rite of ordination held by a sacred college of Kouretes, analogous
to the Kouretes at Ephesus.   We may presume that the banquet
was held, in Crete as at Ephesus, on the sacred mountain.   We
have seen too that the myth of Zagreus retains certain primitive,
and even disgusting, traits which carry us back to very early rites
of tribal initiation.   This myth supplies the remaining details of
the Feast of Tantalus.   We are told that the wicked Titans tore
the child in pieces, put a cauldron on a tripod, and boiled his
limbs, piercing them with spits[1].   The horrid repast ends with an
epiphany of the Thunderer[2].   Zeus was invited to the feast, but
discovering what had been done, blasted the Titans with his bolt[3].
The child was restored to life; his torn limbs were collected, and
he 'emerged whole and entire[4].'

The analogy, or rather identity, of this rite with the death and
resurrection of Pelops can hardly leave a doubt that the Feast of
Tantalus was in essence a ceremony of New Birth, of mock death
and resurrection, and also, in some sense, of Initiation.   It gives
us the ritual which is needed to complete the religion of the
Mother and Child and the Kouretes at the Idaean Cave beneath
the hill of Kronos.

The next point to be considered is, what connection can there
be between an initiation ceremony, such as we have found in the
legend of Pelops, and the inauguration of a New Year?   We
may note, in the first place, that the Eating of Children (τεκνοφαγία) which persistently recurs in the lineage of the house of
Tantalus, is connected with the succession to the kingdom.
Thyestes, son of Pelops, in the course of a strife for the kingdom
with his brother Atreus, is given the flesh of his own children to
eat.   Zeus, the father of Tantalus, does not indeed eat his son
Dionysus, but he caused the Dithyrambos to 'enter his male womb'
and be born again from it.   Kronos swallowed Zeus in the form of

[1] Clem. Alex. *Cohort.* p. 5=Abel, *Orph. frag.* 200.
[2] Was the Thunderer present as a visible thunderbolt on a draped throne such
as those figured above on p. 58?   We are reminded of the famous Throne of
Pelops on the Magnesian mountain-top and the equally famous Sceptre of Pelops
worshipped at Chaeronea, Paus. IX. 40. 11.
[3] Arnob. *adv. nat.* v. 19=Abel, *Orph. frag.* 196.
[4] Macrob. *Somn. Scip.* I. 12=Abel, *Orph. frag.* 205.

a stone and vomited him forth again[1].   Ouranos, father of Kronos, hid his children in the earth.   The motive in the case of these oldest τεκνοφαγίαι is the fear of being superseded by the heir to the kingdom[2].   This same lineage is also the line of transmission of the famous sceptre of Pelops, worshipped at Chaeronea, which is probably nothing but the thunderbolt, marking that the holder of it for the time being is king over the elements[3].   There was no public temple for this sceptre, 'but the man who acts as priest keeps the sceptre in his house *for the year*; and sacrifices are offered to it daily, and a table is set beside it covered with all sorts of flesh and cakes.'   The priest was evidently an annual 'king,' whose *mana* was derived from the sceptre.   As Pausanias says, 'that there is something divine about it is proved by the distinction it confers on its owners.'

The parallelism of these two series of facts—the recurrent τεκνοφαγίαι and the transmission of the sceptre—warrants us in connecting the ritual of the Feast of Tantalus with the succession to an annual or periodic 'kingdom[4].'

These facts suggest that this ritual of New Birth or inauguration at the Mountain Feast can be related to our conception of 'Pelops' as the young Year-God, whose marriage was celebrated in the summer.   The ritual would be appropriate to a seasonal feast of a Kronian (Saturnalian) character, at which the youthful year-god, standing for all young and growing things in nature, was initiated or inaugurated, as 'King' for his Year, under the form of death and resurrection.

In the first place, for the Kronian character of the Feast we have a curious piece of evidence in the text of Pindar itself.

---

[1] See above p. 22 for practical identity of the Κρόνου τεκνοφαγία to the συμφοραί Θυέστου as represented in mimetic dance.

[2] See Prof. Gilbert Murray, *Anthropology and the Classics*, p. 84.

[3] Paus. ix. 40. 11.   The transmission of the sceptre remains an important motive in the Orphic Theogony.   Abel, *Orph. frag.* 85.

[4] Another trait in Pelops' story which may survive from an initiation ceremony is the going down into the sea at night under the open sky to invoke Poseidon (*Ol.* i. 73).   The reason for supposing that this was a piece of ritual is its recurrence in the story of another Olympic hero, Iamos, who goes down into the Alpheus at night to call on Poseidon and Apollo, and is subsequently inaugurated as seer in charge of the oracle (*Ol.* vi. 58).   Pythagoras, when initiated by the Idaean Daktyls, before being purified by the thunderstone, 'lay stretched out on his face *by the sea* at dawn, and *at night by a river*'; see above, p. 57.   This ritual contact with water must have been as essential as contact with fire (thunder): the *mana* of both elements was needed by the king of thunder and of rain.

At line 48 of the *First Olympian*, Pindar describes the cutting up, boiling, and eating of Pelops.   He says this shocking incident was invented by the envious neighbours, who secretly spread the report,

that into bubbling water boiling with fire they had cut him limb by limb with a knife,

$$\tau\rho\alpha\pi\acute{\epsilon}\zeta\alpha\iota\sigma\acute{\iota}\ \tau'\ \grave{\alpha}\mu\phi\grave{\iota}\ \delta\epsilon\acute{\upsilon}\tau\alpha\tau\alpha\ \kappa\rho\epsilon\hat{\omega}\nu$$
$$\sigma\acute{\epsilon}\theta\epsilon\nu\ \delta\iota\epsilon\delta\acute{\alpha}\sigma\alpha\nu\tau o\ \kappa\alpha\grave{\iota}\ \phi\acute{\alpha}\gamma o\nu.$$

Such is the reading of our MSS.   But what sense can be made of it ?   Why should Pindar say they distributed and ate the *last morsels of the flesh* (if we take δεύτατα κρεῶν together), when legend said that only one morsel—the shoulder—was eaten ?   Or (taking ἀμφὶ δεύτατα together[1]), that they ate of the flesh *at the end* of the feast, whereas flesh was usually served first ?   Why, again, are the *tables* mentioned at all ?   We shall not discuss the various editorial emendations, because we believe that the true reading and interpretation are preserved by Athenaeus[2].

The text of Pindar used by Athenaeus read not ἀμφὶ δεύτατα but ἀμφὶ δεύτερα.   This is certain from the interpretation put upon the passage by Athenaeus, which turns on this very word ; for he quotes the lines as proof that 'among the ancients much care and expense were lavished on the "second course" (δεύτεραι τράπεζαι).'   It appears, then, that for some reason Pindar wished to mention the 'second tables'—dessert, in fact—and to avoid the banality of the actual phrase δεύτεραι τράπεζαι, he introduced both words in a different construction—τραπέζαισί τ', ἀμφὶ δεύτερα, 'and at the tables, at the second (course), they divided and ate of thy flesh[3].'

But what is the point of mentioning that Pelops was served up at dessert ?   Athenaeus again supplies the answer.   He is reporting a dinner-party conversation, occasioned by the appearance at table of the δεύτεραι τράπεζαι[4].

[1] Schröder (1908) prints ἀμφὶ δεύτατα between commas.
[2] Athen. XIV. 641 c ὅτι γὰρ ἦσαν καὶ παρὰ τοῖς ἀρχαίοις αἱ δεύτεραι τράπεζαι πολυτελῶς μεμεριμνημέναι, παρίστησιν Πίνδαρος ἐν Ὀλυμπιονίκαις περὶ τῆς Πέλοπος κρεουργίας διηγούμενος· τραπέζαισί τ' ἀμφὶ δεύτερα (ἀμφίδευρα A. corr. Schweigh.) κρεῶν κ.τ.λ.
[3] The wrong correction of δεύτερα to δεύτατα was inevitable ; the converse error, except as a sheer blunder, is inconceivable.
[4] Athen. XIV. 639 B περιηνέχθησαν ἡμῖν καὶ αἱ δεύτεραι καλούμεναι τράπεζαι, πολλάκις ἡμῖν διδόμεναι οὐ μόνον ταῖς τῶν Κρονίων ἡμέραις, ἐν αἷς Ῥωμαίων †παισὶν (? Ῥωμαίοις πάτριόν ἐστιν) ἑστιᾶν τοὺς οἰκέτας, αὐτοὺς τὰς τῶν οἰκετῶν ἀναδεχομένους λειτουργίας. Ἑλληνικὸν δὲ τοῦτο τὸ ἔθος....

When Masurius had finished speaking, the 'second tables,' as they are called, were handed round. These are often served, *not only on the days of the festival of Kronos*, on which it is the Roman custom[1] to feast the slaves, the masters themselves undertaking for the nonce the office of servants. The custom is also Greek. Thus a similar practice prevails in Crete at the Hermaia : the slaves are feasted and make merry, while their masters perform the menial offices.

He goes on to mention similar festivals at which this Saturnalian custom was observed—the Babylonian *Sakaea*, at which a slave was dressed as king; the Thessalian *Peloria* where the sacrifice to Zeus Pelorios was attended by the dressing of tables with a splendid feast to which slaves were admitted and served by their masters, including the king himself[2].

The vegetables, fruits, and cakes served at the 'second tables' were especially associated with the supposed simplicity of the Golden Age of Kronos, and so were characteristic of Kronian or Saturnalian feasts[3]. So this phrase τραπέζαισί τ' ἀμφὶ δεύτερα confirms our suggestion that the Feast of Tantalus was Kronian in character[4].

---

[1] Lydus *de mens.* III. 22 (March 1) ὅτι δὲ πάτριον ἀρχὴν ἐνιαυτοῦ τὸν Μάρτιον οἱ Ῥωμαῖοι παρέλαβον, δῆλον καὶ ἀπὸ τοῦ τὰς...Ματρώνας, τουτέστι τὰς εὐγενίδας, τοὺς οἰκέτας ἐστιᾶν, καθάπερ ἐν τοῖς Κρονίοις τουτὶ πράττειν ἔθος ἦν τοῖς δούλους κεκτημένοις (cf. IV. 42).

[2] Another of Athenaeus' instances is the following from Euripides, *Cretan Women*, frag. 467 N. :

τί γὰρ ποθεῖ τράπεζα; τῷ δ' οὐ βρίθεται;
πλήρης μὲν ὄψων ποντίων, πάρεισι δὲ
μόσχων τέρειναι σάρκες ἀρνεῖά τε δαὶς
καὶ πεπτὰ καὶ κροτητὰ τῆς ξουθοπτέρου
πελάνῳ μελίσσης ἀφθόνως δεδευμένα.

This must describe some important banquet; if it was that of Thyestes, who was a character in the play (Schol. ad Ar. *Ach.* 433), we should again have the δεύτεραι τράπεζαι connected with a τεκνοφαγία. Athenaeus also quotes the Τροφωνίου Κατάβασις of Dikaiarchos, ἥ γε τὴν πολλὴν δαπάνην ἐν τοῖς δείπνοις παρέχουσα δευτέρα τράπεζα προσεγένετο—an instance which may be significant for us, since the Trophoniads are equated with the Idaean Daktyls and Korybants. Plut. *fac. in orb. lun.* XXX., J. E. Harrison, *Prolegomena*, p. 579, and *infra*, chapter XI.

[3] They were also called the Horn of Amaltheia, Athen. XIV. 643 A. See above, p. 186. Compare Plato's description of the vegetarian diet of the City of Pigs (*Rep.* 372). His citizens lie on leaves, reeds, bryony and myrtle boughs as the Idaean Kouretes at Olympia lie on leaves of the wild olive (Paus. V. 7. 7).

[4] Mr Cook draws my attention to the importance in this connection of the agonistic table. On Athenian coins of Imperial date occurs the type of a sacred table on which are an owl, a wreath, and a bust of Athena, and beneath the table the amphora containing presumably the prize oil (Head, *Hist. Num.* p. 326). Some Imperial bronze coins of Delphi (Svoronos, *Bull. Corr. Hell.* (1896), Pl. XXX. nos. 1—8) which clearly refer to the Pythian, as the Athenian to the Panathenaic, Games, show on the reverse a table with wreath, fruits, amphora, and perched near them a crow or raven. The bird, like the bust of Athena, indicates the presence of the god at the vegetarian *dais*. Mr Cook holds that this was originally

THE KRONIAN FESTIVAL OF THE BASILAI.

We are now, perhaps, in a position to identify this mountain Feast with an actual New Year's Festival observed throughout historic antiquity at Olympia—the only Olympic festival we know which was held on the top of a mountain.

Immediately before his description of the shrine of the Mother and child Sosipolis, Pausanias tells us that on the top of the mountain of Kronos, 'the Basilai, as they are called, sacrifice to Kronos at the spring equinox, in the Elean month Elaphios[1].'

With this festival Dr Frazer[2] compares a feast 'not only observed by the Parsis in India and elsewhere, but common to Persians, Arabs, and Turks, it being the day fixed for the computation of the incoming solar year. It corresponds with the vernal equinox and falls about the third week in March. It is called Jamshedi Naoroz, and strictly speaking is "New Year's Day," but in India it is simply a day of rejoicing, and is observed in honour of a Persian king named Jamshed, who first introduced the principles of cultivation, and the proper method of reckoning time on the solar system.' We are reminded of Diodorus'[3] statement that the festivals and sacrifices of Kronos among the Romans commemorated how Kronos became king and introduced among mankind the civilised manner of life.

Everything we know of the sacrifice of the Basilai thus fits the requirements of the Feast of Tantalus. It is a festival of Kronos; it is held on the top of a mountain; its date—the vernal equinox—is the appropriate time for the inauguration of the Year or Sun God under the form of death and resurrection[4]. If we are right in seeing a ritual myth in the story of the mountain banquet, and in

---

a communion table, at which the victor sat and ate the fruit of the God, later degraded into a mere table for prizes.

[1] Paus. VI. 20. 1 ἐπὶ δὲ τοῦ ὄρους (τοῦ Κρονίου) τῇ κορυφῇ θύουσιν οἱ Βασίλαι καλούμενοι τῷ Κρόνῳ κατὰ ἰσημερίαν τὴν ἐν τῷ ἦρι Ἐλαφίῳ μηνὶ παρὰ Ἠλείοις. (Cf. Dion. H. I. 34.)

[2] Pausanias, Vol. IV. p. 75, quoting A. F. Baillie, *Kurrachee (Karachi), past, present, and future*, Calcutta, 1890, p. 190.

[3] V. 66.

[4] Lydus tells us that Oinomaos, king of Pisa, held the contest of horse-driving on the twenty-fourth of March—close to the vernal equinox; but, in the absence of older authority, this statement does not carry much weight. *De mens.* I. 12 οὗτος δὲ (Οἰνόμαος) ἦν βασιλεὺς Πισαίων, ἦγε δὲ τὸν ἱππικὸν ἀγῶνα μηνὶ Μαρτίῳ εἰκοστῇ τετάρτῃ ὑψουμένου τοῦ Ἡλίου. Cf. J. Malalas, *Chronogr.* 173—6.

supposing that this myth, as part of the Olympian legend of Tantalus, reflected some local rite, the Kronian festival of the Basilai is the only one which meets the needs of the case.

It is not improbable that this Kronian feast represents a very ancient seasonal festival of spring, which became attached to the vernal equinox when the sun and the critical dates of his annual course became important. In discussing Salmoneus, we connected his attribute of the slipped fetter (p. 223) with the Kronian custom of releasing slaves and prisoners at new year festivals. We saw too that this custom at Rome, which originally belonged to the Kalends of March, was borrowed by the later Saturnalia of midwinter, and yet retained also at its old date in March. The Attic Kronia show an instructive parallel. At Athens the same Saturnalian custom of feasting slaves and releasing prisoners appears both at the Panathenaea in Hekatombaion—a festival apparently superimposed on the older Kronia[1]—and at the spring festival of Dionysus, the Anthesteria[2].

Proclus[3], more definitely, records the admission of slaves to the festival at the Pithoigia—the first day (Anthesterion 11) of the Anthesteria. This observance is of peculiar interest to us because among the Boeotians, as we know from Plutarch[4], this day was called the day of the Good Spirit, the Agathos Daimon. It was also a day when the souls of the dead were evoked from the grave-jars (*pithoi*); the Opening of the Jars was at once a spring-festival of first-fruits—on that day they broached the new wine—and a temporary release of the spirits of the dead from the prison of the grave[5].

---

[1] Dem. xxiv. 26 εὐθὺς τῇ ὑστεραίᾳ, καὶ ταῦτ' ὄντων Κρονίων καὶ διὰ ταῦτ' ἀφειμένης τῆς βουλῆς, διαπραξάμενος...καθίζεσθαι νομοθέτας διὰ ψηφίσματος ἐπὶ τῇ τῶν Παναθηναίων προφάσει. Plut. vit. Thes. 12 Κρονίου μηνός, ὃν νῦν Ἑκατομβαιῶνα καλοῦσι. Schol. ad Dem. iii. p. 29 ἦν Ἑκατομβαιὼν ὁ καὶ Κρόνιος παρ' Ἕλλησι.
Macrobius, *Sat.* 1. 10. 22, following Philochorus, records the practice of the Attic Kronia: Philochorus Saturno et Opi primum in Attica statuisse aram Cecropem dicit, eosque deos pro Jove Terraque coluisse, instituisseque ut patres familiarum et frugibus et fructibus iam coactis passim cum servis vescerentur.

[2] Dem. xxii. 68 ἐρωτῶν εἰ μάτην τὸ δεσμωτήριον ᾠκοδομήθη. καταφαίην ἂν ἔγωγε, εἰ γ' ὁ πατὴρ ὁ σὸς ᾤχετο αὐτόθεν αὐταῖς πέδαις ἐξορχησάμενος Διονυσίων τῇ πομπῇ. Schol. ad loc., ἔθος ἦν παρὰ τοῖς Ἀθηναίοις ἐν τοῖς Διονυσίοις καὶ ἐν τοῖς Παναθηναίοις τοὺς δεσμώτας ἀφίεσθαι τοῦ δεσμοῦ ἐν ἐκείναις ταῖς ἡμέραις.

[3] Ad Hes. *Op.* 366 ἐν τοῖς πατρίοις ἐστὶν ἑορτὴ Πιθοιγία καθ' ἣν οὔτε οἰκέτην οὔτε μισθωτὸν εἴργειν τῆς ἀπολαύσεως θεμιτὸν ἦν.

[4] *Q. Symp.* viii. 3. For the Pithoigia see J. E. Harrison, *Prolegomena*, p. 32 ff.

[5] For the conjunction of the worship of the Good Daimon and the souls of the dead see next chapter.

When we put these scattered indications together, we conjecture that the Kronian sacrifice of the Basilai at Olympia was one of those old spring festivals of the New Year, at which the resurrection of life in nature was symbolised in various ways[1].

To resume this part of our argument. We find that the story of the eating and resurrection of Pelops at the mountain banquet hangs together with the presence at Olympia, both in legend and in cult, of the Kouretes, attendant on the Mother and Child. Pindar's description preserves a trait which, with the evidence of Athenaeus, points to the Kronian character of the rite. On the hill of Kronos we know of a festival connected with Kronos, which was celebrated at the spring equinox, when the youthful sun comes of age. The sacrifice is conducted by priests called Basilai, or Kings: and the τεκνοφαγίαι characteristic of the house of Pelops are associated with the succession to the kingdom. From these indications we conclude that, while the birth of the new Year God was celebrated in the cult of the infant Sosipolis, his Easter death and resurrection—his initiation or inauguration when he passes from childhood to youth—was marked in ritual by the Kronian festival of the Basilai in March, and in myth by the death and rebirth of the youth Pelops at the mountain banquet of Tantalus.

In the Third *Olympian* Pelops is actually called '*Kronios*'—the very epithet by which the Kouros is invoked in the Cretan hymn :—

> Ἰώ,
> Μέγιστε Κοῦρε, χαῖρέ μοι,
> Κρόνιε.

It is to be wished that Pausanias had recorded more details of the vernal sacrifice of the Basilai on the hill of Kronos. The title Basileus is constantly given to Kronos; at Olympia he seems to have been the arch-basileus of a college of Basilai. Possibly some light may be thrown upon his obscure figure by the Basileus at Priene[2].

An inscription has come to light upon the basis of a statue

---

[1] An Attic spring sacrifice (in Elaphebolion) to Kronos is attested by an inscription *I. G.* 3. 77. 23. Wissowa in Roscher, *Lex.*, s.v. *Saturnus*, col. 438, rejects von Prott's view (*Leges graec. sacrae*, I. 12) that this was borrowed from Rome.

[2] H. v. Gärtringen, *Inschr. v. Priene*, 1906, p. 136, No. 186, gives an inscription from the base of a bronze statue of the second century B.C. found *in situ* at the N.W. corner of the Agora at the entrance to a temple: Βασιλείδης καὶ Καλλινίκη | τὸν

erected to a priest of 'the Basileus and the Kouretes.' Once more we encounter the Kouretes, this time with a Basileus at their head. Further, we learn from Strabo, that Basileus was the title of a 'young man of Priene chosen to take charge of the rites. This young man is manifestly the human Kouros,—related to his Kouretes as the Protokoures is related to the college of Kouretes at Ephesus, and (may we not add?) as the Kronos Basileus at Olympia is related to his Basilai.

The Olympic Games began with a foot-race 'for the kingdom'; the youth who won the race *was* the Basileus. What does this title mean?

The priest at the Laconian Karneia was called *Agetes*, the Leader, and the festival itself, Agetoria[1]. At Argos, Karnos the Ram was called Zeus and *Hegetor*. We are reminded how in ancient days the leader of the annual procession might be a holy Bull or a Goat, and how at Athens the Kouros in Bull form and human form came in procession to the theatre[2]. The young man pursued by the Staphylodromoi, with his wreaths and beast-disguise, was a 'mumming representative of the *daimon*, who went in procession at the festival[3].' We have already seen the Kouros of the Cretan hymn as *Leader of his daimones* (δαιμόνων ἀγώμενος). Was the Basileus simply the βασι-λεύς— 'leader of the march' or 'leader of the step,' that is of the dance of the young men[4]? And is not this dance or march nothing but the *komos*, the procession in which the Olympian victor, attended by his friends and hymned with songs of triumph, visited the altars of the gods? We now understand—what otherwise seems surprising—the fact, implied by Pindar and explicitly

αὐτῶν πάτερα | Ἀπολλόδωρον Ποσειδωνίου | ἱερητεύοντα Βασιλεῖ | καὶ Κούρησιν. Strabo, VIII. 384 καὶ δὴ πρὸς τὴν θυσίαν ταύτην καθίστασι βασιλέα ἄνδρα νέον Πριηνέα τὸν τῶν ἱερῶν ἐπιμελησόμενον. We owe this reference to Mr A. B. Cook. The important word βασιλέα, though found in the MSS. and in editions before Kramer, is now omitted by editors!

[1] Hesych. ἀγητής·...ἐν δὲ τοῖς Καρνείοις ὁ ἱερώμενος τοῦ (τῆς, MSS. corr. Meursius) θεοῦ καὶ ἡ ἑορτὴ Ἀγητόρια. See Nilsson, *Gr. Feste*, p. 121.

[2] See *supra*, p. 209.   [3] See *supra*, p. 234, note 5.

[4] For the derivation of βασιλεύς see E. W. Fays, *Greek* ΒΑΣΙ-ΛΕΥΣ, in Classical Quarterly, v. 1911, p. 117. Prellwitz (*Etym. Wörterb.*) suggests: βασι-: altbaktrisch *jaiti*, Haus, Geschlecht, lit. *gimtis*, natürl. Geschlecht; ἐβάθη· ἐγεννήθη, Hes. Dann βασιλεύς, Geschlechtsherr, wie ahd. *chuning*.

Paus. VI. 22. Near the grave of the suitors of Hippodameia was a sanctuary of Artemis Kordax, so named because the attendants (ἀκόλουθοι) of Pelops, after his victory, τὰ ἐπινίκια ἤγαγον παρὰ τῇ θεῷ ταύτῃ καὶ ὠρχήσαντο ἐπιχώριον τοῖς περὶ τὸν Σίπυλον κόρδακα ὄρχησιν.

stated by the Scholiast[1], that the victor himself *led* the procession
and acted as ἔξαρχος or precentor of the ancient hymn of Archi-
lochos, which was addressed, not to the victor himself, but to the
hero who was his mythical prototype, Herakles.

The Komos or triumphal procession of the victor resembles the
Ovation described by Lydus[2] as a most venerable festival among
the Romans. It was held on new year's day (January 1). The
consul, dressed in white and riding a white horse, led the procession
up the Capitoline hill. Both the dress and the horse assimilated
him to Jupiter, whose victory over the Giants symbolised, in
Lydus' opinion, the victory of the sun over the colds of winter[3].

The Victor and the Hero.

Had we begun this chapter with the statement that the
triumphal procession, or *komos*, was the original kernel of the
Olympic Games, it would have seemed, in the strict sense of the
word, preposterous. But in view of the facts we have analysed
and of the previous discussion of the Dithyramb (p. 205), it will
not perhaps now seem paradoxical to suggest that this procession,
with its sacrifice and eating of a bull[4], its hymn to the hero, and
the concluding feast in the banqueting chamber[5], was the central
rite, to which the foot-race of the Kouretes was a mere preliminary.
The race, whose original purpose was simply to determine who
should be the greatest Kouros or King of his year, developed by
successive accretions into the elaborate athletic sports, which in
later times came to be the central feature of the whole festival.

[1] Pind. *Ol.* IX. 1 τὸ μὲν Ἀρχιλόχου μέλος φωνᾶεν Ὀλυμπίᾳ, καλλίνικος ὁ τριπλόος
κεχλαδώς, ἄρκεσε Κρόνιον παρ' ὄχθον ἀγεμονεῦσαι κωμάζοντι φίλοις Ἐφαρμόστῳ σὺν
ἑταίροις. Christ, *ad loc.* Victor vero ipse vice praecentoris (ἐξάρχου) fungebatur
sodalibus praeeuntis, id quod Pindarus verbo ἀγεμονεῦσαι significavit et scholiasta
hac adnotatione confirmat: κωμάζει δὲ πρὸς τὸν τοῦ Διὸς βωμὸν ὁ νικήσας μετὰ τῶν
φίλων, αὐτὸς τῆς ᾠδῆς ἐξηγούμενος.

[2] *De mens.* III. 3.

[3] The ancient custom was to exchange gifts (στρῆνα) of dried figs and laurel
leaves which were useful for driving away spirits. *Ibid.* 4 ἔνθεν ἂν εἴη δάφνη,
ἐκποδὼν δαίμονες—a phrase which recalls the θύραζε Κῆρες of the Anthesteria,
J. E. Harrison, *Prolegomena*, p. 35.

[4] Schol. ad Pind. *Ol.* v. 7 οἱ γὰρ νικῶντες ἔθυον ἐν τοῖς ἐξ βωμοῖς. Cf. *Nem.* VI. 40
ταυροφόνῳ τριετηρίδι (the Isthmia); frag. ap. vit. Pind. ex schol. Ambros. (Christ,
p. c) πενταετηρὶς ἑορτὰ βουπομπός (the Pythia). That the bull at Olympia was not
only sacrificed but 'distributed' to be eaten (*dais*) appears from Athenaeus I. 5 E:
Empedocles, victorious in the chariot race, disapproving as a Pythagorean of flesh-
eating, made a confectionary bull and διένειμε τοῖς εἰς τὴν πανήγυριν ἀπαντήσασιν.

[5] Paus. v. 15. 12 ἔστι δὲ καὶ ἑστιατόριον Ἠλείοις...τοὺς δὲ τὰ Ὀλύμπια νικῶντας
ἑστιῶσιν ἐν τούτῳ τῷ οἰκήματι.

The Komos, which thus sank to be a mere appendage, retained even in historic times features which show that the personality of the victor was not of primary importance. The elaborate Epinikian ode of the Pindaric type was a late institution. The earlier victors, like Epharmostos, were content with the threefold ringing cry which began, 'Hail, *King* Herakles[1].' Even when Pindar brought the Ode of Victory to its perfection, the victor had still to be satisfied with a personal reference at the beginning and the end. The central portion of the typical Epinikion is occupied, not with the victor's personality and achievements, but with the deeds of his ancestors, those earlier manifestations of the Genius of his house (δαίμων γενέθλιος) who is reimbodied in each successive generation. It is the *daimon*, incarnate for the moment in the victor, who in a great number of Pindar's odes, is really the object of praise and commemoration. In other odes the myth is devoted to the institution or ordinance (τεθμός) of the rite itself. This, as we shall see (p. 327), is the proper and original topic of the myth in a hymn associated with ritual. In the development of the Epinikian ode we may perhaps see an analogy to the development of the drama, which starts from a ritual dithyramb containing an 'aetiological' myth, and later is infused with a new element of saga-history borrowed from epic tradition[2]. In both cases the hymn and the ritual myth come first; the commemoration of ancestors is a secondary importation.

We have spoken of the Olympic victor as the *daimon* of his Year; we have seen him wreathed, and pelted with leaves[3], leading the song and dance of his attendants in the Komos— a Kouros at the head of his Kouretes. We have also found him conceived as the reincarnation of the *daimon* of his house—the Spirit of his dead ancestors, who, as Pindar[4] says, 'listening with such consciousness as the dead may have, hear of his great prowess, on which the delicate dew of song is shed, as of a glory which is their own and which they share with their son.' Finally, we may regard him also as representing the 'local hero,' be he

---

[1] Pind. *Ol.* IX. 1. Hesych. τετράκωμος· μέλος τι σὺν ὀρχήσει πεποιημένον εἰς Ἡρακλέα ἐπινίκιον.

[2] See *infra*, p. 334.

[3] Victors were also pelted with flowers and fruits, Plut. *Symp. Qu.* VIII. 4. 723 c καὶ ῥόδοις καὶ λυχνίσιν, ἔνιοι δὲ καὶ μήλοις καὶ ῥοιαῖς ἔβαλλον ὡς καλοῖς γεραίροντες ἀεὶ τοὺς νικηφόρους.

[4] *Pyth.* v. 98; cf. *Ol.* VIII. 14, *Nem.* IV. 85.

Sosipolis, or Herakles[1], or Pelops. Sosipolis with his cornucopia bears traces of his function as Agathos Daimon, giver of the fruits of earth. The Idaean Herakles has his olive-branch, or apple-bough. Pelops is a figure of saga; yet his legend shows that he slipped into the place of a Year-God, the Sun King of the octennial period.

Fig. 62.

Older than any of these, perhaps, was that nameless Hero, or Heroes, whose altar, painted with a leafy branch, of olive or of bay, was discovered in a round chamber, identified by Curtius with the Gaeum, or sanctuary of Earth, mentioned by Pausanias[2]. The

[1] Milo, the athlete six times victorious at Olympia, led the Krotoniates into battle, wearing his Olympic wreaths and the lion-skin and club of Herakles, Diod. XII. 9. 6.

[2] v. 14. 8. See Frazer on v. 15. 8. No less than twelve coats of plaster were stripped off this altar. Almost every one showed the branch; and on each, as is seen in Fig. 62, was inscribed ΗΡΩΟΡ or ΗΡΩΟΣ or. in one case, ΗΡΩΩΝ. It may be a significant fact that the floor of this round chamber is of earth of a clayey texture, quite different from the sandy soil of the Altis, which has clearly been

worshippers who painted and repainted this altar did not know whether it belonged to one 'hero' or to many: they inscribed it now 'Of the Hero,' now 'Of the Heroes.' Their doubt is instructive. The 'Hero' is not a dead man with a known name and history commemorated by funeral games. His title stands not for a personality, but for an office, defined by its functions and capable of being filled by a series of representatives[1]. At one time Sosipolis might be 'the hero'; at another Pelops, the mythical ancestor of an incoming people; at another the Idaean Herakles or his Dorian homonym. Even as late as Macedonian times, a Philip could build a round shrine—the Philippeum—in deliberate imitation of the old round chamber with the Hero altar, and thus pose as 'the Hero' of Olympia for the time being[2]. In view of these considerations, the establishment of Games and 'hero-worship' in honour of historic personages, like Miltiades or Brasidas, lends no support to the funeral theory of the origin of the Olympic Games. Before any one of these individuals could be worshipped as the Hero of a city, the conception of what the Hero or Saviour of the City is, must first have been clearly defined. The title and functions of a Hero are a blank frame, which may be filled by a succession of representatives, chosen each for his 'year,' or by this or that historic personality, as the changes and chances of time and of politics may determine.

To the analysis of the idea of a Hero the next chapter will be devoted.

brought from Mount Kronios where a similar soil is found. It has been inferred that the sanctuary was transferred from the hill, with some of the sacred soil, to its present site. Dr Frazer regards this inference as uncertain.

[1] The same holds of the octennial kingship—the office to which the winner of the race, according to Dr Frazer's final theory (*G. B.*[3], Part III. p. 104), became entitled. Dr Frazer speaks of *combining* this view with the funeral theory by supposing that 'the spirits of these divine kings...were worshipped with sacrifices at their graves, and were thought to delight in the spectacle of the games which reminded them of the laurels which they had themselves won long ago....' But it must be clearly pointed out that this is *not* the funeral theory as advocated by Prof. Ridgeway, who will have the whole festival start from the obsequies of one individual chief—a historic or quasi-historic personality—whereas Dr Frazer's view (rightly, as we think) makes the office and its functions, not any individual holder of it and his personal exploits, the central factor. This is an essential point of difference between the two theories.

[2] I owe this to Mr Cook, who points out that the Philippeum is built of stone, painted to look like brick, because the old chamber in the Gaeum was of brick.

CHAPTER VIII.

DAIMON AND HERO.

'INCERTUS GENIUMNE LOCI, FAMULUMNE PARENTIS
ESSE PUTET.'

IN the last two chapters we have examined in some detail
two great festivals of the Greeks, the spring Dithyramb, which
according to Aristotle gave birth to the drama, and the Olympic
Games celebrated every fifth year at or after the summer solstice.
We have seen that the primary gist of both these festivals was the
promotion of fertility and that each of them alike gave birth to a
daimon of fertility who took on various names and shapes. The
Dithyramb gave birth to the Greatest Kouros whose matured
form in Crete was that of Father Zeus, but elsewhere he crystallized as Kouros into the figure of Dionysos. At Olympia,
starting again from the Kouretes the *daimon* of fertility took
various heroic shapes as Oinomaos, as Pelops, and finally again
bequeathed something of his nature and functions to the Olympic
Zeus himself.

We have by this time a fairly clear notion of one element in
the nature of a *daimon*. We have seen him to be the product,
the projection, the representation of collective emotion. Normally
and naturally he is attended by the group or thiasos that begets
him, but gradually he attains independent personality. We have
also seen that in primitive communities this collective emotion
focuses around and includes food interests and especially food-
animals and fruit-trees. In consequence of this the *daimon* is
conceived in animal and plant-form, as theriomorph or phytomorph. Dionysos is a bull or a goat, or a tree, or rather the
human Dionysos grows out of the sacrifice of the bull or the
goat, or out of the sanctification of the tree.

But in the case of the Dithyramb and still more vividly in the case of the Olympic games we have been all along conscious of another element as yet not completely analysed, the hero. The Dithyramb has to do with the fertility-*daimon* but the drama which sprang out of it sets before us not the πάθη, the sufferings, the life-history of Dionysos, but the πάθη, the life-histories of a host of heroes, of Agamemnon, of Orestes, of Prometheus, of Herakles, of Hippolytos. Pindar the poet of the Games salutes no *daimon* by name. He asks[1]

'What god, what hero, or what man shall we sing?

If then at one stage of their development in both the drama and the Olympic games the hero-element was dominant, it is all important that we should ask and answer the question,—'what exactly is a hero?'

The question may seem at the first glance superfluous. A hero is surely simple enough. He is just a dead man revered in life, honoured with a mild and modified form of divine honours after death. We have surely done with difficult and dubious conceptions like 'collective representations.' We have got to facts at last, simple, historical facts. All now is plain, concrete, *a posteriori*. 'You must not say that "Minos" represents a dynasty; Minos was a particular man and Dr Ridgeway can discuss his dates and doings. You must not say that Menelaos is a tribal hero; Menelaos was a well-known infantry officer with auburn whiskers[2].' Let us look at facts. It happens that at Athens the record of a succession of hero-kings is unusually full and complete; so to Athens let us turn.

The oldest hero reverenced by Athens was Cecrops. Who was Cecrops? The old Euhemerism knows many things about Cecrops. He was the first king of Athens[3], a native of Egypt, who led a colony to Athens about 1556 B.C. He was a typical culture hero, he softened and polished the rude manners of the inhabitants and, as an earlier Theseus, drew them from their

---

[1] *Ol.* II. 2 τίνα θεόν, τίν' ἥρωα, τίνα δ' ἄνδρα κελαδήσομεν;

[2] See the review of Professor Ridgeway's *Origin of Tragedy* in the Times Literary Supplement, Jan. 26, 1911.

[3] For the classical sources on which the account current in handbooks is based and for monumental evidence see my *Myth. and Mon. Ancient Athens*, p. xxv.

scattered habitations to dwell in twelve small villages. He gave them laws and customs and taught them to cultivate the olive. He introduced the worship of Zeus Hypatos and forbade the sacrifice of living things. 'After a reign of fifty years spent in regulating his newly formed kingdom and in polishing the minds of his subjects, Cecrops died, leaving three daughters Aglauros, Herse and Pandrosos[1].' But in this unblemished career there is one blot, one skeleton in the well-furnished cupboard that even the most skilled Euhemerism cannot conceal. Cecrops the hero-king, the author of all these social reforms, Cecrops the humane, the benevolent, has a serpent's tail.

A serpent's tail is an awkward stumbling-block, but Euhemerism early and late is equal to the occasion. The fact of the snake tail may be damaging, but it is symbolic. Cecrops was twy-formed (διφυής) because, some said, he knew two languages, Greek and Egyptian. Deeper thinkers divined that Cecrops was twy-formed, because he instituted marriage, the union of two sexes. He was arbitrator at the 'strife' of Athena and Poseidon. The women, who exceeded the men by one, voted for Athena, and to appease the wrath of Poseidon they were henceforth disenfranchized[2] and their children were no longer to be called by their mother's name. The women's decision came as a shock to old Cecrops and he forthwith instituted patriarchal marriage. 'At Athens,' says Athenaeus[3], quoting Clearchus the disciple of Aristotle:

'Cecrops was the first to join one woman to one man. Before, connections had taken place at random and marriages were in common. Hence as some think Cecrops was called "Twy-formed" (διφυής) since before his time people did not know who their fathers were, on account of the number of possible parents.'

Scandal and stumbling-block though it was, the serpent's tail was integral and never forgotten. In the *Wasps*[4] old Philocleon,

[1] Lemprière, *Classical Dictionary*, 1827. I quote Lemprière as a typical instance of Euhemerism unabashed, but between him and the less picturesque statements in later Dictionaries, e.g. Seyffert (1908), revised by Prof. Nettleship and Dr Sandys, there is as regards any real understanding of Cecrops little to choose.

[2] S. Aug. *de civit. Dei* 18. 9 ...ut nulla ulterius ferrent suffragia, ut nullus nascentium maternum nomen acciperet.

[3] XIII. 2, §§ 555, and Tzetzes, *Chil.* v. 19. 650. Clearchus like so many of his successors misinterpreted the rigid matriarchal system as licence. See my *Prolegomena*, p. 262.

[4] Ar. *Vesp.* 438

ὦ Κέκροψ ἥρως ἄναξ, τὰ πρὸς ποδῶν δρακοντίδη.

longing to join his dear dikasts and violently held back by the chorus, cries aloud:

Cecrops, hero, King, O thou who at thy feet art serpent-shaped.

The scholiast apologizes and explains, but every Athenian knew that in his serpent's tail was the true nature and glory of the hero.

As serpent-tailed the artist of the delightful archaic terra-cotta[1] in Fig. 63 shows him to us. Half of him is a decorous

FIG. 63.

and civilized statesman. He is bearded, and wears a neat chiton; he holds an olive spray in one human hand, he is *thallophoros*[2]; with the forefinger of the other he touches his lips to enjoin a sacred silence at the birth of a holy child. He stands erect and solemn but he has no feet, only a coiling snake's-tail. So he appears on many a vase-painting and relief; so Euripides[3] figured him at the door of Ion's tent at Delphi: there

> Cecrops with his daughters
> Rolled up his spiral coils, the votive gift
> Of some Athenian.

[1] Berlin Cat. 2537.
[2] See *infra*, p. 366.
[3] *Ion* 1163
          κατ' εἰσόδους δὲ Κέκροπα θυγατέρων πέλας
          σπείρας συνειλίσσοντ', Ἀθηναίων τινὸς
          ἀνάθημα.
The daughters of Cecrops, unlike their father, are never figured with snakes' tails. For female snake-tailed *daimones* see *infra*, p. 280, Fig. 71.

It is at the birth of Erichthonios, the second great Athenian hero, that Cecrops is mostly represented in art, as on the terracotta in Fig. 63. Gaia herself rises in human shape from the earth; she is a massive figure with long heavy hair. She holds the child in her arms, handing him to Athena his foster-mother, to whom he stretches out his eager hands. This birth of the child from the earth symbolizes, we are told, that the race of Erechtheus, the Erechtheidae, ancestors of the Athenians, are autochthonous, home-grown; so it does, but it 'symbolizes,' or rather we prefer to say represents, something much more. This we shall see in the sequel shown in Figs. 64 *a* and *b*.

When the child is born from Earth, Athena his foster-mother gives him into the care of the three daughters of Cecrops. Strange daughters these for a human king, the Dew-Sisters and the bright Spring Water, three reflections as we have seen[1] of the maidens of the Hersephoria. They hide the child in a sacred cista. Two of the sisters in disobedience open the cista. The scene is given in Fig. 64 *a* from a red-figured pelikè[2]. The cista

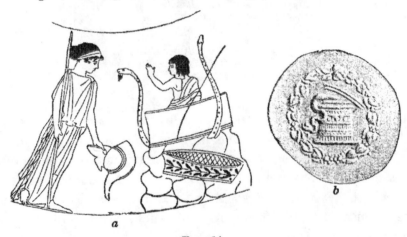

FIG. 64.

stands on piled rocks indicating no doubt the Acropolis. The deed is done, the sacred cista is open. Its lid, it should be noted, is olive-wreathed. From the cista springs up a human child, Athena approaches and the two disobedient sisters[3] hurry away.

---

[1] *Supra*, p. 174, note 1.
[2] British Museum Cat. E. 418, and see my *Prolegomena*, p. 133.
[3] The figures on the reverse are actually those of two epheboi, but the vase is almost certainly a copy from some drawing in which Herse and Aglauros are represented.

They have cause for haste, cause more imminent than a guilty conscience. The design in Fig. 64 *a* shows two guardian snakes, but rooted to the rocks. The child Erichthonios himself is a human child. But the design in Fig. 65 from a cylix by Brygos[1]

Fig. 65.

tells us another and a more instructive tale. The scene, of which only a part is given here, takes place just after the opening of the chest. The two terrified sisters are pursued by a huge snake, a snake so huge that his tail coils round to the other side of the cylix not figured here. He is not one of the guardian snakes, he is the actual dweller in the chest. Cecrops is a snake, Erichthonios is a snake, the old snake-king is succeeded by a new snake-king.

There are no such things as snake-kings. What the myths of Cecrops and Erichthonios tell us is that, for some reason or another, each and every traditional Athenian king was regarded as being also in some sense a snake. How this came to be we might never have guessed but for the story of the cista. In Dionysiac rites the snake in the cista was a constant factor. A whole class of coins of Ephesus known as *cistophoroi*[2] show us

---

[1] Frankfort. In the Städel-Institut; see W. Klein, *Meistersignaturen*, p. 179, and *Wiener-Vorlegeblätter*, Serie VIII. Taf. 2. On the reverse is the sending forth of the Eleusinian 'hero,' Triptolemos, the correlative of Erichthonios.

[2] See Head, *Hist. Num.* p. 461. For cistae and snakes on coins see L. Anson, *Numismata Graeca*, Part I. Cista XIII. 936, where all the known instances are collected.

the sacred cista, its lid half-opened, a snake emerging. A specimen is given in Fig. 64 *b*. The cista of the coin and the cista of Erichthonios are one and the same; the myth arose from a rite.

The carrying of sacred snakes or the figures of snakes was not confined to the worship of Dionysos. It was part of the ceremonial both of the Arrephoria and the Thesmophoria. The scholiast on Lucian[1] tells us that the Arretophoria were the same as the Thesmophoria and

are performed with the same intent concerning the growth of crops and of human offspring. In the case of the Arretophoria, too, sacred things that may not be named and that are made of cereal paste are carried about, i.e. *images of snakes and of the forms of men*[2]. They employ also fircones on account of the fertility of the tree, and into the sanctuaries called *megara* these are cast and also as we have already said, swine,—the swine, too, on account of their prolific character—in token of the growth of fruit and of human beings.

The carrying of snakes is, like the carrying of *phalloi* and the carrying of the life-giving dew, a fertility charm.

In the 'temple of Polias' on the Acropolis there was according to Pausanias[3] besides the image of Athena and the lamp that was always burning another sacred thing, a Hermes of wood said to be *the votive-offering of Cecrops*; it was covered from sight by branches of myrtle. It has long been conjectured that this 'Hermes' was ithyphallic and so reverently veiled. But a simpler explanation is probably right. The 'Hermes' of the old temple was, like the Hermes of Kyllene[4], an αἰδοῖον, possibly snake-shaped. The covering with myrtle boughs recalls the leafage and sprays that so oddly surround the great snake on the Brygos vase, they also recall the olive crown on the cista in Fig. 64 *a*. The notion of these leaf and branch crowned cistae and Hermae is not, I think, concealment, it is rather that the image of the

---

[1] *Dial. Meretr.* ii. 1. The scholion is given in full and discussed in my *Prolegomena*, p. 121.

[2] μιμήματα δρακόντων καὶ ἀνδρῶν σχημάτων. The μιμήματα ἀνδρῶν σχημάτων are undoubtedly φάλλοι, cf. Septuagint, Is. iii. 17. Probably at first the snake was the totemistic vehicle of reincarnation and only later, when the true nature of parentage was known, identified with the φάλλος.

[3] i. 27. 1 κεῖται δὲ ἐν τῷ ναῷ τῆς Πολιάδος Ἑρμῆς ξύλου, Κέκροπος εἶναι λεγόμενον ἀνάθημα ὑπὸ κλάδων μυρσίνης οὐ σύνοπτον.

[4] Due to Dr Frickenhaus, *Erechtheus* in A. Mitt. xxxiii. 1908, p. 171. See also for the whole subject and the analogy to Daktyl cults, Kaibel, *Göttinger Gelehrte Nachrichten*, 1901, 499. It will later (p. 294) appear that Hermes is but a humanized form of the snake life-*daimon*.

life-daimon should be brought into magical contact with the
vegetation he is to revivify.

Once we realise that the traditional kings of Athens were
conceived of as snake-daimons, the 'household-snake' (οἰκουρὸς
ὄφις) of the Acropolis became instantly clear. Herodotus[1] writes
somewhat sceptically:

the Athenians say that they have a great snake which lives in the sanctuary
as the guardian of the Acropolis. They both say this and as if it were really
existing they place monthly offerings before it and the monthly offering is a
honey-cake. And always before, the honey-cake was consumed, but then
(at the Persian invasion) untouched. And when the priestess announced
this the Athenians deserted the city the more readily *because the goddess
herself had forsaken the Acropolis.*

In the days of the old month-year the goddess herself was a
snake. When she took human form the snake became her
'attribute'; it was the 'symbol of wisdom.' When Pausanias[2]
saw the great image of Athena in the Parthenon he noted 'at
her feet lies a shield and near the shield is a serpent.' Who
was the serpent? Pausanias hits the mark, if but tentatively,
'it may be Erichthonios'; it *is* he—the lord and the luck of the
state.

Before we leave the Athenian kings one point remains to be
noted. They are snakes or at least take on the form of snakes,
but they are also 'eponymous heroes.' Cecrops 'gives his name'
to the Cecropidae, Erechtheus to the Erechtheidae. After what
has been said[3] about the Kouros and the Kouroi, Bacchos and
the Bacchoi, it is scarcely necessary to point out that the reverse
is the case: an 'eponymous hero' never 'gives' his name, he always
receives it. Cecrops is the projection of the Cecropidae, Erechtheus of the Erechtheidae; neither is a real actual man, only an
ancestor invented to express the unity of a group.

This comes out very clearly in the case of Ion the 'eponymous
hero' of the Ionians. When we have said 'eponymous hero' we
have exhausted the content of Ion. Save for his birth and childhood, which Euripides makes alive, Ion is for us a shadow-figure.
He is not robust and living like old Cecrops. He never appears
as a snake; the Ionians whom he represented had passed beyond

---

[1] VIII. 41.   [2] I. 24. 7.   [3] *Supra*, p. 48.

the stage of snake-daimons.   Moreover when we come to examine
the birth-story it is but a weak version of the Erichthonios
myth.   Ion takes on the chest and the guardian snakes; they
are canonical.   Ion is a hero, he must wear a hero's swaddling
clothes; as though appropriating the myth he piously recites it,
though for dramatic purposes in question form[1].

> *Ion.*   And did Athena take the child from Earth?
> *Cre.*   Yes, to her maiden arms, she did not bear him.
> *Ion.*   And did she give him as the pictures tell us?
> *Cre.*   To Cecrops' daughters, to be kept not seen.
> *Ion.*   And they methinks opened the goddess' chest?

Ion, like Cecrops, like Erechtheus, is the μέγιστος κοῦρος of his
tribe, but, expressing as he does an artificial rather than natural
group, he is emptied of all vital content.

To resume, the form taken by the traditional hero and also
the king is unquestionably that of a snake, and the snake is used
in phallic ceremonies for the promotion of fertility.   But are we
justified in calling the snake a '*daimon* of fertility'?

It is important to be clear on this point.   Such a notion
contradicts traditional opinion.   The snake we are constantly told
is the vehicle of the dead man, the form in which he is apt to
appear.   The evidence for this death-aspect seems clear and
abundant.   On tombs and funeral 'hero-reliefs' the snake is
constantly present.   On the familiar Sparta hero-reliefs[2] a huge
bearded snake is erect behind the seated heroized pair; on reliefs
of the funeral banquet type[3] a snake appears twined about a tree
or drinks from a cup in the reclining 'hero's' hand.

It is not hard to see reasons why a snake should be associated
with a dead man.   The snake is an uncanny beast gliding in and
out of holes in the earth.   He may well have been seen haunting
old tombs.   It is even possible that, as Plutarch[4] says, the appearance of the spinal cord of a dead man suggested snakes.   Nor is
the association of snake and dead man's soul confined to the

---

[1] Eur. *Ion* 269, cf. *vv.* 21—27.
[2] See Fig. 88 and *Prolegomena*, p. 327.
[3] A number of these monuments are reproduced *op. cit.* in Figs. 97—100, 105,
106, 112, and in connection with these the death-aspect of the snake is discussed.
My present view as to the interpretation of these 'hero-reliefs' will be given
later, p. 307.
[4] *Vit. Cleom.* 39.

Greeks.   It is, Dr Frazer[1] says, a common belief among the Zulus
and other Caffre tribes that the dead come to life and revisit their
old homes in the shape of serpents.   Such semi-human serpents
are treated with great respect and often fed with milk.   Among
the Ba-Ronga[2] the snake is regarded as a sort of incarnation of an
ancestor and is dreaded though never worshipped.   A native
pursuing a snake that had got into the kitchen of a missionary
station accidentally set the building on fire.   All the neighbours
exclaimed that the fire was due to the snake, and the snake was
the *chiko-nembo* or ghost of a man who was buried close at hand
and had come out of the earth to avenge himself.   If a dead man
wants to frighten his wife, he is apt in East Central Africa to
present himself in the form of a snake.   Among the Bahima of
Eukole[3], in Uganda, dead chiefs turn into snakes, but dead kings
into lions.

If the snake then is the symbol or vehicle of the dead man
how can he also be a 'daimon of fertility'?   The two aspects are
incompatible, even contradictory—death and life are not the
same, though mysticism constantly seeks to blend them.   Which
then does the snake represent, death or life?   Is he a good
daimon of life and fertility or an evil *daimon* of mortality and
corruption?

Fortunately, a story told us by Plutarch[4] leaves us in no doubt
as to the significance of the snake and its relation to the dead
man.   After Cleomenes of Sparta had fled to Egypt and there
died by his own orders, Ptolemy, fearing an insurrection, wished to
dishonour the king's body and ordered it to be impaled and
hung up.

A few days after, those who were guarding the impaled body saw a huge
snake (δράκοντα) wound about the head and hiding the face so that no bird of
prey should light on it.   Thereupon a superstitious fear fell on the king and
such a dread that it started the women on various purification ceremonies,
inasmuch as a man had been put to death who was dear to the gods and *of
more than mortal nature.*   The Alexandrians came thronging to the place
and saluted Cleomenes as a hero and the child of the gods, till the learned
men put a stop to it by explaining that as oxen when they putrefy breed bees,

[1] *Adonis Attis Osiris*[2], p. 73.
[2] H. Jumod, *Les Ba-Ronga*, 1898.
[3] J. Roscoe, *The Bahima*, Journal of Anthrop. Inst. xxxvii. (1907).
[4] *Vit. Cleom.* xxxix. ...οἱ παλαῖοι μάλιστα τῶν ζῴων τὸν δράκοντα τοῖς ἥρωσιν
συνῳκείωσαν.

and horses wasps, and beetles come to life from decaying asses, so human carcasses when some of the juices about the marrow congeal and thicken substantially give rise to serpents. And it was because they knew this that the men of old time associated the snake more than any other animal with heroes.

The 'men of old time' were content with no such pseudo-science. They believed, with the pious Alexandrians, not that the snake was the sign and result of putrefaction, but that it was evidence, clear and indefeasible, that the man was of *more than mortal nature* (κρείττονος τὴν φύσιν). Cleomenes had been a hero in our sense in his life, but no one knew that in the religious sense he was a 'hero' till the snake appeared. The snake then is the symbol and the vehicle not of mortality but *immortality*—of something sacred, something in the vaguer sense divine.

The word κρείττων, better, stronger, used by Plutarch is instructive. κρείττονες, Hesychius tells us, is a general term for heroes and for gods, but not all dead men were κρείττονες. This reminds us that the meaning of the word 'hero' is actually not 'dead man,' but, if we may trust Hesychius[1], it means simply 'powerful,' 'strong,' 'noble,' 'venerable.'

The snake then stands for life and *mana*, not for death. In the light of the snake as life-*daimon*, as 'more than mortal,' we understand many birth-stories current in antiquity. A snake was seen lying outstretched by the side of Olympias, mother of Alexander, and Philip from that time on deserted his bride. It may have been, Plutarch[2] concludes, from fear of her enchantments or because 'he dared not violate the sanctity of one wedded to a greater than he.' In like fashion, says Pausanias[3], was Aristomenes the Messenian born, 'for his mother, Nicoteleia, they say, was visited by a *daimon* or a god in the likeness of a serpent.' The same story was told of Aristodama by the Sicyonians.

We have already (p. 148) seen how out of a sacrificed animal, a bull or goat, could arise a god. The case however of the snake is quite different from that of the food animals. So far as we know, the snake was never killed that his *mana* might be eaten. It is well to note that sanctity does not always issue in sacramental

[1] Sub voc. ἥρως· δυνατός, ἰσχυρός, γενναῖος, σεμνός.
[2] *Vit. Alex.* 2.
[3] IV. 14. 7, and Dr Frazer *ad loc.* For other instances of the fatherhood of snakes see *Adonis Attis Osiris*[2], p. 70.

sacrifice. The snake among the Greeks was full of *mana*, was intensely sacred, not because as food he supported life, but because he is himself a life-*daimon*, a spirit of generation, even of immortality. But—and this is all important—it is immortality of quite a peculiar kind. The individual members of the group of the Cecropidae die, man after man, generation after generation; Cecrops, who never lived at all, lives for ever, as a snake. He is the δαίμων γέννης, the spirit, the genius of the race, he stands not for personal immortality in our modern sense, not for the negation of death, ἀθανασία, but for the perennial renewal of life through death, for Reincarnation, for παλιγγενεσία.

The word παλιγγενεσία, 'birth back again,' speaks for itself. It is a much simpler, more primitive thing than we are apt to imagine. We think of Reincarnation as belonging to an elaborate and somewhat stereotyped mysticism, whether Indian or Pythagorean. It is associated in our minds with a grotesque system of purification for the individual soul. Our common sense and the common sense of the normal enlightened Greek rebels against such a doctrine, just as we mentally rebel against the totemist's claim of kinship with beast and plant. The average Athenian, when he was told by Empedokles that he had once been a bird or a tree, was probably as much surprised and disgusted as the theologian of the last century when it was hinted to him that his remoter ancestors were apes.

Reincarnation is, I venture to think, no mystical doctrine propounded by a particular and eccentric sage, nor yet is it a chance even if widespread error into which independently in various parts of the world men have fallen. Rather it is, I believe, a stage in the development of thinking through which men naturally and necessarily pass, it is a form of collective or group thought, and, as such, it is a usual and almost necessary concomitant of totemism. Whether my view in this matter be true or false, thus much stands certain, a belief in Reincarnation is characteristic of totemistic peoples. It is these simple, deep down things that last so long. Reincarnation long held under by Nationalism and Olympianism, reemerged to blossom in Orphism, and constantly to haunt the imagination of a Pindar and a

Plato; to understand this reincarnation we must go back to our savages.

'The theory of conception as a reincarnation of the dead,' writes Dr Frazer[1],

is universally held by all the Central Australian tribes which have been investigated by Messrs Spencer and Gillen; every man, woman and child is supposed by them to be a reembodiment of an ancestral spirit.

Messrs Spencer and Gillen, in the preface to their volume, the *Northern Tribes of Central Australia*, themselves write[2]:

Perhaps the most interesting result of our work is the demonstration of the fact that, in the whole of this wide area, the belief that every living member of the tribe is the reincarnation of a spirit ancestor is universal. This belief is just as firmly held by the Urabunna people, who count descent in the female line, as it is by the Arunta and Warramunga, who count descent in the male line.

And again[3]:

The natives one and all in these tribes believe that the child is the direct result of the entrance into the mother of an ancestral spirit individual.

How the Central Australian came to believe in reincarnation we cannot certainly say, but it is not hard to imagine how such a faith might arise. New young emus, new young kangaroos are born; the savage has no notion of creation, no theory of procreation; he sees the young kangaroo come from the body of its mother, the emu from the emu's egg; the old kangaroos, the old emus, are born back again, there has been a παλιγγενεσία. His rites of initiation constantly obsess him with the notion of re-birth, with a death and resurrection that are of one and the same life. These ceremonies may indeed, it has been well conjectured[4], have for one of their main objects to secure reincarnation. Such rites as circumcision and the knocking out of teeth would thus find a new and simpler meaning. Bones and sinews decay, but a tooth lasts on and would serve, if carefully guarded, as an imperishable bit of the old body, as a focus for

[1] *Totemism and Exogamy*, I. p. 191.
[2] *Northern Tribes*, Introd. p. xi.
[3] *Northern Tribes*, p. 330.
[4] By Dr Frazer, *The Magic Art*, I. 106.

reincarnation, a 'stock of vital energy for the use of the disembodied spirit after death[1].'

It is easy to see how such a belief goes with group-life and
group-thinking. The individual dies, but, as a matter of actual
fact, the group goes on, the totem animal is never extinct. This
totem animal, conceived of as the common life of the tribe, is
projected as it were into the past, the 'Alcheringa' time, and
is there thought of as half man half animal, a figure, if the clan
be a snake clan, strangely like old Cecrops. When a man dies he
goes back to his totem. He does not cease to be, but he ceases
functionally for a time, goes out of sight, by and by to reappear
as a new tribesman. Generation is not, as Plato[2] reminds us,
a straight line stretching after death into an interminable remote
immortality, it is a circle, a κύκλος, always returning upon itself.
Just such was the 'ancient doctrine' of which Socrates[3] reminded
Cebes, which affirmed that 'they who are here go thither and they
come back here and are born again from the dead.'

We have seen[4] how in the *Intichiuma* ceremonies the totem-
group magically secures the multiplication of the totem. The
human-emu sheds his blood, dresses and dances as an emu, that
he may increase and invigorate the supply of bird-emus. If we
bear in mind that recurrent cycle of human life which is
Reincarnation, and if we also bear in mind that to the totemist
the two cycles of life, human and animal or plant, are indissolubly
linked, then we understand without difficulty what otherwise is
so strange and disconcerting, the fact that *Intichiuma* ceremonies
are commemorative as well as magical. The emu man when he
dances as an emu commemorates the deeds of his emu ancestor.
He needs must, because those heroic deeds done in the 'Alcheringa

---

[1] Dr Frazer, *op. cit.* p. 96. Mr Cornford calls my attention to the curious notice
in Lydus (*de mens.* IV. 40), τοὺς μέντοι ὀδόντας οὐκ ἔχοντας φύσεως ἢ πυρὶ ἢ χρόνῳ γοῦν
μακρῷ καταναλίσκεσθαι κατέλιμπανον (οἱ παλαιοὶ) ἐπ' αὐτῆς τῆς πυρᾶς ὡς τὸ λοιπὸν
ἀχρήστους πρὸς τὸν τῆς παλιγγενεσίας λόγον ἀποβλέποντες· σφόδρα γὰρ καὶ αὐτοὶ τὸν περὶ
αὐτῆς παρεδέχοντο λόγον διὰ τὸ αὖθις ὡς ἐδόκει παλιγγενησόμενον ἄνθρωπον μὴ χρήζειν
ἐπὶ τῆς μητρῴας γαστρὸς ὀδόντων.

[2] Plat. *Phaed.* 72 B εἰ γὰρ μὴ ἀεὶ ἀνταποδιδοίη τὰ ἕτερα τοῖς ἑτέροις γιγνόμενα
ὡσπερεὶ κύκλῳ περιιόντα, ἀλλ' εὐθεῖά τις εἴη ἡ γένεσις ἐκ τοῦ ἑτέρου μόνον εἰς τὸ
καταντικρὺ καὶ μὴ ἀνακάμπτοι πάλιν ἐπὶ τὸ ἕτερον μηδὲ καμπὴν ποιοῖτο, οἶσθα ὅτι, κ.τ.λ.

[3] Plat. *Phaed.* 70 c παλαιὸς μὲν οὖν ἔστι τις λόγος, οὗ μεμνήμεθα, ὡς εἰσὶν ἐνθένδε
ἀφικόμεναι ἐκεῖ, καὶ πάλιν γε δεῦρο ἀφικνοῦνται καὶ γίγνονται ἐκ τῶν τεθνεώτων.

[4] *Supra*, p. 124.

time' are but the projection of his own most vital needs, his need of food, his need of offspring.   At his great Eniautos-festival he enacts his ancestors who are his food-animals and thereby brings them back to birth.

To the Central Australian then it is his ancestor who gives him food and offspring and all the wealth he craves.   His way of thinking is not far from the mind of Pindar.   Pindar offends our moral sense, even our taste sometimes, because to him, in the glory of life, Wealth and Plenitude bulk so large, and still worse, as it seems to us, it is inherited wealth which with him seems married to virtue—an alliance unknown to Christianity.   But his view of life, though never quite inspiring, takes on another complexion when we see how deep-rooted it is in things primitive. Any Central Australian at his *Intichiuma* ceremonies would have felt in his bones the nearness of πλοῦτος as well as ἀρετή to the δαίμων γενέθλιος[1].

Theban Pindar may have borrowed his thought from Boeotian Hesiod; both came of a tenacious stock.   Hesiod[2] tells of the men of the Golden Age, the Alcheringa of the Greek, and how after a life of endless feast they fell asleep, and Earth hid them, and thereupon they became δαίμονες, spirits, watchers over men, haunting the land mist-clad,

> Givers of wealth, this kingly guerdon theirs.

In life the king is lord of the Eniautos[3], in death he is the *daimon-hero*.

It may still perhaps be felt that, at least with the Greeks, this totemistic notion of reincarnation, with its corollary that the cycle of man's reincarnation brings with it the renewal of animal and plant life, is matter only of poetry and a vague philosophy.   It is time to enquire whether in actual practice, in definite ritual acts, we have any evidence of the same notion.

---

[1] Cf. such passages as *Ol.* II. 96,
> ὁ μὰν πλοῦτος ἀρεταῖς δεδαιδαλμένος,
and the whole of the fifth Pythian.

[2] *Op.* 125,
> ἠέρα ἑσσάμενοι πάντη φοιτῶντες ἐπ' αἶαν
> πλουτοδόται· καὶ τοῦτο γέρας βασιλήϊον ἔσχον.

[3] It is not a little curious that the scholiast on Hesiod, *Theog.* 112, ὥς τ' ἄφενος δάσσαντο, says Ἄφενός ἐστι κυρίως μὲν ὁ ἀπὸ ἐνιαυτοῦ πλοῦτος.

Are the actual dead, as well as the *daimones* of Hesiod, appealed to as πλουτοδόται, as, like the Olympians, δωτῆρες ἐάων? Cecrops and Erichthonios, we have seen, are connected with ritual snakes, but is the ritual snake connected with the dead? Neither Arrephoria nor Thesmophoria, both ceremonies extremely primitive and both concerned with fertility, have any word to say of ancestors, any hint of a cycle of human reincarnation. We shall find what we seek and more even than we expect in the great Athenian festival of the blossoming of flowers and the revocation of souls, the Anthesteria

THE ANTHESTERIA.

The Anthesteria was a three days' festival celebrated from the 11th to the 13th of Anthesterion, falling therefore at the end of our February, when the Greek spring is well begun. The three days were called respectively *Pithoigia* 'Jar-opening,' *Choes* 'Drinking Cups,' *Chytroi* 'Pots.' Each day had its different form of pot or jar and its varying ceremonial, but the whole festival was, if we may judge from the names of the several days, essentially a Pot-Feast. On the first day, the Pithoigia, the wine-jars were opened, on the second the wine was solemnly drunk, on the third a pot full of grain and seeds, a *panspermia*, was solemnly offered.

I have elsewhere[1] shown, and my view has, I believe, been universally accepted, that beneath the festivities of a Wine-Festival to Dionysos there lay a festival of All-Souls, that in the spring month of February the Athenians, like the Romans at their Feralia, performed ceremonies for the placation of the dead. I was right, I believe, in detecting the All-Souls feast; wrong, however, in supposing that it belonged to a different and lower religious stratum. This mistake I shall now attempt to rectify. I shall try, in the light of the doctrine of reincarnation and the *Intichiuma* ceremonies, to show that the ghost element and the fertility element belong to one and the same stratum of thought, and are, in fact, mutually interdependent.

We begin with the Pithoigia. The *pithos* or great stone jar, frequently half buried in the earth, was the main storehouse of

---

[1] *Prolegomena*, pp. 32—55, to which I must refer for a full statement of sources and for the literature of the Anthesteria.

the ancients both for food and drink, for grain, for oil, for wine. The cellars of the palace of Knossos have disclosed rows of these pithoi. I have elsewhere[1] shown that the pithoi are also grave-jars, out of which the ghosts of dead men might flutter forth and to which they could return as to their homes. But for the present it is as storehouses of food and especially wine that the pithoi concern us. At the Pithoigia these wine-jars were opened for the first time, as the wine made in the autumn would then just be drinkable. Proklos on Hesiod[2] tells us that 'the festival was an ancestral one, and that it was not allowable to prevent either household slaves or hired servants from partaking of the wine.' By this time no doubt it was a family rather than a gentile festival; anyhow it was collective, of the whole house[3], and it was ancient. It was, Proklos says, 'in honour of Dionysos'; he prudently adds 'that is, of his wine.'

Food and drink, and the desire magically to increase and safeguard food and drink, are earlier than the gods. Plutarch[4] in his account of the Pithoigia lets us watch the transit from one to the other. He is speaking of the local Theban Pithoigia over which his father had presided and at which he had been present as a boy.

On the eleventh day of the month (Anthesterion) they broached the new wine at Athens, calling the day *Pithoigia*. And from of old it seems it was their custom to offer some of it as a libation before drinking of it, with the prayer that the use of the drug might be rendered harmless and beneficial to them. But by us (Boeotians) the month is called *Prostaterios*, and it is our custom on the sixth day of the month *to sacrifice to the Agathos Daimon* and then taste the new wine after the West Wind has done blowing.

And again later[5] he says those who are the first to drink of the new wine drink it in Anthesterion after the winter, and we call that day by the name of the Agathos Daimon but the Athenians call it Pithoigia.

The nature of the 'sacrifice is clear. Plutarch uses the

[1] *Proleg.* p. 43.
[2] *Op.* 368 Ἀρχομένου δὲ πίθου. Ἐν ταῖς πατρίοις τῶν Ἑλλήνων ἑορταῖς ἐτελεῖτο καὶ τὰ ἀσκώλια καὶ ἡ πιθοιγία εἰς τίμην Διονύσου, τουτέστι τοῦ οἴνου αὐτοῦ.
[3] Tzetzes ad Hes. *Op.* 366 says ἡ πιθοιγία δὲ κοινὸν ἦν συμπόσιον· ἀνοίξαντες γὰρ τοὺς πίθους πᾶσι μετεδίδουν τοῦ Διονύσου δωρήματος.
[4] *Quaest. Symp.* III. 7. 1 καὶ πάλαι γε (ὡς ἔοικεν) εὔχοντο τοῦ οἴνου πρὶν ἢ πιεῖν, ἀποσπένδοντες ἀβλαβῆ καὶ σωτήριον αὐτοῖς τοῦ φαρμάκου τὴν χρῆσιν γενέσθαι...ἕκτῃ δ' ἱσταμένου νομίζεται θύσαντας ἀγαθῷ δαίμονι γεύεσθαι τοῦ οἴνου μετὰ ζέφυρον.
[5] *Quaest. Symp.* VIII. 3.

word proper to burnt sacrifice ($\theta \acute{v} \epsilon \iota \nu$)[1], but this is no offering to an Olympian, it is simply the solemn pouring out of a little of the new wine, that so the whole may be released from tabu. This 'sacrifice' of the new wine is, to begin with, made to nothing and nobody, but bit by bit a *daimon* of the act emerges, and he is the Agathos Daimon. In what shape and similitude shall we find the Agathos Daimon? Is he a wholly new apparition or an old familiar friend?

The Agathos Daimon. Classical scholars are apt to remember the Good Spirit, the Agathos Daimon or Agathodaimon as he is later called, as a vague 'genius' of some sort invoked at the close of banquets when a little pure wine was drunk, or as a late abstraction appearing like Agathe Tyche in the preamble of decrees. The view I now hope to make clear is that the Agathos Daimon is a very primitive fertility-spirit, a conception that long preceded any of the Olympians. He is indeed the inchoate material out of which, as we shall presently see, more than one Olympian is in part made. But for the present we are interested in him chiefly as the mask or functional form which each individual hero is compelled to wear.

We have first to ask what shape he assumes.

The coin in Fig. 66[2] gives us the clearest possible answer. Here we have a great coiled snake sur-rounded by emblems of fertility, ears of corn and the poppyhead with its multitude of seeds. The snake's name is clearly in-scribed; he is the New Agathos Daimon (NEO. ΑΓΑΘ. ΔΑΙΜ.). On the obverse, not figured here, is the head of Nero; it is he who claims to be the New Agathos Daimon. Cecrops the hero-king was a

FIG. 66.

snake, Nero the Emperor is the new snake: it is not as private individuals that they claim to be fertility-daimons, it is as functionaries. Cecrops the modest old tribal king was content to bring fertility to the Cecropidae, Nero as imperialist claims to be the '*Good Daimon* of the whole habitable world[3].'

---

[1] For the use of $\theta \acute{v} \epsilon \iota \nu$ as distinguished from $\dot{\epsilon} \nu a \gamma \acute{\iota} \zeta \epsilon \iota \nu$ see *Prolegomena*, p. 53 ff.
[2] Head, *Hist. Num.* p. 720.
[3] *C. I. G.* III. 4699 δαίμων ἀγαθὸς τῆς οἰκουμένης.

FIG. 67.

It has long been known of course that the Agathodaimon of Hellenistic days was, as it is generally expressed, 'worshipped in the form of a snake,' but, because his figure appears on late Roman coins of Alexandria and often crowned by the Egyptian *Shent*, it is assumed that the snake-form was late or borrowed from the East. This is true of course of the *Shent*, false of the snake. We shall find abundant evidence of the Agathos Daimon as snake at home in Greece. The special value of the Alexandrian coin-types is that they so clearly emphasize the fertility-aspect of the snake. In Fig. 67 a coin of Nerva[1], better preserved than the coin of Nero, we have the same great fertility-snake, whom but for Nero's coin we should not have certainly known to be the Agathos Daimon; he wears the *Shent* and has ears of corn and somewhat to our surprise he holds in his coils a caduceus.

The snakes are sometimes two in number, a male and female genius who later crystallized into the half-human figures of Agathos Daimon and Agathe Tyche. A marriage was needed magically to compel fertility. In Fig. 68 we have a great *modius* or corn basket placed on the top of an Ionic column.

FIG. 68.

FIG. 69.

In the basket are ears of corn and poppyheads. To either side is a snake; that on the right wears a poppyhead, that on the left a *Shent*. Probably the *Shent*-wearer is the royal or male snake, the bride being poppy-crowned, an earth-*daimon*. On the obverse is the head of Hadrian.

[1] The coins in Figs. 67 to 70 are reproduced by kind permission of Dr George Macdonald from his *Catalogue of Greek Coins in the Hunterian Collection*, Vol. III. Pl. LXXXVI. and LXXXVII.

The modius marks very clearly the function of the snakes as fertility-daimons. The same idea comes out in the manifold attributes of the pair in Fig. 69. That they are regarded here as male and female is doubtful; rather they are the Egyptian and Greek incarnations of the same notion. The snake to the right is all Egyptian. He wears the disk and plumes and carries in his coils the sistrum as well as a poppy-head, he is in fact a *uraeus*. The snake to the left is partly Egyptianized; he wears the *shent*, but in his coils is the kerykeion of the Greek Hermes.

It would almost seem as though the kerykeion had like power in itself with the snakes, and indeed what was it but a staff with a pair of snakes intertwined? On the coin of Claudius in Fig. 70 we have no snakes but a great winged kerykeion, to either side of it ears of corn, the whole tied together in a bunch. Later when we come to the ceremonies of the Chytroi[1] we shall understand why the kery-keion, the 'attribute' of Hermes, had power to compel fertility.

FIG. 70.

From these imperial coins with the figure of the Agathos Daimon two points emerge, both of paramount importance. First, as already noted, the snake-*daimon* is a *collective* representation: he stands for a king or emperor, a functionary of some kind, not a personality. Second, his function is the promotion of fertility. The regular adjective attached to the *daimon* is ἀγαθός, good[2], and the kind of 'goodness' one needs in a Daimon is in the first instance fertility.

So much indeed we might have already guessed from the name, but it was better to have clear monumental evidence. The word ἀγαθός has like δῖος no superlative because it is in itself a superlative, meaning something ἄγαν, something very much[3]. Later of course it was moralized, but to begin with it

---

[1] *Infra*, p. 289.
[2] Menander (Kock 550 ap. Clem. Al. *Strom.* v. 727) was wiser than he knew when he said

    ἅπαντι δαίμων ἀνδρὶ συμπαρίσταται
    εὐθὺς γενομένῳ, μυσταγωγὸς τοῦ βίου
    ἀγαθός· κακὸν γὰρ δαίμον' οὐ νομιστέον
    εἶναι βίον βλάπτοντα χρηστόν.

[3] Stephanos, *Lex.* s.v.

just means as with us 'good' in the sense of 'abundant,' a 'good' lot, ἀγαθὴ δαὶς[1] a good dinner, ἀγαθὰ πράγματα, not matters morally excellent, but 'good' circumstances in peaceful days[2], *res secundae*. We have already[3] seen how in early Hebrew or in Mexican 'good' means 'good to eat.' It is over things 'good to eat' that the Agathos Daimon has his sway. All this, familiar to the student of language, is apt to be forgotten when we come to analyse a religious conception like that of the Agathos Daimon, yet is essential to its realization. This abundance, this 'muchness' of the Agathos Daimon will come out even more clearly when we come to his attribute the cornucopia.

The *Shent*-crowned snakes of Alexandria are late and foreign, can we point to earlier and home-grown snake-daimons of fertility?

On the black-figured cylix[4] in Fig. 71 we find them represented in lovely and quite unlooked-for fashion. The scene is a

Fig. 71.

[1] Hom. *Il.* XXIII. 810 καί σφιν δαῖτ' ἀγαθὴν παραθήσομαι.
[2] Thucyd. III. 82 ἐν μὲν γὰρ εἰρήνῃ καὶ ἀγαθοῖς πράγμασιν.
[3] *Supra*, p. 139.
[4] In Munich, Alte Pinakothek. First published and discussed by Dr Böhlau, *Schlangenleibige Nymphen*. Philologus, N. F. XI. 1. One half of the vase is reproduced and discussed in my *Prolegomena*, p. 259. See also *Delphika* in J. H. S. XIX. 1899, p. 216. But I did not then see the connection with the Agathos Daimon.

vineyard. On the one side, heraldically grouped, are a herd of mischievous goats, the enemies of the vine, bent on destruction, nibbling at the vines. On the other, as though to mark the contrast, under a great spreading vine, are four maiden-snakes. Two hold a basket of net or wicker in which the grapes will be gathered; a third holds a great cup for the grape juice, a fourth plays gladly on the double flute.

It might perhaps be rash to name these gentle snake-bodied vintage nymphs Agathoi Daimones, though Agathoi Daimones they are in form and function. Any Athenian child would have known by what name they best loved to be called. Old Cecrops would not have blushed to own them for his daughters. The

Fig. 72.

Charites so early got them wholly human form they might have looked askance. Anyhow the snake-maidens are own sisters to the three staid matronly women figures on the relief in Fig. 72, the Eumenides of Argos[1], who hold pomegranates in one hand

---

[1] For the Eumenides and their relation to the Semnae and to the Erinyes see *Prolegomena*, pp. 217—256. I have there fully discussed the snake form of the angry ghost, the Erinys, pp. 232—237. See *Delphika*, J. H. S. xix. 1899, p. 230.

and in the other snakes—own sisters too to the ancient fertility goddesses of the Areopagos, the Semnae.

The Agathos Daimon was, like the Roman *numen*, what Dr Warde Fowler[1] has well called a 'functional spirit with will power,' the function being indicated by the adjectival name. As such he was, no doubt, to begin with, sex-less. When sex is later attributed to him he is—perhaps under the influence of patriarchalism—like the Roman genius, always male, a daimon of generation, but on the whole he resists complete personalization. He gets, it is true, as will be seen, a sort of shadowy mother or wife in Agathe Tyche, yet, save for these grape-gathering nymphs and the Eumenides of Argos, we should never have known that the *snake* fertility-*daimon* took female form.

The Agathos Daimon appears again with Tyche at Lebadeia in Boeotia, associated with the strange and almost grotesquely primitive ceremonial of the oracle of Trophonios[2]. When a man would consult the oracle he first of all had to lodge a fixed number of days in a 'certain building' which was sacred to the Agathos Daimon and to Agathe Tyche: when he came back senseless from the oracle he was carried to this same house where he recovered his wits. I suspect that in that house or building dwelt a holy snake, an οἰκουρὸς ὄφις. Pausanias saw in the grotto images with snakes curled about their sceptres, he did not know whether to call them Asklepios and Hygieia or Trophonios and Eileithyia, for he adds, 'they think that snakes are as sacred to Trophonios as to Asklepios.' The suppliant to the oracle when he went down into the dreadful chasm took with him in either hand a honey-cake, surely for a snake's appeasement. Behind all these snake-divinities is the snake-*daimon*, the snake himself, male and female[3].

Boeotia was assuredly a land of snake-cults. The relief[4] in Fig. 73, which is good Attic work of the fourth century B.C., found at Eteonos, attests this. A man carrying a cake, probably a honey-cake, in his uplifted hand approaches a grotto cave; he leads by the hand his little son who hangs back. No wonder, for from the grotto rears out his head a huge snake. A good *daimon* he probably is, but somewhat fearsome.

[1] *The Religious Experience of the Roman People*, 1911, p. 119.
[2] Paus. ix. 39. 3, 5 and 13. See *infra*, chapter xi.
[3] *Infra*, pp. 429—436.   [4] Berlin Museum Cat. 724.

Agathe Tyche we meet again at Elis and with her Agathos
Daimon. only he bears another and a now thrice familiar name,

Fig. 73.

Sosipolis[1]. The people of Elis, Pausanias[2] tells us, had a sanctuary
of Tyche with a colossal image on its colonnade.

Here too Sosipolis has honours (τιμαί) in a small building to the left of
Tyche. The god is painted in the shape in which he appeared in a dream,
as a child, dressed in a chlamys spangled with stars, and in one hand he
holds the horn of Amaltheia.

But what has a child in a spangled chlamys holding a cornucopia to do with our snake-*daimon*? Much, indeed everything; he
is the 'good' snake-*daimon*. We remember[3] that when the child
was placed in the forefront of the Elean army, he changed into a
serpent, and fear fell on the Arcadians and they fled. The Eleans
won a great victory and called the god Sosipolis.

And where the serpent appeared to go down into the ground after the
battle, there they made the sanctuary[4].

Sosipolis at Olympia, it will be remembered, had like Erechtheus and Trophonios the snake's service of the honey-cake.

The Agathos Daimon and Sosipolis are one and the same, and
Sosipolis, it will be remembered, is but another name for Zeus
Soter, Saviour of the city. Now we understand—though this is
of but trifling interest save as a confirmation—the confusion in

[1] *Supra*, p. 240, note 4.   [2] vi. 25. 4.
[3] *Loc. cit., supra*, p. 240.   [4] Paus. vi. 20. 3 and 5.

Greek drinking customs of Zeus Soter with the Agathos Daimon. Suidas[1], in his valuable gloss, says:

> The ancients had the custom after dinner of drinking to the Good Daimon. They gulped down some unmixed wine and said this was to the Good Daimon, but when they were about to separate it was to Zeus the Saviour[2]

The familiar Sosipolis is then in form and function, though not in name, an Agathos Daimon. He is to us especially instructive, because he shows the transition from snake to animal form. Sosipolis changes into a snake. It is a safe mythological rule that a metamorphosis of this kind may always be inverted; the snake takes on the form of a human child. Another point to be noted is, that at Elis and Olympia, when the snake-*daimon* takes on human form, he[3] and his female correlative, Tyche or Eileithyia, appear in the matriarchal relation, as Mother and Son.

Fig. 74.

On the relief in Fig. 74 we see Agathe Tyche holding a child in her arms. The design is carved in low relief on a column in the Hall of the Mystae of Dionysos recently excavated at Melos[4]. Agathe Tyche is clearly here the Good Luck of Melos,

---

[1] s.v. Ἀγαθοῦ Δαίμονος. Ἔθος εἶχον οἱ παλαιοὶ μετὰ τὸ δεῖπνον πίνειν Ἀγαθοῦ Δαίμονος, ἐπιρροφοῦντες ἄκρατον, καὶ τοῦτο λέγειν Ἀγαθοῦ Δαίμονος· χωρίζεσθαι δὲ μέλλοντες Διὸς Σωτῆρος. Suidas adds that the second day of the month was called the day of the Agathos Daimon. The second is one of the few days that are not mentioned as either lucky or unlucky by Hesiod in his calendar.

[2] For the whole discussion of the subject of the final libations at a feast to Agathos Daimon, Agathe Tyche and Zeus Soter see Athenaeus xv. 47, 48, 692, 693. He gives as his authorities Philochoros and Theophrastos, and various poets of the Old and Middle Comedy.

[3] The nominal correlative of Tyche is Tychon, a *daimon* who is but a form of Priapus, see Kaibel, *Daktyloi Idaioi*, in Nachrichten d. k. Gesellschaft d. Wissenschaften zu Göttingen, Phil.-Hist.-Kl. 1901, p. 503.

[4] *J.H.S.* XVIII. 1898, p. 60, Fig. 1, and *A. Mitth.* xv. 1890, p. 248. For Eirene carrying the child Ploutos see my *Mythology and Monuments*, pp. 65—8.

she is the personification or projection, the *genius loci*. The style of the relief is of course late, but it goes back to an earlier prototype and one that to us is instructive. Pausanias[1] saw at Thebes, near to the observatory of Teiresias, a sanctuary of Tyche, and she was carrying the child Ploutos. As he naively observes:

> It was a clever plan of the artists to put Ploutos in the arms of Tyche as his mother or nurse, and Kephisodotos was no less clever; he made for the Athenians the image of Eirene holding Ploutos.

Tyche at Elis has lost, or never had, her prefix Agathe. When the child Ploutos is in her arms the adjective is superfluous, he is her 'Wealth,' her 'Goodness.' When the snake-*daimon* Sosipolis takes human form, he holds the 'horn of Amaltheia,' the cornucopia. The child and the cornucopia of earth's fruits are one and the same. That is clear on the vase-painting[2] in Fig. 35, where Ge rises from the earth, holding in her hands the great cornucopia, out of which uprises the child. The cornucopia is sometimes explained as the 'horn of Amaltheia,' the goat-mother who nursed the infant Zeus. Sometimes it is the horn of the river-bull Acheloös, the great source of fertility[3]. Its symbolism is always the same; fertility, whatever the source. But most of all it stands for the gathered fruits of the year[4]. There was a certain cup, we remember[5], 'called the Horn of Amaltheia and also *Eniautos*.'

Fig. 75.

The relief in Fig. 75[6] may serve to remind us of the snake and human forms of the Agathos Daimon. It is the only instance known to me where they occur together. The monument was found at Epidauros. It is of Roman date[7], a votive offering of

---

[1] ix. 16. 2.   [2] *Supra*, p. 167.   [3] See *Prolegomena*, p. 435, Fig. 135.
[4] Diodorus iv. 35. 4 ὃ προσαγορεῦσαι κέρας Ἀμαλθείας, ἐν ᾧ πλάττουσι πλῆθος ὑπάρχειν πάσης ὀπωρινῆς ὥρας, βοτρύων τε καὶ μήλων καὶ τῶν ἄλλων τοιούτων.
[5] p. 186.   [6] Kabbadias, *Fouilles d'Epidaure*, i. p. 45.
[7] The date is given in the inscription but not the era used. As three eras are in use at Epidauros the exact year cannot be fixed. The lettering is of the 2nd cent. A.D.

a certain priest, a Fire-Bearer, by name Tiberius Claudius Xenokles. The god is represented holding a sceptre in his right hand, a cornucopia in his left. A god we must call him, for the dedication is ἀγαθοῦ θεοῦ, of the Good God. Near Megalopolis Pausanias[1] saw a temple of the Good God; he remarks that 'if the gods are givers of good things to men and Zeus is the supreme god, it may logically be inferred that the term is applied to Zeus.' The inference is somewhat rash. As the relief was found at Epidaurus the epithet is usually explained as a 'title of Asklepios,' but surely the Agathos Theos is only an Olympianized form of the old Agathos Daimon. Over his body still crawls the snake he once was. We follow the snake.

The association of mother, snake, child, and the wealth of harvest fruits comes out strikingly in the Graeco-Roman relief[2] in Fig. 76. We have purposely kept it to the end because it

Fig. 76.

admirably embodies and summarizes the relation of snake, hero and daimon. The seated figure is Demeter, and we are tempted to call the young boy who brings the fruits to her Triptolemos. It is, I think, safer to think of him as the child Ploutos. In Crete Hesiod[3] tells us:

Demeter brought forth Ploutos...and kindly was the birth
Of him whose way is on the sea and over all the Earth.
Happy, happy is the mortal who doth meet him as he goes,
For his hands are full of blessings and his treasure overflows,

---

[1] viii. 36. 5.
[2] Overbeck, *Kunst-Mythologie*, Atlas. Taf.
[3] *Theog.* 969, schol. ad loc. καὶ γὰρ ἡ παροιμία 'πυρῶν καὶ κριθῶν, ὦ νήπιε Πλοῦτε.'

and the scholiast preserves for us the tag:

> Ah for the wheat and barley, O child Ploutos.

The snake behind Demeter is of special interest. In function he was of course an Agathos Daimon, but as to his actual name people were not so sure. Tradition associated him with the hero Kychreus of Salamis.

'At Salamis,' Pausanias[1] tells us, 'there was a sanctuary of Kychreus. It is said that, while the Athenians were engaged in the sea-fight with the Medes, a snake appeared among the ships and God announced that this snake was the hero Kychreus.'

To this sanctuary, when Athens and Megara were fighting for Salamis, Solon went by night and offered to Periphemos and Kychreus *sphagia*, the sacrifice proper to heroes[2].

Kychreus is, perhaps, a somewhat shadowy figure to many of us, but he was in ancient days a hero of high repute. Plutarch solemnly argues that the robber Skiron cannot have been such a very disreputable villain, as he was son-in-law to Kychreus, who had divine honours at Athens. His real home was of course the coast country of the bay, opposite Salamis, of Kychreia, whose other name was Skiros. Of Kychreia and its clansmen Kychreus was eponymous hero, as Cecrops of Cecropia and the Cecropidae. Strabo[3] knew this, and he tells us, on the authority of Hesiod, that

From Kychreia the snake Kychreides had its name, which Kychreus bred, and Eurylochos drove it out because it ravaged the island, but Demeter received it into Eleusis, and it became her attendant.

Others said that Kychreus himself was surnamed Serpent ("Οφις)[4].

All this aetiology is transparent. There was at Kychreia or Salamis, as at Athens, a local 'household' snake (οἰκουρὸς ὄφις). With it, as at Athens, was associated the eponymous hero of the place. The cult of the snake fell into disrepute, the human form of the eponymous hero was preferred. At Eleusis also there was behind the figure of Demeter an old local snake; in the mysteries

---

[1] i. 36. 1; for the various forms of the Kychreus legend see Dr Frazer, *ad loc.*
[2] Plut. *Vit. Thes.* 10: for *sphagia* see *Prolegomena*, pp. 63—73.
[3] ix. §§ 393 ...ὑποδέξασθαι δὲ αὐτὸν τὴν Δήμητρα εἰς Ἐλευσῖνα καὶ γενέσθαι ταύτης ἀμφίπολον. The gist of the killing of the snake by the hero or god will be considered when we come to the Olympians.
[4] Steph. Byz. s. v. Κυχρεῖος πάγος.

the marriage[1] of Demeter with Zeus, who 'took the form of a snake,' was still known, but again the human form of the goddess obtains.   As in Fig. 76, the snake is well behind her; but he is there for all that, and his old fertility functions are shown in the fruit-bearing child, Ploutos.   The little shrine out of which the snake peers is a *heroon*, but the hero is a functionary-*daimon*, not a historic personality.   At Thebes, too, Suidas[2] tells us, 'there is a *heroon* of the Agathos Daimon.

We have dwelt at length on the Agathos Daimon because without a clear notion of him in his twofold aspect as collective representative and as fertility-*daimon* the ceremonies of the Anthesteria lose half their meaning.   Later we shall be able to demonstrate from monumental evidence that it was the form and function of the Agathos Daimon that, not only the mythical kings Cecrops and Erechtheus and Kychreus, but also each and every local hero put on, and that it was only as and because they assumed this guise that they became 'heroes' and won for themselves a cultus.   For the present we must return to the Anthesteria.

The Choes.   The first day of the Anthesteria, the *Pithoigia*, we have seen, was given to the 'sacrifice,' that is to libations of the new wine to the Agathos Daimon at the broaching of the casks.   The second day, the Choes or drinking cups, need not long detain us[3].   It was the natural sequel of the first.   The taboo having been removed from the new wine, a revel set in.   Each man, or at least each householder, was given a *Chous*, a measure of wine: there was a drinking contest ($\dot{a}\gamma\dot{\omega}\nu$), the exact arrangements of which are not clear.   Each man or boy crowned his cup with a garland and brought it to the priestess of the temple of Dionysos in the Marshes[4].

---

[1] See *Prolegomena*, p. 535, and see the great snake coiled round Demeter on the vase in the Museo delle Terme, p. 547, Fig. 156.

[2] s.v. Ἀγαθοῦ Δαίμονος...Καὶ ἐν Θήβαις δὲ ἦν Ἡρῷον Ἀγαθοῦ Δαίμονος.

[3] Most authorities have held that the marriage of the Queen Archon to Dionysos took place on the day of the Choes.   But Dr Frazer (*The Magic Art* I. p. 137) says that the assumption rests on insufficient evidence; he conjectures that it may have taken place in the month Gamelion.   The ceremony was of cardinal importance as a fertility charm, but because of the uncertainty of date I omit all discussion of it in relation to the Anthesteria.

[4] For sources see the Lexica and Dr Martin Nilsson's *Studia de Dionysiis Atticis*, 1900.

The main fact that concerns us as to the Choes is that, spite of the revel and the wine-drinking and the flower-wreathed cups, the day of the Choes was *nefastus*. Photius[1] tells us it was a 'day of pollution,' *in which they believed that the spirits of the dead rose up*: by way of precaution against these spirits from early dawn they chewed buckthorn, a plant of purgative properties, and they anointed their doors with pitch. A new element is here introduced; there are ghosts about and they are feared.

The Chytroi. This coming and going of the ghosts about the city at the Anthesteria is clearly evidenced by the concluding ritual of the third day, the *Chytroi.* The Greeks, Zenodotus[2] tells us, had a proverbial expression said 'of those who on all occasions demand a repetition of favours received.' It was as follows :

> Out of the doors! ye Keres; it is no longer Anthesteria.

And it was spoken, Suidas[3] said,

> inasmuch as there were ghosts going about the city at the Anthesteria.

Year by year, in ever returning cycle as the Anthesteria came round, the ghosts were let loose at the Pithoigia. For three days they fluttered through the city, filling men's hearts with nameless dread, causing them to chew buckthorn and anoint their doors with pitch and close their sanctuaries; then, on the third day, by solemn mandate, they were bidden to depart.

Before we come to the reason of their uprising two points must be noted. First, the ghosts are many, a fluttering crowd; they are collective, addressed in the plural; it is not an individual ancestor of great fame and name who rises from the dead, but *ancestors.* Second, they are feared as well as reverenced. The name Keres, applied to them, is not the equivalent of ψυχαί

---

[1] s.v. μιαρὰ ἡμέρα· ἐν τοῖς Χουσὶν Ἀνθεστηριῶνος μηνός, ἐν ᾧ δοκοῦσιν αἱ ψυχαὶ τῶν τελευτησάντων ἀνιέναι, ῥάμνων ἕωθεν ἐμασῶντο καὶ πίττῃ τὰς θύρας ἔχριον.

[2] *Cent. Paroim.* s.v. Εἴρηται δὲ ἡ παροιμία ἐπὶ τῶν τὰ αὐτὰ ἐπιζητούντων πάντοτε λαμβάνειν. The use of the proverb seems to emphasize the insistent, periodic return of the ghosts.

[3] s.v. θύραζε

θύραζε κῆρες, οὐκ ἔτι Ἀνθεστήρια.
ὡς κατὰ τὴν πόλιν τοῖς Ἀνθεστηρίοις τῶν ψυχῶν περιερχομένων.

'souls'; 'ghosts' is perhaps as close a translation as we can get, for the word carries with it a sense of dread. The word *Keres* is obscure in origin and its career is a downward one, tending always towards evil, disease and death[1]. Among the Greeks, as, it would seem, among many primitive peoples, the fear of the dead seems to precede their worship[2]. The 'feare of things invisible' is, as we have already seen[3], in part 'the naturall seed of Religion.'

This fear of ghosts is natural enough and needs no emphasis. It is not indeed at first a disembodied soul that is dreaded, but rather the whole condition of death, which involves the immediate family and often the whole tribe in a state of contagious infection. But, to totemistic thinkers, the fear is always mixed with a sure and certain hope, the hope of reincarnation. Once the body fairly decayed and the death ceremonies complete, the dead man is free to go back to his totem ancestors and begin again the cycle of life as a new tribesman or a totem animal. This is often clearly indicated by funeral rites[4]. Thus among the Bororo, the dead man is trimmed up with feathers of the parroquet, in order that he may take the form of the parroquet totem. Till the second funeral is over, the dead man among the Hindoos is a *preta*, that is a fearful *revenant*: after that he can enter the world of *Pitaras* or fathers, the equivalents of the Alcheringa totem-ancestors. For this entry, rites of initiation, *rites de passage*, are necessary.

This double nature of the Greek attitude towards the dead is very simply and clearly expressed in the vase-painting in Fig. 77. The design comes from an archaic vase[5] of the 'prothesis' type, a vase used in funeral ceremonies and decorated with funeral subjects. Two mourners stand in attitudes of grief on either side of a

---

[1] I have discussed the development and degradation of the idea of the Keres fully in *Prolegomena*, chapter v.

[2] This was very fully exemplified by Dr Frazer in a series of lectures delivered at Trinity College during the Lent and May terms of 1911 on the 'Fear and Worship of the Dead.'

[3] *Supra*, p. 64.

[4] The social attitude of savages towards death as expressed in funeral rites has been very ably and fully analysed by R. Hertz, *Représentation collective de la Mort*, in Année Sociologique, x. 1905–6, p. 48.

[5] In the Museum at Athens, see *J. H. S.* xix. 1899, p. 219, fig. 4. In discussing this vase before (*Prolegomena*, p. 235) I made the mistake of saying 'Snake and *eidolon* are but two ways of saying the same thing.' I now realize that the two forms express ideas of widely different, almost contradictory import. The ghosts of dead men constantly pass over into the good *daimon*, the collective ancestor, but the ideas are disparate.

grave-mound, itself surmounted by a tall vase. Within the grave-
mound the vase-painter has drawn
what he believes to be there, two
things—in the upper part of the
mound a crowd of little fluttering
Keres, and below the single figure
of a snake.   The Keres are figured
as what the Greeks called εἴδωλα,
little images, shrunken men, only
winged. They represent the shadow
soul, strengthless and vain ; but the
θυμός of the man, his strength, his
life, his μένος, his *mana*, has passed
into the *daimon* of life and reincarnation, the snake.   An εἴδωλον,
an image, informed by θυμός makes
up something approximately not

Fig. 77.

unlike that complex, psychological conception, our modern 'immortal soul.

The central ceremony of the Chytroi, the ceremony that gave
its name to the day, still remains, and it will bring indefeasible
evidence to show that the focus of attention at the Anthesteria
was not on death, not on the εἴδωλον, but on the θυμός, not on
the 'strengthless heads of the dead' but on life through death,
on reincarnation, on the life-*daimon*.   This central ceremony was
the boiling but—significantly—*not the eating* of a pot (χύτρος or
χύτρα) of all kinds of seeds, a *panspermia*.   The scholiast on the
Frogs[1] in commenting on the words 'with the holy Pots says
expressly, quoting Theopompos,

> And of the pot which all the citizens cook, no priest tastes.

And again the scholiast on the *Acharnians*[2], also quoting Theopompos, says

they cooked pots of *panspermia* whence the feast got its name, but of the
pot no one tasted.

[1] Ad Ar. *Ran.* 218 καὶ τῆς χύτρας ἣν ἕψουσι πάντες οἱ κατὰ τὴν πόλιν οὐδεὶς γεύεται
τῶν ἱερέων.   The reading ἱερέων is uncertain.
[2] Ad Ar. *Ach.* 1076 Χύτρους· Θεόπομπος τοὺς διασωθέντας ἐκ τοῦ κατακλυσμοῦ
ἐψῆσαί φησι χύτρας πανσπερμίας ὅθεν οὕτω κληθῆναι τὴν ἑορτήν...τῆς δὲ χύτρας οὐδένα
γεύσασθαι.

The *panspermia* has not, I think, been rightly understood.   In commenting on it before[1], misled by the gift-theory of sacrifice, I took it to be merely a 'supper for the souls.'   No doubt as such it was in later days regarded, when primitive magical rites had to be explained on Olympian principles.   But it was, to begin with, much more.   The ghosts had other work to do than to eat their supper and go.   They took that 'supper,' that *panspermia*, with them down to the world below and brought it back in the autumn a *pankarpia*.   The dead are *Chthonioi*, 'earth-people,' *Demetreioi*, 'Demeter's people[2],' and they do Demeter's work, her work and that of Kore the Maiden, with her Kathodos and Anodos[3]. An Athenian at the Anthesteria would never have needed S. Paul's[4] angry objurgation:

> Thou fool, that which thou sowest is not quickened, except it die : and that which thou sowest, thou sowest not that body that shall be, but bare grain, it may chance of wheat, or of some other grain.

It is sown a *panspermia*, it is reaped a *pankarpia*.

The lexica regularly define *panspermia* and *pankarpia* by each other, and they are right, for fruit *is* seed, but a distinction must be observed.   The living and the dead seem to have as it were a sort of counter-claim on the fruits of the earth.   The live man wants the fruits of the earth that he may eat them and so live ; the dead man wants them as seed that he may take it with him down below and tend it and give it a 'body' and send it back, bring it back as fruit   The autumn is the living man's great time.   Then he takes most of the fruit and grain, eats it and stores it for himself, but even then he saves a little for the dead, offering them ἀπαρχαί, because only so can his seed grow and prosper.   The spring, the Anthesteria, is the dead man's time, for the seeds belong mainly to him.   It is this cycle that haunted the mind of Aeschylus[5], only he abstracts it somewhat,

---

[1] *Prolegomena*, p. 37.   If my present theory, suggested to me in part by Mr Cornford, be right, the cooking of the *panspermia* must be a late invention added when it came to be regarded as a food.

[2] Plut. *de facie in orb. lunae* 28 καὶ τοὺς νεκροὺς Ἀθηναῖοι Δημητρείους ὠνόμαζον τὸ παλαιόν.

[3] For the δρώμενα of the Kathodos and Anodos see *Prolegomena*, p. 123, and for the Anodos of the Maiden, p. 276.   See also *infra*, chapter IX.

[4] 1 Cor. xv. 20 ff.

[5] *Choeph.* 127

κ αὶ γαῖαν αὐτήν, ἣ τὰ πάντα τίκτεται
θρέψασά τ' αὖθις τῶνδε κῦμα λαμβάνει

and Dr Verrall *ad loc.*   For the whole symbolism and for the Roman custom of

making it of Earth the Mother rather than of dead men and
seeds :

> Yea summon Earth, who brings all things to life
> And rears and takes again into her womb.

It is this cycle of reincarnation that makes of the *panspermia*
a thing more solemn and significant than any 'supper of the
souls,' kindly and venerable though that notion be.

The *panspermia* and *pankarpia* appear in many forms and
under other names, as *Kernophoria*, as *Liknophoria*, as *Thargelia*.
The Thargelia are of the first harvest in June. Hesychius[1] defines
thargelos as a 'pot full of seeds.' A *Liknophoria*, the carrying of a
winnowing-basket full of fruits, to which often on monuments a
phallos is added, might take place at any rite when fertility was
desired. It was part of the Eleusinian and other mysteries, it was
practised at marriage ceremonies[2]. Of the *Kernophoria* we have
unusually full particulars. It is specially interesting as showing
the care taken that in a *panspermia* each and every form of seed
should be represented. Athenaeus says of the *Kernos*:

> A vessel made of earthenware, with many little cups fastened on to it in
> which are white poppies, barley, pulse, ochroi, lentils, and he who carries
> it after the fashion of the carrier of the liknon tastes of these things, as
> Ammonius relates in his third book 'On Altars and Sacrifices.'

The Kernophoria was in the autumn, living man's time ; he
tastes of the fruits to get their *mana*.

In previously discussing the *pankarpia* and kindred matters
I was led astray by Porphyry's charming vegetarianism. He
quotes again and again such offerings as these as examples of the
simple life dear to the gods, in the golden days before man tasted
flesh food. Thus Sophocles[3] in the lost *Polyidos*, which must
have dealt with the primitive rites of Crete, says:

planting corn on graves, manifestly to secure the magic of the dead, see *Prolegomena*,
p. 267.

[1] s.v. θάργηλος· χύτρα ἐστὶν ἀνάπλεως σπερμάτων.

[2] Both the *Kernophoria* and the *Liknophoria* are fully discussed and illustrated
in my *Prolegomena*, pp. 160 and 599 and 518—535, 549, and a *Kernos* of which
many specimens have come to light is there reproduced in Fig. 16 : the scene of the
Kernophoria appears on the 'Ninnion' pinax in Fig. 160.

[3] Porphyr. *de Abst.* II. 19 καὶ Σοφοκλῆς διαγράφων τὴν θεοφιλῆ θυσίαν φησὶν ἐν τῷ
Πολυίδῳ

> ἦν μὲν γὰρ οἰὸς μαλλός, ἦν δὲ κἀμπέλου
> σπονδή τε καὶ ῥὰξ εὖ τεθησαυρισμένη·
> ἐνῆν δὲ παγκάρπεια συμμιγὴς ὀλαῖς
> λίπος τ' ἐλαίας καὶ τὸ ποικιλώτατον
> ξουθῆς μελίσσης κηρόπλαστον ὄργανον.

> Wool of the sheep was there, fruit of the vine,
> Libations and the treasured store of grapes
> And manifold fruits were there, mingled with grain
> And oil of olive and fair, curious combs
> Of wax, compacted by the murmuring bee.

Following Porphyry, I explained the *pankarpia* and the *panspermia*, as simple fare for simple-hearted gods. But its gist is really magical, and the rite long preceded any god however primitive and gentle, it preceded even the Agathos Daimon.

The *Anthesteria* was then a feast of the revocation of souls and the blossoming of plants, a feast of the great reincarnation cycle of man and nature. One final point of cardinal importance remains to be noted—the god in whose honour the *panspermia* was offered.

Hermes Chthonios as Agathos Daimon.

The scholiast on the *Frogs*[1], already quoted, makes, in commenting on the *Chytroi*, a second statement of scarcely less interest than the first. Not only does 'no one taste of the Pot' but

> They have the custom of sacrificing at this feast, *not to any of the Olympian gods at all, but to Hermes Chthonios.*

We are thankful to find the Olympians refraining for once; as a rule they are only too ready to lay greedy hands on a magical rite, pervert its meaning and turn it into a 'gift-sacrifice' for themselves. Had Hermes Chthonios been an Olympian we must have postponed the consideration of him to the next chapter, but Hermes Chthonios, it is expressly said, is no Olympian, he is—it is perhaps by now scarcely necessary to state it—our ancient friend, the Agathos Daimon.

Photius[2] tells us in so many words: '*Hermes* a kind of drink—*as of the good Daimon* and Zeus Soter'; but evidence abounds more deep-seated than this hitherto enigmatic yet curiously explicit gloss.

It was the Agathos Daimon who presided over the Pithoigia of the wine-casks; it is Hermes who with magic rhabdos and

---

[1] Ad Ar. *Ran.* 218...θύειν αὐτοῖς ἔθος ἔχουσι τῶν μὲν θεῶν οὐδενὶ τὸ παράπαν, Ἑρμῇ δὲ χθονίῳ.

[2] s.v. Ἑρμῆς πόσεως εἶδος· ὡς ἀγαθοῦ δαίμονος καὶ Διὸς σωτῆρος. I owe this evidence to Professor Murray.

with kerykeion summons the souls from the great grave-pithos on the Jena lekythos[1] in Fig. 78. It is Hermes always who attends Pandora-Anesidora, she of the pithos, when she rises from the earth. Always he carries his kerykeion with the twin twisted snakes, that kerykeion which we saw gathered in the coils of the Agathodaimon on the coins of Alexandria[2], a conjunction now easily understood. We understand now why Hermes, as phallic herm, is god of fertility of flocks and herds, but also, as Psychopompos, god of ghosts and the underworld. He, a snake to begin with and carrying always the snake-staff, is the very *daimon* of reincarnation. Homer, who contrives to forget nearly everything of any religious interest, cannot quite forget *that*; only, for death and life, he, in his beautiful way, puts sleep and waking. When Hermes led the ghosts of the slain suitors to Hades, he held in his hand[3]

FIG. 78.

> His rhabdos fair and golden wherewith he lulls to rest
> The eyes of men whoso he will, and others by his hest
> He wakens.

Under the influence of the epic Hermes is eclipsed; he was never allowed into Olympos save as a half outsider, a messenger; probably, but for the Athenian cult of the Hermae, he could never have forced an entrance at all and his functions would have gone on being filled by the more pliable, upper-air Iris. Even though 'expurgated' by Homer, it is curious to note how as 'messenger' he is almost omnipresent in popular art and literature in many a

---

[1] P. Schadow, *Eine attische Grablekythos* 1897.   See also *Prolegomena*, p. 43.
[2] *Supra*, p. 278, Fig. 67.
[3] *Od.* XXIV. 1—4

...τῇ τ' ἀνδρῶν ὄμματα θέλγει
ὧν ἐθέλει, τοὺς δ' αὖτε καὶ ὑπνώοντας ἐγείρει.

situation, as e.g. the Judgment of Paris, where no 'messenger' is really wanted. He was really there from the beginning as *daimon* or 'luck' of the place or the situation, there long before the gods who made him their 'messenger[1].' If he was only a 'messenger, why did men cry κοινὸς ἑρμῆς 'shares in the Luck,' why does he always 'lead' the Charites, even when they are going no-whither? In later literature which bears his name, in the Hermetic writings and in the magic papyri, he comes to his own again.

In the magic papyri[2] Hermes and the Agathos Daimon are sometimes closely associated, sometimes placed in the relation of father and son, or teacher and disciple, sometimes actually identified. Thus, in one prayer, the Lord Hermes is addressed as 'he who brings together food for gods and men,' and he is employed to

bring about all things for me and guide them by Agathe Tyche and Agathos Daimon[3].

One of the titles of Hermes is *Agathopoios*, and it is said of him as Agathos Daimon that

when he shines forth the earth blossoms, and when he laughs the plants bear fruit, and at his bidding the herds bring forth young[4].

Another prayer runs as follows:

Give me every grace, all accomplishment, for with thee is the bringer of good, the angel standing by the side for Tyche. Therefore give thou means and accomplishment to this house, thou who rulest over hope, wealth-giving Aion, O holy good Daimon. Bring to accomplishment and incline to me all the graces and divine utterances[5].

It is a grave mistake to think that all this is mere late demonology. The magic papyri contain, it is now acknowledged

[1] It is, I think, possible that the 'messenger' may really be a survival of the 'representative' or προστάτης, that is the winner in an *agon*, the πρῶτος Κοῦρος—the individual who stood for the group. When his function was forgotten he might easily lapse into the deputy messenger. Mr Cornford draws my attention in this connection to the fact noted above (p. 276) that the month Anthesterion was in Boeotia called Προστατήριος, possibly it got its name from a festival of Προστατήρια.

[2] Wessely, *Griech. Zauberpapyrus von London und Paris* and *Neue griech. Zauberpapyri* in Denkschr. d. k. Akad., phil.-hist. XXXVI. Wien, 1888 and XLII. 1893.

[3] Πρᾶξόν μοι πάντα καὶ συνρέποις σὺν Ἀγαθῇ Τύχῃ καὶ Ἀγαθῷ Δαίμονι. Reitzenstein, *Poimandres*, p. 21.

[4] ἀνέθαλεν ἡ γῆ σοῦ ἐπιλάμψαντος καὶ ἐκαρποφόρησεν τὰ φυτὰ σοῦ γελάσαντος, ἐξωογόνησε τὰ ζῷα σοῦ ἐπιτρέψαντος—Reitzenstein, *op. cit.* p. 29.

[5] δός μοι πᾶσαν χάριν, πᾶσαν πρᾶξιν, μετὰ σοῦ γάρ ἐστιν ὁ ἀγαθοφόρος ἄγγελος παρεστὼς Τύχῃ. διὸ δὸς πόρον καὶ πρᾶξιν τούτῳ τῷ οἴκῳ κυριεύων ἐλπίδος πλουτοδότα αἰών, ἱερὲ Ἀγαθὲ δαῖμον· τέλει πάσας χάριτας καὶ τὰς εὐθείας φήμας. *op. cit.* p. 29. For φόρος and πρᾶξις in connection with Hermes cf. Aesch. *Choeph.* 808
παῖς ὁ Μαίας ἐπεὶ φορώτατος
πρᾶξιν οὐρίαν θέλων.

on all hands, very primitive stuff[1]. It is noticeable that when Agathe Tyche and Agathos Daimon come together the woman figure in matriarchal fashion precedes the male *daimon*. Indeed in the prayer just quoted the good Daimon is conceived of as an angel or messenger standing as attendant by the side of Tyche. This possibly helps to explain the subordinate function of Hermes as *propolos* or attendant on the greater gods—it is anyhow a mark of early thinking.

Hermes, as Agathos Daimon, was once merely a *phallos*; that he was also once merely a snake, is, I think, a safe conjecture. But it is merely a conjecture: I can point to no actual monument where Hermes is figured as a snake. It is otherwise with another and a greater than Hermes, in whose form the Agathos Daimon chose to masquerade—Zeus.

FIG. 79.

ZEUS KTESIOS AS AGATHOS DAIMON.

Of singular interest is the relief in Fig. 79 found at Thespiae in Boeotia and now in the local museum at Thebes[2]. It dates about the 3rd century B.C. and is clearly inscribed Διὸς Κτησίου, 'Zeus'—we might perhaps translate it—'of household property,' Zeus, not so much of fertility as

[1] Reitzenstein, *op. cit.* p. 28, 129, and R. Foerster, *Hermes in einer Doppelherme aus Cypern.* Jahrbuch d. Inst. 1904, p. 140. 'In diesen Gebeten und Anrufungen dürfen wir nicht so wohl Ergebnisse philosophischer Spekulation als Äusserungen wirklichen Volksglaubens erwarten.'

[2] Inv. No. 330. I owe to the kindness of Dr M. P. Nilsson a photograph of this interesting monument which he has published and fully discussed in the Ath. Mittheilungen, XXXIII. 1908, p. 279, *Schlangenstele des Zeus Ktesios.*

of its stored produce.   Ktesios, Epikarpios and Charitodotes are
titles applied to Zeus in his capacity as the giver of increase[1].
To these might be added Ploutos, Olbios, Meilichios, Philios,
Teleios.   All these are daimons of fertility[2] and like the Agathos
Daimon might naturally be thought of in snake shape.   It was
long ago conjectured by Gerhard[3] that Zeus Ktesios was a snake;
the Thespiae relief brings to his view welcome confirmation.
Snake though he was, to him as to Zeus Olbios (p. 148) a bull was
sacrificed[4].

Zeus Ktesios is not only a snake; to our great delight we
find him also well furnished with Pots.   He was essentially
domestic.   Harpocration[5], quoting Hyperides, says

> They used to set up Zeus Ktesios in storerooms.

In the temple of Zeus at Panamara a votive inscription[6] was
found

> To the household gods, Zeus Ktesios and Tyche and Asklepios.

It is to such primitive *daimones* of the *penetralia* that the Chorus
in the *Choephoroi* of Aeschylus[7] appeal.   It is at the altar of
Ktesios that Cassandra as chattel of the house is bidden to take
her place[8].   Homer[9] must in his queer subconscious way be
thinking of Zeus Ktesios, with perhaps some associations of
Pandora, when he says[9],

> Jars twain upon Zeus' threshold ever stood,
> One holds his gifts of evil, one of good.

---

[1] Plut. *Stoic. Repug.* 30 ὁ Ζεὺς γελοῖος εἰ Κτήσιος χαίρει καὶ Ἐπικάρπιος καὶ
Χαριτοδότης προσαγορευόμενος....

[2] *Prolegomena*, p. 356.

[3] In his brilliant but too little read monograph on Agathos Daimon and Bona
Dea, *Akad. Abhandl.* 1847, II. 45, Anm. 28.

[4] See the decree in Dem. 21. 53 Διὶ κτησίῳ βοῦν λευκόν.

[5] s.v. Κτησίου Διός.   Ὑπερίδης ἐν τῷ πρὸς Ἀπελλαῖον· Κτήσιον Δία ἐν τοῖς ταμιείοις
ἱδρύοντο.

[6] *Bull. de Corr. Hell.* XII. 1888, p. 269, No. 54 καὶ τοῖς ἐνοικιδίοις θεοῖς Διὶ Κτησίῳ
καὶ Τύχῃ καὶ Ἀσκληπίῳ.

[7] v. 786
> οἵ τ' ἔσωθε δωμάτων
> πλουτογαθῆ μυχὸν νομίζετε,
> κλύετε, σύμφρονες θεοί.

[8] Aesch. *Ag.* 1020
> ἐπεί σ' ἔθηκε Ζεὺς ἀμηνίτως δόμοις
> κοινωνὸν εἶναι χερνίβων, πολλῶν μετὰ
> δούλων σταθεῖσαν κτησίου βωμοῦ πέλας.

[9] *Il.* XXIV. 527
> δοιοὶ γάρ τε πίθοι κατακείαται ἐν Διὸς οὐδῷ
> δώρων οἷα δίδωσι κακῶν ἕτερος δὲ ἑάων.

It was indeed side by side with Demeter Anesidora at ancient Phlya[1] that Zeus was worshipped, a fitting conjunction. At Phlya were worshipped also Dionysos Anthios and the Semnae, and at Phlya were mysteries of Eros. In the list of divinities Demeter Anesidora comes first, as was fitting; the Earth sends up her gifts and then man harvests and stores them for his use. It is interesting to find that the actual cult of Zeus Ktesios as well as his name lands us in the storeroom—though to speak of his 'cult' is really a misnomer, as we shall immediately see.

Athenaeus[2], quoting Philemon, makes the following statement:

The *Kadiskos* is the vessel in which they set up Ktesian Zeuses.

He goes on to quote from the *Exegetikon* of Antikleides, a post-Alexandrian writer, some ritual prescriptions for the carrying out of the 'cult' or rather installation.

Put the lid on a new two-eared Kadiskos, crown the ears with white wool and let down the ends of...the thread from the right shoulder and the forehead and place in it whatever you can find and pour into it ambrosia. Now ambrosia is pure water and olive oil and *pankarpia*. Pour in these.

The text is corrupt and therefore it is not quite clear how the wool or thread was arranged on the vase. The vase with its 'ears,' 'right shoulder' and 'forehead' reminds us of the anthropoid vases of the Troad.

But it is the ambrosia that delights and amazes us. Why in the world should *ambrosia* be defined as pure water, olive oil, and *pankarpia*? Why, but because in the *pankarpia* and the oil and the pure living water are the seeds for immortality, for next year's reincarnation? The Olympians took *ambrosia* for their food, but its ancient immortality was of earth's recurrent cycle of growth, not of heaven's[3] brazen and sterile immutability.

Athenaeus[4] has yet another small and pleasant surprise in

---

[1] For the mysteries at Phlya see *Prolegomena*, p. 642, and for Eros as Herm and his close analogies with Hermes see p. 631.

[2] xi. 46. 473 Καδίσκος. Φιλήμων ἐν τῷ προειρημένῳ συγγράμματι ποτηρίου εἶδος. Ἀγγεῖον δ' ἐστὶν ἐν ᾧ τοὺς κτησίους Δίας ἐγκαθιδρύουσιν, ὡς Ἀντικλείδης φησὶν ἐν τῷ Ἐξηγητικῷ, γράφων οὕτως· Διὸς κτησίου σημεῖα ἱδρύεσθαι χρὴ ὧδε. Καδίσκον καινὸν δίωτον ἐπιθηματοῦντα, στέψαντα τὰ ὦτα ἐρίῳ λευκῷ καὶ ἐκ τοῦ ὤμου τοῦ δεξιοῦ καὶ ἐκ τοῦ μετώπου τοῦ κροκίου, καὶ ἐσθεῖναι ὅ τι ἂν εὕρῃς καὶ ἐσχέαι ἀμβροσίαν. Ἡ δ' ἀμβροσία ὕδωρ ἀκραιφνές, ἔλαιον, παγκαρπία. Ἅπερ ἔμβαλε. Kaibel, *supplendum fere* ⟨καθέσθαι τὰ ἄκρα⟩ τοῦ κροκίου.

[3] For the Olympian notion of immortality which is the very contradiction of the old reincarnation, see *infra*, chapter x.

[4] *loc. cit.* Ἑρμῆς, ὃν ἕλκουσ' οἱ μὲν ἐκ προχοιδίου, οἱ δ' ἐκ καδίσκου σ' ἴσον ἴσῳ κεκραμένον.

store for us. 'The comic poet Strattis,' he says, in his *Lemnomeda*
makes mention of the Kadiskos, thus:

Hermes, whom some draw from a prochoidion,
Others, mixed half and half from a Kadiskos.

By the help of the Agathos Daimon we understand the comic
poet Strattis. Hermes is the daimon of *ambrosia* and of *immortality.*

Zeus Ktesios then like Hermes is simply a *daimon* of fertility,
taking snake form—he was not yet a *theos.* His aspect as Ktesios
embarrassed the orthodox theologian and delighted the mystic and
the monotheist. It is pleasant to find[1] that even when translated
to the uttermost heavens he did not disdain the primitive service
of the *pankarpia.*

Ruler of all, to thee I bring libation
And honey-cake, by whatso appellation
Thou wouldst be called, or Zeus, or Hades thou
A fireless offering I bear thee now
Of all earth's fruit, take Thou its plenitude.
For thou amongst the Heavenly Ones art god,
Dost share Zeus' sceptre, and art ruling found
With Hades in the kingdoms underground.

Zeus Ktesios was to the Greeks a house-snake, with a service
of storehouse jars for his chief sanctity. That acute observer
of analogies between Greek and Roman religion, Denys of
Halicarnassos[2], confirms our view and illuminates it further by
Latin custom. Speaking of the Penates brought by Aeneas from
the Troad, he says:

Now these gods are called by the Romans *Penates.* But those who
translate the word into Greek render it, some as 'Patröoi,' some as
'Genethlioi,' some again as 'Ktesioi,' others as 'Mychioi,' others as
'Herkeioi.' Each and all of these translators seem to adopt a word
according to what has occurred to themselves, and they all mean pretty

---

[1] Eur. Nauck frg. (incert.), 912 :

σοὶ τῷ πάντων μεδέοντι χοὴν
πέλανόν τε φέρω, Ζεὺς εἴτ' Ἀίδης
ὀνομαζόμενος στέργεις· σὺ δέ μοι
θυσίαν ἄπυρον παγκαρπείας
δέξαι πλήρη προχυθεῖσαν.

[2] *Ant. Rom.* I. lxvii. 3 τοὺς δὲ θεοὺς τούτους Ῥωμαῖοι μὲν Πενάτας καλοῦσιν· οἱ δ'
ἐξερμηνεύοντες εἰς τὴν Ἑλλάδα γλῶσσαν τοὔνομα οἱ μὲν Πατρῴους ἀποφαίνουσιν, οἱ δὲ
Γενεθλίους, εἰσὶ δ' οἳ Κτησίους, ἄλλοι δὲ Μυχίους, οἱ δὲ Ἑρκείους. ἔοικε δὲ τούτων
ἕκαστος κατά τινος τῶν συμβεβηκότων αὐτοῖς ποιεῖσθαι τὴν ἐπίκλησιν, κινδυνεύουσί τε
πάντες ἀμωσγέπως τὸ αὐτὸ λέγειν. σχήματος δὲ καὶ μορφῆς αὐτῶν πέρι Τίμαιος μὲν ὁ
συγγραφεὺς ὧδε ἀποφαίνεται· κηρύκια σιδηρᾶ καὶ χαλκᾶ καὶ κέραμον Τρωικὸν εἶναι τὰ ἐν
τοῖς ἀδύτοις τοῖς ἐν Λαουινίῳ ἱερά, πυθέσθαι δὲ αὐτὸς ταῦτα παρὰ τῶν ἐπιχωρίων.

much the same. Timaios the historian expresses himself thus as to their form and appearance. The sacred things deposited in the *adyta* at Lavinium are *Kerykeia* of iron and bronze and Trojan pottery, and he said that he learnt this from the natives of the place.

The house-snake of the Romans as guardian of the *penus* is far more familiar to us than the Agathos Daimon or Zeus Ktesios of the Greek storeroom. He appears on countless Graeco-Roman wall-paintings. A good instance is given in Fig. 80[1]. We have

Fig. 80.

the façade of a house in temple-form—the pediment decorated with sacrificial gear, a boucranium, a patera, a sacrificial knife. Within, supposed no doubt to be within the *penetralia*, are the

[1] From the photograph of a Pompeian wall-painting.

family sanctities.   The great fertility-snake in front, all surrounded by herbage and ap-
proaching a small altar, is the
genius of the house in animal
form[1].   Above is the head of the
house himself, the human genius,
to either side of him a dancing
Lar   holding   a   cornucopia.
Similar in feeling is the design
in Fig. 81, from a relief in the
Villa Medici[2].   The snake genius
this time is twined actually
round the household altar and
the head of the house himself
holds the cornucopia.   The snake

Fig. 81.

is omnipresent.   It is not till Rome falls under Greek influence
that we get the family *daimon* abstracted from the hearth and
fully anthropomorphic.   The *Bonus Eventus* of the blue glass
cameo plaque[3] in Fig. 82 is a Greek for all his name[4], a goodly
human youth with no hint of divinity but his patera and corn
ears, a μέγιστος Κοῦρος.

It is of the first importance to note that in Denys's account of
the Greek equivalents of the Penates the renderings are all in the
plural.   The Greek mind, intensely personal, individual, clear cut
as it was, tended to the singular, to Zeus Ktesios, who is a
personality, rather than to Ktesioi, who are vague *daimones*.
It is indeed through the Latin *genii* that we best understand
the Greek *daimones*.   They are at once more impersonal and,
which is almost the same thing, more collective, more generalized,
or rather less specialized.   The genius is essentially as its name
shows the spirit of life, birth, generation[5]; to live a full life is

---

[1] Cf. Servius ad Verg. *Georg.* III. 417 (serpens) gaudet tectis ut sunt ἀγαθοὶ
δαίμονες quos Latini genios vocant.

[2] *Annali dell' Inst.* 1862, Taf. R. 4.

[3] In the British Museum, reproduced from Mr Cyril Davenport's *Cameos*, 1900,
pl. 3, by kind permission of Messrs Seeley.

[4] The cameo seems to reflect the art type adopted by Euphranor; see Pliny *N.H.*
34. 77 Euphranoris simulacrum Boni Eventus dextrâ pateram, sinistrâ spicam ac
papaverem tenens.

[5] Cf. the *lectus genialis.*   Paul the Deacon says (p. 94), Lectus genialis qui
nuptiis sternitur in honorem genii, unde et appellatus, a statement which,
reversed, just hits the mark.

indulgere genio, to live ascetically **is** *defraudare genium*. But though each man had his individual genius, his life-spirit, the genius is essentially of the group; it is as it were incarnate in the

Fig. 82.

father of the family[1] or in the emperor as head of the state. Every department of social life, every *curia*, every *vicus*, every *pagus* had its genius, its utterance of a common life; not only the city of Rome had its *Genius Urbis Romae* but the whole Roman people had its *Genius Publicus Populi Romani*[2].

---

[1] For the family as representing an economic unit and as contrasted with the *gens* which is a kinship unit, see Mr Warde Fowler's most interesting account in his *Religious Experience of the Roman People*, 1911, p. 70.

[2] This point is well brought out in the article s.v. *Genius* in Daremberg and Saglio's *Dictionnaire des Antiquités*, 'il (le génius) était une divinité toute trouvée pour les collectivités de tout ordre.'

THE DIOSCURI AS AGATHOI DAIMONES.

We have not yet done with the singular account by Denys. The mention of *Kerukeia* recalls to us Hermes as Agathos Daimon and the fertility-*kerukeia* of the Alexandrian coins[1]. The Trojan 'pottery' takes us back to the Kadiskoi[2]. Snakes and jars seem indeed to be the natural and characteristic *sacra* of these household *numina* whether Greek or Latin. I have long suspected that the so-called funeral snakes and funeral jars that appear on sepulchral and other monuments have more to do with fertility-daimons than with the dead. On coins of Laconia, Fig. 83,

one frequent symbol of the Dioscuri is a snake-twined amphora. Twins all over the world, as Dr Rendel Harris[3] has abundantly shown, are apt, not unnaturally, to play the part of fertility-*daimones*: they are not only, as the coin shows them, *lucida sidera* but they are gods of all manner of increase; they can make rain, they cause the dew to fall.

FIG. 83.

In connection with the Penates, the Ktesioi and the Kadiskoi, the well-known votive-relief[4] of Argenidas in Fig. 84 is of singular interest. Argenidas has returned from a voyage; his ship is figured in a kind of rocky bay to the right. Argenidas the dedicator stands safe and sound on a plinth in front of his ship. The inscription reads:

Argenidas son of Aristogenidas to the Dioscuri, a vow.

To the left are the twins in human form. In the right hand corner are their earliest ἀφιδρύματα or images, the δόκανα, beams with crossbeams, railings, which to Plutarch's[5] kindly mind represented their brotherly love. Beneath them is written '(Ana)keion.'

---

[1] *Supra*, p. 299.

[2] It is, I think, very probable that the 'Duenos vase,' as suggested by Miss Bennett in an article as yet unpublished, was made like the Kernos to contain in its several compartments different seeds, etc. See also Daremberg and Saglio, s.v. *Kernos*.

[3] *The Cult of the Heavenly Twins*, 1906, p. 26.

[4] Verona Museo Lapidario 555, from a photograph kindly lent me by Dr Rendel Harris.

[5] *De Fratern. amor.* init. τὰ παλαιὰ τῶν Διοσκούρων ἀφιδρύματα οἱ Σπαρτιᾶται δόκανα καλοῦσι. ἔστι δὲ δύο ξύλα παράλληλα δυσὶ πλαγίοις ἐπεζευγμένα καὶ δοκεῖ τῷ φιλαδέλφῳ τῶν θεῶν οἰκεῖον εἶναι τοῦ ἀναθήματος τὸ κοινὸν καὶ ἀδιαίρετον—the word ἀφίδρυμα is untranslatable, it seems to mean anything set up apart, a dedication.

They form as it were a double sanctuary of the 'Lords,' the *Anakes*, a title they share with Cecrops and many another hero.   Between

FIG. 84.

Argenidas and the Dioscuri is a table, on it two tall amphorae. Are they funeral urns containing the ashes of the Dioscuri?   I think not.   They perform, I believe, the function of the Kadiskoi of Zeus Ktesios, and I suspect they contain *ambrosia*, a *pankarpia* or a *panspermia*, for to the right of them is coiled in the air a *daimon*, a snake.   On another relief, in Fig. 85[1], the *dokana* have snakes.   This shows, I think, not that the Dioscuri are dead men, but that they are daimonic; they are, in the strict sense of the word, 'heroes.'

FIG. 85.

The Dioscuri are heroes or *daimones* full of instruction, as another monument[2] in Fig. 86 will show.   The design is from a votive-relief found in Thessaly, of late date and somewhat rough though vigorous workmanship.   It represents the scene familiar

[1] Sparta Cat. 588, from a photograph kindly sent me by Mr Wace.
[2] In the Louvre Museum.   W. Fröhner, *Deux Peintures de Vases Grecs*, 1871, Pl. II., and see my *Mythology and Monuments*, 1890, p. 159, for the simple meal provided in the Prytaneion at Athens for the Dioscuri.

to us as the *Theoxenia*, 'Banquet of the gods.' A couch is set with cushions and coverlet, a table spread with fruit and cakes; below it an altar on which the male worshipper is placing some object. The guests are arriving. The woman lifts her hand to welcome the great Epiphany. The guests are the 'Great Gods,' magnificently galloping down from high heaven on their prancing horses, preceded by Nike with a garland. Above them in the pediment Helios is rising. The inscription reads Θεοῖς

Fig. 86.

μεγάλοις Δανάα ᾿Ατθονειτει[α] 'To the Great Gods Danaa daughter of...'; the reading of the second name is uncertain.

What is the meaning of this absurd, incompatible representation? Simply this. In the *Theoxenia* we have the old magical service of the *panspermia* and the *pankarpia* Olympianized. In the old order the pot of seeds or the liknon full of fruits were in themselves sanctities; they were themselves carried and consecrated as ἀπαρχαί or first-fruits; they were tabooed from man's use that they might be the seed and source of fertility for the coming year. There are as yet no human gods, there is no gift-sacrifice. There are only vague shapes of *daimones* that crystallize gradually into the shape of the Good and Wealthy Daimon who year by year renews himself and refills his cornucopia with earth's produce. But, when the *daimones* take shape as *theoi*, the old service must fit itself to the new conceptions. The ἀπαρχαί and the communal vegetarian *dais* that followed on the release from taboo became feasts held in honour of these *theoi*. These non-existent Olympian magnificences have couches and tables, and oddly combined with the table for the old offering of the *pankarpia* is an altar for burnt sacrifice. To crown the absurdity, the Anakes, 'Lords' of man's life on earth, they who were snake-*daimones* of fertility, are changed into human horsemen who gallop proudly down from the sky to honour a mortal banquet. Mytho-logy makes of them the personal 'sons of Zeus,' but to ritual they are still functionaries, Anakes.

We have purposely brought together the two representations of the Dioscuri (*a*) *the snake-twined amphorae*, (*b*) *the Horsemen descending to the Theoxenia*, because they bring into sharp contrast the two poles as it were of religious thinking. On the one hand we have *daimones*, collective representations of purely functional import, with their ritual of magic; on the other full-blown anthro-poid *theoi*, descending from heaven to their service of *do ut des*. But the Theoxenia[1] is by anticipation; the Olympians, their nature and their ritual, are reserved for the next chapter; we have now to establish finally, not the relation of god to *daimon* but of *daimon* to dead man. This relation, and with it the true nature of a 'hero,' comes out with almost startling clearness in a class of monuments which have puzzled generations of archaeologists, and which I venture to think can only be understood in the light of the Agathos Daimon—I mean the monuments variously and in-structively known as 'Sepulchral Tablets,' 'Funeral Banquets,' and 'Hero Feasts.'

THE 'HERO FEASTS.'

Over three hundred of these 'Hero Feasts' are preserved, so we may be sure they represent a deep-seated and widespread

---

[1] Analogous to the *Theoxenia* of the Dioscuri are the stories of Tantalos (see *supra*, p. 244) and Lycaon who 'entertain the gods.' Behind such myths lies always the old magical δαίς.

popular tradition.   A good typical instance[1] is given in
Fig. 87.

A man reclines at a banquet; his wife, according to Athenian
custom, is seated by his side.   In front is a table loaded with cake
and fruits.   So far we might well suppose that we had, as on
Athenian grave-reliefs, a scene from daily life, just touched with a
certain solemnity, because that life is over.   But other elements
in the design forbid this simple interpretation.   A boy-attendant
to the right pours out wine; that is consistent with the human

Fig. 87.

feast, but a boy to the left brings, not only a basket of ritual
shape, but a pig that must be for sacrifice.

Pindar's question is again much in place:

What god, what hero, what man shall we sing?

The answer is given, I think, by the snake, who with seeming ir-
relevance uprears himself beneath the table.   The banqueter is a
man; the horse's head like a coat of arms marks him as of knightly
rank.   He is in some sense divine; else why should he have
sacrifice and libation?   And yet he is no real god, no Olympian;
rather he is a man masked to his descendants as a daimon, as *the*
Agathos Daimon.   The dead individual grasps a perennial function
and thereby wins immortality, he is *heroized*.

[1] Berlin, Sabouroff Coll.

On past interpretations, beginning with Winckelmann and probably not yet ended with Prof. Gardner[1], it is not necessary long to dwell. All early interpretations fall under four heads. The scenes on the reliefs are explained either as

(a) *Mythological,* e.g. Winckelmann interprets the banqueting scene as the loves of Demeter-Erinys and Poseidon. These mythological interpretations are now completely discredited.

Fig. 88.

(b) *Retrospective and commemorative.* They represent domestic scenes in the daily life of the dead man, and thus are in line with the scenes on ordinary Athenian grave-reliefs. The snake is supposed to be a 'household snake.'

(c) *Representative* of the bliss of Elysium where the dead

Shall sit at endless feast.

[1] I borrow my summary of these views from Prof. Gardner's admirable paper. *A Sepulchral Relief from Tarentum,* in J. H. S., 1884, v. p. 105, where a full bibliography of the subject will be found.

(d) *Commemorative, but of ritual facts*, i.e. of the offerings of meat and drink brought by survivors to the grave of the dead man. This interpretation brings the 'Hero Feasts' almost into line with the well-known Sparta reliefs, where the heroized dead are 'worshipped' by diminutive descendants[1].

Almost but not quite. To bring food and drink to your dead relations, whether from fear or love, is to treat them as though they were the same as when they were alive, creatures of like passions and like potency or impotency with yourself. On the Sparta relief[2] in Fig. 88, they are, like Cleomenes[3], κρείττονες τὴν φύσιν, stronger, greater in their nature, quite other than the humble descendants who bring them cock and pomegranate.

Fig. 89.

How has it come to pass? The relief speaks clearly. They too have taken on the form and function of the Agathos Daimon. A great snake is coiled behind their chair, and the male figure holds in his right hand a huge kantharos, not 'in honour of Dionysos'

---

[1] See Mr A. J. B. Wace, *Sparta Museum Catalogue*, 1906, p. 102, for a full analysis of the 'Totenmahlrelief,' and Dr Rouse's instructive chapter on 'The Dead, the Heroes and the Chthonian Deities,' in his *Greek Votive Offerings*, 1902.

[2] *A. Mitth.* 1877, II. pl. XXII. For the snake's beard which marks him as a half-human *daimon* not a real snake see *Prolegomena*, p. 327.

[3] *Supra*, p. 269.

but because to him as Agathos Daimon libation of the new wine will be made. In his left he holds a pomegranate, the symbol, with its bursting seeds, of perennial fertility.

The relief in Fig. 89[1] shows us another instructive element We have the accustomed banquet scene made very human by the crouching dog under the table. In the background, close to the horse's head, is a tree, and round it is coiled a snake. The tree and the snake wound round it are the immemorial 'symbol' of life. The snake, the Agathos Daimon, is the genius of growing things, guardian of the Tree of Life, from the garden of Eden to the garden of the Hesperides.

In Fig. 89 the foremost of the three banqueting men holds a great horn from which the snake seems about to drink. Is the horn just a drinking-cup, a rhyton, used by the dead man, or has it some more solemn significance, some real connection with the snake? A chance notice in Athenaeus[2] gives us the needful clue. Chamaileon, a disciple of Aristotle, in his treatise 'On Drunkenness' noted that large cups were a characteristic of barbarians and not in use among the Greeks. But he is aware of one exception.

In the various parts of Greece nowhere shall we find, either in paintings or in historical records, any large-sized cup except those used in hero-ceremonies. For example, they assign the cup called *rhyton* only to heroes.

Chamaileon feels that there is a difficulty somewhere, but he explains that the cups of heroes are large because heroes are of 'difficult' temper and dangerous habits. The reason I would suggest is simpler. They 'assign' the rhyton, the great horn, as appropriate to a hero, because the hero as *daimon* had it from the beginning—the rhyton is the cornucopia.

The snake and the great cornucopia, the 'Horn of Amaltheia,' the 'Eniautos' cup[3] are, I think, evidence enough that the banqueting man is conceived of as an Agathos Daimon. It is not necessary to suppose that everywhere he was locally known by

---

[1] From a relief in the local museum at Samos. Inv. 55. See Wiegand, *Antike Skulpturen in Samos*, A. Mitth. 1900, p. 176.

[2] XI. 4. 461 ἐν δὲ τοῖς περὶ τὴν Ἑλλάδα τόποις, οὔτ᾽ ἐν γραφαῖς, οὔτ᾽ ἐπὶ τῶν πρότερον, εὑρήσομεν ποτήριον εὐμέγεθες εἰργασμένον, πλὴν τῶν ἐπὶ τοῖς ἡρωικοῖς. Τὸ γὰρ ῥυτὸν ὀνομαζόμενον μόνοις τοῖς ἥρωσιν ἀπεδίδοσαν. Ὃ καὶ δόξει τισὶν ἔχειν ἀπορίαν, εἰ μή τις ἄρα φήσειε.... In previously discussing this passage (*Proleg.* p. 448) I understood as little as Chamaileon the real significance of the rhyton in the 'Hero-Feasts.'

[3] *Supra*, p. 186.

that exact title.   The name matters little; the functions, as
expressed in the attributes snake and horn, are all important.
Yet in one instance[1], the design in Fig. 90, we have direct evidence

FIG. 90.

of actual names, which, but for the inscription, we should never
have dared to supply.

Aristomache and Theoris dedicated (it) to Zeus Epiteleios, Philios, and to
Philia, the mother of the god and to Tyche Agathe the wife of the god.

Aristomache and Theoris we may see in the two women worshippers.   Probably they are mother and wife of the man who
walks between them.   The inscription teems with suggestion.   It
is Olympian in spirit; the two women pray first and foremost to
Zeus the Accomplisher, no doubt that the wife's marriage may be
fruitful and the mother may see her children's children.   It is
patriarchal, for Zeus has a wife; it is matrilinear, for his mother
is invoked.

But it is the names that most amaze and delight us.   Zeus

---

[1] Jacobsen Coll. Ny Carlsberg, Copenhagen Cat. 95, first published and discussed
by A. Furtwängler, *Ein sogenanntes Todtenmahlrelief mit Inschrift* in Sitzungsberichte d. k. Bay. Akad. d. Wissenschaften, philos.-philolog. Kl. 1897, p. 401.

is not only Epiteleios, he is also Philios[1].   Philios the friendly,
sociable one, is the very incarnation of the *dais*, the communal
meal, he is always ready for the Theoxenia, based as it was on
the old service of the Agathos Daimon.   His mother Philia is but
the feminine counterpart of his name.   It is his wife who unmasks
his Olympian pretensions, and shows him for the earth-born divinity
that he is, his wife and his great cornucopia, for, if his wife be
Agathe Tyche, who is he but the ancient Agathos Daimon?

We have dwelt long on the *daimon* character of the banqueter,
because that is apt to be neglected, but it must not be forgotten
that he has another aspect, that of actual dead man.   On one[2] of
the Sparta grave-reliefs, in Fig. 91 this is certain.   A seated man

holds in the right hand a great
kantharos, in the left a pomegranate.
A large snake in the left-hand corner
marks his *daimon* character, but he
is an actual dead man; against him
his name is clearly written, *Timokles*.
These Sparta reliefs were actual
tomb-stones over particular graves:
the later 'Hero-feast' type with
the reclining banqueter were rather
adjuncts to tomb-stones, set up in
family precincts.   They are however frequently inscribed, sometimes
simply with the name of the dead

Fig. 91.

man or dead woman, sometimes with the additional statement
that he or she is *hero* or *heroine*.   Thus a hero-feast in Leyden[3]
is dedicated 'to Kudrogenes, Hero' (Κυδρογένει Ἥρωι).   On another
in Samos[4] is inscribed 'Lais daughter of Phoenix, Heroine, hail!'
(Λαΐς Φοίνικος Ἡροΐνη χαῖρε).   It is as though we heard the
Chorus chant to the dead Alkestis[5]

> νῦν δ' ἐστὶ μάκαιρα δαίμων·
> χαῖρ', ὦ πότνι', εὖ δὲ δοίης.

[1] For Zeus Philios see *Prolegomena*, p. 359.   To the comedian Zeus Philios was
the 'diner-out' par excellence.
[2] *A. Mitth.* 1879, iv. Taf. viii. p. 292.   Other inscribed instances are figured in
Mr Wace's *Introduction to Sculpture* in the Sparta Museum Catalogue, p. 105.
[3] No. 15; see Prof. Gardner, *op. cit.* p. 116.
[4] No. 60, *Prolegomena*, p. 352, Fig. 106.   [5] Eur. *Alk.* 1003.

In the archaic grave-reliefs of Sparta the dead man is figured as a hero, that is, as we now understand it, he has put on the garb and assumed the functions of an Agathos Daimon. In the ‘Hero Feasts’ of the fourth and succeeding centuries right down through Roman times, the dead man is also heroized, is figured as we have seen with snake and cornucopia. But Athenian grave-reliefs of the fine-period, of the fifth and early fourth centuries B.C., know of no snake no cornucopia[1] no *daimon*-hero. The dead man is simply figured as he was in life; he assumes no daimonic function whether to ban or to bless; he is idealized it may be but not divinized. The cause of this remarkable fact, this submergence of the *daimon*-aspect of the dead man will concern us later. One last form of the Hero-Feast, of special significance for our argument, yet remains to be considered.

The design in Fig. 92 is the earliest known specimen[2] of the

Fig. 92.

so-called ‘Ikarios reliefs.’ The main part of the composition is the familiar ‘Hero Feast,’ the reclining banqueter, the attendant

---

[1] This is the more remarkable as the Athenian grave-reliefs take over, as I have tried to show elsewhere (*Myth. and Mon. Anc. Athens*, p. 590), the art-type of the earlier Spartan monuments. It seems as though, while the art-type is preserved, the snake and cornucopia, the daimonic attributes were *advisedly* expurgated.

[2] Found at the Peiraeus, now in the Louvre. F. Dehneken, *Einkehr des Dionysos*, Arch. Zeit. 1881, p. 272.

cup-bearer, the seated wife, the table laden with fruits and cakes, the rampant snake. But on the left, instead of approaching worshippers, the hero's descendants, we have the Epiphany of a god. A daimon-hero receives *the* daimon, the god Dionysos—ὁ δαίμων ὁ Διὸς παῖς[1].

There were many legends of heroes who 'received' Dionysos. Pegasos received the god at Eleutherae in Boeotia, Ikarios the eponymous hero of the deme Ikaria received him in Attica, Amphictyon at Athens[2]. We cannot say that the banqueter on the relief is Ikarios or Pegasos, nor is it important to give him a name. The cardinal point is that, as the relief shows us, a local, daimonic, hero-cult could and did blend with the worship of the incoming Thracian Dionysos. In the light of the Agathos Daimon of the Pithoigia we see how easy was the fusion. *Daimon* and divinity alike had their wine-jars, their fruitful trees and blossoming flowers, and, best of all, their common animal-form, the holy snake. One daimon receives another and a greater than himself— that is all; but we understand now why Cleisthenes could so lightly take from the hero Adrastos his tragic *choroi* and 'give them as his due[3] to Dionysos.' From one daimon to another they had not far to go.

We have now established the nature of a 'hero' and seen that the two factors, dead man and *daimon*, that go to his making, are, in the light of the primitive doctrine of reincarnation, inextricably intertwined. The *daimon* proper, we have seen, was a collective representation expressing not a personality so much as a function, or at least a functionary, the eponym of a gens, the *basileus* of a state. As each individual man dies, though for a while he may be dreaded as a ghost, his tomb being tended by way of placation, he passes finally to join the throng of vague 'ancestors' who year

---

[1] Eur. *Bacch.* 416. The god's traits as Agathos Daimon, as feaster and as near akin to Eirene who nurtured the child Ploutos, come out very clearly in this chorus.

χαίρει μὲν θαλίαισιν,
φιλεῖ δ' ὀλβοδότειραν Εἰ-
ρήναν, κουροτρόφον θεάν.

Θαλία and Δαίς are figures near akin, ritual communal banquets, and Δαίς we remember (p. 146) was πρεσβίστη θεῶν.

[2] Paus. I. 2. 5, and Dr Frazer, *ad loc.*

[3] Herod. v. 67 Κλεισθένης δὲ χοροὺς μὲν τῷ Διονύσῳ ἀπέδωκε. I advisedly translate ἀπέδωκε 'gave them as his due.' The regular meaning of ἀποδίδωμι is to give to some one what is appropriate to him, to which he has some claim, hence its frequent use in the sense of to 'restore,' 'repay.'

by year at the Anthesteria reemerge themselves and send or rather bring back as flowers and fruit the buried seed. A writer in the Hippocratic Corpus[1] tells us, if any one saw the dead in a dream dressed in white and giving something, it was a good omen, for

'from the dead come food and increase and seeds.'

And as Aristophanes[2] has it:

> When a man dies, we all begin to say
> The sainted one has 'passed away,' has 'fallen asleep,
> Blessed therein that he is vexed no more;
> Yes, and with holy offerings we sacrifice
> To them as to the gods—and pour libations,
> Bidding them send good things up from below.

We have next to establish a further step in our argument. The 'hero' takes on not only the form and general function of the *daimon* but also his actual life-history as expressed and represented in his ritual. This further step is, as will presently be seen, for the understanding of the origin of the drama of paramount importance. We shall best understand its significance by taking a single concrete case that occurs in the mythology and cultus of the quasi-historical hero, Theseus. Theseus is an example to us specially instructive because his cult took on elements from that of Dionysos. He too not only absorbed the functions of an Agathos Daimon but like Pegasos, like Ikarios, like the nameless hero in Fig. 92 'received' the god.

THESEUS AS HERO-DAIMON.

To pass from Cecrops or even Erichthonios to Theseus is to breathe another air. Cecrops is the eponymous hero of the Cecropidae, the Basileus, the imagined head of a *Gens*[3], later misunderstood as a constitutional monarch. He is also a being on whom as medicine-king the fertility of people and crops depended, a snake-daimon. Theseus lays no claim to be autochthonous.

---

[1] *De Somn.* II. p. 14 ...ἀπὸ γὰρ τῶν ἀποθανόντων αἱ τροφαὶ καὶ αὐξήσεις καὶ σπέρματα γίνονται.

[2] *Tagenist.* frg. 1   καὶ θύομέν γ᾽ αὐτοῖσι τοῖς ἐναγίσμασιν
ὥσπερ θεοῖσι καὶ χοάς γε χεόμενοι
αἰτούμεθ᾽ αὐτοὺς τὰ καλὰ δεῦρο ἀνιέναι.

[3] I follow Prellwitz in understanding *Basileus* as 'Geschlechtsherr,' see *Etymologisches Wörterbuch*, 1905, s.v.

A chance poet[1] concerned to glorify the hero may call the Athenians 'Theseidae,' but Theseus is no real eponym. He comes from without; he represents the break with the gentile system, with the *gens* and its Basileus; he stands for democracy. His was the synoikia. Before his days the people of Attica had lived in scattered burghs (κατὰ πόλεις), citadel communities with each a Basileus or archon—a Pandion on the burgh of Megara, a Cecrops on the Athenian Acropolis—with each a city hearth, a Prytaneion. Theseus broke down the old divisions, the ancient Moirai, confusing doubtless many an archaic sanctity. He made one community with one goddess, and in her honour he instituted the festival of the Synoikia, the Feast of Dwelling together[2].

From the mythology of Theseus as representative of the democracy the supernatural has as far as possible been expurgated. The snake, the daimon double of the 'hero,' has ceased to haunt him. Plutarch[3] in his delightful way says at the beginning of his *Life of Theseus*[3]:

'I desire that the fabulous material I deal in may be subservient to my endeavours, and, being moulded by reason, may accept the form of history, and, when it obstinately declines probability and will not blend appropriately with what is credible I shall pray my readers may be indulgent and receive with kindness the fables of antiquity.'

So forewarned, we may be sure that ancient tradition has been freely tampered with by Plutarch as well as by his predecessors. It is the more delightful to find that, though the heroic snake-form is abolished—doubtless as unworthy of the quasi-historical Theseus—his cult preserves intact the life-history of a fertility daimon. One festival only of those associated with him can be considered, but this will repay somewhat detailed examination—the famous *Oschophoria*.

The Oschophoria. Plutarch[4] is our best authority for the Oschophoria and his narrative must be given in full. Theseus has slain the Minotaur, has deserted Ariadne on Naxos, has put in at

---

[1] Soph. *Oed. Col.* 1065   δεινὸς ὁ προσχώρων Ἄρης,
                                        δεινὰ δὲ Θησειδᾶν ἀκμά.
[2] Thucyd. II. 15 ἐπὶ γὰρ Κέκροπος καὶ τῶν πρώτων βασιλέων ἡ Ἀττικὴ ἐς Θησέα ἀεὶ κατὰ πόλεις ᾠκεῖτο πρυτανεῖά τε ἔχουσα καὶ ἄρχοντας....
[3] *Sub init.*
[4] *Vit. Thes.* XXII. Plutarch's account is very likely drawn from Krates περὶ θυσιῶν (circ. 200 B.C.).

Delos and there, parenthetically, instituted the Crane-dance; he turns his ship at last homewards.

'When their course brought them near to Attica both Theseus and the pilot were so overjoyed that they forgot to hoist the sail which was to be the signal to Aigeus of their safe return and he, despairing of it, threw himself from the rock and was killed. But Theseus, on landing, himself performed the sacrifices he had vowed to the gods at Phaleron when he set sail, and meantime *dispatched a messenger* to the city with news of his safe return. *The messenger met with many who were lamenting the death of the king and others who rejoiced as was meet and were ready to receive him* (Theseus) *with kindness and to crown him* on his safe return. *He received the crowns and wound them about his kerykeion* and coming back to the shore, as Theseus had not yet finished his libations, he stopped outside, being unwilling to disturb the sacrifice. When the libations were accomplished *he announced the end of Aigeus, and they with weepings and lamentations hastened up to the city*[1].'

'Hence even now they say, at the Oschophoria, the herald does not crown himself but his kerykeion, and those who assist at the libations utter at the moment of the libations the words *Eleleu, Iou, Iou*, of which the one is a cry used by people when they pour libation and chant the paean, the other expresses terror and confusion[2]. Theseus having buried his father redeemed the vow he had made to Apollo on the seventh day of Pyanepsion; for it was on this day that they came back in safety and went up to the city. The boiling of all sorts of pulse is said to take place because, when they returned in safety, they mixed together what was left of their provisions in one pot in common and consumed them feasting in common together. And they carry out the Eiresione, a branch of olive wound about with wool like the suppliant branch, on that occasion, and laden with all sorts of first-fruits that scarcity may cease, and they sing over it

> Eiresione brings
> Figs and fat cakes,
> And a pot of honey and oil to mix,
> And a wine cup strong and deep,
> That she may drink and sleep.

Some say that these things began to be done on account of the Heracleidae who were thus nurtured by the Athenians, but the greater number agree with the above[3]....And they also celebrate the festival of the Oschophoria which was instituted by Theseus.'

Plutarch begins his account of the actual ceremonies of the Oschophoria with the statement that two of the seven maidens taken by Theseus to Crete were really young men dressed to look like women. On his return to Athens these two young men walked in the procession dressed, he says, like those who now (in the Oschophoria) carry the branches.

---

[1] The passages in italics are those which, if my interpretation be right, have ritual significance, though supposed to be merely historical.

[2] ἐπιφωνεῖν δὲ ἐν ταῖς σπονδαῖς 'Ελελεῦ, 'Ιοὺ 'Ιού, τοὺς παρόντας· ὧν τὸ μὲν σπένδοντες (σπεύδοντες codd. corr. F. M. C.) ἀναφωνεῖν καὶ παιωνίζοντες εἰώθασι, τὸ δὲ ἐκπλήξεως καὶ ταραχῆς ἐστι.

[3] At this point is a digression (XXIII.) in which the ship of Theseus is described. It was preserved by the Athenians down to the time of Demetrios of Phalerum and was probably an old ritual car. See Nilsson, *Archiv f. Religionswiss.* XI. 402, and *Griechische Feste*, 1906, p. 268, note 5.

'These they carry to do honour to Dionysos and Ariadne on account of the legend, or rather because they came back when the fruit-harvest was being gathered in. The Deipnophoroi (carriers of the meal) take part and have a share in the sacrifice, and play the part of the mothers of those on whom the lot fell, for they kept coming to them with provisions, and tales (μῦθοι) are recited because those mothers used to recount tales to cheer up their children and comfort them. Demon also gives the same particulars. And a temenos was set apart to Theseus, and the Phytalidae superintended the sacrifice, Theseus having handed it over to them in return for their hospitality.'

Before discussing this remarkable hodge-podge of ritual and pseudo-history our account of the Oschophoria must be completed from other sources.

Athenaeus[1] in describing the various shapes of vases mentions one called *pentaploa* (the fivefold).

'Philochoros mentions it in the second book of his *Attica*. And Aristodemos in the third book of his *Concerning Pindar* says that during the Skira a contest took place at Athens consisting of a race of epheboi. And that they run holding a fruit-laden vine-branch, which is what is called an *ōschos*. And they run from the sanctuary of Dionysos as far as the sanctuary of Athena Skiras, and he who wins receives the kylix called *pentaploa*, and he feasts with a *choros*. And the kylix is called *pentaploa* inasmuch as it holds wine and honey and cheese and meal and a little oil.'

Proklos also in his *Chrestomathia*[2] has a valuable notice as follows:

'Songs belonging to the Oschophoria are sung among the Athenians. Two youths of the chorus are dressed like women and carry branches of vine laden with fine bunches of grapes, they call such a branch an *ōschē*, and from this the songs get their name, and these two lead the festival.'

After repeating some of the details and the pseudo-history already known to us from Plutarch, Proklos goes on:

'The chorus follows the two youths and sings the songs. Epheboi from each tribe contend with each other in the race, and of these the one who is first tastes of the phiale called *pentaple*, the ingredients of which are oil, wine, honey, cheese and meal.'

---

[1] xi. 62, §§ 495, 496 ...'Αριστόδημος δ' ἐν τρίτῳ περὶ Πινδάρου τοῖς Σκίροις φησὶν Ἀθήναζε ('Ἀθήνησι Mein.) ἀγῶνα ἐπιτελεῖσθαι τῶν ἐφήβων δρόμου· τρέχειν δ' αὐτοὺς ἔχοντας ἀμπέλου κλάδον κατάκαρπον, τὸν καλούμενον ὦσχον. Τρέχουσι δ' ἐκ τοῦ ἱεροῦ τοῦ Διονύσου μέχρι τοῦ τῆς Σκιράδος Ἀθηνᾶς ἱεροῦ, καὶ ὁ νικήσας λαμβάνει κύλικα τὴν λεγομένην πενταπλόαν καὶ κωμάζει μετὰ χοροῦ. Πεντάπλοα δ' ἡ κύλιξ καλεῖται, καθ᾽ ὅσον οἶνον ἔχει καὶ μέλι καὶ τυρὸν καὶ ἄλφιτον καὶ ἐλαίου βραχύ.

[2] *Chrestomath.* 28 ὀσχοφορικὰ δὲ μέλη παρὰ 'Ἀθηναίοις ᾔδετο· τοῦ δὲ χοροῦ δὲ δύο νεανίαι κατὰ γυναῖκας ἐστολισμένοι κλήματα ἀμπέλου κομίζοντες μεστῶν (sic) εὐθάλων βοτρύων (ἐκάλουν δὲ αὐτὸ ὀσχην, ἀφ' οὗ καὶ τοῖς μέλεσιν ἡ ἐπωνυμία) τῆς ἑορτῆς καθηγοῦντο. ἄρξαι δὲ Θησέα πρῶτον τοῦ ἔργου· κ.τ.λ....εἵπετο τοῖς νεανίαις ὁ χορὸς καὶ ᾖδε τὰ μέλη· ἐξ ἑκάστης δὲ φυλῆς ἔφηβοι διημιλλῶντο πρὸς ἀλλήλους δρόμῳ· καὶ τούτων ὁ πρότερος ἐγένετο ἐκ τῆς πενταπλῆς λεγομένης φιάλης, ἣ συνεκιρνᾶτο ἐλαίῳ καὶ οἴνῳ καὶ μέλιτι καὶ τυρῷ καὶ ἀλφίτοις.

Probably most of the ritual details in Plutarch, Athenaeus and Proklos come from Philochoros. Istros[1], who was nearly his contemporary, wrote an account of Theseus in the thirteenth book of his History, and adds the somewhat important detail that the two oschophoroi had to be 'conspicuous both for race and wealth.' The scholiast on Nikander's *Alexipharmaka* says[2] that they had to have both parents alive, and Hesychius[3] adds that they were in the 'flower of their age.

Amid much uncertainty as to detail the main features of the festival stand out clearly. First and foremost the *Oschophoria* is an autumn festival, marking and crowning the end of all the harvests. It is one feature in the great *Pyanepsia* which gave its name to the fourth month of the Attic year, Pyanepsion (Oct. Nov.). *Pyanepsia* meant bean-cooking, and one element in the feast was the common meal out of the common pot, a bean-feast or πανσπέρμια[4], such as that which was eaten, as we saw, in Athens at the Anthesteria on the day of the Chytroi. It required some ingenuity to fit the Bean-Feast on to the slaying of the Minotaur, but Plutarch, or his authority[5], is equal to the occasion. Theseus and his companions, on their return from Crete, being short of provisions, 'mixed together what was left of everything and ate it from a common pot.'

Besides the *pyanepsia* proper, the Bean-Feast, we have two other elements whose gist is clearly analogous, and which are therefore best taken together:

      a. The Eiresione.

      b. The Oschophoria.

The Eiresione[6] was carried also at the earlier harvest-festival

---

[1] Ap. Harpocrat. s.v. ὀσχοφόροι...ὁ δὲ ῞Ιστρος ἐν τῇ ιγ´ περὶ Θησέως λέγων γράφει οὕτως, ἕνεκα τῆς κοινῆς σωτηρίας νομίσαι τοὺς καλουμένους ὀσχοφόρους καταλέγειν β´ τῶν γένει καὶ πλούτῳ κρατούντων. Harpocration defines ὄσχη as κλῆμα βότρυς ἐξηρτημένους ἔχον.

[2] Schol. ad *Alexipharm.* 109 ὀσχοφόροι δὲ λέγονται ᾿Αθήνησι παῖδες ἀμφιθαλεῖς ἁμιλλώμενοι κατὰ φυλὰς οἱ κ.τ.λ.

[3] s.v. ὠσχοφορία. παῖδες εὐγενεῖς ἡβῶντες καταλέγονται οἱ κ.τ.λ.

[4] Athen. xiv. 58, §§ 648 ᾿Εστὶ δὲ τὸ πυάνιον, ὥς φησι Σωσίβιος πανσπερμία ἐν γλυκεῖ ἡψημένη. Probably this was the exact mess eaten at the Pyanepsia. The word πύανον was old-fashioned. Heliodorus (ap. Athen. ix. 71, §§ 406) says, τῆς τῶν πυρῶν ἑψήσεως ἐπινοηθείσης, οἱ μὲν παλαιοὶ πύανον, οἱ δὲ νῦν ὀλόπυρον προσαγορεύουσιν. The most ancient mess was probably of pulse, the more modern of various sorts of grain.

[5] Possibly Krates the friend of Polemon.

[6] I have discussed the Eiresione in detail in connection with the Thargelia, *Prolegomena*, p. 77, chapter iii., Harvest Festivals. I did not then understand the

of the summer first-fruits, the *Thargelia*, which also gave their name to a month *Thargelion*, May—June. The Eiresione is of course simply a portable May-pole, a branch hung about with wool, acorns, figs, cakes, fruits of all sorts and sometimes wine-jars. It was appropriate alike to the early and the late harvest-festival, but for the late harvest after the vintage was over it had naturally to be supplemented by the carrying of other branches, vine-boughs laden with bunches of grapes, an Oschophoria.

This blend of Eiresione and Oschophoria was evidently characteristic of the ceremonies of Pyanepsion. The two ceremonies are represented on the Calendar-frieze[1] of the old Metropolitan Church of Athens (Fig. 93) to mark the month

Fig. 93.

Pyanepsion. A boy carrying the Eiresione is followed by a magistrate, and immediately in front of him is a youth treading grapes and holding in his hand an *öschos*, a branch laden with bunches of grapes. To the right of him is a *kanephoros* carrying no doubt a *pankarpia*.

With the Staphylodromoi of the Karneia[2] in our minds the main gist of the Oschophoria is clear. It is like the race of Olympia, a race of youths, *epheboi*, *kouroi*, with boughs. It has

similar content of the Oschophoria. See also Mannhardt, *Wald- und Feldkulte*, 1877, pp. 214—58, which, spite of its early date, is far the best account both as regards the collection of facts and their interpretation.

[1] J. N. Svoronos, *Der Athenische Volkskalendar*, Sonderabdruck aus Journal Internationale d'archéologie numismatique, 1899, II. 1.

[2] See *supra*, p. 234.

two elements, the actual *agon* the contest, in this case a race, and then, second in time but first in importance, the procession and the *komos*. The somewhat complicated details of the race seem to have been as follows[1]. Two epheboi chosen from each of the ten tribes raced against one another. The ten victors, after being feasted, formed into procession, one of them leading the way as *keryx*, two following, dressed as women and carrying branches, the remaining seven forming, as at Delphi, the *choros*. The prize is, in the Oschophoria, a cup of mingled drinks, manifestly not a thing of money value but of magical intent, a sort of liquid *panspermia*, or *pankarpia*, meet for a vintage feast. The blend of cheese and wine and honey may not commend itself to our modern palates, but Demeter, save for the wine, drank the same in her holy *kykeon*.

The branches were carried, Plutarch conjectures, to do honour to Dionysos 'on account of the myth' (διὰ τὸν μῦθον). The myth of Naxos may have done honour to Dionysos; how it could reflect credit on Theseus or form a suitable element in his cult it is not easy to see. The μῦθος proper[2], the word or tale spoken at a vintage ceremony, would no doubt—when a god had once been projected—do honour to the vintage god and his bride; but Plutarch, or his authorities[3], must of necessity connect it with his hero, so the disreputable legend of Naxos has to be tolerated[4]. But Plutarch suspects the real truth. No Greek as keen about ritual and religion as he was could fail to know that the Oschophoria was part of a vintage festival, but again the awkward hero has to be dragged in, so we have 'or rather *because they came back when the fruit harvest was being gathered in.*'

In his account of the origin of the Olympic games Mr Cornford[5] has made it abundantly clear that the winner issued in the king, who, in one aspect, was but the leader of the *choros*, the head of

---

[1] See Mommsen, *Feste d. Stadt Athen* (1898), p. 285; and for the number seven in the Theseus legend cf. Verg. Æn. VI. 21 septena quotannis Corpora natorum.

[2] For the precise nature of a primitive μῦθος see *infra*, p. 327.

[3] Mommsen thinks that the Oschophoria and the Dionysos myths were attached to Theseus quite late, i.e. after the Persian war. The date of the *contaminatio* is of little importance to my argument.

[4] The mythology of Ariadne cannot here be examined, but it is interesting to note in passing that in the legend of the desertion Theseus and Dionysos are obvious doubles.

[5] See *supra*, chapter VII.

the revelling *komos*. We are never told that the winner in the Oschophoria was called *basileus*, but in Plutarch's pseudo-history the truth comes out. The messenger meets 'many who were lamenting the death of the king and others who rejoiced as was meet and were ready to receive him with kindness and to crown him on his safe return.' The words are in our ears: *Le Roi est mort; Vive le Roi.* Ægeus the old king dies; Theseus the new king reigns. The old Year is over, the new Year is begun. The festival looks back to a time and a place when and where the year ended with the final harvest and the new year began in academic fashion in the autumn[1] or early winter.

In the Oschophoria the winner of the race is, as at Olympia, an *Eniautos-daimon* and a *basileus* in one. He dies as an individual and revives as an eternally recurrent functionary. The contradictory cries *Eleleu Iou Iou* are now clear enough[2]. There is 'terror and confusion' when the old Year, the old King, dies; there is libation, a paean, and a joyful cry when the new Year, the new King, is crowned. One curious detail looks back to still earlier days. At the Oschophoria the herald (ἄγγελος) does not crown himself, he crowns his Kerykeion and his herald's staff with the two snakes entwined. This surely looks back to the time when the *Eniautos-daimon* was a snake or a pair of snakes, and the crown was for the symbol of the snake-*daimon* not for his human correlative.

Another ritual element points to early days—the *Deipnophoroi* or foodbearers who supplied the chosen epheboi with provisions, took part in the ceremony, and then 'played the part of the mothers' of the youths on whom the lot fell (ἀπομιμούμεναι τὰς μητέρας ἐκείνων τῶν λαχόντων). They also recited myths to encourage the youths. We have then as an integral part of the ritual just the two factors always present in matriarchal mythology, the Mother and the Son. The mother brings food, because like Mother-Earth she is essentially the feeder, the Nurturer; the mother speaks words (μῦθοι) of exhortation and consolation such

---

[1] Mr Chambers has shown that this was the case in the bi-seasonal year of central Europe. The winter season began in mid-November, the summer in mid-March. See *The Mediaeval Stage*, vol. I. 110.

[2] It seems impossible to decide that one of these cries definitely expresses joy and the other sorrow. Both vary according to their context.

as many a mother must have spoken in ancient days to a son about to undergo initiation. Such words spoken aloud may have actually been a feature in initiation ritual.

Yet another curious element in the ritual remains. Plutarch and Proklos both tell us that two of the young men who carried the Branches were dressed as women. Plutarch, as we have seen, explains the custom by an aetiological myth of more than usual foolishness. Modern commentators are not much more successful. The common sense or naive school sees in the interchange of dress between the sexes a prolepsis of the 'Arry and Arriet' hilarity of Hampstead Heath. Others think that in the supposed women's dress we may see simply a survival of Ionian priestly vestments. Dr Frazer[1] justly observes that, in an obscure and complex problem like that of the religious interchange of dress between men and women, it is unlikely that any single solution would apply to all the cases[2].

Such a figure of an Oschophoros disguised probably as a woman is, I think, preserved for us in the design in Fig. 94 from the interior of a red-figured cylix[3] of the fine period. The scene takes place before a temple, indicated by the column to the right. A youth or maiden—the doubt is instructive—stands near to a great *lekane* or laver which, as often, stands on a short pillar supported by a basis. The horned object on the basis is probably part of a basket of a type not uncommon in ritual use. The same shape of basket is carried by the boy on the relief in Fig. 87. The youth or maiden has hair elaborately long, and on the head is a diadem

---

[1] *Adonis, Attis and Osiris*, Appendix IV., on *Priests dressed as Women*. See also Mannhardt, *Wald- und Feldkulte*, p. 253, and *Baumkultus*, 203. Prof. Murray reminds me that Pentheus in his woman's robe imitated "the gait of Ino or of Agave my mother," Eur. *Bacch.* 925.

[2] Of the general problem of interchange of dress a solution is offered in chapter XI. In the particular case before us it seems to me just possible that the two youths disguised as women may represent really a woman and a youth, a mother and a young son. The parts of women in rural mimes are still to-day taken in Greece by men disguised. Men assumed women's parts in the classical theatre: the reason for this, to our minds, ugly practice is obscure, but the facts remain. If we suppose the two first figures of the procession of Branch-Bearers (preceded only by the herald) to have been Mother and Son, their dress might not be clearly distinguishable. Dionysos the son *par excellence* was effeminate in guise and gait. The Son before he leaves his Mother is a woman-thing. The racers would race either naked or but lightly clad, but the two who became *personae* might, once the contest over, assume ritual garb as Mother and Son.

[3] See Hauser, *Philologus*, LIV. (1895), p. 385.

with leaf-sprays. The robe is manifestly a ritual vestment: its
elaborate decoration reminds us of the robe worn by Demeter at
Eleusis on the Hieron vase[1]. The *lekane* is filled with water. The
youth (or maiden) is, it may be, about to plunge the great bough
into the water. Is it for a rain-charm, or will he asperge the
people? We cannot say. One thing, and perhaps only one, is
certain: the figure, be it maid or man, is a Thallophoros, possibly
an Oschophoros, though no grape-bunches are depicted.

The moral of Plutarch's clumsy aetiological tale is clear; had
it been made for our purpose it could scarcely have been clearer.

Fig. 94.

It embodies the very act of transition from the periodic festival
with its *Eniautos-daimon* to the cult of the individual hero; from,
in a word, the functionary to the personality. It is along this
well-trodden road that each and every hero, each and every god,
must travel before the parting of their ways.

There is competition among the saga-heroes as to who shall
seize the function-festival for his own. Plutarch, as usual, is
instructive through his very *naïveté*. Some said that the ceremonies of Pyanepsion '*began to be done on account of the*

[1] *Prolegomena*, p. 556, Fig. 158.

Heracleidae[1] who were thus nurtured by the Athenians, but the greater number agree with the above.'

Theseus, the individual hero, for reasons political now lost to us, won and survived, though when we read the shifts to which Plutarch is put to 'do him honour' we feel his triumph is a sorry one. But honest Plutarch[2] knew and cannot conceal that the rites were really in the hands not of an individual hero, but a group, a *gens*, the *Phytalidae*, the 'Plant-Men.' Very fitly did such a group hold presidency over harvest ceremonies: their function was to promote the fertility of all growths fit for human food. The group of the Phytalidae project of course an eponymous hero Phytalos, *Plant Man*. Phytalos received Demeter into his house, as Ikarios 'received' Dionysos; she gave him for guerdon the gift of the fig-tree[3]. Translated into the language of fact, this means that the group of the Plant-Men at one time or another began cultivating the fig, a tree which seems long to have preceded in Greece the culture of the vine.

Pausanias[4] saw—and the sight is for us instructive—the sepulchre of Phytalos, and on it was an inscription:

Here the lordly hero Phytalos once received the august
Demeter, when she first revealed the autumnal fruit
Which the race of mortals names the sacred fig;
Since when the race of Phytalos hath received honours that wax not old.

Phytalos is lord (ἄναξ) and hero (ἥρως), and he has a tomb (τάφος), but does even the wildest Euhemerist dream that he ever existed? The writer of the epitaph knew that he was the merest eponym; it is the *race* (γένος) of Phytalos, not the individual hero, that has deathless honours.

The climax of a preposterous aetiology is reached by Plutarch[5] in commenting on the Phytalidae. He knows of them and their local presidency; knows of their tribal contribution to the ceremonial house by house feast which Theseus took to himself; and what does he say? 'The Phytalidae superintended the sacrifice, *Theseus having handed it over to them in return for their hospitality.*' Very handsome of him, for it was the *gens* of the Phytalidae who

---

[1] For Herakles as arch-hero see *infra*, p. 364.   [2] *Op. cit.* XXIII. *sub fin.*
[3] Paus. I. 37. 2.   [4] I. 37. 2, trans. Frazer.
[5] Ἐξηρέθη δὲ καὶ τέμενος αὐτῷ καὶ τοὺς ἀπὸ τῶν παρασχόντων· τὸν δασμὸν οἴκων ἔταξεν εἰς θυσίαν αὐτῷ τελεῖν ἀποφοράς· καὶ τῆς θυσίας ἐπεμελοῦντο Φυταλίδαι, Θησέως ἀποδόντος αὐτοῖς ἀμοιβὴν τῆς φιλοξενίας.

first received or purified him on his entry into Athens. The real functional tribal eponym, Phytalos, fades before the saga-personality Theseus.

Theseus indeed marks, as already noted, the period of transition between the group and the individual, the functionary, the *basileus* and the individual historic or saga-chief. Theseus is a king's son, but he lets go the kingship (βασιλείαν ἀφείς). He is the hero of the new democracy whose basis is individuality. It is this swift transit from the group to the individual, from the function to the person, that is, as will later become clear, at once the weakness and the strength of the religion of the Greek. The individual is a frail light bark to launch· upon a perilous sea. But the Sibyl bade the Athenian, who let the kingship slip, take courage:

> The wine-skin wins its way upon the waves[1]

Theseus, then, the saga-hero, the quasi-historical personality, took ·on the life-history, the year-history of a fertility-*daimon*, that *daimon* himself, figured by the youth with the Eiresione, having assimilated another *daimon*, him of the grape—Dionysos. It remains to ask—What are the factors, the actual elements, the events in the life-history of an *Eniautos-daimon*[2]? What is his *mythos*? And first, what precisely do we mean by a *mythos*?

THE MYTHOS.

A myth is to us now-a-days a 'purely fictitious narrative[3].' When we say a thing is 'mythical' we mean it is non-existent. We have travelled in this matter far from ancient thinking and

---

[1] Plut. *Vit. Thes.* XXIV.

ἀσκὸς γὰρ ἐν οἴδματι ποντοπορεῦσαι.
Τοῦτο δὲ καὶ Σίβυλλαν ὕστερον ἀποστοματίσαι πρὸς τὴν πόλιν ἱστοροῦσιν ἀναφθεγξαμένην·
Ἀσκὸς βαπτίζῃ· δῦναι δέ τοι οὐ θέμις ἐστίν.

[2] To avoid misunderstanding I ought perhaps to state clearly at this point that the phrase ἐνιαυτὸς δαίμων is so far as I know never used by the Greeks. They called their year-daimones by different names in different places. In Boeotia he was *Agathos Daimon*, in Crete *Megistos Kouros*, at Eleusis *Plouton*. Our earliest literary evidence for Eniautos as a definite personality is probably Pindar, *Paean*, I. 5 Ὁ παντελὴς Ἐνιαυτός, Ὧραί τε Θεμιγόνοι. See *infra*, chapter XI.

[3] See the excellent definition in Murray's *English Dictionary*. 'A purely fictitious narrative usually involving supernatural persons, actions or events, and embodying some popular idea concerning natural or historical phenomena.' A myth is essentially 'popular,' i.e. collective, not the product of an individual brain, it has to do with *daimones*, i.e. involves the 'supernatural,' it blends the historical and the natural in a way to be observed later.

feeling. A *mythos* to the Greek was primarily just a thing spoken, uttered by the *mouth*[1]. Its antithesis or rather correlative is the thing done, enacted, the *ergon* or work. Old Phoinix says to Achilles 'Thy father Peleus sent me to thee to teach thee to be both

> Of words the speaker and of deeds the doer[2].'

From sounds made by the mouth, to words spoken and thence to tale or story told the transition is easy. Always there is the same antithesis of speech and action which are but two different ways of expressing emotion, two forms of reaction; the *mythos*, the tale told, the action recounted, is contrasted with the action actually done. It is from this antithesis that the sense of unreality, non-existence gradually arises.

This primary sense of *mythos* as simply the thing uttered, expressed by speech rather than action, can never, so long as he reads his Homer, be forgotten by the literary student. But when we come to *myth* in relation to religion, myth contrasted with ritual, we are apt to forget this primary and persistent meaning, and much confused thinking is the result. The primary meaning of myth in religion is just the same as in early literature; it is the spoken correlative of the acted rite, the thing done; it is τὸ λεγόμενον as contrasted with or rather as related to τὸ δρώμενον[3].

Let us take the simplest possible instance in a rite already described[4], in which—the instances are rare—we have recorded both act and myth. In the Grizzly Bear Dance of the North American Indians the performers shuffle and shamble about like a bear in his cave waking from his winter sleep. That is the

---

[1] Our word *mouth* and μῦθος are connected, cf. also μύζω—all come from the root μύ, lat. *mu*—to make an audible sound by opening or closing the lips, cf. n.h.d. Mücke, μυῖα, a 'hummer,' and μύω, μύστης; see Prellwitz, *Etymologisches Wörterbuch*, 1905, s.v.

[2] *Il.* IX. 443

μύθων τε ῥητῆρ' ἔμεναι πρηκτῆρά τε ἔργων.

[3] Passages dealing with δράμενα and λεγόμενα are collected by Bergk, *Griechische Literaturgeschichte*, 1884, vol. III. p. 4, but he does not distinguish between the myth proper and the aetiological myth. Thus in Paus. II. 37. 2 τὰ λεγόμενα ἐπὶ τοῖς δρωμένοις means clearly the story current to account for the rites, whereas in Galen, *de usu part.* VI. 14 ὅλος ἦσθα πρὸς τοῖς δρωμένοις τε καὶ λεγομένοις ὑπὸ τῶν ἱεροφάντων, the λεγόμενα are clearly the myth proper, spoken at the moment of the performance. Bergk well remarks that the word *drama* is never used of these δρώμενα but that Aristotle connects the two in the *Poetics* (3. 3) ὅθεν καὶ δράματα καλεῖσθαί τινες αὐτά φασιν ὅτι μιμοῦνται δρῶντες.

[4] *Supra*, p. 112.

action, the δρώμενον. They also at the same time chant the words:

> I begin to grow restless in the spring.
> I take my robe,
> My robe is sacred,
> I wander in the summer.

These are the λεγόμενα, the things uttered by the mouth, the *myths*. As man is a speaking as well as a motor animal, any complete human ceremony usually contains both elements, speech and action, or as the Greeks would put it, we have in a rite τὰ δρώμενα and also τὰ ἐπὶ τοῖς δρωμένοις λεγόμενα.

It is necessary to emphasize this point because that great genius Robertson Smith has here led many of us his weaker followers astray.

'Strictly speaking,' he says[1], 'mythology was no essential part of ancient religion for it had no sacred sanction and no binding force on the worshippers.'

To Robertson Smith a myth was the ancient equivalent of that hated thing, a dogma, only unguarded by sanctions. Had it been granted him to tarry awhile among the Iowa Indians or among the Zuñis he would have told another tale. An Iowa Indian when asked about the myths and traditions of his tribe said[2]:

These are sacred things and I do not like to speak about them, and it is not our custom to do so except when we make a feast and collect the people and use the sacred pipe.

A pious man would no more tell out his myths than he would dance out his mysteries. Only when the tribe is assembled after solemn fasting, and holy smoking, only sometimes in a strange archaic tongue and to initiate men or novices after long and arduous preparation, can the myth with safety be uttered from the mouth; such is its sanctity, its *mana*.

In discussing the 'Aetiological Myth[3]' of the *Hymn to the Kouretes* we noted briefly that a myth is not to begin with and necessarily 'aetiological.' Its object is not at first to give a reason; that notion is part of the old rationalist fallacy that saw in primitive man the leisured and eager enquirer bent on research, all alive *rerum cognoscere causas*. When the Grizzly Bear dancer

---

[1] *Religion of the Semites*, 1889, p. 19.
[2] Dorsey, *Eleventh Annual Report of the American Bureau of Ethnology*, 1889–90, p. 430. I owe this reference to the admirable chapter on 'Mythology' in Prof. Ames's *Psychology of Religious Experience*, 1910.
[3] *Supra*, p. 13.

utters his myth, says the words, 'I begin to grow restless in the spring,' he is not explaining his action—that, if he has any gift of observation and mimicry should be clear enough—he only utters with his mouth what he enacts with his shambling, shuffling feet, the emotions and sensations he feels in relation to the 'most Honourable One,' the Bear. It is not until he becomes shy and shamefaced instead of proud and confident in his pantomime, that, seeking an excuse, he finds it in his myth turned aetiological. When the Kouretes lose faith in their power to rear a child εἰς ἐνιαυτόν they go on uttering their myth, but they put it in the past tense and interpolate an explanatory conjunction marking the decay of faith:

For here the shielded Nurturers took thee a child immortal.

We have previously[1] analysed in detail the motor or active factor in a rite, the δρώμενον[2], we have seen that in its religious sense it was not simply a thing done but a thing *re*-done or *pre*-done; it was commemorative or magical or both. We have also noted that it was a thing done under strong emotional excitement and done collectively. All this applies equally to the other factor in a rite, the myth. In the religious sense a myth is not merely a word spoken; it is a re-utterance or pre-utterance, it is a focus of emotion, and uttered as we have seen collectively or at least with collective sanction. It is this collective sanction and solemn purpose that differentiate the myth alike from the historical narrative and the mere *conte* or fairy-tale: a myth becomes practically a story of magical intent and potency.

Possibly the first *muthos* was simply the interjectional utterance *mū*; but it is easy to see how rapid the development would be from interjection to narrative. Each step in the ritual action is shadowed as it were by a fresh interjection, till the whole combines into a consecutive tale. Thus to take again a simple instance; in the Rutuburi dance described above[3] we have a sequence,

The Blue Squirrel ascends the tree and whistles.
The plants will be growing and the fruit will be ripening,
And when it is ripe it falls to the ground,

[1] *Supra*, p. 42.
[2] It is worth noting that the actual word δρώμενον when it becomes the equivalent of 'rite' shows that the tendency must have been to emphasize the motor element.
[3] *Supra*, p. 112.

and this sequence is as it were the life-history of the plant or the animal to be magically affected; it is the plot of the δρώμενον, for, says Aristotle[1], in a most instructive definition,

> by myth I mean the arrangement of the incidents.

When we realize that the myth is the plot of the δρώμενον we no longer wonder that the plot of a drama is called its 'myth.'

It would be convenient if the use of the word *myth* could be confined[2] to such sequences, such stories as are involved in rites. Anyhow the primitive myth, the myth proper, is of this nature, and it is one form of the myth proper that we have now to consider, the plot or life-history of the *Eniautos-daimon*. What are its elements and its characteristics? What if anything did it contribute to the plots (μῦθοι) of the dramas enacted at the Great Dionysia? If these dramas arose from the Spring δρώμενα some analogies between their respective 'myths' must surely be observable.

The Eniautos-Mūthos.

The elements of the Eniautos myth are few and simple[3]; its main characteristic is its inevitable, periodic monotony. This comes out clearly in the δρώμενα of the Oschophoria. The principal factors are:

(a) A contest (ἀγών). In this case and also in the Karneia and in the Olympic Games the contest is a race to decide who shall carry the boughs and wear the crown.

(b) A *pathos*, a death or defeat. In the Theseus myth this appears in the death of the old king. The *pathos* is formally announced by a *messenger* (ἄγγελος) and it is followed or accompanied by a *lamentation* (θρῆνος).

(c) A triumphant Epiphany, an appearance or crowning of the victor or the new king, with an abrupt change (περιπέτεια

---

[1] *Poet.* VI. 6 λέγω γὰρ μῦθον τοῦτον τὴν σύνθεσιν τῶν πραγμάτων.

[2] Mr van Gennep proposes this in his interesting paper *Was ist Mythus?* (Internationale Wochenschrift für Wissenschaft, Kunst und Technik, Sept. 1910, p. 1167). His definition of myth is as follows: 'Der Mythus ist eine Erzählung, die allgemeine und regelmässig wechselnde und sich wiederholende Erscheinungen darstellt und deren Bestandteile sich in gleicher Sequenz durch religiösmagische Handlungen (Riten) äussern.'

[3] I omit the presentation or *prologue* introducing the plays as not ritually essential and as not noted in the Oschophoria, but it is interesting to find that in Mr Chambers' analysis of the Mummers' play (*op. cit.* I. p. 211) he divides it into three parts: the Presentation, the Drama, the Quête. See also Prof. Murray, *infra*, p. 359.

from lamentation to rejoicing.   In the Theseus rite, we have the actual *mūthoi* which marked this shift, *Eleleu Iou Iou*[1].

The δρώμενον may of course take a somewhat simplified form. Thus the Kathodos and Anodos of Kore[2] omits the *agon*, but probably in all cases where a human representative had to be chosen, a leader or king, the contest element was present. It is surely a fact of the highest significance that the Greek word for actor is *agonistes*, contester.   The shift from sorrow to joy was integral because it was the mimetic presentation of the death of the Old Year, the birth of the New.   To seek for a *threnos* we need not go to a hero's tomb.

To have a fixed ritual form imposed is, like the using of a beautiful, difficult rhythm—an impediment to the weak, a great and golden opportunity to the strong.   But a ritual form, however solemn and significant, does not, and did not make great drama.   We see that clearly enough in the folk-plays, that, as they were before the drama, so have long out-lasted it.   With extraordinary tenacity the old form maintains itself as in the Carnival plays observed by Mr Dawkins[3] in Thrace and by Mr Wace[4] in Thessaly and Macedonia.   They are nothing but the life-history of a fertility-*daimon*; the story is more complete than in the Oschophoria; it takes the *daimon* from the cradle to the grave and back again, to life and marriage.   Mr Wace from many scattered and fragmentary festivals constructs the full original somewhat as follows:

An old woman first appears nursing her baby in her arms, and this child is in some way or other peculiar.   He grows up quickly and demands a bride. A bride is found for him, and the wedding is celebrated, but during the wedding festivities he quarrels with one of his companions, who attempts to molest the bride, and is killed.   He is then lamented by his bride, and miraculously restored to life.   The interrupted festivities are resumed, and the marriage is consummated.

[1] *Supra*, p. 318.

[2] Such simplified δρώμενα are the Thesmophoria, where we hear of no *agon*, the Charila at Delphi (*infra*, p. 416), the summoning of Dionysos by trumpets from the abyss at Lerna.   Sometimes the *agon* is apparently the chief element in the rite as at the Lithobolia at Eleusis.   Sometimes it is softened to a mere λοιδορία, as in the Stenia.

[3] R. M. Dawkins, *The Modern Carnival in Thrace and the Cult of Dionysos*, J. H. S. xxvi. 1906, p. 191.   Mr Dawkins' attention was drawn to this festival by Mr G. M. Vizyenos, a native of Viza (the ancient Βιζύη), which is about two hours west of Haghios Gheorghios, where the festival is now celebrated.   Mr Vizyenos had seen the festival as a boy some forty years before it was observed by Mr Dawkins.

[4] In a paper to be published in the forthcoming *Annual* of the British School, of which Mr Wace has very kindly allowed me to see a proof.

To attempt a close parallel with the ancient cult of Dionysos is, I think, scarcely worth while, though analogies like the baby in arms or in the cradle to Liknites are obvious. We are dealing with material that long preceded and long outlasts the worship of any Olympian, the *disjecta membra* of the life-history of a year-god or fertility-*daimon*. He is a babe; he has, probably at his initiation, a death and resurrection; he is married. The cycle of his life is eternally monotonous, perennially magical.

The monotony of these folk-plays is almost intolerable, and if we were asked to see in them the germ of all the life and splendour and variety of Attic drama we might rightly rebel; but we are not. What the δρώμενα of the *Eniautos-daimon* gave to Attic drama was, not its content, but its ritual form, a form which may be *informed* by beauty or by ugliness, according as it is used by an imagination clean or coarse.

That the form is really the life-history of a fertility-*daimon*, and its intent, like the ritual of the *daimon*, strictly magical is shown beyond doubt by the concluding words of the Thracian ceremony:

Barley three piastres the bushel. Amen, O God, that the poor may eat! Yea, O God, that poor folk may be filled.

That the *daimon* impersonated is the *Eniautos-daimon* is no less clear. At one point in the concluding ceremonies Mr Dawkins tells us:

All the implements used were thrown high into the air with cries 'Καὶ τοῦ χρόνου,' 'Next year also.'

It would be tedious and unprofitable for our argument to multiply instances of these folk-plays which last on in the remoter corners of Europe to-day[1]. They are tenacious of life because they are still held to be magical—the playing of them brings

---

[1] They have been collected and discussed by Mr E. K. Chambers in his invaluable book *The Mediaeval Stage*, 1903, vol. i. Book ii. Folk Drama. Everywhere, he points out, we have the contest, our *agon*, which in the eighth century crystallized into the *Conflictus Veris et Hiemis*, and the death and resurrection mime from which, in the form of the Easter trope *Quem Quaeritis*, mediaeval drama sprang. The subject has been so fully and admirably treated by Mr Chambers that I will only note here that we could have no simpler or more significant instance of a death and resurrection δρώμενον than the *Quem Quaeritis* with its *mythos* in dialogue:
  Quem quaeritis in sepulchro, [o] Christicolae?
  Iesum Nazarenum crucifixum, o caelicolae.
  Non est hic, surrexit sicut praedixerat.
  Ite, nuntiate, quia surrexit de sepulchro.
The function of the ἄγγελος is here specially clear. The *agon* is absent.

luck to the village for the season, and they are popular because they invariably end with a *quête*. They are intolerant of development because of their periodic nature, and fixed factors—the fight, the death, the resurrection, on which this 'luck' inherently and essentially depends.

The *mythos*, the plot which is the life-history of an Eniautos-daimon, whether performed in winter, spring, summer or autumn, is thus doomed by its monotony to sterility. What is wanted is material cast in less rigid mould; in a word λεγόμενα not bound by δρώμενα, plots that have cut themselves loose from rites. The dithyramb, which was but the periodic festival of the spring *renouveau*, broke and blossomed so swiftly into the Attic drama because it found such plots to hand; in a word—*the forms of Attic drama are the forms of the life-history of an Eniautos-daimon; the content is the infinite variety of free and individualized heroic saga—in the largest sense of the word 'Homer'*.[1]

THE HOMERIC SAGA.

We are perhaps tired of being told that Æschylus[2] said his tragedies were 'slices from the great banquets of Homer,' and we feel the ugly metaphor is worthier of the learned and ingenious *Diners* who record it than of the poet on whom it is fathered. Yet the metaphor is instructive. The plots of Attic drama are things cut off (τεμάχη). They are *mythoi* that have worked themselves loose from the cults of which they were once the spoken utterance[3], and are thereby material to be freely moulded at the artist's will.

[1] Following Dieterich rather than Prof. Ridgeway, I had long vaguely held that the *threnos* and *peripeteia* of Greek tragedy arose from mysteries based on the death and resurrection of the year rather than from the tomb-ritual of any mere historical hero. But I date my definite enquiry into the daimonic origin of these forms from a lecture *On the Form and Technique of Greek Tragedy* delivered by Prof. Murray at Oxford in the Easter term of 1910. For detailed and to me conclusive evidence I am now able to refer to the Excursus which Prof. Murray has with great kindness appended to this chapter and which embodies the result of his independent investigations. By the kindness of Dr M. P. Nilsson I have just received a pre-print of his valuable monograph, *Der Ursprung der Tragödie*, which appears in Ilberg's Neue Jahrbücher für das klassische Altertumsgeschichte und deutsche Literatur, xxvii. 9, p. 609.

[2] Athen. viii. 39. 347 οὐδ' ἐπὶ νοῦν βαλλόμενος τὰ τοῦ καλοῦ καὶ λαμπροῦ Αἰσχύλου, ὃς τὰς αὑτοῦ τραγῳδίας τεμάχη εἶναι ἔλεγε τῶν Ὁμήρου μεγάλων δείπνων.

[3] I am aware of course that these 'tied' *mythoi*, even while they were tied, attached to themselves a certain amount of floating historical legend. This has been very well shown by Mr Chambers (*op. cit.*) in his account of the various local elements of folk story attracted by the Mummers' play, vol. i. p. 211.

It may have surprised some readers that in our long discussion of 'heroes' there has been no mention of Homer, who sings heroic deeds. The reason is clear. If my contention be right that the cult of the collective daimon, the king and the fertility-spirit is primary, Homer's conception of the hero as the gallant individual, the soldier of fortune or the gentleman of property, is secondary and late. It has again and again been observed that in Homer we have no magic and no cult of the dead. Our examination of the Anthesteria has shown us that, for Greece as for Central Australia, the two were indissolubly connected. Homer marks a stage when collective thinking[1] and magical ritual are, if not dead, at least dying, when rationalism and the individualistic thinking to which it belongs are developed to a point not far behind that of the days of Perikles. Homer's attitude towards religion is sceptical, Ionian[2].

What is meant by the 'individualism' of Homer is seen very clearly in the case of the *androktasiai* or 'man-slayings.' Dr Bethe[3] has shown beyond the possibility of a doubt that the somewhat superabundant *androktasiai* which appear as single combats in the *Iliad* really reflect not the fights of individual heroes at Troy, but the conflicts of tribes on the mainland of Greece. When the tribes who waged this warfare on the mainland pass in the long series of Migrations to Asia Minor and the islands, the local sanctities from which they are cut loose are forgotten, and local daimones, eponymous heroes and the like become individualized Saga-heroes. Achilles and Alexandros are tribal heroes, that is collective conceptions, of conflicting tribes in Thessaly. Hector before, not after, he went to Troy was a hero-daimon in Boeotian Thebes; his comrade Melanippos had a cult in Thebes, Patroklos whom he slew was his near neighbour, like him a local daimon. It is the life-stories of heroes such as these, cut loose by the Migrations from their local cults, freed from their monotonous periodicity, that are the material of Attic drama, that form its free and plastic plots.

[1] The connection of collective thinking with magic and of individualism with the Olympian system will be discussed in the next chapter.

[2] For this whole subject and the contrast of Homer's attitude with that of Æschylus see Prof. Murray, *Rise of the Greek Epic*, Ionia and Attica.

[3] *Homer und die Heldensage. Die Sage vom Troischen Kriege*, in Sitzungsberichte d. k. Pr. Ak. d. Wissenschaften, phil.-hist. Kl., 1902. English readers will find the ἀνδροκτάσιαι fully discussed on the basis of Dr Bethe's researches in Prof. Murray's *Rise of the Greek Epic*, p. 195. Prof. Murray accepts Dr Bethe's conclusions and adds much to their significance.

The enquiry of the date of this influx of heroic saga belongs to the Homeric Question and is beyond alike my scope and my competence. When and how the old forms of the daimon-drama were replenished by the newly imported Ionic epos can only be conjectured. If conjecture be permissible I should imagine that the Pot-Contests (χύτρινοι ἀγῶνες) of the Anthesteria were, from time immemorial, of the old daimon type. When Peisistratos ordained the recitation of "Homer" at the Panathenaea, the influence of the epos on the rude dramatic art of the time must have been immediately felt, and it only needed the birth of an Æschylus to make him seize on the τεμάχη that lay so close to hand. He or his predecessors took of necessity the prescribed form, the life-history of the daimon, and filled it with a new content, the story of a daimon de-daimonized; an Agamemnon who though he was a tribal daimon at home was an individual hero before the walls of Troy.

The local daimons of Thessaly and Boeotia and the Peloponnese were *de*-daimonized by the Migrations; that is easily understood. But once the fashion set, once the rationalizing story-telling tendency started, once the interest in the local daimon and his magical efficacy diminished, and even those stationary daimons whose tribes never migrated, became de-daimonized, individualized. Hippolytos, son of Theseus, is a clear and very instructive case. He has a local cult at Trozen, later by some shift of population taken in at Athens, but to the drama he is wholly human, the hero of a widespread folk-tale. Yet even drama cannot wholly forget the daimon-functionary, and Euripides[1], by the mouth of Artemis, tells us the manner of his cult.

> Yea and to thee, for this sore travail's sake,
> Honours most high in Trozen will I make,
> *For yokeless maids before their bridal night*
> *Shall shear for thee their tresses.*

Pausanias[2] confirms Euripides; he tells us that at Trozen

A precinct of great renown is consecrated to Hippolytos son of Theseus; it contains a temple and an ancient image....There is a priest of Hippolytos

---

[1] *Hipp.* 1424:

τιμὰς μεγίστας ἐν πόλει Τροζηνίᾳ
δώσω· κόραι γὰρ ἄζυγες γάμων πάρος
κόμας κεροῦνταί σοι, δι' αἰῶνος μακροῦ
πένθη μέγιστα δακρύων καρπουμένῳ.

[2] I. 32. 1, Frazer.

at Trozen who holds office for life, and there are annual sacrifices. Further, they observe the following custom. Every maiden before marriage shears a lock of her hair for Hippolytos, and takes the shorn lock and dedicates it in the temple.

Hippolytos is indeed, in a sense that has hitherto escaped us, the *Megistos Kouros*, 'He of the Shorn-Hair[1]'—the *daimon* of initiation ceremonies, of the *rite de passage* from virginity to virility. The plot, the *mythos* of the *Hippolytos* utters things older and deeper than any ugly tale, however ancient, of Potiphar's wife.

In the relief[2] in Fig. 95 we have a monument of Hippolytos.

Fig. 95.

He is figured as a young hero with a horse, a knight like the daimones of the Hero-Feasts. His dog is with him to mark him as a human huntsman. But the hero-daimon is not forgotten.

---

[1] With his accustomed generosity Mr Cook allows me to cite in advance his view that κόρος κόρη are from the same root as κείρω. This had of course been guessed by the ancients, see *Et. Mag.* κουρά· ἀπὸ τοῦ κείρω κέκαρμαι κορὰ καὶ κουρά, and for modern supporters of the view see Collitz-Bechtel, *Gr. Dial. Inschr.* I. 143, No. 373 ται κόρφαι, and F. Solmsen in the *Zeitschrift f. vergleich. Sprachforschung*, 1888, xxix. 128 f. This derivation I had known and from cowardice rejected. It strongly supports, as Mr Cook kindly points out, my contention that the Kouretes were the young initiates of the tribe. On the third day of the Apatouria, called κουρεῶτις, the κοῦροι had their hair cut and were enrolled in the phratries. Full references will be found in Mr Cook's forthcoming book in section 1 of chapter I. in connection with the 'hair festival' of the Komyria. I venture to apply Mr Cook's argument in the case of Hippolytos as *Megistos Kouros* of Trozen. For Herakles and his connection with hair-cutting see *infra*, p. 379.

[2] Found at Aricia but of Attic workmanship, now in the Torlonia Museum. See Blenkenberg, *Et Attisk Votiv-relief*, Festskrift til J. L. Ussing, 1900.

Just in front of the horse is a low altar, an *eschara*, the kind in use for 'heroes'; a worshipper approaches. Moreover the figures in the background show clearly to what company Hippolytos belongs. Asklepios who, as we shall see in the next chapter, was but a daimon half crystallized into a god, Aphrodite Pandemos to the left, and between them the temple of Themis[1].

In the case of Hippolytos we know precisely where was his local cult, and from his ritual we can partly see how the tragedy of Euripides arose from his annual *muthos*. More often the con-

Fig. 96.

nection escapes us. We have the record of a local cult and we have the finished dramatic figure but the links are lost. The relief in Fig. 96 presents us with the two factors baldly and blankly juxtaposed without attempt at reconciliation. To the left we have a warrior like Hippolytos leading a horse, to the right the daimon-snake. The artist himself was probably at a loss to establish a connection; anyhow he does not attempt it. The horseman takes no notice of the snake; the snake, serenely

[1] For these local divinities of the south slope of the Acropolis see *Prolegomena*, p. 354.

coiled, is indifferent to the horseman. They are of two alien worlds.

If with this relief to help us we bear in mind these two factors, the old daimonic, magical ritual which lent the *forms*, the new 'Homeric' saga which lent the heroic *content*, the relation of the drama to the worship of Dionysos and also to the worship of the dead becomes, I think, fairly clear. The plays were performed in the theatre of Dionysos, in the precinct of the god, his image was present in the theatre, the chorus danced round his altar, his priest sat in the front and central seat among the spectators. In the face of facts so plain it seems to me impossible that the drama had its roots elsewhere than in the worship of Dionysos[1]. Aristotle is right, 'tragedy arose from leaders of the Dithyramb[2].' Of any connection with the tomb and obsequies of an actual dead Athenian hero there is not a particle of evidence. But, Dionysos is a daimon, he is *the* daimon, of death and resurrection, of re-incarnation, of the *renouveau* of the spring, and that *renouveau*, that reincarnation, was of man as well as nature. In the Anthesteria, the Blossoming of Plants and the Revocation of Ghosts are one and the same, but they are universal, of ancestors, not of one particular dead ancestor.

We left the problem of one scene (Fig. 31) on the Hagia Triada sarcophagos unsolved and the solution now comes of itself. The figure standing in front of the building is not, I think, a god, not Dionysos Dendrites, nor is he a man, a particular dead individual who is having a funeral at the moment. Rather he is a daimon-hero, and the building before which he stands is a heroon, like the heroon of the Agathos Daimon at Thebes. He may be a dead king, if so he is worshipped as a functionary, a fertility-daimon not as an individual; he is like Cecrops, like Erichthonios. He is certainly I think a *kouros* like in youth and

---

[1] For a full statement of this, Prof. Ridgeway's view, see his *Origin of Tragedy*, 1910.

[2] *Supra*, p. 32. The difficult question of *when* and *how* the incoming Thracian *daimon* Dionysos came to dominate the local Agathos Daimon I leave here un-answered. I have elsewhere (*Proleg.* pp. 557 and 571) suggested that Dionysos may have come to Athens by way of Delphi and Eleusis. For the possible influence of the Mysteries on drama see A. Dieterich's 'epoch-making' *Die Entstehung der Tragödie* in Archiv f. Religionswissenschaft, 1908, p. 164.

strength to the *kouroi* who approach him with offerings, only stiff
and somewhat xoanon-like as becomes one who is a daimon not
a man. Over his forehead hangs a long single curl which may
well characterize him as ephebos[1]. Near him is his holy tree, sign
and symbol of the life and function of an Agathos Daimon. To
him, as Eniautos-daimon, are brought offerings of young bulls
and a new-moon boat, not a service of *do ut des*, not as gifts to
persuade, but rather magically to *induce*[2] him: and, in his honour
with like intent, is played out the *renouveau* of bird and tree,
the mimic drama of the Dithyramb.

We have watched the making of a daimon-hero out of vaguer
sanctities; in the next chapter we shall see the daimon-hero
crystallize, individualize into a god.

[1] See *supra*, p. 337, note 1.

[2] Even, perhaps, magically to bring him to life. The figure of the Kouros, as
noted above, has a stiff, half-lifeless look. We may compare the figure of Pandora
the Earth-Goddess as she appears on the Bayle cylix in the British Museum (see
my *Myth. and Mons. of Anc. Athens*, p. 450, Fig. 50). The 'Birth' and 'Making'
of Pandora are but mythological presentations of the *renouveau* of earth in the
spring. For the analogous Anodos vases see *infra*, p. 418.

Note to p. 260. For the whole subject of the cult of heroes see *Le culte des Héros
et ses conditions sociales*, with a preface by M. H. Hubert in the *Travaux de l'année
sociologique*. See also for the blend of ritual agon and epic recitation A. Berriedale
Keith, *The Sanskrit Drama in its Origin, Development, Theory and Practice*, 1924.
Also for the relation between Attic tragedy and puberty initiations see Egill Rostrup,
Attic Tragedy in the Light of Theatrical History, 1923. And for the psychological
aspect of the question see A. Winterstein, *Zur Entstehungsgeschichte der griechischen
Tragödie* published as *Separatabdruck aus Imago*, 1922, Heft 4.—The blend of the
cults of the various Eniautos-daimons with those of local heroes and their contribution to the 'dances' of Dionysos is convincingly set forth by Dr Leaf in his analysis
of Herodotus, v. 67; see his *Homer and History*, pp. 265—275.

EXCURSUS ON THE RITUAL FORMS PRESERVED IN GREEK TRAGEDY.

THE following note presupposes certain general views about the origin and essential nature of Greek Tragedy. It assumes that Tragedy is in origin a Ritual Dance, a *Sacer Ludus*, representing normally the Aition, or supposed historical Cause, of some current ritual practice: e.g. the *Hippolytus* represents the legendary death of that hero, regarded as the Aition of a certain ritual lamentation practised by the maidens of Trozên. Further, it assumes, in accord with the overwhelming weight of ancient tradition, that the Dance in question is originally or centrally that of Dionysus, performed at his feast, in his theatre, under the presidency of his Priest, and by performers who were called Διονύσου τεχνῖται. It regards Dionysus in this connection as an 'Eniautos-Daimon,' or vegetation god, like Adonis, Osiris, etc., who represents the cyclic death and rebirth of the Earth and the World, i.e., for practical purposes, of the tribe's own lands and the tribe itself. It seems clear, further, that Comedy and Tragedy represent different stages in the life of this Year Spirit; Comedy leads to his Marriage Feast, his κῶμος and γάμος, Tragedy to his death and θρῆνος. See Mr Cornford's *Origin of Attic Comedy*[1].

These conceptions, it will be seen, are in general agreement with the recent work of Dieterich (*Archiv für Religionswissenschaft*, XI. pp. 163—196), also with that of Usener (*ib.* VII. pp. 303—313), as developed by Dr Farnell (*Cults*, vol. v. p. 235, note A), and the indications of the Macedonian mummeries described by Mr Dawkins and others. I must also acknowledge a large debt to Prof. Ridgeway's Tomb-theory, the more so since I ultimately differ from him on the main question, and seek to show that certain features in tragedy which he regards as markedly foreign to Dionysus-worship are in reality natural expressions of it.

It is of course clear that Tragedy, as we possess it, contains many non-Dionysiac elements. The ancients themselves have warned us of that. It has been influenced by the epic, by hero cults, and

---

[1] It is worth remarking that the Year-Daimon has equally left his mark on the New Comedy. The somewhat tiresome foundling of unknown parentage who grows up, is recognized, and inherits, in almost every play of Menander that is known to us, is clearly descended from the foundling of Euripidean tragedy who turns out to be the son of a god and inherits a kingdom. And that foundling in turn is derived from the Year-Baby who grows up in such miraculous fashion in the Mummers' Play. These babies are always bastards and always divine; also they are generally twins. One need only recall the babies of the *Ichneutae*, the *Ion*, the *Augê*, the *Alopê*, the *Oedipus* (esp. *O. T.* 1086—1109); the twins of Antiopê and Melanippê, of Alcmena, and Leda, and Leto, and Iphimedeia and Rhea Silvia. In Menander the foundlings are prevailingly twins.

by various ceremonies not connected with Dionysus. Indeed the actual Aition treated in tragedy is seldom confessedly and obviously Dionysiac. It is so sometimes, as sometimes it is the founding of a torch-race or the original reception of suppliants at some altar of sanctuary. But it is much more often the death or *Pathos* of some hero. Indeed I think it can be shown that every extant tragedy contains somewhere towards the end the celebration of a tabu tomb. This point we must gladly concede to Professor Ridgeway. I wish to suggest, however, that while the content has strayed far from Dionysus, the forms of tragedy retain clear traces of the original drama of the Death and Rebirth of the Year Spirit.

Dieterich has already shown that a characteristic of the Sacer Ludus in the mysteries was a Peripeteia, or Reversal. It was a change from sorrow to joy, from darkness and sights of inexplicable terror to light and the discovery of the reborn God. Such a Peripeteia is clearly associated with an Anagnorisis, a Recognition or Discovery. Such formulae from the mysteries as Θαρσεῖτε, Μύσται, τοῦ θεοῦ σεσωσμένου—Ηὑρήκαμεν, συγχαίρομεν—Ἔφυγον κακόν, ηὗρον ἄμεινον, imply a close connection between the Peripeteia and the Anagnorisis, and enable us to understand why these two elements are regarded by Aristotle as normally belonging to Tragedy. Now Peripeteia of some kind is perhaps in itself a necessary or normal part of any dramatic story. But no one could say the same of Anagnorisis. It must come into Greek tragedy from the Sacer Ludus, in which the dead God is Recognized or Discovered.

So far Dieterich. But we may go much further than this. We have the actual testimony of Herodotus.

A well-known passage in Hdt. 5, 67 tells how at Sicyon they used to honour 'Adrastus' instead of Dionysus, celebrating his πάθεα with tragic choruses. Ordinary people, therefore, in their tragic choruses, may be supposed to have celebrated the πάθεα of Dionysus.

Now it is strange that, while we have such masses of material about Dionysus-worship, we are never explicitly told what these πάθεα were. We are faced therefore with two questions: (1) Why is the 'fate' of Dionysus so hidden? (2) What was it? The answer to both is the second book of Herodotus.

(1) The 'fate' of Dionysus was ἄρρητον and was kept unspoken through εὐφημία. Herodotus is explicit. In speaking of the mourning for Osiris which took place at the Feast of Isis he says: τὸν δὲ τύπτονται (= mourn) οὔ μοι ὅσιόν ἐστι λέγειν 2, 61.

2, 132 ἐπεὰν δὲ τύπτωνται τὸν οὐκ οὐνομαζόμενον ὑπ' ἐμεῦ θεὸν ἐπὶ τοιούτωι πρήγματι...

2, 170 ταφαὶ τοῦ οὐκ ὅσιον ποιοῦμαι ἐπὶ τοιούτωι πρήγματι ἐξαγορεύειν τοὔνομα. In 2, 86 there is similar language about the mummy of this god whose name must not be mentioned in connection with death. The god in question was of course Osiris. Now apparently it was not forbidden in Egypt to mention Osiris' death; but to Herodotus Osiris is Dionysus, and if he treats the death of Osiris as ἄρρητον that must be because the death of Dionysus was so.

Cf. 2, 144 Ὄσιρις δέ ἐστι Διόνυσος κατ᾽ Ἑλλάδα γλῶσσαν.

2, 42 Ὀσίριος, τὸν δὴ Διόνυσον εἶναι λέγουσιν (where observe the apologetic τὸν δή, 'whom of course'). In other passages Herodotus simply uses the name 'Dionysus' for 'Osiris.'

We need not therefore be surprised that we have no direct statement about the fate of Dionysus, or even that no tragedy ever depicts that fate. It was ἄρρητον.

But (2) can we tell what it must have been? Can we, for example, argue that the πάθος of Dionysus was the same in kind as that of Osiris? Yes. Herodotus again is explicit. He says of the Osiris Feast in the month Athyr τὴν δὲ ἄλλην ὁρτὴν ἀνάγουσι τῶι Διονύσωι, πλὴν χορῶν, κατὰ ταὐτὰ σχεδὸν πάντα Ἕλλησι 2, 48. The Egyptians did not have τραγικοὶ χοροί, 'but in almost all other respects the ritual was identical.' At any rate the gist of the δρώμενον was the same. Thus we may conclude that the fate of Dionysus, in Herodotus' time as well as later, was a *Sparagmos*: doubtless he had, like the other Year-Daemons, a special enemy; was torn in pieces, scattered over the fields, lost, sought for, discovered and recognized, just as Osiris was. This forms the normal pattern for the fate of the Year-Daimon; the other representatives of that being go through similar experiences, but Dionysus, the most typical of them, has the most typical and complete cycle of πάθεα. Cf. Frazer, *Attis Adonis Osiris* pp. 244 ff.; esp. 267 on the *Sparagmos*.

If we examine the kind of myth which seems to underlie the various 'Eniautos' celebrations we shall find:

1. An *Agon* or Contest, the Year against its enemy, Light against Darkness, Summer against Winter.

2. A *Pathos* of the Year-Daimon, generally a ritual or sacrificial death, in which Adonis or Attis is slain by the tabu animal, the Pharmakos stoned, Osiris, Dionysus, Pentheus, Orpheus, Hippolytus torn to pieces (σπαραγμός).

3. A *Messenger*. For this Pathos seems seldom or never to be actually performed under the eyes of the audience. (The reason of this is not hard to suggest, and was actually necessary in the time when there was only one actor.) It is announced by a messenger. 'The news comes' that Pan the Great, Thammuz, Adonis, Osiris is dead, and the dead body is often brought in on a bier. This leads to

4. A *Threnos* or Lamentation. Specially characteristic, however, is a clash of contrary emotions, the death of the old being also the triumph of the new: see p. 318 f., on Plutarch's account of the Oschophoria.

5 and 6. An *Anagnorisis*—discovery or recognition—of the

slain and mutilated Daimon, followed by his Resurrection or Apotheosis or, in some sense, his Epiphany in glory. This I shall call by the general name *Theophany*. It naturally goes with a *Peripeteia* or extreme change of feeling from grief to joy.

Observe the sequence in which these should normally occur: *Agon, Pathos, Messenger, Threnos, Theophany*, or, we might say, *Anagnorisis* and *Theophany*.

First, however, there **is a** difficulty to clear away. Peripeteiai are of course common in tragedy: both from joy to grief, as in *O.T.* 920 ff., where the Corinthian Stranger seems to come as a blessed answer to prayer but really brings calamity, or the similar scene in Soph. *El.* 665; and from grief to joy, as in various Recognition scenes, such as Soph. *El.* 1210 ff., *I.T.* 770—850. But in the ritual there seems to have been a special final Peripeteia, from grief to joy, in connection with the Anagnorisis and Theophany. Now our tragedies normally, or at least commonly, end with a comforting Theophany but not with an outburst of joy.—No, but it looks as if they once did. We know that they were in early times composed in tetralogies consisting of three tragedies and a Satyr-play.

This is no place to discuss the Satyr-play at length. But those who have read Miss Harrison's article on the Kouretes (*B.S.A.* xv. and Chapter I. above) will recognize that the Satyrs are the πρόπολοι δαίμονες in the rout of Dionysus, especially associated with his 'initiations and *hierourgiai*'—that is, exactly with our Sacer Ludus of Dionysus. Strabo, pp. 466—8, makes this pretty clear. Hence comes their connection with the dead and with the anodos of Korê. The subject could easily be illustrated at length, but probably the above point, as it stands, will hardly be disputed. The Satyr-play, coming at the end of the tetralogy, represented the joyous arrival of the Reliving Dionysus and his rout of attendant daimones at the end of the Sacer Ludus.

It has however been argued, and by so high an authority as Mr Pickard-Cambridge[1], that the Satyr-play though very early associated with tragedy was not so in its first origin. He points out that no Satyr-plays are attributed to Thespis, that it is difficult to make out tetralogies for any writer before Aeschylus, and that it was Pratinas who πρῶτος ἔγραψε Σατύρους (Suidas). I take this to mean that Pratinas was the first person to *write words* for the rout of revelling masquers to learn by heart. Thespis, like many early Elizabethans, had been content with a general direction: 'Enter Satyrs, in revel, saying anything.' I do not, however, wish to combat this view. It would suit my general purpose equally

[1] In a public lecture at Oxford in 1910. It may be worth mentioning that the new fragments of Sophocles' *Ichneutae* (Oxyrhynchus Papyri, vol. ix.) are markedly tragic in metre and diction.

well to suppose that the Dionysus-ritual had developed into two divergent forms, the Satyr-play of Pratinas and the tragedy of Thespis, which were at a certain date artificially combined by a law. In any case there must have been close kindred between the two. The few titles of tragedies by Thespis which are preserved by tradition are unfortunately not well attested: but even if they are all forgeries by Heraclides Ponticus it is perhaps significant that he thought such names plausible. They are Ἱερεῖς, Ἤιθεοι, Πενθεύς, Φόρβας ἢ Ἆθλα ἐπὶ Πελίᾳ. All bear the mark of the initiation *drômenon* or Sacer Ludus. *The Priests*; *The Youths*, or Kouroi; *Pentheus*, the torn Dionysus; *Phorbas*, the battling King who slew or was slain—to a reader of the present volume these tell their own tale. And after all Aristotle has told us that Tragedy ἐκ τοῦ Σατυρικοῦ μετέβαλεν (*Poet.* 4). It 'developed out of the Satyric' —at the very least, from something akin to the Satyrs. I therefore continue—provisionally—to accept as a starting-point some tragic performance ending in a Satyr-play.

Now we know that in the historical development of Tragedy a process of differentiation occurred. The Satyr-play became more distinct and separate from the tragedies and was eventually dropped altogether; and, secondly, the separate Tragedies became independent artistic wholes.

This process produced, I conceive, two results. First, the cutting-off of the Satyr-play left the tragic trilogy without its proper close. What was it to do? Should it end with a threnos and trust for its theophany to the distinct and irrelevant Satyr-play which happened to follow? or should it ignore the Satyr-play and make a theophany of its own? Both types of tragedy occur, but gradually the second tends to predominate.

Secondly, what is to happen to the Anagnorisis and Peripeteia? Their proper place is, as it were, transitional from the Threnos of tragedy to the Theophany of the Satyr-play; if anything, they go rather with the Satyrs. Hence these two elements are set loose. Quite often, even in the tragedies which have a full Theophany, they do not occur in their proper place just before the Theophany, yet they always continue to haunt the atmosphere. The poets find it hard to write without bringing in an Anagnorisis somewhere.

Before tracing the Forms in detail, let us take some clear and typical instances of the sequence of all the five elements together, Agon, Pathos, Messenger, Threnos, Theophany. I take three plays which, though not early, are very strict in structure, and I begin with the *Bacchae*. For, if there is any truth in this theory at all, our one confessedly Dionysiac play ought to afford the most crucial test of it.

The latter half of the *Bacchae* divides itself thus:

787—976. A long Agon, divided by a Choric dance, 862—911. Dionysus pleads with Pentheus in vain, then at 819 begins to exert the Bacchic influence upon him till Pentheus follows him into the house, already half-conquered: after the Chorus, the two come out, the Contest already decided and Pentheus in his conqueror's power; they go out to the mountain.

Chorus, then 1024—1152 Pathos, Σπαραγμός of Pentheus, narrated by a Messenger and received with violent clash of emotion.

1153—1329. Elaborate Threnos, which consists first of a mad dance of triumph ἀντὶ θρήνου, then of a long Threnos proper, and contains in the midst of it—exactly in the proper place—the collection of the fragments of Pentheus' body and the Anagnorisis of him by Agave.

1330, or rather in the gap before 1330. Epiphany of Dionysus.

Now, when we remember that Pentheus is only another form of Dionysus himself—like Zagreus, Orpheus, Osiris and the other daimons who are torn in pieces and put together again—we can see that the *Bacchae* is simply the old Sacer Ludus itself, scarcely changed at all, except for the doubling of the hero into himself and his enemy. We have the whole sequence: Agon, Pathos and Messenger, Threnos, Anagnorisis and Peripeteia, and Epiphany. The daimon is fought against, torn to pieces, announced as dead, wept for, collected and recognized, and revealed in his new divine life. The *Bacchae* is a most instructive instance of the formation of drama out of ritual. It shows us how slight a step was necessary for Thespis or another to turn the Year-Ritual into real drama.

Hippolytus.

902—1101. Clear and fierce Agon between Theseus and Hippolytus.

Short Chorus, Threnos-like.

1153—1267. Σπαραγμός of the Hero by his own horses: Pathos, narrated by a Messenger.

Short Chorus, hymn to Cypris ἀντὶ θρήνου.

1283—end. Epiphany of Artemis, curiously mixed with the Threnos, and bringing with it the Anagnorisis (1296—1341).

We are just one step further from the original ritual. For who was Hippolytus? He was, ritually, just another form of the same Year-Daimon, who is torn to pieces and born again. When we remember the resurrection of Hippolytus in legend, we shall suspect that in an earlier form of the Hippolytus-*drômenon* there may have been a resurrection or apotheosis of the hero himself together with his protectress Artemis. Drama has gained ground upon ritual. Hippolytus has been made a mortal man. And we now have a Theophany with Artemis immortal in the air and Hippolytus dying on the earth.

Andromache.

547—765. Agon between Peleus and Menelaus.

An interrupting scene containing the appearance of Orestes and flight of Hermione; Chorus.

1070—1165. Pathos—stoning—narrated by Messenger.

1166—1225. Threnos.

1226. Theophany of Thetis, bringing comfort.

The Theophanies of Euripides almost always bring comfort, and thus conserve an element of the old Peripeteia from grief to joy. The sequence in the *Andromache* is very clear, but has one interrupting scene. This interrupting scene will find its explanation later. For the present we merely notice that it is concerned with Orestes and that it falls naturally into the following divisions: 802—819, Nurse as Exangelos or Messenger from within; 825—865, Threnos of Hermione; 879—1008, Appearance of Orestes, who saves and comforts Hermione, and expounds the death of Neoptolemus, which is the Aition of the play. See below p. 356.

The above cases are merely illustrations of the way in which the Dionysus ritual has adapted itself to the reception of heroic myths. The chief modification is that other persons and events are put into the forms which originally belonged to the Daimon. In the *Bacchae* it is Pentheus who is torn, but Dionysus who appears as god. In the *Hippolytus* it is not Hippolytus who appears as god but Artemis, his patroness. In the *Andromache* the persons are all varied: it is Peleus and Menelaus who have the contest; it is Neoptolemus who is slain and mourned; it is Thetis who appears as divine. This substitution of persons undoubtedly occurs and is certainly very curious. I suspect that it comes from the fact, noticed above, that the real death of Dionysus himself was ἄρρητον and though it had to be somehow shown in the *Sacer Ludus* it could only be shown δι' αἰνιγμῶν. It may well be, for instance, that when Drama became public entertainment rather than religious celebration, objection was felt to an actual public mention or representation of the God's death.

We will now consider the various Forms, and see how far they are constant or usual, and what modifications they undergo. And first for the most crucial of them, the Theophany. This subject has been excellently treated by Eric Müller, *De Deorum Graecorum Partibus Tragicis*, Giessen, 1910.

THEOPHANY.

We all know that most of the extant plays of Euripides end with the appearance of a god (*Hipp., Andr., Suppl., Ion, El., I. T., Hel., Or., Bac., I. A., Rhes.*). But it has not been observed that in this, as in so many of his supposed novelties, Euripides is following the tradition of Aeschylus. The reason of this is, first, that the technique of Aeschylus is not so clear-cut and formal as that of Euripides. His gods do not so definitely proclaim themselves as such, and probably did not appear from quite so effective a *μηχανή*. Second, and more important, Aeschylus was still operating with trilogies, not with single plays, so that his Theophanies are normally saved up to the end of the trilogy and then occur on a grand scale.

To take the extant plays first:

The Oresteia has no gods till the *Eumenides* (unless we count a vision of the Furies at the end of the *Choephoroi*), but then we have a great Theophany of Apollo, Athena and the Furies in procession together.

The Supplices trilogy, *Supplices, Aegyptii, Danaides*: we know that this ended with an epiphany of Aphrodite, whose speech, founding the institution of marriage based on consent, is preserved (Nauck, fr. 44). This is evidently a full-dress Theophany in the style afterwards followed by Euripides, in which the god solemnly founds an institution and gives the Aition of the performance.

The Persae trilogy consisted of the *Phineus, Persae, Glaucus (Pontius?)*, that is, it seems not to have been a continuous treatment of one subject leading up to one final Epiphany, like the Oresteia and the Danaid-trilogy. It falls apart into separate plays, and each play will be found to have in it some divine or supernatural apparition.

Persae: the Hero or, as he is called, the God (*θεός* 644, etc., *δαίμων* 642) Darius is evoked from his sacred tomb.

Phineus: the end, or at any rate the *dénouement*, of the play consisted in the chasing away of the Harpies by the Sons of the North-wind—that is, in a great apparition of winged supernatural shapes.

Glaucus Pontius: it contained, probably at the end, a prophecy spoken by Glaucus; and in it Glaucus, half-man, half-beast, appeared rising from the sea. (N. 26.) This seems like a regular Theophany with a prophecy. (If the third play was the other *Glaucus*, called *Potnieus*, then we have no evidence.)

Prometheia Trilogy. This stands somewhat apart for two reasons. First, its Aition is not any Year-ritual or Tomb-ritual but definitely the institution of the Torch-race at the Prometheia. Secondly, all the characters are divine, so that there can hardly be question of an epiphany in the ordinary sense. The reconstruction of the trilogy is still doubtful, but it seems unlikely that the ultimate reconciliation of Prometheus and Zeus can have been dramatically carried out without some appearance of Zeus in his glory.

Theban Trilogy. *Laius, Oedipus, Septem.* Here we possess the third play and it ends not in a Theophany but in a Threnos[1]. That is, it belongs to the first type mentioned on p. 345 above. The Satyr-play belonged to the same cycle of saga. It was called Sphinx. It would be interesting to know how Dionysus and his train were brought into connection with the Sphinx and Oedipus and whether there was any appearance of the God as deliverer or bringer of new life. In any case the same conjunction appears on the Vagnonville Crater; a Sphinx is sitting on a χῶμα γῆς which Satyrs are hammering at with picks, as though for the Anodos of Korê. (See J. E. Harrison, *Delphika*, J.H.S. XIX. 1899, p. 235, and *Prolegomena*, p. 211, fig. 45; cf. also the krater in *Monumenti dell' Inst.* II. pl. LV.)

Thus we find that of the five trilogies of Aeschylus which are represented in our extant plays, two end with a final epiphany, one has an epiphany in each play, one is uncertain but most likely had a grand final appearance of Zeus in state; one ends with a Threnos.

What of the fragmentary plays? I will not attempt to discuss them at length, but will merely mention those which *prima facie* seem to have contained an epiphany. I refer throughout to Nauck's *Fragmenta*.

Amymône: the heroine attacked by satyrs Ποσειδῶνος δὲ ἐπιφανέντος ὁ Σάτυρος μὲν ἔφυγεν. Epiphany of Poseidon.

Bassarai: 2nd of the Lycurgus trilogy, *Edoni, Bassarai, Neaniskoi*. The *Neaniskoi* I take to be the converted *Edoni*; they form a band of Kouroi initiated into the worship of Dionysus. Thus the whole trilogy had probably an epiphany at the end, with Dionysus instituting his own ritual worship. But also the separate plays seem to have had epiphanies.

Edôni: king Lycurgus acts the part of Pentheus: Dionysus is on the stage, as in the *Bacchae*, fr. 61: he makes an earthquake, as in the *Bacchae*, fr. 58: and, since his enemy Lycurgus was ultimately confounded, it is practically certain that in the end, as in the *Bacchae*, he appeared in glory.

Bassarai: Orpheus, a rebel of a different sort, was torn to pieces by the Maenads (Bassarids) for worshipping the Sun, αἱ δὲ Μοῦσαι συναγαγοῦσαι ἔθαψαν Eratosth. *Catast.* 24. This suggests a great epiphany of the Muses. The play must have been very close to the original Dionysiac ritual, like the *Bacchae*. The Daimon (Dionysus-Orpheus) is torn to pieces, collected and recognized, mourned for, and then revealed in glory.

Other Dionysiac plays are *Pentheus*, of which we are definitely told that its plot was the same as that of Euripides' *Bacchae*; *Dionusou Trophoi*, plot not known: evidently the nursing of the young Year-Daimon in some form (see above, p. 13); and lastly, *Bacchae*.

See also, for other Year-Daimon plays, the *Kréssai*, and the *Nemea-Hypsipyle* trilogy below.

Ixîon: perhaps the third play of the same trilogy as the *Perrhaebides*. The last scene seems to have shown Ixîon bound by Zeus to the burning wheel in the sky. See Diod. Sic. 4. 69. 3, *ap.* N. This would give a great epiphany of Zeus and the gods.

---

[1] I do not mean by this to suggest that the final scene is spurious. On the contrary. The Aition is the grave-ritual of Eteocles and Polynices, and the last scene is quite correct and normal in stating that Aition.

Eurôpê or *Kâres*: see N. The play seems to have ended by the arrival through the air of the gods Sleep and Death, bearing the body of Europa's son, Sarpêdôn, for burial in his native land.

Kabîri: plot uncertain, but we know that the Kabiri themselves made an appearance. Plutarch, *ap.* N. 97.

Memnon: at the end Memnon is slain by Achilles. His goddess mother, Eôs, goes to Zeus and obtains the gift of immortality which she brings to him. Epiphany of Eôs. Proclus, *ap.* N.

Niobé: no direct evidence, but it is difficult to see how this plot can have been completed without the appearance of a god.

Pentheus: same plot as the *Bacchae*. Epiphany of Dionysus. See above.

Xantriai, '*The Rending Women*': possibly another name for the *Pentheus*: in any case it seems to have dealt with the same story.

Semele or *Hydrophoroi*. The 'Water-bearers' are those who try to put out the conflagration of the palace owing to the epiphany of Zeus.

Toxotides: Actaeon transformed into a stag. Probably epiphany of Artemis.

Phineus: see above, p. 348.

Psychostasia: the epiphany here was famous and elaborate. Zeus appeared on the 'theologeion,' Thetis on one side of him and Eos on the other, weighing the souls of Achilles and Memnon. Pollux, 4. 130. Eos, we are told, came down on a γέρανος.

Óreithuia: she was carried off by Boreas. The passages from Longinus and John of Sicily about the extravagance or ἀτοπία of the poet suggest that Boreas appeared in person when he 'stirred the sea by blowing with his two cheeks.'

The following are less clear.

Heliades: their transformation into poplars was foretold or explained. This suggests an epiphany. Such things are usually done by a divine being.

The Achilles trilogy, *Myrmidones*, *Nereides*, *Phryges* or *Hector's Ransom*. In the first Thetis seems to have appeared to provide the arms, in the second the Chorus consists of Nereids and it is difficult to imagine the play without Thetis. In the third we know that Hermes appeared at the beginning. It seems possible that the council of the gods described in *Il.* XXIV. as insisting on the ransoming of Hector made an appearance.

Hoplôn Krisis, the Adjudgement of the Arms of Achilles: it appears from N. 174 that Thetis was summoned to come with her attendants to preside over the trial. No doubt she came.

Lastly, there are some plays in which our supposed Year-Daimon makes his epiphany not as a celestial god but as a ghost or a hero returned from the grave. It is obvious that he is quite within his rights in so appearing: he is essentially a being returned from the dead, and his original ritual epiphany was a resurrection.

Persae: after the Pathos narrated by the Messenger comes a Thrênos and an *evocation of the dead king or god*, Darius, see p. 348.

Krêssai: the subject seems to have been the restoration to life of Glaucus, son of Minos, by Polyidus. (This Glaucus, restored to life by snakes, may well have been a form of Year-Daimon.)

Psychagôgoi: the plot is unknown, except that the title is said to have denoted 'persons who by charms of some sort resurrect the souls of the dead.' Bekk. *Phryn.* p. 73, 13.

Nemea and *Hypsipyle* probably belong to a trilogy on the death and heroization of Archemorus-Opheltes, who is a typical Year-Daimon, appearing as a Snake or a Baby. (See p. 214.)

We do not know whether there was an appearance of Heracles at the end of Aeschylus' *Philoctetes*, as there was in that of Sophocles. But it is perhaps worth remembering that Aeschylus was supposed to have revealed 'certain lore of the mysteries' in the *Toxotides, Hiereiai, Sisyphus Petrocylistes, Iphigenia* and *Oedipus*. The extremely close connection between the mysteries and the Year-daimon will be in the minds of all who have read the present volume.

A numerical tabulation of the above results would be misleading, both because most of the conclusions are only probabilities, and still more because we cannot generally constitute the trilogies to which the various lost tragedies belong. If we could, the final Theophanies would probably be still more numerous. There remain outside the above plays some 23 of which our knowledge is so scanty that no *prima facie* conclusions can, as far as I can see, be drawn. But it can hardly be disputed that in a surprising number of Aeschylus' tragedies we have found signs of either a definite epiphany of a god or the resurrection of a dead hero, or lastly the direct worship of a Year-Daimon. We cannot be certain, but we may surmise that some such epiphany or resurrection was quite as common in Aeschylus as in Euripides.

I will leave out the question of such Epiphanies in the fragments of Sophocles: the evidence would take very long to state. His extant plays will be briefly treated below. In general the result is that in this, as in so many other particulars, Sophocles is influenced more by the Ionian Epic and less by the Attic Sacer Ludus than the other two tragedians. It is just the same with the other Forms. Sophocles deliberately blurs his outlines and breaks up his Agôn and Messenger and Prologue into what we may almost call continuous dramatic conversation; Euripides returns to an extreme clarity and articulateness and stiffness of form in all three. The discussion of Euripides' technique is of course another story, but so much will, I think, hardly be denied either by his friends or his enemies.

Passing on, then, to Euripides, what is it that he did about his epiphanies? In especial, why is he ridiculed by comedy for his use of the *Deus ex machina*, if Aeschylus really used such epiphanies as much or more?

The answer, I think, is not that he invented the introduction of gods: he clearly did not: but that, *more suo*, he introduced them in a sharply defined manner, always at the end of the play, and, it would seem, with some particularly smooth and effective machinery. (Perhaps an invention made about the year 428, see Bethe, *Prolegomena*, pp. 130—141.) The general purpose for which he used them—(1) to console griefs and reconcile enmities and justify *tant bien que mal* the ways of the gods, and (2) to expound the Aition of the play, and the future fates of the characters—was, I believe, part of the tradition. In these respects his gods play exactly the parts of Athena in the *Eumenides* or Aphrodite in the *Danaides*, probably even of Zeus in the *Prometheus Unbound*.

The Theophanies in the extant plays of Euripides are as follows:

Hippolytus: Artemis appears, (1) comforts and reconciles Theseus and Hippolytus, and (2) founds the ritual of Hippolytus at Trozên.

Andromache: Thetis appears, (1) sheds comfort on the suffering Peleus and Andromache, and (2) orders that Neoptolemus be laid in his tabu tomb at Delphi.

Supplices: Athena appears, (1) comforts the Argives by foretelling the expedition of the Epigoni to conquer Thebes, and (2) bids Theseus consecrate the brazen tripod at Delphi which is witness to the oath of eternal friendship to Athens sworn by the Argives.

Ion: Athena appears, (1) comforts Ion and Creusa, and (2) ordains the founding of the four Attic tribes.

Electra: the Dioscoroi appear, (1) condemn the law of vengeance, comfort Electra and Orestes, and (2) expound the origin of the Areopagus, of the Oresteion in Arcadia, and of the tabu tombs of Aegisthus and Clytemnestra (cf. Paus. II. 16. 7).

Iphigenia Taurica: Athena appears, (1) appeases Thoas, promises comfort to Orestes, and (2) founds the worship of Artemis-Iphigenia at Halae and Brauron.

Helena: the Dioscoroi appear, (1) appease Theoclymenus, (2) found the worship of Helen (in conjunction with their own), explain the name of the island Helene, and promise immortality to Menelaus.

Orestes: Apollo appears, striking (as I hope to show elsewhere) his hearers into a trance; (1) makes peace between Menelaus and Orestes, (2) explains the origin of the Oresteion in Arcadia and of the Areopagus and proclaims the worship of Helen.

Bacchae: Dionysus appears, (1) judges his enemies, consoles Cadmus and (2) establishes his worship. See above.

Iph. Aul.: end lost: Artemis seems to have appeared, (1) saved Iphigenia, comforted Agamemnon, and (2) doubtless ordained the Brauron rite.

Rhesus: the Muse, mother of Rhesus, appears, (1) laments her son, and (2) establishes his worship as an 'anthropodaimon.'

If this were free and original composition the monotony would be intolerable and incomprehensible: we can understand it only when we realize that the poet is working under the spell of a set traditional form.

The Euripidean plays which do not end with a god are the following: *Cyclops, Alcestis, Medea, Heracleidae, Hecuba, Heracles, Troades, Phoenissae.*

These require special consideration. It is no part of my case to argue that all plays necessarily conform to the same type. The sacer ludus of a Torch-race, like the Prometheia, or the sacer ludus of some Altar of Sanctuary like the various Suppliant Plays, has no particular reason for conforming to the scheme of the Dionysus-play, except the influence of custom and analogy. But we shall find even in these plays which have no obvious Theophanies some curious traces of the Theophany-form.

The *Cyclops* is a Satyr-play, and does not come into question.

The *Alcestis* is, I think, also in form a Satyr-play. (See Argument, also Dieterich, *Pulcinella*, p. 69.) Yet we must note that it ends with a Resurrection.

Medea: it ends with a scene in which Medea appears on a height (Schol. *ad* 1317), and then rides through the air uttering prophecies and founding the rite of her children's worship. When we remember that Medea was really a goddess, and that she and her children received worship in Greece, we can see that this scene is really a faded or half-humanized Theophany. Cf. the treatment of Hippolytus.

Heracleidae: who is, in the ritual sense, the 'hero' of the *Heracleidae*? Without doubt Eurystheus; it is the Ἄγος of his death and his sacred grave or 'place of burial' (1040 ff.) that constitute the Aition of the play. The end in our MSS. seems to be incomplete, but it clearly contains the foundation by the Hero himself of his own tabu ritual. This is not far removed from the original daimon-rite or theophany.

Hecuba: it ends with the prophecies of the fey and dying Thracian hero, and his announcement of the Aition of the *Kunos Sêma* (1273).

Heracles: Theseus is of course not a god, but he is a worshipped hero: and his function in this play is just that of the ordinary *Deus*. He comforts Heracles, sends him away from Thebes, describes his future life, and lastly ordains his worship with its proper honours and ritual. (See esp. 1322—1340: just like a speech *ex machina*.)

Troades: it ends with a pure Threnos. See above. It is interesting to note that the Theophany, omitted here, comes by its rights at the beginning of the play.

Phoenissae: a curious question arises. The play apparently ends with a Threnos, which is legitimate enough. But the last scene also contains the driving out of Oedipus to Mt Kithairon. Now Oedipus was a daimon who haunted Mt Kithairon. (See Roscher; also my Introd. to Sophocles' *Oed. Rex*.) He goes out to Kithairon in this play, 1751 f. Also in *Oed. Rex*, 1451 ff. he expresses his wish to go out to 'yonder Kithairon that is called mine own.' When we remember that the connection of Oedipus with the Attic Colônus is probably a late Attic invention (*Phoen.* 1704 ff.) and reflect on the curious 'passing' of Oedipus in the *Coloneus*, a suspicion occurs that the true ritual end of the Oedipus-dromenon was the supernatural departure of the hero-daimon to his unknown haunt on the mountain. In this case the sending forth to Kithairon—otherwise almost unmotived—is again a faded remnant of what we have called the Theophany-form. This argument is strengthened by the generally admitted fact that the pair Oedipus-Jocasta are a vegetation pair, like Adonis-Aphrodite, Hippolytus-Artemis, etc. But it cannot be pursued further here.

To sum up, we find that the tragedies of Euripides usually end with a Theophany of a markedly formal and ritual character, closely suiting our conception of the Sacer Ludus of Dionysus, as daimon of the Year-Cycle of death and rebirth; further, that in those tragedies which do not end in a confessed Theophany there are at any rate curious resemblances to the typical Theophany-form; furthermore, the evidence of the extant and fragmentary plays of Aeschylus, though often uncertain, seems to show that a Theophany of a similar sort was also usual in them, either at the end of a trilogy or in the separate plays. About Sophocles we shall say something later: the evidence is not very conclusive, but the indications are not at all inconsistent with the above results.

Let us now consider the other forms, especially the group

AGON, PATHOS, MESSENGER, THRENOS.

Pathos and Messenger almost always go together; the Agon is doubtless less characteristically ritual than the other parts, as arguments and spirited dialogue scenes naturally tend to occur in any drama. With respect to the Agon and Threnos we will chiefly notice how they stand in relation to the Messenger, and how far the supposed original order of sequence is preserved in each play.

Euripides being the clearest and most definite in his ritual forms, we will take him first.

Alcestis: being a Satyr-play it need not conform to the tragic type. It has, however, in the proper place the Agon (Heracles and Death), Threnos and Resurrection.

Medea: typical, with the necessary modifications. Agon, Medea against herself 1020—1080. (The scene before has also been an Agon, Medea out-witting Jason.) Pathos and Messenger 1121—1230; quasi-Threnos in the frightful scene (1251—1292) where the children are murdered behind the barred door: quasi-Theophany, as explained above. (There cannot be a real Threnos because that is definitely forbidden by Medea 1378 ff. We may conjecture that there was no θρῆνος in the Corinthian rite: cf. Paus. II. 3. 6 and Schol. *Med.* 273. If it was intended to mitigate infant mortality, this would be natural.)

Heracleidae: see above on Eurystheus. The Pathos-Messenger (799—866) announces the battle and the capture of Eurystheus: there then follows an Agon-scene, apparently out of its order; the end is incomplete, but it contained the establishment of the funeral rite by Eurystheus himself, as Hero.

Hippolytus: typical. Agon, Messenger with Pathos, Threnos, Anagnorisis, Theophany. See above.

Andromache: typical: same order. See above.

Hecuba: the Messenger comes early in the play, hence we cannot have a Theophany immediately following it. In compensation a Ghost appears at the beginning. We have Agon between Odysseus and Hecuba-Polyxena (218—440): Messenger with Pathos 484—582: then Threnos in Hecuba's speech. Then the course of the play interrupts. On the end see above, p. 353.

Supplices: clear sequence. Agon between Herald and Theseus-Adrastus (399—597); Messenger announcing the Battle 634—777; then Threnos. This Threnos is enormously developed and practically includes the rest of the play up to the Theophany, except that it is interrupted by the Euadne scene. (That curious scene seems to have been inserted to fill up the interval while the slain men are cremated and their bones made ready for burial. But it must, no doubt, have some ritual explanation also.)

Heracles: the sequence is peculiar. The Messenger bursts out from the ruined house at 909. The scene before has been the divine apparition of Lyssa, which, however, is quite different in character from the regular Theophanies. I am inclined to think that technically the attack of Lyssa upon Heracles is an Agon; see below on the *Iph. Aul., Persae* and *Septem.* The scene before has certainly been an Agon between Heracles and Lycus (cf. 789, 812). Thus we get the sequence Agon (Agon), Pathos and Messenger,

Threnos, and, clearly, Anagnorisis 1089—1145: then, instead of a god, Theseus appears, *ex machina* as it were: see above.

Ion: typical. Great Agon scene, Creusa against Apollo 859—922, or one may perhaps count it as lasting till 1047; then Pathos-Messenger 1106—1228, brief Threnos 1229—1250; then second Agon 1250—1394 and Anagnorisis 1395—1549 (with Peripeteia): then Theophany.

Troades: the form in many ways peculiar, but the latter part has the sequence: Agon of Helen against Hecuba-Menelaus 860—1060; Choric ode, then Messenger 1123—1155, then great Threnos to the end.

Electra: Agon of Electra and Clytemnestra 997—1146: then the Messenger is omitted, the Pathos is αὐτάγγελον, announced by the shriek of Clytemnestra and the return of the murderers with bloody swords 1147—1176: then Threnos (with a Repentance-scene which forms a spiritual Anagnorisis and Peripeteia), then Theophany. The Messenger-form, omitted here, has occurred earlier in the play 761—858.

Iphigenia Taurica: the end is clear: Agon, Thoas and Iphigenia 1152—1233: Messenger (with a kind of Anagnorisis 1318, 1361): no Threnos, unless we may take the Chorus' two lines of lamentation, 1420, 1421, as an atrophied Threnos: Theophany. The real Threnos of the play has come earlier, as it tends to come in plays about Orestes.

Helena: Agon with Theoclymenus (I take the diplomatic contest with these dangerous barbarians to be a clear form of Agon) 1186—1300: continued in 1369—1450: then Messenger 1512—1618: no Threnos is possible; instead we have a brief Agon, Theoclymenus against the Servant at the door 1621—1641: then Theophany.

Phoenissae: there are two Messengers, each with a double speech. We take at present only the second. The great Agon of the play has occurred much earlier, 446—637, between Eteocles and Polynices. The sequence at the end is merely Messenger 1356—1479, Threnos 1485—1580, and 1710—end, interrupted by an Agon between Creon and Antigone. As Aitia we have the burial arrangements of Eteocles and Polynices and the expulsion of Oedipus to Mt Kithairon—perhaps a faded Theophany, see above. The tabu tombs of the two princes form also the end of the *Septem*. The general structure of the *Phoenissae* is highly formal under its cover of Epic expansion, but we will not discuss it here.

Orestes: in the conclusion of the play I think we must recognize the Phrygian as an Exangelos. That is, his dramatic function is to relate what has taken place inside the house. The lyrical form is merely chosen for variety's sake. This gives us the sequence: Messenger combined with Threnos: Agon between Orestes and Menelaus: Theophany of Apollo. There has been an ordinary Messenger earlier 852—956: also a Threnos 960—1012. Also an Evocation of the dead Agamemnon, much atrophied 1225—1240. (These atrophied evocations of Agamemnon are of course derived from the great evocation in the *Choephori*: one would like to know if that scene itself is softened down from some still more complete predecessor, in which Agamemnon actually rose from the tomb.)

Bacchae: absolutely typical: see above.

Iphigenia Aulidensis: the end is lost, but the present traces suggest a pretty typical sequence: Agon, Achilles pelted by the troops, argument between Achilles and Clytemnestra 1337—1432: Threnos of Iphigenia 1475—1531: Messenger 1532—? Then perhaps Threnos, certainly Theophany.

Rhesus: the Hêniochos is clearly a Messenger. So we end with the sequence Agon 675—727, fight of Diomedes and Odysseus with the Guards: Messenger 728—819, continuing into a short Agon between Hêniochos and Hector 820—881: then Theophany combined with Threnos.

But let us consider one particular point more closely. If we notice the plays in which Orestes occurs we shall find that that hero always produces a peculiar disturbance in the Forms. Now Orestes is traditionally a figure of strongly marked type—the beloved hero who is reported dead and then returns in triumph. I strongly suspect that his reported death, lamentation and reappearance alive were in origin exactly parallel to the reported death, lamentation and reappearance alive of the Daimon, Dionysus, Osiris, etc. In Sophocles the false death is described in detail: it is a σπαραγμός, like that of Hippolytus, and at the Pythian games! As Orestes became thoroughly humanized, the supernatural element dwindled away. But we shall see that his appearance, though it mostly comes early in the play and does not count—so to speak—as a real final Theophany, is apt to come in conjunction with Messenger and Threnos and Invocation of the Dead. It bears traces of its original theophanous glory.

Usener has argued on other grounds (*Archiv, l.c.* pp. 332 ff.) that Orestes at Delphi was a winter daimon and 'Doppelgänger' to Dionysus, as Neoptolemus was to Apollo. And it is worth noting that the same line of thought possibly supplies a clue to a puzzling and tiresome scene in Euripides' *Electra*, 771—858. The ritual described in the messenger's speech seems extraordinarily like a reflection of a *Bouphonia* at an Eniautos festival. Orestes is made to act as *Daitros* for the communal *Dais* (see p. 142)—one might say, as some reminiscence of a daimon of the New Year who in human form slays the Old Year in bull form. As such he is recognized (*v.* 852 ἐγνώσθη δ' ὑπὸ | γέροντος...) and they crown and lead him with acclamation (*v.* 854 στέφουσι δ' εὐθὺς σοῦ κασιγνήτου κάρα | χαίροντες ἀλαλάζοντες). However this may be, Orestes is the most typical of Greek tragic heroes and occurs in more (extant) plays than any other. See my *Orestes and Hamlet, a Study in Traditional Types*, Proceedings of British Academy 1912.)

Iph. Taur.: besides the final sequence we have an opening Orestes-sequence: Threnos for Orestes 136—235: Messenger announcing Pathos (*Stoning*) of Orestes: then Appearance of Orestes, in a great scene 472—900, involving an Agon and an Anagnorisis and Peripeteia.

Eur. *Electra*: after Prologue, we have Threnos 112—212 (on Orestes and Agamemnon): then Appearance of Orestes, with Agon leading to Anagnorisis 487—595. Oddly enough this is followed by an Evocation of the Dead, and a Messenger. The various elements of the death and resurrection of the Daimon are all there, but scattered and broken since the conception which held them together has been lost.

We noticed above in the *Andromache* (p. 347) that the interrupting Orestes-scene came with a sequence Messenger, Threnos,

Epiphany of Orestes, and that, much in the manner of a *deus ex machina* he (1) saved and consoled Hermione, and (2) announced the Aition of the play.

In the *Orestes* the hero does not return from the dead, and the sequence is quite confused, but our supposed original Daimon-Orestes appears possibly to have left two rather curious traces. 1. He is shown at the beginning of the play *lying like a dead man* (83 ἀθλίωι νεκρῶι· νεκρὸς γὰρ οὗτος κτλ., 385 τίνα δέδορκα νερτέρων;), is *roused by the women wailing round him* and rises. 2. At the end, just before the full-blooded Theophany of Apollo, we see Orestes appearing on the roof of the Palace, a place generally appropriated to divine beings. See also below on the *Choephori* and Soph. *Electra*.

Turning from Euripides to the less formal tragedians, we shall not of course expect to find in them the same clear-cut sequences of unmistakable Agon, Messenger-Pathos, Threnos, Anagnorisis, Theophany. But I think we shall find that these Forms, a little less stark and emphatic, a little more artistically modified, are usually present in both Aeschylus and Sophocles.

Aeschylus:

Supplices: we have seen that the whole trilogy ended in a typical Theophany, so we need not expect one here. But we have a clear Agon (Maidens against Herald) 826—910, followed by arrival of the Basileus with a Peripeteia; then Messenger (Danaus as Messenger 980—1014); then not exactly a Threnos, but a song of prayer (1018—end).

Persae: the Forms come early. Messenger 249—514, Threnos 515—597, Evocation of dead 'god' 598—680: epiphany 681—842. The rest to the end is Threnos. This gives us a perfect typical sequence, except that the Agon seems to be absent. If we look for it in its proper place we shall find it, not acted indeed but described. In 176—214 we have Atossa's dream of the Agon between Europe and Asia, the Agon which was actually taking place but could not be represented on the stage. Cf. *Alc., Heracles, Iph. Aul.*

Septem: here also the Agon takes place 'off,' after 718. Then Messenger 792—822: then Threnos 831—1009, and, instead of a Theophany, an enactment of the Aition of the ritual. (Grave-worship of Eteocles and Polynices.)

Prometheus: a passionate little scene between Prometheus and the Chorus just before 940 might possibly be described as an Agon, though the greater Agon comes earlier; then 944—1035 Messenger (Hermes, cf. 943) mixed with Agon: then, as substitute for the Theophany, a supernatural earthquake involving the cleaving of Earth and the revealing of Hell.

Agamemnon: in this trilogy the full Theophany is reserved for the last play and consequently the sequence in the individual plays is upset and confused. We have, however, Messenger 550—680: Agon of Clytemnestra and Agamemnon 810—975: then the Cassandra scene, foretelling the Pathos; then Pathos αὐτάγγελον, another Agon and Threnos.

Choephori: as in other Orestes-plays we have a Threnos and Anagnorisis quite early 165—244: Evocation of dead 315—510: Agon (Orestes and Clytemnestra) 674—930, with a Messenger (Exangelos) in the midst of it 875—886, combined with Pathos αὐτάγγελον: Threnos, consisting of mixed joy and woe and culminating in long speeches over the dead bodies 935—1047: lastly a Vision of the Furies, which may possibly have involved a real epiphany.

Eumenides: Agon 566—680, or perhaps to 750, with Athena making an Aition-speech in the style of a *Deus ex machina* in the middle 681—710: then new Agon with a reconciliation (886 ff.) and Peripeteia; then great Procession of gods. No Messenger. The whole play is really the Theophany of the Oresteia trilogy.

Sophocles:

It is especially interesting to see how Sophocles has broken down the stiff lines of the ritual Theophany into scenes of vague supernatural grandeur.

Oedipus Rex: fairly clear end. Agon (short but involving Anagnorisis and Peripeteia) between Oedipus and the Herdsman 1123—1185: Exangelos or Messenger with Pathos 1223—1296: then Threnos with suggestion of Oedipus' flight to Kithairon to become a daimon (1451 ff.).

Oedipus Coloneus: Agon between Oedipus and Polynices 1254—1396: slight Threnos and last speech of Oedipus. This last speech is very supernatural; it consists of prophecies and Aitia, and is spoken amid continuous lightning and thunder (1514 f.): then Messenger 1579—1666, and final Threnos over Oedipus' passing. A faded Theophany is pretty visible here.

Antigone: enormous Agon scene, Creon v. Antigone, then v. Haemon, then v. Antigone again 384—943: Tiresias bringing a kind of Discovery (?) and Peripeteia 988—1114: Messenger with Pathos 1155—1256, small Threnos: Second Messenger (Exangelos) 1278 and greater Threnos. The Aition is the same as that of the *Septem*, some Theban hero-ritual commemorating the children of Oedipus and their unhallowed ends—the buried living and the unburied dead.

Ajax: a curious question suggests itself. All the latter part of the play, 1046—1401, is occupied with an Agon (in three stages, ending in a reconciliation) about the burial of Ajax. It is triumphantly decided that he is to be buried. Is that the end? Or was he really buried? Was there not some great final pomp representing the burial?—In considering the prolonged emphasis laid on this burial question in the *Ajax*, we should remember that among the dromena of the Aianteia was a πομπή and that the funeral bier of Ajax μετὰ πανοπλίας κατεκοσμεῖτο. (Hesych., vid. Pauly s. *Aianteia*.) The play is close to the old hero-cult; and perhaps the hero-cult itself not quite unrelated to some 'Year-ritual,' if the dead hero re-appeared in the spring flower that was marked with his name.

In any case the sequence is rather curious: Theophany at beginning 1—133. Later on we get a much atrophied Messenger 719—783, who foretells the Pathos which then proceeds to follow 815—865. Then a scene of search and Anagnorisis 866—890: then Threnos 891—1040: then the great Agon, Reconciliation and—on some scale or other—Heroic Funeral.

Electra: an Orestes-play, with the usual special characteristics. It begins, after the Prologue, with a Threnos 86—250, then an Agon 328—471 (Chrysothemis) and a greater Agon 516—633 (Clytemnestra): then an Invocation of the dead Agamemnon 634—659: this is answered by the arrival of the Messenger announcing the death of Orestes 660—763, short Agon and Threnos 822—870: then, after Agon which is almost part of the Threnos, 871—1057, Appearance of Orestes, with Anagnorisis, Peripeteia and final settlement of the play. On the death, lamentation, and discovery alive of Orestes, see p. 356.

Trachiniae: the same question arises here as in the *Ajax*. The burning of Heracles on Mt Oeta was in ancient tradition and art closely associated with his Apotheosis. Was this burning and apotheosis represented on the stage? It definitely is so in Seneca's imitation, *Herc. Oet.* ad fin. In any case, whether represented or not, I think it must have been suggested to the minds of all spectators. The sequence is fairly typical: Agon of Hyllus and Deianira 734—820, Messenger (Exangelos) 870—946, Threnos, interrupted by the Appearance of Heracles, his Self-Lamentation and Burning—i.e. Apotheosis.

Philoctetes: this play has a definite Theophany at the end, but otherwise its sequence is rather far from any type. One might divide it thus: Agon 865—1080, including an Anagnorisis 895—926: Threnos 1081—1217: fiercer Agon (Odysseus v. Neoptolemus and Philoctetes) 1222—1302: Reconciliation 1308—1408: Theophany 1400—1471.

PROLOGUES.

We have hitherto considered the Forms that come towards the end and build up the conclusion of a tragedy. In any true work of art the end is always specially important and significant. It is the last act that chiefly determines the character of a play. It is the end of the verse that best indicates the metre. But there is one important form which belongs necessarily to the beginning.

Dieterich is doubtless right in comparing the Prologue of tragedy with the Prorrhêsis of the hierophant before a sacred Drômenon. What such a prorrhêsis was like we can only guess. There are a few small phrases of ritual preserved: there is the parody of a prorrhêsis given by the Hierophant in the *Frogs*, 354 ff.; there are a few lines spoken by Iphigenia as priestess before her tabu procession starts (*I. T.* 1226 ff.). It certainly gave orders for Euphemia, or solemn silence: it probably also said something about the sacred dance which was to follow. '*Make room for a Dance of Mystae! And do you begin the singing and the all-night dances that are meet for this festival*' (Ar. *Frogs*, 370 f.). When the nature of the dance was something obviously dictated by the occasion—e.g. when it was the celebration of a particular Festival on the proper day—there was no need for any further explanation. But as soon as anything like tragedy began, the case was different. The sacred dance of Dionysus might be about Agamemnon, or Oedipus, or the Daughters of Danaus, or what not. Consequently there was need of a *Pro-logos*, of something *spoken before*. The word suggests prose rather than verse. We know that the sacred Herald proclaimed— in an audience which had no knowledge of what play or what poet was coming—'*O Theognis, lead on your Chorus!*' (Ar. *Ach.* 11). We know that—in a certain Proagon, whatever that was—Sophocles led on his Chorus in black. What was the poet supposed to do when he 'led on' his Chorus? Did he just bow and retire, leaving the audience to guess as best they could from the play itself what it was all about? Or did he use this opportunity and tell them? Any- how the prologos is defined as 'all the part before the dancers come on,' and it seems quite likely that originally it was not regarded as part of the sacred dance at all, but was something informal spoken by the poet. If our knowledge were a little fuller we should very likely be told who πρῶτος ἔγραψε προλόγους, and be able to assume that when Aeschylus 'led on' his Chorus for the *Persae* and the *Suppliant Women* he told the audience what the play was to be. Then the development would be like that of the Dithyramb, of Comedy, of the Satyr-play, perhaps of the Apotheosis-scenes at the end: a Form that was first merely improvised or built up by scenic effects without written verses, grew gradually to be 'written' and regarded as an integral part of an artistic whole. Mediaeval prologues and clown-scenes would afford good parallels, and we should understand why Euripides was so proud that οὑξιὼν πρώτιστά μοι τὸ γένος ἂν εἴπεν εὐθὺς τοῦ δράματος. He, more than either of his predecessors, made a character in the play do all the Prologue for him, and that in a thorough and clear manner. For clearness, σαφηνεία, was to the age of the Sophists the first virtue of λέξις.

But this is conjectural: what development is traceable in our extant remains? I think we can see that the Prologue, still rather fluid in the hands of Aeschylus, grew first in the direction of mere drama, and then turned aside towards a definite religious form.

For instance, in Aeschylus we have the stages:

1. No written Prologue: *Supplices* and *Persae*;

2. Simple Prologue of one speaker: *Agamemnon*, *Choephori* (with Pylades dumb);

3. Complete exposition-scene with two or more characters:

Septem: Eteocles and Messenger.

Eumenides: Pythia: change of Scene: Apollo, Orestes and Ghost. (Unless indeed the Dance in the strict sense begins by the Chorus being seen within about *v.* 35.)

Prometheus: the elaborate scene with Kratos and Bia has apparently been introduced to meet the need of nailing the gigantic figure on the rock.

In Sophocles stage (1) disappears altogether, and so practically does (2). All the plays without exception begin with regular exposition-scenes involving two or more characters. It is noticeable, however, that two of the latest plays, *Trachiniae* and *Philoctetes*, start this exposition-scene with a quasi-Euripidean Prologue, addressed confessedly or half-confessedly to the audience. That is, Sophocles regularly works in stage (3), but in his latest work begins to be influenced by a further stage. What this is we shall find in Euripides.

Euripides has practically always an exposition-scene—so much is a natural concession to the growing complexity of drama—but in front of the exposition-scene he has a formal speech addressed to the audience by one quiet and solitary figure; a figure, also—and this is what I wish to emphasize—which is either confessedly supernatural or at least somehow charged with religious emotion.

Let us take first the plays which happen to omit the exposition-scene altogether. To do so is, of course, a kind of archaism: a return to a less complex kind of drama, in which the sacred dance followed immediately on the Prologue-speech. It occurs, if we disregard the *Cyclops* as not being a tragedy, in only two dramas, and those naturally enough the very two that are most formal and nearest to their respective forms of Sacer Ludus, the *Bacchae* and the *Supplices*. The *Bacchae* has been already dealt with: the Sacer Ludus behind all the Suppliant Plays seems to me to have been a ritual only second in its influence on tragedy to that of the Year-cycle itself. I will not now discuss the subject at length, but I can understand the origin of the Suppliant Plays best as a ritual intended to keep alive the right of sanctuary attached to some particular altar or tomb or the like, very much as we keep alive the control over a right of way. On one day in the year some fugitives take refuge at the altar, some pursuer tries to drag them away, and some high authority, god or king or people, forbids him. This is notoriously a very common motive in Greek tragedy, and was used, as recent finds have shown us, in the romantic comedy of the fourth century. (Pap. Ox. VI. 855, a scene which I should now explain differently.) I suspect that this ritual is also at the back of various rites which have generally been interpreted as survivals of human sacrifice, rites in which some one is pursued with weapons and is supposed to be killed unless he reaches a certain place of refuge.

However that may be, let us consider the actual Prologue-speakers. We may start with *Alcestis*, Apollo (and Death): *Hippolytus*, Aphrodite: *Hecuba*, the Ghost of Polydorus: *Ion*, Hermes: *Troades*, Poseidon (and Athena): *Bacchae*, Dionysus: all these are supernatural. Next observe *Heracleidae*, Iolaus suppliant at an altar: *Andromache*, the heroine suppliant at an altar: *Supplices*, Aithra, surrounded by a band of women suppliant at an altar: *Heracles*, Amphitryon and Megara, suppliants at an altar: *Helena*, the heroine suppliant at an altar: *Iph. Taur.*, the half-divine priestess of a strange and bloodstained Temple rising from a dream of death. The religious half-supernatural atmosphere is unmistakable.

The only exceptions are *Medea, Phoenissae, Electra, Orestes*, though in the two last the exception is more apparent than real. We must remember the curious traces of the daimon that cling about Orestes. In any case, both openings produce a decidedly uncanny atmosphere— the lonely woman in the night uttering curses against her mother, and the woman sitting alone by her brother who is mad and perhaps dead.

There remain two peculiar cases, the *Rhesus* and *Iphigenia in Aulis*. We know that the *Rhesus* had in Alexandrian times three different Prologues, while the *Iphigenia* has two in our present MSS. I will not discuss them further than to point out that they seem to represent a new form of Prologue, which starts with a lyric scene. The lyric Prologues of both are very similar and exceedingly beautiful, and I may say in passing that I have long been inclined to think that we have in them the hand of the original producer of *Iphigenia*, Euripides the younger. In the *Iph. Aul.*, according to our MSS., the Prologue proper follows the lyrical scene. This order seems to be taken from the New Comedy! Menander usually made his expository Prologue the second scene of the play.

What is the explanation of these facts? It seems to me that the old Sacer Ludus has reasserted itself: the Prologue, after passing into a mere dramatic exposition-scene between ordinary people, returns again to be a solemn address spoken to the audience by a sacred or mysterious figure. The differences are, first, that it is now integral in the whole play as a work of art, and secondly, that it has been markedly influenced by the speech of the god at the end. It is the same story with other elements of the drama. The language and metre get freer in Sophocles, and return to formality in Euripides. The dialogue becomes irregular and almost 'natural' in Sophocles, and then returns to a kind of formal antiphony of symmetrical speeches or equally symmetrical *stichomythiae*. The Chorus itself first dwindles to a thing of little account and then increases again till it begins once more to bear the chief weight of the tragedy. Something like the old hierophant reappears at the beginning, something like the old re-risen god at the end; and, as we have seen, it is in plays of Euripides, and most of all in the very latest of his plays, that we find in most perfect and clear-cut outline the whole sequence of Contest, Tearing-asunder, Messenger, Lamentation, Discovery, Recognition, and Resurrection which constituted the original Dionysus-mystery.

Thus the death of Dionysus is ἄρρητον. It was blasphemous, if not impossible, to speak seriously of the death of the Life of the World. This fact seems to me to have had important consequences, differentiating Dionysus from the other Year-Daimons and incidentally explaining some peculiarities of Greek Tragedy.

The ordinary Year-Daimon arrived, grew great and was slain by his successor, who was exactly similar to him. But Dionysus did not die. He seemed to die, but really it was his enemy, in his dress and likeness, it was Pentheus or Lycurgus who died while Dionysus lived on in secret. When the world seemed to be dead and deprived of him, he was there in the ivy and pine and other evergreens; he was the secret life or fire in wine, or other intoxicants. By this train of ideas Dionysus comes to be regarded not as a mere vegetation-spirit or Year-Daimon, but as representing some secret or mysterious life, persisting through death or after death.

An outer shape dominated by tough and undying tradition, an inner life fiery with sincerity and spiritual freedom; the vessels of a very ancient religion overfilled and broken by the new wine of reasoning and rebellious humanity, and still, in their rejection, shedding abroad the old aroma, as of eternal and mysterious things: these are the fundamental paradoxes presented to us by Greek Tragedy. The contrasts have their significance for other art also, perhaps for all great art. But aesthetic criticism is not the business of the present note.

G. M.

CHAPTER IX.

FROM DAIMON TO OLYMPIAN.

(HERAKLES. ASKLEPIOS. GAIA TO APOLLO AT DELPHI.)

Ἄπολλον, Ἄπολλον,
ἀγυιᾶτ᾽, ἀπόλλων ἐμός.

ON the very threshold of Olympos, one foot within the portals yet never quite inside, stands the hero of all heroes, the 'young dear hero,' Herakles[1]. The reason of his tarrying there is simple and instructive. It is not that in his labours and his banquetings he is too human, too 'heroic' in the saga sense; it is that he is a daimon, and a daimon-hero has much ado to fit his positive functions and yet shadowy shape into the clear-cut inert crystal of the Olympian.

HERAKLES AS FERTILITY AND YEAR-DAIMON.

Homeric saga did for Herakles all it could.

'And as to Hermes and Herakles,' says Pausanias[2], 'the poems of Homer have given currency to the report that the first is a servant of Zeus and leads down the spirits of the departed to Hades, and that Herakles performed many hard tasks.'

Why should Hermes and Herakles be linked together? What has the young messenger with golden rod and winged sandals to do with the lusty athlete? A second question brings an answer to the first. What were Hermes and Herakles before 'Homer' made of one the 'servant of Zeus' and of the other the 'hero' of the labours? Pausanias himself tells us; they were both 'Herms.'

[1] Usener, *Sintflutsagen*, p. 58, supposes an old Greek diminutive καλος = Latin *culus*, and adduces the hypokoristic form Ἡρυκάλος. See Hèsych. s.v. τὸν Ἡρακλέα Σώφρων ὑποκοριστικῶς, cf. *Hercules*.
[2] VIII. 32. 4.

The Athenians, he says[1], zealous in all matters of religion, were 'the first to use the square-shaped images of Hermes.' The Arcadians were 'specially partial[2]' to the square form of Hermes. Hermes was a Herm, but not only Hermes, also Apollo Aguieus and Poseidon and Athena Ergane and Helios and—which concerns us most for the moment—Herakles. Art too bears out the testi-

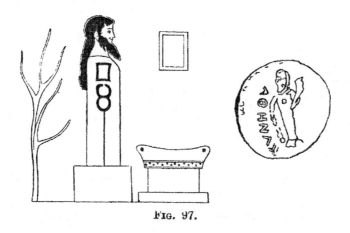

FIG. 97.

mony of Pausanias. In the vase-painting, Fig. 97, we have Hermes in Herm form[3]. The Herm is marked by the kerykeion, the staff with double snakes. Behind the Herm is a little tree, for Hermes is a fertility-daimon; in front an altar and, suspended on the wall, a votive pinax. Side by side with the Herm of Hermes we figure a Herm of Herakles[4], from a bronze coin of Athens. More human than the Hermes, Herakles has arms; in one he holds a great cornucopia which marks him as Agathos Daimon, in the other his characteristic club

We talk and write glibly of the 'club' of Herakles as his 'characteristic attribute' and thereby miss the real point. The 'club' of Herakles is not to begin with a thing characteristic of Herakles, a ῥόπαλον, the rude massive weapon of a half-barbarian hero; it is a magical bough, a κλάδος[5] rent from a living tree.

[1] iv. 33. 4.

[2] viii. 48. 6.

[3] Conze, *Heroen und Göttergestalten*, Taf. 69. 2. The Herm on the original is ithyphallic.

[4] See Roscher, s.v. *Herakles*, 2157, and see Overbeck, *Gr. Plastik*[4], ii. 25.

[5] This was long ago pointed out to me in a letter from Dr Walter Headlam, but neither he nor I then saw its full significance. It was also observed by Mr A. B. Cook in *J.H.S.* 1894, xiv. p. 115.

The Orphic Hymn[1] going back, as so often, to things primitive thus addresses Herakles:

'Come, Blessed One, bring spells for all diseases,
Drive out ill fates, wave in thy hand thy branch;
With magic shafts banish the noisome Keres.'

Herakles is, like Theseus, Thallophoros. Hermes as Herm has a tree in his sanctuary; Herakles as Herm carries a bough.

The people of Trozen knew the truth about the 'club of Herakles,' and their simple faith seemed over credulous to Pausanias[2]. He says:

And there is here a Hermes called Polygios. They allege that Herakles placed his club against this image and this club, which was of wild olive, took root in the earth, if anyone likes to believe it, and sprouted up afresh, and the wild olive tree is still growing. They say that Herakles found the wild olive at the bay of Saron and cut the club from it.

Hermes Polygios[3] seems to be some old xoanon about which grew a wild olive stunted and club-like in some part of its shape. One thing is clear, the 'club' of Herakles was connected, though after the inverted fashion of an 'aetiological' myth, with the living growth of a tree.

The bough in the right hand tells then the same story of fertility as the cornucopia in the left. The cornucopia and its significance are now familiar[4] and need not detain us. Only one point is important, the Athenian coin is of high evidential value because it shows the cornucopia as a cultus attribute. Later when 'Homer' and his saga had completely humanized Herakles, when the saga-individuality of the hero became articulate and his

---

[1] XII. 14 ἔλθε μάκαρ, νούσων θελκτήρια πάντα κομίζων,
    ἐξέλασον δὲ κακὰς ἄτας, κλάδον ἐν χερὶ πάλλων,
    πτηνοῖς τ' ἰοβόλοις κῆρας χαλεπὰς ἀπόπεμπε.

[2] II. 31. 10 ...καὶ ἦν γὰρ κοτίνου τοῦτο μὲν (τὸ ῥόπαλον) ὅτῳ πιστά, ἐνέφυ τῇ γῇ καὶ ἀνεβλάστησεν αὖθις, καὶ ἔστιν ὁ κότινος πεφυκὼς ἔτι,..

[3] The etymology of Polygios is uncertain. Usener (*Rhein. Mus.* LVIII. 167) suggests Πολύγυιος, and would make of the Hermes a τετράχειρ. Maass (*De Aeschyli Supplicibus commentatio*, 1890, p. xiii, note 1) explains as Πολ-ύγιος 'sanitate pollens,' and compares Ἀκακήσιος. S. Eitrem (*Rhein. Mus.* LXII. 1909, p. 333), quoting Prof. Torp, derives Πολύγιος from Πολυλύγιος, and compares Asklepios Agnitas, Artemis Lygodesma, and the Hermes of the Hymn (v. 410) and the miracle of the withies. I dare not build upon this most interesting but unproved suggestion.

[4] I may add to what was said above pp. 311, 312 about the cornucopia on grave-reliefs, an interesting fact that had escaped me. Dr Pfuhl, in his article *Das Beiwerk auf den ost-griechischen Grabreliefs* in Jahrb. d. Inst. XXI. 1905, section VI. das Füllhorn, points out that in no less than five instances on grave-reliefs the cornucopia appears erected on a pillar as an adjunct to the ordinary parting scenes. The specimen is in the British Museum, Cat. 704, from Smyrna.

functions as a daimon were forgotten, the cornucopia became cumbersome. Tradition held to it as we see in the design in Fig. 98. It could not, like the branch, be transformed from a fertility-emblem into a weapon; it had to be accounted for; it called aloud in fact for an aetiological myth. The cornucopia, men said, did not originally belong to Herakles, it was the guerdon of one of his great labours; he broke it off from the bull-headed river Acheloös.

Dejaneira speaks.

Fig. 98.

> 'A river was my lover, him I mean
> Great Acheloös, and in threefold form
> Wooed me, and wooed again. A visible bull
> Sometimes, and sometimes a coilèd, gleaming snake,
> And sometimes partly man, a monstrous shape
> Bull-fronted, and adown his shaggy beard
> Fountains of clear spring water glistening flowed[1].'

The vase-painting[2] in Fig. 99 reads like a commentary on Dejaneira's words. It just gives us the needful clue. Here is the great daimon of fertility in his familiar form, half man, half bull. And, as on countless coins the bull-man is the local river-god, so from his mouth flow the fertilizing streams, for is he not παγκρατὴς γάνους, 'Lord of all that is wet and gleaming[3]'? And, that there be no mistake, a great cornucopia lies parallel above the life-giving waters[4].

Nowhere perhaps does the fertility-daimon come so vividly before us as in the words of Dejaneira. We see him shifting from

---

[1] Soph. *Trach.* 9 ff.   [2] *Arch. Zeit.* xvi. (1883), Taf. 11.

[3] Such are the θεοὶ γανάεντες invoked by the Danaid chorus at the close of the *Supplices* of Aeschylus (v. 993). They leave the praises of the Nile and implore the local gods

> ποταμοὺς οἳ διὰ χώρας
> θελεμὸν πῶμα χέουσιν
> πολύτεκνοι.

[4] Life-giving and also land-making. For the story of Alkmaion and the new alluvial earth deposited at the mouth of the Acheloös see *Prolegomena*, pp. 220, 221.

one familiar shape to another; he is now, like Agathos Daimon, like Zeus Ktesios, a 'gleaming snake,' now a 'visible bull[1],' as he appeared to the women of Elis who wooed him to come to them 'with his bull-foot,' and now a monstrous shape bull-fronted (βούπρῳρος) like Zeus Olbios[2]. Nowhere else moreover is he, the fertility-daimon, so clearly the bridegroom, rejected indeed for saga purposes, but rejected only for his fully humanized form, for another fertility-daimon, Herakles. Herakles breaks off the horn of the fertility-daimon and carries away his bride. So understood the monstrosities of the story become real and even beautiful.

Fig. 99.

In the wooing of Dejaneira, whether by Acheloös the river-god or by Herakles the hero-daimon, we have a *mythos* that embodies the marriage, the ἱερὸς γάμος, of the queen of the land with the fertility-daimon, reflecting a ritual like that of the marriage of the Queen Archon at Athens with Dionysos. It is the old wedlock of the Earth and Sky, of thirsty Argos and the rain of heaven which fills the wells and rivers of earth. We wonder no longer that the Dithyramb, the spring mystery babe, is laid at his birth in the stream of

Acheloös' roaming daughter,
Holy Dirke, virgin water[3].

---

[1] In some places naturally the fertility-daimon was not a goat, but a bull. See *supra*, p. 165. The goat, like the bull, might be associated with the cornucopia. Amaltheia, whose horn was the original cornucopia, was of course a goat. Below the reclining figure of a goat-headed 'Tityros' in the Museum of Fine Arts at Boston is a cornucopia. See P. Baur, *Tityros*, in American Journal of Archaeology, ix. 1905, Pl. v.

[2] *Supra*, p. 148, Fig. 26.   [3] Eur. *Bacch.* 519.

But if this wedlock of earth and living water be the first stage, there is in the Herakles-myth as told in the *Trachiniae* a second stage.   Herakles is not only a seasonal fertility-daimon; he is manifestly[1] a daimon of the Sun-Year.   His Twelve Labours occupy a Great Year, μέγας ἐνιαυτός.   The divisions of this cycle were somehow set forth in the 'ancient tablet' from Dodona which he gave to Dejaneira before he set forth on his last Labour, in the twelfth year.   This twelfth year was not 12 months but 14, that is, it had the two intercalary months necessary to equalize approximately the moon and sun cycles.   The sacrifice that, together with the death of Herakles on the pyre, crowned the great calendar festival, the Eniautos-festival, had a like symbolism.   Twelve 'perfect bulls' stood for the twelve years, but in all the victims were a hundred, to save the face of the hundred moons in the octennial moon-cycle.

It may be that neither Sophocles nor his predecessors in shaping the legend, Peisander and Panyasis, were actually aware that Herakles was a daimon of the Sun-Year, but more, much more, than conscious knowledge goes to the making of poetry. Anyhow, the chorus, the maidens of Trachis at their first entry[2], strike a note strangely appropriate.   They would fain know where tarries the son of Alkmena.   To whom do they appeal?

> 'Thou whom Night as the stars die bringeth to birth
>   And layeth to bed all ablaze,
> Helios, Helios, speak: where over the earth
>   Move his wandering ways?'

In orthodox fashion the maidens explain that their appeal is to Helios because he is all-seeing.

> 'Speak, O thou of the seeing eye[3].'

But the real reason lies deeper; the Sun and only the Sun knows where Herakles is, for Herakles is a daimon of the Sun-Year[4].

---

[1] See Dr Verrall, *The Calendar in the Trachiniae of Sophocles*, Class. Rev. x. 1896, p. 85, to which I must refer for details of a somewhat complicated argument. No one will tax Dr Verrall with a *parti pris* for Sun-Myths.   He says expressly 'Our proposition is simply that, in respect of the chronological framework, the story presented in the *Trachiniae* exhibits, and is founded upon, a certain calendar and certain institutions relating to the calendar which existed when the story was first thrown into this shape.'

[2] *v.* 94.   [3] *v.* 101.

[4] In just the same fashion, as I have tried to show elsewhere (*Helios-Hades*, Class. Rev. xxii. (1908), p. 15), Demeter appeals to Helios to know who has ravished her daughter, and Helios himself is the ravisher as Helios-Hades.

In much of his mythology that cannot be examined here, Herakles is but the humanized double of Helios[1]. It is from the sun he borrows his tireless energy. As the young sun he fights with Hades the setting sun at Pylos. As again the rising sun he rescues Alcestis from the shades. If such cases seem to any to be dubious, there is one adventure that admits of no alternative interpretation. Helios, Apollodorus tells us, so admired the courage of Herakles in shooting at him, that he gave to the hero a golden cup in which he might cross the ocean. Helios had but one cup to give, the golden cup in which he himself sailed and slept at sunset.

> Surely the Sun has labour all his days,
> And never any respite, steeds nor god,
> Since Eos first, whose hands are rosy rays,
> Ocean forsook, and Heaven's high pathway trod;
> All night across the sea that wondrous bed
> Shell-hollow, beaten by Hephaistos' hand,
> Of wingèd gold and gorgeous, bears his head
> Half-waking on the wave from eve's red strand
> To the Ethiop shore, where steeds and chariot are,
> Keen hearted, waiting for the morning star[2].

After the magical words the vase-painting in Fig. 100 is more like a blasphemy than an illustration. Yet it is instructive. The *human* Herakles was never meant to sail in the sun's boat, but orthodox anthropomorphism demands it; room or no room, in he must go, to sail but not to sleep.

HERAKLES AS IDAEAN DAKTYL.

The Herakles of the *Trachiniae* as fertility and Year-daimon helps us to understand another aspect of the hero that much embarrassed the piety of Pausanias[3]. At Thespiae he visited the

---

[1] I would guard against misunderstanding. Herakles takes on the form of an Eniautos-daimon, and therefore has solar elements, but these do not exhaust his content. The same is true of Apollo, Odysseus, Orpheus and Dionysos, and indeed of almost all gods and daimones. The reaction against certain erroneous developments of solar mythology has led, as I have long pointed out, to the neglect of these elements.

[2] Mimnermos, frg. of *Nanno*. I borrow this translation from Prof. Murray's *History of Greek Literature*, p. 81.

[3] IX. 27. 6. The nature of the Thespian cult of Herakles and his character as an Idaean Daktyl have been convincingly demonstrated by Dr Kaibel in his brilliant monograph, *Daktyloi Idaioi* in Nachrichten d. k. Ges. d. Wiss. zu Göttingen, phil.-hist. Kl. 1901, p. 506 ff. For Herakles as Eniautos-daimon the responsibility is mine. The phallic daimon is long-lived. Dr Usener has convincingly shown in his *Der heilige Tychon*, 1907, that Priapos may survive in the hagiology of a Christian Saint.

sanctuary of Herakles and heard the story of the fifty daughters
of Thestios. Pausanias cannot reconcile a
legend so discreditable with what he knows
of Herakles son of Amphitryon, so he
suggests another and an earlier Herakles.

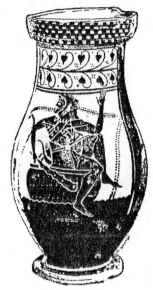

'I judged the sanctuary to belong to the
Herakles who is called one of the Idaean Daktyls,
the same of whom I found sanctuaries at Erythrae
in Ionia and at Tyre. Nor are the Boeotians
ignorant of this name of Herakles, for they say
themselves that the sanctuary of Mycalessiau
Demeter is entrusted to the Idaean Herakles.'

What manner of daimon this Herakles,
this Daktyl, was is made abundantly clear
from this very cult of Mycalessian Demeter
to which Pausanias refers. At Mycalessos
close to the Euripos Demeter had a
sanctuary.

Fig. 100.

They say that it is closed every night and opened again by Herakles, who
is said to be one of the so-called Idaean Daktyls. Here a miracle is exhibited.
Before the feet of the image they place whatever fruits the earth bears in
autumn and these keep the bloom upon them the whole year round[1].

It is a *pankarpia*. Such magical fruits, with upon them a bloom
that is perennial rather than immortal, does the Eniautos-daimon
carry in his Eiresione and hold for ever in his cornucopia.

Herakles, the Idaean Daktyl, brought fertility to plants but
also to man. His cornucopia is for fruits, but sometimes it holds
phalloi[2]. That is why his cult is at Thespiae: he and every
fertility-daimon is but another Eros[3]. Because Eros is human
there is excess and ugliness waiting to shadow and distort nature's
lovely temperance. The saga of the daughters of Thestios was
ugly and polygamous, but the cult was magical and austere. At
the sanctuary of Herakles at Thespiae Pausanias[4] tells us

A virgin acts as his priestess till her death.

---

[1] Paus. IX. 19. 5 ...ὅσα ἐν ὀπώρᾳ πέφυκεν ἡ γῆ φέρειν ἃ διὰ παντὸς μένει τεθηλότα
ἔτους.

[2] See the bronze Gallo-Greek statuette in Dr A. Coulson's collection at Noyon.
Gazette published by him, *Hermes Phallophore*, Gazette Arch. 1877, pl. 26. The
liknon, whose function is the same as that of the cornucopia, often contains a *phallos*
as well as fruits. See *Prolegomena*, Figs. 148 and 149.

[3] For Eros as Herm and his kinship with Priapos see *Prolegomena*, p. 631.

[4] IX. 27. 6.

Herakles then, till saga caught and transformed him, was an Idaean Daktyl and as such own brother to the Kouretes, the Korybantes and the Satyrs[1]. We wonder no longer that it was Herakles the eldest of the Idaean Daktyls who founded the Olympic games. It is not merely that there may have been early immigrants from Crete, it is certainly not because Herakles was the strong man of the Twelve Labours, it is because Herakles, the Idaean Daktyl, was as Megistos Kouros the fertility-daimon of the year. Therefore he was Kladophoros, Thallophoros[2]. Hero-daimon though he be, with branch and cornucopia, with Twelve Labours like the Sun and, Sun-like, sailing in a golden cup, yet no effort is spared to make of Herakles a regular Olympian. In literature he has his apotheosis, on vase-paintings he is formally 'received into Olympos,' brought by Athena his patron up to the very throne of Zeus[3]. Tradition even said that Hera passed him through her robe to make him by adoption her real son[4]. Yet though he is always being 'received' and 'adopted' he never attains real godhead[5].

Why is this? What is it that eternally bars the gate of Olympos? We shall find the answer in a study of his twofold ritual.

RITUAL OF HERAKLES AS YEAR-DAIMON.

The failure of Herakles to gain admission to Olympos is the more remarkable because we have clear evidence that he was worshipped in part with the same ritual as the Olympians themselves. Pausanias[6] when visiting the sanctuary of Herakles at Sekyon observes as follows.

They say that Phaistos when he came to Sekyon found them devoting offerings (ἐναγίζοντας) to Herakles as to a hero. But Phaistos would do nothing of the kind but would offer burnt offering (θύειν) to him as to a god. And even now the Sekyonians, when they slay a lamb and burn the thighs upon the altar, eat a portion of the flesh as though it were a sacrificial victim, and another part of the flesh they devote (ἐναγίζουσι) as though to a hero.

---

[1] For the Satyrs see *infra*, p. 423.

[2] Paus. v. 7. 7. See *supra*, p. 366. Therefore, too, I think he was *Epitrapezios*, for the winner in the *agon* was regularly feasted. The ugly saga-figure of Herakles as glutton and wine-bibber, so popular in comedy and Satyric plays, and not wholly absent from tragedy, has probably this beautiful origin. Thus hardly did saga deal with cultus. Like *Dais* (*supra*, p. 146), *Thaleia* is no mere goddess of banqueting and revels, she is the daimon of the magical fertility-feast.

[3] For instances see Roscher, *Herakles*, 2239.

[4] Diod. Sic. iv. 40.　　　　　　　　　[5] See *Prolegomena*, p. 347.

[6] ii. 10. 1. For details as to the ritual of ἐναγίζειν see *Prolegomena*, p. 55 ff.

Phaistos it may be was the eponymous hero of Phaistos in Crete, and from Crete he may have brought to Sekyon[1] the ritual of an Ouranian Zeus. That ritual common to all Olympians was of course *burnt* sacrifice; the worshipper ate part, the rest was a gift-sacrifice, etherialized by burning, that so in the form of a sweet savour it might reach the gods of the upper air. We have seen[2] in the rite of the *panspermia* practised on the day of the *Chytroi* that of the *panspermia* no man tasted, it was made over, tabued to Hermes Chthonios, it was an ἐναγισμός, a thing *tabu*. The reason in the case of the vegetarian sacrifice is clear, the seeds are wanted as seeds, that they may reappear as fruits in autumn. The same applies in the case of animal sacrifice, though to us the reasoning is less obvious. The flesh is made over, buried, or wholly burnt; it is *tabu*, because it is wanted to fertilize the ground, like the pigs buried with the snakes and fir-cones at the Thesmophoria[3].

Herodotus[4] was evidently puzzled by the two-fold nature of Herakles. Finally he comes to the conclusion that

> Those of the Greeks do most wisely who have set up a double worship of Herakles and who offer burnt sacrifice to the one as an immortal and with the title Olympian, and to the other devote offerings as to a hero.

The first of these wise Greeks who set up the double worship of Herakles were the Athenians. Diodorus Siculus[5] draws an instructive contrast between the practice at Athens and that of Opous and of Thebes: he says

> Menoitios, having sacrificed a boar and a bull and a ram, ordered them to *make a yearly sacrifice* at Opous and to do honour to Herakles as a hero. The Thebans did much the same, but the Athenians were the first to honour Herakles as a god with burnt sacrifices.

To give Herakles his fitting honours (τιμαί) as a hero Menoitios ordered a *yearly* sacrifice. The fact is cardinal; and

---

[1] In Hesiod's days Sekyon was called Mekone. A change of name implies usually some change in population. Such may lie at the back of Hesiod's strange story about how Prometheus tricked Zeus. The ethnology of the ritual shift from ἐναγίζειν to θύειν I must leave to others of wider competence.

[2] *Supra*, p. 291.

[3] *Supra*, p. 266.

[4] II. 44 καὶ δοκέουσι δέ μοι οὗτοι ὀρθότατα Ἑλλήνων ποιέειν, οἳ διξὰ Ἡράκλεια ἱδρυσάμενοι ἔκτηνται, καὶ τῷ μὲν ὡς ἀθανάτῳ Οὐλυμπίῳ δὲ ἐπωνυμίην θύουσι, τῷ δὲ ἑτέρῳ ὡς ἥρωϊ ἐναγίζουσι.

[5] IV. 39 κάπρον καὶ ταῦρον καὶ κριὸν θύσας ὡς ἥρωι κατέδειξε κατ᾽ ἐνιαυτὸν ἐν Ὀποῦντι θύειν καὶ τιμᾶν ὡς ἥρωα τὸν Ἡρακλέα—τὸ παραπλήσιον δὲ ποιησάντων καὶ τῶν Θηβαίων, Ἀθηναῖοι πρῶτοι τῶν ἄλλων ὡς θεὸν ἐτίμησαν θυσίαις τὸν Ἡρακλέα.

yet, because the notion of the Eniautos-daimon lay undetected, its true significance is never seen. Here and there a careful writer[1] will note that the hero-sacrifice is yearly, but in perfunctory fashion for completeness sake. The reason for the yearly recurrence is never given, it is not even asked. Once the Eniautos-daimon comes to his own, and once it is recognized that it is his mask which each and every individual dead man eventually puts on, once it is seen that he, not the individual dead man, is the real 'Strong One,' 'Venerable One,' the essential 'Hero,' on whom the luck and life of the year depend, then the need for honours that shall be yearly is instantly evident.

We need not multiply instances. Not only to Herakles are the yearly dues paid but to a host of others whom we think of merely or mainly as the heroes of saga, to Tereus[2], Melampous[3], Neoptolemos[4], Achilles, Tleptolemos. Tleptolemos is specially interesting. From Pindar[5] we should never guess that Tleptolemos had yearly dues or indeed that he was anything but a magnificent ancestor of Diagoras to whom sacrifice was done 'as to a god.' But the scholiast lets out a fact instructive to us if somewhat compromising to Pindar. He tells that there was a yearly *panegyris* and *agon* in honour of Tleptolemos and called by his name, but he adds

It was by way of compliment that Pindar transferred to Tleptolemos the *agon* performed in honour of Helios.

[1] Dr Nilsson in his *Griechische Feste*, 1906, p. 454, quotes Stengel as observing that 'wohl alle Heroenopfer jährlich wiederkehrten,' but so little does he see the importance of the fact or the real gist of a 'hero' that in the preceding sentence he says 'eine vollständige Behandlung (der Heroen-Kulte) gehört nicht in die Heortologie.' Rohde in his brilliant *Psyche*, 1894, deals in detail with the yearly *agones* for the dead, but with no hint of why they are yearly. Deneken in his admirable article, *Heros*, in Roscher's *Lexicon*, does not, I think, even mention the fact. In this matter I have been myself an equal offender. In discussing (*Prolegomena*, pp. 55—76 and 326—359) the ritual of the dead and of heroes and its chthonic character, I never even observed, much less understood, the fact that this ritual was *annual*.

[2] Paus. I. 41. 9 θύουσιν ἀνὰ πᾶν ἔτος.

[3] Paus. I. 44. 5 καὶ θύουσι τῷ Μελάμποδι καὶ ἀνὰ πᾶν ἔτος ἑορτὴν ἄγουσι.

[4] καὶ οἱ (Νεοπτολέμῳ) κατὰ ἔτος ἐναγίζουσιν οἱ Δελφοί.

[5] *Ol.* VII. 77

τόθι λύτρον συμφορᾶς οἰκτρᾶς γλυκὺ Τλαπολέμῳ
ἵσταται Τιρυνθίων ἀρχαγέτᾳ
ὥσπερ θεῷ
μήλων τε κνισάεσσα πομπὰ καὶ κρίσις ἀμφ' ἀέθλοις.

Schol. *ad loc.* ἐγκωμιαστικῶς δὲ ὁ Πίνδαρος τὸν ἀγῶνα Ἡλίῳ τελούμενον εἰς τὸν Τληπόλεμον μετήγαγε; and again more forcibly ἐψεύσατο δὲ ὁ Πίνδαρος· οὐ γὰρ Τληπολέμῳ ὁ ἀγὼν ἐπιτελεῖται, τῷ δὲ Ἡλίῳ τιθέασι τὸν ἀγῶνα, ὡς Ἴστρος φησὶν ἐν τῇ περὶ τῶν Ἡλίου ἀγώνων· Ῥόδιοι τιθέασιν Ἡλίου ἐν Ῥόδῳ γυμνικὸν στεφανίτην ἀγῶνα.

The ritual of a hero was that of a year-daimon and hence often of a sun-daimon, and this explains why heroes were worshipped at sunset. This was much more than a mere poetical way of expressing that the hero's life was westering. It was magical. You emphasize death that you may ensure resurrection. At Elis Pausanias[1] tells us

> Achilles had not an altar but a cenotaph erected in consequence of an oracle. At the beginning of the festival on a fixed day *about the setting of the sun* the women of Elis perform other ceremonies in honour of Achilles and it is their custom to bewail him.

The women of Elis we remember[2] 'summoned' the bull-daimon in the spring. Here we have them raising a *threnos* over the dead day and the dead year[3].

The notion that to the hero the sacrifice must be yearly went on into historical times. It is this yearly character and this only that explains the nature of the offerings. Thucydides is evidence of both. Hard pressed in the Peloponnesian War, the Plataeans thus appeal to the Lacedaemonians:

> 'Cast your eyes upon the tombs of your fathers slain by the Persians and buried in our land. Them do we honour year by year with a public gift of raiment and other wonted offerings and *of whatsoever the earth brings forth in its season, of all these things we bring to them the firstfruits*[4].'

. The Plataeans themselves—or at least Thucydides—do not really understand. He thinks it is because the earth is just a 'friendly land' to the dead heroes. It really is that they, the ancestors, have a *pankarpia* which they, like the Australian ancestors of the Alcheringa time, may turn into a *panspermia*. This is their perennial function as Year-daimones.

Much that remains valid has been written as to the distinction between a chthonic and Olympian ritual, between the consecrations (ἐναγισμοί) of heroes, chthonic divinities and the burnt offerings (θύματα) of the Olympians, between the low-lying *eschara* and the high stone *bomos*. It has been seen and rightly that heroes and chthonic divinities have a common ritual, save that to heroes

---

[1] vi. 23. 3.   [2] *Supra,* p. 205.

[3] For the relation of the setting-sun to Hades see my *Helios-Hades*, Class. Rev. xxii. 1908, p. 12, and for sun-aspects of Achilles see Otto Seeck, *Geschichte des Untergangs der antiken Welt*, 1902, vol. ii. p. 579.

[4] Thucyd. iii. 58 ...οὓς ἐτιμῶμεν κατὰ ἔτος ἕκαστον δημοσίᾳ ἐσθήμασί τε καὶ τοῖς ἄλλοις νομίμοις, ὅσα τε ἡ γῆ ἡμῶν ἀνεδίδου ὡραῖα πάντων ἀπαρχὰς ἐπιφέροντες εὖνοι μὲν ἐκ φιλίας χώρας. See also Porphyry (*de Abst.* iv. 22) who says that Draco laid it down as an eternal ordinance that heroes as well as gods should receive offerings of 'yearly pelanoi.'

as being more recent in sanctity wine is offered. All this is true, but not the whole, nor even I think the main truth. The real distinction is that heroes and chthonic divinities are Year-daimones who die to rise again. The Olympians are, and, as will presently[1] be seen, it is nowise to their credit, Immortals (ἀθάνατοι). It is as Year-daimones that Heroes have chthonic ritual with all its characteristic apparatus of low-lying altars, of sunset sacrifices, and above all of the *pankarpia*.

HERAKLES AS ALEXIKAKOS OF EPHEBOI.

We return to Herakles whose content is not yet exhausted.

FIG. 101.

The relief[2] on Fig. 101 shows us the Hero in front of his own Heroon, a small shrine on a stepped basis and consisting only of four pillars and a roof. The shrine is not large enough to hold the great humanized hero, and probably at first it held no figure at all, only a sacred pot, a *kadiskos*, with a *panspermia*, or perhaps again a slab with a holy snake. Around the shrine is a sacred grove as befits a daimon of fertility. The worshippers approach bringing a bull. The bull will be sacrificed to the hero whose animal shape he once was[3]. The character of a Herakleion is shown very clearly in Fig. 102, from a Lower Italy amphora[4]. The design also emphasizes in singular fashion the somewhat strained relations between saga and daimon-cult. The scene is from a lost tragedy the plot of which is preserved for us by Hyginus[5]. Haemon is bidden to kill Antigone; he saves her and she bears

---

[1] *Infra*, chapter x.

[2] A. Frickenhaus, *Das Herakleion von Melite*, A. Mitt. xxxvi. 1911, Taf. ii. 2. The reliefs in Figs. 101 and 104 are reproduced by kind permission of Dr Frickenhaus.

[3] Cf. *C.I.G.* 1688, 32 τοῦ βοὸς τιμὰ τοῦ ἥρωος ἑκατὸν στατῆρες Αἰγιναῖοι. I do not feel certain whether this is to be construed 'the price of the Hero-Ox' or 'the price of the ox of the hero,' but in any case hero and ox are intimately linked.

[4] In the Ruvo coll., *Mon. d. Inst.* x. 1848, Tav. xxvi., and Klugmann, *Annali*, 1848, p. 177.

[5] Fab. lxxii. ...hunc Creon rex, quod ex draconteo genere omnes in corpore insigne habebant, cognovit. cum Hercules pro Haemone deprecatur ut ei ignosceret non impetravit.

a child to him.   The child grown to manhood comes to the games
at Thebes and is recognized as of royal race by the mark on his
body.   Herakles begs Creon to pardon Haemon but his prayer is
refused.   Haemon kills himself and Antigone.

FIG. 102.

The story is of great interest because of the recognition by
some body-mark of the child as belonging to the 'dragon's seed.'
To this we shall later[1] return, but for the present it is the figure of
Herakles that concerns us.   In the saga he, for some reason not
given, asks Creon a favour.   He is no daimon; he is just one mortal
of royal race asking a boon of another.   But art is more conservative.   Herakles was *the* hero of Thebes and on the amphora his
heroon, marked by his name[2], bulks proportionately large.   He,
not Creon, for all Creon's kingly sceptre, is the Hero to be
intreated.   It is a strange instructive fusion and confusion of two
strata of thinking.

On the reverse of the Ruvo amphora in Fig. 103 we have the
same heroon.   In it is seated the figure of a woman with mirror
and toilet-box after the fashion of an Attic grave-relief.   She is
the correlative of the Herakles on the other side; she by dying
is heroized.   By that time any individual dead man or woman
might be heroized.   The two sides of the vase give us a strange
blend of daimon-cult, of saga, and of daily life.

[1] *Infra*, p. 434.
[2] Haemon, Antigone, Creon, and the local nymph Ismene are also all clearly
inscribed.   The other figures are uncertain and unimportant.

The relief[1] in Fig. 104 enables us to give to the figure of Herakles a local habitation and a name. The inscription on the basis of the little shrine is clear—'Of Herakles Alexikakos[2].' As 'Defender from Evil' Herakles was worshipped in the deme of Melite, the Pnyx region of Athens. Again the hero stands close to and overtopping his little shrine. The shrine is surmounted by a great krater on a pedestal. Krater and pedestal together are about half the height of the shrine itself. Whom is Herakles to defend from evil? The worshipper only approaches; an *ephebos*, like in age and stature to Herakles himself, save that he wears cloak and petasos. Is there any link between the great krater and the youth and Herakles 'Defender from Evil'? It happens that, in very singular and instructive fashion there is, and by a happy

FIG. 103.

chance we know it.

Photius[3] in a priceless gloss thus explains the word οἰνι[α]στήρια 'wine-doings':

A libation to Herakles performed by the *epheboi* before the cutting of their hair.

Photius gives as his authority a play of Eupolis, the *Demoi*. We should guess therefore that the custom was Athenian, but

---

[1] *A. Mitt.* xxxvi. 1911, Taf. ii.

[2] For Herakles in Melite, see my *Primitive Athens*, pp. 146—152. Dr Frickenhaus holds that the triangular precinct with the wine-press, excavated by Dr Dörpfeld, and by him explained as the old sanctuary of Dionysos-in-the-Marshes, is the Herakleion in Melite. I followed Dr Dörpfeld, and this is not the place to re-examine a question mainly topographical, but if Dr Frickenhaus's most interesting theory be true, and we have a Herakleion close to the old orchestra, it may, as Prof. Murray suggested to me, throw an odd light on the Herakles disguise assumed by the Dionysos of the *Frogs*. Both are Kouroi; both, as will immediately be seen, have a wine-service. So the shift from one to another is not as great as it seems.

[3] s.v. οἰνι[α]στήρια· σπονδὴ τῷ Ἡρακλεῖ ἐπιτελουμένη ὑπὸ τῶν ἐφήβων πρὶν ἀποκείρασθαι. Εὔπολις Δήμοις.

fortunately we know it for certain. Hesychius[1], explaining the same word *oinisteria*, says:

At Athens those who are about to become *epheboi* before the lock of hair is cut bring to Herakles a measure of wine and when they have poured libation they give to drink to those who come with them. And the libation is called *oinisteria*.

Athenaeus[2] adds the authority of Pamphilos and says that the great cup of wine offered was called an *oinisteria*.

Fig. 104.

To Herakles as to the Agathos Daimon at the Pithoigia[3] is offered a libation of wine. To Herakles as to Hippolytos[4] is offered the shorn lock, because he is the Greatest Kouros, *Herakulos* 'the young, dear hero.' In the light of the offering of the lock, the sign and the vehicle of the bloom of youth, some of the *athla* of Herakles which have seemed insignificant, not to say ignoble, are instantly understood. He the Greatest Kouros swings his *klados*, his branch from the tree of life, against a pygmy ker, with shrunken body and distorted face. It is youth against noisome disease and death. He the Greatest Kouros lifts his

---

[1] s.v. οἰνιστήρια· Ἀθήνῃσι οἱ μέλλοντες ἐφηβεύειν πρὶν ἀποκείρασθαι τὸν μαλλὸν εἰσφέρουσιν (ειν MS.) Ἡρακλεῖ μέτρον οἴνου καὶ σπείσαντες τοῖς συνελθοῦσιν ἐπεδίδουν πίνειν· ἡ δὲ σπονδὴ ἐκαλεῖτο οἰνιστήρια.

[2] XI. 494 οἰνιστήρια· οἱ μέλλοντες ἀποκείρειν τὸν σκολλὸν ἔφηβοι φησὶ Πάμφιλος εἰσφέρουσι τῷ Ἡρακλεῖ μέγα ποτήριον οἴνου ὃ καλοῦσιν οἰνιστηρίαν καὶ σπείσαντες τοῖς συνελθοῦσι διδόασι πίνειν.

[3] *Supra*, p. 288.   [4] *Supra*, p. 337.

klados to slay the shrivelled ugly figure leaning on his stick and inscribed γῆρας, Old Age[1].

> We blossom like the leaves that come in spring,
>   What time the sun begins to flame and glow,
> And in the brief span of youth's gladdening
>   Nor good nor evil from the gods we know,
> But always at the goal black Keres stand
> Holding, one grievous Age, one Death within her hand[2].

We understand also now why constant emphasis is laid on the fact that Herakles was *initiated*. On a cinerary urn in the Museo delle Terme[3] Herakles leaning on his club stands in the presence of Demeter and fondles the sacred snake that is twined about her. The scholiast on the *Ploutos*[4] of Aristophanes tells us that the mysteries at Agrae were founded in order that Herakles might be initiated. He is the prototype, the projection, of the initiate youth, he as Alexikakos defends the boy in his *rite de passage* to and through the perils of manhood[5]. Later the initiation into the tribe is viewed as initiation into a 'mystery.'

And, finally, we see the reality and significance of what has hitherto seemed a somewhat frigid conceit, the marriage of Herakles and Hebe. In the Nekuia[6] Odysseus sees Herakles in Hades and is perplexed, for orthodoxy demanded that Herakles should be in Olympos feasting with his bride Hebe. Odysseus, or rather the poet, betrays his embarrassment:

> Next Herakles' great strength I looked upon—
> His shadow—for the man himself is gone
> To join him with the gods immortal ; there
> He feasts and hath for bride Hebe the fair.

Herakles the *Ephebos, the* Kouros, is fitly wedded to *Hebe*,

---

[1] See the two vases reproduced in *Prolegomena*, Figs. 17 and 18. When I discussed them (*op. cit.* pp. 166, 174) I did not at all understand the significance of Herakles as Greatest Kouros.

[2] Mimnermos, 2.

[3] Helbig Cat. 1168. Lovatelli, *Ant. Mon. illustr.* p. 25 ff. tav. II.—IV. Reproduced *Prolegomena*, p. 547, Figs. 155, 156.

[4] Ad *v.* 845.

[5] In previously discussing the initiation of Herakles (*Primitive Athens*, 1906, p. 147) I have, I think, over-emphasized the fact that he was always regarded as an immigrant; foreign elements entered undoubtedly into his cult, but I now believe him to be in the main home-grown.

[6] Hom. *Od.* XI. 601.

maiden-youth in its first bloom, who is but the young form of Hera Teleia[1], *the* Kore.

Herakles, it is abundantly clear from his cornucopia, is Agathos Daimon; but if so, we naturally ask where is his characteristic snake? He has no kerykeion, no snake-twined staff; his body never ends, like that of Cecrops, in a snake's tail. Olympos did not gladly suffer snakes, and Herakles, aiming at Olympos, wisely sloughed off his snake-nature. While yet in his cradle he slew the two snakes that attacked him and his twin brother Iphikles[2]. We shall later[3] see the significance of this snake-slaying which is common to many heroes and which culminates as it were in the myth of the slaying of the Python of Apollo.

Another hero-daimon Saviour and Defender like Herakles was less prudent; he kept his snake and stayed outside Olympos, the great Hero-Healer with the snake-twined staff, Asklepios.

ASKLEPIOS AND TELESPHOROS.

Asklepios is a god but no Olympian; his art-type is modelled on that of Zeus; he is bearded, benign, venerable; he is, in fact, the Zeus of daimon-heroes. He never becomes an Olympian because he remains functional rather than personal, he is always the Saviour-Healer.

On the snake-aspect of Asklepios it is needless to dwell, it is manifest[4]. When it was desired to introduce the cult of the god from Epidauros[5], a sacred snake was sent for whether to Rome or Athens. In art as a rule the snake is twined about his staff, but

---

[1] For Hebe as Ganymeda and her ancient cult at Phlius see *Prolegomena* p. 325. For the relations of Hebe to Hera, and of both to Herakles, I may refer forward to Mr Cook's *Zeus*.

[2] Herakles slaying the snakes appears on silver coins of Thebes and on red-figured vases. See Roscher, *Lexicon*, s.v. *Herakles*. The origin of the twin nature of so many 'heroes' of Daktyl type has been explained by Dr Kaibel, *op. cit.*, and does not here concern us.

[3] *Infra*, pp. 429—436.

[4] For details as to the snake-origin of Asklepios see my *Prolegomena*, p. 342. Fick, in Bezzenberger's *Beiträge*, 1901, p. 313, suggests that the difficult name *Asklepios* is connected with σκαλαπάζω, to turn round and round. Hesychius explains σκαλαπάζει as ῥέμβεται—he coils or rolls round.

[5] Paus. VIII. 8. 4, II. 10. 3, III. 23. 7.

in the relief[1] in Fig. 105 the simple truth is patent: the god in

Fig. 105.

human form leans on his staff awaiting his worshippers, the holy
snake behind him is his equal in stature and in majesty.   It was
in the precinct of Asklepios at Epidauros that the relief in Fig. 75
was found, dedicated to the Agathos Theos[2] with his cornucopia
and sacred snake.

But if the snake-aspect of Asklepios is evident and, I believe,
now accepted, there are two other elements in his cult that show
him to be a fertility-daimon and that have hitherto not I think
been rightly understood, the figure of Telesphoros and the snake-
twined omphalos.

On many coins of Asia Minor of Roman date, and especially
on those of Pergamos there appears in connection with Asklepios

---

[1] Athens, Central Museum Cat. 1407. In previously publishing this relief
(*Prolegomena*, p. 342) I did not understand the relation of the snake to the Agathos
Daimon.
[2] *Supra*, p. 285.

types the figure of a child or dwarf wearing a cloak and high
peaked hat. The three coins[1] in Fig. 106 are typical. In the
central coin of the three we have a sacred tree and round it is
coiled a snake. An emperor salutes the holy beast. Between
the snake and the emperor is the figure of the child Telesphoros.
To the right, on a coin of Pergamos, the same child occupies the
whole field; on the left, again a coin of Pergamos, he stands in a
shrine of the same type as the Herakleion in Fig. 102.

Fig. 106.

Numismatists have long ago found for the child *daimon* the
right name: he is Telesphoros[2], but just because the needful clue
was missing, the name lacked its true meaning. Telesphoros, we
are told, was the 'daimon of convalescence.' Telesphoros is
wrapped in a cloak because invalids when convalescent wear
shawls. For his peaked hat as yet no such satisfactory explanation
has been found. The blunder is an odd one, for to pronounce the
adjective *telesphoros* is to call up the missing noun:

$$\text{ἔνθα παρ' αὐτῷ μεῖνα τελεσφόρον εἰς ἐνιαυτόν}^{3}.$$

Asklepios, with his staff and venerable beard, is Old Father
Christmas, Telesphoros is the Happy New Year[4]. Under the
influence of patriarchy and Zeus the venerable type of the
Eniautos-daimon obtains, and, save in remote Asia Minor, the
Kouros form is forgotten. At Pergamos he lives on clad like the
infant Dioscuri[5] in pointed cap and hooded cloak.

---

[1] *Num. Chron.* Serie iii. Vol. ii. Pl. 1.
[2] Warwick Wroth, *Telesphoros*, J.H.S. 1882. See especially p. 297 for the
curious bronze statuette of Telesphoros with peaked hood. The upper part when
lifted off discloses a *phallos*, symbol of regeneration.
[3] Hom. *Od.* xiv. 292. For ἐνιαυτός and τελεσφόρος see *supra*, p. 183.
[4] For similar child-figures see *supra*, pp. 187 and 188.
[5] Cf. the children wearing peaked hats in votive terra cottas to the Anakes. See
my *Myth. and Mon. Anc. Athens*, p. 154, Fig. 32.

The snake-twined omphalos. We connect Asklepios with the snake but not with the omphalos, yet on the coin[1] of Pergamos in Fig. 107 the association is clear. On the obverse we have the

FIG. 107.

head of the god, of the usual bearded benevolent Zeus-like type, on the reverse a netted omphalos round which coils a great snake with upreared head. The mention of the omphalos brings Delphi instantly to our minds, but it must be clearly noted that the omphalos is not at Delphi only. The omphalos is of Ge rather than of Apollo, and wherever there is worship of Mother-Earth there we may expect the omphalos. We find it at Eleusis, clearly figured on the Ninnion pinax[2], the centre of the whole design. We meet it again at Phlius[3]. Asklepios himself then is a snake-daimon, twined round the omphalos of Ge. He is but the daimon of the fertility of the Earth. As such he never passes wholly to the upper air of the Olympians. He remains a Saviour and a Healer, loved of the dream-oracle, very near to earth and to man.

Herakles then and Asklepios, though as Saviours and Healers they are greater than any Olympians, never became really Olympianized. Their function is to make us feel how thin and chill, for all their painted splendour, are these gods who live at ease in the upper air, how much they lose when they shake off mortality and their feet leave the earth who was their mother.

We now pass to the examination of a god who was perhaps more Olympian than any Olympian, more serene, more radiantly splendid, more aloof, more utterly in the fullest sense of the word *superior*. By a fortunate chance we shall study him where his cult and figure are brought into direct contrast and even conflict

[1] *Num. Chron.* III. vol. II. Pl. 1, p. 23.
[2] See *Prolegomena*, p. 559, Fig. 160.
[3] Paus. II. 13. 7.

with the old sanctities of Earth and her *daimones* at Delphi, where

> Phoibos, *on Earth's mid navel o'er the world*
> *Enthronèd*, weaveth in eternal song
> The sooth of all that is or is to be[1].

THE SEQUENCE OF CULTS AT DELPHI FROM GAIA TO APOLLO.

It happens that, as to the cults of Delphi, we have a document of quite singular interest, no less a thing than an official statement from the mouth of the local priestess of the various divinities worshipped at Delphi, and—a matter of supreme importance—the traditional order of their succession. Delphi was the acknowledged religious centre of Greece, and nowhere else have we anything at all comparable in definiteness to this statement. Thrice familiar though the passage is, it has not I think been quite fully understood. It must therefore be examined somewhat in detail. The prologue of the *Eumenides* spoken by the priestess of Apollo opens thus:

> First in my prayer before all other gods
> I call on Earth, primaeval prophetess.
> Next Themis on her mother's mantic throne
> Sat, so men say. Third by unforced consent
> Another Titan, daughter too of earth,
> Phoibe possessed it. She for birthday gift
> Gave it to Phoibos, and he took her name.
>
> With divination Zeus inspired his soul,
> And stablished him as seer, the fourth in time,
> But Loxias speaks the mind of Zeus his sire[2].

Such are the opening words of the prologue to the *Eumenides*, and they are more truly of prologue[3] character than perhaps at first appears. They set forth or rather conceal the real *agon* of

[1] Eur. *Ion*, 5.
[2] Æsch. *Eum.* 1—8 and 17—19

> Πρῶτον μὲν εὐχῇ τῇδε πρεσβεύω θεῶν
> τὴν πρωτόμαντιν Γαῖαν· ἐκ δὲ τῆς Θέμιν,
> ἣ δὴ τὸ μητρὸς δευτέρα τόδ' ἕζετο
> μαντεῖον, ὡς λόγος τις· ἐν δὲ τῷ τρίτῳ
> λάχει θελούσης οὐδὲ πρὸς βίαν τινός,
> Τιτανὶς ἄλλη παῖς χθονὸς καθέζετο
> Φοίβη· δίδωσιν δ' ἣ γενέθλιον δόσιν
> Φοίβῳ· τὸ Φοίβης δ' ὄνομ' ἔχει παρώνυμον.
>
> . . . .
>
> τέχνης δέ νιν Ζεὺς ἔνθεον κτίσας φρένα,
> ἵζει τέταρτον τόνδε μάντιν ἐν χρόνοις
> Διὸς προφήτης δ' ἐστὶ Λοξίας πατρός.

[3] For function of Prologue see Prof. Murray, *supra*, p. 359.

the play, the conflict between the new order and the old, the daimones of Earth, the Erinyes, and the *theoi* of Olympos, Apollo and his father Zeus, and further necessarily and inherently the conflict of the two social orders of which these daimones and *theoi* are in part the projections—matriarchy or, as it is better called, the matrilinear system and patriarchy. The conflict between the daimones of Earth and the Olympian Apollo will be discussed in the present chapter; the conflict of the two social orders as reflected in mythology must be reserved for the next.

The statement of Æschylus is necessarily somewhat *ex parte.* He is a monotheist and moreover he is 'all for the Father.' In dealing with the religion of Delphi he is confronted with the awkward fact that Zeus at Delphi had no official cult, the oracle was in the hands of Apollo. Moreover that oracle was actually delivered by a woman seated over a cleft in the Earth and inspired not only by the laurel she chewed but by mephitic vapours that rose from the earth. In all this Zeus was—nowhere. Yet the supremacy of Zeus was to Æschylus the keystone of his beautiful faith in a right that was beyond might, a thing to be preserved even in the face of seeming facts. A lesser soul would have turned obscurantist, would have juggled with facts; a more conventional mind would have accepted orthodox tradition and claimed that Apollo conquered by force. That to Æschylus was no conquest at all. The solution he gives us in the prologue is utterly Æschylean and in a sense strangely modern. There has been not a fight but a development[1], not even, as in the *agon* of the play, a reconciliation and sudden conversion, but a gradual emergence and epiphany of godhead from strength to strength, from Gaia to Zeus. And, an interesting thing, Æschylus, as will shortly appear, was right. He gives us by the mouth of his priestess a sequence of cults which not only existed at Delphi

---

[1] The same notion of development comes out in the *Prometheus*, as has been well observed by Miss Janet Case (*Class. Rev.* 1902, p. 195). It has not, I think, been recognized in the *Supplices*, but Prof. Murray points out to me that the keynote of the play is the transition from violence to persuasion. Ares, who is βλάβη —violence and hurt personified—must give way to Aphrodite as Peitho. So only can the Danaides, fertility-nymphs like the Semnae, bring peace and prosperity to the barren land. See also for the same idea in the story of Io, *Rise of the Greek Epic*[2], p. 291.

but is found as a regular religious development over a great part of the civilized world.

The chronological sequence at Delphi was as follows:

       (1)   Gaia,
       (2)   Themis,
       (3)   Phoibe,
       (4)   Phoibos.

Zeus is not given as fifth, he is the crown and climax of all. Phoibos reigns, fourth in time but only as vice-gerent, as '$\Delta\iota\grave{o}s$ $\pi\rho o\phi\acute{\eta}\tau\eta s$,' not of course prophet in our sense, but utterer, exponent of his father's will[1].

Gaia is transparent. She stands for Earth and the powers of the Earth; her sanctuary, the omphalos, will have to be considered in detail later. Themis is a conception so dominant, so integral to religion that her full consideration is reserved for our final chapter. In the figure of Themis, if we are right, we have the utterance, the projection and personification, of *the* religious principle itself. She will not be considered now because she is not really a link in the chain. Rather she is a figure who shadows and attends each of the others. She is the daughter and bye-form of Gaia. She delivers oracles, $\theta\acute{e}\mu\iota\sigma\tau\epsilon s$, *ordinances*, rather than prophecies in our sense, for both Phoibe and Phoibos; she even ultimately ascends to high heaven and becomes the counsellor and wedded wife of Zeus himself. This will I hope be made clear in the final chapter; for the present the reader is asked to substitute provisionally for the order:

(1) Gaia,		(1) Gaia and Themis,
(2) Themis, this shortened succession		(2) Phoibe and Themis,
(3) Phoibe,		(3) Phoibos and Themis.
(4) Phoibos,		

Gaia then is the Earth and Phoibos is of course Phoibos-Apollo. The reason of his double title will appear later. But who is Phoibe? Phoibos and Phoibe are seen, from the practical identity of name, to be beings of the same order, beings of brightness and purity[2]. It is odd that their real nature should have escaped commentators. Once stated it is simple and so

---

[1] See Dr Verrall's *Eumenides*, note to *vv.* 17—19; and for the prologue generally, his *Introduction*, p. xii.

[2] Cf. $\phi o\iota\beta o\nu o\mu\epsilon\hat{\iota}\sigma\theta a\iota$ to live in ritual purity; see *Prolegomena*, p. 394.

obvious. It has only lain so long concealed because of a dominant anthropomorphism. Phoebus is still to-day the Sun[1].

> Hark, hark, the lark at heaven's gate sings,
> And Phoebus 'gins arise.

And if Phoibos be the Sun, who is Phoibe but the Moon?

Æschylus gives no hint of the Moon nature of Phoibe. To him and to his commentators she seems simply a Titaness, one of the old order used as a bridge between Gaia and Phoibos-Apollo. But Latin poets, unconfused by anthropomorphism, never forget. Vergil[2] writes

> Iamque dies caelo concesserat: almaque curru
> Noctivago Phoebe medium pulsabat Olympum,

and again Ovid[3] with an eye on the mantic Apollo,

> Auguribus Phoebus, Phoebe venantibus adsit.

But we are not left to Latin poets for evidence. We have the direct statement of Plutarch[4]—no better authority could be desired—that, according to Orphic tradition, the oracle at Delphi was held by Night and the Moon. This point is important for our sequence and must be clearly established. The statement occurs in the curious account given of one Thespesios[5]—an oddly magical name—and his spiritual adventures in the underworld.

Thespesios and his guide arrive at a certain place—the topography is necessarily vague, where three daimones are seated at the angles of a triangle, and then

The guide of the soul of Thespesios told him that Orpheus got as far as here, when he went to fetch the soul of his wife, and, from not clearly remembering, he published to mortals a false report that *the oracle at Delphi was shared by Apollo and Night*, whereas in no respect was there community between Night and Apollo. 'But *this* oracle,' said the guide, 'is held in common by Night and the Moon, not issuing out of the earth at any one place, nor having one particular seat, but it wanders everywhere among men in dreams and visions. Hence dreams receive and spread abroad a blend, as you see, of what is simple and true with what is complex and misleading.' 'But the oracle,' he continued, 'of Apollo you cannot see clearly. For the

---

[1] The sense in which Phoibos may be said to 'be' the Sun will be explained later (p. 392). To avoid misunderstanding it may be stated in advance that equivalence is not meant. Phoibos stands for the Sun-aspect of Apollo; and Apollo has other aspects. Hence Phoibos is not the equivalent of Helios, still less is Apollo. The same applies to Phoibe, Artemis and the Moon.

[2] *Æn.* x. 215.   [3] *Amores*, III. 2. 51.

[4] *De ser. num. vindict.* XXII.

[5] His real name was Aridaeus. Thespesios was a new name given him. The whole account reads strongly like the account of an initiation ceremony.

earthiness of the soul will not relax nor permit it to soar upwards but keeps it down tight, held by the body.' Thereon leading him up to it, the guide sought to show Thespesios the light from the tripod which as he said shone through the bosom of Themis on to Parnassos. But much desiring to see it he could not for its brightness, but as he went by he heard the shrill voice of a woman uttering in verse, both other things and, as it seemed, the day of Thespesios' death. And the daimon said that that was the voice of the Sibyl who sang of what was to be *as she was borne round in the face of the moon.* And though he desired to hear more he was pushed away in the contrary direction by the swirl of the moon as though in a whirlpool, so that he only heard distinctly a little.

The story of Thespesios is instructive. It reflects theological embarrassment. Local primitive tradition knew that the oracle at Delphi was of Earth and Night. Like the oracles of Amphiaraos, of Asklepios, and of the Panagia of Tenos to-day, it was a dream-oracle, that came to you while sleeping on holy ground. The suppliants were probably like the Selloi at Dodona χαμαιεῦναι, Couchers-on-the-ground. But an overdone orthodoxy demanded that about Apollo there should be nothing earthy' and no deed or dream of darkness. A bridge, as with Æschylus, was built by way of Phoibe, who is always half of earth and half of heaven. To save the face of the resplendent Sun-God the Sibyl is set in the Face of the Moon[1].

Such mild obscurantism was dear to the gentle Plutarch but it would scarcely have availed but for a clear tradition of the Moon's sometime dominance at Delphi. And it would seem at Delos also. A bronze coin of Athens shows us in the field a copy of the cultus statue of Apollo made by Tektaios and Angelion for the sanctuary at Delos[2]. Apollo holds on' his outstretched hand three figures whom we may call Moirae, Horae, Charites, as we will[3]. They are, like all these triple figures, moon-phases, for, as we remember, according to Orpheus[4] 'the *Moirae* are the divisions (τὰ μέρη) of the Moon[5].' On Delos dwelt Artemis and Apollo, in whom the Persians recognized their own Sun and Moon. Apollo as the Sun, on Delos as at Delphi,

---

[1] Plut. *loc. cit.* ...ἐν τῷ προσώπῳ τῆς σελήνης περιφερομένην. Plutarch says (*de defect. orac.* xiii.) that some called the moon an ἄστρον γεῶδες, others ὀλυμπίαν γῆν, so that she was well adapted as a transition from earth to heaven.

[2] Paus. ix. 35. 3.

[3] Pausanias, *loc. cit.*, says the Apollo of Delos held Charites in his left hand. See the Athenian coin with Apollo and Charites on p. 444. For the shift between Moirae, Horae and Charites, see *supra*, pp. 189—192.

[4] *Supra*, p. 189, note 4.

[5] Hence they are children of Night, as in the Orphic Hymn to the Moirae, which begins Μοῖραι ἀπειρέσιοι Νυκτὸς φίλα τέκνα μελαίνης.

succeeded to, took over, a service of the Moon. We no longer
wonder why Thespesios at the place of the oracle found 'three
daimones seated in triangular pattern[1],' nor why the light and
Fate of the Moon 'shone through the bosom of Themis on to
Parnassos[2].'

We have dwelt on the moon-character of Phoibe because, as
in the sequence of cults enumerated by the priestess it has not
been recognized, some insistence was needed. This sequence is
now clearly before us, Earth, Moon, Sun. To our delight, though
it should not be to our surprise, the same sequence that we met
at Olympia[3] we now meet at Delphi, and this sequence it would
appear is, for agricultural peoples, world-wide.

For long, perhaps too long[4], scholars have reacted against
sun-mythology and moon-mythology. The reaction was of course
brought about by the learned absurdities perpetrated in the name
of these two great lights. The old error of Naturism[5] was to
suppose that sun or moon or dawn or wind exhausted the content
of a god. The new truth, born of psychology and sociology, is to
recognize that, into the content of every man's experience and
hence of every man's divinities, enter elements drawn not only
from earth but from sun and moon.

Mr Payne, in his remarkable, and to me most illuminating,
History of the New World, called America[6], was, I believe, the first
to call attention to this sequence of the gods. His testimony is
specially valuable as arising out of a study of the religious facts
of the New World, not the Old. After a long and interesting
account of the great Earth Goddess of Mexico, he thus continues:

Having thus surveyed the principal objects of worship belonging to the
region of earth we pass on to consider next those belonging to the upper air

---

[1] Plut. *loc. cit.* ἕωρα δὲ τρεῖς δαίμονας ὁμοῦ καθημένους ἐν σχήματι τριγώνου. We are
reminded of Hekate and the crossways.
[2] Plut. *loc. cit.*   [3] *Supra*, p. 237.
[4] I have long protested against the excesses of this reaction. See *Athenaeum*
(No. 4301), April 2, 1910, p. 404, in which I tried to indicate that each god, 'each
and every divine name, is but as it were a focus round which conceptions cluster
from heaven above as well as earth below.' The sequence of these theological
conceptions I owe to Mr Payne, and their special relation to the calendar largely
to Mr Cornford.
[5] The errors of the old Naturism have been admirably exposed by Prof. Durkheim
in his *Examen critique des systèmes classiques sur les origines de la pensée religieuse*,
2nd article in Revue Philosophique, 1909, p. 142.   [6] Vol. I. p. 474.

or firmament; and lastly the heavenly bodies. If our conclusions are correct, the cultivator has universally followed the same order in his theological speculations. Beginning with the gods of the earth, he has advanced to the atmospheric powers or gods of the weather, powers which are at first conceived as dwelling on particular mountains, but are ultimately disengaged from the earth, and formed into a distinct class. He next infers that these important powers are subject to powers higher still, powers which regulate the winds and the rains, compelling them to recur at regular intervals. and through them exercising an ultimate control over the production of food and whatever else affects human life and fortune on earth. These powers are the sun, the moon and the stars. When this point has been reached the cycle is complete. No further progress, none at least on the old lines, is possible.

Mr Payne carefully guards his statement against all excess:

When it is said that man has begun by worshipping the terrestrial powers and has advanced successively to the worship of the atmospheric and the celestial, it is by no means meant that he does not, in the very earliest stages of advancement, recognize the wind and the rain, the sun and the moon, as objects exercising influence over his fortunes; for such objects naturally awaken even in the savage mind the instincts of fear and veneration. What is meant is that the atmospheric and stellar powers take a prominent place in the incorporated family of men and gods, bound together by the covenant of sacrifice at a later period than the gods of the earth. The recognition of these powers as benevolent ones belongs to the stage of artificial food-production.

As to the sequence moon and sun rather than sun and moon and the cause of this sequence Mr Payne is equally explicit[1]:

The worship of the moon naturally precedes that of the sun, because a connection is traced between the lunar phenomena and the food-supply in an earlier stage than that in which a connection is traced between the food-supply and the solar phenomena. The different seasons of the year bring with them different supplies of natural force....The approach and duration of the periods in which these different supplies are provided is measured by the successive re-appearances and gradual changes of the moon. Hence apparently the savage naturally regards the moon as the cause of these successive supplies of food[2].

To all the beneficent aspects and relations of the moon as insisted on by all authorities we may add perhaps, in the making of man's early religion, some touch of spectral terror of the remote dull staring thing:

Setebos, Setebos, Setebos,
Thinketh he dwelleth in the cold of the moon.

In Mr Payne's sequence one step on the ladder from earth to heaven is what may be called the 'weather.' He adopts in fact without knowing it a distinction at which the Stoic philosophers arrived and which is very convenient for religion, the distinction

[1] *Op. cit.* i. p. 493.
[2] In some parts of the world the successive moons or months are called by the name of the plants that appear in them.

between τὰ μετάρσια and τὰ μετέωρα. The Stoic writer Achilles[1], going back probably to Poseidonios, writes thus:

Τὰ μετέωρα are distinguished from τὰ μετάρσια thus: τὰ μετέωρα are the things in heaven and the ether, as e.g. the sun and the other heavenly bodies and ouranos and ether: τὰ μετάρσια are the things between the air and the earth, such as winds.

The gist of the distinction lies in the difference between *aer* and *aither*; τὰ μετέωρα are the holy blaze of *aither* which is uppermost, τὰ μετάρσια, thunder, rain, clouds, wind, are of the damp cold *aer*, the lower region of earthy mist. Of all the heavenly bodies the moon with her dew and mists is most akin to τὰ μετάρσια.

From the sequence of Æschylus τὰ μετάρσια are missing. He was probably only half conscious of the moon and sun elements in Phoibe and Phoibos, and of the disorderly phenomena of the weather as sanctities he took no account. In our previous chapters on the *Thunder-Rites* and on *Bird-Magic* we have seen how early and large a place τὰ μετάρσια held in Greek religion, but τὰ μετάρσια were among the elements that Olympian religion tried, though somewhat vainly, to discard. Even however at Delphi traces remain, for we find the weather birds perching at either side of the omphalos of Gaia, and Zeus is obliged to acknowledge them as his eagles.

In the light then of comparative religion Æschylus is seen to be right. At Delphi, as elsewhere, broadly speaking man's reactions and hence his interests or emotions focus first on earth as a source of food, then successively on the moon and sun as fertilizers and regents of the season. In every rite and every mythological figure these elements must be reckoned with. In analysing a god we must look for traits from earth, from 'weather,' from moon, from sun. The earth stage will show him as a snake or a bull or a tree or in human form as Megistos Kouros or Thallophoros. The moon[2] will give him horns afresh,

---

[1] περὶ σφαίρας. The fragment is printed in the *Uranologie* of Petavius, Paris, 1680. My quotation is borrowed from O. Gilbert's valuable work, *Die Meteorologischen Theorien d. Gr. Altertums*, 1907, p. 8.

[2] Moon-elements are found in nearly all goddesses and many heroines: in Athena, Artemis, Hekate, Persephone, Bendis; in Antiope, Europa, Pasiphaë, Auge, and a host of others. Sun-elements in Odysseus, Bellerophon, Perseus, Talos, Ixion, Phaethon. Sun and moon symbols are the bull, the golden dog, the Golden Fleece, the Golden Lamb, etc., etc. In fact, if our contention be true, there is scarcely any mythological figure that does not contain sun and moon elements, and scarcely any of which the content is exhausted by sun and moon.

the sun will lend him a wheel or a chariot or a golden cup. Such a view is not sun-mythology or moon-mythology, it is common human psychology. What a man attends to, feels about, provided it be socially enforced and perpetuated, that is his religion, thence are his gods.

But what Æschylus envisaged as a divine sequence, and what modern psychology and anthropology know to be a necessary development, looked quite otherwise to the popular mind. A gradual evolution seen from beginning and end only is apt to be conceived as a fight between the two poles. So it was at Delphi. The natural sequence of cults from Gaia to Apollo was seen by the man in the street as a fight between Earth and the Sun, between Darkness and Light, between the dream-oracle and the truth of heaven. All this for ritual reasons that will appear later crystallized in the form of a myth, the slaying of the Python by Apollo.

Æschylus has given us the peaceful evolution. The fight, though probably a fiction, is of great importance to us because it helps us to realize one cardinal factor in the making of an Olympian. Euripides[1] gives us the fight in two traditional forms: first the slaying of the snake, and second the dream-oracle of Earth and Night as against Phoibos the Sun. The chorus of captive maidens, handmaidens to Iphigeneia, think with longing of Delos and tell of Apollo's birth there and his passing to Delphi. Euripides as was natural in an Athenian, accepts the version that Apollo came from Delos, not from Crete.

> Oh fair the fruits of Leto blow;   Strophe.
> A Virgin, one, with joyous bow,
> And one a Lord of flashing locks,
>   Wise in the harp, Apollo:
> She bore them amid Delian rocks,
>   Hid in a fruited hollow.
>
> But forth she fared from that low reef,
> Sea-cradle of her joy and grief,
> A crag she knew more near the skies
>   And lit with wilder water,
> That leaps with joy of Dionyse:
>   There brought she son and daughter.

[1] *I. in T.* 1235.

Then comes the slaying of the snake, as in some way necessary—
Euripides does not say why—if Apollo is to come to his own.
The snake, the guardian of the old Earth oracle, is killed, but the
general apparatus of the cult, the cleft in the earth, the tripod
and the omphalos, is kept.

> And there, behold, an ancient Snake,   Strophe 1245.
> Wine-eyed, bronze-gleaming, in the brake
> Of deep-leaved laurel, ruled the dell,
>   Sent by old Earth from under
> Strange caves to guard her oracle,
>   A thing of fear and wonder.
>
> Thou, Phoebus, still a new-born thing,
>   Meet in thy mother's arms to lie,
> Didst kill the Snake, and crown thee King
>   In Pytho's land of prophecy;
> Thine was the tripod and the chair
> Of golden truth; and throned there,
> Hard by the streams of Castaly,
>   Beneath the untrodden portal
> Of Earth's mid-stone there flows from thee
>   Wisdom for all things mortal.

Phoibos as a new-born child slays the snake. We are reminded
inevitably of the young New Year, of Telesphoros; we remember
also that the hero-kings of Athens were thought of as snakes.
But these questions must wait. For the death of her snake and
the banishment of Themis which goes with it, Earth takes revenge,
she sends up dream-oracles.

> He slew the Snake; he cast, men say,   Antistrophe.
> Themis, the child of Earth, away
> From Pytho and her hallowed stream;
>   Then Earth, in dark derision,
> Brought forth the Peoples of the Dream
>   And all the tribes of Vision.
>
> And men besought them; and from deep
> Confusèd underworlds of sleep
> They showed blind things that erst had been
>   And are, and yet shall follow.
> So did avenge that old Earth Queen
>   Her child's wrong on Apollo.

Clearly the oracle abolished by Apollo, the particular Themis
banished by the god, was just the sort that Orpheus attributed
to Delphi and the existence of which at Delphi was denied by
the orthodox guide of Thespesios[1]; it was of Earth and Night; like
that of Asklepios it was of dream and snakes. The chorus puts

---

[1] *Supra*, p. 388.

it as though this kind of oracle was started by Earth in revenge
to 'spoil the trade of Delphi[1].'   It was of course there from the
beginning, and the snake is its representative.

> Then swiftly flew that conquering one
> To Zeus on high and round the throne
> Twining a small indignant hand,
>   Prayed him to send redeeming
> To Pytho, from that troublous band
>   Sprung from the darks of dreaming.
>
> Zeus laughed to see the babe, I trow,
> So swift to claim his golden rite;
> He laughed and bowed his head, in vow
> To still those voices of the night.
> And so from out the eyes of men
> That dark dream-truth was lost again;
> And Phoebus, thronèd where the throng
>   Prays at the golden portal,
> Again doth shed in sunlit song[2]
>   Hope unto all things mortal.

It is a strange hymn, its gods concerned with hope and
petty jealousy.   It reflects the Delphi of the day which stood for
greed and lying and time-serving and obscurantism.   But because
Euripides is poet more even than moralist, it is redeemed and
made beautiful by the background in which move the two ancient
protagonists Night and Day.   Still, Euripides the mystic did not,
could not, wholly love Apollo, who stood more and more for clear
light and truth and reason and order and symmetry and the
harmony of the heavenly bodies and all the supposed Greek
virtues.   He knew of a god whose rites and whose beauty were
of darkness; when Pentheus asks Dionysos:

> How is thy worship held, by night or day?

the god makes answer:

> Most often night: 'tis a majestic thing
> The darkness[3].

Literary tradition then is unanimous as to the sequence of
cults from Gaia to Apollo.   Æschylus explains it as a peaceful
and orderly development, Euripides as a fight.   We have now to

[1] See Prof. Murray, *Iphigeneia in Tauris*, p. 103.
[2] v. 1279   ἀπὸ δ' ἀλαθοσύναν νυκτωπὸν ἐξεῖλεν βροτῶν,
                   καὶ τιμὰς πάλιν θῆκε Λοξίᾳ,
                   πολυάνορι δ' ἐν ξενόεντι θρόνῳ θάρση βροτοῖς
                           θεοφάτων ἀοιδαῖς.
There is no 'sunlit' in the original, but Prof. Murray divines that it is the young
Sun-God who climbs to his father's throne.
[3] Eur. *Bacch.* 485.

see what light is thrown on the situation and on the character of the ultimately dominant Olympian by an examination of the actual ritual at Delphi and the evidence of monuments. We begin with the cultus of Gaia.

Of a ritual of Gaia under that name we have, it must be clearly understood at the outset, no evidence. But of her chief sanctity, the omphalos, we know much, and it is through our understanding of the omphalos that we shall come to realize the relation between Earth and Apollo and their ultimate hostility, as figured in the slaying of the Python. It is of the first importance to be clear about the omphalos, but it is not from Æschylus that we shall learn its real nature, though it is only when that nature is understood that we can feel the full beauty and reality of the *agon* in his *Eumenides*.

The Omphalos.

By the time of Æschylus the omphalos was regarded as simply a holy Stone which, by pious consent, was held to be the centre of the earth; it was a fetich-thing, supremely sacred, to which the suppliant clings. This holy Stone is naturally in the innermost shrine. Thither, when the priestess[1] has ended her ordering and invocation of the Delphian divinities, she goes, and there she finds Orestes, clinging to the omphalos, horribly polluting its sanctity by his touch. The scene, *mutatis mutandis*, is figured on many vase-paintings, one of which is given in Fig. 108[2]. It brings the conical holy Stone clearly before us; it is covered with fillets, a refuge for the suppliant. Its sanctity is clearly established, but what was the cause of this sanctity? In a word what did the omphalos really stand for, really mean?

The name *omphalos* is little or no help. Like its correlative *umbilicus* it came to mean *navel*, but originally it only meant any sort of boss or thing that bulged, the boss of a shield or a phialè, an island that stands up on the 'nombril' of the sea[3]. Fortunately

---

[1] Æsch. *Eum.* 39

ἐγὼ μὲν ἕρπω πρὸς πολυστεφῆ μυχόν·
ὁρῶ δ' ἐπ' ὀμφαλῷ μὲν ἄνδρα θεομυσῆ,
ἕδραν ἔχοντα προστρόπαιον.

[2] O. Jahn, *Vasenbilder, Orestes in Delphi*, 1839, Taf. I. The vase was formerly in the Lamberti collection.

[3] Later it may have been connected with ὀμφή, as the place of sacred utterance.

we are not left to philology. We know what an omphalos actually *was*, and we have traditions as to what it was believed to be. These traditions seem at first to contradict the monumental

Fig. 108.

evidence, but, as we shall see immediately, both tradition and monumental facts, are equally true and equally essential to any right understanding.   We begin with the monumental facts.

Few, Pausanias[1] tells us, ever entered the adyton ; few therefore saw the real omphalos.   Pausanias himself does not seem to have seen it, for, in enumerating the contents of the adyton, he makes no mention of the omphalos.   But, outside the temple near the altar of the Chians and the famous stand of the krater of Alyattes, king of Lydia, there was another omphalos which Pausanias[2] did see and thus describes :

What the people of Delphi call the *omphalos* is made of white stone and is said by them to be at the centre of the whole earth, and Pindar in one of his odes agrees with this.

Pausanias it would seem, before he entered the temple, saw *an* omphalos and *à propos* of it gives the current tradition about *the* omphalos which he did not see.   On the vase-painting[3] in Fig. 109 which represents the slaying of Neoptolemos, an egg-shaped omphalos is seen in the open air under a palm tree.

[1] x. 24. 5.
[2] x. 16. 2 τὸν δὲ ὑπὸ Δελφῶν καλούμενον ὀμφαλόν, λίθου πεποιημένον λευκοῦ τοῦτο εἶναι τὸ ἐν μέσῳ γῆς πάσης κ.τ.λ.
[3] *Annali d. Inst.* 1868, Tav. d' Agg. E.

This outside omphalos has been found by the French excavators[1]

FIG. 109.

just on the very spot where Pausanias saw it, and is shown in Fig. 110. As he described it, it is not *a* stone but 'made of white stone.' It

FIG. 110.

is covered with an *agrenon*, a net of fillets copied here in stone. We have then simply a holy Stone, and the evidence of Pausanias and the vases is confirmed. The discovery of an actual omphalos, we are told, is 'exceedingly interesting,' but we are not one jot better off than we were as to its meaning. The old question faces us. What is the reason of its sanctity?

We turn to literary tradition and literary tradition comes as a salutary shock. It is to Varro we owe a tradition as to the omphalos that is of capital importance. Epimenides

[1] By kind permission of the Director of the Ecole Francaise I was allowed to publish it in the *Bulletin de Correspondance Hellénique*, 1900, p. 254, Fig. 2. But as the title of my article—*Aegis-Agrenon*—shows, its object was only to discuss the decoration. I had previously (*Delphika*, J. H. S. xix. 1899, p. 225) discussed the value of the omphalos itself, and to this article I must refer for many details. A number of illustrations of omphaloi will be found in Prof. Middleton's article in *J. H. S.* 1888, p. 296 ff. By far the best account of the omphalos known to me is that by Dr G. Karo in Daremberg and Saglio's *Dictionnaire des Antiquités Grecques et Romaines*, s.v. omphalos. By the kindness of Prof. Svoronos I have just received his monograph on οἱ ὀμφαλοὶ τῶν Πυθίων, but not in time to utilize his researches.

of Phaistos—having an omphalos of his own in Crete, though
he did not assign this as the reason—impiously denied that the
omphalos at Delphi was the centre of the earth[1]. Varro[2] agrees
with him, and not only, he says, is the omphalos at Delphi not
the centre of the earth but the human navel is not the centre
of the human body.   He then goes on to say that

> What the Greeks call the *omphalos* is something at the side of the temple
> at Delphi, of the shape of a *thesaurus*, and *they say it is the tumulus of Python*.

The omphalos then according to *literary* tradition is not a fetich-
stone but a grave-mound, and moreover, for this is cardinal, it is
not a grave-mound commemorating a particular dead man, it is
the grave-mound of a sacred snake, *the* sacred snake of Delphi.

The testimony of Varro does not stand alone.   Hesychios[3] in
explaining the words Τοξίου βουνός, 'Archer's Mound,' says:

> It is of Apollo in Sikyon, but according to a better tradition it is the
> place in Delphi called *Napè* (ravine).   For there the snake was shot down.
> *And the omphalos of Earth is the tomb* (τάφος) *of the Python*.

Monumental fact then says that the omphalos is a holy Stone,
tradition says it is the grave of a daimon-snake.   Which is right?
Happily both.   The question once fairly stated almost answers
itself.   A holy Stone is not a grave, but a holy Stone may stand
upon a grave, and such a complex of tomb and tombstone is the
omphalos.

Tomb and tombstone, grave-mound and stele are known to us,
of course, from Homer.   When Sarpedon was carried to the rich
land of wide Lycia his kinsmen and clansmen buried him

> With mound and stele—such are dead men's dues[4].

Grave-mounds are found all over the world.   They are, when
the ground is soft, the simplest form of sepulture; you dig a hole,
heap a mound, plant a stone or memorial pillar to mark the spot.
You may have the mound without the stone, or the stone without
the mound, but for a complete conspicuous tomb you want both.

---

[1] Plut. *de defect. orac.* i.   The myth here related is purely aetiological to account
for the birds on the omphalos.   It does not here concern us.

[2] *De ling. Lat.* vii. 17 Praeterea si quod medium id est umbilicus, ut pilae, terrae,
non Delphi medium.   Sed terrae medium non hoc sed quod vocant Delphis in
aede ad latus est quiddam ut thesauri specie, quod Graeci vocant ὀμφαλόν, quem
Pythonos aiunt tumulum.

[3] s.v. Τοξίου βουνός.

[4] *Il.* XVI. 675 τύμβῳ τε στήλῃ τε· τὸ γὰρ γέρας ἐστὶ θανόντων.

Is this then all? Is the omphalos simply the heaped-up grave
of a local hero marked by a commemorative pillar? Are we driven
at last by facts, back to common-sense and Euhemerism? A
thousand times 'No.' The omphalos is a grave compounded of
mound and stele; yet the grave contains no dead man but a
daimon-snake; the stele is, as we shall immediately see, a thing
not commemorative but magical.

Varro tells us the omphalos is like in shape to a *thesaurus* or
treasury. It is now recognized that the 'treasury' of which Varro
is speaking is not, as was formerly supposed, a beehive tomb, a
thing like the 'Treasury' of Atreus, but merely a money-box of
the beehive tomb shape[1]. Two of these are reproduced in Fig.
111 *a* and *b*. Their shape is that of a blunt cone, and their likeness

a   *b*

FIG. 111.

to the omphalos is clear. On the one (*a*) just below the hole for
the money, is a shrine with Hermes holding purse and kerykeion;
near him his cock. On the other (*b*) stands a figure of Fortuna
or Agathe Tyche with cornucopia and rudder. They are there, as
the god and goddess of money, but it will not be forgotten[2] that
in early days they were daimones of the fertility of the earth.

[1] H. Graeven, *Die thönerne Sparbüchse in Altertum* in Jahrbuch d. Inst. XVI.
1901, p. 160, Figs. 27, 29. Specimen (*a*) was formerly in the Castellani collection;
(*b*) is in the Cabinet de médailles of the Bibliothèque Nationale, No. 5230.
[2] pp. 284 and 296.

But, though Varro is probably only thinking of money-boxes, these money-boxes reflect the shape and to some extent the function of other and earlier 'Treasuries,' the familiar beehive tombs. Pausanias[1] thus describes the 'Treasury' of Minyas, to him the great wonder of the world:

It is made of stone; its shape is round, rising up to a rather blunt top, and they say that the topmost stone is the keystone of the whole building.

We are reminded of the omphalos-form, and it seems others saw the analogy too, for Aristotle[2] tells us that

What are called *omphaloi* are the midmost stones in vaulted buildings.

A beehive tomb must of necessity have a central keystone, but the 'Treasuries' which abound in Greece proper have no keystone that is in any way like an omphalos. For a real and instantly convincing analogy we must go to Asia Minor. In Fig. 112 we have

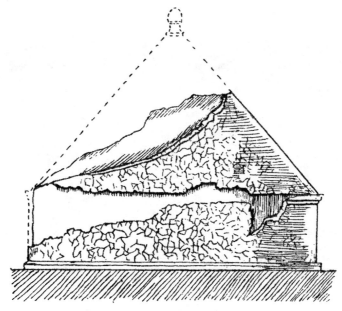

FIG. 112.

a view of the so-called 'Tomb of Tantalos' on Mt. Sipylos, before it was excavated[3]. The dotted lines indicate of course a restoration

[1] ix. 38. 3 ...σχῆμα δὲ περιφερές ἐστιν αὐτῷ, κορυφὴ δὲ οὐκ ἐς ἄγαν ὀξὺ ἀνηγμένη... τῶν δὲ ἀνωτάτω τῶν λίθων φασὶν ἁρμονίαν παντὶ εἶναι τῷ οἰκοδομήματι.

[2] *De mund.* vi. 28 οἱ ὀμφαλοὶ δὲ λεγόμενοι οἱ ἐν ταῖς ψαλῖσι λίθοι, οἱ μέσοι κείμενοι.

[3] Texier, *Description de l'Asie Mineure*, vol. ii. pp. 253, 254, Plate cxxx., Fig. 14. For evidence as to the restoration see the text. Numerous *phalloi* were found round the tombs, of just the right size to serve as keystones. They are omphalos-shaped.

but a certain one—the keystone of the great vault is a terminal cone like the Delphic omphalos; the chamber of death was crowned by the primitive symbol of life. It is no stele commemorating an individual man, still less is it a mere architectural or decorative feature; it is there with solemn magical intent to, ensure, to induce, the renewal of life, reincarnation.

The 'Tomb of Tantalos' is of great importance because it fixes beyond a doubt the nature of an omphalos stone. But if Asia Minor is felt to be too remote we have evidence, though somewhat less explicit, nearer home. On the road from Megalopolis to Messene, Pausanias[1] saw a sanctuary of certain goddesses called *Maniae*, which name he believed to be a title of the Eumenides. With the sanctuary was associated the story of the madness of Orestes.

Not far from the sanctuary is a mound of earth of no great size and set up upon it is a finger made of stone. And indeed the name of the mound is Finger's Tomb.

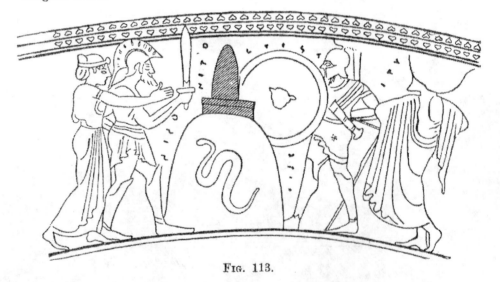

Fig. 113.

Pausanias goes on to recount a purely aetiological myth about Orestes in his madness biting off one of his fingers.

What 'Finger's Tomb' must have looked like may be seen in Fig. 113 the design from a black-figured lekythos[2]. We have the

---

[1] VIII. 34. 2 ...οὐ πόρρω δὲ τοῦ ἱεροῦ γῆς χῶμά ἐστιν οὐ μέγα, ἐπίθημα ἔχον λίθου πεποιημένον δάκτυλον, καὶ δὴ καὶ ὄνομα τῷ χώματί ἐστι Δακτύλου μνῆμα.
[2] In the Naples Museum. For full details see my *Delphika* in J.H.S. XIX. 1889, p. 229.

mound of earth covered in this case by *leukoma*. The mound is surmounted by a conical stone painted black and, roughly, finger-shaped. It stands on a basis of black stone. Bury the mound out of sight in earth, and you have an omphalos on a basis like those in the vase-paintings. The figures on either side approach as though for some solemn ritual; probably of oath-taking.

We have translated the words Δακτύλου μνῆμα as 'Finger's Tomb' because they were undoubtedly so understood by Pausanias and the people who told the aetiological myth about Orestes. But the true gist of the monument is better realized if we translate 'Daktyl's monument.' In discussing Herakles the nature of the Daktyls[1] became evident. They are fertility-daimones. Daktyl's monument is *mutatis mutandis* the same as the 'Tomb of Tantalos.'

The funeral mound in Fig. 113 is marked by a great black snake. A white mound marked by a snake is indeed on vase-paintings the normal form of a hero's tomb. A good instance is shown in

FIG. 114.

Fig. 114 from a black-figured amphora[2]. Here we have the funeral mound of Patroklos. Above the mound is a pigmy *eidolon*, the hero's ghost; on the mound is the hero-snake whose meaning is now[3] to us amply clear. To its special significance in relation to the omphalos we shall return when we come to the myth of the slaying of Python.

The covering of white stucco served a double purpose. It preserved the mound from the weather and also made it conspicuous. A tomb was necessarily *tabu*, and the more conspicuous it was, the safer for the chance passer-by. In Fig. 115 from an Attic

[1] *Supra*, p. 370.
[2] Gerhard, *Auserlesene Vasenbilder*, III. Taf. 199. Berlin, Cat. 1867, No. 1902.
[3] *Supra*, chapter VIII.

lekythos[1] the mound is covered with *leukoma* but the precaution
has failed. A passer-by has transgressed the *tabu*. Out from the

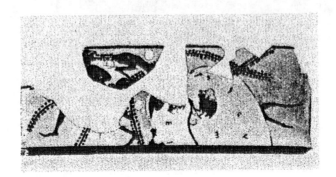

Fig. 115.

grave-mound darts a huge snake, the offended daimon, the Erinys
of the tomb.

The ordinary grave-mound, as seen in Figs. 113, 114, is
covered with *leukoma* on which is painted a snake, but it has as a
rule no surmounting cone. It is not a complete omphalos-tomb.
On many Athenian lekythoi we have a representation of the
mound and the stele. A fine example[2] is given in Fig. 116. The

Fig. 116.

[1] Remains of actual tombs covered with λεύκωμα have come to light. That it
was in use in Athens we know from Solon's prescription of it (Cicero, *de leg.* II. 26).
For the whole question see Winnefeld, *Jahrbuch d. Inst.* 1891, p. 197, Taf. IV., by
whom the vase in Fig. 115 was first published.
[2] Now in the National Museum, Athens. See Prof. Bosanquet, *Some early
Funeral Lekythoi*, J. H. S. XIX. 1899, Pl. II. p. 169.

commemorative stele stands on a high stepped basis. Apparently behind it is a large egg-shaped grave-mound.

It is tempting to see in the stele a survival or transformation of the surmounting cone, but the vase-painting in Fig. 117[1] forbids

Fig. 117.

this supposition. When a vase-painter wanted to draw a cone he was well able to do so. It is not clear from the drawing whether the cone stood by the side of the mound or passed through it emerging into sight at the top, but in any case we have a well-defined cone not a stele. The intent is therefore magical not commemorative, though as we saw in considering the *Intichiuma* ceremonies the two are to the primitive mind not wholly sundered[2].

The sceptical reader will probably by this time demand a plain answer to a long-suppressed question. By collecting and combining scattered evidence, literary and monumental, it has been made possible and indeed practically certain that the omphalos was a cone surmounting a grave. We have further had abundant evidence that cones did surmount graves. Well and good. But such monuments, we found, were called the 'Tomb of Tantalos' or 'Finger's Tomb.' Can we point to any grave-mound surmounted by a cone which we can fairly associate with an omphalos? Happily

[1] From an Athenian white lekythos in the possession of Mr Cook, by whose most kind permission it is figured here. The drawing was made for me by Mrs Hugh Stewart.

[2] *Supra*, p. 124.

we can, and this final evidence clinches our whole argument. It also casts new light on the relations between Gaia and Apollo.

APOLLO AGUIEUS.

The bronze coin[1] in Fig. 118 is from Byzantium. On the obverse

is the head of Apollo; on the reverse an object which, in the light of what has been already seen, is not hard to explain. It is a mound surmounted by a tall narrow cone-shaped pillar, round which near the top is a wreath. The cone with the wreath looks somewhat like a cross, and might be mistaken for this

Fig. 118.

Christian symbol. We are however able to trace the type back to earlier coins where all likeness to the cross disappears.

In Fig. 119 we have placed side by side for comparison (a) a

a   b   c

Fig. 119.

coin of Megara, (b) a coin of Apollonia in Illyria, (c) a coin of Ambrakia in Epiros. All three show the slender obelisk or cone of our Byzantium coin, but it stands on a basis not a mound, and has slightly variant adjuncts. The Megara coin (a) is of special interest, for Byzantium was a colony of Megara and doubtless derived its coin-types from the mother-city. The obelisk here is decorated with two dependent fillets and what seems to be a wreath seen sideways, it is certainly *not* a cross; to either side in the field is a dolphin. On the coin of Apollonia (b) the pillar tapers slightly to either end and has a wreath only. The coin of Ambrakia (c) has two fillets dependent from the point of the obelisk, and here a surprise awaits us.

The filleted obelisk on the coins of Ambrakia is the symbol

---

[1] In the possession of Mr Cook, and published by his kind permission from a drawing made for me by Mrs H. Stewart. For previous discussion of the type see Pauly-Wissowa, s.v. *Aguieus*, p. 912.

and vehicle of a god thrice familiar, Apollo Aguieus, 'He of the Ways.' Harpocration[1] thus describes him:

Aguieus is a pillar tapering to the end, which they set up before the doors. And some say they are proper to Apollo, others to Dionysos, others to both.

It is usually thought that Harpocration is blundering when he attributes the Aguieus pillar to Dionysos. Now that its real nature as a fertility-symbol is understood he is seen to be right. The pillar was neither Apollo nor Dionysos, it preceded and entered into the nature of both.

A good specimen of an actual Aguieus-pillar[2] is still extant and is given in Fig. 120. It is cone-shaped, and on it are a number of pegs on some of which hang votive wreaths. About two-thirds of the way up as on the coin of Megara a fillet is twined round the pillar. Round the vase are sculptured figures of Apollo himself in human form dancing round his own Aguieus pillar. Opposite him is Pan playing on the syrinx. To their piping dance the three Horae. It is a strange conjunction of old and new, the human-shaped

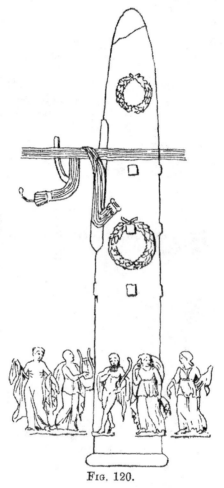

Fig. 120.

[1] s.v. Ἀγυιᾶς· ἀγυιεὺς δέ ἐστι κίων εἰς ὀξὺ λήγων, ὃν ἱστᾶσι πρὸ τῶν θυρῶν· ἰδίους δὲ εἶναί φασιν αὐτοὺς Ἀπόλλωνος, οἱ δὲ Διονύσου, οἱ δὲ ἀμφοῖν.

[2] Now in the Villa Albani. See Panofka, *Dionysos und die Thyiaden*, 1852, Taf. III. No. 9. Panofka explains the pillar as Dionysos, and refers to the Dionysos Stylos of Thebes (Clem. Alex. *Strom.* I. 346). But the cones were before the human-shaped god, and it is only by their monumental context that they can be assigned to one or another. In the present case the lyre-playing Apollo points to Aguieus. Further, we know from Clement (*Strom.* I. 348) that according to the author of the *Europia*, in the temple of Apollo at Delphi there was a high pillar on which were hung tithes and spoils votive to him.

Ὄφρα θεῷ δεκάτην ἀκροθίνιά τε κρεμάσαιμεν
σταθμῶν ἐκ ζαθέων καὶ κίονος ὑψήλοιο.

But the description is too vague to be decisive evidence.

divinities still as it were adhering to the old sanctity from which they sprang.

The cone with the dancing Horae throws light I think on one form of the triple Hekate, as shown in Fig. 121[1]. Three maidens dance round a central half-humanized column. The type which occurs frequently is usually and rightly explained as Hekate, and the triple Charites who dance round the column are triple because of the three phases of the Moon. As such they are clearly shown in another Hekateion relief at Budapest, where on the head

FIG. 121.

of the midmost figure is a great crescent. Further this relief shows clearly that the triple maidens were, to begin with, of earth. One of them like the Semnae, like the Erinyes, holds a coiled snake. The Horae or Seasons of the Moon, her *Moirae*, are preceded by the earlier Horae, the Seasons of Earth's fertility, at first two, spring for blossoming, autumn for fruit, then under the influence of a moon-calendar three. These earliest Horae dance as was meet round the old fertility-pillar.

The scholiast on the *Wasps*[3] as well as Suidas[4] both state that the cone-shaped Aguieus is Dorian, and the statement according to the scholiast has the authority of Dieuchidas of the fourth century B.C. who wrote chronicles of Megara. The point is interesting because the coins cited all come from Dorian colonies, and since Prof. Ridgeway's[5] investigations Dorian now spells for us not late Hellenic but primitive 'Pelasgian.'

[1] In the Museum at Prague. For these Hekateia see my *Mythol. and Mon. of Anc. Athens*, p. 379.

[2] *Archäol. epigr. Mitt. aus Oestr.* IV. Taf. VI.

[3] v. 875 ὦ δέσποτ' ἄναξ γεῖτον Ἀγυιεῦ τοὐμοῦ προθύρου προπύλαιε.

[4] s.v. Ἀγυιαί...ἀγυιεὺς δέ ἐστι κίων...as in Harpocration. He adds ἔστι δὲ ἴδιον Δωριέων· εἶεν δ' ἂν οἱ παρὰ τοῖς Ἀττικοῖς λεγόμενοι ἀγυιεῖς οἱ πρὸ τῶν οἰκιῶν βωμοί· ὡς Σοφοκλῆς μετάγων τὰ Ἀθηναίων ἔθη εἰς Τροίαν φησὶ
Λάμπει δ' ἀγυιεὺς βωμὸς ἀτμίζων πυρὶ
σμύρνης σταλαγμούς, βαρβάρους εὐοσμίας.
καὶ ἀγυιεὺς ὁ πρὸ τῶν αὐλείων θυρῶν κωνοειδὴς κίων ἱερὸς Ἀπόλλωνος καὶ αὐτὸς θεός.

[5] *Who were the Dorians?* in Anthropological Essays presented to E. B. Tylor, 1907, p. 295, but for another view see Mr C. Hawes, *B.S.A.* XVI. 1909–10, p. 265.

Suidas speaks of the Aguieus pillars as 'altars' (βωμοί).   As
an altar in our sense, as a place for burnt-offering, the obelisk could
scarcely serve, but, when it stood on a grave-mound or on a basis,
mound or basis would serve as altar while wreaths and *stemmata*
as on the coins would be hung on the obelisk.   In this connection
it is instructive to note that on a black-figured vase-painting[1]
Fig. 122 we have an omphalos-like structure decorated with diaper
pattern, and against it is clearly written 'Βωμός.'   The primitive
altar was not a stone structure raised high above the earth but
rather a low mound of earth, a grave-mound.   This is shown very
clearly in the vase-painting on another vase[2], where there is no

Fig. 122.

doubt that the omphalos-like structure is a grave-mound.   The
scene is the slaying of Polyxena over the very tomb of Achilles
into which her blood is seen flowing.   Near the omphalos-altar is a
low hearth, an *eschara*.

The pillar of Aguieus stood before the entrance of the Athenian
house[3].   This comes out very clearly in the absurd scene of the
sacralization of the Court in the *Wasps*[4].   The chorus of old
dikasts solemnly invoke the god of the place:

'O Pythian Phoebus, and Good Fortune,
O speed this youth's design
Wrought here, these gates before;
Give us from wanderings rest
And peace for evermore,
Ieie Paian.'

[1] *Munich Cat.* 124; Gerhard, *Auserlesene Vasenbilder*, 223.
[2] A 'Tyrrhenian' amphora in the British Museum.   H. B. Walters, *J. H. S.*
XVIII. 1898, Pl. xv. p. 284.
[3] Three examples of Aguieus-pillars are still *in situ* beside house-doors at
Pompeii.   Another, inscribed Μῦς με ἴσατο, is in the Corfu Museum.   See J. Six in
A. Mitt. XIX. 1894, 340—345.
[4] *v.* 869.   I have ventured to interpolate 'Good Fortune' in Mr Rogers' translation, of which I make use.   Apollo as Aguieus is essentially Agathos-Daimon.
He probably had the old honey-service instead of wine, and this I think is referred
to in the words (*v.* 878) ἀντὶ σιραίου μέλιτος μικρὸν τῷ θυμιδίῳ παραμίξας.

And Bdelycleon, while the Paean is sung, looks up to the conical pillar of Aguieus who was also Patroos and prays for his father:

'Aguieus, my neighbour, my hero, my lord! who dwellest in front of my
    vestibule gate,
I pray thee be graciously pleased to accept the rite that we new for my
    father create.'

Apollo Aguieus is often interpreted as a sun-pillar and with some measure of truth. In front of the ordinary Athenian house there stood not only an Aguieus but a Hekateion. Philocleon[1] is filled with the bright hope that the oracles will come true and each Athenian will someday build

Before his own door in the porch a Courtlet,
A dear little Courtlet like a Hekateion.

Aguieus the sun will guard and guide him by day, Hekate the Moon by night. So the scholiast on Plato[2] understands Apollo and Hekate. They are both ἐνόδιοι δαίμονες 'Way-Gods,' lighting the wayfarer, the first business of moon and sun to primitive man.

By '*daimon* of the ways' he means Artemis or Selene; Apollo also is called Of the Ways (Aguieus), because they both fill the ways with light, the one, the Sun, by day, the other by night. Therefore they set them up in the roads.

The triple Hekateia as we have seen show a pillar surrounded by three dancing figures[3]. The pillar of life has become a pillar of light. Aguieus is Phoibos.

Aguieus the pillar is often confused with the Herm. The wife of Mnesilochos goes out to met her lover and talks to him, near the Aguias, under a bay-tree. The scholiast[4] explains Aguieus as a herm. 'They give this name to a four-square Apollo.' In intent there is obviously no difference, but the form was unlike and they were probably developed by different peoples. Hermes remained in cultus phallic to the end; Aguieus, at least at Delphi, was by historical times expurgated, possibly because he early took

---

[1] Ar. *Vesp.* 804.
[2] *Legg.* 914 B ἐνοδίαν δαίμονα τὴν Ἄρτεμιν ἤτοι τὴν Σελήνην φησίν, ἐπεὶ καὶ ὁ Ἀπόλλων Ἀγυιεύς, καὶ γὰρ ἄμφω τὰς ὁδοὺς πληροῦσι φωτός, ὁ μὲν ἡμέρας ὁ ἥλιος ἡ δὲ νυκτός. διὸ καὶ ἰδρύουσι τούτους ἐν αὐταῖς.
[3] *Supra*, p. 408.
[4] Ar. *Thesm.* 489 παρὰ τὸν Ἀγυιᾶ, Schol. ἀγυιεὺς οὕτω καλούμενος Ἀπόλλων τετράγωνος.

on as 'birthday gift' from Phoibe the fertility of the moon rather than the earth.

On the red-figured vase-painting in Fig. 123[1] we see the

Fig. 123.

Olympian Apollo seated on the omphalos[2]. The scene is certainly at Delphi, for the figure approaching on the left and holding a sheathed sword is Orestes balanced to the right by Pylades. Apollo looks triumphant holding lyre and laurel branch, and if we think of him as dethroning Gaia from her ancient seat we find his intrusion hard to bear, but, remembering Aguieus, it may be that the seated Olympian is no *parvenu* but only the fully humanized form of the ancient fertility cone, surmounting the grave-mound.

The grave-cone took shape in Aguieus, but naturally the omphalos-cult was not confined to Delphi or associated only with Apollo. It might arise anywhere where there was a hero-grave or a worship of Earth-Spirits[3]. We have seen that Asklepios had

[1] Raoul Rochette, *Mon. Méd.* pl. 37. Naples Museum, Heydemann Cat. 108.
[2] For the type in sculpture see Mr Wace's article in *B.S.A.* 1902–3 (ix.), p. 211.
[3] An instructive parallel to the omphalos-cult I believe to be the ceremonial of the Latin *mundus*, covered by the *lapis manalis*. But the examination of this would take me too far for present limits. I will only note that the two elements of the omphalos-cult, ghosts or fertility, are very clearly present, though their connection is not expressly stated. Varro (*ap.* Macrob. I. 16. 18) says 'Mundus cum patet, deorum tristium atque inferum ianua patet.' Plutarch, *Vit. Rom.* 11, notes that the mundus was, as it were, the *penus* or storehouse of the new city, ἀπαρχαί τε πάντων ὅσοις νόμῳ μὲν ὡς καλοῖς ἐχρῶντο, φύσει δὲ ὡς ἀναγκαίοις, ἀπετέθησαν ἐνταῦθα. As often with the Latins, we have the social fact presented clearly because unmythologized. For 'Mundus patet' see Mr Warde Fowler, *Roman Festivals*, p. 211, and for Tellus and the Manes see his *Religious Experience of the Roman People*, 1911, p. 121.

a snake-twined omphalos[1]; there was probably an omphalos in Cyprus[2]; we shall meet another in Athens. At Phlius[3], that home of archaic cults, there was an omphalos which, in emulation of Delphi, was reputed to be the midmost point of the whole Peloponnese, a pretension obviously absurd. It stood near the ancient house of divination of Amphiaraos, where was a dream-oracle.

At Argos an inscription[4] has come to light which tells how the προμάντιες and προφῆται of Apollo Pythios

established, in accordance with an oracle, the omphalos of Ga and the colonnade and the altar...and they arranged a *thesauros* in the oracular shrine.

Obviously this complex was a correct copy of the Delphic installation and would have no interest for us, but that it probably supplanted or somehow rearranged a more ancient sanctuary. When the Danaides in the *Supplices* of Æschylus land at Argos they betake themselves as suppliants to a hill (πάγος)[5] whereon was an altar and about it somewhere the symbols of the gods, or rather, as we should put it, the sanctities that preceded any definite divinities. They are called by Danaos the ἀγώνιοι θεοί, gods of the agon or assembly. The chorus, more justly, alludes to them as daimones.

The chorus, holding their suppliant branches, which are, Danaos says, 'images of holy Zeus[6],' that is of Zeus *Aphiktor*[7], Zeus the 'Suppliant,' pray, as they needs must, and as Æschylus would himself desire, first and foremost to Zeus. But, seated as they are, on the holy mound, they have to get into touch with the local sanctities. Hence a sort of sacramental litany follows, expounding and emphasizing, and as it were displaying, their forms and functions.

---

[1] *Supra*, p. 384.

[2] Hesych. γῆς ὀμφαλός· ἡ Πάφος καὶ Δελφοί.

[3] Paus. II. 13. 7.

[4] Vollgraff, *Bull. Corr. Hell.* 1903, p. 274 Ἕσσαντο [τὸν] ἐκ μαντῆας Γᾶς ὀμφαλὸν καὶ τ[ὰ]ν περίστασιν καὶ τὸ φράγμα καὶ τὸν βωμόν...καὶ θησαυρὸν ἐν τῷ μαντήῳ κατεσκεύασσαν.

[5] Æsch. *Supp.* 179
ἄμεινόν ἐστι παντὸς εἴνεκ', ὦ κόραι,
πάγον προσίζειν τῶνδ' ἀγωνίων θεῶν.

[6] *v.* 181
ἀλλ' ὡς τάχιστα βᾶτε, καὶ λευκοστεφεῖς
ἱκετηρίας ἀγάλματ' αἰδοίου Διός...

[7] Prof. Murray, *Rise of the Greek Epic*[2], p. 291, has shown that Zeus Aphiktor is a 'projection' of the rite of Supplication.

Zeus duly invoked, Danaos continues, pointing to some symbol:

Da. Next call ye upon yonder son of Zeus.
Cho. We call upon the saving rays of the Sun.
Da. And pure Apollo banished, a god, from heaven[1].

Unless we realize the background the passage is not easy to understand, but, if we suppose an omphalos-sanctuary, all is clear. Danaos at the word 'yonder' (τόνδε) points to the Aguieus-pillar that marks the top of the mound. It is the symbol of the young son (ἶνις), the *kouros* of Zeus[2]. But the chorus do not quite catch his point. They answer conventionally, and perhaps with a trace of Egyptian reminiscence, 'Yes, of course, Apollo the Sun with his saving rays.' Well and good, says Danaos, but the point just now is that you appeal to a god who was, like yourselves, banished, and who, though counted as impure, was intensely, savingly pure, and the source of life, health and salvation. The holy stone he points to is, like the omphalos, like the stone on which Orestes sat at Gythion[3], like the black stone of the Mother[4], kathartic and apotropaic. It is an earlier sanctity and purity than the purity of the Sun.

Among the local sanctities precedence is given to the Apollo-stone which, if we are right, crowns the mound. Other sanctities appropriate to the circumstances of the Danaides are, the trident[5] of the sea-god who has brought them hither, and the kerykeion of the herald-god who is the protector and vehicle of all suppliants[6]. We seem to see before us the social sanctities on their way to be divinities. Supreme among them is the relation to Ga, Ga *Bounis*[7],

---

[1] Æsch. *Supp.* 202

> Δα. καὶ Ζηνὸς ἶνιν τόνδε νῦν κικλήσκετε.
> Χο. καλοῦμεν αὐγὰς ἡλίου σωτηρίους.
> Δα. ἁγνόν τ' Ἀπόλλω φυγάδ' ἀπ' οὐρανοῦ θεόν.

The MSS. have ὄρνιν. Following Kiehl (Bamberger) and Prof. Tucker and Dr Headlam I read ἶνιν. If the reading ὄρνιν be correct, the reference must be to an eagle.

[2] For Apollo as *Kouros* see end of chapter.

[3] Paus. III. 22. 1.

[4] The scholiast on Pind. III. 77 tells of the Mother-stone for which Pindar founded a shrine. For the prophetic, kathartic and prophylactic properties of these holy stones in connection with the omphalos see my *Delphika*, J.H.S. XIX. p. 237. The phallos-stone being specially the vehicle of life was specially able to revivify and heal all sickness and misfortune.

[5] v. 208   ὁρῶ τρίαιναν τήνδε σημεῖον θεοῦ.
Probably (see *supra*, p. 171) an ancient *bidens*-mark—as in the Erechtheion.

[6] Æsch. *Supp.* 210   Δα. Ἑρμῆς ὅδ' ἄλλος τοῖσιν Ἑλλήνων νόμοις.
                          Χο. ἐλευθέροις νῦν ἐσθλὰ κηρυκευέτω.

[7] v. 742   ἰὼ γᾶ βουνῖτι, ἔνδικον σέβας.

'Earth of the Mound,' to whom the Danaides, the Well-Nymphs, ever appeal. Even Zeus is to them 'Child of Earth,' hence Olbios and Ktesios[1]. It is scarcely possible to breathe the religious atmosphere of the play save as we see it enacted against the background of the omphalos-sanctuary.

We go back to Delphi and view the omphalos with new eyes. When the priestess passes into the inmost sanctuary of Gaia, she finds Orestes clinging to the life-stone and about him the aveng-ing ghosts, the fell Erinyes. They have come, it seemed to Æschylus—his mind all out of focus through his beautiful mono-theism and his faith in God the father—from afar, hunting the fugitive. But of course they, the ghosts, were there in the grave-sanctuary from the first. Like the Semnae they dwell in a chasm of the earth, and over the chasm stood, it may be, the life-stone, for they, the ghosts, year by year, bring, in the cycle of reincarnation, new-old life to man and to the earth, from which they spring and to which they return. They are from the beginning what Æschylus makes them ultimately become, spirits of life, fertility-ghosts. By the mouth of Clytemnestra[2] he blackens their ritual:

'How oft have ye from out my hands licked up
Wineless libations, sober offerings,
On the low hearth of fire, banquets grim
By night, an hour unshared of any god.'

Yet these same wineless libations, these sober offerings, were the due of the Eumenides at Argos, the snake-maidens, and of the Semnae at Athens:

The firstfruits offered for accomplishment
Of marriage and for children[3].

Æschylus seems to have seen only the evil of the Earth-Spirits, only the perennial damnation of the blood-feud. It is impossible to avoid regret that he did not see that these Earth-Spirits were for blessing as for cursing, and that he stooped to the cheap

---

[1] *v.* 859 ὦ βᾶ, Γᾶς παῖ, Ζεῦ; *v.* 509 τελειότατον κράτος, ὄλβιε Ζεῦ; for Zeus Olbios see *supra*, p. 148, *v.* 428 γένοιτ᾽ ἂν ἄλλα κτησίου Διὸς χάριν; for Zeus Ktesios see *supra*, p. 297.

[2] Æsch. *Eum.* 106.

[3] *v.* 837. For the practical identity of the *ritual* of the Erinyes, the Eumenides, and the Semnae, see *Prolegomena*, pp. 239—256. That the Semnae were ghosts as well as fertility spirits is quite clearly shown by the customs connected with the δευτεροπότμοι. *Op. cit.* p. 244.

expedient of maligning his spiritual foes. What in his inspired way he *did* see, both in the *Supplices* and the *Eumenides*, was that the old forces of the Earth must be purged from forcefulness, from violence and vengeance, before Earth could in plenitude bring forth her increase.

It remains to ask, 'What do we know of the ritual of Gaia at Delphi?' Of ritual to Gaia *under that name* and definitely stated to have been carried on at the omphalos-sanctuary, the answer, as previously indicated, is, 'Nothing.' But it happens that we have from Plutarch a fairly full account of three manifestly primitive festivals which took place at Delphi every nine years, and these festivals, on examination, turn out to be three acts in one dramatic or rather magical ceremony, whose whole gist is to promote the fertility of Earth. They are in short three factors in, or forms of, a great Eniautos-Festival.

THE ENNAETERIC FESTIVALS AT DELPHI.

In his *Greek Questions* Plutarch[1] asks, What is Charila among the Delphians?' His answer begins as follows:

There are three Nine-Year Festivals that the Delphians keep in the following order. One they call Stepterion, the next Herois, the third Charila.

All that Plutarch states is that these three festivals were each celebrated every nine years and that their sequence was as given. Whether they were all enacted at the same time—on, e.g. three successive days, or at successive periods in the year, cannot be decided certainly. The order is not of great importance, as in the cyclic monotony of the life of an Eniautos-daimon it matters little whether death follows resurrection or resurrection death. We shall begin therefore with the festival, the intent of which is clearest and to us most instructive, the second in order, the *Herois* or 'Heroine,' reserving for the end the festival with which Plutarch begins, the *Stepterion*.

The Herois. This is a delightful festival to investigate, because

---

[1] *Q. Gr.* XII. Τίς ἡ παρὰ Δελφοῖς Χαρίλα; τρεῖς ἄγουσι Δελφοὶ ἐνναετηρίδας κατὰ τὸ ἐξῆς, ὧν τὴν μὲν Στεπτήριον καλοῦσι, τὴν δ' Ἡρωΐδα, τὴν δὲ Χαρίλαν.

we have only one source for it, Plutarch[1] himself. And he, though it is but little, tells us just enough for its understanding.

> Most of the ceremonies of the *Herois* have a mystical reason which is known to the Thyiades, but, from the rites that are done in public, one may conjecture it to be a 'Bringing up of Semele.'

The Herois was a woman's festival. Plutarch of course could not be present at the secret ceremonies of the Thyiades, but his friend Thyia, their president, would tell him all a man might know. Part of the ceremonial he says was public.

Charila. The third of the ennaeteric festivals, the *Charila*, is the manifest counterpart of the *Herois*, and again Plutarch is our sole but sufficient source. After recounting the aetiological myth he gives us the ritual facts[2].

> The king presided and made a distribution in public of grain and pulse to all, both strangers and citizens. And the child-image of Charila is brought in. When they had all received their share, the king struck the image with his sandal, and the leader of the Thyiades lifted the image and took it away to a precipitous place and there tied a rope round the neck of the image and buried it, where they buried Charila when she hanged herself.

Charila is manifestly, whether enacted in spring or autumn, a festival of the type of 'Carrying out the Death.' Charila is beaten and hanged and buried in some chasm. The nearest analogies in Greece are the pharmakos ceremonies and the 'Driving out of Hunger[3].' Like the *Herois* the *Charila* was managed by the Thyiades and was therefore a woman's festival.

It is however the *Herois* that most instructs us. It never seems to have occurred to Plutarch, as it would to a modern mythologist, that, because a festival was called *Herois*, it must have to do with a mortal 'heroine.' From the rites known to him he promptly conjectured that it was a 'Bringing up of Semele.' Semele, it is acknowledged, is but a Thraco-Phrygian form of Gaia. The 'Bringing up of Semele' is but the Anodos of Gaia or of Kore the Earth-Maiden. It is the return of the vegetation or Year-spirit in the spring.

---

[1] *Qu. Gr.* XII. τῆς δὲ Ἡρωΐδος τὰ πλεῖστα μυστικὸν ἔχει λόγον ὃν ἴσασιν αἱ Θυιάδες, ἐκ δὲ τῶν δρωμένων φανερῶς Σεμέλης ἄν τις ἀναγωγὴν εἰκάσειε.

[2] *Loc. cit.* προκάθηται μὲν γὰρ ὁ βασιλεύς, τῶν ἀλφίτων καὶ τῶν χεδρόπων ἐπιδιδοὺς πᾶσι καὶ ξένοις καὶ πολίταις, κομίζεται δὲ τῆς Χαρίλας παιδικὸν εἴδωλον...

[3] *Prolegomena*, p. 106.

Why then is the festival called *Herois*? Because *Herois* is but the feminine of *Hero*, Strong One, Venerable One, and as it was the business of all *Heroes* to be Good Daimones and to bring fertility, so, and much more, was it the business of all Heroines. Again we have the ancestral dead, the collective dead women at their work of fertilization by way of reincarnation, and again they crystallize into one figure, *Herois*.

That fertilization was indeed the business of Heroines and that they were expected to do it regularly for the Eniautos-festival is plainly evidenced by an inscription[1] of about the third century B.C. It was found in the precinct of Artemidoros in Thera, cut into a small basis or rock-altar on which statues seem to have stood. It runs as follows in two hexameter lines:

> Heroines they are who bring the new fruit to the Year-Feast,
> Come then to Thera's land and accomplish increase for all things.

We remember well enough that the spirits of the Earth, the ghosts, can be summoned for cursing. The ghost of Clytemnestra[2] hounds up her Erinyes, herself the leader of the pack. Althaea[3] beats upon the Earth with her hands to rouse the Curse; the priest of Demeter[4] at Pheneus in Arcadia smites the Earth with rods to summon the underground folk when there is swearing to be done by the holy *Stones*. But we are apt to forget, perhaps because Homer and sometimes Æschylus forgot, that there was a ritual which summoned these underground folk to bless and not to curse.

At Megara, near the Prytaneion, Pausanias[5] saw

a rock which they name *Anaklethra*, 'Place of Calling up,' because Demeter, if anyone believe it, when she was wandering in search of her daughter called her up there.

---

[1] *I.G.* vol. xii. (1904) fasc. iii. Supp. Thera, Res Sacrae, No. 1340.

> ['Ηρωισ]σαι καρπὸν νέον
> [ε]ἰς ἐνιαυτὸν ἄγουσιν,
> δεῦτε [κ]αὶ ἐν Θήρας χθονὶ
> με[[ς]ο[να] πάντα τελοῦσαι.

The text is restored by Wilamowitz. For ἡρῶισσαι, an emendation that seems practically certain, he compares *Anth. Pal.* vi. 225, and Ap. Rhod. iv. 1309. Both are references to Libyan heroines, and the relations of Thera to Cyrene in Libya were of course close. In the epigram a tithe of the winnowed harvest is offered to the heroines. I have again to thank Mr Cook for referring me to the important evidence of this Thera inscription.

[2] Æsch. *Eum.* 115.   [3] *Il.* ix. 529.

[4] Paus. viii. 15. 2 ...τελετῇ ῥάβδοις κατὰ λόγον δή τινα τοὺς ὑποχθονίους παίει.

[5] i. 43. 2 ...'Ανακλήθραν τὴν πέτραν ὀνομάζουσι...ἐοικότα δὲ τῷ λόγῳ δρῶσιν ἐς ἡμᾶς ἔτι αἱ Μεγαρέων.

As to the aetiological myth Pausanias is rightly sceptical. Happily he adds:

The women of Megara to this day perform rites that are analogous to the story told.

Did the 'Bringing up of Semele' take place at an omphalos-sanctuary? At Delphi we cannot say for certain. It is possible that in the fragmentary Paean, 'For the Delphians,' Pindar[1] may allude to some such ceremonial. He goes gladly to Pytho we are told:

to Apollo's grove, nurse of wreaths and feasts, where oft by the shadowed omphalos of Earth the maidens of Delphi beat the ground with swift feet, as they sing of the son of Leto.

But the reference is too vague to be of much use as evidence.

At Athens we are more fortunate. Pindar we remember[2], in his spring Dithyramb, bids the very Olympians come to the omphalos[3] of Athens, where, as on an altar, incense smokes and where many feet are treading. So insistent is he on the flowers and the 'fragrant spring' that we can scarcely doubt that his song was written for the Anthesteria. We are sure it was written for a 'Bringing up of Semele,' for:

Then, then are flung over the immortal Earth lovely petals of pansies, and roses are amid our hair; and voices of song are loud among the pipes, *the dancing-floors are loud with the calling of crowned Semele*[4].

On Gaia worship as seen in 'The Bringing up of Semele' much light is thrown by the familiar 'Anodos' vases[5]. The design in Fig. 124[6] shows the Anodos. We have a great mound of earth artificially covered in with a thick coat of white. On it

---

[1] Paeans, frg. vi. 15, Grenfell and Hunt, *Oxyrhynch. Pap.* Part v. p. 41.

> κατέβαν στεφάνων
> καὶ θαλιᾶν τρόφον ἄλσος Ἀπόλ-
> λωνος, τόθι Λατοΐδαν
> θαμινὰ Δελφῶν κόραι
> Χθονὸς ὀμφαλὸν παρὰ
> σκιόεντα μελπ(ό)μεναι
> ποδὶ κροτέο(ντι γᾶν θοῷ).

[2] *Supra*, p. 203.

[3] Pind. frg. 75. 3
> πολύβατον οἵτ' ἄστεος
> ὀμφαλὸν θυόεντα...

[4] v. 20
> ἀχεῖ τ' ὀμφαὶ μελέων σὺν αὐλοῖς,
> ἀχεῖ τε Σεμέλαν ἑλικάμπυκα χοροί.

[5] For the 'Anodos' type of vases see my *Prolegomena*, pp. 276—285 and p. 640, where most of the important specimens are figured. The subject can only here be briefly resumed, so far as it affects the immediate argument.

[6] Krater, Berlin, 2646. *Mon. d. Inst.* xii. tav. 4.

are painted a tree, leaf-sprays and a tortoise. From the top of
the mound rises a tree. In the midst rises up the figure of a
woman. It is a grave-mound, an omphalos-sanctuary, and she
who is the spirit of the earth incarnate rises up to bring and be
new life. The tree that springs from the mound is, like the cone,
a symbol and vehicle of life. Probably it marked the earlier stage

Fig. 124.

in which the earth as mother was all-sufficing. On another Anodos
vase[1] the uprising woman is inscribed (*Phe*)*rophatta*, but in most
instances of the type she is nameless, she is the Earth-Kore reborn
in spring. On the Pherophatta vase Hermes Psychopompos, he
who summoned the Keres from the pithos, stands near with
uplifted rhabdos. On the vase in Fig. 124 the Earth-Mother
clearly rises from an artificial mound, and this is doubtless a
grave. On yet another vase, a black-figured lekythos[2], she rises,
not out of a mound but within the precinct of a sanctuary marked
by two columns, and from her head are branching trees. The
grave *is* a sanctuary.

On the Pherophatta vase we have clearly the influence of

[1] Krater, Albertinum Mus. Dresden. *Jahrb. d. Inst.* 1893, p. 166.
[2] Bibliothèque Nat. Paris, Cat. 298, Milliet et Giraudon, Pl. LII B.

Eleusis; Pherophatta is the Eleusinian Kore, not the Thraco-Phrygian Semele, though their nature is one and the same. The uprising we note is here eagerly greeted by a *choros* of goat-daimones with hoofs and high pointed horns. Tityroi we might call them, though perhaps it is safest they should be nameless[1]. But on the vase in Fig. 124 it is horse-daimones, Satyrs, with but one goat-daimon, who attend the uprising. Moreover seated near the hill is Dionysos himself with his thyrsos waiting for his Mother to rise up. We have before us unquestionably the 'Bringing up of Semele.'

Tradition said that Dionysos fetched his mother up from the underworld. Apollodorus[2] sketching the history of the worship of Dionysos ends it thus:

Finding that he was a god, men paid him worship, but he went and fetched his mother up out of Hades, gave her the title of Thyone and went up with her into heaven.

The hasty Assumption of the mother, viewed as history, strikes us as abrupt and unmeaning. It is of course simply an Olympianized saga-*mythos* of the old ritual of the 'Bringing up of Semele.' Semele, Earth, never could or did go to heaven, but she rose up out of earth. She needed no son to bring her, her son was indeed the fruits of the earth, the child Ploutos[3]. But, when patriarchy came in, and the Mother takes the lower place, someone has to 'fetch her up.' Moreover she must rise not only up from earth but up to high heaven. There is no one but her son to do all this. Later, Orpheus as lover 'fetches up' Eurydike, Earth, the 'wide-ruler,' the 'broad-bosomed.' He fails, because she must perennially return to Hades that she may rise again next spring.

In actual ritual at Athens the Son as well as the Mother is summoned. And the Mother is summoned in her two-fold aspect of Mother and Maid rather than Mother and Daughter. In the ritual scene in the *Frogs*[4], at the bidding of the Hierophant, the chorus chant the Saviour Maid who—be it noted—comes first

---

[1] Goat-daimones are also figured on the krater published by Dr Harting, *Röm. Mitt.* XII. 1899, p. 88, 'Die Wiederkehr d. Kore.' The figure of Kore rises on this vase straight from the ground. There is no omphalos-mound. The throng of ithyphallic goat-daimones seem to be dancing a regular dance. The focus of interest is clearly on them rather than on the figure of Kore.

[2] III. 5. 3. 3.

[3] *Supra*, p. 167.   [4] *vv.* 373—396.

and hence is not daughter—and then, with changed measure, the Fruit-bearing Mother[1]. Next the Hierophant says:

Now call Him hither, the Spirit of Spring[2].

And then follows the hymn to Iacchos, the young Dionysos of the mysteries:

Iacchos, O Iacchos.

The scholiast[3] on the passage gives valuable information.

'Some,' he says, 'account for the words κάλει θεόν thus. In the *agones* at the Lenaia of Dionysos, the Torchbearer, holding the torch, says, "Call ye the god," and those present call aloud in answer, "Son of Semele, Iacchos, Wealth-Giver."'

The ceremony of calling the god at Athens went on at the Lenaia, probably on the ancient orchestra, the round dancing-place close to the agora. Its central altar may well have been the omphalos, though of this there is no certain evidence. Manifestly the Son of Semele, the Earth-goddess, is but the impersonation, the projection of the fruits of the Earth. Like the child in the cornucopia he *is* Wealth, *Ploutos*. Beginning as a child in the religion of Mother and Son, he ends in later patriarchal days as a white-haired old man[4].

The functional identity of and the easy shift between Mother and Son, Earth and He of the Earth, Semele and Semeleïos, is shown in vase-paintings. On far the greater number Semele herself rises through the mound or out of the level earth, but sometimes the heads of both Mother and Son are seen rising side by side[5]. Two instances are known to me in which the Son rises alone through the mound. One of these is reproduced in Fig. 125[6].

---

[1] v. 383   ἄγε νῦν ἑτέραν ὕμνων ἰδέαν, τὴν καρποφόρον βασίλειαν,
Δήμητρα θεάν.

[2] v. 395   νῦν καὶ τὸν ὡραῖον θεὸν παρακαλεῖτε δεῦρο.
The adjective ὡραῖος is quite untranslateable. It means blooming in spring. As the word ὥρα is primarily the season of spring, my translation may perhaps pass. Eros too is ὡραῖος as the life-spirit (see *supra*, p. 187). The ritual instruction κάλει τὸν θεόν is good comic material later in the play (v. 479).

[3] Ad v. 479 τό τε 'κάλει θεὸν' τινὲς οὕτως ἀποδεδώκασιν· ἐν τοῖς Ληναϊκοῖς ἀγῶσι τοῦ Διονύσου ὁ δαδοῦχος κατέχων λάμπαδα λέγει, καλεῖτε θεόν· καὶ οἱ ὑπακούοντες βοῶσι Σεμελήϊε Ἴακχε πλουτοδότα. Later when people did not understand the 'summoning' of the Spring-Spirit they thought the Olympian was called 'πρὸς ἀρωγήν.' Σεμελήϊε probably meant to begin with just 'Earth-One,' not Son of Semele.

[4] As on a kalpis in the British Museum, Cat. E. 229, where, absurdly enough, the white-haired Hades-Plouton holds a huge cornucopia.

[5] *Prolegomena*, p. 407, Fig. 130.

[6] In the Hope collection at Deep-dene. See *Jahrbuch d. Inst* 1890, p. 120, note 17. In the collection of Greek Antiquities at Stockholm I saw a late red-figured vase, the design of which seemed, as far as memory served me, almost identical with this. There may be others of the same type as yet unnoted.

The Son uprising is attended by a figure of Nīke. Maenads as well as Satyrs await his rising. From the artificial mound a leafed spray is blossoming.

Fig. 125.

The attendants that wait on the rising figure are of high importance. They not only await but often actively aid the uprising. On the vase[1] in Fig. 124 they are idle though keenly interested spectators. In the Pherophatta vase they dance,

Fig. 126.

probably by way of magical induction. On the vase in Fig. 126 they are drastic. Each of the two Satyrs holds a great pick.

[1] Hydria, now, M. Hébert kindly informs me, in the Musée Cinquantenaire at Brussels. Fröhner, *Choix de Vases Grecs*, Pl. VI. 24.

They have hacked open the ground to help the Earth-Maiden to rise. It is impossible to say for certain that the *dromena* of the 'Bringing up of Semele' included the hacking of the earth with picks, but some action of the sort may well have been part of the ritual of an agricultural people. The earth in some few favoured regions brings forth her fruit in due season without man's help, but in Greece, with its thin stony soil, man must help her. Long before he invented the plough, and long after in places where no plough could go, he used the pick[1].

But these horse-tailed daimones are no mere mortal agriculturists. They are Satyrs; their function is magical rather than actual. That function is clearly shown by the two figures of Erotes, one to either side, that balance and complete them. In bygone days, before the facts of parentage were known, the Earth was thought of as mother and husbandless, sufficient herself for all her child-bearing, or vaguely fertilized by the dead spirits of men buried in her bosom. But, when she first appears in mythology, she is attended by a throng of male daimones, and they are Daktyls, Tityroi, Satyroi, Korybantes, all, according to Strabo, we remember[2], substantially the same, all the projection of marriageable youth, of the band of Kouroi. Their earliest cultus-shape is the Daktyl fertility-cone. Their last and loveliest form is that of the winged spirits, the Erotes, who on the vase before us wait the uprising of the Mother, and who on the great Hieron vase[3] cluster about the goddess of growth and increase, Aphrodite. But the form of fertility-daimones known to the early *dromenon* was probably that of Satyrs, and down to late days it is Satyrs in the Satyr play[4] who attend the Theophany of the god.

In the cults of Delphi there is not a word of Satyrs. The *Herois* festival is conducted by women. It is Maenads not Satyrs who on the peaks of Parnassos dance round Dionysos. This may well be mainly because the religion of the Thracian Dionysos came to Delphi in a form in which, as already noted[5], the Maenads, the Mothers, were most emphasized, and the child was a babe and only potentially a Kouros. But I would conjecture that at Delphi expurgation was at work; the old meaning of the omphalos

---

[1] E. Hahn, *Die Entstehung d. Pflugkultur*, 1909, p. 9, Der Hackbau.
[2] *Supra*, p. 14.   [3] *Prolegomena*, p. 634, Fig. 170.
[4] See Prof. Murray, *supra*, p. 343.   [5] *Supra*, p. 40.

was at first advisedly ignored, then forgotten. The religion of Apollo with its 'Nothing too much' may well have protested against the religion of Dionysos with its inherent ecstasy and possible licence.

We have seen Aguieus as the symbol of life standing on the earth-mound. It is to the cult of Apollo as emerging from that of Gaia and more and more sharply differentiated from hers that we must now turn. We shall best understand it by examining the myth of the slaying of the Python, and this brings us to our third ennaeteric festival, the *Stepterion*.

THE SLAYING OF THE PYTHON.

Æschylus, as already observed, will have none of the slaying of the snake. Our chief literary source is the Homeric Hymn to the Pythian Apollo. Art adds very little to our knowledge, though coins frequently represent the slaying of the Python near the tripod, and vases, though rarely, show the infant Apollo shooting from his mother's arms at the huge monster issuing from a rocky cave. One monument, however, the Pompeian fresco in Fig. 127[1], is of some religious interest because it shows us the

FIG. 127.

Python in relation to the omphalos. The beast, wounded and bleeding, is still coiled round it. Moreover behind the omphalos is a high pillar which gives a grave-like look to the whole complex. On the pillar are hung, not wreaths, but the bow and quiver of the

[1] From a photograph.

god. To celebrate the Python's death there is to be a *Bouphonia*. The priestess with the sacred double-axe in her hand brings up the bull. Apollo has cast aside his laurel-branch and is preparing to chant a Paean to himself. Artemis looks on in the background.

Of much more importance than any monument of art is the account we have from Plutarch of the ritual of the *Stepterion*.

The Stepterion[1]. In the *Greek Questions*[1] Plutarch does not state the actual ritual of the *Stepterion*. He makes allusive mention of it and attempts a rather confused and feeble explanation. He has evidently not made up his mind as to what the real gist of the festival is.

Now the Stepterion would seem to be an imitation of the fight of the god against the Python and of his flight to Tempe after the fight, and of his banishment. Some say that he took flight, being in need of purification after the murder, others say that he was following hard on the Python who was wounded and escaping, and that he failed by a little to be in at the death. For he came up with the Python when he was just dead of his wound, and his son, whose name they say was Aix, had just performed for him his funeral rites. Of such events or of something of this sort is the Stepterion an imitation.

Plutarch, confused in his mind though he seems to be, is about right. The Stepterion was not exactly an 'imitation' of an actual fight with a particular monster the Python, but it was an imitation or rather a perpetual reenactment of 'something of this sort.' In another passage, though half unconsciously, he himself lets out the truth.

In his discourse on the *Cessation of the Oracles*[2] Plutarch gives vent to his distress about the unworthy stories that are told of the gods, their rapes, their wanderings, their hidings, their banishments, their servitudes.

'These,' he says, 'are not of the gods, but they are the sufferings of *daimones* and their changes and chances which are commemorated on account of their virtue and force.'

It may be incidentally observed that no one of Plutarch's day

[1] The sources for the Stepterion are given in Nilsson's *Griechische Feste*, 1906, p. 150. Dr Nilsson rightly criticizes my previous explanation of the rite as based on the slaying of the snake, but his own explanation is not to me satisfactory. By far the best account of the Stepterion is given by Dr H. Usener, *Heilige Handlung. Ilion's Fall*, in Archiv f. Religionswissenschaft, 1904, pp. 317—328, to which I refer for all details, e.g. the Doloneia and the figure of Aix, which do not affect my present argument. I owe much to Dr Usener's argument, though I cannot accept all his conclusions.

[2] XVI. ...οὐ θεῶν εἰσιν, ἀλλὰ δαιμόνων παθήματα καὶ τύχαι μνημονευόμεναι δι' ἀρετὴν καὶ δύναμιν αὐτῶν.

could well have put the matter more clearly and truly. These 'wanderings' and 'hidings' and the like are not of the θεοί, not of the fixed Olympian personalities, but of the recurrent cycles of the daimones, and they are commemorated just because of their magical 'virtue and force.' In another moment we feel Plutarch will be using the expression 'functional daimon.'

Being himself a priest at Delphi Plutarch takes, as an instance of how things are misunderstood, the festival of the *Stepterion*, according to him an extreme case. Æschylus, we are told, is utterly wrong when he says

'And pure Apollo, banished, a god, from Heaven[1].'

And furthest of all from the truth are the theologians at Delphi who hold that once a fight took place there between the god and a serpent about the oracle, and who allowed poets and story-writers to present this at dramatic performances in the theatres, as though they were bent on contradicting what is actually done in the most sacred rites.

Here he is interrupted, most fortunately for us, by a question from one of his audience, a certain Philip, who wants to know exactly what these 'most sacred rites' are, which dramatic authors, when they represent a fight as taking place between Apollo and the snake, contradict. Plutarch answers:

Those rites I mean which are in connection with the oracular shrine, which quite recently the state (Delphi) celebrated, admitting into them all the Hellenes beyond Pylae and going in procession as far as Tempe.

It is these rites that contradict the notion of a fight with a serpent.

For the hut that is set up here, over the threshing-floor, every nine years, is not just some hole like the lair of a serpent, but *is the imitation of the dwelling of a tyrant or king*, and the attack made in silence upon it along what is called the Doloneia...they accompany the youth, both of whose parents are alive, with lighted torches, and when they have set fire to the hut and overturned the table they fly without looking back through the doors of the sanctuary. Finally the wanderings and the servitude of the boy and the purifications that take place at Tempe make one suspect that there has been some great pollution and some daring deed[2].

---

[1] *Supra*, p. 413.

[2] *De def. orac.* 15 ...ἥ τε γὰρ ἱσταμένη καλιὰς ἐνταῦθα περὶ τὴν ἅλω δι᾽ ἐννέα ἐτῶν, οὐ φωλεώδης τις δράκοντος χειά, ἀλλὰ μίμημα τυραννικῆς ἢ βασιλικῆς ἐστιν οἰκήσεως, ἥ τε μετὰ σιγῆς ἐπ᾽ αὐτὴν διὰ τῆς ὀνομαζομένης Δολωνείας ἔφοδος† ἐν ᾗ (Reiske, μή MSS.) Αἰολάδαι† (αἰολὰ MSS.) τὸν ἀμφιθαλῆ κόρον ἡμμέναις δᾳσὶν ἄγουσι καὶ προσβαλόντες τὸ πῦρ τῇ καλιάδι καὶ τὴν τράπεζαν ἀναστρέψαντες ἀνεπιστρεπτὶ φεύγουσι διὲκ θυρῶν τοῦ ἱεροῦ· καὶ τελευταῖον αἵ τε πλάναι καὶ ἡ λατρεία τοῦ παιδὸς οἵ τε γιγνόμενοι περὶ τὰ Τέμπη καθαρμοὶ μεγάλου τινὸς ἄγους καὶ τολμήματος ὑποψίαν ἔχουσι. After ἔφοδος is a lamentable lacuna. It has not been successfully filled, so I attempt no translation. Fortunately the loss does not affect the main argument, i.e. that the Stepterion was no imitation of the slaying of the Python.

Clearly Plutarch has here no belief in the aetiological myth which in the *Quaestiones* he doubtfully accepts. It is often assumed that the hut which was burned contained a serpent[1], but of this there is no evidence. Had Plutarch known of any such serpent he would never have argued as he did, and no one was better acquainted than Plutarch with the details of Delphic ritual. We must give up the serpent. The Stepterion consisted of a secret attack with lighted torches on a hut[2], which though apparently it is made of wood or reeds had somehow—a piece of purple drapery and a wreath would do it—the semblance of a king's palace. The boy who lit the fire fled to Tempe, was purified and feasted there, and returned in triumph crowned and carrying a laurel branch.

We know that boy with both his parents alive. He carries the Eiresione; he is the young New Year. But the burning of the hut? It is the old, old Eniautos-festival, but enacted here at the end of a Nine-Years Year, one of the periods arranged to fit together the course of Sun and Moon[3]. *Le Roi est mort*, so his kingly palace is burnt, the table of his first-fruits overturned[4]; and the celebrants fly as the slayers of the holy ox fled at the Bouphonia[5]. They have incurred an *agos*. The cry of Ie Paian is heard[6]. *Vive le roi*; the new, young king appears from Tempe or from anywhere[7], crowned and bearing his branch.

It is from Ælian[8], in his account of the ceremonies at Tempe, that we get the fullest details of the carrying of the laurel branch, and it is through Ælian that we realize that this bringing in of the new laurel, this carrying it and wearing it in wreaths, gave to the Festival its name 'Stepterion, Festival of Wreathers[9].'

---

[1] I was misled by this myself in treating of the *Stepterion* before, *Prolegomena*, p. 113.

[2] The hut at Delphi does not of course stand alone. The burning of the booths at the Tithorea festival, followed by departure in haste, is a close parallel. See Paus. x. 32. 17. At Tithorea the festival was held twice a year—once in the spring, once in the autumn.

[3] *Supra*, p. 223.   [4] *Supra*, p. 426.   [5] *Supra*, p. 142.

[6] Ephoros (*F.H.G.* I. 225, p. 70, quoted by Strabo IX. p. 422) the Euhemerist says that Python was a χαλεπὸς ἀνήρ; it is he who speaks of the σκηνὴ τοῦ Πύθωνος, and he says that when the man called *Drako* was shot down they cried ἰὲ παιάν.

[7] The appearance from Tempe is probably due to some local shift of cults, and does not concern us.

[8] *Var. Hist.* III. 1.

[9] I was quite wrong (*Prolegomena*, p. 113, note 4) in my previous adoption of the form Σεπτήριον, but I still think there may be connection with the enigmatic στέφη and στέφειν of Æsch. *Choeph.* 94, Soph. *Ant.* 431, *Elek.* 52, 458.

After a long account of the beauties of Tempe Ælian thus writes:

And it was here the Thessalians say that Apollo Pythios by command of Zeus purified himself after he had shot down the snake of Pytho who guarded Delphi while he still held the oracle. So Apollo made himself a crown of the laurel of Tempe, and taking in his right hand a branch of this same laurel came to Delphi and took over the oracle, he who was son of Zeus and Leto. And there is an altar in the very place where he wreathed himself and bore away the branch. And to this day the Delphians send high-born boys in procession there, and one of them is *architheoros*. And they, when they have reached Tempe and made a splendid sacrifice, return back, after weaving themselves wreaths from the very laurel from which the god made himself a wreath....And at the Pythian games the wreaths given to the actors are made of the same laurel.

Apollo on vases and coins carries the bough, he is thallophoros. A good example is shown in the design in Fig. 128 from an

Fig. 128.

Etruscan Cista[1]. Apollo is seated close to his omphalos on which is perched a mantic bird. He holds a huge bough. A warrior approaches to consult the oracle.

But if there was no snake, how did the story of the snake get in? Very simply I think. At Pytho there were holy snakes, or a snake used for mantic purposes. The tradition as to this that the snake guarded the oracle for Gaia, is very strong. The

[1] *Monimenti dell' Inst.* viii. Tav. xxv.—xxx.

people of Epiros had a snake-cult which they believed to be derived from Delphi, and which we may suppose was, if not actually derived, at least analogous.   Ælian[1] thus describes it:

> The people of Epiros sacrifice in general to Apollo, and to him they celebrate their greatest feast on one day of the year, a feast of great magnificence and much reputed.   There is a grove dedicated to the god, and it has a circular enclosure and within are snakes, playthings surely for the god.   Now only the maiden priestess approaches them, and she is naked (γυμνή), and she brings the snakes their food.   These snakes are said by the people of Epiros to be descended from the Python at Delphi.   Now if when the priestess comes near them the snakes are seen to be gentle, and if they take to their food kindly, that is taken to mean that there will be a plentiful year and free from disease; but if they frighten her, and do not take the honey-cakes she offers them, then they portend the reverse.

The snake here is not slain by Apollo, it is taken on peaceably as a plaything (ἄθυρμα).   The snake has a maiden priestess. The omen, as at Athens, is by food.   When the snake of Pytho, feminine of course at first, as guardian of Gaia, had to be killed, he became a male serpent, a foeman worthy of Apollo's steel[2]. But all this goes to show the harmlessness of the local *genius loci*, and does not explain how men came to think he had to die. The clue is given by the 'kingly palace' at the nine-years Festival, the Stepteria.   Minos reigned for nine years[3].   The king as daimon incarnate of the Year reigned at Delphi for nine years. At the end he is killed or deposed.   And—this is the important point—the king as hero-daimon *is envisaged as a snake*.   Cecrops was a snake, Kychreus was a snake[4].   The old snake dies, the young snake lives.

KADMOS AND JASON AS SNAKE-SLAYERS.

The myth of the slaying of the snake is not of course confined to Delphi, though only at Delphi is it the deed of a god.   Kadmos slays the snake of Ares, and his snake-slaying is singularly instructive.

The chorus in the *Phoenissae*[5] tell the story of how Kadmos

---

[1] *De Nat. An.* XI. 2.
[2] The Homeric Hymn has, however (*v.* 300), δράκαινα.   Euripides (*I. in T.* 1245) has δράκων.
[3] *Od.* XIX. 179 ἐννέωρος βασίλευε Διὸς μεγάλου ὀαριστής.   See Prof. Murray, *Rise of the Greek Epic*[2], p. 156, note 1.
[4] *Supra*, p. 287.   [5] Eur. *Phoen.* 638.

followed the heifer, and guided by her came to the fertile Aonian land, to the fount of Dirke.

> There the snake of Ares, savage guard,
> O'er the flowing fount kept watch and ward,
> There the beast his bloody eyeballs rolled,
> Thither on a time came Kadmos bold
> Seeking lustral water. By the might
> Of maiden Pallas he the snake did smite,
> With a rock upon its head
> Bloody stained, and straight he shed
> All its teeth upon the earth,
> Up there sprang an armed birth.
> Not for long were they. Bloody strife
> Sent them back to *earth that gave them life.*

The snake, though the chorus regard him as a terrible monster, is the guardian of the well, is really the *genius loci,* the Agathos Daimon of the place. As such he appears on the vase[1] by Assteas reproduced in Fig. 129.   Kadmos has come up

Fig. 129.

to the well, the snake ramps out at him, and in terror he drops his water-jar and picks up a great stone.   With the help of the stone and the goddess *Athene* who stands near he will presently

[1] Naples Museum, Cat. 3226. From a photograph.

slay the snake. Above is seated to the right *Thebe*; above
Kadmos, and rather inappropriately remote behind a hill, is
Krenaie the well-nymph; above

Athene the old river-god *Ismenos*
stands holding his sceptre.   All
about the snake are blossoming
trees and plants.   This is not I
think mere landscape painting, it
marks the snake as a fertility-
daimon.

But the fertility character
of the snake comes out most
clearly in the snake who guards
the golden fruit of the Hesperides.
On the vase-painting[1] in Fig. 130
we have the tree and the great
snake coiled round it, and at the
foot wells out from a cave in
the earth a spring with double
mouths.   Here we have the real
old cultus-complex, tree and well
and snake-daimon guarding both.

Fig. 130.

The tree and all green things come from the earth bedewed
by living water.   So on the Acropolis at
Athens there was an olive tree, a holy snake,
a well.   Snake and tree are seen on the
familiar Athenian coin in Fig. 131.   The well
is not yet there, for when Poseidon took it
over he had to create it with his trident and
to salt it.

Fig. 131.

Another vase-painting in Fig. 132 is instructive, because it shows how easily, once
the story-telling instinct is at work, the meaning and the
conjunction of the old sanctities is forgotten.   We have the
garden and the Hesperid nymphs, the great tree with the golden
fruit, and the snake twined about it.   But the holy well is sundered from the tree and the snake, the Hesperids are just

---

[1] I regret that I am unable to trace the sources of the vases in Figs. 130
and 132.   They are reproduced from lantern slides long in my possession.

water-carrying maidens, and the whole scene, charming though it
is, has lost its daimon-glamour.   It is just that daimon-glamour,

Fig. 132.

that haunting remembrance of things ancient, felt rather than
understood, that a poet[1] keeps, when he is gone

> To the strand of the Daughters of the Sunset,
>   The Apple-tree, the singing and the gold ;
> Where the mariner must stay him from his onset,
>   And the red wave is tranquil as of old :
>   Yea, beyond that Pillar of the End
>   That Atlas guardeth, would I wend ;
> Where a voice of living waters never ceaseth
>   In God's quiet garden by the sea,
> And Earth, the ancient life-giver, increaseth
>   Joy among the meadows, like a tree.

Now a snake, like the daimon of the tree and well is not a
monster to be slain, he is a genius to be cherished.   Only a
total misunderstanding of his nature, or rather his functions, could
make him a curse to be killed.   But there are two things to be
remembered.   He, the fertility-daimon, if angered had his evil
side, which comes out clearly in the Erinyes[2].   He, or rather at
Delphi she, the angry Earth, could blast as well as bless.   Moreover, as we have seen, the snake-daimon king was in all probability
supposed to die each nine years.   So that there was both the
notion of an evil, hostile snake, and also probably a dead king-
snake, to start the myth of the slaying of Python.

On a Kyrenaic vase[3]—a class in which things primitive are
apt to survive—in Fig. 133 there is, I think, some reminiscence of
the snake-king.   The scene is probably Kadmos slaying the snake,
but it might be any hero slaying any snake without local determination.   The building from which the snake issues is usually

---

[1] Eur. *Hipp.* 742.
[2] For the angry snake as Erinys or avenging ghost see *Prolegomena*, pp. 232 ff.
[3] Puchstein, *Arch. Zeit.* 1881, p. 238.

interpreted as a well-house and may be such, but it is, I think, more like 'the imitation of the dwelling of a tyrant or king[1].'

Fig. 133.

It will be remembered that on grave reliefs we have the hero in human form standing with or without his horse—a saga-figure drawn from reality—and by his side his daimon-form, a coiled snake. Now it is not a little curious that in a few grave reliefs, an instance[2] of which is given in Fig. 134, we have a man killing a snake. This does not, I think, refer to any actual incident in the man's life, does not imply that a man died of the bite of a snake. It is simply the old type misunderstood and made into a pseudo-fact. A man and a snake side by side on a tombstone. What does it mean? We do not really know, we have forgotten. It must mean something. Well then the man must be killing the snake. Something like this happened in mythology. There was a snake at Delphi probably painted on the omphalos, and, it may be, a real snake used for divination. There came to be a human god Apollo, side by side with the snake. What was Apollo the bright and beautiful doing with

Fig. 134.

---

[1] *Supra*, p. 426. [2] Sparta Cat. 565.

the old snake? Well, he had better be killing it. So he was. He was *Pythoktonos* as he was *Sauroktonos.*

The Kadmos myth tempts to another conjecture. It must frankly be admitted that it is only a conjecture—but I hope a probable one—that Kadmos who is a snake-slayer is also himself a snake. When, at the close of the *Bacchae*[1], Dionysos bids Kadmos depart from Thebes, he says to him:

> 'For thou must change and be a Serpent Thing
> Strange, and beside thee she whom thou didst bring
> Of old to be thy bride from Heaven afar,
> Harmonia, daughter of the Lord of War,'

and Kadmos knows that the dragon-shape is upon him; he says to Agave, 'I must

>   lead my spouse, mine own
> Harmonia, Ares' child, discorporate
> And haunting forms, dragon and dragon mate.'

We know now what lies behind these metamorphoses. A man is turned into what he really was. Kadmos is turned into a snake because he was a Snake-man, *the* snake-man, head and king of a Snake-group. The snake was the blazon of the Spartoi. Pausanias[2] saw the grave of Epaminondas at Mantinea, and thus describes it:

Over his tomb stands a pillar and there is a shield on it upon which is wrought a dragon.

The Spartoi of Thebes were the 'sown men,' that earth-born dragon's brood from which Pentheus sprang, set always, as we shall later see, when moralized, in some sort of antithesis to the Olympians. So in the *Bacchae*[3]

> Dark and of the dark impassioned
> Is this Pentheus' blood : yea fashioned
> Of the Dragon, and his birth
> From Echion child of Earth.
> He is no man, but a wonder ;
>   Did the Earth-Child not beget him
>   As a red Giant to set him
> Against God, against the Thunder?

And now we see that the mysterious sequel to the dragon-slaying is quite simply explained. Both Kadmos and Jason, when they have slain the dragon, sow his teeth, and up from the earth springs a crop of armed men. The Spartoi had the snake for

[1] *v.* 1330 ff.   [2] VIII. 11. 8.   [3] *v.* 537 ff.

their blazon; they had also marked, probably tattooed on their bodies from childhood, a lance. Whether the two-fold symbols of snake and lance were owing to the fusion of two groups or not we cannot determine, but the fact is certain; hence the alternative of dragon or armed man. Aristotle[1] in dealing with *anagnorisis* speaks of 'the lance which the earth-born bear.' Dio Chrysostom[2] writes of 'the lance which is said to be the sign of their race among the Spartoi at Thebes'; and Julian[3] even more explicitly says:

> The lance is said to be imprinted on the Spartoi by their mother.

But why the teeth? In a previous chapter[4] we have noted the savage custom of knocking out a boy's tooth at puberty ceremonies and its possible significance. We have seen the tooth preserved on the Roman pyre. The tooth because it is practically indestructible, and perhaps also because it looks like a gleaming white seed-corn, is the symbol and supposed vehicle of reincarnation.

Jason, as well as Kadmos and Apollo, slew a dragon and sowed the dragon's teeth. The scene is set before us with a strange and magical splendour by Apollonios Rhodios[5]. On it a curious light is cast by the vase-painting[6] in Fig. 135. In the background is the tree with the golden fleece. Near at hand Athena with her owl, as guardian of the hero. She should of course be Hera, but the vase-painter is a good Athenian patriot. A magnificent dragon ramps up to the left—there will be splendid sowing with that dragon's teeth. So far all is on sound conventional saga lines, but where is the dragon-slaying hero? Where indeed? The vase-painter seems to have remembered in some odd haunting way that the dragon-slayer is of the dragon's seed. He is being born anew from his jaws.

The slaying of the snake then, based on the ritual death of the old snake king, gradually got moralized. It came to symbolize

---

[1] *Poet.* 16 λόγχην ἣν φέρουσι γηγενεῖς. Aristotle instances the lance as one of the 'congenital' (σύμφυτα) tokens. It is more probable that it was a tattoo-mark imprinted in infancy.

[2] 4. 23.   [3] p. 81 c.   [4] pp. 272, 273.   [5] III. 1178 ff.

[6] In the Vatican collection; from a photograph. The swallowing of the hero has so far as I know never been explained. There is no literary tradition, and the vase is a ἅπαξ λεγόμενον among monuments. For the myth of Jonah and the whale which is clearly analogous see W. Simpson, *The Jonah Legend*, 1899.

and re-emphasize as a fight what Æschylus saw to be a development and succession, the passage from the old Earth-cult to the
later completely humanized Apollo-worship. Whether behind the
story of the fight there lay also some historical fact such as the
incursion of a new tribe either from North or South bringing
a more advanced form of worship I cannot determine[1]. Tradition

Fig. 135.

pointed on the one hand to the coming of Apollo from Crete, on
the other from Delos.

The snake-killing is but one aspect of Apollo's content; we must
now pass to another, closely connected indeed but which adds
fresh elements to our conception.

---

[1] No critic can be more deeply conscious of the ethnographical weakness of this
book than is the writer. I have attempted to get light from ethnography, but
have not so far succeeded; I look forward to the achievements of others better
equipped.

APOLLO AS PHOIBOS.

We have seen Apollo as Aguieus, the old fertility-cone.   But it is not as Aguieus that he conquers the Earth-snake and submerges the ancient Themis of the dream-oracle.   It is not as Aguieus that he stands for light and reason, for justice and moderation.   As Aguieus he is indeed in some sense Phoibos the Pure or the Purifier, for the conical stone, as a life-stone, was kathartic: what gives life heals from disease[1].   It is however, as will immediately be seen, the second stage in the succession, the passage from Earth to Sun by way of Moon, from Gaia to Phoibos by way of Phoibe, that lifts Apollo to Olympos.   What definite ritual evidence have we of this?   If the *Herois*, the *Charila*, the *Stepterion* all find their utterance, their projection, in Gaia and her Snake, what is the festival, the ritual, that finds its utterance, its projection, in the name and nature of Phoibos?   It is the *Daphnephoria.*

The Daphnephoria.   We have seen that under the name Stepterion there was a Daphnephoria at Delphi, but our fullest evidence as to the festival comes to us not from Delphi but from Thebes.   When Pausanias[2] visited Thebes, he saw the dragon's well and the field where Kadmos sowed the teeth.   He saw also a hill sacred to Apollo, who bore the title of *Ismenian* from the river Ismenos which, as we have already seen[3], was near at hand.   After describing the temple of Apollo Ismenios he says:

> The following custom is, I know, still observed at Thebes. A boy of distinguished family and himself well-looking and strong is made the priest of Ismenian Apollo *for the space of a year* (ἐνιαύσιος).   The title given him is Laurel-bearer, Daphnephoros, for these boys wear wreaths made of laurel leaves.

Now if this were all we should naturally say—Here, as in the Stepterion, is the same old fertility-spirit who belongs to the seasonal service of Gaia; the boy carries a laurel Eiresione, and

---

[1] For the connection between life and resurrection gods, i.e. what I should call Eniautos-daimones, and gods of healing, I can now refer to Baudissin's interesting book, *Adonis und Esmun. Eine Untersuchung zur Geschichte des Glaubens an Auferstehungsgötter und an Heilgötter*, 1911.   The book deals largely with Semitic religion, and specially with Jahwe as the 'living' God, and because living, the Healer of diseases.   Asklepios, who raises from the dead, is a close parallel.

[2] IX. 10. 4.   [3] p. 431.

we are not a step the further. Fortunately we know more particulars of the Daphnephoria and they take us straight from earth to heaven, from Gaia to Phoibos.

Proklos quoted by Photius[1] gives us the ritual of the Daphnephoria in quite exceptional detail, as follows. After telling us that it was an enneateric festival and of the same order as the Parthenia, and after giving its aetiological myth, he proceeds to enumerate the ritual facts.

They wreathe a pole of olive wood with laurel and various flowers. On the top is fitted a bronze globe, from which they suspend smaller ones. Midway round the pole they place a lesser globe binding it with purple fillets—but the end of the pole is decked with saffron. By the topmost globe they mean the sun to which they actually compare Apollo. The globe beneath this is the moon; the smaller globes hung on are the stars and constellations, and the fillets are the course of the year—for they make them 365 in number. The Daphnephoria is headed by a boy, both whose parents are alive, and his nearest male relation carries the filleted pole to which they give the name *Kopo*. The Daphnephoros himself, who follows next, holds on to the laurel, he has his hair hanging loose, he wears a golden wreath and he is dressed out in a splendid robe to his feet and he wears light shoes. There follows him a *choros* of maidens holding out boughs before them to enforce the supplication of the hymns. The procession of the Daphnephoria is to the sanctuary of Apollo Ismenios and Him-of-the-Hail.

Our sequence of cults is uttered in visible ritual form with a clearness, an actuality, beyond anything we might have dared to hope. We have an Eiresione of the Earth, the flowers of the Earth, and it is carried to the sanctuary of a Weather-God, *Him-of-the-Hail*, probably in this case with a view to magical aversion rather than induction. We have the Moon with her purple fillets half-way up the pole, and at the top the saffron-decked globe of the golden Sun Phoibos himself. The ladder from Earth to Heaven is complete.

[1] *Bibl. cod.* 239, p. 321 (= Schol. ad Clem. Alex. *Protrept.* p. 9) καὶ ἡ αἰτία...ἡ δὲ δαφνηφορία· ξύλον ἐλαίας καταστέφουσι δάφναις καὶ ποικίλοις ἄνθεσι· καὶ ἐπ' ἄκρου μὲν χαλκῆ ἐφαρμόζεται σφαῖρα, ἐκ δὲ ταύτης μικροτέρας ἐξαρτῶσι· κατὰ δὲ τὸ μέσον τοῦ ξύλου περιθέντες ἐλάσσονα τῆς ἐπ' ἄκρῳ σφαίρας καθάπτουσι πορφυρᾶ στέμματα· τὰ δὲ τελευταῖα τοῦ ξύλου περιστέλλουσι κροκωτῷ. βούλεται δ' αὐτοῖς ἡ μὲν ἀνωτάτω σφαῖρα τὸν ἥλιον, ᾧ καὶ τὸν Ἀπόλλωνα ἀναφέρουσιν, ἡ δὲ ὑποκειμένη τὴν σελήνην, τὰ δὲ προσηρτημένα τῶν σφαιρίων ἄστρα τε καὶ ἀστέρας, τὰ δέ γε στέμματα τὸν ἐνιαύσιον δρόμον· καὶ γὰρ καὶ τξε ποιοῦσιν αὐτά. ἄρχει δὲ τῆς δαφνηφορίας παῖς ἀμφιθαλής, καὶ ὁ μάλιστα αὐτῷ οἰκεῖος βαστάζει τὸ κατεστεμμένον ξύλον, ὃ κωπὼ καλοῦσιν. αὐτὸς δὲ ὁ δαφνηφόρος ἑπόμενος τῆς δάφνης ἐφάπτεται, τὰς μὲν κόμας καθείμενος, χρυσοῖν δὲ στέφανον φέρων καὶ λαμπρὰν ἐσθῆτα ποδήρη ἐστολισμένος, ἰφικρατίδας τε ὑποδεδεμένος· ᾧ χορὸς παρθένων ἐπακολουθεῖ προτείνων κλῶνας πρὸς ἱκετηρίαν τῶν ὕμνων· παρέπεμπον δὲ τὴν δαφνηφορίαν εἰς Ἀπόλλωνος Ἰσμηνίου καὶ Χαλαζίου.

It is difficult for us perhaps to realize how pregnant was to the ancient world this shift from Gaia to Phoibos, from a focus of attention that was on the coming and going of the fruits of the earth and the disorderly and fearful phenomena of the weather, to a contemplation of the fixed and orderly procession of the heavenly bodies. Time was to primitive man always a coloured various thing, with festivals of spring and harvest for purple patches, but, through the calendars of moon and sun, it became also a recurrent rhythmical pattern[1].

Aguieus is the fertility of the Earth; the gist of *Phoibos* is the Sun-calendar with all its attendant moralities of law and order and symmetry and rhythm and light and reason, the qualities we are apt too readily to lump together as 'Greek.' But what of *Apollo* ?

We have seen that Apollo Aguieus, who by a strange and terrible irony became to Cassandra her 'Destroyer,' was in reality the Lord of Life. Can we more closely determine what kind of life ? For once philology may, I think, safely guide us—to a goal desired but unlooked for.

APOLLO AS KOUROS.

Apollo's name has an earlier form Apellon[2]. From this rather than the form in *o* we must start. The Doric month *Apellaios* frequently occurs at Delphi where it begins the year and can safely be equated with the Attic Hekatombaion. Now seasonal festivals, it would seem, were before months and frequently lent to the months their names. The month of Apellaios is the month in which the festival of the Apellaia occurred. But what are the Apellaia ? The word ἀπελλάζειν is, Hesychius tells, Laconian for ἐκκλησιάζειν. It means therefore to 'hold' or 'summon' or 'be

---

[1] See *supra*, p. 184, for the importance of 'periodicity' in the development of civilization. Dr Troels-Lund (trans. by Leo Bloch) in his *Himmelsbild und Weltanschauung im Wandel der Zeiten*, 1908[3]—a book too little known in England probably because of its popular form—has shown in very interesting fashion that a period of enlightenment goes *pari passu* with an increased interest in astronomy. See also Otto Seeck, *Geschichte d. antiker Welt*, 1902, Band II. Anhang, *Der Sonnenglaube*.

[2] For the form *Apellon* see Pauly-Wissowa s.v. *Apollo*, and Usener, *Götternamen*, p. 305. The short *e* for *o* is, according to Herodian, *ap.* Eustath. 183. 10, *ad Il.* II. 103, characteristically 'Doric.'

member of' an assembly.　Most significant of all Hesychius has the gloss

ἀπελλάκας· ἱερῶν κοινωνούς, sharers of sacred rites:

and again

ἀπελλαί· σηκοί, ἐκκλησίαι, ἀρχαιρεσίαι, folds, assemblies, elections.

Is Apollo the god of the fold and those within the fold?　Is he the Good Shepherd? or the arch-politician?

It has long been conjectured, partly from the evidence adduced and partly from the supposed nature of Apollo Karneios, that Apollo was the god of flocks and herds.　But Apollo is surely not more, nor indeed half so much, god of flocks and herds as Hermes. We have no Apollo *Kriophoros* nor *Moschophoros*.　Apollo will prove, I think, to be the god of the fold (σηκός), but it is a fold of human sheep.　The nature of the fold and the sheep shepherded by Apollo will be found, I believe, in an inscription[1] found in the French excavations at Delphi dealing with the organization and regulations of the phratria of the Labyadae.

The inscription gives us a rare glimpse into the inner life of an ancient group.　It records regulations for the various initiation ceremonies, the successive *rites de passage* through which a member of the group must pass, and the offerings that must be made by him or on his behalf, 'from the cradle to the grave.'

Among the ceremonies prescribed[2] occur certain offerings called respectively ἀπελλαῖα and δάραται[3].　We know from Athenaeus[3] that δάρατος is a kind of unleavened bread made in Thessaly.　The δάραται then are offerings of cakes.　The inscription further divides these δάραται into two kinds, γάμελα and παιδῆια, that is obviously what we should call wedding-cakes and christening-cakes.　So much for the δάραται, but what of the ἀπελλαῖα?　On what occasion are they offered?

---

[1] Homolle, *Inscriptions de Delphes*, in Bull. de Corr. Hell. xix. 1895, p. 5, Règlements de la Phratrie des Λαβυαδαι.

[2] The inscription at the end of the fifth century B.C. begins ταγε[υ]σέω δι[καίως κ]ατὰ τοὺς νόμους τὰς [π]ό[λ]ιος καὶ τοὺς τῶν Λαβυαδ[ᾶν] πὲρ τῶν ἀπελλαίων καὶ τᾶν δαρατᾶν, I will perform aright the office of *tagos* in accordance with laws of the state and of the Labyades with respect to the *apellaia* and the *daratai*.　Both city (πόλις) and group (Labyadae) are concerned in the enactments.　We stand as it were on a bridge between old and new.

[3] iii. p. 110 D Νίκανδρος δὲ ὁ Κολοφώνιος ἐν ταῖς Γλώσσαις τὸν ἄζυμον ἄρτον καλεῖ δάρατον.　114 B Σέλευκος μὲν δράμιν ὑπὸ Μακεδόνων οὕτως καλούμενον, δάρατον δ' ὑπὸ Θεσσαλῶν.　Hesych. s.v. δαράτῳ· ἀζύμῳ.

Among the ancients, as among ourselves, a man's christening, his reception as a child into the congregation, was a family festival. So also was his marriage. Neither concerned the state. But there was another occasion, more solemn, charged with a civic importance beyond that of either christening or marriage, and that was his reception into the body of grown men as a full-grown *kouros*. Then and not till then the youth became ἀπελλάξ, a 'sharer in sacred rites'; then and not till then could he enter the ἀπέλλαι, the 'folds,'. the 'assemblies,' the 'elections.' The ἀπελλαῖα I believe[1] to be the offerings made at puberty initiation. Apellaios is the month of these rites and these offerings, Apellon is the projection of these rites; he, like Dionysos, like Herakles, is the arch-ephebos, the Megistos Kouros.

Apollo was Phoibos of the unshorn hair[2], and now remembering his double Herakles Alexikakos we understand why. Plutarch[3] tells us that in the days of Theseus

It was the custom for those who were passing from childhood to manhood to go to Delphi and offer there the firstfruits of their hair to the god. Theseus went there, and there is, they say, a place at Delphi that is called the Theseion after him. He only shaved the forepart of his head, as Homer says was the practice of the Abantes, and this sort of tonsure was called *Theseis* after him.

The tonsure may have varied with each group. All that concerns us is that He-of-the-Unshorn-Hair is youth incarnate, youth just about to be initiated.

When Pentheus will insult the Bacchos what outrage does he choose[4]?

First shear that delicate curl that tangles there,

and the daimon, the Greatest Kouros, makes answer,

I have vowed it to my God; 'tis holy hair.

[1] I follow here Mr Homolle, *op. cit.* p. 45. The *Apellaia* are equated by Mr Homolle with the Ionian Apatouria. 'C'est l'hommage de la majorité, et l'offrande reçue fait de l'enfant un homme et de l'incapable un citoyen.' This view of the *Apellaia* is accepted by Dr Nilsson, *Griechische Feste*, p. 465, note 2. But for the view that Apollo-Apellon is the projection of the ceremonial I am alone responsible. For the Apatouria and other festivals in which traces of puberty-initiation survive, see the concluding chapter.

[2] *Il.* xx. 39 Φοῖβος ἀκερσεκόμης.

[3] *Vit. Thes.* v. ἔθους δὲ ὄντος ἔτι τότε τοὺς μεταβαίνοντας ἐκ παίδων ἐλθόντας εἰς Δελφοὺς ἀπάρχεσθαι τῷ θεῷ τῆς κόμης. The word μεταβαίνειν marks the *rite de passage*.

[4] *Eur. Bacch.* 493 Πε. πρῶτον μὲν ἀβρὸν βόστρυχον τεμῶ σέθεν.
Δι. ἱερὸς ὁ πλόκαμος· τῷ θεῷ δ' αὐτὸν τρέφω.

It is youth incarnate, youth with the unshorn hair[1], who leads the Bacchants to the mountains,

> And sets them leaping, as he sings,
> *His tresses rippling to the sky.*
> And deep beneath the Maenad cry
> His proud voice rings:
> 'Come, O ye Bacchae, come.'

Fɪɢ. 136.

¹ 150 τρυφερόν <τε> πλόκαμον εἰς αἰθέρα ῥίπτων.

On a curious and beautiful early Greek mirror[1], in Fig. 136, we see the two gods standing, each on a basis, face to face. Apollo holds his laurel spray. He is a typical ephebos, wearing but a chlamys and with his unshorn hair coiled in a krobylos. Dionysos, always more effeminate, less remote from the Mother, wears a long chiton. They are both calendar gods; the sun, a disk with the head of an ephebos, shines impartially between them. But the place seems to belong to Dionysos. A great vine is to either side of the bases and above is a panther. Perhaps Apollo as Delphinios may claim the dolphins.

There came then to Delphi, tradition tells us, two Kouroi, the greatest Kouroi the world has ever seen, Apollo and Dionysos. Were they, who seem so disparate, really the same? So far as

FIG. 137.

they are Kouroi and Year-Gods, yes. But they are Kouroi and Year-Gods caught and in part crystallized at different stages of development. Apollo has more in him of the Sun and the day, of order and light and reason, Dionysos more of the Earth and the Moon, of the divinity of Night and Dreams. Moreover, Apollo is of man's life, separate from the rest of nature, a purely human accomplishment; Dionysos is of man's life as one with nature, a communion not a segregation.

The vase-painting[2] in Fig. 137 may serve as the résumé of a

[1] Gerhard, *Etruskische Spiegel*, ccxcii.
[2] Hermitage Cat. 1807. See *Prolegomena*, p. 391, Fig. 124.

long and complex chapter.   We are at Delphi, and Dionysos the elder Kouros holds the place.   About him are his Maenads and his Satyrs.   He welcomes the younger Kouros with his laurel bough, grasping him by the hand.   Between them stands the holy tree, for they are both branch-bearers, and beneath them is the omphalos of Gaia, mother of both.

We have watched Apollo in his transit from earth to heaven. We have seen that he like Dionysos was an Eniautos-daimon and a Megistos Kouros.   But Apollo, unlike Dionysos, is a genuine, unmistakable Olympian.   Wherein lies the difference?   In a word, what is it to be an Olympian?   The enquiry will be attempted in the next chapter.

APOLLO OF DELOS.

Note to p. 396. For the omphalos recently discovered at Delphi and his new interpretation of the whole subject, to which I subscribe, see Mr A. B. Cook's *Zeus*, vol. II. pp. 169 ff.

Note to p. 418. To the Anodos monuments must now be added the Minoan intaglio from Thisbe published by Sir Arthur Evans, *J.H.S.* 1925, p. 15, Fig. 16.

Note to p. 439. For the derivation here suggested I am inclined to substitute the 'apple' etymology of Dr Rendel Harris. For the whole question see Mr A. B. Cook's *Zeus*, vol. II. pp. 493—501 and Dr Rendel Harris, 'Apollo at the Back of the North Wind,' *J.H.S.* 1925, p. 229, and his *Apollo's Birds* in Bulletin of the John Rylands Library, 1925.

CHAPTER X.

THE OLYMPIANS.

ἄτοπον δ' ἂν εἴη εἴ τις φαίη φιλεῖν τὸν Δία.

οὐ γὰρ τοὺς Τυφῶνας ἐκείνους οὐδὲ τοὺς Γίγαντας ἄρχειν ἀλλὰ τὸν πατέρα θεῶν καὶ ἀνθρώπων.

In the *Peace*[1] of Aristophanes, when Trygaeus is trying to win Hermes to his side, he tells him that there is a most serious and alarming plot being hatched against all the gods. Hermes asks what it is all about and Trygaeus answers

> 'Why there's Selene and that old villain Helios
> Have been plotting away against you for ever such a time,
> To betray Hellas into the hands of the barbarians.'

Hermes asks why they should do that and Trygaeus explains

> 'Why, by Zeus, it's because
> *We* sacrifice to *you*, but those barbarians
> To *them*, and of course that's why they'd like
> To ruin us altogether, that they may get
> For themselves the feasts that ought to belong to the gods.'

The 'barbarians' on whose behalf the Moon and Sun are plotting are, of course, the Persians. Herodotus[2] in an instructive passage tells us of the manner of their worship.

The Persians to my knowledge observe the following customs.
It is not their habit to set up images, temples and altars; rather they charge them who do so with folly, and this, I think, is because they do not hold like the Greeks *that the gods are of human natures*. It is their practice to ascend to the tops of mountains, and there they do sacrifice to Zeus, and they call the whole circle of heaven Zeus (Δία). They sacrifice to the sun and the moon, to the earth and to fire and water and the winds. To these and these only have they sacrificed from the beginning.

Herodotus, like Trygaeus, clearly thought that the nature-gods of the Persians were quite distinct from the *human*-nature gods of the Greeks. He could not possibly, at his stage of thinking, realize that all gods are, in the sense explained in the last chapter,

---

[1] *v.* 403 ff.

[2] I. 131 ...ὅτι οὐκ ἀνθρωποφυέας ἐνόμισαν τοὺς θεοὺς κατά περ οἱ Ἕλληνες εἶναι...

nature-gods, and all, because they are born of man's reaction towards the outside world, are by equal necessity *human*-nature gods; that it is in fact a question of degree, of stage of development rather than of definite distinction. Apollo the typical Olympian was, as we have just seen in the last chapter, of Earth and of the Sun, as well as of that human-nature which in him, as Kouros, as Ephebos, emerged resplendent. A detailed examination would probably show that the same was true in great part of each and every Olympian.

The Greek Gods, in their triumphant humanity, kicked down that ladder from earth to heaven by which they rose. They reflected, they represented the mood of their worshippers, which tended always to focus itself rather on what was proper to humanity than on what was common to man and the rest of the universe. The Greek of the time of Aristophanes or even of Herodotus had probably no very clear idea that the Apollo he worshipped was a Sun-god. But the Persians as outside observers were more acute. The scholiast on the passage from the *Peace*[1] just quoted observes,

The barbarians honour the sun and the moon as Herodotus relates. And probably they reverence both sun and moon more than all the other gods. On this account they refrained from ravaging both Delos and Ephesos. For the sun is held to be Apollo and Artemis to be the moon.

Whatever may have been the view of the unthinking public, the educated man, as well as the barbarous Persian, knew that in past days the Greeks themselves had worshipped Nature-powers. Plato in the *Kratylos*[2] makes Sokrates say

'The earliest inhabitants of Greece accounted those only to be gods whom the barbarians now worship, the sun and moon and earth and the constellations and heaven.'

And again in the *Laws*[3], when the Athenian asks the Cretan Kleinias how he could show that the gods existed, Kleinias answers,

'Why first of all there is the earth and the sun and the constellations and the whole universe and the fair order of the seasons and the division of them into years and months. And then there is the fact that all men, Hellenes and barbarians alike, account them to be gods.'

[1] Ad v. 410 ...ὁ μὲν γὰρ ἥλιος Ἀπόλλων ἐνενόμιστο ἡ δὲ Ἄρτεμις σελήνη. See *supra*, p. 192.
[2] 397 c.			[3] 886 A.

Here we seem to be in a midway position. The Nature-powers, earth and sun and stars, are gods, but they are also evidence that there are gods. Divinity is in process of extrusion from nature.

The Pythagorean writer of the *Epinomis*[1] speaks very clearly as to the precedence due to the Nature-powers.

> As to the gods, Zeus and Hera and all the rest, let each man lay down a law for himself as he will, and let this be binding, but as to the visible gods, who are greatest and most to be honoured...these must be reverenced with due rites and sacrifices and festivals.

To doubt the existence of these is the wildest impiety.

Everywhere then we find among thinking men the consciousness that behind the recognized Olympians were Nature-powers. It was, of course, as already observed, impossible for a Greek of that day to recognize the simple psychological fact that a god was neither of the two, neither a man nor a nature-power but rather the outcome of both, the expression of man's focus of attention on nature.

We think and write of the gods of the Greeks as anthropo-*morphic*, 'of human form' or 'shape.' The clumsy word is too narrow; its associations are rather of art than religion. The word used by Herodotus ἀνθρωποφύης 'of human growth' or 'nature' is wider and better. It has more life-blood about it, more of the real nature and function of the god, less of the outer semblance. Yet even the wider word must not be glibly used. Still less must we assume off-hand that the shift from nature-god to human-nature god is necessarily an advance. The process needs careful scrutiny and the result some detailed analysis. We shall find that the complete human-nature god is, roughly speaking, what we call an Olympian. What then are his characteristics? It will be seen in the sequel that they are strangely, significantly negative, that an Olympian is in fact in the main the negation of an Eniautos-daimon.

(1) *The Olympian sheds his plant or animal form.* Of this we have already had abundant evidence. Zeus Ktesios was once a snake[2]. Zeus Olbios in local worship long preserved his bull's

---

[1] 984 D—985 D. The close of the long passage is resumed rather than translated.

[2] *Supra*, p. 297.

head[1]. But imagination boggles at a bull-headed Zeus seated in Olympos. Yet for all that the remembrance of the bull-nature never dies out. It lives on in mythology.

Fig. 138.

On the beautiful archaic metope of Selinus[2] in Fig. 138 we have Europa seated on the bull.

No whit like other bulls is he, but mild and dear and meek;
He has a wise heart like a man's, only he cannot speak.

[1] *Supra*, p. 148.   [2] From a photograph.

Moschos[1] of course, in his lovely idyll, thinks that Zeus took upon him the form of a bull, but, in the light of Zeus Ktesios and the Bull Dionysos, we know this to be a mere late aetiological inversion. The Sun-God of Crete in Bull-form wooed the moon-goddess, herself a cow; their child is the young bull-god the Minos-Bull, the Minotaur. Kadmos sought Europa in Boeotia, in Cowland—and what did he find?

> Kadmos hither came from Tyrian town;
> Lo! untired before him laid her down
> The heifer, that made clear the god's command
> And bade him dwell there in the fertile land[2].

And, that there may be no mistake, Mnaseas[3] tells us that on either flank of the heifer was

> 'a white sign like the circle of the moon.'

Sometimes the animal form of the god lives on as in mythology; more often perhaps it survives in the supposed 'attribute' of the god. Thus on the familiar coin of Kaulonia in Fig. 139 we have Apollo in full human form. Standing beside him is a stag, an animal 'sacred to' him as to his sister Artemis. Such sanctities are not lightly forgotten. On the outstretched arm of the god is a little winged figure, usually interpreted as a wind. It is, I think, more probably the daimon of the god, his *Kratos*, his power, his *mana*

FIG. 139.

made visible. In his other hand the god as Thallophoros holds a sacred bough. In high Olympos the gods cease to carry boughs, instead they carry wine-cups. They feast more freely than they function.

The shedding of plant and animal form marks of course the complete close of anything like totemistic thinking and feeling. It is in many ways pure loss. The totemistic attitude towards animals may, as based on ignorance, beget superstition, but it is

---

[1] *Id.* ii. 105.
[2] Eur. *Phoen.* 638.
[3] Schol. Eur. *Phoen.* 638
ἔνθα δὲ προσπελάσας συλλάμβανε βοῦν ἐρίμυκον
τὴν ἥ κεν νώτοισιν ἐπ' ἀμφοτέροισιν ἔχῃσι
λευκὸν σῆμ' ἑκάτερθε περίτροχον ἠΰτε μήνης.

full of beautiful courtesies. There are few things uglier than a lack of reverence for animals. The well-born, well-bred little Athenian girls who danced as Bears to Artemis of Brauronia, the Bear-Goddess, could not but think reverently of the great might of the Bear. Among the Apaches to-day, Bourke[1] states, 'only ill-bred Americans, or Europeans who have never had any "raising," would think of speaking of the Bear or indeed of the snake, the lightning or the mule, without employing the reverential prefix "Ostin," meaning "old man," and equivalent to the Roman title "Senator."'

In art this exclusion of animal and plant life from the cycle of the divine is sometimes claimed as a gain. Rather it leaves a sense of chill and loneliness. Anyone who turns from Minoan pottery with its blossoming flowers, its crocuses and lilies, its plenitude of sea life, its shells and octopuses and flying fish, anyone who turns from all this life and colour to the monotonous perfection of the purely human subjects of the best red-figured pottery, must be strangely constituted if he feels no loss. He will turn eagerly for refreshment from these finished athletes and these no less accomplished gods, to the bits of mythology wherein animals still play a part, to Europa and her bull, to Phrixos and his ram, to Kadmos and his snake, and he will turn also to the 'attributes' of the humanized Olympian, he will be gladdened by Athena's owl and by the woodpecker of Zeus; glad too that Dionysos' Dendrites still deigns to be a tree and Apollo to carry his living branch. The mystery gods it should be noted here, though it has been observed before[2], are never free of totemistic hauntings, never quite shed their plant and animal shapes. That lies in the very nature of their sacramental worship. They are still alive with the life-blood of all living things from which they sprang.

(2) *The Olympian refuses to be an Earth-daimon.* In discussing the sequence of cults from Gaia to Apollo it has been seen that, even when he has left totemistic ways of thinking behind him, when he has ceased to base his social structure on

---

[1] *On the Border with Crook,* p. 132. I borrow this quotation from Mr Cook's delightful article on *Descriptive Animal Names in Greece,* Class. Rev. VIII. (1904), p. 384.

[2] *Supra,* p. 129.

supposed kinship with animals and plants, man tends, in his search after food, to focus his attention first on earth[1] and only later on heaven. His calendar is at first seasonal, based not on observation of the heavenly bodies but on the waxing and waning of plants, of the fruits of the earth. The worship of Earth in a word comes before the worship of Heaven.

This worship of Earth and the daimonic powers of the earth is, we have also seen, closely and even inextricably mixed with the cult of the dead. The daimonic power of the dead is figured under the form of a snake. The situla in Fig. 140 from Daphnae[2] recalls this earth-snake to our minds. He is clearly a daimon of fertility; to his right hand springs up a tree. He is winged, for he is in part a daimon of the powers of the air, but he is emphatically a snake. That there may be no mistake not only

Fig. 140.

has he, like Cecrops, a snake's body, but in either hand he holds a snake.

When the Olympians mounted from Olympos to the upper air they were, it seems, ashamed of their earth-origin and resolved to repudiate their snake-tails. This is very clearly seen on the vase-painting[3] in Fig. 141. To the right is an old Earth-daimon just like the daimon on the Daphnae situla. He is winged, and his body ends in two snake-coils. He is obviously as benevolent and as civilized as Cecrops himself. But he is earth-born, and Zeus of the upper air, the completely human Zeus, will have none

[1] For a full examination of the religion of Earth and its relation to phallic cults see A. Dieterich, *Mutter Erde*, 1905; and for the transition from Earth- to Heaven-worship, S. Wide, *Chthonische und Himmlische Götter*, in Archiv f. Religionswiss. 1907, p. 257.

[2] Brit. Mus. Cat. B. 104.

[3] Gerhard, *Auserlesene Vasenbilder*, III. 237.

of him, will blast him with his thunder-bolt. We seem to hear
the kindly, courteous old earth-daimon cry, and cry in vain,

ἰὼ θεοὶ νεώτεροι.

The animosity of the wholly human Olympians against the
earth-born daimones takes definite and instructive form in the
myth of the *Gigantomachia*. The word *giant* brings to our minds
the picture of a man of monstrous size and probably cannibal
habits, but the 'giants' of the Greeks are nowise in this sense
'gigantic.' Pentheus is a 'bloody giant[1],' but his stature is like
that of other mortals. He is the typical 'giant,' earth-born, seed
of Echion. The Greek giants have one characteristic mark and
even this scarcely separates them from ordinary mortal men: they

Fig. 141.

are Earth-born, γηγενεῖς, and as such they fight with primitive
weapons wrested from earth, with huge blocks of stone and trees
uptorn by their roots. They are the actual and special children
of Earth herself. Again and again on vases and reliefs when in
the great fight with the Olympians the earth-born ones are in
danger, the figure of Gaia rises up from the ground to implore
mercy for her sons[2].

In this connection it is important to note the form given
to them in art[3]. On black-figured vases and early reliefs, such
as the pediment of the Megara Treasure-house at Olympia, they

---

[1] Eur. *Bacch.* 573; see *supra*, p. 434.
[2] See Roscher, *Lexicon*, s.v. *Gaia*.
[3] For the whole subject of the Giants see Dr Maximilian Mayer's brilliant
Die Giganten und Titanen, 1887. Following the *Etymologicum Magnum*, s.v.
γίγαντες, he holds that γῆ and γίγας are from the same root. I follow in the
main his view of the contrast between Giants and Titans, but he is in no way
responsible for the views I deduce from this contrast.

are simply armed men, hoplites, like the crop of men who sprang
at Thebes from the dragon's teeth.   On later and more learned
monuments, as for example red-figured vases and the great Altar
of Pergamos, they are men with bodies ending in serpents' tails.
They are, even to the detail of the added wings, creatures just
like the opponent of Zeus in Fig. 141.   They prove to be in fact
nothing but the gods, or rather the snake-tailed daimones, of the
early population.   They began like the daimon on the Daphnae
vase and like Cecrops and Kadmos as fertility-daimones, as Agathoi
Daimones.   When the human-shaped Olympians triumph they
become evil monsters to be overthrown.   Their kingdom is of
this earth.

(3) *The Olympian refuses to be a daimon of air and sky.*
Mythology tells us not only of a Gigantomachia but of a Titanomachia.   The Titans cannot be very precisely delimited from the
Giants.   They too are in some sense Earth-born[1].   Titaia was a
title of Earth, Titias was own brother to Kyllenos, and the nature
of Hermes Kyllenios we know, and both were *paredroi* of the
Mother and both were Idaean Daktyls[2].   The Earth-born Tityos
is a figure that needs no comment.   Priapos, Lucian[3] tells us, was
either 'one of the Titans or of the Idaean Daktyls[4].'   Picus and
Faunus, says Plutarch, 'either Satyrs or Titanes.'

But, and this is the interesting point, the Titans, unlike the
Giants, seem early to have left their earth-nature behind them
and climbed one step up the ladder to heaven.   Fertility-daimones
they remain, but rather as potencies of sky than earth.   A little
south of Sikyon Pausanias[5] saw the town of Titane, the town,
according to the natives, where Titan first dwelt.

They say that he was brother to the Sun, that the place took its name
Titane from him.   I think that Titan was great at marking the seasons of
the year and the time when the sun gives increase to and ripens the fruit
of trees.

---

[1] For the primitive Daktyl and phallic nature of the Titans see Kaibel, *Daktyloi
Idaioi*, 1902.

[2] See Kaibel, *op. cit.*, pp. 489—492.

[3] *De Salt.* 21, speaking of the invention of the armed dance by Priapos, τῶν
Τιτάνων οἶμαι ἕνα ἢ τῶν Ἰδαίων Δακτύλων.

[4] *Vit. Num.* 15 οὓς τὰ μὲν ἄλλα Σατύρων ἄν τις ἢ Τιτάνων γένει προσεικάσειε.   From
lack of understanding of the nature of the Titanes Τιτάνων has been emended into
Πανῶν.

[5] ii. 11. 5.

The notion that Titan is a Sun-power lives on, like Phoebus, in English poetry.

> And Titan, tired in the mid-day heat,
> With burning eye did hotly over-look them[1].

But it would be a mistake to suppose that Titan is always and merely the Sun. Empedokles[2] is nearer the truth because less specialized. To him Titan is the *aither*, the whole region of the *meteora*.

> Gaia and billowy ocean and air with its moisture,
> And Æther, the Titan, embracing the All in a circle.

Special Titans specialize into Sun-Gods. The Titan Sisyphos who climbs the steep of heaven rolling his stone before him, only to fall adown the steep and climb it again next morning, is the Sun, the Titan Phaethon is the Sun, the Titaness Phoebe is the Moon, but Titan himself is rather Ouranos, the whole might of the upper air.

Art has left us no representations of the Titanomachia as distinguished from the Gigantomachia—but in literature it is abundantly clear that the Titans are Ouraniones. In Homer and Hesiod they, unlike the Giants, are always gods, Τιτῆνες θεοί[3]. They are constantly being driven down below the earth to nethermost Tartarus and always re-emerging. The very violence and persistence with which they are sent down below shows that they belong up above. They rebound like divine india-rubber balls. Their great offence in Olympian eyes is that they will climb up to high heaven, which the human-shaped Olympians had arrogated to themselves. The fight between Titans and Olympians always takes place in mid air. In the Theogony[4] the Titanomachia is but a half-humanized thunderstorm, where Zeus as much and perhaps more manifestly than his opponents is but a Nature-Power.

---

[1] Shakespeare, *Venus and Adonis*, 177.

[2] Diels, *F.V.S.* 38

> γαῖά τε καὶ πόντος πολύκυμων ἠδ' ὑγρὸς ἀήρ
> Τιτὰν ἠδ' αἰθὴρ σφίγγων περὶ κύκλον ἅπαντα.

A kindred figure to Titan is Akmon (Sk. açman), the personified vault of heaven.

[3] Hes. *Theog.* 630

> Τιτῆνές τε θεοὶ καὶ ὅσοι Κρόνου ἐξεγένοντο.

Hom. *Il.* xiv. 278   θεοὺς ὀνόμηνεν ἅπαντας.

[4] v. 675 ff., trans. Prof. Murray, τοὺς ὑποταρταρίους, οἳ Τιτῆνες καλέονται.

The new gods stood on Olympos and the Titans on the older religious seat, Thessalian Othrys.

And the Titans opposite had made strong their lines and both sides put forth their might. And there was a terrible cry from the boundless sea, and shattering of the earth, and the broad sky groaned and high Olympos was shaken from his foundations with the rush of immortal things, and the quaking and the noise of feet upon the steeps came down unto cloudy Tartaros.... And the armies met with a great shout and Zeus held back his fury no more. Down from Olympos and heaven he came in one sweep of thunders that ceased not; and the bolts went winged from his mighty hand and the life-bearing Earth cracked with the burning and around him the fathomless forest roared in fire and all Earth seethed and the streams of Okeanos and the unharvested sea, and a hot blast beset the earth-born Titans, a flame unspeakable blazed in holy aether and the flash of thunderbolt and lightning blinded their eyes mighty though their strength was, and a wondrous heat laid hold of Chaos[1]. And it seemed, to see with the eyes and to hear the great din with the ears, that Earth and broad heaven crashed together. For such a mighty din had been if earth were in ruin and heaven hurtling above her. Such was the din what time the gods met in battle.

The stuff of which Zeus is made is clear enough. He too was a Titan, he too was Ouranos and Aither, and his nature retains more of τὰ μετάρσια than of τὰ μετέωρα. But he has emerged into humanized form, and his old form is made to appear, not like the chrysalis from which he evolved himself, but rather as an alien foe opposed. It is strange and interesting that Zeus, king and father of all the other Olympians, should be the last to shed his elemental nature. He who is always boasting that he is Father and Councillor remains to the end an automatically explosive thunderstorm[2]. He has none of the achieved serenity of the Sun-god Apollo.

We are accustomed to think of the Titans as criminals, rebels against high heaven condemned for their sin of ὕβρις to languish in Tartarus. It is well to look at things from the other side, the side set before us in the *Prometheus* of Æschylus.

---

[1] Chaos is the space between Earth and Heaven. See schol. *ad Theog.* 116 ἤγουν τὸν κεχυμένον ἐν τῷ μεταξὺ γῆς καὶ οὐρανοῦ.

[2] M. Salomon Reinach in his *Orpheus*, 1909, p. 5, has well pointed out that the same explosiveness attaches to the Hebrew Father-God, Jahveh. It is difficult to do justice to Jahveh unless we remember the primitive elements his figure absorbs. The account of Uzzah and the ark in 2 Samuel vi. 4—7 shocks our moral sense. Uzzah caught hold of the Ark to prevent it falling—'for the oxen shook it.' The intent was innocent, even praiseworthy, but 'the anger of the Lord was kindled against Uzzah; and God smote him there for his error: and there he died by the ark of God.' Such a God makes worship difficult. But if we remember that the ark was itself a centre of tabu, automatically explosive, like a thunderstorm, and that the human Jahveh is a later addition, our antipathy in part disappears.

Prometheus is the arch-Titan and he is son of Gaia. The chorus who sympathize with him are nature-powers, Okeanids of the old order. There is perhaps nothing in all ancient poetry more lovely than the coming of the Okeanid chorus. Prometheus, hurt and bitter of heart, hears in the air a flutter of bird-wings. He is afraid. He is so badly hurt that all the world is pain and fear to him—

πᾶν μοι φοβερὸν τὸ προσέρπον[1].

The Okeanids sing softly to him their song of sympathy and gentleness, in that measure which in itself is a healing—

μηδὲν φοβηθῇς· φιλία γὰρ ἅδε τάξις πτερύγων θοαῖς
ἁμίλλαις προσέβα τόνδε πάγον.

It is the eternal healing of *dis*passionate nature as against the angry clash of irreconcilable human wills and egotisms.

The chorus laments the new rulers, the new helmsmen of the world's ship, just as the Erinyes bemoan the coming of the νεώτεροι θεοί—

νέοι γὰρ οἰακονόμοι κρατοῦσ᾽ Ὀλύμπου, νεοχμοῖς δὲ δὴ νόμοις
Ζεὺς ἀθέτως κρατύνει,
τὰ πρὶν δὲ πελώρια νῦν ἄϊστοῖ[2].

'He has destroyed the old portentous ones.' The expression 'portentous ones,' πελώρια, is noticeable and repays investigation.

We think of the Okeanids as Ocean-nymphs, sea-nymphs, but we do not think quite rightly, nor does the notion sea-nymph at all exhaust their content. Okeanos is much more than Ocean and of other birth.

This comes out clearly in the unforgettable scene at the beginning of the 20th *Iliad*[3]. Zeus summons all the gods to his council on Olympos and Themis ranges round to collect them. She fetches the rivers and they all hurry up and do on their human shapes and sit them down in the polished colonnades.

There was no River came not up, save only Ocean, nor any nymph, of all that haunt fair thickets and springs of rivers and grassy water-meadows.

Why did not Ocean come? The sea-god came[4],

Nor was the Earth-shaker heedless of the goddess' call, but from the salt sea came up after the rest and set him in the midst.

---

[1] Æsch. *Prom. Vinct.* 128 ff.   [2] *v.* 150 ff.
[3] Hom. *Il.* xx. 4 ff.   [4] *v.* 13.

Homer[1] is loud and instant to tell us that no river might rank with Zeus.

Not even King Acheloios is match, nor yet the great strength of deep-flowing Ocean, from whom all rivers flow and every sea, and all springs and deep wells: yet even he hath fear of the lightning of great Zeus and his dread thunder, when it pealeth out of heaven.

Homer here, as often, doth protest too much. Okeanos fears no Zeus and will not attend his councils—and why? Because he himself is not Ocean but the stream of Ouranos, high heaven itself, an earlier unhumanized Zeus. Okeanos, says the *Etymologicum Magnum*[2], is a title of Ouranos.

As a potency of the old order he is the enemy of Zeus, the friend of Prometheus. And he comes, not like a sea-god mounted on a dolphin but on a four-legged bird with winnowing wings. The bird comes in so clumsily that he must be integral. It beats the air with its pinions eager to be back in its heavenly home. And again, the Okeanids come, not swimming and floating through the waves but borne on the breeze, for they too are daimones of the upper air—

$$\kappa\rho\alpha\iota\pi\nu\circ\phi\acute{o}\rho\circ\iota\ \delta\acute{e}\ \mu'\ \ddot{e}\pi\epsilon\mu\psi\alpha\nu\ \alpha\ddot{v}\rho\alpha\iota^3.$$

The gods who came to Prometheus in his sorrow are the old nature-gods whom he as Titan invoked, *aither*, the swift-winged winds, the springs of heaven-born rivers—

$$\dot{\omega}\ \delta\hat{\iota}\circ\varsigma\ \alpha\dot{\iota}\theta\grave{\eta}\rho\ \kappa\alpha\grave{\iota}\ \tau\alpha\chi\acute{v}\pi\tau\epsilon\rho\circ\iota\ \pi\nu\circ\alpha\grave{\iota}$$
$$\pi\circ\tau\alpha\mu\hat{\omega}\nu\ \tau\epsilon\ \pi\eta\gamma\alpha\grave{\iota}\ \pi\circ\nu\tau\acute{\iota}\omega\nu\ \tau\epsilon\ \kappa\upsilon\mu\acute{\alpha}\tau\omega\nu$$
$$\dot{\alpha}\nu\acute{\eta}\rho\iota\theta\mu\circ\nu\ \gamma\acute{\epsilon}\lambda\alpha\sigma\mu\alpha,\ \pi\alpha\mu\mu\hat{\eta}\tau\acute{o}\rho\ \tau\epsilon\ \gamma\hat{\eta}^4.$$

That is poetry, but it is also theology, sound if obsolete, but obsolete only to revive in philosophy, the philosophy of Sokrates hung in mid-air; the philosophy of those Ionians who, borrowing it may be their doctrine from the βάρβαροι, the Persians, saw in the elemental nature-powers the beginning of things. Most of all the sun is not forgotten by the old Titan-god:

$$\kappa\alpha\grave{\iota}\ \tau\grave{o}\nu\ \pi\alpha\nu\acute{o}\pi\tau\eta\nu\ \kappa\acute{v}\kappa\lambda\circ\nu\ \dot{\eta}\lambda\acute{\iota}\circ\upsilon\ \kappa\alpha\lambda\hat{\omega}\cdot$$
$$\ddot{\iota}\delta\epsilon\sigma\theta\acute{e}\ \mu'\ \circ\dot{\iota}\alpha\ \pi\rho\grave{o}\varsigma\ \theta\epsilon\hat{\omega}\nu\ \pi\acute{\alpha}\sigma\chi\omega\ \theta\epsilon\acute{o}\varsigma^5.$$

---

[1] *Il.* xxi. 195.

[2] s.v. Ὠκεανός· ὁ οὐρανὸς νενόμισται. Ὠκεανός is connected with ai, açayānas—surrounding; it is the stream of ether engirdling the universe; it is ceaseless, recurrent (ἀψόρροος), unwearied (ἀκάματος), essentially Titanic. See E. H. Berger, *Mythische Kosmographie der Griechen*, 1904, pp. 1 and 2.

[3] Æsch. *Prom. Vinct.* 132.

[4] v. 88.   [5] v. 92.

The Gigantes are children of Earth, the Titanes are children of Earth and Heaven, with a leaning towards Heaven. The Gigantomachia stands for the triumph of the humanized Olympian over the powers of Earth, over the snake-tailed monster; the Titanomachia stands for the triumph, partial only, of Olympianism over that higher form of Naturism which is Ouranianism[1]. It would scarcely have been possible to figure Sun and Moon as lawless monsters, but Ouranos included in his compass τὰ μετάρσια as well as τὰ μετέωρα, and in the conduct of τὰ μετάρσια and the weather-daimones generally there was much that might cause a willing enemy to blaspheme. Thunder and lightning, wind and rain, storm and tempest might fitly be classed as *peloria*, portents.

The chorus of Okeanids, we have seen, lament that

He has destroyed the old portentous ones.

The word *peloria* covers, I think, both Earth-powers and Sky-powers, both Giants and Titans; but it is not a little interesting to find that quite early the word differentiated itself into two forms. Dr Osthoff[2] has shown that πέλωρ and τέρας—monster and portent—are one and the same. An examination of the uses of the two words shows that they are practically identical, only that—and this is for us the important point—πέλωρ tends to specialize towards what is earth-born, and τέρας in the form τείρεα tends to be used of heavenly signs.

Thus πέλωρ is one regular term for an earth-born monster and specially for a snake. Gaia herself in Hesiod[3] is Γαῖα πελώρη, the Python in the Homeric Hymn to Apollo[4] is πέλωρ,

---

[1] The chorus of Okeanids say emphatically (v. 164)

ὁ δ' ἐπικότως ἀεὶ
θέμενος ἄγναμπτον νόον,
δάμναται οὐρανίαν
γένναν.

[2] *Etymologische Beiträge zur Mythologie und Religionsgeschichte*, in Archiv f. Religionswiss. 1904, p. 51. Both πέλωρ and τέρας go back to a guttural form *qϵρας. Hesychius has the form τέλωρ· πελώριον, μακρόν, μέγα and τελώριος, μέγας, πελώριος. Euripides (*Androm.* 1033) uses the form κέλωρ,

ὅτε νιν Ἀργόθεν πορευθεὶς
Ἀγαμεμνόνιος κέλωρ, ἀδύτων ἐπιβὰς
κτεάνων ματρός,

where κέλωρ is obviously not 'a poetic word' for son. Orestes is the daimon household snake, the Ktesios turned Erinys.

[3] *Theog.* 159.　　　　　　　　　[4] *v.* 374.

but to Euripides[1] he is γᾶς πελώριον τέρας. The portent sent by Persephone from below the earth is Γοργείη κεφαλὴ δεινοῖο πελώρου, but it is also Διὸς τέρας, as though by afterthought. Hades himself is *Pelorios*. One of the earth-born men sprung of the dragon's seed was, according to Hellanikos[2], called Pelor. The rest of the five were Oudaios, He of the Soil, Hyperenor, the Overweening, Echion, Snakeman, and Chthonios, Earthman, surely a significant company.

Finally, what is very interesting for us, we know of an ancient festival celebrated in honour of these primitive earth-potencies and called by their name *Peloria*. Athenaeus[3], in discussing the ancient rites to which it was the custom to admit slaves, writes thus:

Baton of Sinope, the orator, in his work on Thessaly and Haemonia, says plainly that the Roman Saturnalia was essentially a Greek festival and alleges that it was called by the Thessalians *Peloria*.

Baton then goes on to give an aetiological myth to the effect that the festival, which was a sacrifice held in common by the Pelasgians, was instituted in honour of one Peloros who brought the news of the sudden emergence, owing to an earthquake, of the vale of Tempe. A table spread with all manner of delicacies was set for Peloros, hence the name of the feast—to which strangers and slaves were made welcome—and

Even to this day the Thessalians celebrate this as their chief festival and call it Peloria[4].

The primitive character of the Peloria has been already[5] discussed. What concerns us now is the name. It is abundantly clear that by the time of Athenaeus, and probably long before, the meaning of the word *Peloria* had been lost—the feast was said to be held in honour of Zeus Peloros. No one knew that the festival was in honour of just those old earth-portents whom Zeus destroyed. If we want to realize the sanctities reverenced at the old Thessalian festival we must go back not to Zeus but to the old Earth-daimon, winged and snake-tailed, who on the vase-painting in Fig. 141 smiles as he confronts the thunderbolt of Zeus.

The Olympians then stand first and foremost as a protest

[1] *I. in T.* 1248. [2] Schol. Apoll. Rhod. III. 1178.
[3] XIV. 45. 639. [4] 640. [5] *Supra*, p. 251.

against the worship of Earth and the daimones of the fertility
of Earth.   So far they command our respect and even our
sympathy.   As long as man is engaged in a hand to hand struggle
for bare existence, his principal focus of attention must be on food.
The magical inducement of the recurrent fertility of the earth is
his first and well-nigh his last religious duty.   But, as civilization
advances, and he is freed from the more urgent necessities, his
circle of needs enlarges and the focus of his attention widens.
The old intense interest in food and fertility slackens.   Moreover
a worship of the powers of fertility, which includes all plant and
animal life, is broad enough to be sound and healthy, but, as man's
attention centres more and more intently on his own humanity,
such a worship is an obvious source of danger and disease.   Instinctively a healthy stock will purge its religion from elements
exclusively phallic.   This expurgation ranks first and foremost
among the services Olympianism rendered to Greece[1].   The fight
of the Gods against the Giants had right as well as might on
its side.

But, if the fight of the Gods against the Earth-born Giants be
just and right, the same can scarcely be said of the fight against
the Titans.   These powers of the upper air, these gods of storm
and lightning, these μετάρσια may be, because not understood,
lawless, but they are nowise impure and their worship can scarcely
degrade.   Moreover, though the μετάρσια were, as being wholly
unintelligible and apparently irresponsible, the appropriate objects
of magic, the μετέωρα with their ordered comings and goings,
risings and settings, waxings and wanings, tempted man up the
steep road of exact observation.   Measurements led him to mathematics, in a word, to science.   The Olympians would have done well
had they, while renouncing or at least reforming Earth and τὰ
μετάρσια, clung to and developed the worship of τὰ μετέωρα.
It has already been observed[2] that, in the course of the advance
of European civilization, each new period of enlightenment has

---

[1] See Kaibel, *Daktyloi Idaioi*, 1902, p. 512, for expurgation in Homer, and
Prof. Murray, *Rise of the Greek Epic*[2], 1911, pp. 143 ff.   The process of expurgation
probably long preceded its literary expression.   For the general moral gain and the
softening of manners see *Greek Epic*[2], p. 257, where Prof. Murray quotes Plutarch's
significant words which head this chapter as motto, *Vit. Pelop.* XXI., a human
sacrifice is opposed on the grounds ὡς οὐδενὶ τῶν κρειττόνων καὶ ὑπὲρ ἡμᾶς ἀρετὴν
οὖσαν οὕτω βάρβαρον καὶ παράνομον θυσίαν· οὐ γὰρ τοὺς Τυφῶνας ἐκείνους οὐδὲ τοὺς
Γίγαντας ἄρχειν ἀλλὰ τὸν πατέρα θεῶν καὶ ἀνθρώπων.

[2] *Supra*, p. 439.

been accompanied or rather expressed by new progress in the study of astronomy.

Why then did the orthodox Olympian religion, spite of the protests of philosophers, renounce τὰ μετέωρα? I would hazard a conjecture, distinctly marking the fact that it is at present little more than a conjecture, of which confirmation, however, seems to grow apace. By the mouth of Herodotus and Aristophanes we have seen that, to the popular mind, the worship of nature-powers, the elements and the heavenly bodies, earth, air, water, fire, Sun and Moon, was characteristic of 'the barbarians,' and in the sixth century B.C. barbarian of course spelt Persian. 'That old villain Helios' is intent on betraying the Olympians; he is caught Medizing. Is it not possible that some, indeed much of the acrimony felt, the contumely heaped on meteoric philosophy is due, not to the rage of the common man against the thinker, but to the natural resentment of the patriot? Sokrates in his basket contemplating τὰ μετέωρα is not only, or chiefly, the fantastic philosopher, he is the pilloried Persian.

We may take it as an axiom[1] that philosophy arises out of religion. Greek philosophy arose, we are told, in Ionian Naturism. Starting from our axiom we are bound to ask, 'Out of what religion was it that Ionian Naturism arose?' Not from Olympianism. The doctrines of Thales, of Herakleitos, of Anaximenes, of Anaximander, given that they arose from a religion at all, must have arisen from a religion concerned with the elements, Water, Fire, Air, Earth. For such a religion we look in vain to Greece. That philosophy arose in the sixth century B.C., just the century when Asia Minor was riddled through and through with Persian infiltrations.

The history of art tells, I think, the same tale. Up to the time of the Persian wars Greek art was all that we call archaic. It was traditional and hieratic. Then comes the sudden awakening to an almost complete naturism. We write and lecture on the outburst of new life that followed on the struggle with a great Oriental potency. Is it not at least as likely that in art as in

---

[1] For a full exposition and analysis of this principle, to me indisputable and axiomatic, I may be allowed to refer to Mr F. M. Cornford's forthcoming work, *From Religion to Philosophy*.

philosophy 'Naturism' received a fresh impulse from Persia[1] and both had a common source, Persian religion? The Olympians are, as will presently be shown[2], essentially *objets d'art*.

We shall find confirmation of this view if we look at another movement of the sixth century B.C., the movement known as Orphic[3]. Orphic religion contains within itself much that is indigenous. Its main *fond* is primitive Ægean religion, with all those factors of naturism and magic already described in detail. But what differentiates it out from the rest of the popular religion of Greece is, I have long believed, certain imported elements of Oriental and mainly Iranian nature-worship and formal mysticism[4]. The Greek spirit always tended to humanize and individualize its daimones into personal gods, Iranian mysticism kept them disintegrated and dispersed in the medium of nature from which they sprang. Divinities so dispersed are the natural medium and vehicle of magic, of sacramentalism, of each and every form of mysticism.

Orphism did just what the Olympian religion failed or refused to do. It reformed the religion of Earth, but by strengthening the powers of Heaven, not by disallowing them; it fought the Giants but joined forces with the Titans[5]. This it was, I think, enabled to do through its reinforcement by Iranian naturism and mysticism. To confirm this view the main position of Orphic

[1] This is not the place to discuss the character of Persian art. Its characteristic naturalism may be well studied in the sculptures from Persepolis, excavated by M. and Mme Dieulafoy, and now in the Louvre. The possible influence of Persia in producing Pheidian and post-Pheidian naturalism in art was first suggested to me *à propos* of his discoveries at Memphis by Prof. Flinders Petrie. It was a conversation with him that first led me to the idea that Persian nature-worship might underlie Ionian philosophy.

[2] *Infra*, p. 478.

[3] Orphism as a whole is advisedly excluded from the present book, which aims only at an examination of certain social origins of Greek religion.

[4] For these foreign elements in Orphism see especially Dr Eisler, *Weltenmantel und Himmelszelt*, 1910. For Persian influence in Egypt in the sixth and fifth centuries B.C. see W. Flinders Petrie, *Personal Religion in Egypt*, p. 40 ff. For prehistoric relations between Iran and Asia Minor as evidenced by the Boghazköi excavations see Winckler in *Mitteilungen d. deut. Orient.-Gesellschaft*, 1907, No. 35, pp. 1—71, and Garstang, *Land of the Hittites*, 1910. For a good résumé of the Persian elements in Orphism see Dr Wünsch's review of Dr Eisler's book in *Archiv f. Religionswiss.* 1911, p. 536.

[5] Persian religion laid, as is well known, special stress on Fire-worship, and along with this went a minute attention to ritual purity, and a sharp distinction drawn between light and darkness, good and evil—a distinction foreign to the primitive Greek mind. We owe our devil to the Persians.

religion must briefly be resumed. Only so can we feel to the full the weakness and deadness of Olympian negations.

The broad foundation of Orphic religion, as of all mysticism, was a pantheistic naturism. All things are sprung from Earth and Heaven. This doctrine is best voiced in the priceless fragment of the *Melanippe the Wise* of Euripides[1]. Melanippe has borne two children to the god Poseidon. They are exposed, by the god's command, but saved by divine interposition and found, in the usual fashion, suckled by wild kine. They are brought to the king. He calls a seer who pronounces it to be a portent, and orders expiation by the burning of the children. Melanippe is called and ordered to carry out the sentence. She recognizes and pleads for them, an odd, advanced plea. She urges that there are no such things as portents and then, while her children are still under sentence of burning, in strange Euripidean fashion, expounds the immutable order of nature—a tradition received by her from her half divine mother, Hippo, the daughter of the wise old Cheiron on Mt Pelion.

This is the statement:

It is not my word, but my mother's word[2]
How Heaven and Earth were once one form, but stirred
And strove and dwelt asunder far away:
And then, rewedding, bore unto the day
And light of life all things that are, the trees,
Flowers, birds and beasts and them that breathe the seas,
And mortal Man, each in his kind and law.

A primitive and beautiful cosmogony, meet material for mysticism, but why, it may be asked, claim it as Orphic? Such it was held by tradition to be, at least in Alexandrian times. Apollonius Rhodius[3] tells how, just before the Argo sailed, the heroes fell to quarrelling, and Jason sought to stay them from their strife, and Orpheus lifted up his voice and essayed to sing.

He sang how Earth and Heaven and Sea were joined
Of old together in one form, and next
How that they parted after deadly strife
Asunder. How, in ether, Sun and Moon
And stars keep each their ever steadfast course,
And how uprose the mountains, and the rivers
Rippled and rushed, and creeping things were born.

[1] Nauck, *Frg.* 484, trans. Murray.
[2] A much-quoted line. Cf. Plato, *Symp.* 177 A, and Eur. *Hel.* 513. It is used of something having the force of ancient tradition. As a preface it makes us expect some weighty pronouncement.
[3] I. 494.

Different though the style is, vaguer and more Ouranian the outlook, it is clear that here, as in Melanippe, we have the old Orphic cosmogony which lent to Empedokles his *Neikos* and *Philia*, and to philosophy in general τὸ ποιοῦν and τὸ πάσχον. It is a cosmogony that knows no Olympians. To Melanippe Earth and Sky are the causes, the beginnings, of all things. The Olympians are there; they may be, as Helen said, 'to blame' (αἴτιοι), but they are only spokes in the great wheel[1] of nature, not the driving force that sets and keeps her going, not αἰτίαι[2].

Varro[3] tells us expressly that

Earth and Sky, as the mysteries of Samothrace teach, are the Great Gods,

and Samothrace was the natural bridge between Orientalized Asia Minor and the mainland. Most conclusive of all is the avowal of the Orphic mystic, his avowal of race and parentage. He claims to be the child of no Olympian, he goes back to potencies earlier, more venerable:

I am the child of Earth and of Starry Heaven[4].

The avowal of the initiate Orphic does not end here. A second clause is added, not wholly untinged, I think, by protest:

But my race is of Heaven (alone)[5].

The creed he adopts is definitely opposed to that of Xenophanes[6]:

From earth all things rise, and all things in earth have their ending.

Again Xenophanes says:

All things are earth and water that grow and come into being;

and again:

For we all are born of earth and are born of water,

where the fire element is intentionally disallowed.

---

[1] *Infra*, p. 523.
[2] *Il*. III. 164 οὔ τί μοι αἰτίη ἐσσί, θεοί νύ μοι αἴτιοί εἰσιν.
[3] *De Ling. Lat.* v. 58 Terra enim et Caelum ut Samothracum initia docent, sunt Dei Magni.
[4] *Petelia Tablet.* See *Prolegomena*, p. 574.
[5] αὐτὰρ ἐμὸν γένος οὐράνιον. Even if we take the αὐτάρ as having but slight adversative force and translate 'moreover' the emphasis is the same.
[6] Diels, *Frg.* 27, 29 and 33. Prof. Burnet, *Early Greek Philosophy*[2], p. 135, thinks that certain expressions used by Xenophanes 'can only be meant to make the heavenly bodies ridiculous.' But though Xenophanes may have distrusted the worship of the heavenly bodies, he revered Ouranos as a whole.

It is almost as though the initiate Orphic would say, By nature, by birth, I spring from my mother Earth, but by adoption and grace I am made the child of Heaven.   Manifestly a distinction is drawn between the two great cosmic powers, and preference given to Ouranos.

But we have other definite evidence that the religion of Orpheus emphasized just what the Olympian religion disallowed, the worship of the heavenly bodies.   Tradition accounted Orpheus a Sun-worshipper.   Eratosthenes[1] thus writes:

> He (Orpheus) did not honour Dionysos but accounted Helios the greatest of the gods, whom also he called Apollo.   And rising up early in the morning he climbed the mountain called Pangaion and waited for the rising of the sun, that he might first catch sight of it.   Therefore Dionysos was enraged and sent against him his Bassarids, as Æschylus the poet says.

In worshipping Helios, Orpheus only followed the custom of his native Thrace.   Sophocles in the *Tereus*[2] makes one of his characters say:

> O Helios, name
> To Thracian horsemen dear, O eldest Flame!

Maximus of Tyre[3] said that the Paeonians reverenced Helios, and the Paeonian image of Helios is a small disk on a long pole.

Orpheus, Eratosthenes tells us, called Helios also Apollo, and the later Orphics who went by the name of Pythagoreans always worshipped Apollo.   It was revealed in the mysteries that Apollo and Helios were the same.   That is clear from a passage in the lost *Phaethon* of Euripides[4].   The rash Phaethon has fallen, killed by a lightning flash from the Sun, and his bride thus reproaches the slayer:

> Thou hast destroyed me, O bright Helios,
> Me and this man.   O rightly among mortals
> Apollo, yea, Destroyer, art thou called
> By such as know the Silent Names of spirits.

Side by side with the Olympian movement which tended entirely to humanize the gods, we have then a movement of return to Nature-Worship.   This movement arose in the sixth century, and was, broadly speaking, contemporary with the rise of Ionian philosophy, itself, if our contention be just, based in part on

---

[1] *Catast.* 24. p. 140.   [2] Soph. *Frg.* 523.
[3] 8. 8 ...δίσκος βραχὺς ὑπὲρ μακροῦ ξύλου, something like, no doubt, the pole and globe carried in the Daphnephoria.   See *supra*, p. 438.
[4] Nauck, *Frg.* 781 ὅστις τὰ σιγῶντ' ὀνόματ' οἶδε δαιμόνων.

Persian naturism. Is it rash to suppose that Orphism owed its main impulse to the infiltration of Persian religious doctrine? that in religion as in politics there was 'Medizing'? Tradition said, and it is a tradition that has been too long forgotten, that when Cyrus consulted the oracle of the head of Orpheus at Lesbos, there came to him in answer words as singular as significant. 'Mine,' said the oracle to the Persian, 'O Cyrus, are also thine[1].'

Moreover, and this I think is an important point, Orphism was always discredited at Athens. Spite of its high moral tone, spite of the fact that it was recognized as a purer and reformed phase of Dionysiac religion[2], it was never popular in high places. Is it not at least possible that some of its discredit arose from political, racial prejudice?

To resume. In discrediting certain elements of Earth-Worship Olympianism did well. In disallowing the worship of the Heavenly bodies Olympianism did ill. Save for the Persian War, or rather the Persian infiltration, this backward step need perhaps never have been taken.

(4) *The Olympians refuse the functions of the Eniautos-daimon.* As to the making of Greek theology, Herodotus[3] has left us a notable statement, much discussed but not as yet, I think, fully elucidated.

> But as to the origin of each particular god, whether they all existed from the beginning, what were their individual forms, the knowledge of these things is, so to speak, but of to-day and yesterday. For Hesiod and Homer are my seniors, I think, by some four hundred years and not more. And it is they who have composed for the Greeks the generations of the gods, *and have given to the gods their titles and distinguished their several provinces and special powers and marked their forms.*

There were gods before the Olympians of Homer and Hesiod, but they were without titles, they were undistinguished in their

---

[1] Philostr. *Heroic.* v. 3. 704 τὰ ἐμὰ ω Κῦρε καὶ σά. See *Prolegomena,* p. 466. A commentator on Statius also notes the analogy between the Persian and the Pythagorean nature-gods as contrasted with the anthropomorphic Greek divinities. See Lutatius Plac. *ad* Stat. *Theb.* iv. 516 (Abel, *Frg.* 282). He contrasts 'hos deos cognitos qui coluntur in templis' with 'alium principem...de cujus genere sunt sol et luna.' Of this last he says 'Persae etiam confirmant...maximis in hoc auctoribus Pythagora et Platone.'

[2] See *Prolegomena,* p. 456, and especially Diodorus, iii. 65, where it is said of Orpheus πολλὰ μεταθεῖναι τῶν ἐν τοῖς ὀργίοις.

[3] ii. 53 ...οὗτοι δέ εἰσι οἱ ποιήσαντες θεογονίην Ἕλλησι καὶ τοῖσι θεοῖσι τὰς ἐπωνυμίας δόντες καὶ τιμάς τε καὶ τέχνας διελόντες καὶ εἴδεα αὐτῶν σημήναντες.

functions, undiscriminated in their forms. We know now what manner of beings these pre-Olympian potencies were; they were Year-daimones, all alike in shape and function, all apt to take on plant or animal shape, the business of each and all monotonously one, to give food and increase to man and make the year go round. But the Olympian will have none of this, he shakes himself loose of the year and the produce of the year. In place of his old *function*, his τιμή, his γέρας, he demands a new honour, a service done to him, himself as a personality. Instead of being himself a sacrament he demands a sacrifice.

This shift of meaning in τιμή[1] from function that must be performed to honour claimed marks the whole degradation of the Olympian. The god like the man who substitutes privilege for function, for duty done, is self-doomed and goes to his own place. 'If any will not work neither let him eat.' Sentiment, tradition, may keep up the custom of gift-sacrifice for a while, but the gods to whom the worshipper's real heart and life goes out are the gods who work and live, not those who dwell at ease in Olympos. They are Year-daimones, and the type and model of them all is the old hard-working Helios, the unwearied one, whether he toils to mount the heavens day by day or, in human form as Herakles, to cleanse the earth for man from monsters.

> Surely the Sun has labour all his days,
> And never any respite, steeds nor god[2].

The real true god, the Eniautos-daimon, lives and works for his people; he does more, he dies for them. The crowning disability and curse of the new theological order is that the Olympian claims to be *immortal* (ἀθάνατος). In examining sacrament and sacrifice we have seen that the Year-daimon in the form of a Bull lived his year-long life that he might die, and died that he might live again. His whole gist and nature was absorbed and expressed by the cycle of periodic reincarnation. Out of this cycle came all his manifold, yet monotonous life-history, his Births, his Re-births, his Appearances and Disappearances, his Processions

---

[1] For this observation on the shifting use of τιμή I am indebted to Mr Cornford, and may refer to his forthcoming book *From Religion to Philosophy.* Mr Cook points out to me that Zeus never quite shook off his year-aspect, see *Iliad* ii. 134 ἐννέα δὴ βεβάασι Διὸς μεγάλου ἐνιαυτοί. Zeus indeed, alone among the Olympians, is a Sky and Weather-god to the end.

[2] See *supra,* p. 370.

and Recessions, his Epiphanies, his Deaths, his Burials, his Resurrections, his endless Changes and Chances[1].

All this, all life and that which is life and reality—Change and Movement[2]—the Olympian renounces.   Instead he chooses Deathlessness and Immutability—a seeming Immortality which is really the denial of life, for life is change.   This brazen lifeless immutability impressed the imagination of Pindar[3].   Tinged with Orphism though he was, he did not hear how hollow it rang:

> Of one race, one only are men and gods ; both of one mother's womb, we draw our breath : but far asunder is all our power divided, and parts us— here there is nought and there in strength of bronze, a seat unshaken, eternal, abides the heaven above.

He sees the beauty and the fertility of Earth's recurrent cycle mirrored in man:

> Even so, for a sign thereof, Alcimidas shows clear the mark of his race, close kin to the fruitful cornlands : whose alternation now gives from the soil life in abundance to man and now again takes rest to lay hold upon strength.

But he cannot see that the Olympian who will not die to live renounces life, he desiccates and dies.   Such is the very nature of life that only through the ceaseless movement and rhythm of *palingenesia* is immortality possible.   Athanasia, eternity through not dying, is almost a contradiction in words.

Together with this conception of a dead and barren immortality there grew up the disastrous notion that between god and man there was a great gulf fixed, that communion was no more possible.   To attempt to pass this gulf was *hybris*, it was *the* sin against the gods.   Pindar again lends himself to this pitiless, fruitless doctrine.   The dull, melancholy mandate runs through his odes:

> Seek not thou to become a god[4].

In this mandate we see the door closed finally on the last remnants of totemistic thinking ; it is the death warrant of sacramentalism. The only possible service now is gift-sacrifice ; and by that service alone, history has shown, the soul of man cannot live.

---

[1] See *supra*, pp. 425, 426.

[2] H. Bergson, *La Perception du Changement*, Conférences faites à Oxford 1911, p. 28 'si le changement est réel et même constitutif de toute realité....'

[3] *Nem.* vi. *sub init.*

[4] *Supra*, p. 128.

In a fashion more sad and dreary and degraded still the complete separation of man and god utters itself in another and, to sacramentalism, a blasphemous thought. The gods are jealous gods; there is φθόνος. The gods begrudge a man a glory that may pale their own splendour. To the mystery-god Dionysos φθόνος is unknown:

> No grudge hath he of the great,
> No scorn of the mean estate;
> But to all that liveth, his wine he giveth,
> Griefless, immaculate[1].

So too Plato[2], by a beautiful instinct, when he tells of the great procession of the gods and daimones through high heaven, will exclude no one save only φθόνος himself:

> And any one may follow who can and will, for jealousy stands ever without the heavenly choir.

Zeus is but the great leader of an equal band, but the Megistos Kouros[3], he is no jealous god.

So far then our conception of the Olympian is mainly negative. He refuses the functions of the totemistic daimon, he sheds his animal or plant form. He will not be a daimon of Earth, nor yet even of the Sky; above all he refuses to be a Year-daimon with his function of ceaseless toil. He will not die to rise again, but chooses instead a barren immortality. He withdraws himself from man and lives remote, a 'jealous god.'

But these negations, instructive though they are, do not exhaust the content of the Olympian. We feel instinctively that in some ways an Olympian is more vivid, more real than any shapeless, shifting nature-daimon. If we met Zeus or Apollo in the street we should know them and greet them. To put it simply, the Olympian, for all his negations, has personality, individuality. It will repay us to investigate rather closely what we mean by personality and individuality.

It has been from the outset a cardinal principle of this book that the god is the reflection, the projection of man's emotions socially reinforced. We saw in the first chapter that the divine

---

[1] Eur. *Bacch.* 421.
[2] *Phaedr.* 247 B ...φθόνος γὰρ ἔξω θείου χοροῦ ἵσταται and again, in the *Timaeus* (29 E), Plato, aristocrat though he is, knows that in the sphere of the good there are no class distinctions. ἀγαθῷ δὲ οὐδεὶς περὶ οὐδενὸς οὐδέποτε ἐγγίγνεται φθόνος.
[3] *Supra*, p. 12, note 1.

figures of the Kouros and the Mother were but the projections of social conditions essential to a Matrilinear group[1]. Further, in considering totemistic societies[2], we have seen that their main characteristic was solidarity, lack of differentiation. Man had not yet separated himself out from nature, and the individual man has but slight consciousness of himself as distinguished from his group. Such a social state of things has its religious counter-part, its religious projection, in undifferentiated forms like the daimon of the group, the functionary, uttering and embodying the collective life of the group[3].

But as the group system disintegrates, the individual emerges, and further, not only does the individual emerge from the group, but the human individual is more and more conscious of his sharp distinction from animals and plants, from the whole of nature that surrounds him. This twofold emergence of the individual from the group, of the human individual from the nature-world around him, is inevitably mirrored in the personality, in the individuality of the Olympian gods.

We are still too apt to put the cart before the horse, to think of the group as made up of an aggregate of individuals rather than of the individuals as a gradual segregation of the group. It is only by an effort of imagination that we realize that plurality, the group, comes first. A simple illustration from language may serve to make clear this point.

In many North American, Central Asian, and Pacific languages two plurals are in use, the Inclusive and Exclusive, or, as they are perhaps better called, the Collective and Selective Plurals. The Collective 'we' includes all persons present, the 'Selective' a smaller selected group, to which the speaker belongs. The proper use of this plural is essential to the successful missionary, otherwise doctrinal scandal may ensue:

When the formula 'We have sinned' occurs in prayer, the exclusive form must be employed, for the supplicant would otherwise be including the Almighty among those to whom sin is imputed. The same expression occurring in a sermon, takes the inclusive form; for the audience would otherwise be excluded from the category of sinners and would understand the preacher's meaning to be 'We, the clergy, have sinned but not you, the people[4].'

---

[1] pp. 38—42.   [2] pp. 118—127.   [3] pp. 271—273.
[4] Payne, *op. cit.* 188.

Again, and still more instructively, we have among the Apache Indians and the British Columbian tribes a collective as well as a selective singular. The collective singular denotes the person as a member of the group. Thus if the question be asked 'Who will help?' the answer would be the collective 'I,' that is 'I for one' or 'I among others.' But if the question be 'Who is the mother of this child?' the answer will be the selective 'I,' that is I and nobody else.

Now 'this sharp distinction occurs,' Mr Payne[1] observes, 'with a frequency which indicates it as answering to a substantial need of daily life. The Apache Indians for example, one of the wildest peoples in America, would scarcely have invented and rigorously preserved this idiom unless it were indispensable to their intercourse: and the same may be said of the British Columbian tribes in whose languages it is even more conspicuous. *The collective*, it should be noted, *is the ordinary form, and the selective the exception.*'

No more interesting illustration could be adduced of the sense of solidarity naturally pervading the food-group and of the weak sense of individuality in separate members.

It will be apparent whither the argument is tending. Now-a-days we think of the plural number in language as made up of a number of singular units, as a complexity rather than a simplicity. That is because we reason back from a segregation already accomplished and that seems to us instinctive. But the facts of language show that the plural and all other forms of number in grammar arise not by multiplication of an original 'I' but by selection and gradual exclusion from an original collective 'we.' This 'we' represents the aggregate personality of the food-group, and therefore includes the undifferentiated 'I' of the speaker of the time being[2]. The procedure is from synthesis to analysis, from the group to the individual.

Dr Tylor, the great exponent of Animism, sees in the conception of the human soul 'the very *fons et origo*[3] of the conception of spirit and deity in general':

'Spiritual beings,' he says, 'are modelled by man on his primary conception of his own human soul[4].'

---

[1] *History of the New World*, ii. p. 188.
[2] Mr Payne, from whom (*op. cit.* vol. ii. p. 186) I borrow this interesting observation, adds, 'to borrow terms from the philosophy of Quantity, if thought and language are regarded as two related variables, the "I" does not represent their prime ratio but their ultimate one.' I am no mathematician but I append the illustration in case it may be significant.
[3] *Primitive Culture*[3], ii. 247.
[4] *Op. cit.* ii. p. 184.

Broadly speaking this remains true, but, in the light of modern psychology and sociology, it needs some restatement. For the individual human soul we must substitute that thing at once more primitive and perhaps therefore more complex—the group-soul. The god is projected, not by the thinking or the feeling of one man, but by such part of his thinking and feeling as he has in common with other men, such emotions and ideas as are represented by his customs and enshrined in his language:

'It seems,' again says Prof. Tylor[1], 'as though the conception of a human soul *when once attained to by man* served as a type or model on which he framed not only his ideas of other souls of lower grade, but also his ideas of spiritual beings in general, from the tiniest elf that sports in the long grass up to the heavenly Creator and Ruler of the world, the Great Spirit.'

Profoundly true if only the words italicized '*when once attained to by man*' be carefully borne in mind. A more intimate knowledge of savage thinking has brought to light a stage of thinking more primitive, more inchoate, than animism, a stage which we may call Animatism, or better I think Zoïsm[2], a stage in which man has not yet got his own individuality clear, but is intensely conscious of life lived, of power felt, though not yet of isolated personality. This state of group-thinking or rather group-living is reflected in totemism and in the vague daimones that emerge from totemistic thinking[3].

Until man learns to think of himself sharply as an individual, that is until the hold of the group is weakened, he will not sharply individualize his gods. They will be not clear cut personalities but functional daimones. Now it would seem at first that a clear cut personality is a higher and better thing than a vague impersonal daimon or functionary. So he is from the point of view of art and intellect, but all experience goes to show that his emotional appeal, save to the very highly educated, is feebler. The sight of a great discoverer or great thinker will touch the imagination of a few, but, if you want to move the great heart of the people to hysteria, to almost frenzy, you must

[1] *Op. cit.* ii. p. 110. The italics are my own.
[2] I borrow this term—and welcome it is a substitute for the inelegant form 'Animatism'—from Mr Cook.
[3] For the indeterminate stage preceding Animism see especially A. C. Kruijt, Het Animisme in den Indischen Archipel, 1906, a book I unfortunately know only through the analysis in the *Revue de l'Histoire des Religions*, by R. Hertz, 1909, p. 352. Mr W. McDougall's 'Defence of Animism' (*Body and Mind*, 1911) appeared after this section of my book was written, and I have not had leisure to study it with the needful attention.

produce a daimon-functionary, as little individualized as may be, you must crown a king. The reason is clear, the king, the daimon-functionary, is the utterance of the group and each individual in the group claims him as in part himself.

The highly personalized, individualized god is fashioned on the highly personalized, individualized self, and the essence of the sense of self is separateness[1], or consciousness of the severance of one self from other selves[2], and of that self as subject and distinct from objects. Now primitive consciousness for the most part lacks this sense of segregation, because it is mainly absorbed in activities, in 'doing things.' The things of which the savage is mainly conscious are not envisaged as external objects, they are parts of his doing, of his 'warm stream of human consciousness.' We have already[3] seen this in the case of weapons and tools which are felt as extensions of personality. Your stick is part of your act of brandishing, or of your sense of walking. You are not conscious of it as a stick till you let it fall. The sense of action, of relation, is vivid and submerges subject and object. This comes out very clearly in certain aspects of primitive language.

It used to be thought that language began with nouns, the names of things, to which later were added qualifying adjectives. Still later, it was held, these separate nouns were joined by verbs expressing relations between subject and object, and these again were qualified by adverbs. Modern linguistic tells quite another and, for psychology and primitive religion, a very instructive tale. Language, after the purely emotional interjection, began with whole sentences, *holophrases*[4], utterances of a relation in

[1] See *supra*, p. 86. Separateness, individuality, is a characteristic of *life*, but it is eternally combated by the tendency to reproduce other life which prevents complete individuality. See Prof. Bergson, *L'Évolution Créatrice*, p. 14, ' on peut dire que si la tendance à s'individuer est partout présente dans le monde organisé, elle est partout combattue par la tendance à se réproduire.' Hence the Eniautos-daimon resisted complete individualization.

[2] The correlative of this, the process of individualizing the soul, is very clearly stated by M. Lévy-Bruhl in his *Les Fonctions Mentales dans les Sociétés Inférieures*, p. 430, ' Quand l'individu humain prend une conscience claire de lui-même en tant qu'individu, quand il se distingue formellement du groupe auquel il se sent appartenir, alors les êtres et les objets extérieurs commencent aussi à lui apparaître comme pourvus d'âmes ou d'esprits individuels, durant cette vie et après la mort.'

[3] *Supra*, p. 86.

[4] For this illustration from language I am indebted to Mr E. J. Payne's sections on language in his *History of the New World*, 1899, vol. II. p. 114 ff. In the discussion of personalization that follows from it I owe much to Mr Crawley's *Idea of the Soul*, 1909, p. 35.

which subject and object have not yet got their heads above water but are submerged in a situation. A holophrase utters a holopsychosis. Out of these *holophrases* at a later stage emerge our familiar 'Parts of Speech,' rightly so called, for speech was before its partition. A simple instance will make this clear.

The Fuegians[1] have a word, or rather holophrase, *mamihlapi-natapai*, which means '*looking-at-each-other,-hoping-that-either-will-offer-to-do-something-which-both-parties-desire-but-are-unwill-ing-to-do.*' This holophrase contains no nouns and no separate verbs, it simply expresses a tense relation—not unknown to some of us, and applicable to any and every one. Uneducated and impulsive people even to-day tend to show a certain holophrastic savagery. They not unfrequently plunge into a statement of relations before they tell you who they are talking about. As civilization advances, the holophrase, overcharged, disintegrates, and, bit by bit, object, subject and verb, and the other 'Parts of Speech' are abstracted from the stream of warm conscious human activity in which they were once submerged.

'The analogy,' as Mr Crawley observes, 'between the holophrase and the primitive percept and concept is close. In both we start with masses which are gradually divided in the one case by perception becoming analytical, in the other by an attempt on the part of the articulating muscles to keep pace with this mental analysis.'

The holophrase shows us man entangled as it were in his own activities, he and his environment utterly involved. He has as yet no 'soul,' but he has life, and has it more abundantly.

Is the savage then impersonal? Does he tend to employ only generalized abstract terms denoting that indefinable though wholly palpable thing 'relation'? Far from it. He is intensely personal. Language again is the best evidence.

A New Caledonian expressing the fact that some fruit was not high enough for the native palate, said not 'it-not-yet-eatable,' but 'we-not-yet-eatable[2].'

Egotism could scarcely go further. The thing eaten is regarded as a mere appendage to, as in fact part of, the personality of the eater. It is indeed actually an essential factor in that activity, that eating or not-eating of which he is intensely conscious. A faint survival of this egotistic plural is observable in the 'we' of the modern writer, which absorbs the reader's personality; when

---

[1] Crawley, *op. cit.* p. 34.   [2] Crawley, *op. cit.* p. 37.

the writer becomes doubtful of a sympathetic union he naturally lapses into the exclusive ' I.'

Language then would seem to throw light on two points. First, primitive man, submerged in his own reactions and activities, does not clearly distinguish himself as subject from the objects to which he reacts, and therefore has but slight consciousness of his own separate soul and hence no power to project it into 'animated nature.' He is conscious of life, of *mana*, but not of individual spirits; his faith may be described as Animatism or Zoïsm[1] rather than as Animism, his ritual will be that of magic, which is, as we have seen, but the manipulation of *mana*. His sacrifice, if sacrifice he performs, will be a sacrament partaken of, not a gift offered to a person. Second, man felt himself at first not as a personality separate from other persons, but as the warm excited centre of a group; language tells us what we have already learnt from ritual, that the 'soul' of primitive man is 'congregationalized[2],' the collective daimon is before the individual ghost, and still more he is before the Olympian god.

The savage we have seen is never impersonal, never abstract. His whole being, his whole personality, is as it were involved, submerged in action, but he does not personify. The act of personifying involves the realization of subject and object, the vivid consciousness of the subject as an individual, a person, and then the projection of that personality over into an object realized as distinct. It is as far as possible from that *holopsychosis*, that *symbiosis* of which the holophrase is the expression. The one is emotional, the other highly intellectual. As M. Lévy-Bruhl[3] has well said:

Connaître en general c'est objectiver; objectiver, c'est projeter hors de soi, comme quelque chose d'étranger, ce qui est à connaître.

To know, it would seem, is at least in part to purge perception from egoistic emotion, from sympathy; it is to view dispassionately.

---

[1] Some new term is much needed. I prefer Mr Cook's Zoïsm; see *supra*, p. 472. Animatism is suggested by Mr Marett (*Threshold of Religion*, p. 15), 'It (the attitude of a Kaffir towards a thunderstorm) is Animism in the loose sense of some writers, or, as I propose to call it, *Animatism*, but it is *not* Animism in the strict scientific sense that implies the attribution, not merely of personality and will but of "soul" or "spirit" to the storm.' Mr Clodd in his *Pre-animistic Stages in Religion*, Fortnightly Review, 1909, p. 1133, suggests *Naturism*.

[2] p. 48.

[3] *Les Fonctions Mentales dans les Sociétés Inférieures*, p. 452.

Here we seem to trace one cause of the chill remoteness of the Olympians. They are objects to a subject, they are concepts thrown out of the human mind, looked at from a distance, things *known*, not like the mystery gods *felt* and lived. The more clearly they are envisaged the more reasonable and thinkable they are, the less are they the sources, the expression, of emotion.

We touch here on the very heart and secret of the difference between the Olympian and the mystery-god, between Apollo and Zeus on the one hand and Dionysos on the other: a difference, the real significance of which was long ago, with the instinct of genius, divined by Nietzsche[1]. The Olympian has clear form, he is the '*principium individuationis*' incarnate; he can be thought, hence his calm, his *sophrosyne*. The mystery-god is the life of the whole of things, he can only be felt—as soon as he is thought and individualized he passes, as Dionysos had to pass, into the thin, rare ether of the Olympian. The Olympians are of conscious thinking, divided, distinct, departmental; the mystery-god is the impulse of life through all things, perennial, indivisible.

Above the intellectualized Olympians was set, by Homer and by Æschylus alike, the dominant figure of Moira[2], division, partition, allotment, and rightly, for it is by dividing, by distinguishing, by classifying, that we know. This impulse to divide is reflected in Moira, and the departmental Olympians are, so far as they are *thought*, but specialized Moirai. As has been well said:

Chaque mythologie est, au fond, une classification, mais qui emprunte ses principes à des croyances religieuses, et non pas à des notions scientifiques.

---

[1] *Die Geburt der Tragödie*, p. 116, 'erste aus dem Geiste der Musik heraus verstehen wir eine Freude an der Vernichtung des Individuums. Denn, an den einzelnen Beispielen einer solchen Vernichtung, wird uns nur das ewige Phänomen der dionysischen Kunst deutlich gemacht, die den Willen in seiner Allmacht gleichsam hinter dem *principio individuationis*, das ewige Leben jenseit aller Erscheinung und trotz aller Vernichtung, zum Ausdruck bringt,' and again, p. 23, 'man möchte selbst Apollo als das herrliche Götterbild des *principii individuationis* bezeichnen'; for the emotional, unifying tendency of Dionysos see p. 24.

[2] The meaning of this figure of Moira and the inherent scepticism of the Olympians was also in his inspired way divined by Nietzsche, *op. cit.*, p. 69, '...dies alles erinnert auf das stärkste an dem Mittelpunkt und Hauptsatz der äschyleischen Weltbetrachtung, die über Göttern und Menschen die Moira als ewige Gerechtigkeit thronen sieht. Bei der erstaunlichen Kühnheit, mit der Äschylus die olympische Welt auf seine Gerechtigkeitswagschalen stellt, müssen wir uns vergegenwärtigen, dass der tiefsinnige Grieche einen unverrückbar festen Untergrund des metaphysischen Denkens in seinen Mysterien hatte, und dass sich an den Olympiern alle seine skeptischen Anwandelungen entladen konnten.'

Les panthéons bien organisés se partagent la nature, tout comme ailleurs les clans se partagent l'univers[1].

The Olympians are then but highly diversified Moirai and the Moirai are departments, they are the spatial correlatives of the temporal Horai. The wheel of Dike moves through time, Moira operates in space. The distinction is of cardinal importance. Prof. Bergson[2] has shown us that *durée*, true time, *is* ceaseless change, which is the very essence of life—which is in fact ' l'Évolution Créatrice, and this is in its very essence one and indivisible.

La durée réelle est ce que l'on a toujours appelé le temps, mais le temps perçu comme indivisible.

We cannot understand this perhaps through the eye, trained to spatial perception, but we can imagine it through the ear.

Quand nous écoutons une mélodie, nous avons la plus pure impression de succession que nous puissions avoir—une impression aussi éloignée que possible de la simultanéité—et pourtant c'est la continuité même de la mélodie et l'impossibilité de la décomposer qui font sur nous cette impression. Si nous la découpons en notes distinctes, en autant 'd'avant' et 'd'après' qu'il nous plaît, c'est que nous y mêlons des images spatiales et que nous imprégnons la succession de simultanéité ; dans l'espace seulement, il y a distinction nette de parties extérieures les unes aux autres.

It is this 'durée,' figured by the Greek as Dike, the Way[3], that the mystic apprehends; in the main stream and current of that life of duration, he lives and has his being. Moira and all the spatial splendours of her Olympians are to him but an intellectual backwater.

Finally, the Olympians not only cease to be sources of emotion but they positively offend that very intellect that fashioned them. They are really so many clear-cut concepts, but they claim to have objective reality. This is the rock on which successive generations of gods have shattered. Man feels rightly and instinctively

[1] MM. Durkheim et M. Mauss, *De quelques Formes Primitives de Classification— Contribution à l'Étude des Représentations Collectives.* L'Année Sociologique, 1901— 1902, p. 1. In this monograph, which in its relation to the study of religious origins is simply 'epoch-making,' the authors seek to establish that logical classification arises from social. This is analogous to the philosophical position of Prof. Durkheim, who holds that the ' categories' are modes of collective rather than individual thinking ; see his *Sociologie Religieuse et Théorie de la Connaissance* in Rev. de Métaphysique, xvii. 1909, p. 733. For Moira as the principle of classification I am entirely indebted to Mr Cornford, and, for the full analysis and significance of the conception, may refer to his forthcoming *From Religion to Philosophy*, chapter i.

[2] *La Perception du Changement*, 1911, p. 27.

[3] For the significance of Dike see *infra*, pp. 516—528.

that a god is a real thing—a real thing because he is the utterance of a real collective emotion, but, in progress of time, man desiccates his god, intellectualizes him, till he is a mere concept, an *eidolon*. Having got his *eidolon*, that *eidolon* fails to satisfy his need, and he tries to supply the place of the vanished *thymos*, the real life-blood of emotion, by claiming objective reality.

There is another submerged reef waiting to wreck the perilous bark of divinity. Man's first dream of a god began, as we saw, in his reaction towards life-forces not understood. Here again we begin with the recognition of, or rather the emotion towards, a truth. There *is* a mystery in life, life itself which we do not understand, and we may, if we choose, call that mystery by the name of god, but at the other end of the chain of evolution there is another thing, a late human product which we call goodness. By a desperate effort of imagination we try to link the two; we deny evolution and say that the elementary push of life is from the beginning 'good[1],' that God through all his chequered career is immutably moral, and we land ourselves in a quagmire of determinism and teleology[2]. Or, if we are Greeks, we invent a Zeus, who is Father and Councillor and yet remains an automatic, explosive Thunderstorm[3].

Such in general is the progress of a god—from emotion to concept, from totem-animal to mystery-god, from mystery-god to Olympian. But the Greek, and perhaps only the Greek, went one step further, and that step brought a certain provisional salvation. It is a step, at all events, so characteristic of the Greek mind, that it claims our attention.

This brings us to our last point.

(5) *The Olympian became an objet d'art.* We have been told to satiety that the Greeks are a people of artists. Something we mean by this, but what? It is manifest that their gods, Apollo, Artemis and Athene, are works of art in a sense that our own are

---

[1] So, as Mr Cornford points out to me, the Greeks themselves came to identify φύσις which is life, nature, with a moral ideal; they confused what ought to exist with what does. See Ar. *Pol.* a 5, 1255 *b*, 2.

[2] See G. Santayana, *The Life of Reason*, 1905, p. 169, on 'the mythical identification of the God which meant the ideal of life, with the God which meant the forces of nature.' This was one element in the mistake made by Plato when he equated τὸ ἕν with τἀγαθόν.

[3] See *supra*, p. 455.

not. We feel instinctively that, however much we may quarry for the origin of Greek religion, and strive to reconstruct it, and see its influence on life and on literature, the broad fact remains that the strength of the Greek temperament lay rather in art than in religion. The full gist of this fact cannot appear till, in the last chapter, we have examined the figure of Themis, but one point is immediately clear and immediately relevant.

M. Bergson[1] has shown us that the function of science is to aid and direct *action* to provide tools for life. It begins with and only very slowly emerges from practice. Man acts that he may live, by adjusting himself to his environment. Man thinks that he may the better act. But here and there arises an individual, and once there has arisen a race, in whom nature has linked less clearly the faculty of perception with the faculty of action. We all know that the artist is 'unpractical[2],' and that is what we mean. When an artist looks at a thing, it is at that thing whole, that he may see it for the love of it. When the man of action looks at a thing he analyses it, classifies it, sees it dismembered; he sees the joints carved for his eating, not the whole live animal—he sees what he can use and eat.

Therefore to the Greek his god, however remote and detached, is never quite a mere cold concept. His Olympian is alive, seen whole, and seen with keen emotion, loved for himself not for the work he does, not merely as a means of living. But it was only to the Greek that the Olympian lived, a great and beautiful reality. Seen through Roman eyes, focussed always on action, he became the prettiest and emptiest of toys.

So far we have looked at the Olympians as individuals, as luminously distinct personalities. But they are not only individuals; they form a group, and as a group they claim to be considered. This brings us to our last consideration, to the figure of Themis.

[1] p. 47 'Originellement, nous ne pensons que pour agir. C'est dans le monde de l'action que notre intelligence a été coulée,' and see *supra*, p. 473.

[2] H. Bergson, *La Perception du Changement*, Conférences faites à l'Université d'Oxford, 1911, p. 11, 'L'artiste est, au sens propre du mot, un "distrait,"' and see *op. cit.* p. 13. See also Prof. J. A. Stewart's beautiful section on 'The doctrine of Ideas as expressing aesthetic experience' in *Plato's Doctrine of Ideas*, 1909, p. 135. 'Aesthetic experience *is* a condition in which concentration, often momentary, never long maintained, *isolates* an object of consciousness: the object stands there itself, alone, peerless,' and for a suggested psychological explanation, the temporary inhibition of 'synapses,' see *op. cit.* p. 142, note.

CHAPTER XI.

THEMIS.

Θόρε κ᾿ ἐc Θέμιν καλάν.

In discussing the sequence of the gods at Delphi, we left, it will be remembered[1], the figure of Themis unformulated. Before we can consider the Olympians as a group, her significance must be examined.

At Delphi Themis comes next in order after Gaia, and in the *Prometheus Bound* Æschylus[2] makes her but another form of Gaia. Prometheus says that the future was foretold to him by his mother,

> Themis,
> And Gaia, one in nature, many-named.

By Æschylus, in both plays, Themis is in fact envisaged as the oracular power of Earth. As such she is figured in the design in Fig. 142 from a red-figured cylix[3].

Aigeus, the childless king, comes to the oracle at Delphi to ask how he may have a son. Within the temple is the tripod and seated on it is not any one particular Pythia, but Themis herself, the spirit, the projection of the oracle. Gods might come and go, Gaia and Phoibe and Phoibos, but Themis who, as we shall presently see, is below and above all gods abides there seated. She holds in one hand a phiale of it may be holy water, and in the other a spray of laurel. She is thallophoros.

At Athens[4] the priestess of Themis had a seat in the Dionysiac theatre and another seat bears the inscription 'Two Hersephoroi

---

[1] *Supra*, p. 387. [2] *Prom. Vinct.* 209.
[3] Berlin Cat. Gerhard, *Auserlesene Vasenbilder*, cccxxviii.
[4] *C.I.A.* iii. 318, 350. See *Myth. and Mon. Ancient Athens*, p. 274.

of Ge Themis.' Themis had a sanctuary on the south slope of the Acropolis near to that of Ge Kourotrophos and Demeter Chloe[1]. At Rhamnus[2] she was worshipped by the side of Nemesis. At Trozen, whence her cult may have come to Athens with Aigeus, there was an altar to the Themides[3]. In Thessaly[4] there was a worship of Themis with the title *Ichnaios*, the 'Tracker,' which links her with Nemesis and Erinys. At none of these places is there any mention of her prophetic function; but at Olympia

FIG. 142.

Pausanias[5] tells us of a Gaion or sanctuary of Ge, at which there was an altar of Themis.

> In olden days they say that there was also an oracle of Ge here. On what is called the *Stomion* (opening or mouth) there is an altar to Themis.

But if Themis be but the projection, the impersonation of Earth and of the prophetic powers of Earth, why should she be above and beyond all other gods? First a minor point must be made clear. Themis is in a sense prophecy incarnate, but it is

---

[1] Paus. I. 22. 1.　　　　[2] *C.I.A.* II. 1570.
[3] Paus. II. 31. 5. It is probable that, as O. Gruppe, *Gr. Mythologie*, II. p. 585, conjectures, Theseus and Themis were connected, and both came together from Trozen. Themis may have been the goddess of the old Kalaureia Amphictyons.
[4] Strabo, IX. 435.　　　　[5] v. 14. 10.

only in the old sense of *prophecy*, utterance, ordinance, not in the later sense of a forecast of the future[1]. A closer examination of the word Themis and its cognates will show that in her nature is more even of ordinance than of utterance. It will repay us at the outset to examine her functions in Homer, though Homer has but dim consciousness of their significance.

In Homer Themis has two functions. She convenes and dissolves the assembly; she presides over the feast. Telemachos[2] adjures the assembly at Ithaka

By Olympian Zeus, and by Themis, who looseth and gathereth the meetings of men.

Zeus himself cannot summon his own assembly. He must

bid Themis call the gods to council from many-folded Olympos' brow. And she ranged all about and bade them to the house of Zeus[3].

Themis presides over the banquet. When Hera enters Olympos, the gods rise up to greet her and hold out their cups in welcome, and she takes the cup of Themis who is first. And, when Themis would ask what troubled her, Hera makes answer,

'Ask me not concerning this, O goddess Themis; thyself knowest it, how unweening is his heart and unyielding. But do thou begin the equal banquet of the gods in the halls[4].'

It is the meed of Themis to convene and dissolve the agora[5]; it is hers too to preside over the equal, sacramental feast.

We think of Themis as an abstraction, as Law, Justice, Right, and, naturally, we are surprised that she who is above Zeus himself should be set to do the service of a herald, an office surely meeter for Hermes or Iris. Why, we ask, with Hermes and Iris at hand, ready to speed over earth and sea with messages and mandates, should Themis have to execute just this one office of convening the assembly? To preside over the banquet may be an honourable

---

[1] *Supra*, p. 387.
[2] Hom. *Od.* II. 68

　　　λίσσομαι ἠμὲν Ζηνὸς Ὀλυμπίου ἠδὲ Θέμιστος,
　　　η τ' ἀνδρῶν ἀγορὰς ἠμὲν λύει ἠδὲ καθίζει.

[3] Hom. *Il.* xx. 4—6.
[4] Hom. *Il.* xv. 87—95

　　　ἀλλὰ σύ γ' ἄρχε θεοῖσι δόμοις ἔνι δαιτὸς ἐίσης.

For the Equal Feast see *supra*, pp. 145 and 157.

[5] Aristides (I. p. 837) doubtless referring to Homer says, ἐκκλησίαι καὶ βουλευτήρια ἃ θεῶν ἡ πρεσβυτάτη συνάγει Θέμις. Hesychius gives Themis the title of Ἀγοραία.

function, but to 'range about all over,' fetching up gods and demi-gods, is no more a mark of supremacy. The solution of this obvious difficulty will give us a clue not only to the nature of Themis herself but to the source and mainspring of Greek, and incidentally of every other, primitive religion.

The Greek word *Themis* and the English word *Doom* are, philology tells us, one and the same; and it is curious to note that their development moves on exactly parallel lines. *Doom* is the thing set, fixed, settled; it begins in convention, the stress of public opinion; it ends in statutory judgment. Your private doom is your private opinion, but that is weak and ineffective. It is the collective doom, public opinion, that, for man's common convenience, crystallizes into Law. Themis like *Doom* begins on earth and ends in heaven. On earth we have our Doomsday, which, projected into high heaven, becomes the Crack of Doom, the Last Judgment.

We have seen that Themis at Trozen was worshipped in the plural, that there was an altar to the Themides. Out of many dooms, many public opinions, many judgments, arose the figure of the one goddess. Out of many *themistes* arose Themis. These *themistes*, these fixed conventions, stood to the Greek for all he held civilized. They were the bases alike of his kingship and of his democracy. These *themistes* are the ordinances of what must be done, what society compels; they are also, because what must be will be, the prophecies of what shall be in the future; they are also the dues, the rites, the prerogatives of a king, whatever custom assigns to him or any official.

The Greek attitude towards Themis and the *themistes* comes out very vividly in the account of the Cyclopes[1]. The Cyclopes are the typical barbarians, and how do they show it? They are not irreligious, far from it, they are notably pious, trusting entirely in the divine mercy and not tilling the earth.

> A people proud to whom no law is known,
> And, trusting to the deathless Gods alone,
> They plant not and they plough not, but the earth
> Bears all they need, unfurrowed and unsown:

[1] Hom. *Od.* IX. 106

Κυκλώπων δ' ἐς γαῖαν ὑπερφιάλων, ἀθεμίστων
ἱκόμεθ'......
τοῖσιν δ' οὔτ' ἀγοραὶ βουληφόροι οὔτε θέμιστες,

trans. Mackail.

> Barley and wheat, and vines whose mighty juice
> Swells the rich clusters when the rain of Zeus
> Gives increase; and among that race are kept
> No common councils nor are laws in use.

That is what is wrong with the Cyclopes: they reverence the gods, they are earth-worshippers, and earth for them brings forth her increase, but they are ἀθέμιστες, they have no customs, no conventions, binding by common consent, they have no agora. That for the Greek was the last desolation. We hear the chorus in remote barbarian Tauri cry[1]

> O for a kind Greek market-place again!

Not only were the Cyclopes god-fearing and god-trusting exceedingly, but they excelled in family life. To each Cyclops his house was his castle, each Cyclops was master in his own patriarchal home.

> For on the high peaks and the hillsides bare
> In hollow caves they live, and each one there
> To his own wife and children deals the law,
> Neither has one of other any care.

The only Themis was of the hearth and home, and to the Greek that was no Themis at all. Themis was the use and wont of full-grown men, citizens, made effective in the councils of the agora.

Themis was of course at first of the tribe, and then she was all powerful. Later when the tribal system, through wars and incursions and migrations, broke up, its place was taken less dominantly, more effectively, by the *polis*[2]. The *polis* set itself to modify and inform all those primitive impulses and instincts that are resumed in Earth-worship. It also set itself, if unconsciously, as a counterbalance to the dominance of ties of near kinship. Antigone[3] stands for kinship and the dues of Earth, Creon for patriarchalism incarnate in the Tyrant and for the Zeus religion that by that time had become its expression.

We no longer wonder why in Homer Themis convenes the assembly. She is no herald like Hermes, no messenger like Iris,

---

[1] *Supra*, p. 116.

[2] For the emergence of the *polis* from the *débris* of the shattered group-system see Prof. Murray, *Rise of the Greek Epic*[2], pp. 31, 37.

[3] This has been very ably worked out by Dr Zielinski in his *Der Gedankenfortschritt in den Chorliedern der Antigone* in Festschrift für Theodor Gomperz, 1901. See also his *Exkurse zu den Trachinierinnen*, Philologus LV. 1896, pp. 491, 577.

she is the very spirit of the assembly incarnate.   Themis and the actual concrete agora are barely distinguishable.   Patroklos comes running to the ships of godlike Odysseus,

Where were their agora and themis[1]?

Here the social fact is trembling on the very verge of godhead. She is the force that brings and binds men together, she is 'herd instinct,' the collective conscience, the social sanction.   She is *fas*, the social imperative.   This social imperative is among a primitive group diffuse, vague, inchoate, yet absolutely binding. Later it crystallizes into fixed conventions, regular tribal customs; finally in the *polis* it takes shape as Law and Justice.   Themis was before the particular shapes of gods; she is not religion, but she is the stuff of which religion is made.   It is the emphasis and representation of herd instinct, of the collective conscience, that constitutes religion.

But it will immediately and most justly be asked, What is this?   If Themis be the source and well-spring of religion, are we not turning religion into mere morality?   Themis is herd-instinct, custom, convention slowly crystallized into Law and abstract Right; well and good.   We all acknowledge that custom, manners, *mores*, are the basis of *morals*, that ἤθεα, haunts and habits, are the material of *ethics*.   If we doubted it language is at hand with proof irrefragable.   But surely religion and ethics are not, cannot be, the same.   There is about the very word religion an atmosphere, a warmth, an emotional lift quite other and even alien to the chill levels of ethics.   An Ethical Society is not a Salvation Army.

The protest is entirely just.   But mark our definition.   It is not herd instinct, not the collective conscience, not the social imperative that constitutes religion; it is the emphasis and representation of this collective conscience, this social imperative. In a word Themis is not religion, she is the stuff of which religious representations are made.   That is why in the ordered sequence of the gods at Delphi we gave Themis no place.   She is the substratum of each and every god, she is in a sense above as well as below each and every god, but herself never quite a

---

[1] Hom. *Il.* xi. 807 ἵνα σφ' ἀγορή τε θέμις τε.

full-fledged divinity. In the passage already quoted[1] when Patroklos runs to the ships, we have seen her hover on the verge of divinity, and it is not a little curious that Homer here, in his odd semi-conscious way, seems to feel that the gods grow out of the assembly. Patroklos comes to the place

where was their assembly and their themis, *whereby also were the altars of their gods established.*

These are the θεοὶ ἀγοραῖοι, ἀγώνιοι.

Religion has in it then two elements, social custom, the collective conscience, and the emphasis and representation of that collective conscience. It has in a word within it two factors indissolubly linked: ritual, that is custom, collective action, and myth or theology, the representation of the collective emotion, the collective conscience. And—a point of supreme importance—both are incumbent, binding, and interdependent.

Now it is in this twofold character and incumbency of religion that its essence lies, and here too are found the characteristics that delimit it from its near neighbours, morality and art. Morality is the social conscience made imperative upon our actions, but morality unlike religion, save on questions involving conduct, leaves our thoughts free. Art, which is also, like religion, a representation of the social conscience[2], has no incumbencies. She imposes no obligation on either action or thought. Her goddess is Peitho not Themis.

We accept then Prof. Durkheim's[3] illuminating definition:—

Les phénomènes dits religieux consistent en croyances obligatoires connexes de pratiques définies qui se rapportent à des objets donnés dans les croyances.

It is of interest to note that Prof. Durkheim in his definition never overtly says the word collective. The note and characteristic

---

[1] Hom. *Il. loc. cit.*

ἵνα σφ' ἀγορή τε θέμις τε
ἦην, τῇ δὴ καί σφι θεῶν ἐτετεύχατο βωμοί.

[2] This subject I hope to discuss later in another connection.

[3] E. Durkheim, *De la Définition des Phénomènes Religieux* in L'Année Sociologique, II. 1898, p. 1, and see also *Représentations Individuelles et Représentations Collectives* in Revue de Métaphysique et Morale, VI. 1898, p. 273, and *Sociologie Religieuse et Théorie de la Connaissance* in the same review, XVII. 1909, p. 733. This last paper is the *Introduction* to M. Durkheim's forthcoming book on *Les Formes Élémentaires de la Pensée et de la Vie Religieuse*. M. Durkheim's views as to the origin of religion have been sympathetically stated by M. Henri Hubert in his preface to the French translation of Chantepie de la Saussaye's *Manuel d'Histoire des Religions*, 1904. For English readers there is a short account of M. Durkheim's position in the last chapter of Mr Marett's *Threshold of Religion*.

of what is religious is that it is 'obligatoire.' But when we come to analyse 'obligatoire' there is for man quâ his humanity only one source of what is 'obligatoire,' and that is the social conscience. His body obeys natural law and his spirit is bound by the social imperative. The moral constraint upon him is of Themis not of Physis, and, because of this constraint, man is a religious animal.

In the early days of group civilization man is altogether a religious animal, altogether under the sway of Themis, of the collective conscience. His religion, his representation, is that of a totem animal or plant, a mere projection of his sense of unity with his group and with the outside world. The obligation is so complete, so utterly dominant, that he is scarcely conscious of it. As the hold of the group slackens and the individual emerges, the field of religion is bit by bit narrowed. Man's latest religious representation is of that all but impossible conception, the god as individual. The god as individual passes over, as we have seen in the last chapter, into the *objet d'art*.

A definition however illuminating always desiccates its object. To think of religion as consisting in 'des croyances obligatoires connexes de pratiques définies' chills its very life-blood. Religious faith and practice is intensely obligatory, but it is also eagerly, vividly, chosen, it is a great collective *hairesis*. Religion sums up and embodies what we feel together, what we care for together, what we imagine together, and the price of that feeling together, that imagining together, the concessions, the mutual compromises, are at first gladly paid.

It is when religion ceases to be a matter of feeling together, when it becomes individualized and intellectualized, that clouds gather on the horizon. It is because religion has been regarded as a tissue of false hypotheses that it has commanded, will always command, the animosity of the rational thinker. When the religious man, instead of becoming in ecstasy and sacramental communion one with Bacchos, descends to the chill levels of intellectualism and asserts that there is an objective reality external to himself called Bacchos, then comes a parting of the ways. Still wider is the breach if he asserts that this objective reality is one with the mystery of life, and also with man's last projection, his ideal of the good.

In the light of the new definition it is instructive to examine the old. Until recent times definitions of religion have usually included some notion of a relation of the human soul to a god; they have been in some sense theological. Thus M. Reville[1]:

La religion est la détermination de la vie humaine par le sentiment d'un lien unissant l'ésprit humain à l'ésprit mystérieux dont il reconnait la domination sur le monde et sur lui-même, et auquel il aime à se sentir uni.

Here, though the word God is cautiously avoided, the idea of a god, and even a personal god, the object of love, is present.

This idea that religion may be defined as a relation to a god is sufficiently refuted by the simple fact that one of the most important and widespread of religions, Buddhism, knows no god. Religion is to the Buddhist not prayer, the worship of an external being, but the turning in upon himself, the escape from the sorrow that comes of desire, the gradual attainment of Nirvana. Yet no one will deny to Buddhism the name of religion.

But if it be felt that Buddhism is a strange exception, it is important to note that theology is in all other religions not essential and integral, but rather a phase, a stage marking a particular moment in development. At the outset of the present book advisedly no definition of religion was attempted. The aim was to examine actual religious facts. It was seen in the early chapters that such religious facts were, collective emotion, *mana*, magic, sacramentalism. All these existed long before they blossomed into the figure of a god. That vague and inchoate thing 'sanctity' was there long before it did on shape and personality. As Prof. Durkheim[2] well says:

La notion de la divinité, loin d'être ce qu'il y a de fondamental dans la vie religieuse, n'en est en realité qu'un épisode secondaire. C'est le produit d'un processus spécial en vertu duquel un ou deux des caractères religieux se concentrent et se concrétisent sous la forme d'une individualité plus ou moins définie.

Feeling the futility of defining religion in terms of theology, scholars have resorted to things vague,—to a 'sense of the supernatural,' or to an 'instinct for mystery,' the apprehension of a sort of *nescio quid*, an unknown 'infinite,' behind the visible world. Such were the definitions of Max Müller, which, to the modern psychologist and anthropologist, seem unreal to the point of

---

[1] *Prolégomènes à l'Histoire des Religions*, p. 34.
[2] *Définition des Phénomènes Religieux.* L'Année Sociologique, 1898, p. 13.

grotesqueness.   We   may   take   Max   Müller's[1]   definition   as
typical :

> Religion is a mental faculty or disposition which, independent of, nay in
> spite of sense and reason, enables man to apprehend the Infinite under different
> names and under varying disguises.

Here we have the old Intellectualist fallacy in full force.   The
protests of a host of scholars who felt the inadequacy and frigidity
and unreality of this Intellectualism induced Max Müller[2] to
modify his definition as follows :

> Religion consists in the perception of the infinite under such manifestations
> as are able to influence the moral character of man.

Here we have a dim inkling of the truth.   The notion of
social obligation as an element in religion begins to creep in.

Max Müller's 'infinite' was re-stated and re-emphasized by
Herbert Spencer[3], but with a characteristic rationalist corollary.
According to him the essence and kernel of all religions was not
only the sense of mystery, but an instinctive desire and demand
to penetrate this mystery; man desired to know the unknown, the
unknowable.

> Here is an element which all creeds have in common.   Religions diametri-
> cally opposed in their overt dogmas are yet perfectly at one in the tacit
> conviction *that the existence of the world with all it contains and all which
> surrounds it is a mystery ever pressing for interpretation.*

In the light of present anthropological knowledge the picture
called up for us by Herbert Spencer of the lonely individualistic
savage lost in contemplation of the All, and waking from his trance
eager to start on his career of elementary science, 'rerum cognoscere causas,' is, if natural and illuminating at the time it was
written, now, in the light of a more familiar intimacy with the
savage mind, inadequate and even misleading.   Wonder and awe,
as we have seen in discussing the Thunder-god[4], were elements that
went to the making of religion, but the main objects of his cult,
i.e. the main foci of his attention, were his food-plants and his food-
animals; if he was an Australian his witchetty grubs, his emus,
his kangaroos.   If he was a North American Apache, his bears.

---

[1] *Introduction to the Science of Religion*, 1882, p. 13.   The definition was put
forward verbally in 1873.
[2] *Natural Religion* (Gifford Lectures, 1888), pp. 188, 193.
[3] *First Principles*, 1875, p. 44.
[4] *Supra*, p. 64.

He was concerned, not to lie prostrate in wonder before the mystery of their life, still less to embark on scientific enquiry into the causes of that life, but to make them grow and multiply that he might eat them and grow and multiply himself.

Has man then no sense of mystery, no consciousness of something greater than himself to which he owes obedience, to which he pays reverence? Yes. The instinct of those who, in framing the old definitions of religion, included 'mystery' and 'the infinite,' was right—though their explanations wrong. The mystery, the thing greater than man, is potent, not only or chiefly because it is unintelligible and calls for explanation, not because it stimulates a baffled understanding, but because it is *felt* as an obligation. The thing greater than man, the 'power not himself that makes for righteousness,' is, in the main, not the mystery of the universe to which as yet he is not awake, but the pressure of that unknown ever incumbent force, herd instinct, the social conscience. The mysterious dominant figure is not Physis, but Themis[1].

If then we would understand religion, we must get behind theology, behind, for the Greeks, the figures of the Olympians, and even the shadowy shapes of the daimones, and penetrate to the social conscience, and first and foremost to its earliest and perhaps most permanent expression[2], to social structure—the organized system of relationships.

This brings us back to the Olympians. Of what social structure are they the projection?

Undoubtedly they represent that form of society with which we are ourselves most familiar, the patriarchal family. Zeus is the father and head: though Hera and he are in constant unseemly conflict, there is no doubt about his ultimate supremacy. Hera

---

[1] It will later (p. 516) be seen that Themis casts her shadow over Physis till the two are scarcely distinguishable.

[2] For the importance of social structure I may refer to the Presidential address of Dr W. H. R. Rivers to the Anthropological Section of the British Association, 1911, p. 9. His words are a landmark in the history of anthropological study, and are specially relevant to all enquiries as to the origin of religious forms. 'If then social structure has this fundamental and deeply seated character, if it is the least easily changed and only changed as the result either of actual blending of peoples or of the most profound political changes, the obvious inference is that it is with social structure that we must begin the attempt to analyse culture.'

is jealous, Zeus in frequent exasperation, but none the less finally dominant. The picture is intensely modern, down to the ill-assorted, incongruous aggregate of grown-up sons and daughters living idly at ease at home and constantly quarrelling. The family comes before us as the last forlorn hope of collectivism. Its real original bond is a sex-tie between husband and wife; its real function the rearing of helpless children. For this rearing the husband is, save for the highest forms of civilization, useless at home, his function is to be a food-seeker abroad and to come back with his beak full of worms. Once the children grown up, and the sex-tie grown weak, the family falls asunder for sheer lack of moral molecular cohesion.

Olympos is in Northern Thessaly. We are so obsessed by the literary Homeric Olympos that we are apt to forget that Olympos was, to begin with, an actual northern mountain. Zeus, father of gods and men, Zeus the sky-god, with all the heavy fatherhood of Wuotan, is a Northerner, or at least has been profoundly modified by Northern racial influence. As the Father, though perhaps not wholly as the Sky-God, he is the projection of northern fatherhood. He, or rather his fatherhood, came down from the north with some tribe, or tribes, whose social system was patri-linear[1]. Hera was indigenous and represents a matrilinear system; she reigned alone at Argos, at Samos, her temple at Olympia is distinct from and far earlier than that of Zeus. Her first husband, or rather consort, was Herakles. The conquering Northerners pass from Dodona to Thessaly. Zeus drops his real shadow-wife, Dione, at Dodona, in passing from Thessaly to Olympia, and at Olympia Zeus, after the fashion of a conquering chieftain, marries Hera, a daughter of the land[2]. In Olympos Hera seems merely the jealous and quarrelsome wife. In reality she reflects the turbulent native princess, coerced, but never really subdued, by an alien conqueror.

---

[1] To discuss the racial question I have not the necessary equipment nor is the archaeological material as yet adequate. But, following Dr Rivers, *supra*, p. 490, note [2], I believe that a change of social structure indicates either racial change or some profound political upheaval. It is, I think, *probable* that the indigenous population whose social structure was matrilinear was not Indo-European at all but belonged to the same race as the Hittites of Asia Minor and that the memory of them survives in the mythological Amazons. To this question I hope to return on another occasion. The subject has been already discussed in Dr Walther Leonhard's *Hittites und Amazonen*, 1911.

[2] For a full discussion of this question we may look to Mr Cook's forthcoming *Zeus*.

Now in Homer, once alive to the fact of an earlier background against which is set the Northern patrilinear family, traces of primaeval sanctities are not hard to find. When Themis summons the Olympian agora, we remember[1] that she not only summons the Olympian family, but she has to 'range round' to find the earlier nature-potencies, the gods of spring and stream. Hastily they do on their human shapes; we catch them at the very moment of hurried, uneasy metamorphosis. But, though they do on human shapes, they are no part of the great human, patrilinear, family.

Again, ritual is always conservative. In the archaic ritual of the oath we see the contrast between new and old. When Menelaos is about to engage with Paris, he says[2] to the Trojans

Bring ye two lambs, one white ram and one black ewe for Earth and Sun, and we will bring one for Zeus.

The Trojans, Southerners of Asia Minor, use the old sympathetic ritual of the Horkos. The primitive Horkos or barrier or division is between Earth and Sky, and Earth the Mother is, as we shall presently see, before Sky, the Father. The Achaeans, the Northerners, have no Horkos proper, but they bring a ram for the anthropomorphic Zeus.

If then we would understand the contrast between the Olympians and their predecessors we must get back to the earlier Themis, to the social structure that was before the patriarchal family, to the matrilinear system, to the Mother and the Tribe, the Mother and the Child and the Initiated young men, the Kouretes.

MATRILINEAR STRUCTURE.

We are back where we began. It may be well to recall what has been so long out of sight. The relief in Fig. 143 from the Capitoline altar[3] sets the old matrilinear social structure very clearly before us.

To the left the Mother is seated. Her child has been taken away from her. Seated on a rock in the middle of the picture he

---

[1] *Supra*, p. 482. [2] Hom. *Il.* III. 104.
[3] Overbeck, *Kunstmythologie*, Atlas III. 24.

is suckled by the goat Amaltheia. Over him, dominating the
whole scene, two Kouretes clash their shields. Mother, Child,
Initiated youths, these are the factors of the old social group.
The father, Kronos, is...nowhere. We hear the words of the Hymn:

'For here the shielded Nurturers took thee, a child immortal, from Rhea,
and, with noise of beating feet, hid thee away[1].'

From art-representations Kronos the father is singularly,
saliently, absent. We remember the detailed representation of
the birth of the child, on the Milan relief[2]; the mother giving
birth to the child, the child set on the throne, the child on the

Fig. 143.

back of the prancing goat; always the mother and child, and the
animal form of the mother with its totemistic remembrance, but
never the father. The conclusion is very clear. The myth is a
presentation, a projection of the days when, at first, the facts of
fatherhood were unknown, and later, but little emphasized; when
the Themis of the group was the mother, as mother of the initiate
youth to be. Themis as abstract Right, or as statutory Law,
sanctioned by force, would surely never have taken shape as a

[1] *Supra*, p. 7.			[2] *Supra*, p. 60. Fig. 9.

woman; but Themis as the Mother, the supreme social fact and focus, *she* is intelligible.

It may seem strange that woman, always the weaker, should be thus dominant and central. But it must always be observed that this primitive form of society is matri*linear* not matri*archal*. Woman is the social centre not the dominant force. So long as force is supreme, physical force of the individual, society is impossible, because society is by cooperation, by mutual concession, not by antagonism.

Fig. 144.

Moreover, there is another point of supreme importance. In primitive matrilinear societies woman is the great social force or rather central focus, not as woman, or at least not as sex, but as mother, the mother of tribesmen to be. This social fact finds its projection in the first of divine figures, in Kourotrophos—'Rearer of Sons.' The male child nursed by the mother is potentially a *kouros*, hence her great value and his. When Agamemnon bids Menelaos slay all his foes root and branch, he says

'Let not one escape sheer destruction, spare not even that which a mother bears in her womb, for it is a *kouros*[1].'

[1] Hom. *Il.* VI. 58

ὅν τινα γαστέρι μήτηρ
κοῦρον ἐόντα φέροι.

Prof. Murray kindly drew my attention to this passage. Hence the custom, common to many lands, of placing a male child in the bride's lap that she may become Kourotrophos. See D. S. Stuart, *The Prenuptial Rite in the New Callimachos*, Journal of Classical Philology, VI. 1911.

Kronos the Father emerges into prominence when patriarchy becomes dominant. He then is figured as a sort of elder Zeus. He appears on another face of the Capitoline altar[1] reproduced in Fig. 144. Like Zeus he is seated on a chair with arms. Unlike Zeus he is veiled. Rhea approaches bearing the swaddled stone. It is a strange, almost grotesque, blend of old and new.

Kronos as a father is respectable, even venerable. But patriarchy, once fully established, would fain dominate all things, would invade even the ancient prerogative of the mother, the right to rear the child she bore. Standing before the Hermes of Praxiteles I have often wondered why a figure so beautiful should leave the imagination unsatisfied, even irritated. It is not merely that the execution is late and touched with an over facility; it is, I think, that the whole conception, the motive, is false. Hermes, the young male, usurps the function of the mother, he poses as Brephotrophos. He is really *Kouro*trophos. The man doing woman's work has all the inherent futility and something of the ugly dissonance of the man masquerading in woman's clothes.

Kronos stands always for the old order, before Zeus and the Olympians; he hates his father Ouranos but reverences and takes counsel with Earth his mother. Another trait links him with the earlier pre-patriarchal order. Unlike Zeus, Kronos is not addressed as father. He is not father but 'king,' king upon earth in the older Golden Age.

> O king Kronos and Zeus the Father[2].

It is not a heavenly kingdom imagined, it is a definite reign upon earth. Kronos is never, never could be, translated to the skies. The reason is, I think, clear: Kronos is *the* king, he is the projection of the old medicine king. He is like Picus, like Salmoneus. He reigns as τύραννος in an ancient fortress, a τύρσις[3], not as Father in the open δώματ' Ὀλύμπου. It is as king that he is constantly confused with Moloch who is *Melek, the* King[4].

Kronos the king represents the old matrilinear days and is

---

[1] Overbeck, *Kunstmythologie*, Atlas III. 24.

[2] Julian, *Conviv.* 317 D, ὦ βασιλεῦ Κρόνε καὶ Ζεῦ πάτερ.

[3] Pind. *Ol.* II. 124 ἔτειλαν Διὸς ὁδὸν παρὰ Κρόνου τύρσιν. For turris, τύρσις and τύραννος and their possibly Mongolian origin see *Rev. Arch.* 1904, p. 414.

[4] This illuminating suggestion, which immediately commends itself, was made to Dr Frazer by Professor Kennett. See *Adonis, Attis and Osiris*, Appendix, p. 401.

therefore closely linked with Gaia. It has been already[1] shown
how on the slopes of the hill Kronion at Olympia was the sanctuary
of the Mother and Child, Sosipolis and Eileithyia. The same
conjunction obtains at Athens. When the cult of Olympian Zeus
was brought by Peisistratos to Athens, with him came Kronos and
Rhea, and with him came Gaia[2], for Rhea is but the Mountain
Mother, the Asia Minor wilder form of Gaia.

As king, Kronos is also daimon of the year. He stands for
the cycle of reincarnation. Plato, in the *Politicus*[3], makes a most
instructive comparison between the Age of Kronos and his own
age, the Age of Zeus. His account of the Age of Kronos seems
haunted by reminiscences not only of totemism but of matrilinear
social structure. Above all things, it is the age of the Earth-Men,
sown and re-sown[4].

'There were divine daimones who were the shepherds of the various species
and herds of animals, and each was entirely sufficient for those whom he
shepherded. So that there was no wildness nor eating of each other, nor
any war, nor revolt amongst them....In those days God himself was their
shepherd....Under him there were no governments nor separate possessions
of women and children. For all men rose again from the earth remembering
nothing of their past. And such things as private property and families did
not exist, but Earth herself gave them abundance of fruits from trees and
other green things, spontaneously, and not through husbandry. And they
dwelt naked in the open air, for the temperature of the seasons was mild.
And they had no beds, but lay on soft couches of herb which grew abundantly out of the earth. Such, Socrates, was the life of men in the days of
Kronos.'

Plato seems conscious that, in the days of Kronos, the ruler of
each department was more herdsman or shepherd than king. The
ancient *Basileus* was indeed, as already has been hinted, a person
half daimon, half man, essentially a functionary, and almost wholly
alien to our modern, individualistic notion of king. Given that
Kronos was such a daimon king, it is clear that he rules over the
early earth-born race, that his kingdom is in quite a special way
of this earth. He stands for the Earth and her seasonal year
rather than for any cycle of Sun and Moon.

The etymology of his name is not quite certain, but the ancient
guess which connects it with the verb κραίνω is probably right.

[1] *Supra*, p. 240. [2] Paus. I. 18. 7.
[3] 271 E, 272 A.
[4] Plato, *op. cit.* 272 E καὶ τὸ γήϊνον ἤδη πᾶν ἀνήλωτο γένος, πάσας ἑκάστης τῆς
ψυχῆς τὰς γενέσεις ἀποδεδωκυίας, ὅσα ἦν ἑκάστῃ προσταχθέντα, τοσαῦτα εἰς γῆν σπέρματα
πεσούσης..., and see also *Timaeus* 42 D, 83 D. The whole thought is that expressed
in ritual by the Anthesteria. *Supra*, p. 292.

Kronos is the Fulfiller, the Accomplisher. In what sense he is the Accomplisher is clear from the words of the Chorus in the *Trachiniae*[1] :

ἀνάλγητα γὰρ οὐδ' ὁ πάντα κραίνων βασιλεὺς
ἐπέβαλε θνατοῖς Κρονίδας·
ἀλλ' ἐπὶ πῆμα καὶ χαρὰ πᾶσι κυκλοῦσιν οἷον "Αρκτου
στροφάδες κέλευθοι.

Kronos is the Accomplisher of the full circle of the year. His nature and his name alike make easy his identification with Chronos[2]. He is not the Sun or the Moon, but the circle of the Heavens, of Ouranos, husband of Ge ; of Ouranos, in whose great dancing-place the planets move,

And God leads round his starry Bear[3].

Kronos indeed, so far as he is a Year-god, marks and expresses that earlier calendar of Hesiod, in which Works and Days are governed by the rising and setting of certain stars and constellations, Sirius, Orion, the Pleiades, and by the comings and goings of migratory birds, the swallow, the cuckoo, and the crane[4]. But though man looks to these heavenly and atmospheric *terata* to guide his sowings and reapings, his real focus of attention is still earth. And inasmuch as his social structure is matrilinear, she is Mother-Earth ; Father-Heaven takes as yet but a subordinate place. When, nowadays, we speak of God as 'Father' we mean of course no irreverence, but we strangely delimit the sources of life. The Roman Church, with her wider humanity, though she cherishes the monastic ideal, yet feels instinctively that a male Trinity is non-natural, and keeps always the figure of the divine Mother.

[1] v. 126.
[2] Thus Proklos on Plato, *Kratylos*, 61 νοῦς γάρ ἐστιν ὁ βασιλεὺς Κρόνος...αὐτὸς εἰς ἑαυτὸν ἐπεστραμμένος, ὅς γε καὶ τοὺς ἀπ' αὐτοῦ προκύψαντας εἰς ἑαυτὸν αὖθις ἐπέστρεψεν καὶ ἐνεκολπίσατο καὶ ἐν ἑαυτῷ σταθερῶς ἵδρυσεν, and the fragment of Kritias (Diels, *F.V.S.*[2], p. 618. 21)

ἀκάμας τε Χρόνος περί τ' ἀενάῳ
ῥεύματι πλήρης φοιτᾷ τίκτων
αὐτὸς ἑαυτόν.

Kronos and Chronos were of course in meaning, as in form, entirely distinct to begin with. Chronos is an Orphic figure derived from the Iranian Time-God Zrvan. His figure cannot be discussed here. See R. Eisler, *Weltenmantel und Himmelszelt*, 1910, index s.v. Kronos, Chronos, and Zrvan, and also for Kronos and Eniautos, W. Schultz, "Αὗτος in *Memnon*, 1910, p. 47.
[3] W. Raleigh.
[4] *Supra*, p. 97. Since I wrote the chapter on bird magic and the τείρεα there has appeared an interesting paper dealing in part with the association of constellations and birds by Dr M. P. Nilsson, *Die älteste Zeitrechnung. Apollo und der Orient* in Archiv f. Religionswiss., 1911, xiv. p. 423.

The particular forms taken by a people's mythology or theology can, as before said, only be understood in the light of its social structure. The matrilinear stage had long been buried and forgotten, and hence the figures of Dionysos and his mother Semele, and his attendant Satyrs, the figures of Rhea with her effaced husband Kronos and the band of the Kouretes, had lost their real significance. To the mythologist it is sufficient evidence of a matrilinear state of society in Greece, with its attendant tribal initiations, that such a social structure is seen thus clearly reflected in mythology. But, to a mind trained rather in historical than mythological method, such evidence may seem less convincing. We have therefore now to ask : what evidence is there, apart from mythological representations, of the existence of a social structure in which the mother, the male-child, and the tribe were the main factors ?

We turn, of course, first and foremost to the Apatouria, the festival of enrolment in the phratriai, but we turn only to be at the outset disappointed. The name itself is manifestly patriarchal. Apatouria is *Homopatoria*[1], the festival of those who have *the same fathers*. It is celebrated κατὰ τὰ πάτρια, according to paternal usage. On the third day was celebrated the festival of the κουρεῶτις, of the shearing of the hair, the significance of which has been already[2] noted in connection with Herakles and Apellaios. But here again we can detect no special relation to the Mother. A chance biographical notice in one of the 'Lives[3]' of Homer gives us the needful clue, and makes us suspect and indeed feel practically certain that the festival of The Same Fathers originally belonged to the Mothers[4].

When Homer was sailing to Greece, he put in at Samos. And the people there chanced at the moment to be celebrating the Apatouria. And one of the Samians, who had seen him before in Chios, when they beheld Homer

---

[1] So definitely the scholiast to Aristoph. *Acharn.* 146 οἱ δέ φασιν ὅτι τῶν πατέρων ὁμοῦ συνερχομένων διὰ τὰς τῶν παίδων ἐγγραφὰς οἷον ὁμοπατόρα λέγεσθαι τὴν ἑορτήν· ὁποίῳ τρόπῳ λέγομεν ἄλοχον τὴν ὁμολέκτρον καὶ ἄκοιτιν τὴν ὁμόκοιτιν οὕτω καὶ Ὁμοπατόρια Ἀπατόρια.

[2] *Supra*, pp. 378 and 441; for hair shearing in general see Dr Frazer, *Pausanias*, vol. III. p. 279.

[3] Westermann, *ps.-Herod. Biogr.* 29, p. 15.

[4] The connection of Athena with the ἐφῆβοι, her κοῦροι, and their relation to initiation ceremonies have been ably examined by Miss Dorothy Lamb, of Newnham College, in an essay as yet unpublished. See also *Addenda*.

arriving at Samos, went and told the clansmen, and made a panegyric about Homer. Aud the clansmen ordered him to bring Homer. And the man who had met him said to Homer—'Stranger, the city is celebrating the Apatouria, and the clansmen bid you come and feast with them.' And Homer said he would, and he went along with his host. And, as he went, he lighted on the women who were sacrificing at the crossways to Kourotrophos. And the priestess looked at him in anger, and said to him, 'Man, begone from the sanctities[1].'

The festival has become that of the 'Same Fathers,' but the sacrifice is by women and to the Mother, the Rearer of Children. It is by the Crossways, for the Mother has taken on her Moon-Aspect, as Eileithyia, as Hekate. It is strange indeed, at the sacrifice for the 'Same Fathers,' that no man might be present, but if the festival were once of the Same Mothers all is clear.

The Apatouria, the festival of the 'Same Fathers,' is late and patriarchal. It is interesting to find that, late though it is, the Apatouria finds—as in early days all social structure must—its mythological reflection and representation in a myth, that of the *Tritopatores*[2]; figures the interpretation of which, because they neglect to examine social structure, has caused mythologists much trouble and perplexity.

Of the Tritopatores Suidas[3], quoting Phanodemos, says:

The Athenians only both sacrifice and pray to them for the birth of children when they are about to marry.

The scholiast[4], commenting on the word *Tritogeneia*, recalls a phrase that sounds like an echo of this prayer, and throws new light on it:

'May my child be τριτογενής.'

The father prays to the Tritopatores that his child may be

---

[1] 'ἄνερ, ἀπὸ τῶν ἱερῶν.'

[2] I follow the explanation of Dr G. Lippold in his *Tritopatreis*, A. Mitt. xxxvi. 1911, p. 105. Dr Lippold scarcely seems to see the great importance in relation to Athenian social structure of his own convincing interpretation.

[3] s.v. Τριτοπάτορες. For the older explanation of Tritopatores see *Prolegomena*, p. 179.

[4] Schol. BT *ad* Hom. *Il.* viii. 39

καὶ παροιμία

παῖς μοι τριτογενὴς εἴη, μὴ τριτογένεια.

It is very likely, as Dr Lippold points out, that the two concluding words are not original, but have been added, as often in similar cases, to make up a desired hexameter.

τριτογενής. Tritogeneia, we remember, was the Athena who sprang from her father's head:

> Tritogeneia, the daughter of Zeus the Counsellor,
> Born from his sacred head, in battle-array ready dight,
> Golden all glistering[1].

Tritogeneia is not 'she who is born on the third day,' nor yet 'she who was born from the head of her father,' nor yet 'she who was born of the water of the brook Triton'; she is she who was *true* born, and to be true born is in patrilinear days to be born in wedlock of your lawful father. Hesychius[2], defining the word Τριτοκούρη, says:

> She for whom everything has been accomplished as to marriage. Some define it as 'a true virgin.'

The outrageous myth of the birth of Athena from the head of Zeus is but the religious representation, the emphasis, and over emphasis, of a patrilinear social structure. When an Athenian prayed to the Tritopatores, it was not for children merely, but for true born children, children born with him for their father.

The Apatouria, then, is the festival of those who have the same father, and of these the Tritopatores and Tritogeneia are the mythical expression. Now we realize why the god and goddess, who presided over the Apatouria, were Zeus and Athena, Father and Father-born daughter. As, in the old matrilinear days, Kronos the father was ignored, so, by the turn of the wheel, the motherhood of the mother is obscured, even denied; but with far less justice, for the facts of motherhood have been always patent. Athena is the real Kourotrophos, but for patrilinear purposes she is turned into a diagram of motherless birth.

As patrons of the Apatouria, Zeus and Athena bear the titles *Phratrios* and *Phratria*. The phratria is the *brotherhood* of those who have the same father. It has nothing to do with the ἀδελφοί, those who have the same mother, the ὁμογάστριοι[3]; it is of the

---

[1] *Hom. Hym.* xxviii. 4
Τριτογενῆ, τὴν αὐτὸς ἐγείνατο μητίετα Ζεὺς
σεμνῆς ἐκ κεφαλῆς πολεμήϊα τεύχε' ἔχουσαν.

[2] s.v. Τριτοκούρη· ᾗ πάντα συν(τε)τέλεσται τὰ εἰς τοὺς γάμους· τινὲς δὲ γνησία παρθένος. The origin of the stem τρῖτο is not known; all that is clear is that it must mean 'true,' 'genuine.'

[3] Gaius (*Inst.* iii. 10), in true patrilinear fashion, thus defines *agnatus* and *consanguineus*: 'legitima cognatio est ea quae per virilis sexus personas coniungitur.

patrilinear, not the matrilinear structure. When, in the *Eumenides*[1], the Erinyes ask of Orestes, slayer of his mother,

> What *brotherhood* will give him holy water?

Apollo is ready with his answer:

> This too I tell you, mark how plain my speech,
> The mother is no parent of her 'child,'
> Only the nurse of the young seed within her.
> The male is parent, she as outside friend
> Cherishes the plant, if fate allows its bloom.
> Proof will I bring of this mine argument.
> A father needs no mother's help. *She* stands,
> Child of Olympian Zeus, to be my witness,
> Reared never in the darkness of the womb,
> Yet fairer plant than any heaven begot.

This alliance of the three Olympians of the *Eumenides*, Zeus, Apollo, Athena, brings us to a curious point. The bond, we feel, is non-natural; the three gods stand together not because there is any primitive link, any common cultus, but as projections, representations of patriarchy, pushed to the utmost. They are a trinity of *Phratrioi, Patröoi.* Where else, we ask, are these three disparate divinities thus unequally yoked together? The answer is clear and brings immediate light; in Homer and in Homer only[2].

Achilles, sending forth Patroklos in his armour, prays[3]

> Would, O father Zeus and Athene, and Apollo, would that not one of all the Trojans might escape death, nor one of the Argives.

Hector names Apollo and Athene as linked together for special adoration[4]:

> Would that I were immortal and ageless all my days, and honoured, like as Athene is honoured and Apollo;

Itaque eodem patre nati fratres agnati sibi sunt, qui etiam consanguinei vocantur, nec requiritur an etiam matrem eaudem habuerint.' So subtle and persistent is the suggestion of name that there are persons even to-day who think that in some mysterious way they are more descended from their father than their mother. For the whole question see P. Kretschmer, *Die Griechische Benennung des Bruders*, Glotta II. p. 210.

[1] 559 ποία δὲ χέρνιψ φρατέρων προσδέξεται; and see also Eur. *Or.* 552, and *Frg.* 1048.

[2] As long ago remarked by Mr Gladstone, who brought together all the evidence in a book too little read now-a-days, his *Juventus Mundi*, 1869, p. 266 (Section viii. Athene and Apollo). We cannot of course adopt Mr Gladstone's solution. He held that Apollo and Athene were each in a special way the *Logos* of Zeus. The question is also raised by Prof. Murray, *Rise of the Greek Epic*[2], p. 69, note 3.

[3] Hom. *Il.* XVI. 97.

[4] Hom. *Il.* VIII. 540.

and again[1], even more significantly, he links Zeus, Athene, and Apollo together as the typical happy family:

> Would that indeed I were for ever as surely the son of aegis-bearing Zeus, and that my mother were lady Hera, and that I were held in such honour as Apollo and Athene, as verily this day is to bring utter evil on all the Argives!

Apollo and Athena then are linked together as *Phratrioi* and this conjunction is found in the patrilinear Homer and in the *Eumenides* where all the emphasis is patriarchal. Elsewhere Apollo is linked with quite another goddess, with Artemis, and in this conjunction we see a survival, though altered and disfigured, of matriarchal structure. In Homer a great effort is made to affiliate Artemis as one of the patriarchal family, but, in her ancient aspect as Πότνια θηρῶν, she is manifestly but a form of the Great Mother: at Delphi, where Apollo reigns supreme, his 'sister' Artemis is strangely, significantly absent. What has happened is fairly obvious. Artemis, as Mother, had a male-god as son or subordinate consort, just as Aphrodite had Adonis. When patriarchy ousted matriarchy, the relationship between the pair is first spiritualized as we find it in Artemis and Hippolytos; next the pair are conceived of in the barren relation of sister and brother. Finally the female figure dwindles altogether and the male-consort emerges as merely son of his father or utterer of his father's will—Διὸς προφήτης.

This is curiously and instructively shown in the history of the Eiresione. Originally of course the Eiresione was, as we have seen[2], a sanctity *per se*, a branch carried magically to promote fertility. In historical times, in the Thargelia, Daphnephoria, etc. it was associated with the worship of, it was 'sacred to,' Apollo[3]. This is natural enough for Apollo, as Aguieus and as Kouros, was the young male divinity, the source of fertility. In the Thargelia

---

[1] Hom. *Il.* XIII. 827.

[2] *Supra*, p. 220.

[3] Also at the Eiresione of Samos, which was associated with the primitive swallow song. See (Hdt.), *Vit. Hom.* p. 17 f. ap. Suidam, s.v. Ομηρος...ἥδετο δὲ τὰ ἔπεα τάδε (ἃ καλεῖται Εἰρεσιώνη) ἐν τῇ Σάμῳ ἐπὶ πολὺν χρόνον ὑπὸ τῶν παίδων, ὅτ' ἀγείροιεν ἐν τῇ ἑορτῇ τοῦ Ἀπόλλωνος. In the song given by Suidas occur the lines

> νεῦμαί τοι νεῦμαι ἐνιαύσιος ὥστε χελιδών
> ἕστηκ' ἐν προθύροις ψιλὴ πόδας· ἀλλὰ φέρ' αἶψα
> †πέρσαι τῷ Ἀπόλλωνος γυιατιδος
> εἰ μέν τι δώσεις·

but the ceremony was really to Kourotrophos. See Suidas, *loc. cit.* ...εἶτα ἀφίκετο (Ὅμηρος) εἰς Σάμον καὶ εὗρε γυναῖκα Κουροτρόφῳ θύουσαν κ.τ.λ.

and the Daphnephoria the figure of the Mother is effaced, though it may be that in the two pharmakoi, female as well as male, as in the two Oschophoroi[1] and the Daphnephoroi, her figure really survives. But in another service of the Eiresione the Mother holds her own, even to the exclusion of the Son, the ceremony of the *Korythalia*.

Hesychius[2] defining *Korythalia* says,

> A laurel wreathed : some call it *Eiresione*.

The *Etymologicum Magnum*[3] gives further and most instructive particulars. It thus defines the word *Korythale*:

> The laurel-bough placed before the doors. Because branches which the call *koroi* blossom.

So too Chrysippos:

> Let some one from within give me lighted torches and woven *koroi* unmixed with myrtle. For poets call branches, diversely, shoots and saplings and *koroi*. And others *when their sons and daughters come to maturity, place laurel-boughs before the doors in ceremonies of puberty and marriage.*

The *Korythalia*, 'Youth Bloom,' expresses just that oneness of man and nature that is so beautiful and so characteristic of primitive totemistic thinking. For them it was expressed in ceremonial, in the carrying of branches, for us it survives in 'poetry.'

> Thy wife shall be as the fruitful vine, upon the walls of thine house.
> Thy children like the olive-branches, round about thy table[4].

And at Athens in prose, for Demades[5], the orator, is reported to have said

> The epheboi are the spring of the *demos*.

But the *Korythalia* tells us more, it is the matriarchal form of the Eiresione. We know the divinity projected, represented by the *Korythalia*. She was no Kouros, she was Artemis *Korythalia*.

---

[1] *Supra*, p. 324.

[2] s.v. κορυθαλία· δάφνη ἐστεμμένη τινὲς τὴν εἰρεσιώνην.

[3] s.v. κορυθάλη· ἡ πρὸ τῶν θυρῶν τιθεμένη δάφνη· ὅτι οἱ κλάδοι (οὓς κόρους καλοῦσι) θάλλουσιν ὡς καὶ Χρύσιππος· Ἀλλὰ δᾷδας ἡμμένας μοι δότω τις ἔνδοθεν, καὶ κόρους πλεκτοὺς ἀκραιφνεῖς μυρρίνης—οἱ γὰρ ποιηταὶ ἀνάπαλιν τοὺς κλάδους καὶ ὄξους καὶ ὀρπηκας λέγουσι. τινὲς δὲ ὅτι ἡβησάντων τῶν νέων καὶ θυγατέρων, δάφνας προετίθουν ἐφήβοις καὶ γάμοις εἰς τὸ δίκρον.

[4] Psalm cxxviii. 3, 4.

[5] *ap.* Athen. III. 55. 99 καὶ Δημάδης δὲ ὁ ῥήτωρ ἔλεγε...ἔαρ δὲ τοῦ δήμου τοὺς ἐφήβους; cf. the *ver sacrum* of the Latins.

And, if as to her nature there was any doubt, she had another festival which marks her function, the *Tithenidia*, the festival of nurses and nurslings. Call her Orthia[1], or Korythalia, or Hyakinthotrophos[2], or Philomeirax[3], it is all one; she is Kourotrophos, the Rearing Mother, nurse of the Kouroi to be[4].

Kourotrophos and the Lady of the Wild Things are but the forms of the ancient mother served by the Kouretes and she survives in the figure of Artemis, the Huntress sister of Apollo.

Of this we have curious ritual evidence.

At Messene, near to a temple of Eileithyia, Pausanias[5] saw

a hall of the Kouretes, where they sacrifice without distinction all animals, beginning with oxen and goats and ending with birds: they throw them all into the fire.

Why this singular service to the Kouretes? Why indeed, unless we remember that they were the ministrants, the correlatives of the Great Mother, the 'Lady of the Wild Things.' To her the sacrifice of all living things is manifestly, if hideously, appropriate.

And to her it was offered. Lucian[6], in his account of the Syrian goddess at Hieropolis—manifestly but a form of the Great Mother—tells how, in the court of the sanctuary, were kept all manner of beasts and birds.

Consecrated oxen, horses, eagles, bears and lions, who never hurt anyone, but are holy and tame to handle.

But of these tame beasts and birds in one day in the year there is a holocaust.

'Of all the festivals,' Lucian[7] says, 'the greatest that I know of they hold in the beginning of the spring. Some call it the *Pyre*, some the *Torch*. At this festival they do as follows. They cut down great trees and set them up in the courtyard. Then they bring in goats and sheep and other live beasts, and hang them up on the trees. They also bring birds and clothes and vessels of gold and silver. When they have made all ready, they carry the victims round the trees and set fire to them and straightway they are all burned.'

By a fortunate chance we know that this sacrifice of all living things, so appropriate to the Mother, was also made to Artemis

[1] The etymology of Orthia is still uncertain, but the scholiast on Pindar, *Ol.* III. 54, is probably right in his guess as to the meaning: ὅτι ὀρθοῖ εἰς σωτηρίαν ἢ ὀρθοῖ τοὺς γεννωμένους.

[2] For ὑακινθοτρόφος see Collitz-Bechtel, *Samm. Gr. Dialekt.* 3501, 3502, 3512; the title occurs in Knidos. For Hyakinthos as *iuvencus=adulescentulus*, see Dr S. Wide, *Lakonische Kulte*, p. 290.

[3] Paus. VI. 23. 8.   [4] *Supra*, p. 494.   [5] IV. 32. 9.
[6] *De Syria Dea*, 41.   [7] *Op. cit.* 49.

with the title of Laphria, who was, Pausanias[1] tells us, substantially
the same as the Ephesian Mother. At Patrae, which was in-
habited by dispossessed Calydonians, a yearly sacrifice to Artemis
was celebrated. After describing the altar surrounded by a circle
of green logs of wood and approached by an inclined plane of
earth, and also the procession of the virgin priestess in a car
drawn by deer, Pausanias comes to the sacrifice itself, which, he
says, is not merely a state affair, but popular also among private
persons. It is sad reading.

> For they bring and cast upon the altar living things of all sorts, both
> edible birds and all manner of victims, also wild boars and deer and fawns
> and some even bring the cubs of wolves and bears, and others full grown
> beasts. And they lay on the altar also the fruits of cultivated trees. Then
> they set fire to the wood. I saw indeed a bear and other beasts struggling to
> get out of the first force of the flames and escaping by sheer strength. But
> those who threw them in drag them up again on to the fire. I never heard
> of anyone being wounded by the wild beasts[2].

Such was the savage service of the Kouretes and of the
Mother and of that last survival of the Mother, the maiden 'sister'
of Apollo the Kouros.

Of matrilinear structure there is evidence stronger still and
better concealed in an obscure ceremony, the significance of which
has only lately been made out[3], the festival of Things Insolent or
Things Unwonted, Things beyond and outside their Moira, the
Hybristika.

The Hybristika.

Plutarch, in his treatise on the *Virtues of Women*[4], tells of
the brave fight made by the women of Argos against Cleomenes,
under the leadership of the poetess Telesilla. This fight was the
alleged *aition* of a curious festival.

> Some said the fight was on the seventh day of the month, others that it
> was on the day of the new moon of the month which is now called the fourth,
> but which was formerly called *Hermaios*, on which day they still celebrate the
> *Hybristika*, and clothe women in men's chitons and chlamydes and men in
> the peploi and veils of women.

The learned Plutarch realises that this festival belonged to a
whole class in which women counterfeited men and *vice versa*.
He cites as a further instance the Argive law that women who

---

[1] iv. 32. 6.   [2] vii. 18. 12.
[3] By Mr W. R. Halliday in his illuminating monograph, *A Note on Herodotos
vi. 83 and the Hybristika*, in B.S.A. xvi. 1909–10, p. 212.
[4] *De Mulier. Virt.* 4.

were brides should wear beards. The *aition* he gives was that the scarcity of males caused the women to admit slaves as husbands. The singular customs of the Hybristika marked, he thinks, the contempt of the freeborn bride.

The name τὰ ὑβριστικά means things outrageous, *insolent* in the etymological sense, things against use and wont. Now why, in a primitive society, should Themis who rules over all things be wantonly and yet systematically outraged? What lies behind this world-wide outrage of the exchange of clothes between the sexes, which survives to-day among the 'Arries and 'Arriets of Hampstead Heath?

The answer that till quite lately has been accepted as most satisfactory is, that the transfer of clothing marks the shift from matriarchy to patriarchy. The priest of Herakles at Cos[1] had to wear woman's clothes when he sacrificed. It is tempting to suppose that once there had been a woman priestess of some native goddess Omphale, and that when patriarchy obtained a priest usurped the office of the priestess but still wore her ritual gear. The theory is ingenious and indeed points the way to the more satisfactory solution suggested by Mr Halliday. That solution he arrived at by the only safe road, by examining in their entirety all the various occasions on which the change of clothes takes place.

The rite of the change of clothes—for a formal rite it is, not a wanton eccentricity—is observed on occasions seemingly the most dissimilar, at circumcision, at marriage, at mourning after a death. At circumcision Egyptian boys are dressed as girls. Among the Nandi, before boys are circumcised, the young girls pay them a visit and give them some of their own garments and ornaments, and similarly the girls are given the clothes and ornaments of boys on a like occasion.

The borrowed plumage is returned when the girls and boys are respectively admitted into the new social status for which circumcision has qualified them[2].

Achilles on Skyros was disguised as a girl[3], Dionysos was brought up by Ino and Athamas as a maiden[4].

[1] Plut. *Quaest. Gr.* LVIII. Διὰ τί παρὰ Κῴοις ὁ τοῦ Ἡρακλέους ἱερεὺς ἐν Ἀντιμαχίᾳ γυναικείαν ἐνδεδυμένος ἐσθῆτα καὶ τὴν κεφαλὴν ἀναδούμενος μίτρᾳ κατάρχεται τῆς θυσίας;
[2] Mr Halliday, *op. cit.* p. 214.   [3] Apollod. III. 13. 8.   [4] Apollod. III. 4. 3.

The rites of puberty, the rites of marriage, are, like all other primitive rites, *rites de passage* : their object is to afford a safe passage in the perilous transit from one age or condition to another. Man feels, though he does not yet know, that life *is* change, and change is beset with dangers. The first crisis of life is the change of puberty, from boyhood to manhood. Manhood, among primitive peoples, seems to be envisaged as ceasing to be a woman : the notion is quite natural. Man is born of woman, reared of woman. When he passes to manhood, he ceases to be a woman-thing[1] and begins to exercise functions other and alien. That moment is one naturally of extreme peril ; he at once emphasizes and disguises it. He wears woman's clothes. The same applies at marriage.

The focus of attention at puberty and in marriage is on sex. The *rite de passage* is from one sex to another. Hence the change of clothes. But what is effective and salutary for one crisis may be effective and salutary for another. Hence the fact, perplexing at first, that at mourning for death—another *rite de passage*—the Lycians changed clothes with the opposite sex. In fact the ceremony of change of clothes might easily come to be observed whenever it was desirable to ' change the luck.' Among the Nandi

> Once every seven-and-a-half years, some say four years after the circumcision festival, the Saket-ap-eito ceremony takes place. The country is handed over from one age to another. At the conclusion of the ceremonies, the men of the preceding age take off their warriors' garments and put on those of old age. The defence and well-being of the community are thereby handed over to their successors.

Here the *rite de passage* is not from sex to sex but from age to age. The general characteristics of each periodic festival, such as the Carnival, the Saturnalia, are always the same, a complete upset of the old order, a period of licence and mutual hilarity, and then the institution of the new. As Mr Halliday points out, the last survival is the servants' ball of the old-fashioned country Christmas.

Behind the Hybristika and many another primitive Greek rite there lies a rite of initiation, the rite of the making of a *Kouros*. When tribal conditions are broken up, the family takes the place

---

[1] See *supra*, p. 36.

of the group. What were once puberty rites change, as we have already seen[1], into other forms of initiation, as medicine or seer or member of some secret society. A very singular instance of this is preserved to us in the rites of Trophonios at Lebadeia which are known to us in exceptional detail, and which cast considerable light on the figure of Themis as she shifts from being a projection of the social structure to her final form as a divinity of prophecy.

THE ORACLE OF TROPHONIOS.

The sources of our knowledge of the ritual of Trophonios are three:

1. The account of Pausanias when he visited Lebadeia.

2. The treatise of Plutarch on the *Daimon of Sokrates*, in which he recounts the experiences of a young philosopher who went down into the chasm of Trophonios to find out what the Daimon of Sokrates was.

3. Plutarch's treatise on the *Face in the Orb of the Moon*, in which he relates the rite of Trophonios to other ceremonies, and thereby lets out their real nature.

(1) The account of Pausanias[2] is familiar, and also too long to be quoted *in extenso*; it must for the most part be resumed. After a description of the city of Lebadeia, which in splendour equalled the most flourishing cities of Greece, and after stating that Trophonios was in form and function analogous to Asklepios, Pausanias describes the procedure of consulting the oracle. The consultation is preceded by various rites of purification and sacralization. The applicant lodges for a stated number of days in a certain building sacred to the Agathos Daimon and to Agathe Tyche. He bathes only in the river Herkyna, he sacrifices to various divinities, among them of course Trophonios and Demeter with the title Europa, whom they call the nurse of Trophonios, obviously a divinity of the Ge-Kourotrophos type. He feeds on sacrificial flesh, and omens are taken from the victims, especially from the flesh of a ram sacrificed over a pit to Agamedes.

Next comes the actual descent:

The way in which he goes down is this. First, during the night two citizen boys about thirteen years old lead him to the river Herkyna and anoint him

---

[1] *Supra*, p. 52.   [2] IX. 39. 1—14.

with oil and bathe him. The boys are called *Hermai*, and they wash him and do all necessary things for him. Then the priests take him not straight to the oracle, but to certain springs of water which are close to each other. Here he must drink what is called the water of Lethe, that he may forget all he has hitherto had in mind. Next he drinks of another water, the water of Memory, and by it he remembers again what he sees down below. Then having seen it and worshipped and prayed he comes to the oracle itself dressed in a tunic of linen, girded with fillets and wearing the boots of the country.

Then follows a detailed account of the actual structure of the oracular chasm. It is artificial and shaped like a pot for baking bread in. It is about eight ells deep. The consultant goes down by a ladder.

When he has gone down he sees a hole between the ground and the stone-work. Its breadth seems to be two spans and its height one. He then lays himself down on his back, and holding in either hand barley-cakes mixed with honey, he pushes his feet through the hole first and then follows himself, trying to squeeze his knees through the hole. When he has got his knees through the rest of his body is immediately pulled in, and shoots along as a man might be caught and dragged along by the swirl of a mighty and swift stream. The future is not revealed to all in the same way. To one it is given by sight, to another by hearing. They return through the hole feet foremost.

Next comes a story of the sad and instructive fate of a sacrilegious consultant, and then Pausanias concludes:

When a man has come up from Trophonios, the priests again take him and set him on what they call the throne of Memory, which stands not far from the shrine, and when he is seated there they ask him as to what he has seen and heard. When he has told them they give him over to his friends, and they carry him, still overwhelmed with fear and unconscious of himself and where he is, to the same building where he stayed before, the house of Agathos Daimon and Agathe Tyche. Later on his wits return to him and the power to laugh will come back again. I do not write from hearsay. I have myself consulted Trophonios, and have seen others who have done it.

It is important that Pausanias states what he knows from personal experience. No one who has read Pausanias will incline to credit him with hysteria.

(2) Plutarch's account of the experiences of Timarchos[1] adds certain details to the picture, and greatly emphasizes the importance of the revelations imparted. When Timarchos after the accustomed preliminaries entered the chasm,

thick darkness was about him. He prayed and lay a long while upon the ground uncertain whether he was waking or dreaming. But it seemed to him that he felt a sharp blow on his head with a great noise, and that through the

[1] *De Genio Socr.* XXII.

sutures of his skull his soul was let loose.   And, as his soul went forth, it was mixed with pure and pleasant and lightsome air, and it seemed for the first time to take breath, and seemed to expand and be more spacious than before, like a sail swollen with the wind.

Then follows a long account of the revelation vouchsafed to Timarchos, which included the whole cosmos and the daimones pervading the cosmos, all of which was explained by an invisible voice Finally,

The voice ceased speaking, and Timarchos turned round to see who was the speaker. But a sharp pain seized his head, as though his skull were being pressed together, so that he lost all sense and understanding. In a little while he recovered and found himself in the mouth of the cave of Trophonios, where he had first lain down[1].

Sokrates, when he was told all this, was much annoyed that he had not heard about it before Timarchos died, so that he might have questioned him on his experiences. We share the annoyance of Sokrates.

In the *Hybristika* we saw that the *rite de passage* was emphasized, expressed, represented by a change of clothes.   In the rites of Trophonios the transit from one state to another is still more drastically enacted.   After purification the suppliant goes down into a chasm, slips through a hole feet foremost, is swirled away, has a vision, comes back through the hole reversed. Without exaggeration, he may surely be said to have accomplished a *rite de passage*.   In the rites of Trophonios we seem to see the thing presented pictorially, physically, geographically; the rites are, as M. van Gennep[2] would say, preliminal, liminal, postliminal.

But it may fairly be asked, Are we justified in comparing the rites of Trophonios to rites of initiation?   Are they not expressly and merely certain curious ceremonies in relation to the consultation of a primitive oracle?

It may be noted in passing that the suppliant was attended by boys who were citizens, and that they were about thirteen years of age, that is they had just attained puberty.   But happily we have evidence more definite.

(3) In his treatise on the *Face in the Orb of the Moon,*

---

[1] Plut. *de Genio Socr.* XXII. *sub fin.*

[2] *Les Rites de Passage*, 1909, p. 14 'le schéma complet des rites de passage comporte en théorie des rites *préliminaires* (séparation), *liminaires* (marge) et *postliminaires* (agrégation).'

Plutarch[1] tells us that the moon is daimon-haunted, but that certain of the better sort of daimones do not always stay in the moon.

They come down hither in order to take charge of oracles, and they are present at, and take part in, the highest of orgiastic initiatory rites, and they are chasteners and watchers over wrong doings and they shine as saviours in battle and at sea…. *Of the best of these daimones those of the age of Kronos said they themselves were. And the same of old were the Idaean Daktyls in Crete and the Korybantes in Phrygia and the Trophoniads in Lebadeia of Boeotia* and countless others in various places all over the habitable world, of whom the sacred rites and honours and titles remain.

Plutarch could not put the matter more plainly. The same daimones preside over oracles and over rites of initiation; Trophoniads, Idaean Daktyls and those of the age of Kronos are all substantially the same. The statement is for us a priceless illumination. But we ask what is really meant by this bringing together of things apparently so remote and alien, oracles, institutions for looking into the future, and rites of initiation, purely social institutions?

MNEMOSYNE AND ANAMNESIS.

At the outset, it must be remembered that oracles were, down to late days, places to be consulted for advice as to the present as much and more than for knowledge of the future; they were essentially places of counsel for practical purposes. But even so there remains a certain gulf to be bridged between the social and the oracular. The bridge is easily crossed if we examine the analogy of primitive initiation rites.

We saw in the first chapter[2] that the cardinal rite of tribal initiation was a mimetic Death and Resurrection. By every sort of pantomime the notion was enforced that the boy had died to his old life, had put away childish things, had in a word a new social status and soul. We also saw that tribal initiation was the prototype of all social rites, that the rites at birth, marriage, the

---

[1] *De fac. in orb. lun.* xxx. οὐκ ἀεὶ δὲ διατρίβουσιν ἐπ' αὐτῇ οἱ δαίμονες ἀλλὰ χρηστηρίων δεῦρο κατίασιν ἐπιμελησόμενοι, καὶ ταῖς ἀνωτάτω συμπάρεισι καὶ συνοργιάζουσι τῶν τελετῶν, κολασταί τε γίνονται καὶ φύλακες ἀδικημάτων καὶ σωτῆρες ἔν τε πολέμοις καὶ κατὰ θάλατταν ἐπιλάμπουσιν…ἐκ δὲ τῶν βελτιόνων ἐκείνων οἵ τε περὶ τὸν Κρόνον ὄντες ἔφασαν αὐτοὺς εἶναι, καὶ πρότερον ἐν τῇ Κρήτῃ τοὺς Ἰδαίους Δακτύλους, ἔν τε Φρυγίᾳ τοὺς Κορύβαντας γενέσθαι, καὶ τοὺς περὶ Βοιωτίαν ἐν Λεβαδείᾳ Τροφωνιάδας, καὶ μυρίους ἄλλους πολλαχόθι τῆς οἰκουμένης· ὧν ἱερὰ καὶ τιμαὶ καὶ προσηγορίαι διαμένουσιν.

[2] *Supra*, p. 18.

making of a medicine man, death itself, were only *rites de passage*, the transit from one state to another. Change which is life itself is emphasized, represented. To consult an oracle you need a *rite de passage* just as much as to be made a member of a tribe. To know is to be in touch with *mana*, not to be *entheos*, for the *theos* is not yet formulated and projected, but to be sanctified, to pass inside the region of *tabu*; hence the preliminary purification. Lethe is but an attenuated Death; Mnemosyne, renewed consciousness, is a new Life.

We distinguish between the objective and the subjective. So did primitive man; indeed a creature who did not for practical purposes make some such distinction would not long survive. But we know definitely that the subjective world, though it can influence our actions as strongly as the objective, has its only reality within us. The savage gives to the world of his imagination, of his feelings, emotions, dreams, a certain outside reality. He cannot quite distinguish between a conception and a perception. He makes another world with a sort of secondary reality, supersensuous but quite real. To this supersensuous world go all his remembrances of the past, all his hopes and imaginings for the future.

And so the supersensuous world grows big with the invisible present and big also with the past and the future, crowded with the ghosts of the dead and shadowed with oracles and portents of the future. It is this supersensuous, supernatural world which is the eternity, the other world, of primitive religion; not an endlessness of time but a state removed from full sensuous reality, a world in which anything and everything may happen, a fairyland of heaven and hell, a world too peopled with demonic ancestors and liable to a 'once upon a time-ness' denied to the present[1].

Thus, to consult an oracle, a veritable, almost physical, *rite de passage* is indispensable. The suppliant must pass out of the actual, sensible, 'objective' world, into that other world of dream, of ecstasy, of trance, with its secondary reality, the world in which emotions, hope and fear, and imaginations, are blended with what we should call subjective hallucinations. He needs a *rite d'agrégation* to assimilate him, and when he would return to the normal

---

[1] See my paper on *The Influence of Darwinism on the Study of Religions*, pp. 499—501 in the Darwin Memorial Volume, 1909. The view there expressed as to the content of the primitive supersensuous world is entirely based on Dr P. Beck's *Erkenntnisstheorie des primitiven Denkens* in Zeitschrift f. Philosophie und philos. Kritik, 1903, p. 172, and 1904, p. 9.

sensuous world with its other and almost alien reality he needs a *rite de ségrégation*.

That Memory, the mere remembering of facts, should be the Mother of the Muses is a frigid genealogy. The usual explanation offered is that memory is the faculty which enables you to remember and repeat long epic poems. But the Mnemosyne of initiation rites, the remembering again, the ἀνάμνησις, of things seen in ecstasy when the soul is rapt to heavenly places, she is surely now, as ever, the fitting Mother of all things musical. We are told again and again that Plato 'borrowed much of his imagery' from the mysteries, but it is no external borrowing of a mere illustration. Plato's whole scheme alike of education and philosophy is but an attempted rationalization of the primitive mysticism of initiation, and most of all of that profound and perennial mysticism of the central *rite de passage*, the death and the new birth, social, moral, intellectual. His borrowings of terminology, his φύλακες, his ἀνδρεία, his κάθαρσις, ἔκπληξις, ἀνακάλυψις, even his μελετᾶν ἀποθνήσκειν, are but the outer signs of a deep inward and spiritual debt.

Plato, in his accustomed way, just slightly alters the word, giving us a more strictly accurate term *Anamnesis* for the mythological Mnemosyne, but with no intention of concealing his borrowing. What has so long lain hidden from us must have been patent to every initiated Greek, and especially to every Orphic. On the tablet[1] hung round the neck of the dead initiated man, was inscribed an instruction that reflects, though in slightly different form, the ritual of Trophonios:

> Thou shalt find to the left of the House of Hades a Well-spring,
> And by the side thereof standing a white cypress.
> To this Well-spring approach not near.
> But thou shalt find another by the Lake of Memory,
> Cold water flowing forth, and there are guardians before it.

At Lebadeia the supplicant must drink of Lethe, he must present a clean sheet for the revelation to come. But Lethe was only *Katharsis*[2], the negative side, and gradually this negative

[1] *Prolegomena*, pp. 574 and 660. I have there fully discussed the Mnemosyne of the Orphic tablets and drawn attention to the analogy of the rites of Trophonios, but I did not then understand their relation to rites of social initiation.

[2] For another view of Katharsis as the restoration of equilibrium see Prof. Margoliouth's *Poetics of Aristotle*, 1911, p. 59.

side fell away and came even to be regarded as a forbidden evil, a denial of the new life of Mnemosyne[1].

The evidence then, not only of the rites of the Kouretes but also of such rites as the *Hybristika* and the oracular rites of Trophonios, shows us clearly that some primitive conceptions of Greek religion, and hence inevitably of Greek philosophy, were based on group-institutions, the social structure of which was of the matrilinear type. We return to the point from which we set out, the rites and representation of the Palaiokastro Hymn. We shall find there to our surprise and satisfaction that this dominance of social structure is not only evident but even strongly emphasized.

THEMIS, DIKE AND THE HORAE.

Our first chapter was devoted to the consideration of the Hymn of the Kouretes. We noted then that in subject as in structure the Hymn fell into three parts, (1) The Invocation, (2) the Aetiological Myth, (3) the Resultant Blessings. The first and second parts we considered in detail. We saw how the Kouros invoked was a projection of his worshippers the Kouretes, and we noted that he was invoked for the year, that he was in fact the vehicle and incarnation of the fruits and blessings of the year. His growth to maturity, his entry on the status of ephebos[2], caused the growth and maturity of the natural year.

We then passed to the consideration of the aetiological myth and saw that in it was reflected and projected that matrilinear structure of society in which the Mother and the Son, the Son grown to maturity, were the prominent facts. The third factor, the Resultant Blessings, had to be held over till the figure of Themis had been discussed, and now awaits consideration.

After the birth of the Kouros and that yearly coming which reflects his yearly re-birth the Hymn tells us[3]

---

[1] This notion of Mnemosyne, of Death and Resurrection, is almost like a dim imaginative forecast of modern philosophical speculation. Prof. Bergson has shown us that Consciousness 'signifies above all memory,' 'all consciousness is memory; all consciousness (what he elsewhere calls *durée*) is a preservation and accumulation of the past in the present,' and again 'all consciousness is an anticipation of the future,' 'consciousness is above all a hyphen, a tie between the past and future.' See *Life and Consciousness* in Hibbert Journal, Oct. 1911, pp. 27 and 28.

[2] Too late for incorporation in chapter I., I find that, if we may trust the *Etymologicum Magnum* (s.v. Δίκτη), there was at Dikte a Διὸς ἄγαλμα ἀγένειον, obviously the image of Zeus as *Kouros*.

[3] *Supra*, p. 8.

The Horai began to be fruitful year by year and Dike to possess mankind, and all wild living things were held about by wealth-loving Peace.

Then the Invocation is repeated, the Kouretes bid their Kouros, who is but themselves,

'Leap for full jars, and leap for fleecy flocks, and leap for fields of fruit, and for hives to bring increase.'

And

'Leap for our Cities, and leap for our sea-borne ships, and leap for our young citizens and for goodly Themis.'

In the light of ancient magic we understand leaping for flocks, fields and beehives. In the light of the Eniautos-daimon we understand leaping for the Horai, the Seasons, who bring the great Year-Festival. In the light of the Greatest Kouros and rites of initiation we even understand leaping for young citizens, but when it comes to the last leap of all, high in the air, for goodly Themis, we stand amazed. If we examine the figures of Dike and the Horai our surprise may change to understanding and even admiration.

Themis is the mother of the Horai. Speaking of the weddings of Zeus, Hesiod[1] says,

> Next led he goodly Themis, and she bore
> The Hours, Eunomia, Dike, blooming Peace.

It is then two of the Horai, the Seasons, who, at the birth of the Kouros, bring the new and splendid order to the earth[2].

Pindar[3] gives the same genealogy when he tells of the glories of Corinth :

Where doth Eunomia reign and her sister, secure foundation of cities, Dike and her foster sister Eirene, guardians of wealth for men, golden daughters of Themis of the Fair-Counsels.

And again in the fragment of the first Paean[3], written for Thebes for the festival of the Daphnephoria :

'Iē.
Lo the Year in its accomplishment and the Horai born of Themis have come to the horse-loving city of Thebes, bringing Apollo's garland-loving feast. May he long time crown the race of the citizens with the flowers of temperate Eunomia.'

[1] *Theog.* 901.
[2] For the Horai and the Age of Innocence see Prof. Bosanquet, *B.S.A.* VIII. p. 354 : but, as Mr Cornford suggests to me, the notion may be that of the inauguration of a new Great Year, like Empedocles' world-periods, beginning with a reign of Philia and Justice; cf. Plato, *Politicus,* 270.
[3] Grenfell and Hunt, *Oxyrhynchus Papyri,* vol. v. p. 25; and for connection with Daphnephoria see p. 16.

The sentiment is strangely like the Hymn of the Kouretes. Apollo takes the place, as well he might[1], of the Greatest Kouros.

The Dike then of the Hymn is one of the Horai and is the daughter of Themis. To us she seems like a slightly more abstracted Themis. In her other form she is Justice, that is, she is Convention, public usage, the social conscience, Themis regarded as an abstraction. But to regard Dike thus is to lose sight of her aspect as one of the Seasons, and indeed to mis-conceive her origin and very essence.

Dike in her origin is very like Themis, only always a little more alive, less stationary. In common Greek parlance, preserved chiefly in the normal use of the accusative, she is the 'way of life,' normal habit.

$$\beta\rho\acute{\epsilon}\mu\epsilon\iota\ \delta'$$
$$\dot{a}\mu a\chi\acute{\epsilon}\tau o\upsilon\ \delta\acute{\iota}\kappa a\nu\ \ddot{\upsilon}\delta a\tau o\varsigma\ \dot{o}\rho o\kappa\tau\acute{\upsilon}\pi o\upsilon^2.$$

'The clatter of horse's hooves roars in the way of, after the fashion of, an unconquerable mountain-beating torrent.'

$$\kappa\acute{o}\mu\eta\varsigma\ \delta\grave{\epsilon}\ \pi\acute{\epsilon}\nu\theta o\varsigma\ \lambda a\gamma\chi\acute{a}\nu\omega\ \pi\acute{\omega}\lambda o\upsilon\ \delta\acute{\iota}\kappa\eta\nu^3.$$

My hair dishevelled like a colt's wild mane.

Again, Pindar[4] says he will have no share in the loud boast of the guileful citizen:

$$\phi\acute{\iota}\lambda o\nu\ \epsilon\ddot{\iota}\eta\ \phi\iota\lambda\epsilon\hat{\iota}\nu\cdot$$
$$\pi o\tau\grave{\iota}\ \delta'\ \dot{\epsilon}\chi\theta\rho\grave{o}\nu\ \ddot{a}\tau'\ \dot{\epsilon}\chi\theta\rho\grave{o}\varsigma\ \dot{\epsilon}\grave{\omega}\nu\ \lambda\acute{\upsilon}\kappa o\iota o\ \delta\acute{\iota}\kappa a\nu\ \dot{\upsilon}\pi o\theta\epsilon\acute{\upsilon}\sigma o\mu a\iota,$$
$$\ddot{a}\lambda\lambda'\ \ddot{a}\lambda\lambda o\tau\epsilon\ \pi a\tau\acute{\epsilon}\omega\nu\ \dot{o}\delta o\hat{\iota}\varsigma\ \sigma\kappa o\lambda\iota a\hat{\iota}\varsigma.$$

'A friend to a friend, a foe to a foe, like a wolf will I leap upon him, heading now here, now there.'

Like a wolf, like a foal, like water. Here we have the difference between $\theta\acute{\epsilon}\mu\iota\varsigma$ and $\delta\acute{\iota}\kappa\eta$. The one, $\theta\acute{\epsilon}\mu\iota\varsigma$, is specialized to man, the social conscience, the other is the way of the whole world of nature, of the universe of all live things. The word $\delta\acute{\iota}\kappa\eta^5$ has in it more life-blood, more of living and doing; the word $\theta\acute{\epsilon}\mu\iota\varsigma$ has more of permission to do, human sanction shadowed always by *tabu*; *fas* is unthinkable without *nefas*.

---

[1] *Supra*, p. 439.   [2] Æsch. *Septem*, 84.
[3] Soph., Nauck, *Frg.* 598.   [4] *Pyth.* II. 155.
[5] Mr Cornford points out to me that in some compounds, e.g. ἔνδικος, δίκη keeps the notion of 'way' after she has, as a personality, submerged it in retribution and vengeance. Aristotle (*Pol.* B. 3. 1262 a 24), Mr Cook reminds me, uses δίκαιος of Pharsalian horses who, apparently, breed true. The commentators, *ad loc.*, note that in the land of the just, τίκτουσιν...γυναῖκες ἐοικότα τέκνα τοκεῦσι. Xenophon (*Cyr.* VIII. 3. 38) uses δίκαιος of a soil that repays cultivation.

We speak of the δίκη of a wolf, a foal, a torrent, not of its θέμις; but man, as well as nature, has his ways, his habits, so we speak of the δίκη of men; and with this human use a notion not merely of habit but of right, due habit, comes in. To lie soft' is the δίκη, not merely the *habit*, but the *due* of old men[1]. Odysseus, Penelope[2] says to Medon, was

'One that wrought no iniquity toward any man, nor spake aught unright-eous in the township, *as is the way of divine kings.*'

Dike then is the way of the world, the way things happen, and Themis is that specialized way for human beings which is sanctioned by the collective conscience, by herd instinct. A lonely beast in the valley, a fish in the sea, has his Dike, but it is not till man congregates together that he has his Themis.

And now we begin to understand the link between Dike and the Horai. Dike we have seen is the way of life of each natural thing, each plant, each animal, each man. It is also the way, the usage, the regular course of that great animal the Universe, the way that is made manifest in the Seasons, in the life and death of vegetation; and when it comes to be seen that these depend on the heavenly bodies, Dike is manifest in the changes of the rising and setting of constellations, in the waxing and waning of the Moon and in the daily and yearly courses of the Sun.

In one passage at least, in the *Medea*[3] of Euripides Dike stands for the course, even the circular course of the whole cosmos. In the general reversal of all things

> Upward go the streams of the living rivers,
> Dike and all things are turned about.

Only so do we understand how Dike seems sometimes to take on the semblance of the Moon, sometimes of the Sun. In the Hymn to the Moon in the Magic Papyri[4], where so much that is

---

[1] Hom. *Od.* XXIV. 255

εὐδέμεναι μαλακῶς· ἡ γὰρ δίκη ἐστὶ γερόντων.

[2] *Od.* IV. 690

οὔτε τινὰ ῥέξας ἐξαίσιον οὔτε τι εἰπὼν
ἐν δήμῳ· ἥτ᾽ ἐστὶ δίκη θείων βασιλήων.

[3] *v.* 410   ἄνω ποταμῶν ἱερῶν χωροῦσι παγαὶ
καὶ δίκα καὶ πάντα πάλιν στρέφεται.

[4] Par. Pap. Abel, 292, verses 7 and 49. For the moon-aspect of Moira, Dike, Tyche, Ananke, etc., see Dieterich, *Abraxas*, p. 102.

ancient is enshrined, the Moon is addressed not only as Moira, but as Dike.

> ἄστρασι κωμάζουσα Δίκη καὶ νήματα Μοιρῶν,
> Κλώθω καὶ Λάχεσις ἠδ' Ἄτροπος εἰ τρικάρανε,

and again,

> ...σὺ γὰρ δυσάλυκτος Ἀνάγκη
> Μοῖρά τ' ἔφυς...Δίκη σύ,

and in the prooemium of Parmenides[1] the Ways of Day and Night are closed by mighty doors, and of these

> Dikè Avenging keeps the keys that fit them.

In Homer the Gates of Heaven are turned on their hinges by the Horai. The Ways, the Paths, the Goings of Day and Night could never have been guarded by Themis.

We have yet to note another distinction between Themis and Dike. Iamblichus in his *Life of Pythagoras*[2] makes an instructive statement as to their relative positions.

'Men,' he says, 'knowing that all places alike have need of justice, fable that Themis occupies the same position in the realm of Zeus as Dike in that of Plouton and as Law occupies in cities, so that he who does not act aright with respect to what is ordained should seem to be thereby committing injustice at one and the same time against the whole universe.'

Iamblichus[3] seems to have discerned, if rather dimly and confusedly, the real state of the case. Human custom and law, *Nomos*, was a fact of this actual world. Themis in Heaven and Dike in Hades were fictions, mythological projections. He gives no hint why Themis should be in Heaven, Dike in Hades. An enquiry into the cause will repay us. But first we must establish the fact.

Themis is constantly associated with Zeus; she hangs about

---

[1] Diels, *F.V.S.* p. 114, *v.* 11

> ἔνθα πύλαι Νυκτός τε καὶ Ἤματος εἰσὶ κελεύθων
> . . . . .
> αὐταὶ δ' αἰθέριαι πλῆνται μεγάλοισι θυρέτροις,
> τῶν δὲ Δίκη πολύποινος ἔχει κληῖδας ἀμοιβούς.

Dr Otto Gilbert in his *Die Daimon des Parmenides*, Archiv f. Gesch. d. Philosophie, xx. p. 25, has conclusively shown that the vision of Parmenides is a Hades-journey. The poet goes with the Sun-chariot through the gates of the West (κάθοδος) and passes through the house of Night to the gate of the ἄνοδος where Dike is. The Heliads go to the upper world. Parmenides stays with Dike below.

[2] ix. 46 ...τοὺς γὰρ ἀνθρώπους...μυθοποιεῖν τὴν αὐτὴν τάξιν ἔχειν παρὰ τῷ Διὶ τὴν Θέμιν καὶ παρὰ τῷ Πλούτωνι τὴν Δίκην καὶ κατὰ τὰς πόλεις τὸν Νόμον, ἵνα ὁ μὴ δικαίως ἐφ' ἃ τέτακται ποιῶν ἅμα φαίνηται πάντα τὸν κόσμον συναδικῶν.

[3] He may be quoting a dictum of Pythagoras.

him like a sort of moralized Kratos and Bia.   The nurse says of Medea[1],

> 'Did ye hear her cry
> To them that guard man's faith forsworn,
> Themis and Zeus?'

It was the boast of Ægina that more than any other city she honoured

> Saviour Themis who sitteth by Zeus, God of Strangers[2].

Hesiod as we have seen makes her succeed Thetis as second wife of Zeus.

The real truth comes out in the fragment of a hymn of Pindar's[3] in which he describes this Olympian wedding.

And first did the Moirai[4] lead Heavenly Themis of the Good Counsels with golden horses along the springs of Okeanos, up the holy ladder of Olympos, along the shining way.

She who was of earth, she who was Earth herself, leaves her home and goes the way of all things divine, up to Olympos.   But, in the very pomp and pageant of her going, we feel she is entering on an alien kingdom.   Hers are human conventions, and it is only by constraint of the Moirai that she goes skyward, there to wed Zeus and to summon his councils.

Not less clearly and with more inherent propriety does Dike belong to Hades, the kingdom of Plouton.   When Antigone[5] is

---

[1] Eur. *Med.* 169

ἐπιβοᾶται
Θέμιν εὐκταίαν Ζῆνά θ'.

And again, 208

τὰν Ζηνὸς ὁρκίαν Θέμιν.

[2] Pind. *Ol.* viii. 21

ἔνθα Σώτειρα Διὸς ξενίου
πάρεδρος ἀσκεῖται Θέμις.

[3] Christ, *Frg.* 29, 30, *v.* 7.   This hymn, like the Paean quoted above, may very probably have been written for the Daphnephoria to accompany the procession of the Κοπο.   See *supra*, p. 439.

[4] In a lyric fragment (Bergk, *adesp.* 139) the Fates are made to escort the three Horai, Eunomia, Dike and Eirene.

Κλωθὼ Λάχεσίς τ' εὐώλενοι
κοῦραι Νυκτός,
εὐχομένων ἐπακούσατ', οὐράνιαι χθόνιαί τε δαίμονες·
ω πανδείμαντοι, πέμπετ' ἄμμιν
ῥοδόκολπον Εὐνομίαν λιπαροθρόνους τ' ἀδελφάς, Δίκαν
καὶ στεφανηφόρον Εἰράναν.

[5] Soph. *Ant.* 450.

charged with transgression she thus contrasts the law of Zeus and that of the underworld gods.

> 'Yes, for it was not Zeus who heralded
> That edict, no nor she who dwells below,
> Dike, who gave such laws for mortal men.'

Of course, at the time of the general migration to Olympos, a great effort is made to assure the assumption into heaven of Dike as well as Themis. The notion obtained to a certain extent in Olympianized Orphic circles. Dike becomes as a double of Themis assessor of Zeus. So the Orphic Hymn[1].

> Sing the all-seeing eye of Dike fair
> Who sits upon the holy throne of Zeus.

Demosthenes[2] pleads with his citizens to honour Eunomia and Dike holy and unswerving,

Whom Orpheus, who instituted our most sacred mysteries, declares to be seated by the throne of Zeus.

Orphic literature might proclaim Dike as assessor of Zeus in the highest heavens, but Orphic popular art, like primitive philosophy, knew that her real home was in Hades, by the side of Plouton. On the well-known underworld vases of Lower Italy of which a specimen[3] is given in Fig. 145 a group of figures occurs in the right-hand corner, of which the interpretation is fortunately certain. A seated youth bids farewell to another youth about to start on his journey to the upper world. The seated youth is Theseus.

> ...Sedet aeternumque sedebit
> Infelix Theseus[4].

The youth about to return to the upper world bears a significant name, 'He who runs round,' *Peirithoös*. His periodic cycle leads him inevitably upwards.

By the side of Theseus a woman is seated holding a drawn sword. She is Dike in her later Orphic aspect of Vengeance. Of this happily there is no doubt, as on the fragment of a vase[5] with

[1] LXII.　　　[2] c. *Aristogeit.* xxv. 11, and see *Prolegomena*, p. 507.
[3] Munich, Jahn Cat. 849. *Wiener Vorlegeblätter*, Serie E, Taf. I. For the whole series see *Prolegomena*, p. 601.
[4] Verg. *Æn.* VI. 617.
[5] Carlsruhe, Cat. 258, Hartung, *Arch. Zeit.* p. 263, Taf. XIX., and *Wiener Vorlegeblätter* E, Taf. VI. 3. See also my *Myth. and Mon. Ancient Athens*, p. cxlviii., Fig. 39.

similar design the figure is inscribed ΔIKH. What has this Dike with the drawn sword, this Vengeance incarnate, this denizen of Hades, to do with that Dike we already know, the fixed order of the world, the Way of Nature? The fragment of another vase-painting[1] may help us to understand. It is reproduced in Fig. 146, and is obviously a portion of a design similar to that in Fig. 144, though of earlier and much finer workmanship.

To the right is the palace of Hades and in it is seated Persephone. To her left we may safely restore Plouton. To her

FIG. 145.

right stands 'Hekata' with two blazing torches. Close to the palace, as usual, is the figure of Orpheus as Thracian musician or priest. Above him to the left a door, just ajar, leading evidently to the upper air. Close to the door, with her hand upon it, is a winged figure. Above the right wing are letters read variously AIKA and ΔIKA. Dr Dieterich[2] would read ΔIKA, and sees in the winged figure Dike warding the gates of Hades a reminiscence

---

[1] Jalta, Coll. Ruvo, *Monumenti Antichi d. Accademia dei Lincei*, vol. XVI. Tav. III.

[2] *Archiv f. Religionswiss.* XI. 1908, p. 159.

of the Dike who appears as gate-warden of Hades in the prooemium of Parmenides[1].

But to this interesting suggestion there is one obvious objection. If the winged figure be Dike, she is a duplication. Below, in the left-hand corner, is a seated figure with hand upraised, attentive to what goes on above her. Against her is her name ΔIKA, Dike. Of the winged figure a simple explanation lies to hand[2]. The inscription ΔIKA is close to a fracture. By supplying

Fig. 146.

the letters εὐρυ we get Eurydike. The figure who turns at the door is Eurydike herself. Her wings present no difficulty. She is in Hades and hence is conceived of as an *eidolon*.

Moreover—and this is for us the important point—in the light of Eury-dike we understand Dike herself. Eurydike, She of the Wide-Way, is, like Eurysternos, but the ordered form of Earth herself, in her cyclic[3] movement of life and death, her eternal wheel

---

[1] *Supra*, p. 518, note 1.

[2] I offered this explanation in the *Archiv f. Religionswissenschaft*, 1909, p. 411, in a note entitled *Dike oder Eurydike*. Before his lamented death, Dr Dieterich wrote acknowledging my suggestion with the utmost courtesy and kindness, but he pronounced it to his mind 'unwahrscheinlich.'

[3] It is perhaps scarcely needful to note that the Greek philosopher never 'escaped from the wheel'; *revolution* was as near as he could get to *l'Évolution Créatrice*.

of palingenesia. She, the young green Earth, has, as we have seen[1], her yearly Anodos, as Kore, as Semele, as Eurydike. At first she rises of her own motion and alone, as we have seen on many a vase-painting[2]. Later, when the physical significance of her rising is no longer understood, when patriarchy has supplanted matrilinear earth-worship, a human and patrilinear motive is provided. She needs a son or a lover to fetch her up, to carry her down. So we get the rape of Persephone by Hades, of Basile by Echelos, of Helen by Theseus and Peirithoös, the descent of Dionysos to fetch his mother Semele, and, latest and loveliest, the love-story of Orpheus and Eurydike. Here on the Orphic vase-painting we have a reminiscence of the fact that Eurydike really and primarily returned to the upper world alone. Orpheus is there, but he sings on, untouched by, irrelevant to, her going. Dike then, like her prototype Eurydike, represents the eternal cycle of the life of the earth, the temporal sequence of the Horai.

In the light of Dike we understand another element in the underworld vases which has long puzzled scholars. In the palace of Plouton (Fig. 145), above alike the figure of Plouton and Persephone, is suspended a wheel. This wheel has been strangely misunderstood.

We think instinctively of the Wheel of Fortune, and we think rightly. Fortune (Tyche) is the goddess who brings—brings forth, brings to accomplishment. But we add to this notion the notion of retribution.

> Turn Fortune, turn thy Wheel, and lower the proud,

or again,

> He hath put down the mighty from their seat.

Just such a degradation awaited Dike. From being the order of the world, the way of the world, she became the Avenger of those who outstep and overpass the order of the world. But this notion of Vengeance is secondary, not primitive; the wheel to the early Greek would carry no such suggestion.

The powers of the sky were divided in antiquity as we have seen[3] into τὰ μετάρσια and τὰ μετέωρα, the 'weather' and the heavenly bodies. The two are well shown side by side on the

---

[1] *Supra*, p. 418.   [2] *Supra*, pp. 419 and 422.
[3] *Supra*, p. 392.

Gallic altar[1] in Fig. 147.　The thunder and the thunder-god have everything to do with Kratos and Bia, but have no lot or part in Dike; hers is the regular course of the heavenly bodies symbolized by the rotation of the wheel.

FIG. 147.

The Paeonians we remember[2] worshipped the sun in the form of a disk.　At the Daphnephoria[3], sun and moon and stars were represented by globes.　On the archaic Greek mirror in Fig. 136 the sun is a rayed disk with the head of a Kouros.　But these represent rather the stationary aspect of the sun than his perennial motion, his ceaseless *way*.　The going of the sun is drastically represented by the little votive solar chariot[4] in Fig. 148.　The chariot has six wheels and is drawn by one horse.　It contains the solar disk itself.　It is of course the wheel in motion that has

FIG. 148.

power magically to compel the sun to rise.　The wheels in sanctuaries[5] were turned by ropes with the like intent.

[1] In the Maison Carrée at Nismes.　See Gaidoz, *Le Dieu Gaulois du Soleil*, Rev. Arch. VI. 1885, p. 187, Fig. 26.
[2] *Supra*, p. 465.　　　　　　　　　[3] *Supra*, p. 438.
[4] Found at Trundholm.　Sophus Müller, *La Représentation solaire de Trundholm*, Antiquités Scandinaves, Copenhague, 1903, pp. 303—321; and J. Dechelette, *Le Culte du Soleil aux Temps Préhistoriques*, in Rev. Arch. 1909, XIV. p. 94.　For the whole subject see Gaidoz, *Le Dieu Gaulois du Soleil*, in Rev. Arch. 1884, p. 33.
[5] See *Prolegomena*, p. 591.

And here in Greek art representations a curious point may be noticed. The actual wheel, whether solid or spoked, does not appear in Greek symbolism till late. But what we may call the spokes of the wheel and the indication of its going are represented very early in the ornament known as the Swastika[1]. The Swastika has been variously interpreted as a 'croix gammée' and as a reduced simplified kind of wheel. It is really not quite either; it is a symbol combining motion and direction. It is the four points of the compass in motion.

To the Greeks it undoubtedly stood at one time for the Sun. On coins of Thrace we find Mesembria thus written ΜΕΣ卐, Mid-Sun or Mid-Day-town[2]. But on other coins we may with equal probability conjecture that the *swastika,* or rather *triskeles,* represents the Moon. In Fig. 149 we have two Syracusan coins.

Fig. 149.

The three winged legs indicate swift motion. In the coin to the right the rudimentary body, or belly, from which the legs spread has become a human face, a Gorgoneion which symbolizes rather Moon than Sun[3].

The origin of the Swastika is still much disputed. It is found at Hissarlik in the remains of the Second City; it abounds on geometric ware and on the archaic pottery of Cyprus, Rhodes, and Athens. The name we give it is of course Sanskrit: *swastika* is from *su,* well, and *asti,* it is. When the direction of the croix

---

[1] The literature of the ritual wheel and the Swastika is immense. See especially W. Simpson, *The Buddhist Praying Wheel,* 1896, in which the results of most of the earlier literature are collected. Also Goblet d'Alviella, *La Migration des Symboles,* 1891; and M. Goblet d'Alviella's recent work, *Croyances, Rites, Institutions,* 1911, vol. I. chapter 1, *Moulins à prières, Roues magiques et circumambulations.* On p. 80 of the same book is given a very full bibliography of the literature of the Swastika and the cross.

[2] See Prof. Percy Gardner's 'Ares as a Sun-God,' and 'Solar Symbols,' in *Num. Chron.* N.S. vol. xx. p. 12.

[3] For the *triskeles* and *tetraskeles* on coins see Mr Anson's *Numismata Graeca,* part IV. Religion, Pl. xv.—xix. The *triskeles* occurs with special frequency on the coins of Lycia, land of sun-worship.

gammée is to the right it is *swastika*, all is well; when, as much
more rarely, the direction is to the left, 卍, it is *sauvastika*, and
all is evil. The idea is of course not confined to the East. It
lives on to-day in Scotland, as *deisul*, 'sunwise,' and *widershins*.
In college Combination Rooms port wine is still passed round
according to the way of the Sun.

The notion of following the course of the sun is world-wide.
Starting no doubt in practical magic, it ended in a vague feeling
of 'luck.' But it is in India and China that the idea most
developed on the moral side, and India and China best help us
to the understanding of Dike as the *way* of the world and also
as Right and Justice.

The Praying Wheels of the Lamas and of Buddhism generally
have long been the butt of missionaries and of ignorant Anglo-
Indians. But they enshrine a beautiful and deeply religious
thought. When the Lama sets his wheel a-going, it is not merely
that he gets the prayers printed upon it mechanically said. He
finds himself in sympathetic touch with the Wheel of the Universe; he performs the act *Dharma-chakra-pravartana*, 'Justice-
Wheel-Setting in motion.' He dare not turn the wheel contrari-
wise; that were to upset the whole order of Nature. The wheel
moves along and indeed symbolizes the course of *ṛta*. This *ṛta*
rules all the periodic events of nature. It is indeed periodicity
incarnate. The Dawn-Maidens shine in harmony with *ṛta*. The
sun is called the wheel of *ṛta* with twelve spokes, for the year's
course has twelve months. The fire of sacrifice is kindled 'under
the yoking of *ṛta*,' which means under the world order[1].

In man's activity *ṛta* is moral law. In things intellectual it is
satya, truth. Untruth, it is instructive to find, though it is sometimes *asatya*, is more often expressed by *anṛta*. Among the Greeks
too Dike was closely companioned by Aletheia. We remember[2]
that, when Epimenides slept his initiation sleep in the cave of
Diktaean Zeus,

he met with the gods, and with divine intercourse, and with Aletheia
and Dike.

[1] Maurice Bloomfield, *The Religion of the Veda*, 1908, pp. 126, 127.
[2] *Supra*, p. 53.

Parmenides[1] makes Dike reveal

> the unshaken heart of fair-rounded Truth.

Greeks and Indians alike seem to have discerned that the divine Way was also the Truth and the Life.

This notion of the Way, which is also the Right, seems to have existed before the separation of Indian from Iranian. The Vedic *ṛta* is the same word as the Avestan *asha* (*areta*) and the Cuneiform Persian *arta*. Varuna of the Veda, and Ahura Mazda of the Avesta, are divinities closely akin, and

One of the most interesting parallels between Veda and Avesta is that both gods are described as 'the spring of the ṛta, or righteousness.' Varuna is *khā̆rtasya* (Rig-Veda, 2. 28. 5); Ahura Mazda is *ashahe khāo* (Yasna, 10. 4). The words are sound for sound the same[2].

The emphasis of Iranian religion was always strongly on the moral conflict between right and wrong, as figured by the struggle between light and darkness. Dike, who was the *way* of the world, became in Orphic hands Vengeance on the wrong doer, on him who overstepped the *way*. I would again suggest that it is possible that this moral emphasis was due to Persian influence[3].

Closely analogous to Dike and to *ṛta* is the Chinese *tao*, only it seems less moralized and more magical. *Tao* is like Dike the *way*, the way of nature; and man's whole religion, his whole moral effort, is to bring himself into accordance with *tao*. By so doing he becomes a microcosm, and by sympathetic magic can control the world. The calendar not only indicates natural facts, but it prescribes moral doings. *Tao*, like *ṛta*, is potent in all three spheres, in outside nature, in the relation of man to his gods, in the relation of man to man or morality proper; but *Tao*, unlike *ṛta* and Dike, does not seem to include intellectual truth, a matter which does not much concern the magic-ridden Chinaman.

If Dike is the *way*, the order of the going of life, it is not hard to see how she should develop into Vengeance, how her figure

---

[1] Diels, *F.V.S.*[2], p. 115. *v.* 10

χρέω δέ σε πάντα πυθέσθαι,
ἠμὲν ᾿Αληθείης εὐκύκλεος ἀτρεμὲς ἦτορ
ἠδὲ βροτῶν δόξας.

[2] Maurice Bloomfield, *The Religion of the Veda*, 1908, p. 126.

[3] The cuneiform tablets discovered at Pterium (Boghazkoï) show that the syllables *arta*=*ṛta*=*asha* were known as elements in personal names, e.g. *Arta*-shavara, *Arta*tama, as early as 1600 B.C.

should be hard to distinguish from that of Nemesis and even Adrasteia, she from whom none may run away. On coin types the figures of Dike, Nemesis, Tyche, Adrasteia, are only distinguishable by the places at which they are minted, and that only in cases where it is known from literature or inscriptions that particular cults existed. In Fig. 150 *a* a coin of Alexandria[1], struck by Antoninus Pius (A.D. 139—140), we have a seated figure holding in her right hand the scales, in her left the cornucopia. Because she holds the scales she is usually called Dikaiosyne, but the cornucopia is more appropriate to Agathe Tyche, or Fortune. In Fig. 150 *b*, a coin of Markianopolis[2] in Moesia, struck by

a *b*

Fɪɢ. 150.

Heliogabalus, we have a standing figure again holding the scales in her right. In her left is a measuring-rod, at her feet a wheel. Numismatists call her inelegantly 'Nemesis Æquitas,' but why not Dike or Tyche? It is not that there is a late 'syncretism' of these divine figures; they start from one conception and differentiate.

With the Way and the Wheel in our minds we return to Dike in Hades. She sheds a new light on certain other denizens. All the noted criminals are victims of the wheel, they are all of the old order of palingenesia. It is not so much that Olympian, patriarchal malice, condemns these elder potencies of mother-Earth to eternal Hell[3], as that they are forced by their own cyclic nature to die, to go below the bosom of earth, that they may

---

[1] G. Macdonald, *Cat. Hunterian Coll.* 1905, vol. ɪɪɪ. pl. ʟxxxvɪɪɪ. 28, p. 459. Reproduced by Dr Macdonald's kind permission.

[2] H. Posnansky, *Nemesis and Adrasteia*, 1890, pl. ɪ. No. 15. For Tyche with the scales see Bergk, *Adespot.* 139 Τύχα μερόπων ἀρχά...καὶ τὸ τεᾷ πλάστιγγι δοθέν...

[3] A view I have previously expressed (see *Prolegomena*, p. 607), but which I now see requires restatement.

rise again.   Each and all of them must say with the initiated Orphic:

'I have sunk beneath the bosom of Despoina, Queen of the Underworld[1].'

Each and all must be born anew with the New Birth of the world.   Such is the Way.

In Fig. 146, beneath the palace of Plouton, are the Erinyes with snakes in their hair.   But they are not ministers of Vengeance.   The inscription calls them (Eu)menides, and near them, the goddesses of new life, is a little upspringing tree.   Plouton himself is not the sullen terror of the underworld, he is the Wealth that rises up from the Earth in spring.   Hekate, with her torches, is not the spectre of the night, she is the life-giving

Fig. 151.

moon that waxes and wanes, the very spirit of palingenesia. Theseus is made by the orthodox to sit for ever on the rock, but Dike, the Way, lets Peirithoös, the Wheel, return to the upper air. Ixion on his wheel is not tormented; by the might of Dike he, the Sun-God, is ceaselessly turning.   It is his function, not his fate.   Herakles goes down to Hades, not once to fetch up Cerberus, but day by day at sunset, that he may rise again on the morrow[2].

This notion of Dike explains sometimes a grouping of criminals that might otherwise be unmeaning.   In Fig. 151 we have a design from a black-figured amphora[3].   The Danaides are filling their cask, and by their side is Sisyphos rolling his pitiless stone up

---

[1] Δέσποινας δ' ὑπὸ κόλπον ἔδυν χθονίας βασιλείας.   See *Prolegomena*, p. 594.
[2] So Orpheus must always return that he may reemerge.   When the real function of Eurydike is forgotten, the story of her looking back is invented to account for her return.
[3] Munich, Jahn Cat. 153.   See *Prolegomena*, p. 617.

the hill. Sisyphos is the ancient Titan, the Sun himself. His labour is no penalty, it is the course of Dike, it is periodic, eternally incumbent. So too with the Danaides; they are well-nymphs, but also projections of the ancient rain-making ceremonies, they carry water to make rain[1]. Their labour too is ceaseless, periodic. They are part of the eternal *dike* of nature.

The design in Fig. 152 is from the Castle Howard[2] krater

Fig. 152.

signed by Python. It shows in striking contrast the Olympian order of things. Zeus is there, Zeus of the sky, but unlike the old Titan Sisyphos who 'has labour all his days' Zeus lives at ease, remote. He has ceased to *be* a thunderstorm, instead he orders one. The Danaides are now Hyades, Rain-nymphs. They still pour water from their hydriae, but they have mounted to high heaven, and they have ceased to be recurrent, periodic; they no longer ceaselessly pour water into leaky vessels. To Olympian theology, in its ignorance and ineptitude, 'recurrent' had come to spell 'fruitless'; the way of life was envisaged as an immutable sterility and therefore rejected.

[1] I owe this interpretation to Mr A. B. Cook; it is a marked advance on my old view (*Prolegomena*, p. 621) that the Danaides were merely well-nymphs.

[2] Now in the British Museum, Cat. F. 149. For details of the subject, the quenching of the great pyre of Alkmena, see *J. H. S.* XI. p. 225.

Dike then, the Way, rules in the underworld, she and her subjects, the year and day daimones. She is there of necessity, as the Living Way, the course of Nature, before Orphic theology placed her there as the spirit of Vengeance. Regarding Dike as the Way, the order of living, of Nature, we see at once that she, eldest and chief of the Horai, might well be invoked by the Kouretes to welcome the Year. But here we come straight up against our final difficulty, a difficulty we have ignored in considering *ṛta* and *asha* and *tao*, but that has all the time been dogging our steps. Why does man make this strange confusion between moral right and natural law? Why is Themis the mother of Dike, and why must the Kouretes, if they want a good harvest, 'leap' not only for Dike and the Horai but for 'goodly Themis'?

Deep-rooted in man's heart is the pathetic conviction that moral goodness and material prosperity go together, that, if man keep the *ṛta*, he can magically affect for good nature's ordered going. When the Olympians became fully humanized, and sacramentalism was replaced by gift-sacrifice, the notion slightly altered its form. The gods it was now felt were bound in honour to bestow on their faithful worshippers a *quid pro quo*. The idea is no-wise confined to the Greeks. The Psalmist, whose sheltered outlook on life was traditional and religious rather than realistic, says confidently,

'I have been young, and now am old,
And yet saw I never the righteous forsaken,
Nor his seed begging their bread[1].'

Hesiod[2] *mutatis mutandis* cherishes the same conviction,

Whoso to stranger and to kinsmen deal
Straight judgments, ne'er o'erpassing Justice' bounds,
Their city flowers, and their folk blossometh,
And in their land is Peace the Nurse of children.
Never on them doth Zeus bring grievous war.
Famine and strife are far from men who deal
Straight judgments, feast and song are all their toil.
For them earth bears rich food; the mountain oak
Rears high her acorns, midway holds her bees.
The fleecy sheep go heavy with thick wool,
And wives bear children like unto their sires.
All good things blossom; never need they tempt
The barren sea, for them earth bears her grain.

[1] Ps. xxxvii. 25.   [2] *Op.* 225.

The hymn to the Kouretes echoes the sentiments of Hesiod, save that the sea-going Cretans have learnt to 'leap for their ships.'

Then, when the social life finds its focus in the figure of a king, on his goodness and the justice of his ruling, on his Dike, his Way, the prosperity of his people depends. He himself must be free from blemish, morally and physically (ἀμύμων), and he must uphold right judgments (εὐδικίας). Odysseus[1] tells Penelope that she need fear no breath of blame, her fame goes up to wide heaven.

'As doth the fame of a blameless king, one that fears the gods and reigns among men, many and mighty, maintaining right, and the black earth bears wheat and barley, and the trees are laden with fruit, and the sheep bring forth and fail not, and the sea gives store of fish, and all out of his good guidance, and the people prosper under him.'

This sympathy, this almost identity of the Way of Man and the Way of Nature, comes out very beautifully in the Golden Lamb chorus of the *Electra* of Euripides[2]. The chorus goes back in spirit to the First Sin, the bloodfeud of the drama. This was to them, in their tribal way of thinking, *the* First Sin of the entire world; and after it, the whole order of the universe was changed. Atreus, as king, had a mascot, a Golden Lamb, on which the luck of the tribe depended. Thyestes stole the Lamb and thereby claimed and won the kingship.

> Then, then the world was changed,   [Strophe 2
> And the Father, where they ranged,
> Shook the golden stars and glowing,
> And the great Sun stood deranged
> In the glory of his going.
>
> Lo from that day forth, the East
> Bears the sunrise on his breast,
> And the flaming Day in heaven
> Down the dim ways of the west
> Driveth, to be lost at even.
>
> The wet clouds to Northward beat;
> And Lord Ammon's desert seat
> Crieth from the South, unslaken
> For the dews that once were sweet,
> For the rain that God hath taken.

[1] Hom. *Od.* xix. 111
εὐδικίας ἀνέχῃσι, φέρῃσι δὲ γαῖα μέλαινα
πυροὺς καὶ κριθάς κ.τ.λ.   (trans. Butcher and Lang.)
For the whole subject of the king as source of medicine see Dr Frazer, *Lectures on the Early History of the Kingship*, 1905, *passim*. For Oedipus as medicine king see Professor Murray's translation of *Oedipus, King of Thebes*, p. 88, note to verse 21.

[2] *vv.* 699—746. For the origin of the myth see Professor Murray's note to his translation of the *Electra*, p. 94. For the Lamb as mascot see Mr A. B. Cook, *Zeus*, ch. i. § 6 (f), iv.

The reversal of nature is complete. Not only τὰ μετέωρα in their ordered goings, but even τὰ μετάρσια, the 'weather,' is upset.

Then in the Antistrophe comes a note, surely Euripidean, of scepticism. Can man really affect nature, is Themis really potent over Physis?

> 'Tis a children's tale, that old   [Antistrophe 2
>   Shepherds on far hills have told;
> And we reck not of their telling,
>   Deem not that the Sun of gold
> Ever turned his fiery dwelling,
>
>   Or beat backward in the sky,
>   For the wrongs of man, the cry
> Of his ailing tribes assembled,
>   To do justly, ere they die.
> Once, men told the tale, and trembled;
>
>   Fearing God, O Queen: whom thou
>   Hast forgotten, till thy brow
> With old blood is dark and haunted.
>   And thy brethren, even now,
> Walk among the stars, enchanted.

Because Electra slew her mother, will the moon change her course or veil her face? The chorus refuse to believe it. Such a doctrine is contrary to all experience, though it accords, it would seem, with common sense, that is with accepted tradition. Why did men ever accept a doctrine disproved day by day, and from the outset preposterous? For a reason put very simply by the Greeks. Because *Themis was the mother of Dike*; the social conscience, the social structure, gave birth, not of course to the order of nature, but to man's conception, his representation, of that order[1].

To man in the totemistic stage of thinking, Dike and Themis, natural order and social order, are not distinguished, not even distinguishable. Plants and animals are part of his group[2], factors in his social structure. It is not that he takes them under his protection; they are his equals, his fellow-tribesmen; naturally they obey the same law, or rather, for definite law is not yet, they are part of the same social structure, they follow the same social custom. If one member of that body suffer, or prosper, all the

---

[1] This position will be more fully established in Mr F. M. Cornford's *From Religion to Philosophy*.

[2] *Supra*, p. 120.

other members suffer or prosper with him.   The oneness of group life and collective consciousness makes this axiomatic.

When a man, living in a totemistic social structure, believes that, by observing his group-customs, he can help the crops to grow, this nowise requires explanation.   Such a faith, indeed, is of the essence of totemistic thinking.   What *does* seem strange is that, when group-thinking or emotion makes way for individual reason, a faith disproved by even the most superficial observation should still be upheld.   The reason is of course simple.   Religious beliefs, as we have seen, are but presentations, projections, of θέμιστες, of utterances, ordinances, of the social conscience.   Begotten by one social structure, they long survive its dissolution. We believe that a pestilence or a famine is consequent on some national wrong-doing, not because we have observed facts and noted such a sequence, but because we once thought and lived totemistically and the habits of totemistic thinking still cling. Moreover they take shape in dogmas and in ritual, faithfully and blindly[1] handed down from generation to generation.

To any rational thinker it is at once clear that Dike, Natural Order, and Themis, Social Order, are not the same, nay even they are not mother and daughter; they stand at the two poles remote and even alien.   Natural Law is from the beginning; from the first pulse of life, nay even before the beginning of that specialized movement which we know as life, it rules over what we call the inorganic.   Social Order, morality, 'goodness' is not in nature at the outset; it only appears with 'man her last work.'

A strange mystery it is that Nature, omnipotent but blind, in the revolutions of her secular hurryings through the abysses of space, has brought forth at last a child, subject still to her power, but gifted with sight, with knowledge of good and evil, with the capacity of judging all the works of his unthinking Mother[2].

The mystic will claim that life is one indivisible movement[3],

---

[1] So remote is ritual from reason that Dr Beck (*Nachahmung*, p. 165) gives the following suggestive, though I think inadequate, definition of ritual: 'So entstand der Kultus und die Mythologie nach meiner Theorie aus gedeuteten Gewohnheitshandlungen.   Kultisch nennen wir aber nur Handlungen die ihrem Erfolg nach unzweckmässig waren.'

[2] Bertrand Russell, 'The Free Man's Worship,' *Independent Review*, 1903. Reprinted in *Philosophical Essays*, 1910, p. 59.

[3] H. Bergson, *La Perception du Changement*, Conférences faites à Oxford, p. 18, 'Nous devons nous représenter tout changement, tout mouvement, comme absolument indivisibles.'   *Op. cit.* p. 2, 'Mon état d'âme en avançant sur la route du temps s'enfle continuellement de la durée qu'il ramasse; il fait, pour ainsi dire, boule de neige avec lui-même.'

one, if he prefers it, ever accumulating snowball. We gladly
agree. But to say that Alpha is Omega, the end is as the
beginning, that life and force are the same as moral good, and
to label the mystical marriage of the two 'God,' is to darken
counsel. It is to deny that very change and movement which
is life, it is to banish from a unified and sterilized universe
'l'Évolution Créatrice.'

The religious man who in the supposed interests of morality
maintains this creed is, it may be, *splendide mendax*. He is more ;
he is one in heart and soul with his brother the antique medicine
priest, the Koures. With him he leaps on high, crowning his
magical invocation of Spring and the Seasons with the cry

$$\theta\acute{o}\rho\epsilon\ \kappa'\ \grave{\epsilon}\varsigma\ \Theta\acute{\epsilon}\mu\iota\nu\ \kappa\alpha\lambda\acute{\alpha}\nu.$$

Note to p. 511. For new material as to Orphism see Michael Tierney, 'A new
ritual of the Orphic Mysteries' in *The Classical Quarterly*, April 1922, p. 77.

Note to p. 513. The well-spring of Ennoia I hope shortly to show is of Oriental
provenance. But my evidence is as yet incomplete.

Note to p. 535. For a possible modern survival of the ritual of the Kouretes in
the dance of the Seises in Seville Cathedral see my *Epilegomena*, p. 26, note 2, and
for the magical leaping dance still carried on at Echternach on Whit-Tuesday see
my *Reminiscences*, Hogarth Press, 1925. For the dance of Herodias' daughter as a
ritual survival of the dance of the Eniautos-daimon see my paper on the 'Head of
John Baptist,' *Classical Review*, 1916, p. 216. This includes a brief notice of the
Vertep daimon plays of White Russia.

PREFACE TO THE SECOND EDITION

IT WAS, I confess, with grave misgivings that I began the revision of *Themis*. Much water had flowed, was still flowing swiftly under the archaeological bridge. I feared that my work might have to be 'scrapped,' or at least—to borrow the drastic phrase of a young reviewer—that 'nine-tenths of the book would be better away.' It is difficult justly to appraise one's own work, but I have tried to be dispassionate and I have decided to let *Themis* stand, substantially unaltered.

I see now what I scarcely realized in the first excitement of writing that, though prompted and indeed forced upon me by a great archaeological discovery, the book is really addressed not so much to the specialist as to the thinker generally. It is in a word a study of herd-suggestion, or, as we now put it, communal psychology. Its object is the analysis of the Eniautos- or Year-Daimon, who lies behind each and every primitive god; of the Eniautos-Daimon and of his ritual. That the gods and rituals examined are Greek is incidental to my own specialism.

My own sobriety and soundness of judgment I might well doubt, but I have confidence in that of Dr Walter Leaf. In his *Homer and History* he has to my great satisfaction and pleasure accepted the Eniautos-Daimon as an integral factor of pre- and post-Homeric religion. My faith in the Daimon is further confirmed by a happy coincidence. By far the most important accession to this second edition is the new material which Professor Gilbert Murray has added to his excursus. At the moment of sailing for America he wrote to me: 'I really think that the evidence of Herodotus

Book II makes the business (i.e. the Osirian or daimonic nature of Dionysos and his πάθη) so clear as almost to destroy its interest.' Yes, the controversy once so burning is now at rest. This victory is to me tinged with sadness, for the protantagonist of the Eniautos-Daimon, Professor Ridgeway, has gone where the noise of battle is for ever hushed.

But though the main argument of *Themis* stands, I think, secure, this is not to say she is flawless, and I would offer some words of explanation and apology.

My critics have blamed me, and justly, for my intemperate antipathy to the Olympians. Reading *Five Stages of Greek Religion* I see more clearly the debt we owe to these Olympians for 'slaying the old blind dragon' still unreasonably dear to me. Moreover the psychology of Freud has taught me that the full-blown god, the Olympian, has a biological function which could never be adequately filled by the *daimon*. I have therefore already in my *Epilegomena* chanted a half reluctant palinode. Disciple as I am in this matter of Nietzsche, I ought never to have forgotten that humanity needs not only the intoxication of Dionysos the daimon (who is the escape into the suffering will behind phenomena), but also, and perhaps even more, that 'appeasement in form' which is Apollo the Olympian.

To the orthodox among my contemporaries, and to the younger reactionaries, *Themis* has appeared dangerous. Their fear is justified. A hand was laid upon their ark. A cultured policeman, a member of the Working Men's College, whom I was privileged to entertain at Cambridge, said to me, 'I used to believe everything they told me, but, thank God, I read the *Golden Bough*, and I've been a free-thinker ever since.' I am no obscurantist and I am proud to have lived to hear the same said of *Themis*. I proffer my 'dangerous' *Themis* to a new generation, better fitted than my own to safe-guard its own mentality.

Chiefest among the joys that long life brings to the scholar and researcher is this—that he lives to hail new lights on his horizon, lights that he himself could never have lit. Of the importance of communal psychology I was already well—some said too well—aware. *Themis* however was already in print when I came to know Dr Rivers and to grasp the importance of the intensive study of the social unit. In 1924 when Dr Rivers' *Social Organization*, edited by W. J. Perry and prefaced by Professor G. Elliot Smith, came to me for review I felt in reading it that almost terrified excitement and delight which always herald the advent of new truth. A younger generation nurtured on our old evolutionism, our comparative mythology, and, even, on our communal psychology, had mounted on our shoulders and seen *new* lands to be explored by *new* methods. The lure of the unknown, the voice of the eternal charmer, was again in our ears, and one aged Athenian, at least, could not play the deaf adder.

Perhaps I was prejudiced, for I found to my joy that most of my own old heresies that had seemed to my contemporaries so 'rash' were accepted by the new school, almost as postulates. Such heresies were: that gods and religious ideas generally reflect the social activities of the worshipper; that the food-supply is of primary importance for religion; that the *daimon* precedes the full-blown god; that the Great Mother is prior to the masculine divinities. But the real delight was to find that these notions which for me, with my narrow classical training, had been, I confess, largely *a priori* guesses had become for the new school matter of historical certainty, based on definite facts, and substantiated by a touch-and-handle knowledge and a sort of robust common-sense to which I could lay no claim. To find myself thus out-dated was sheer joy.

Fourteen years have passed since the appearance of *Themis*. Between the two editions lies the great war which shattered much of academic tradition, scattered my fellow-workers all over Europe to be killed or drilled, and drove me, for I am no Archimedes, to fly from Greece and seek sanctuary in other languages and civilisations—Russian, Oriental, and, finally, Scandinavian—bringing with them no bitter tang of remembrance. For nearly ten years

I never opened a Greek book. It may be that the bibliographic notes appended to each chapter show in consequence some lacunae. Such lacunae can however easily be filled by reference to the index of that mine of learning *Zeus.*

I would also ask all serious students to consult Adolphe Reinach's review of—or rather treatise on—my first edition. It appeared in the *Revue de l'histoire des Religions* (1914) and its fifty pages are charged with valuable references. Adolphe Reinach fell in the battle of the Marne. My thanks for his searching yet sympathetic criticism I lay upon his grave.

The long interlude has anyhow brought this gain: my eyes are now cleared from the mists of old and obsolete controversy, and I come back with energy renewed by the contact of new material, of other minds, and newer methods. What remains to me of years and strength I hope to devote to re-examining, in the light shed by the new 'diffusionist' school, Orphic Mysteries, and, especially, Orphic eschatology. Some soundings in these perilous waters I have already made. But for the most part I must set sail in seas as yet for me uncharted. 'It may be that the gulfs will wash us down.'

J. E. H.

INTRODUCTION

THE title of this book and its relation to my *Prolegomena* may call for a word of explanation.

In the *Prolegomena* I was chiefly concerned to show that the religion of Homer was no more primitive than his language. The Olympian gods—that is, the anthropomorphic gods of Homer and Pheidias and the mythographers—seemed to me like a bouquet of cut-flowers whose bloom is brief, because they have been severed from their roots. To find those roots we must burrow deep into a lower stratum of thought, into those chthonic cults which underlay their life and from which sprang all their brilliant blossoming.

So swift has been the advance in science or rather in historical imagination, so complete the shift of standpoint, that it has become difficult to conceive that, in 1903, any such protest was needed. Since the appearance of Professor Murray's *Rise of the Greek Epic* we realize how late and how enlightened was the compromise represented by these Olympians. We can even picture to ourselves the process by which their divinity was shorn of each and every 'mystical or monstrous' attribute.

When in 1907 a second edition of my book was called for, its theories seemed to me already belated. My sense of the superficiality of Homer's gods had deepened to a conviction that these Olympians were not only non-primitive, but positively in a sense non-religious. If they were not, for religion, starting-points, they were certainly not satisfactory goals. On the other hand, the cultus of Dionysos and Orpheus seemed to me, whatever its errors and licenses, essentially religious. I was therefore compelled reluctantly to face the question, what meaning did I attach to the word *religion*? My instinct was to condemn the Olympians as *non*-religious, because really the products of art and literature though posing as divinities. Could this instinct stand the test of examination, or was it merely a temperamental prejudice masquerading as a reasoned principle?

The problem might have continued ineffectively to haunt me, and probably to paralyse my investigations, had not light come rather suddenly from unexpected quarters, from philosophy and social psychology. To France I owe a double debt, indirect but profound, and first and foremost to Professor Henri Bergson.

It is characteristic always of a work of genius that it casts, as it were, a great search light into dark places far beyond its own immediate province. Things unseen before or insignificant shine out in luminous projection. The sudden flash may dazzle, the focus be misleading or even false; but the light is real. New tracks open out before us, and we must needs set forth through the long uncharted shadows.

It is no part of Professor Bergson's present programme, so far as I understand it, to analyse and define the nature and function of religion. But when, four years ago, I first read his *L'Évolution Créatrice*, I saw, dimly at first, but with ever increasing clearness, how deep was the gulf between Dionysos the mystery-god and that Olympos he might never really enter. I knew the reason of my own profound discontent. I saw in a word that Dionysos, with every other mystery-god, was an instinctive attempt to express what Professor Bergson calls *durée*, that life which is one, indivisible and yet ceaselessly changing. I saw on the other hand that the Olympians, amid all their atmosphere of romance and all their redeeming vices, were really creations of what Professor William James called 'monarchical deism.' Such deities are not an instinctive expression, but a late and conscious representation, a work of analysis, of reflection and intelligence. Primitive religion was not, as I had drifted into thinking, a tissue of errors leading to mistaken conduct; rather it was a web of practices emphasizing particular parts of life, issuing necessarily in representations and ultimately dying out into abstract conceptions. A statement like this when condensed is necessarily somewhat cryptic. In the concrete instances to be adduced from Greek religion, it will become I hope abundantly clear. I may add that, save perhaps for a few sentences in the last two chapters, every word of my book is, I hope, intelligible without any understanding of Professor Bergson's philosophy.

My second debt is to a thinker whose temperament, manner and method are markedly different, and whose philosophy is, I believe, in France, accounted as alien to that of Professor Bergson, Professor Émile Durkheim.

In the light of *L'Évolution Créatrice, Matière et Mémoire* and *Les Données Immédiates de la Conscience* I had come to see the real distinction between the mystery-god Dionysos and the Olympians. In the light of Professor Durkheim's *De la Définition des Phénomènes Religieux, Représentations Individuelles et Représentations Collectives* and *Sociologie Religieuse et Théorie de la Connaissance*, I saw why Dionysos, the mystery-god, who is the expression and representation of *durée*, is, alone among Greek divinities, constantly attended by a thiasos, a matter cardinal for the understanding of his nature. The mystery-god arises out of those instincts, emotions, desires which attend and express life; but these emotions, desires, instincts, in so far as they are religious, are at the outset rather of a group than of individual consciousness. The whole history of epistemology is the history of the evolution of clear, individual, rational thought, out of the haze of collective and sometimes contradictory representations. It is a necessary and most important corollary to this doctrine, that the form taken by the divinity reflects the social structure of the group to which the divinity belongs. Dionysos is the Son of his Mother because he issues from a matrilinear-group.

These two ideas, (1) that the mystery-god and the Olympian express respectively, the one *durée*, life, and the other the action of conscious intelligence which reflects on and analyses life, and (2) that, among primitive peoples, religion reflects *collective* feeling and *collective* thinking, underlie my whole argument and were indeed the cause and impulse of my book. I felt that these two principles had altered my whole outlook on my own subject, and that, in the light of them, I must needs reexamine the whole material—a task at present only partially achieved.

I am however no philosopher and still more no sociologist.

All this intellectual stir and ferment might for me have remained sterile or at least have taken no definite form, but for an archaeological discovery, the finding at Palaikastro of the *Hymn of the Kouretes*. In commenting on this Hymn, discovered in the temple of Diktaean Zeus, I found to my delight that we had in it a text that embodied this very group-thinking, or rather group-emotion towards life, which I had begun to see must underlie all primitive religious representations. The Hymn sung by the Kouretes invoked a daimon, the greatest Kouros, who was clearly the projection of a thiasos of his worshippers. It accompanied a magical dance and was the vehicle of a primitive sacramental cult. In the detailed analysis of the Hymn we should come, I felt, to understand the essence of a mystery-religion and incidentally the reason also why the Olympians failed to satisfy the religious instinct. The Hymn of the Kouretes furnished for my book its natural and necessary plot.

In the pages that follow, subjects apparently unconnected will come in for discussion. We shall have to consider, for example, magic, *mana*, *tabu*, the Olympic games, the Drama, Sacramentalism, Carnivals, Hero-worship, Initiation Ceremonies and the Platonic doctrine of Anamnesis. All these matters, seemingly so disparate, in reality cluster round the Hymn, and can really only be understood in connection with the two principles already laid down. If the reader will be good enough to hold these two clues firmly in his hand, the windings of the labyrinth will be to him no perplexity. The course is plain before us as follows.

Chapter I is devoted to the analysis of the Hymn. The Kouretes are found to represent the initiated young men of a matrilinear group. The Daimon they invoke is, not the Father of Gods and Men, but the Greatest Kouros. He springs from the social emphasis of the rite of initiation, the central ceremony of which was a *dromenon* or enaction of the New Birth into the tribe. Among primitive peoples the child, by his first natural birth, belongs to his mother, his life is of her life. By his Second Birth at Initiation, he is made one with the life of his group, his 'soul is congregationalized,' he is received into his church, his thiasos. The new life emphasized is group life. The unity of the group is *represented* by the figure of the Daimon. The Kouros stands for the unity of the Kouretes, the Bacchos for the thiasos of Bacchoi.

Since the religious conception of a Daimon arises from a *dromenon*, it is of the first importance to be clear as to what a *dromenon* is. The second chapter is devoted to its psychological analysis. The *dromenon* in its sacral sense is, not merely a thing done, but a thing *re*-done, or *pre*-done with magical intent. The magical dance of the Kouretes is a primitive form of *dromenon*, it commemorates or anticipates, in order magically to induce, a New Birth. The Dithyramb, from which the drama arose, was also a *dromenon* of the New Birth. In the drama then we may expect to find survivals of a ritual akin to that of the Kouretes. Further, the *dromenon* is a thing which, like the drama, is collectively performed. Its basis or kernel is a *thiasos* or *choros*.

So far attention has been concentrated on Professor Durkheim's principle that religious representation arises from *collective* action and emotion. This emotion necessarily has its objects, and they prove to be such as occur in other primitive societies. I have studied especially two rites: (1) the Rite of the *Thunders* and (2) the *Omophagia* (Chapters III, IV, and V). The Thunder-Rite emphasizes man's reaction towards, and, in a sense, his desire for union with, the most striking manifestation of force in the universe around him. The emotions that arise out of similar reactions are expressed in such savage terms and conceptions as *Mana, Orenda, Wa-kon'-da*. In Greek religion this stage, owing to the Greek tendency to swift impersonation, is much obscured, but traces of it survive in such conceptions as Kratos and Bia, Styx, Horkos, μένος, θυμός and the like. Such sanctities, such *foci* of attention precede divinities and even daimones, and it is the manipulation of such sanctities that issues in the notions and practices of magic and *tabu* discussed in Chapter IV.

Magic, it is seen, though it may imply a large amount of mistaken science, arises primarily from a *dromenon*, a rite which emphasizes, and aims at inducing, man's collective desire for union with or dominion over outside powers. The kernel and essence of magic is best seen in the second Kouretic rite of initiation, the sacramental feast of the Omophagia. Sacraments lie at the heart of religion and sacraments can only be understood in the light of totemistic thinking, which may long survive any definite totemistic social structure. To the meaning of the word *sacrament* Chapter V is devoted.

Totemism, it is found, is the utterance of two kinds of unity and solidarity, that of man with his group of fellow men, and that of the human group with some group of plants or animals. Sacramentalism stands for the absorption by man of the *mana* of nonman. Gift-sacrifice implies the severance of man from that outside *mana* which man has externalized, objectified into a god. Totemistic thinking knows no god; it creates sanctities but not divinities. These animal and plant group-sanctities live on in the plant and animal forms the mystery-god can assume at will.

The Omophagia was a *dais* or communal meal. Since food is the main source or at least support of life, sacraments among primitive peoples tend to take the form of meals, though other means of contact, such as rubbing and washing, are in use. As food was primitive man's main focus of interest, it was soon observed that most food-supplies were seasonal and therefore recurrent. Hence arose the seasonal *dromenon* with its attendant sacrifice. In Greece the chief seasonal *dromenon* seems to have been in the spring; its object, the magical inducement of fresh life, for man, for other animals and for plants. A particular form of this spring rite was the Dithyramb. In Chapter VI this is discussed in connection with the famous Hagia Triada sarcophagos.

From the spring *dromenon* with its magical intent of the renewal of the year, arose two of the main factors in Greek religious life and indeed in Greek civilization: (1) the *agones* or athletic contests, and (2) that other contest significantly bearing the same name, the *agon* of the drama. Different though they seem, and different as in fact they became, they arose from the same root, the spring *dromenon* conceived of as a conflict, a dramatic setting forth of the natural happening of the spring. This *drama* might with equal appropriateness be represented as a Death followed by a Rebirth or as a contest followed by a victory. Chapter VII, by Mr Cornford, deals with the greatest of the athletic *agones* of Greece, the Olympic Games, as arising from a race of the Kouretes. The victor in the race became the daimon of the year, or, to give him a Greek name, the Eniautos-Daimon. In the victor is incarnate at once the daimon of the group and the 'luck' of the year. It is this δαίμων γέννης who is the real object of commemoration in Pindar's *Odes*; hence the prominence of mythical elements. The particular hero is commemorated rather as functionary than as individual personality.

And here I owe to the reader an apology, or at least an explanation, for the introduction of a new term. I am well aware that no such conjunction as Eniautos-Daimon exists in Greek. I did not set out to invent any such word, nor did I even foresee its employment; it simply grew on my hands from sheer necessity. Dr Frazer, following Mannhardt, gave us 'Tree-Spirit, Corn-Spirit, Vegetation Spirit,' and the use of these terms has incalculably enlarged our outlook. My own debt to Dr Frazer is immeasurable. But even 'Vegetation Spirit' is inadequate. A word was wanted that should include not only vegetation, but the whole world-process of decay, death, renewal. I prefer 'Eniautos' to 'year' because to us 'year' means something definitely chronological, a precise segment as it were of spatialized time; whereas *Eniautos*, as contrasted with *etos*, means a *period* in the etymological sense, a cycle of waxing and waning. This notion is, I believe, implicitly though not always explicitly, a cardinal factor in Greek religion. Beyond it, to anything like our modern notion of non-recurrent evolution, the Greek never advanced. I prefer the word *daimon* to 'spirit' because, as I try to show (in Chapter VIII), *daimon* has connotations unknown to our English 'spirit.'

At this point, before passing to the second great development from the spring-festival, the drama, recent controversy compelled a halt. Euhemerists of all dates, and quite recently. Professor Ridgeway, have maintained that agonistic festivals and drama alike take their rise, not in magical ceremonial nor in the worship of a god or daimon, but in funeral ceremonies at the grave of some historical individual, a dead hero or chieftain. Totemism, vegetation spirits and the like are, according to Professor Ridgeway, secondary phenomena; the primary principle is the existence of the individual soul after death and the necessity for placating it. Now it is indisputable that, at agonistic festivals and in the drama, *heroes* are commemorated. For his emphasis of this fact and its relations to the *origines* of drama we all owe a deep debt to Professor Ridgeway. But the analysis of the term *hero* goes to show that the main factor in a hero is that very being whom Professor Ridgeway would reject or ignore, the Eniautos-Daimon himself. Chapter VIII is devoted to the analysis of the term *hero*, with results as follows.

The *hero* on examination turns out to be, not a historical great man who happens to be dead, but a dead ancestor performing his due functions as such, who may in particular cases happen to have been a historical great man. As hero he is a functionary; he wears the mask and absorbs the ritual of an Eniautos-Daimon. The myths of the *heroes* of Athens, from Cecrops to Theseus, show them as kings, that is as functionaries, and, in primitive times, these functionaries assume snake-form. The daimon-functionary represents the permanent life of the group. The individual dies, but the group and its incarnation the king survive. *Le roi est mort, vive le roi.* From these two facts, of group permanency and individual death, arose the notion of reincarnation, *palingenesia*. Moreover, since the group included plants and animals as well as human members, and these were linked by a common life, the rebirth of ancestors and the renewed fertility of the earth went on *pari passu*. Hence the *Intichiuma* ceremonies of Central Australians, hence the Revocation of ghosts at the Athenian *Anthesteria*. Gradually, as the group focussed on its king, the daimones of fertility, the collective ancestors, focussed on to an Agathos Daimon, a spirit of fertility, again figured as a snake.

The later Attic heroes Ion and Theseus, unlike the earlier Cecrops and Erechtheus, do not assume snake-form. None the less they are functionaries rather than individual personalities—Ion a mere eponym, a group projection of the Ionians, and Theseus a *hero* because, as his mythology makes manifest, he took on the ritual and functions of the Eniautos-Daimon. This is clearly evidenced by his festival the Oschophoria, which can be reconstructed, partly from the recorded *mythos*, partly from the *dromena*. The principal factors are the *agon* or contest, the *pathos* a defeat or death, the triumphant reappearance or rebirth, the Epiphany. In a word the ritual of the Eniautos-Daimon is substantially the same as the ceremony of death and resurrection enacted as a rite of tribal initiation. This ritual with its attendant *mythos* lives on in the Mummers' Play and Carnival festivals still performed at spring time all over modern Europe. At Athens, reinvigorated by the Homeric saga, it issued in the splendid human diversity of the Attic drama.

What then is the relation between the Homeric saga, which furnishes obviously the plots of Attic dramas, and the ancient ritual of the Eniautos-Daimon as embodied in the Dithyramb or Spring-Dance? The answer is given in Prof. Murray's Excursus. A detailed examination of the plays and fragments extant shows that, while the content of the plots comes from the saga, the ritual forms in which that content is cast derive straight from the *dromena* of the Eniautos-Daimon. Such forms are the Prologue, the Agon, the Pathos, the Messenger's Speech, the Threnos, the Anagnorisis and the final Theophany. Certain of these ritual forms also survive in shadowy fashion in the Games, but here they are well-nigh submerged by a growing athleticism. In the drama literary art by some blind yet happy instinct felt their value and held to them tenaciously.

Thus the ritual of the Eniautos-Daimon, who was at once the representation of the life of the group and the life of nature, issued in agonistic festivals and in the drama. We have now to watch another process, by which the daimon is transformed into a god and finally, for the Greeks, into that form of godhead which we call Olympian. To an analysis of this process the three concluding chapters are devoted.

In Chapter IX the case of Herakles who tried and failed to be a god is examined. The reason of his failure is found to be instructive. Spite of all efforts to make him *athanatos* he remains an Eniautos-Daimon, doomed by function and attributes to a yearly death and resurrection. He is also doomed to eternally recurrent Labours and cannot join the Olympians who 'dwell at ease.' He remains, like Asklepios, the typical half human *Saviour*. Asklepios, from the extraordinary spread of his cult, took rank as a god, but his snake-form enshrines his old daimon nature and prevents his becoming an Olympian. His younger form, Telesphoros, marks him clearly as Eniautos-Daimon.

Having seen how and why two daimones failed to become Olympians we have next to watch the transformation of one who succeeded, Apollo.

In the evolution of the Eniautos-Daimon we noted the influence of periodicity; the succession of the seasons was always important because they brought food to man. So far man's eyes are bent on earth as the food-giver. In his social structure the important features are Mother and Son, and, projecting his own emotions into nature round him, he sees in the earth the Mother as food-giver, and in the fruits of the earth her Son, her Kouros, his symbol the blossoming branch of a tree. The first divinity in the sequence of cults at Delphi is Gaia.

But before long he notices that Sky as well as Earth influences his food supply. At first he notes the 'weather,' rain and wind and storm. Next he finds out that the moon measures seasons, and to her he attributes all growth, all waxing and waning. Then his goddess is Phoibe. When later he discovers that the Sun really dominates his food supply, Phoibe gives place to Phoibos, the Moon to the Sun. The shift of attention, of religious focus, from Earth to Sky, tended to remove the gods from man; they were purged but at the price of remoteness. Apollo begins on earth as Agueius and ends in heaven as Phoibos.

Ritual at Delphi, as elsewhere, lagged behind myth and theology. Of the three great Ennaeteric Festivals, two, the *Charila* and the *Herois*, are concerned with the death and resurrection, the Kathodos and Anodos, of the Earth; they are essentially Eniautos Festivals. The third festival, the *Stepterion*, speaks still more clearly. It is the death of the Old Year envisaged as a snake, followed by the birth of the New as a Kouros carrying a branch. The same Kouros, representing Apollo in the *Daphnephoria*, carries a pole from which are hung the moon and sun. The God is thus manifestly a year-daimon. As the Son of his Father and as the god to whom the *epheboi* offered the first-fruits of their hair, he is also the Greatest Kouros. But unlike Dionysos, the other Greatest Kouros, he is a complete Olympian. Wherein lies the difference? An answer is attempted in Chapter X.

It is characteristic of an Olympian, as contrasted with a mystery-god like Dionysos, that his form is rigidly fixed and always human. The Zeus of Pheidias or of Homer cannot readily shift his shape and become a bird, a bull, a snake, a tree. The Olympian has come out from the natural facts that begot him, and has become 'idealized.' The mystery-god was called a bull because he really was a bull—a bull full of vital *mana*, eaten at a communal feast. He died and was re-born, because the world of life which he embodies really dies and is re-born. But as the reflecting worshipper began to idealize his god, it seemed a degradation, if not an absurdity, to suppose that the god was a beast with the brute vitality of a beast. He must have human form and the most beautiful human form; human intellect and the highest human intellect. He must not suffer and fail and die; he must be ever blessed, ageless and deathless. It is only a step further to the conscious philosophy which will deny to God any human frailties, any emotions, any wrath or jealousy, and ultimately any character whatever except dead, unmeaning perfection, incapable of movement or change.

Then at last we know these gods for what they are, intellectual conceptions merely, things of thought bearing but slight relation to life lived. Broadly speaking, these Olympians represent that tendency in thought which is towards reflection, differentiation, clearness, while the Eniautos-Daimon represents that other tendency in religion towards emotion, union, indivisibility. It might almost be said that the Olympians stand for articulate consciousness, the Eniautos-Daimon for the sub-conscious.

Chapter XI brings us back to the Hymn. Whatever the difference between the religion of the Eniautos-Daimon and that of the Olympians, the forms of both these religions depend on, or rather express and represent, the social structure of the worshippers. Above the gods, supreme, eternally dominant, stands the figure of Themis. She is social ordinance, the collective conscience projected, the Law or Custom that is Right.

Una superstitio superis quae reddita divis.

The social structure represented by the Olympians is the same as that of the modern family, it is patrilinear. The figure of Dionysos, his thiasos, and his relation to his mother and the

Maenads, is only to be understood by reference to an earlier social structure, that known as matrilinear. But the all-important point is not *which* particular structure is represented, but the general principle that social structure and the collective conscience which utters itself in social structure, underlie all religion. Themis conditions not only our social relations, but also our whole relation with the outside world. The Kouretes bid their daimon come 'for the Year'; they also bid him, that crops and flocks may prosper, 'leap for fair Themis.'

Ancient faith held, and in part modern religion still holds, that moral excellence and material prosperity must go together, that man by obeying Themis, the Right, can control the Way of Nature. This strange faith, daily disproved by reason, is in part the survival of the old conviction, best seen in totemism, that man and nature form one indivisible whole. A breach of Themis would offend your neighbours and produce quarrels; quite equally it would offend the river or the earth and produce floods or famine. His emotion towards this unity the Greek uttered at first in the vague shape of a daimon, later, more intellectually, in the clear-cut figure of an Olympian god. But behind Gaia the Mother, and above even Zeus the Father, stands always the figure of Themis.

Such in brief is the argument. And here it would be perhaps discreet to pause. I have neither desire nor aptitude for confessional controversy. As my main object is to elucidate Greek religion, it would be both safe and easy to shelter myself behind the adjective 'primitive' and say that with modern religion I have no concern. But I abhor obscurantism. It is to me among the deadliest of spiritual sins. Moreover, the human mind is not made in water-tight compartments. What we think about Greek religion affects what we think about everything else. So I cannot end a book on Greek religion without saying simply how the writing of it has modified my own views.

I have come to see in the religious impulse a new value. It is, I believe, an attempt, instinctive and unconscious, to do what Professor Bergson bids modern philosophy do consciously and with the whole apparatus of science behind it, namely to apprehend life as one, as indivisible, yet as perennial movement and change.

But, profoundly as I also feel the value of the religious impulse, so keenly do I feel the danger and almost necessary disaster of each and every creed and dogma. For the material of religion is essentially the uncharted, the ungrasped, as Herbert Spencer would say, though with a somewhat different connotation, the 'unknowable.' Further, every religious dogma errs in two ways. First, it is a confident statement about something unknown and therefore practically always untrustworthy; secondly, if it were right and based on real knowledge, then its subject-matter would no longer belong to the realm of religion; it would belong to science or philosophy. To win new realms for knowledge out of the unknown is part of the normal current of human effort; but to force intellectual dogma upon material which belongs only to the realm of dim aspiration is to steer for a backwater of death. In that backwater lies stranded many an ancient galley, haunted by fair figures of serene Olympians, and even, it must be said, by the phantom of Him—the Desire of all nations—who is the same yesterday, to-day and for ever. The stream of life flows on, a saecular mystery; but these, the *eidola* of man's market-place, are dead men, hollow ghosts.

As to religious ritual, we may by degrees find forms that are free from intellectual error. The only intelligible meaning that ritual has for me, is the keeping open of the individual soul—that bit of the general life which life itself has fenced in by a separate organism—to other souls, other separate lives, and to the apprehension of other forms of life. The avenues are never closed. Life itself, physical and spiritual, is the keeping of them open. Whether any systematized attempt to remind man, by ritual, of that whole of life of which he is a specialized fragment can be made fruitful or not, I am uncertain.

My other debts are many.

To Dr Verrall, who in a single sentence gave me material for my second chapter. The reader will probably feel more grateful for his single sentence—an inspired bit of translation—than for the commentary that attends it.

To Mr Arthur Bernard Cook, who has spared time from his own valuable work to read through the greater part of my proofs. He has also, with a generosity as rare as it is characteristic, allowed me to borrow many suggestions from his forthcoming book *Zeus*, the appearance of which will, I know, mark an epoch in the study of Greek Religion. My sense of Mr Cook's great kindness is the deeper, because on some fundamental points we see differently.

Mr Francis Macdonald Cornford has again carried through for me the tedious task of proof-correcting. My chief debt to him is however for his chapter on *The Origin of the Olympic Games*. The conclusions he had independently arrived at in a course of lectures on Pindar, given at Trinity College during the Michaelmas Term of 1910, came as a quite unlooked for confirmation of my own views. This confirmation was the more valuable since it reached me at a time when my own argument was still inchoate and my conviction halting. My whole book—especially its last two chapters—owes much to Mr Cornford's constant help on points which will be developed more fully in his forthcoming work, *From Religion to Philosophy.*

My thanks are also offered to

Mrs Hugh Stewart and Miss Ruth Darwin for much kind help in the drawing of illustrations and the making of the index;

My College, which, by releasing me from teaching work, has given me the leisure necessary for writing;

The British School of Athens for permission to republish some part of my article on *The Kouretes and Zeus Kouros*, which appeared in the Annual, 1908–1909;

The German Archaeological Institute, the École Française of Berlin and Athens, and the Hellenic Society for permission to reproduce plates, and Messrs Macmillan for kindly allowing me the use of blocks from my *Mythology and Monuments of Ancient Athens*, now out of print;

The University Press for undertaking the publication of my book, and especially their skilful proof-reader, whose care has saved me from many errors.

And last I would thank my critics.

They have kindly warned me that, in the study of Alpha there is danger lest I lose sight of Omega. Intent on *origines*, on the roots of things, I fail to gather in, they tell me, the tree's fair, final fruit and blossom. I thank them for the warning, but I think they have not read my *Prolegomena*, or at least its preface. I there confess, and still confess, that I have little natural love for what an Elizabethan calls 'ye Beastly Devices of ye Heathen.' Savages, save for their reverent, totemistic attitude towards animals, weary and disgust me, though perforce I spend long hours in reading of their tedious doings. My good moments are when, through the study of things primitive, I come to the better understanding of some song of a Greek poet or some saying of a Greek philosopher.

It is because he has taught me to perceive, however faintly, this 'aroma of mysterious and eternal things' that I have asked leave to dedicate my most unworthy book to a scholar who is also a poet.

JANE ELLEN HARRISON.

NEWNHAM COLLEGE, CAMBRIDGE.
New Year's Eve, 1911.

ADDENDA ET CORRIGENDA.

p. 3, l. 1. 'But Palaikastro...is not Dikte.' At the moment of going to press I receive, by the kindness of Monsieur Toutain, a pre-print of his article, *L'Antre de Psychro et le Δικταῖον ἄντρον* (Rev. de l'Histoire des Religions, LXIV. 1911, Nov.— Dec.). The Diktaean cave of antiquity is not, according to M. Toutain, the cave excavated by Mr Hogarth at Psychro, but has yet to be sought in the easternmost part of Crete, near to the recently discovered temple at Palaikastro. I hope that M. Toutain is right, as it would relieve my argument of some embarrassments, but, till a cave comparable to that at Psychro comes to light near Palaikastro, nothing can be certain.

p. 12, l. 12. 'The Kouros, the young Zeus.' The Etymologicum Magnum, s.v. Δίκτη, says, 'ἐνταῦθα δὲ Διὸς ἄγαλμα ἀγένειον ἵστατο. λέγεται καὶ Δίκταιον.'

p. 32, l. 2. 'Tragedy...originated with the leaders of the dithyramb.' It is worth noting that Solon in a lost elegy is reported to have connected the earliest tragedies with Arion, the supposed originator of the dithyramb. τῆς δὲ τραγῳδίας πρῶτον δρᾶμα Ἀρίων ὁ Μηθυμναῖος εἰσήγαγεν ὥσπερ Σόλων ἐν ταῖς ἐπιγραφομέναις Ἐλεγείαις ἐδίδασκε. See the commentary of John the Deacon on Hermogenes, Περὶ μεθόδου δεινότητος, published by H. Rabe, *Aus Rhetoren-Handschriften*, in Rhein. Mus. LXIII. 1908, p. 150. Dr Nilsson in his valuable *Der Ursprung d. Tragödie* (Neue Jahrbücher, XXVII. 1911, p. 611, note 1), which by his kindness has just reached me, questions the tradition. For the historical relation of the Dithyramb to hero-cults see Dr W. Schmid, *Zur Geschichte des griechischen Dithyrambus*, Tübingen, 1901, a monograph which I regret to say has only just come to my knowledge.

p. 56, note. To the bibliography of the thunder-stone must now be added Dr Chr. Blinkenberg's able monograph, *The Thunder Weapon in Religion and Folk-Lore*, which has just appeared in the Cambridge Archaeological and Ethnographical Series, 1911.

p. 69, note 1. Omaha initiations. By Miss Fletcher's great kindness I have now received her splendid monograph, *The Omaha Tribe*, which she publishes in connection with Mr Francis la Flesche (himself a member of the tribe) in the 27th Annual Report of the Bureau of American Ethnology, 1911.

p. 82, l. 24. *For* krtya *read* krtya.

p. 93, l. 6. 'Behold God's Son.' This and all translations from Euripides are by Professor Gilbert Murray. Other translations he has kindly made for me are acknowledged in their place. For the remainder I am myself responsible.

p. 113, l. 32. 'The Persian Artemis.' See Mr M. S. Thompson's article, *The Asiatic or Winged Artemis*, J. H. S. XXIX. 1909, p. 286.

p. 206, l. 12. 'Tragedy, the Goat-Song.' I wish entirely to withdraw my explanation of τραγῳδία as 'spelt-song' first suggested in the *Classical Review*, 1902, p. 331, and further amplified in relation to *Bromios* and the supposed title *Braites* in my *Prolegomena*, pp. 414—422. All three interpretations fall together. Since my ill-starred attempt, two other etymologies of *tragedy* have appeared. Mr Louis H. Gray, in the *Classical Quarterly*, VI. 1912, p. 60, proposes to derive τραγῳδία from an Indo-Germanic base *tereg* (of which τραγο would be the second 'full grade'), with the meaning strong, terrible; tragedy would be the 'singing of bold or terrible things,' comedy would be the 'singing of revelrous things.' A weak point of this suggestion is that *tereg* appears to have left in Greek no other cognates, and is the 'bold or terrible one' a fitting description of a goat? Professor Margoliouth, *The Poetics of Aristotle*, 1911, p. 61, points out that, with reference to the voice, the verb τραγίζειν means 'to be cracked,' i.e. when at puberty the voice changes to harshness and irregularity of pitch. A tragic song is then a song of *irregular pitch*, full of—in the Greek sense—*anomalies*. This would suit Plutarch's account of the Dithyramb (*infra*, p. 156). I would gladly avail myself of any derivation that might connect tragedy with puberty and initiation-ceremonies, but I fear τραγῳδία and τραγίζειν alike ultimately derive from the canonical τράγος, and that it is to some ceremonial connected with a goat that we must look for the origin of the word.

p. 214, l. 18. 'No material evidence.' Dr Pfister in his *Reliquienkult im Altertum*, 1909, p. 396 and *passim*, shows convincingly that the evidence of excavation is dead against Euhemerism. 'Im allgemeinen wird man behaupten dürfen dass wenn die Griechen einmal die "Graber" ihrer Heroen aufgegraben hätten, sie in den weitaus meisten Fällen keine Gebeine gefunden haben würden. Die "Graber" waren alte Kultstätten.' Dr Pfister's testimony is doubly valuable as he has no theoretical axe to grind.

p. 271. 'Reincarnation'—'παλιγγενεσία.' See now Dr Torgny Segerstedt's important article on metempsychosis, *Själavandringslärans ursprung*, in Le Monde Orientale, Archive pour l'Histoire et l'Ethnographie de l'Europe orientale et de l'Asie, Uppsala, 1910, pp. 43—87, known only to me at present through the review in *Rev. de l'Histoire des Religions*, LXIII. 1911, p. 215. In the early Upanishads the dead go the moon, which then waxes; when the moon wanes the dead are reincarnated on the earth, a doctrine strangely akin to that of Plutarch, noted *infra*, p. 511. The custom of carrying the bride over the threshold is, according to Dr Segerstedt, connected with the burial of ancestors below the threshold and also anthropophagy of dead kin. The dead here and in many other customs are regarded as sources of fertility.

p. 333, note 1. 'The death and resurrection mime.' For analogies in the Rig Veda see Dr L. von Schroeder's illuminating *Mysterium und Mimus im Rig Veda*, 1908. For the analogy of the spring Zagmuk festival see Dr C. Fries, *Das Zagmukfest auf Scheria und der Ursprung des Dramas* (Mitt. d. Vorderasiatischen Gesellschaft, 1910), which contains much valuable material and many suggestions, though I am not yet satisfied that his main contention is established.

p. 373, note 1. 'How Prometheus tricked Zeus.' See Ada Thomsen, *Der Trug des Prometheus*, in Archiv f. Religionswiss. XII. 1909, p. 460.

p. 479, l. 8. 'M. Bergson has shown.' See now *L'Intuition Philosophique*, Revue de Métaphysique, XIX. 1911, pp. 809—827.

p. 486, note 3. 'M. Durkheim's views.' See now G. Davy, *La Sociologie de M. Durkheim* in Rev. Philosophique, XXXVI. pp. 42—71 and 160—185.

JANE ELLEN HARRISON, 1850-1928

"The Year Spirit, born young again every spring, has entered into your soul, and taught us all alike to feel ourselves the companions and sharers of your youthfulness."

So wrote Walter Leaf in the address of farewell sent to Jane Harrison by various friends when she left Cambridge for Paris. And in re-reading it, there come to my mind his other words of farewell, the verses in his book on Troy addressed to the memory of three friends, three great Cambridge scholars, Maitland, Butcher, and Verrall:

Χαίρετε κἀν φθιμένοις κεφαλαὶ φίλαι· οὐ γὰρ ἔτ' Ἄρης
   Χαίρειν τοὺς ζωοὺς ὀβριμόεργος ἐᾷ....
Εὕδετε νήδυμον ὕπνον. Ἐγὼ δ' ἐπὶ γήραος οὐδῷ
   Ὑμᾶς δακρύω καὶ σοφίην φθιμένην.

"Be glad among the departed, beloved faces; for Ares with brutal deeds suffers no gladness now among the living. . . . Sleep your deep sleep, while I on the threshold of old age shed tears for you and for learning lost."

Leaf, Verrall, Butcher, Maitland, four of the greatest names of English scholarship are commemorated together in those verses, and Jane Harrison belonged to the same generation and the same brilliant group of friends.

Δακρύω σοφίην φθιμένην. Certainly one has a sense

of learning or at least of scholarship irreparably lost: the focus of study seems to be changing, and it is quite possible that there will never again be scholars who know Greek as Verrall, Butcher, and Leaf knew it.   In any case it seems as if the personal acquirement of each of these men, built up by the study and keen observation of fifty years, had just passed away and ceased.   There is no Verrall now; no Walter Leaf, and no Jane Harrison.   That particular union of skill and power, the fruit of long labour in understanding, appreciating, interpreting the wisdom and beauty of the past, is gone.   "Vanity of vanities, saith the Preacher; all is vanity . . . because man goeth to his long home and the mourners are about the streets."

If all is vanity, I should like to answer the Preacher, if all is vanity, why did he take the trouble to write down so carefully his own exquisite and penetrating thoughts?   Why, above all, did he work them up into a form of such magical beauty?   Is not the very existence of the book a confession that, amid all his preaching of the vanity of things, he had faith in the value of philosophic thought, and above all faith in the immediate and enduring value of beauty?   And is not that the reason why, as a matter of fact, one rises from reading that last chapter of Ecclesiastes, not depressed but inspired?

If I try to think what was most characteristic of Jane Harrison's work, as compared with that of contemporary scholars, I think perhaps it is that, though she was capable of much steady grind and long research among potsherds and heavy volumes of German, she was always in pursuit of one or the other of two things: either of some discovery which was not a mere fact, but which radiated truth all about it, or of some creation or fresh revelation of beauty. It was said of a certain great Scotch savant that to him all facts were born free and equal. To her it was much the reverse. If the fact had a living message she embraced it and loved it; if it had not, it was entirely unimportant to her. She had the real artist's indifference to the things that were not serving her purpose, though of course she had the scholar's patience in searching through wastes of apparently unrepaying material for the sake of a result to which they might lead. In the preface to the *Prolegomena*, after explaining that she is approaching Greek religion through the facts of ritual and not through literature, she writes:

> "I would guard against misapprehension. Literature as a starting point, and especially the poems of Homer, I am compelled to disallow; yet literature is really my goal. I have tried to understand primitive rites, not from love of their archaism, nor yet wholly from a single-minded devotion to science, but with the definite hope that I might come to a better understanding of some forms of Greek poetry. Religious convention compelled the tragic poets to draw their plots from traditional mythology, from stories whose religious content and motive were already in Homer's days obsolete. A knowledge of, a certain sympathy with . . . this primitive material is one step towards the realisation of its final form in tragedy. It is then in the temple of literature, if but as a hewer of wood and drawer of water, that I still hope to serve."

The sense of literary style was present in all her work. Her lectures had a combination of grace and daring, of playfulness and dignity, which made them unlike any others. Her private letters were, not by study but as it were by instinct, works of art; completely spontaneous and informal, they somehow could not help bubbling with wit and striking out good

phrases. I take the first few that come to my hand
out of a bundle:

> "I am cross to-day and feel there is no such person as Dikê. I
> denied myself a lovely lace tea-jacket because it was costly, and
> instantly afterwards lost two £5 notes. What a comfort it is that
> the things that really matter can't be stolen; things like Iasion."

Iasion was the poem of Theocritus (κῶμος, Id. III)
about which we were writing. Again, some acquain-
tance of mine had attacked her unfairly, and I had
expressed my indignation to her and also in what I
meant to be a kindly expressed but truthful letter to
him. I received the answer:

> "Your curses are sweeter than honey and the honey-comb. I
> hate that man's mind. I wish I had seen that kind truthful letter;
> I expect the insults were unspeakable. By the way I am so relieved
> you did not catch a worse cold. I saw with consternation that
> you had no Jaeger boots. I almost asked after them, but my
> manners are so good."

Again when I could not come somewhere because
one of my children had whooping cough:

> "Oh dear, Oh dear, those accursed children. I begin to under-
> stand how right Elisha was and how really kind and wise was the
> action of the two She-Bears. All the same I hope it isn't poor little
> Basil; whooping cough does so shake a baby to bits. I will go
> to the Verralls and get more gruesome details.

Or again when I had ventured on the correction
of a tense in some translation of hers:

> "I will not be told that ἐγχυτριεῖν is the future of ἐγχυτρίζειν.
> I knew that before you were born, but not being a pedant I object
> to the meretricious prestige that some people attach to the present
> infinitive."

In her published writings one can see a constant
interest in beauty, as well, of course, as in discovery.
The writing is sometimes careless. She took little

interest in mere correctness for correctness sake. But when the hunt is up and she is off in full cry after some new fact or interpretation, the sentences seem to rush and glow.   There is no extraneous ornament; there is no polemic against other scholars, such as so often defaces the style of learned books; it is the joy of the chase conveyed sympathetically to the reader and exactly expressed.   The same sense of style and beauty gives rise to one habit of hers which has been much condemned by critics.   When she quoted Greek poetry she always liked to translate it into verse: thus the famous passage in Sophocles, καὶ τὰν ἄβατον θεοῦ φυλλάδα μυριόκαρπον ἀνήλιον ἀνήνεμόν τε πάντων χειμώνων becomes:

> "Footless, sacred, shadowy thicket, where a myriad berries grow,
>   Where no heat of the sun may enter, neither wind of the winter
>   blow,
>   Where the Reveller Dionysus with his nursing nymphs will go."

(The translation is D. S. MacColl's.)   Critics say: "This is wanton.   The translation is not exact, yet you mean your argument to be scientific.   Why can you not give the Greek text and add a literal prose translation for the benefit of those who do not know Greek?"

And her answer, I think, would be: "Because no prose can ever be an exact translation of poetry.   It leaves out what to me matters most.   What matters most is the atmosphere and the beauty; and a verse translation, with luck, may give me, not indeed exactly the same atmosphere as the original but an atmosphere that will resemble and suggest it."

It would, of course, be much safer to use prose. But, as always, she rejects the safe course, because she is not seeking to avoid blame, she is seeking to discover or express truth, or the nearest possible approach to truth.

There was one peculiarity about the way in which she sought and found beauty which is illustrated by the sentence already quoted from the *Prolegomena*. She liked to find it where it had not been noticed before. She did not really like "the beastly devices of the heathen," but she loved to work among them and understand them and eventually to discover the spiritual beauty latent beneath their uncouth helplessness. She had a rare power of insight and imaginative sympathy; and, it seemed to me, she did not much care for the kind of art that did not demand from a spectator the exercise of that power. A well-written hymn to Zeus the supreme judge, the father of gods and men, left her cold. Athena the armed virgin, the seeker of wisdom, whose vote in the court is always cast on the side of mercy, was too obvious in her beauty, and slightly repelled her. But a smiling dragon with a blue beard, or a man and woman poorly carved on a stele, bearing a speechless sacrifice to a great snake, called for understanding, for sympathetic interpretation, and always got it. She loved, and doubtless idealised, the thought or desire that could not express itself; she loved to help it out, to strip it of its mere externals and expound the aspiration that lay at its heart. She would try to penetrate the real purpose or meaning of a horrible practice like omophagia, or the tearing and devouring of live beasts, and almost forget the fact in the idea, or in what she supposed to be the idea, which informed it. This is doubtless one reason why Russian literature appealed to her so strongly. I remember her weeping over a little story of Tolstoy's about the "Three Old Men."

The three were hermits on an island in the Black Sea, very pious indeed and humble and loving to all men, but terribly ignorant. A bishop goes in a steamer to see them and teach them a few prayers, but finds them too old and stupid to learn. At last he gets—or thinks he has got—one very short and simple prayer into their heads, and leaves the island, feeling rather contemptuous. When night falls he sees a bright light advancing swiftly over the sea behind the steamer; it is the old men who have come, walking on the waves, to beg him to be patient with their great stupidity and teach them the prayer again. Jane Harrison saw that magic light and that unconscious possession of miraculous power in things that were stupid, ugly, primitive and helpless to express themselves.

Mrs. Salter writes of her as a lecturer: "She had an admirable dramatic sense and knew just how to lead an audience to expect a particular point and then give them what they expected"—or perhaps did not expect. "One small instance comes back to me. We were gradually led to expect a revelation, and then with a slightly hushed voice Jane heralded as 'an exquisitely lovely creature' the appearance on the screen of a peculiarly hideous Gorgon, grinning from ear to ear."

There is a vase painting of Helen on p. 323 of the *Prolegomena*, of which she spoke to me with the same hushed voice of admiration. I commend it to your respectful notice.

One must not forget, however, the obvious and undeniable beauty of her own speaking and lecturing. A lecture of hers, apart from its matter or its originality, was always a delightful artistic performance. The language and the articulation were as finished as they were unaffected. And again to quote Mrs. Salter, "Jane had an additional advantage in that she could throw herself in as part of the show in a way that is hardly possible for a man. She was always delightful to look at, and I remember among other things how skilfully she used her beautiful hands."

I have been speaking of her constant search for beauty; perhaps even more characteristic was her search, continual and ever-increasing, for what shall I call it? Not exactly truth, but a particular kind of truth; the kind that radiates and illumines the world as a whole. She felt towards everything that she studied as Tennyson felt towards the flower in the crannied wall. Any black-figured or red-figured vase at which she worked might reveal to her not only its date and style and perhaps its maker, but also, if she only saw it the right way, the secret of secrets, what God and man really are. It is extraordinarily interesting to look at her work from this point of view.

After *Myths of the Odyssey* and *Introductory Studies in Greek Art* there came in 1890, when she was forty years old, her first really important work, *Mythology and Monuments of Ancient Athens.* It was written in conjunction with Mrs. Verrall. It is a thoroughly sound and exact treatise in archæology. It is unusually interesting, perhaps it has more style and personality than most books of archæology—(I note, for example, the phrase: "this is to me not a demonstration but that surer thing, a conviction.") It is full of personal gratitude to Dörpfeldt. But it is indisputably what it calls itself, a book on the *Mythology and Monuments of Ancient Athens.* That limited subject is thoroughly mastered; the evidence is scrupulously cited, and in spite of the phrase quoted above, personal conviction is not often preferred to demonstration.

In 1903 came what I can only call a work of genius, the *Prolegomena to Greek Religion*. Not an account of Greek Religion, you will observe. I doubt if she would have had the patience to write a systematic account of Greek Religion; at any rate, that was not her desire. She had some "prolegomena," some things to say to students of Greek Religion at the outset of their studies, which would make them see the subject in a new light. She is no longer writing on a definite limited subject; there is no particular mass of material that she has to master under penalty of incompleteness, no rigid line beyond which she must not wander, under penalty of being irrelevant. She is going to tell us, out of the wide range of her expert knowledge, some things that we ought to know before we begin to read the regular books.

The first point is that we must escape from the tyranny of the fully articulate and finished literary accounts, and wring a deeper and truer evidence from the inarticulate and half-understood rituals which the Greeks really practised. We must study the things done at the festivals, especially the three great Athenian festivals Diasia, Anthesteria, Thargelia, and discover the stuff of religion that was there before the Olympians, before anthropomorphism, before theology. This opening leads on naturally to the admirable discussions on the Keres and the Making of a Goddess. Some details in these first half-dozen chapters are, I think, probably wrong. But the method they follow was both original and profoundly right. It is not too much to say that they have transformed the whole approach to the study of Greek religion. No competent student writing after the *Prolegomena* operates with the same conceptions and problems in his mind as were almost universally accepted before the *Prolegomena*. It is a book which, in the current phrase, made an epoch.

The second half of the *Prolegomena* seems to me to be an attempt, gallant, imaginative, learned, but premature, to grapple with a problem for whose solution the materials were not yet extant. Yet it is interesting to see how, even with the imperfect understanding of the worships of Dionysus and Orpheus which was the best attainable in 1903, Jane Harrison contrived, not indeed to analyse those worships exactly, but to wrest from them a kind of real religion for mankind; and how similar in the main that was to the religion which she expounded later on in *Themis*, when the new anthropological evidence was in her hands. It is easy here to say either of two things. The sceptic will say that she was, for psychological reasons, determined to bring out a certain result, whatever the evidence or whatever the subject she might be studying. The believer will claim for her that most surprising of intellectual gifts, the power of divining the truth from a mass of imperfect and imperfectly analysed evidence. Both, in a sense, are right. She had an extraordinary power of finding grist for her mill in whatever material came before her. Such a power, or at least such a habit, is often characteristic of the "crank," because the "crank," being possessed by something that we call a "fad," is always exaggerating its importance and finding imaginary support for it where real support does not exist. But it also belongs to the great thinker, or the possessor of some large and fruitful idea. Think how, when Darwin had formed in his mind the idea of Evolution, he found evidence for it in all regions of life, not because he was determined to find it, but because the evidence was really there. The flower in the crannied wall has a thousand secrets to yield to one who possesses any one of the thousand keys.

No one, of course, has all the keys. No one has or, I suppose, can have in his mind the complete answer to the question "what God or man is." Yet it seems to be a condition not merely of human progress but of any satisfactory spiritual life that one should go on seeking for it. Certainly Jane Harrison did so. Her next important book, *Themis*, marks to my mind a great advance on the *Prolegomena*, both in the light it throws on Greek Religion and in its contribution to religious thought outside classical antiquity. *Themis* had a less favourable reception than the *Prolegomena*, chiefly, I think, for two reasons. First it was too full of new ideas, or rather of new lights which made all the material on which they fell look different. Secondly, the author never succeeded in explaining each separately and in order, and then showing one after another the effects of each. She began straight off with all of them: the tribal initiations; the year-festivals with their projection, the Eniautos Daimon; God as the projected desire; and *Themis* as the tribal custom. All these conceptions are based on fact: all throw real light on the whole field of Greek religion, and are indeed almost indispensable to its understanding; but they were new to most scholars, and it required a strong mind so to readjust its conception of a material already known, named, and pigeon-holed, so as to take in all of them. I think there was also, in conservative or orthodox circles, rather more dislike of *Themis* as a "dangerous book" than there had been of the *Prolego-mena*. Opposition, as usual in such cases, concen-trated on irrelevant or absurd objections, particularly on a pretence that the Eniautos Daimon was a new god, instead of a new and convenient name for a well-recognised class of beings, formerly called Vegeta-tion Spirits, Corn Spirits and the like.

Themis was rather slow in coming to its kingdom; by the time a second edition was wanted the author had left Cambridge, dispersed her Greek library, and devoted her ever-fresh intellect to divers new languages and new philosophies. She did little to *Themis* in the way of correction or re-writing; she preferred to put out in 1921 a little book of 40 pages called *Epilegomena*. They gave shortly the main things that she wanted to say *after* all her books on Greek religion were finished and sent out to the world.

The point I wished to emphasise was this. In the *Prolegomena* we had a book which was based on facts of Greek archæology, and was really about Greek religion, or at least about the conceptions necessary for understanding Greek religion, though, all through, and especially in the latter part, the writer kept thinking of the bearing of those conceptions on the problem of religion as it now is or of life as a whole. In *Themis* there is a mass of new evidence; but very little of it is Greek evidence taken from the facts of Greek religion. It is evidence from modern anthropology and modern philosophy, from the most primitive and the most highly cultivated forms of human intelligence, throwing light on Greek religion not so much for its own sake, as for the sake of the religious adventures and aspira-tions of the human mind everywhere. Greek religion, like other Greek things, has an illustrative power so strange and pervasive. When the *Prolegomena* told us about *devotio*, and the Keres and Helen's tree and the Making of a Goddess, we did not immediately feel that our own minds were peopled with such beings or filled with such preoccupations. But in *Themis* you can from time to time hardly help a suspicion that the writer is speaking *mutato nomine de te:* the herd-emotion, the projection of desire, the primitive conception of sacrament, the sanctity of *Themis* and her relation to *Dike*, are ideas still haunting our minds just because they arise so far back in the history of the race. They belong to the roots and not the branches, and therefore their influence is everywhere.

And if this is true of *Themis*, it is even more markedly true of the slight but interesting *Epilegomena*. The things that Jane Harrison had to say at the end of her studies of Greek religion are scarcely about Greek religion at all. It is not based on new Greek texts or the discoveries of Greek scholars. The brief last chapter, indeed, is entitled "The Religion of To-day." If we look back to the *Prolegomena* we find in the Introduction expressions of obligation, made, of course, with boundless generosity, to many Greek scholars, but only to Greek scholars. The Introduction to *Themis*, besides mentioning various Greek scholars, payed special thanks to Bergson and Durkheim; the preface to the *Epilegomena* mentions only the psychologists Jung and Freud and the Russian philosopher Soloviov. We see thus that Jane Harrison's subject of study has expanded steadily; from the Mythology and Monuments of Athens to the religion that lay beneath all the monuments and mythology of Greece, and thence to the things that have lain and still lie implicit in all forms of religion and beneath the tide of temporal change. I will not attempt to criticise or estimate the value of her actual philosophy of religion, except to say that I think her best when she throws out passing flashlights and less good when she settles down to a definite discussion or exposition. But one point of fact is perhaps worth noticing.

All through the eighteenth and nineteenth centuries, and probably at most other periods, the human reason, when trying to escape from the dogmas of its traditional religion, has usually found its way to deism, monotheism. They settled down to a belief in one eternal father, "Jehovah, Jove or Lord" or, of course, Allah. They rejected polytheism, myths, consorts of God or sons of God. It is interesting historically, if not philosophically, that Jane Harrison took quite a different course. Like William James, she entirely rejects what she calls "monarchical deism," she will hear nothing of any immortal god; but she does passionately believe in a being—or at least accept the worship of a being—who labours for man, is man, suffers and dies for man, and though dead shall rise again. If, as some of the fathers say, all religious language is necessarily nothing but metaphor, attempting to indicate by human words what is admittedly inexpressible, it is interesting to see how in this fearlessly and almost recklessly sceptical mind the orthodox Christian metaphor finds such warm hospitality in the end.

But on this whole subject she herself has spoken in the Introduction to *Themis*:

"Such in brief is the argument. And here it would be perhaps discreet to pause. I have neither desire nor aptitude for confessional controversy. As my main object is to elucidate Greek religion, it would be both safe and easy to shelter myself behind the adjective 'primitive' and say that with modern religion I have no concern. But I abhor obscurantism. It is to me among the deadliest of spiritual sins. Moreover, the human mind is not made in water-tight compartments. What we think about Greek religion affects what we think about everything else. So I cannot end a book on Greek religion without saying simply how the writing of it has modified my own views.

"I have come to see in the religious impulse a new value. It is, I believe, an attempt, instinctive and unconscious, to do what Professor Bergson bids modern philosophy do consciously and with the whole apparatus of science behind it, namely to apprehend life as one, as indivisible, yet as perennial movement and change. But, profoundly as I also feel the value of the religious impulse, so keenly do I feel the danger and almost necessary disaster of each and every creed and dogma. For the material of religion is essentially the uncharted, the ungrasped, as Herbert Spencer would say, though with a somewhat different connotation, the 'unknowable.' Further, every religious dogma errs in two ways. First, it is a confident statement about something unknown and therefore practically always untrustworthy; secondly, if it were right and based on real knowledge, then its subject-matter would no longer belong to the realm of religion; it would belong to science or philosophy. To win new realms for knowledge out of the unknown is part of the normal current of human effort; but to force intellectual dogma upon material which belongs only to the realm of dim aspiration is to steer for a backwater of death. In that backwater lies stranded many an ancient galley, haunted by fair figures of serene Olympians, and even, it must be said, by the phantom of Him—the Desire of all nations—who is the same yesterday, to-day and for ever. The stream of life flows on, a sæcular mystery; but these, the *eidola* of man's market-place, are dead men, hollow ghosts.

"As to religious ritual, we may by degrees find forms that are free from intellectual error. The only intelligible meaning that ritual has for me, is the keeping open of the individual soul—that bit of the general life which life itself has fenced in by a separate organism—to other souls, other separate lives, and to the apprehension of other forms of life. The avenues are never closed. Life itself, physical and spiritual, is the keeping of them open.

Whether any systematised attempt to remind man, by ritual, of that whole of life of which he is a specialised fragment can be made fruitful or not, I am uncertain."

This passage seems to me to expound with great felicity the curious combination of doubt and faith, of eager search for truth and rooted scepticism as to the possibility of discovering it, which was characteristic of Jane Harrison's mind. It is a kind of inverted Platonism; or rather it goes dead against Plato's doctrine and strongly in accord with his practice. Plato finds reality only in the eternal and unchangeable, and mere fitful imitations of reality in the material and changing world. Yet Plato's method of teaching is never to lay down a dogma, practically never to assert a definite clear-cut result; always to search for truth by means of dialogue, with thought answering thought and suggestion improving on suggestion: till he ends perhaps in a parable or metaphor, perhaps in a confessedly unsolved problem, but practically never in a demonstrated conclusion. It is not an arrival; it is a search, stimulating to further search.

So it certainly was with Jane Harrison: a search stimulating to further search; and, we may add, a search which was, and rejoiced in being, a work of co-operation and mutual help. Her pupil, Mrs. Hugh Stewart, writes:

"I have not yet tried to define what she was to myself as a teacher, partly because she never treated you as a pupil. Age and status were no barriers in friendship or discussion. You were treated on equal terms intellectually.

I think the spell lay in the impression that she was sharing with you something new and vital. (I have only felt the same at other times listening to a scientific discoverer lecturing). . . . She laid a mass of evidence before us, following up the latest trail: poets, scholiasts, early Fathers. Unless you were well grounded in sound classical learning it was rather indigestible fare for a student . . . But it was intensely stimulating to be treated as a scholar by a scholar. She was not interested in imparting knowledge, but she made you want to learn what she was learning. That was why she taught the Greek language only to a few exceptional people; but when, after the war, she returned qualified as lecturer in Russian, she taught the rudiments to all her Russian pupils by the method she had evolved for herself."

"Age and status were no barriers." That absence of barriers between Jane Harrison and her various young friends was due in part, I think, to her lack of any consciousness of age in herself or others. When an old savant and a young student begin to talk about a learned subject, the one is apt to think "This young man will not want to listen to an old fogey like me" and the other, "This old man knows that I know nothing about the subject; how can I talk to him?" They think of themselves instead of the real subject. But she seemed to be quite free from these thoughts and inhibitions. Like the heroes and heroines of Greek mythology she had no particular age. She was engaged in a search, and she liked to have fellow-searchers. They helped her to clear her own mind, they cheered her, and they always might make a useful suggestion. I think she also definitely preferred the society of the young, because they were less likely to have fixed views and established orthodoxies, and therefore, less likely to be critical of her or displeased with her. She had also, I think—it comes out in her delightful Reminiscences— a keen remembrance of how she herself had been snubbed and silenced in her youth by elders who were not a bit wiser than herself, but merely failed to understand her. She was determined always to understand; or at least never to condemn that which she did not understand. She had fought all through life for the freedom of the young, especially of young women, and she was determined not to spoil that freedom by trying to dictate what use should be made of it. Another point to be remembered is that, with all her fame and influence, she never became an accepted orthodox authority. She was always frowned upon by a fair number of important persons: she was always in spirit a little against the government, against orthodoxy. And, thus since orthodoxy is the belief of the established authorities, she never went over, as most successful writers do, from the ranks of the young to those of the old.

I always felt, besides, that she loved young people; she dearly wished to be loved by them; and was terribly afraid of losing their intimacy and confidence, being left behind in the race, and becoming like many old people whom she had known long ago, still able to repeat formulae but no longer able to think.

That fear was certainly never realised. Amid the considerable bodily weaknesses that affected her later years, the freshness of her mind, her wit, her sense of beauty, her power of giving and inspiring affection, remained a constant wonder and a source of delight. Her friends could still laugh, as they had laughed thirty and perhaps forty years ago, at the eager welcome which she gave to a new discovery or hypothesis. She had always been over-hospitable to the ideas of others. If she was not swept away by every wind of vain doctrine, she at least liked to have plenty of winds blowing round her and seemed refreshed by their movement. But, the truth is, there were powerful forces always keeping her safe. In her own special subject, her knowledge of Greek literature and archæology was so wide and so intimate that vain doctrines had as a rule not much chance with her. She could not be imposed upon there. And in the wider problems of life, she was guarded by a native sanity and the ineradicable habits left by an old-fashioned and somewhat severe education, with its good manners, its fastidious taste, its personal dignity and power of self-control. These things remained, like the original writing in a palimpsest, clear and indelible beneath the superficial and fast-fading script of the last new philosopher or psychologist.

There are many, of course, who knew her better than I, particularly the chosen companion of her latest years. They can give impressions which will be much more valuable. To me personally the main impressions which remain of my old and dear friend are her vitality, her passion for the things of the intellect, her ever ready sympathy, and the unbounded generosity with which she estimated the work of others and more than repaid every contribution to her own.

INDEXES

I. GREEK WORDS.

II. LATIN WORDS.

III. PASSAGES QUOTED.

IV. GENERAL INDEX.